D1121441

Political Ideologies and Political Philosophies

Second Edition

To Photini, wife and companion,
for her generosity, patience and encouragement

Political Ideologies and Political Philosophies

Second Edition

Edited by

H.B. McCullough

Okanagan University College

TEP

THOMPSON EDUCATIONAL PUBLISHING, INC.
Toronto

Main entry under title:

Political ideologies and political philosophies

2nd ed.
Includes bibliographical references.
ISBN 1-55077-065-9

1. `Political science - Philosophy, 2. Political science - History. I. McCullough, H. B., 1944-

JA83.P58 1995   320.5   C94-932206-7

Photographs: Courtesy of the Bettman Archives.
Printed and bound in Canada.
1 2 3 4   99 98 97 96 95

Table of Contents

Acknowledgements

The editor would like to express his thanks to the numerous individuals who offered assistance in the preparation of the second edition of this book. In particular, he would like to thank Professors Thomas H. Greene of the University of Southern California and Angus Taylor of the University of Victoria for their advice on ways to improve the chapters on Conservatism and Marxism respectively. He would also like to express his gratitude to Mr. Kelly Beardmore for his suggestion on a way to improve the chapter on Feminism and to Dr. Carl Hodge for recommendations on the glossary. A special note of thanks is owed Ms. Mary Ellen Holland and Dr. Howard Reimer for their perceptive comments. Finally the editor would like to thank Dr. P.S. Mamo for his willingness to discuss and review substantive aspects of the book.

Introduction

The demise of the Soviet Union has led many to believe that communism is dead and that liberalism—in one of its forms—alone is triumphant. Yet such a belief is too readily formed and pays insufficient attention to the vicissitudes of history amply demonstrated in Edward Gibbon's *The Decline and Fall of the Roman Empire*. There Gibbon contrasts the wisdom and virtue governing the Roman Empire from the death of Domitian to the accession of Commodus with the darkness of Tiberius, the fury of Caligula, the feebleness of Claudius, the profligacy and cruelty of Nero and the beastliness of Vitellius. To say, in light of this prodigious work, that ideological convergence has occurred once and for all, as suggested by the end of history school of thought, is simply far-fetched.

What is true is that the twentieth century will close with the recognition of the sustainability of several ideologies including conservatism and liberalism and the recognition of the sociopathic nature of others, including fascism. However once one departs from these ideologies the going gets rougher and one's prognosis for such ideologies as environmentalism, communitarianism, feminism, and even communism becomes much less clear and confident.

The articles that follow are not meant to prejudge how the dust will settle on any of this; rather, they are meant to afford students and professors alike an opportunity to read primary sources in tandem with seminal secondary sources to facilitate the construction of a coherent and plausible political theory. A decent political theory will not give equal weight to every ideology, but should be able to explain why individuals have been tempted to adopt ideologies that should be rejected as well as to explain why other individuals have accepted ideologies that are incomplete yet plausible.

Whether the political theory constructed is largely a matter of domestic ideology, and thereby bounded by the constraints of international politics, or whether it has both a domestic and international dimension, does not seem to matter a great deal. It may just be that political theory and international relations will have to work together, rather than separately and hegemonically. Whichever way the story goes here, political theory will remain alive and well.

A word or two is now in order on the differences between political theories, political philosophies and political ideologies. The term "political theory" seems best reserved for the theoretically guided empirical study of power, justice, human nature and constitutional arrangements as they relate to the allocation and re-allocation of scarce goods and as they relate to conflict and conflict resolution. The term "political philosophy," whilst sharing the same focus as political theory, seems best reserved for that which is more theoretical and less empirical. Here the positions of Hobbes, Locke, Rousseau and Rawls spring to mind. Often the operative constraints of their positions are those of rational conduct under the terms of a social contract or social compact. Productive philosophical work has been done in this area in recent times by others in addition to Rawls, including Robert Nozick and David Gauthier, who have made effective use of some discoveries in the theory of choice and in the field of economics. Undoubtedly in this philosophical work there is some reflection of the empirical, but this is unashamedly dwarfed by the *a priori* and the normative. The operative word here is "unashamedly" for the *a priori* does bring with it the advantage of logical certainty.

Finally, the term "political ideologies," whilst sharing the same focus as political philosophies and political theories, seems best reserved for the normative, descriptive and unreflective study of these topics. This latter characteristic of ideologies explains why the term "ideology" has such a tendentious ring to it, its unreflectiveness giving rise to a dogmatism and intransigence that reflective individuals find offensive.

More important than a semantic analysis of the above terms is the establishment of a future line of research for scholars working in the general area of political theory. The suggestion here is that work in political theory proceed apace, alert to the acute need for empirical work that helps assess the autonomy of the state, the impact of individual choice, and the opportunity costs associated with pursuing some ideals such as liberty or security. As Kant maintains, observations without theories are blind. Therefore conjecture and hypothesis-generation need to occur in the study of politics if understanding in this field is to take place. The words of Charles Darwin in the nineteenth century make this point with unavoidable clarity:

> About thirty years ago there was much talk that geologists ought only to observe and not to theorize, and I well remember someone saying that at this rate a man might as well go into a gravel-pit to count the pebbles and describe the colours. How odd it is that anyone should not see that all observations must be for or against some view if it is to be of any service (Darwin, 1903, p.195).

So too the study of politics calls for a theory which has within its scope a number of things including human nature, justice, power and constitutional arrangements. But this will have to be a theory backed up by empirical data. It is with this in mind that one should understand the following extractions of political philosophies and ideologies, providing as they do the normative judgements, ideals, biases, historical observations and philosophical constraints of the last four hundred years that need to be taken into account in constructing a political theory. Studying the primary sources and some secondary sources on this subject is merely the first step—albeit an important one—in the march towards a much better understanding of politics. Only when this takes place will there be, if at all, a real convergence of political ideas.

The following selections have been grouped according to ideals and this has perforce resulted in some roughness of classification. But it is reassuring to note that others, besides myself, e.g. Sterba (Peffer 1992; Sterba 1992), have grouped five conceptions (libertarian, socialist, welfare liberal, feminist and communitarian) of social justice according to the ideals of liberty, equality, fairness, androgyny and the common good respectively. That other ideals (racial purity, national purity, faith and tradition) are commonly left undiscussed is often, though not always, testimony to the gratuitous assumption of some that conflict involving such ideals is non-existent. But a brief reminder of the faith of settlers on the West Bank in the Middle East, or of emergent nationalism in the Balkans, or of conflicts involving the use of the environment in the late twentieth century, belies the truth of this assumption.

The approach taken herein is to mark political ideologies and philosophies according to ideals—ideals which function as criteria of classification, the justification of these criteria being the profoundly important role which normative matters play in political views. It is hoped that such classification will facilitate the construction of a good political theory.

In any anthology questions arise about the choice of extracts. As for the choice of particular articles in this volume, their inclusion is based either on their own merit or on the widespread influence that they have had in the literature up to the present time. As with the first edition, a choice had to be made concerning the historical starting point. It seems defensible to use 1660, the year of the founding of the Royal Society of London, as a temporal touchstone to mark the beginning of modern science, and in many ways a new era in politics. Using this date has deep implications for the construction of the present work for it means that the writings of such influential thinkers as Plato, Aristotle, Augustine, Aquinas, Machiavelli and Hobbes are excluded. In defence, let it simply be said that in a larger work they would have been included. As for omissions after 1660 of individuals like Kant, the defence lies in the issue of immediate relevance or duplication. Many of these individuals, including Kant, have political views deserving of careful study, something which regrettably will have to be deferred to another time.

A word or two should be said at the pedagogical level. There exists a need for students studying the humanities and social sciences to read primary sources. By so doing they receive the opportunity to make their own critical judgement. Exposing students to primary sources in political thought, therefore, forms part of the rationale of the present work.

Finally the editor would like to say that those who make extensive use of the material contained herein should be encouraged to consult the biographies of many of the contributors. A peak into the life of an Emma Goldman, a Mary Wollstonecraft, a Peter Kropotkin, or a Chico Mendes can become in its own way truly inspirational.

References

F. Darwin and A.C. Seward, eds. *More Letters of Charles Darwin*. London. 1903. Vol. I, 195.

Peffer, Rodney,G. "Sterba's Reconciliation Project: A Critique," *Journal of Social Philosophy* XXIII (1992), pp. 132–144.

James P. Sterba, "Reconciliation Reaffirmed: A Reply to Peffer," *Journal of Social Philosophy* XXIII (1992), pp. 145–49.

1

Classical Liberalism

The Ideal of Rights

Embedded in the spirit of classical liberalism is the concept of rights. This core paradigm includes the premise of a human being's right to life, liberty and property. According to both John Locke and Thomas Paine, these rights are "natural"; in fact, the concept of natural rights forms the foundation upon which these scholars construct the philosophy of civil rights. Building on their thesis of civil rights, Adam Smith, the father of modern economics, gives a decidedly economic twist to the language of Locke and Paine, focusing not on rights but instead upon the theory of the invisible hand as well as the theory of comparative advantage. Notwithstanding Smith's strong preference for descriptive and explanatory idioms, rights-oriented concepts—both prescriptive and evaluative—are never far below the surface of his discourse. As an example, Smith very cleverly offers a rational defence of the wholesale merchant investing his capital close to home. In the process of his argument, Smith presupposes rights which investors have in virtue of the rationality of their actions. That Smith does not explicitly talk of such rights should not detract one from seeing that they form part of the economic philosophy in whose name he speaks.

As with Smith, so too with John Stuart Mill. The story is sometimes told that he, like other utilitarians such as Jeremy Bentham and James Mill, bases his ethical discourse solely upon the notion of utility rather than rights. There is truth in this line of analysis, but one should see that in developing his political philosophy, the later Mill makes rights play a secondary role without reducing them to units of utility. This is evident in Mill's principle of liberty which reads roughly as follows: the sole end for which humankind is warranted in interfering with the liberty of action of any of its number is self-protection. Nominalizing the language here one could properly talk of "warrants" or "entitlements" or better yet, "rights". Whatever the story Mill goes on to tell, these rights cannot be eliminated; rather, they are part of the discourse needed to construct a political philosophy however they might be connected to notions as rich as those of individuality, human happiness, and utility-maximising.

Despite their differences, each of the above mentioned writers (John Locke, Thomas Paine, Adam Smith and John Stuart Mill) believes that rights secured by a social contract play an important role in establishing and maintaining a secure political environment. This is particularly true of the right to liberty both in the political and economic spheres. In the event that the government flagrantly betrays the governed, the air of civility which the social contract brings can always be trumped by the right to rebellion, itself grounded in the right to liberty. What one sees in the case of classical liberals is a preoccupation with rights, especially that of the right to liberty, first found in the state of nature and then in civil societies.

Of Property

John Locke

JOHN LOCKE *(1632-1704) was one of the three great British empiricists along with Bishop George Berkeley and David Hume. His two major works were, in epistemology,* An Essay Concerning Human Understanding, *and, in politics,* Two Treatises on Government.

Though the earth and all inferior creatures be common to all men, yet every man has a property in his own person; this nobody has any right to but himself. The labour of his body and the work of his hands we may say are properly his. Whatsoever, then, he removes out of the state that nature hath provided and left it in, he hath mixed his labour with, and joined to it something that is his own, and thereby makes it his property. It being by him removed from the common state nature placed it in, it hath by this labour something annexed to it that excludes the common right of other men. For this labour being the unquestionable property of the labourer, no man but he can have a right to what that is once joined to, at least where there is enough, and as good left in common for others.

28. He that is nourished by the acorns he picked up under an oak, or the apples he gathered from the trees in the wood, has certainly appropriated them to himself. Nobody can deny but the nourishment is his. I ask, then, When did they begin to be his—when he digested, or when he ate, or when he boiled, or when he brought them home, or when he picked them up? And 'tis plain if the first gathering made them not his, nothing else could. That labour put a distinction between them and common; that added something to them more than Nature, the common mother of all, had done, and so they became his private right. And will any one say he had no right to those acorns or apples he thus appropriated, because he had not the consent of all mankind to make them his? Was it a robbery thus to assume to himself what belonged to all in common? If such a consent as that was necessary, man had starved, notwithstanding the plenty God had given him. We see in commons which remain so by compact that 'tis the taking any part of what is common and removing it out of the state nature leaves it in, which begins the property; without which the common is of no use. And the taking of this or that part does not depend on the express consent of all the commoners. Thus the grass my horse has bit, the turfs my servant has cut, and the ore I have dug in any place where I have a right to them in common with others, become my property without the assignation or consent of anybody. The labour that was mine removing them out of that common state they were in, hath fixed my property in them.

29. By making an explicit consent of every commoner necessary to any one's appropriating to himself any part of what is given in common, children or servants could not cut the meat which their father or master had provided for them in common without assigning to every one his peculiar part. Though the water running in the fountain be every one's, yet who can doubt but that in the pitcher is his only who drew it out? His labour hath taken it out of the hands of Nature, where it was common, and belonged equally to all her children, and hath thereby appropriated it to himself.

30. Thus this law of reason makes the deer that Indian's who hath killed it; 'tis allowed to be his goods who hath bestowed his labour upon it, though before it was the common right of every one. And amongst those who are counted the civilised part of mankind, who have made and multiplied positive laws to determine property, this original law of nature, for the beginning of property in what was before common, still takes place; and by virtue thereof, what fish any one catches in the ocean, that great and still remaining common of mankind, or what ambergris any one takes up here, is, by the labour that removes it out of that common state nature left it in, made his property who takes that pains about it. And even amongst us, the hare that any one is hunting is thought his who pursues her during the chase. For being a beast that is still looked upon as common, and no man's private possession, whoever has employed so much labour about any of that kind as to find and pursue her has thereby removed her from the state of nature wherein she was common, and hath begun a property.

31. It will perhaps be objected to this, that if gathering the acorns, or other fruits of the earth, &c., makes a right to them, then any one may engross as

much as he will. To which I answer, Not so. The same law of nature that does by this means give us property, does also bound that property too. "God has given us all things richly" (I Tim. vi. 17), is the voice of reason confirmed by inspiration. But how far has He given it to us? To enjoy. As much as any one can make use of to any advantage of life before it spoils, so much he may by his labour fix a property in; whatever is beyond this, is more than his share, and belongs to others. Nothing was made by God for man to spoil or destroy. And thus considering the plenty of natural provisions there was a long time in the world, and the few spenders, and to how small a part of that provision the industry of one man could extend itself, and engross it to the prejudice of others—especially keeping within the bounds, set by reason, of what might serve for his use—there could be then little room for quarrels or contentions about property so established.

32. But the chief matter of property being now not the fruits of the earth, and the beasts that subsist on it, but the earth itself, as that which takes in and carries with it all the rest, I think it is plain that property in that, too, is acquired as the former. As much land as a man tills, plants, improves, cultivates, and can use the product of, so much is his property. He by his labour does as it were enclose it from the common. Nor will it invalidate his right to say, everybody else has an equal title to it; and therefore he cannot appropriate, he cannot enclose, without the consent of all his fellow-commoners, all mankind. God, when He gave the world in common to all mankind, commanded man also to labour, and the penury of his condition required it of him. God and his reason commanded him to subdue the earth, i.e., improve it for the benefit of life, and therein lay out something upon it that was his own, his labour. He that, in obedience to this command of God, subdued, tilled, and sowed any part of it, thereby annexed to it something that was his property, which another had no title to, nor could without injury take from him.

33. Nor was this appropriation of any parcel of land, by improving it, any prejudice to any other man, since there was still enough and as good left; and more than the yet unprovided could use. So that in effect there was never the less left for others because of his enclosure for himself. For he that leaves as much as another can make use of, does as good as take nothing at all. Nobody could think himself injured by the drinking of another man, though he took a good draught, who had a whole river of the same water left him to quench his thirst; and the case of land and water, where there is enough of both, is perfectly the same.

34. God gave the world to men in common; but since He gave it them for their benefit, and the greatest conveniences of life they were capable to draw from it, it cannot be supposed He meant it should always remain common and uncultivated. He gave it to the use of the industrious and rational (and labour was to be his title to it), not to the fancy or covetousness of the quarrelsome and contentious. He that had as good left for his improvement as was already taken up, needed not complain, ought not to meddle with what was already improved by another's labour; if he did, it is plain he desired the benefit of another's pains, which he had no right to, and not the ground which God had given him in common with others to labour on, and whereof there was as good left as that already possessed, and more than he knew what to do with, or his industry could reach to.

35. It is true, in land that is common in England, or any other country where there is plenty of people under Government, who have money and commerce, no one can enclose or appropriate any part without the consent of all his fellow-commoners: because this is left common by compact, i.e., by the law of the land, which is not to be violated. And though it be common in respect of some men, it is not so to all mankind; but is the joint property of this country, or this parish. Besides, the remainder, after such enclosure, would not be as good to the rest of the commoners as the whole was, when they could all make use of the whole; whereas in the beginning and first peopling of the great common of the world it was quite otherwise. The law man was under was rather for appropriating. God commanded, and his wants forced him, to labour. That was his property, which could not be taken from him wherever he had fixed it. And hence subduing or cultivating the earth, and having dominion, we see are joined together. The one gave title to the other. So that God, by commanding to subdue, gave authority so far to appropriate. And the condition of human life, which requires labour and materials to work on, necessarily introduces private possessions.

36. The measure of property nature has well set by the extent of men's labour and the convenience of life. No man's labour could subdue or appropriate all; nor could his enjoyment consume more than a small part; so that it was impossible for any man this way, to entrench upon the right of another, or acquire to himself a property to the prejudice of his neighbour, who would still have room for as good and as large a possession (after the other had taken out his) as before it was appropriated. Which measure did confine every man's possession to a very moderate proportion, and such as he might appropriate to himself

JOHN LOCKE (1632-1704)

JOHN LOCKE was an English philosopher and political thinker. His best-known works in the field of political thought were the *First and Second Treatises on Government* (1689).

Locke is widely regarded as having been one of the first to articulate the basic principles of modern liberalism. He believed that humans were able to rise above the hypothetical "state of nature" by forming basic political agreements, or "social contracts" with one another. The result of these contracts was what Locke called "civil society." He believed that a state's sovereignty was located in the citizens of that state and not within the authority of a ruler. Authority to govern was only granted to rulers or governments because citizens permitted it in order to achieve certain common aims.

Locke's rights-based theories have been interpreted as both a defence of the "Glorious Revolution" in England in 1680, and as having laid the groundwork for the US Constitution. His contributions to the field of epistemology are also widely studied today. The *Essay Concerning Human Understanding* (1690) is Locke's most lasting work in this area.

without injury to anybody, in the first ages of the world, when men were more in danger to be lost by wandering from their company in the then vast wilderness of the earth than to be straitened for want of room to plant in. And the same measure may be allowed still without prejudice to anybody, as full as the world seems. For supposing a man or family in the state they were at first peopling of the world by the children of Adam or Noah; let him plant in some inland vacant places of America, we shall find that the possessions he could make himself, upon the measures we have given, would not be very large, nor, even to this day, prejudice the rest of mankind, or give them reason to complain or think themselves injured by this man's encroachment, though the race of men have now spread themselves to all the corners of the world, and do infinitely exceed the small number that was at the beginning. Nay, the extent of ground is of so little value without labour, that I have heard it affirmed that in Spain itself a man may be permitted to plough, sow, and reap, without being disturbed, upon land he has no other title to but only his making use of it. But, on the contrary, the inhabitants think themselves beholden to him who by his industry on neglected and consequently waste land has increased the stock of corn which they wanted. But be this as it will, which I lay no stress on, this I dare boldly affirm—that the same rule of propriety, viz., that every man should have as much as he could make use of, would hold still in the world without straitening anybody, since there is land enough in the world to suffice double the inhabitants, had not the invention of money, and the tacit agreement of men to put a value on it, introduced (by consent) larger possessions and a right to them; which how it has done I shall by-and-bye show more at large.

37. That is certain, that in the beginning, before the desire of having more than man needed had altered the intrinsic value of things, which depends only on their usefulness to the life of man; or had agreed that a little piece of yellow metal which would keep without wasting or decay should be worth a great piece of flesh or a whole heap of corn, though men had a right to appropriate by their labour, each one to himself, as much of the things of nature as he could use, yet this could not be much, nor to the prejudice of others, where the same plenty was still left to those who would use the same industry.

Before the appropriation of land, he who gathered as much of the wild fruits, killed, caught, or tamed as many of the beasts as he could; he that so employed his pains about any of the spontaneous products of nature as any way to alter them from the state which nature put them in, by placing any of his labour on them, did thereby acquire a propriety in them. But if they perished in his possession without their due use; if the fruits rotted, or the venison putrefied before he could spend it, he offended against the common law of nature, and was liable to be punished; he invaded his neighbour's share, for he had no right further than his use called for any of them and they might serve to afford him conveniences of life...

46. The greatest part of things really useful to the life of man, and such as the necessity of subsisting made the first commoners of the world look after, as it doth the Americans now, are generally things of short duration, such as, if they are not consumed by use, will decay and perish of themselves: gold, silver, and diamonds are things that fancy or agreement have put the value on more than real use and the necessary support of life. Now, of those good things which nature hath provided in common, every one hath a right, as hath been said, to as much as he could use, and had a property in all he could effect with his labour—all that his industry could extend to, to alter from the state nature had put it in, was his. He that gathered a hundred bushels of acorns or apples had thereby a property in them; they were his goods as soon as gathered. He was only to look that he used them before they spoiled, else he took more than his share, and robbed others; and, indeed, it was a foolish thing, as well as dishonest, to hoard up more than he could make use of. If he gave away a part to anybody else, so that it perished not uselessly in his possession, these he also made use of; and if he also bartered away plums that would have rotted in a week, for nuts that would last good for his eating a whole year, he did no injury; he wasted not the common stock, destroyed no part of the portion of goods that belonged to others, so long as nothing perished uselessly in his hands. Again, if he would give his nuts for a piece of metal, pleased with its colour, or exchange his sheep for shells, or wool for a sparkling pebble or a diamond, and keep those by him all his life, he invaded not the right of others; he might heap up as much of these durable things as he pleased, the exceeding of the bounds of his just property not lying in the largeness of his possessions, but the perishing of anything uselessly in it.

47. And thus came in the use of money—some lasting thing that men might keep without spoiling, and that, by mutual consent, men would take in exchange for the truly useful but perishable supports of life.

48. And as different degrees of industry were apt to give men possessions in different proportions, so this invention of money gave them the opportunity to continue and enlarge them; for supposing an island, separate from all possible commerce with the rest of the world, wherein there were but a hundred families—but there were sheep, horses, and cows, with other useful animals, wholesome fruits, and land enough for corn for a hundred thousand times as many, but nothing in the island, either because of its commonness or perishableness, fit to supply the place of money—what reason could any one have there to enlarge his possessions beyond the use of his family and a plentiful supply to its consumption, either in what their own industry produced, or they could barter for like perishable useful commodities with others? Where there is not something both lasting and scarce, and so valuable to be hoarded up, there men will not be apt to enlarge their possessions of land, were it never so rich, never so free for them to take; for I ask, what would a man value ten thousand or a hundred thousand acres of excellent land, ready cultivated, and well stocked too with cattle, in the middle of the inland parts of America, where he had no hopes of commerce with other parts of the world, to draw money to him by the sale of the product? It would not be worth the enclosing, and we should see him give up again to the wild common of nature whatever was more than would supply the conveniences of life to be had there for him and his family.

49. Thus in the beginning all the world was America, and more so than that is now, for no such thing as money was anywhere known. Find out something that hath the use and value of money amongst his neighbours, you shall see the same man will begin presently to enlarge his possessions.

50. But since gold and silver, being little useful to the life of man in proportion to food, raiment, and carriage, has its value only from the consent of men, whereof labour yet makes, in great part, the measure, it is plain that the consent of men have agreed to a disproportionate and unequal possession of the earth—I mean out of the bounds of society and compact; for in governments the laws regulate it; they having, by consent, found out and agreed in a way how a man may rightfully and without injury possess more than he himself can make use of by receiving gold and silver, which may continue long in a man's possession, without decaying for the overplus, and agreeing those metals should have a value.

Source: John Locke. *Of Civil Government Second Treatise.* Originally published in 1689.

Of the Dissolution of Government

John Locke

He that will with any clearness speak of the dissolution of government ought in the first place to distinguish between the dissolution of the society and the dissolution of the government. That which makes the community and brings men out of the loose state of nature into one politic society is the agreement which everybody has with the rest to incorporate and act as one body, and so be one distinct commonwealth. The usual and almost only way whereby this union is dissolved is the inroad of foreign force making a conquest upon them; for in that case, not being able to maintain and support themselves as one entire and independent body, the union belonging to that body which consisted therein must necessarily cease, and so every one return to the state he was in before, with a liberty to shift for himself and provide for his own safety, as he thinks fit, in some other society. Whenever the society is dissolved, it is certain the government of that society cannot remain. Thus conquerors' swords often cut up governments by the roots and mangle societies to pieces, separating the subdued or scattered multitude from the protection of and dependence on that society which ought to have preserved them from violence. The world is too well instructed in, and too forward to allow of, this way of dissolving of governments to need any more to be said of it; and there wants not much argument to prove that where the society is dissolved, the government cannot remain—that being as impossible as for the frame of a house to subsist when the materials of it are scattered and dissipated by a whirlwind, or jumbled into a confused heap by an earthquake.

212. Besides this overturning from without, governments are dissolved from within.

First, when the legislative is altered. Civil society being a state of peace amongst those who are of it, from whom the state of war is excluded by the umpirage which they have provided in their legislative for the ending all differences that may arise amongst any of them, it is in their legislative that the members of a commonwealth are united and combined together into one coherent living body. This is the soul that gives form, life, and unity to the commonwealth; from hence the several members have their mutual influence, sympathy, and connection; and, therefore, when the legislative is broken or dissolved, dissolution and death follows; for the essence and union of the society consisting in having one will, the legislative, when once established by the majority, has the declaring and, as it were, keeping of that will. The constitution of the legislative is the first and fundamental act of society, whereby provision is made for the continuation of their union under the direction of persons and bonds of laws made by persons authorized thereunto by the consent and appointment of the people, without which no one man or number of men amongst them can have authority of making laws that shall be binding to the rest. When any one or more shall take upon them to make laws, whom the people have not appointed so to do, they make laws without authority, which the people are not therefore bound to obey; by which means they come again to be out of subjection and may constitute to themselves a new legislative as they think best, being in full liberty to resist the force of those who without authority would impose anything upon them. Everyone is at the disposure of his own will when those who had by the delegation of the society the declaring of the public will are excluded from it, and others usurp the place who have no such authority of delegation.

213. This being usually brought about by such in the commonwealth who misuse the power they have, it is hard to consider it aright, and know at whose door to lay it, without knowing the form of government in which it happens. Let us suppose then the legislative placed in the concurrence of three distinct persons:

(1) A single hereditary person having the constant supreme executive power, and with it the power of convoking and dissolving the other two within certain periods of time.

(2) An assembly of hereditary nobility.

(3) An assembly of representatives chosen *pro tempore* by the people. Such a form of government supposed, it is evident,

214. First, that when such a single person or prince sets up his own arbitrary will in place of the laws which are the will of the society declared by the legislative, then the legislative is changed; for that

being in effect the legislative whose rules and laws are put in execution and required to be obeyed. When other laws are set up, and other rules pretended and enforced than what the legislative constituted by the society have enacted, it is plain that the legislative is changed. Whoever introduces new laws, not being thereunto authorized by the fundamental appointment of the society, or subverts the old, disowns and overturns the power by which they were made, and so sets up a new legislative.

215. Secondly, when the prince hinders the legislative from assembling in its due time, or from acting freely pursuant to those ends for which it was constituted, the legislative is altered; for it is not a certain number of men, no, nor their meeting, unless they have also freedom of debating and leisure of perfecting what is for the good of the society, wherein the legislative consists. When these are taken away or altered so as to deprive the society of the due exercise of their power, the legislative is truly altered; for it is not names that constitute governments but the use and exercise of those powers that were intended to accompany them, so that he who takes away the freedom or hinders the acting of the legislative in its due seasons in effect takes away the legislative and puts an end to the government.

216. Thirdly, when, by the arbitrary power of the prince, the electors or ways of election are altered, without the consent and contrary to the common interest of the people, there also the legislative is altered; for if others than those whom the society has authorized thereunto do choose, or in another way than what the society has prescribed, those chosen are not the legislative appointed by the people.

217. Fourthly, the delivery also of the people into the subjection of a foreign power, either by the prince or by the legislative, is certainly a change of the legislative, and so a dissolution of the government; for the end why people entered into society being to be preserved one entire, free, independent society, to be governed by its own laws, this is lost whenever they are given up into the power of another.

218. Why is such a constitution as this the dissolution of the government in these cases is to be imputed to the prince is evident. Because he, having the force, treasure, and offices of the state to employ, and often persuading himself, or being flattered by others, that as supreme magistrate he is incapable of control—he alone is in a condition to make great advances toward such changes, under pretence of lawful authority, and has it in his hands to terrify or suppress opposers as factious, seditious, and enemies to the government. Whereas no other part of the legislative or people is capable by themselves to attempt any alteration of the legislative, without open and visible rebellion apt enough to be taken notice of, which, when it prevails, produces effects very little different from foreign conquest. Besides, the prince is such a form of government having the power of dissolving the other parts of the legislative, and thereby rendering them private persons, they can never in opposition to him or without his concurrence alter the legislative by a law, his consent being necessary to give any of their decrees that sanction. But yet, so far as the other parts of the legislative in any way contribute to any attempt upon the government, and do either promote or not, what lies in them, hinder such designs, they are guilty and partake in this which is certainly the greatest crime men can be guilty of one toward another.

219. There is one way more whereby such a government may be dissolved, and that is when he who has the supreme executive power neglects and abandons that charge, so that the laws already made can no longer be put in execution. This is demonstratively to reduce all to anarchy, and so effectually to dissolve the government; for laws not being made for themselves, but to be by their execution the bonds of the society, to keep every part of the body politic in its due place and function, when that totally ceases, the government visibly ceases, and the people become a confused multitude, without order or connection. Where there is no longer the administration of justice for the securing of men's rights, nor any remaining power within the community to direct the force to provide for the necessities of the public, there certainly is no government left. Where the laws cannot be executed, it is all one as if there were no laws; and a government without laws is, I suppose, a mystery in politics, inconceivable to human capacity and inconsistent with human society.

220. In these and the like cases, when the government is dissolved, the people are at liberty to provide for themselves by erecting a new legislative, differing from the other by the change of persons or form, or both, as they shall find it most for their safety and good; for the society can never by the fault of another lose the native and original right it has to preserve itself, which can only be done by a settled legislative, and a fair and impartial execution of the laws made by it. But the state of mankind is not so miserable that they are not capable of using this remedy till it be too late to look for any. To tell people they may provide for themselves by erecting a new legislative, when by oppression, artifice, or being delivered over to a foreign power, their old one is gone, is only to tell them they may expect relief when it is too late and the evil is past cure. This is in effect no more

than to bid them first be slaves, and then to take care of their liberty; and when their chains are on, tell them they may act like freemen. This, if barely so, is rather mockery than relief; and men can never be secure from tyranny if there be no means to escape it till they are perfectly under it; and therefore it is that they have not only a right to get out of it, but to prevent it.

221. There is, therefore, secondly, another way whereby governments are dissolved, and that is when the legislative or the prince, either of them, act contrary to their trust.

First, the legislative acts against the trust reposed in them when they endeavor to invade the property of the subject, and to make themselves or any part of the community masters or arbitrary disposers of the lives, liberties, or fortunes of the people.

222. The reason why men enter into society is the preservation of their property; and the end why they choose and authorize a legislative is that there may be laws made and rules set as guards and fences to the properties of all the members of the society to limit the power and moderate the dominion of every part and member of the society; for since it can never be supposed to be the will of the society that the legislative should have a power to destroy that which every one designs to secure by entering into society, and for which the people submitted themselves to legislators of their own making. Whenever the legislators endeavor to take away and destroy the property of the people, or to reduce them to slavery under arbitrary power, they put themselves into a state of war with the people who are thereupon absolved from any further obedience, and are left to the common refuge which God has provided for all men against force and violence. Whensoever, therefore, the legislative shall transgress this fundamental rule of society, and either by ambition, fear, folly, or corruption, endeavor to grasp themselves, or put into the hands of any other, an absolute power over the lives, liberties, and estates of the people, by this breach of trust they forfeit the power the people had put into their hands for quite contrary ends, and it devolves to the people, who have a right to resume their original liberty and, by the establishment of a new legislative, such as they shall think fit, provide for their own safety and security, which is the end for which they are in society. What I have said here concerning the legislative in general holds true also concerning the supreme executor, who having a double trust put in him—both to have a part in the legislative and the supreme execution of the law—acts against both when he goes about to set up his own arbitrary will as the law of the society. He acts also contrary to his trust when he either employs the force, treasure, and offices of the society to corrupt the representatives and gain them to his purposes, or openly pre-engages the electors and prescribes to their choice such whom he has by solicitations, threats, promises, or otherwise won to his designs, and employs them to bring in such who have promised beforehand what to vote and what to enact. Thus to regulate candidates and electors, and new-model the ways of election, what it is but to cut up the government by the roots, and poison the very fountain of public security? For the people, having reserved to themselves the choice of their representatives, as the fence to their properties, could do it for no other end but that they might always be freely chosen, and, so chosen, freely act and advise as the necessity of the commonwealth and the public good should upon examination and mature debate be judged to require. This those who give their votes before they hear the debate and have weighed the reasons on all sides are not capable of doing. To prepare such an assembly as this, and endeavor to set up the declared abettors of his own will for the true representatives of the people and the lawmakers of the society, is certainly as great a breach of trust and as perfect a declaration of a design to subvert the government as is possible to be met with. To which if one shall add rewards and punishments visibly employed to the same end, and all the arts of perverted law made use of to take off and destroy all that stand in the way of such a design, and will not comply and consent to betray the liberties of their country, it will be past doubt what is doing. What power they ought to have in the society who thus employ it contrary to the trust that went along with it in its first institution is easy to determine; and one cannot but see that he who has once attempted any such thing as this cannot any longer be trusted.

223. To this perhaps it will be said that, the people being ignorant and always discontented, to lay the foundation of government in the unsteady opinion and uncertain humor of the people is to expose it to certain ruin; and no government will be able long to subsist if the people may set up a new legislative whenever they take offense at the old one. To this I answer: Quite the contrary. People are not so easily got out of their old forms as some are apt to suggest. They are hardly to be prevailed with to amend the acknowledged faults in the frame they have been accustomed to. And if there be any original defects, or adventitious ones introduced by time or corruption, it is not an easy thing to get them changed, even when all the world sees there is an opportunity for it. This slowness and aversion in the people to quit their old constitutions has in the many revolutions which have been seen in this kingdom, in this and former ages, still kept us to, or after some interval of fruitless attempts still brought us back again to, our old legislative of king, lords, and commons; and whatever provocations have made the crown be taken from some of our princes' heads, they never carried the people so far as to place it in another line.

224. But it will be said this hypothesis lays a ferment for frequent rebellion. To which I answer:

First, no more than any other hypothesis; for when the people are made miserable, and find themselves exposed to the ill-usage of arbitrary power, cry up their governors as much as you will for sons of Jupiter, let them be sacred or divine, descended or authorized from heaven, give them out for whom or what you please, the same will happen. The people generally ill-treated, and contrary to right, will be ready upon any occasion to ease themselves of a burden that sits heavy upon them. They will wish and seek for the opportunity, which in the change, weakness, and accidents of human affairs seldom delays long to offer itself. He must have lived but a little while in the world who has not seen examples of this in his time, and he must have read very little who cannot produce examples of it in all sorts of governments in the world.

225. Secondly, I answer, such revolutions happen not upon every little mismanagement in public affairs. Great mistakes in the ruling part, many wrong and inconvenient laws, and all the slips of human frailty will be born by the people without mutiny or murmur. But if a long train of abuses, prevarications, and artifices, all tending the same way, make the design visible to the people, and they cannot but feel what they lie under and see whither they are going, it is not to be wondered that they should then rouse themselves and endeavor to put the rule into such hands which may secure to them the ends for which government was at first erected, and without which ancient names and specious forms are so far from being better that they are much worse than the state of nature or pure anarchy—the inconveniences being all as great and as near, but the remedy farther off and more difficult.

226. Thirdly, I answer that this doctrine of a power in the people of providing for their safety anew by a new legislative, when their legislators have acted contrary to their trust by invading their property, is the best fence against rebellion, and the probablest means to hinder it; for rebellion being an opposition, not to persons, but authority which is founded only in the constitutions and laws of the government, those, whoever they be, who by force break through, and by force justify their violation of them, are truly and properly rebels; for when men, by entering into society and civil government, have excluded force and introduced laws for the preservation of property, peace, and unity amongst themselves, those who set up force again in opposition to the laws do *rebellare*—that is, bring back again the state of war—and are properly rebels; which they who are in power, by the pretence they have to authority, the temptation of force they have in their hands, and the flattery of those about them, being likeliest to do, the properest way to prevent the evil is to show them the danger and injustice of it who are under the greatest temptation to run into it.

227. In both the forementioned cases, when either the legislative is changed or the legislators act contrary to the end for which they were constituted, those who are guilty are guilty of rebellion; for if any one by force takes away the established legislative of any society, and the laws of them made pursuant to their trust, he thereby takes away the umpirage which every one had consented to for a peaceable decision of all their controversies, and a bar to the state of war amongst them. They who remove or change the legislative take away this decisive power which nobody can have but by the appointment and consent of the people, and so destroying the authority which the people did, and nobody else can, set up, and introducing a power which the people has not authorized, they actually introduce a state of war which is that of force without authority; and thus by removing the legislative established by the society—in whose decisions the people acquiesced and united as to that of their own will—they untie the knot and expose the people anew to the state of war. And if those who by force take away the legislative are rebels, the legislators themselves, as has been shown, can be no less esteemed so, when they who were set up for the protection and preservation of the people, their liberties and properties, shall by force invade and endeavor to take them away; and so they putting themselves into a state of war with those who made them the protectors and guardians of their peace, are properly, and with the greatest aggravation, *rebellantes*, rebels.

Source: John Locke. *Second Treatise of Government.* Originally published in 1690.

The Wealth of Nations

Adam Smith

ADAM SMITH *(1723-1790) was the father of economics. He was born in Scotland and educated at Glasgow and Oxford University. He served as professor of logic and then professor of moral philosophy at the University of Glasgow. In retirement he wrote his now famous* Wealth of Nations, *from which the present selection is taken.*

Of Restraints Upon the Importation from Foreign Countries of Such Goods as Can Be Produced at Home

By restraining, either by high duties or by absolute prohibitions, the importation of such goods from foreign countries as can be produced at home, the monopoly of the home market is more or less secured to the domestic industry employed in producing them. Thus the prohibition of importing either live cattle or salt provisions from foreign countries secures to the graziers of Great Britain the monopoly of the home market for butcher's meat. The high duties upon the importation of corn, which in times of moderate plenty amount to a prohibition, give a like advantage to the growers of that commodity. The prohibition of the importation of foreign woollens is equally favourable to the woollen manufacturers. The silk manufacture, though altogether employed upon foreign materials, has lately obtained the same advantage. The linen manufacture has not yet obtained it, but is making great strides towards it. Many other sorts of manufacturers have, in the same manner, obtained in Great Britain, either altogether or very nearly, a monopoly against their countrymen. The variety of goods of which the importation into Great Britain is prohibited, either absolutely, or under certain circumstances, greatly exceeds what can easily be suspected by those who are not well acquainted with the laws of the customs.

That this monopoly of the home market frequently gives great encouragement to that particular species of industry which enjoys it, and frequently turns towards that employment a greater share of both the labour and stock of the society than would otherwise have gone to it, cannot be doubted. But whether it tends either to increase the general industry of the society, or to give it the most advantageous direction, is not, perhaps, altogether so evident.

The general industry of the society never can exceed what the capital of the society can employ. As the number of workmen that can be kept in employment by any particular person must bear a certain proportion to his capital, so the number of those that can be continually employed by all the members of a great society must bear a certain proportion to the whole capital of that society, and never can exceed that proportion. No regulation of commerce can increase the quantity of industry in any society beyond what its capital can maintain. It can only divert a part of it into a direction into which it might not otherwise have gone; and it is by no means certain that this artificial direction is likely to be more advantageous to the society than that into which it would have gone of its own accord.

Every individual is continually exerting himself to find out the most advantageous employment for whatever capital he can command. It is his own advantage, indeed, and not that of the society, which he has in view. But the study of his own advantage naturally, or rather necessarily, leads him to prefer that employment which is most advantageous to the society.

First, every individual endeavours to employ his capital as near home as he can, and consequently as much as he can in the support of domestic industry; provided always that he can thereby obtain the ordinary, or not a great deal less than the ordinary profits of stock.

Thus, upon equal or nearly equal profits, every wholesale merchant naturally prefers the home trade to the foreign trade of consumption, and the foreign trade of consumption to the carrying trade. In the home trade his capital is never so long out of his sight as it frequently is in the foreign trade of consumption. He can know better the character and the situation of the persons whom he trusts, and if he should happen to be deceived, he knows better the laws of the country from which he must seek redress. In the carrying trade, the capital of the merchant is, as it were, divided between two foreign countries, and no part of it is ever necessarily brought home, or placed under his own immediate view and command. The capital which an Amsterdam merchant employs in carrying corn from Konnigsberg to Lisbon, and fruit and wine from Lisbon to Konnigsberg, must generally

ADAM SMITH (1723-1790)

ADAM SMITH is regarded today as the founder of modern economics. He was the son of a Scottish customs official who, according to popular lore, was kidnapped by gypsies when he was four years old. Smith studied at Glasgow College and at Oxford University, and returned to Glasgow to teach there for thirteen years. Following this, Smith moved to France to tutor a young Scottish nobleman. This latter position, while well-paying, was apparently not much of an intellectual challenge for Smith. Consequently, he began writing the book that would change the way the world viewed economics.

The *Inquiry into The Nature and Causes of the Wealth of Nations* (1776) revolutionized the field of political economics and is still regarded as one of the most important works on the subject ever written. Smith disputed the prevailing belief that nations remained economically powerful by keeping domestic wealth securely within their own political borders. Instead, Smith advocated trade with other nations as a way of promoting what he believed to be healthy economic competition. Nations were economically prosperous, he argued, insofar as their citizens were able to have access to goods and services. Prior to Smith's time the commonly-held view was that a nation's wealth was increased by the selling of commodities abroad in exchange for gold or silver. Smith held that the pursuit of economic gain, instead of being socially divisive, was actually productive, since self-interest could motivate individuals to discover the form of employment and/or commerce for which they are best suited.

Smith gave extensive thought to concepts such as labour and taxation, and defended the "*laissez faire*" theory of the marketplace. This theory holds that if a market economy is not placed under excessive legislative or governmental controls, it will establish its own equilibrium in which, as Smith explained, "every individual is continually exerting himself to find out the most advantageous employment for whatever capital he can command." In the end, the removal of restrictions upon trade would be governed by the "invisible hand" of the market which, through competition, would determine prices for goods and services. The result would be an overall increase in a nation's production and wealth.

Smith's ideas about capital, labour and taxation, and how they should best be put to use within an economic marketplace set the foundations for the nineteenth century's debate on political economy. With the advent of industrialization in the modern world, Smith's theories about *laissez faire* competition took hold and were embraced as governments began to loosen their control over the economic life of their countries. Adam Smith's writings are still widely studied today, and the field of political economy, which he originated, is still a vibrant academic discipline in institutions world-wide.

be the one-half of it at Konnigsberg and the other half at Lisbon. No part of it need ever come to Amsterdam. The natural residence of such a merchant should either be at Konnigsberg or Lisbon, and it can only be some very particular circumstances which can make him prefer the residence of Amsterdam. The uneasiness, however, which he feels at being separated so far from his capital generally determines him to bring part both of the Konnigsberg goods which he destines for the market of Lisbon, and of the Lisbon goods which he destines for that of Konnigsberg, to Amsterdam: and though this necessarily subjects him to a double charge of loading and unloading, as well as to the payment of some duties and customs, yet for the sake of having some part of his capital always under his own view and command, he willingly submits to this extraordinary charge; and it is in this manner that every country which has any considerable share of the carrying trade becomes always the emporium, or general market, for the goods of all the different countries whose trade it carries on. The merchant, in order to save a second loading and unloading, endeavours always to sell in the home market as much of the goods of all those different countries as he can, and thus, so far as he can, to convert his carrying trade into a foreign trade of consumption. A merchant, in the same manner, who is engaged in the foreign trade of consumption, when he collects goods for foreign markets, will always be glad, upon equal or nearly equal profits, to sell as great a part of them at home as he can. He saves himself the risk and trouble of exportation, when, so far as he can, he thus converts his foreign trade of consumption into a home trade. Home is in this manner the centre, if I may say so, round which the capitals of the inhabitants of every country are continually circulating, and towards which they are always tending, though by particular causes they may sometimes be driven off and repelled from it towards more distant employments. But a capital employed in the home trade, it has already been shown, necessarily puts into motion a greater quantity of domestic industry, and gives revenue and employment to a greater number of the inhabitants of the country, than an equal capital employed in the foreign trade of consumption: and one employed in the foreign trade of consumption has the same advantage over an equal capital employed in the carrying trade. Upon equal, or only nearly equal profits, therefore, every individual naturally inclines to employ his capital in the manner in which it is likely to afford the greatest support to domestic industry, and to give revenue and employment to the greatest number of people of his own country.

Secondly, every individual who employs his capital in the support of domestic industry, necessarily endeavours so to direct that industry that its produce may be of the greatest possible value.

The produce of industry is what it adds to the subject or materials upon which it is employed. In proportion as the value of this produce is great or small, so will likewise be the profits of the employer. But it is only for the sake of profit that any man employs a capital in the support of industry; and he will always, therefore, endeavour to employ it in the support of that industry of which the produce is likely to be of the greatest value, or to exchange for the greatest quantity either of money or of other goods.

But the annual revenue of every society is always precisely equal to the exchangeable value of the whole annual produce of its industry, or rather is precisely the same thing with that exchangeable value. As every individual, therefore, endeavours as much as he can both to employ his capital in the support of domestic industry, and so to direct that industry that its produce may be of the greatest value; every individual necessarily labours to render the annual revenue of the society as great as he can. He generally, indeed, neither intends to promote the public interest, nor knows how much he is promoting it. By preferring the support of domestic to that of foreign industry, he intends only his own security; and by directing that industry in such a manner as its produce may be of the greatest value, he intends only his own gain, and he is in this, as in many other cases, led by an invisible hand to promote an end which was no part of his intention. Nor is it always the worse for the society that it was no part of it. By pursuing his own interest he frequently promotes that of the society more effectually than when he really intends to promote it. I have never known much good done by those who affected to trade for the public good. It is an affectation, indeed, not very common among merchants, and very few words need be employed in dissuading them from it.

What is the species of domestic industry which his capital can employ, and of which the produce is likely to be of the greatest value, every individual, it is evident, can, in his local situation, judge much better than any statesman or lawgiver can do for him. The statesman who should attempt to direct private people in what manner they ought to employ their capitals would not only load himself with a most unnecessary attention, but assume an authority which could safely be trusted, not only to no single person, but to no council or senate whatever, and which would nowhere be so dangerous as in the hands of a man who had folly and presumption enough to fancy himself fit to exercise it.

To give the monopoly of the home market to the produce of domestic industry, in any particular art or manufacture, is in some measure to direct private people in what manner they ought to employ their capitals, and must, in almost all cases, be either a useless or a hurtful regulation. If the produce of domestic can be brought there as cheap as that of foreign industry, the regulation is evidently useless. If it cannot, it must generally be hurtful. It is the maxim of every prudent master of a family never to attempt to make at home what it will cost him more to make than to buy. The tailor does not attempt to make his own shoes, but buys them of the shoemaker. The shoemaker does not attempt to make his own clothes, but employs a tailor. The farmer attempts to make neither the one nor the other, but employs those different artificers. All of them find it for their interest to employ their whole industry in a way in which they have some advantage over their neighbours, and to purchase with a part of its produce, or what is the same thing, with the price of a part of it, whatever else they have occasion for.

What is prudence in the conduct of every private family can scarce be folly in that of a great kingdom. If a foreign country can supply us with a commodity cheaper than we ourselves can make it, better buy it of them with some part of the produce of our own industry employed in a way in which we have some advantage. The general industry of the country, being always in proportion to the capital which employs it, will not thereby be diminished, no more than that of the above-mentioned artificers; but only left to find out the way in which it can be employed with the greatest advantage. It is certainly not employed to the greatest advantage when it is thus directed towards an object which it can buy cheaper than it can make. The value of its annual produce is certainly more or less diminished when it is thus turned away from producing commodities evidently of more value than the commodity which it is directed to produce. According to the supposition, that commodity could be purchased from foreign countries cheaper than it can be made at home. It could, therefore, have been purchased with a part only of the commodities, or, what is the same thing, with a part only of the price of the commodities, which the industry employed by an equal capital would have produced at home, had it been left to follow its natural course. The industry of the country, therefore, is thus turned away from a more to a less advantageous employment, and the exchangeable value of its annual produce, instead of being increased, according to the intention of the lawgiver, must necessarily be diminished by every such regulation.

By means of such regulations, indeed, a particular manufacture may sometimes be acquired sooner than it could have been otherwise, and after a certain time may be made at home as cheap or cheaper than in the foreign country. But though the industry of the society may be thus carried with advantage into a particular channel sooner than it could have been otherwise, it will by no means follow that the sum total, either of its industry, or of its revenue, can ever be augmented by any such regulation. The industry of the society can augment only in proportion as its capital augments, and its capital can augment only in proportion to what can be gradually saved out of its revenue. But the immediate effect of every such regulation is to diminish its revenue, and what diminishes its revenue is certainly not very likely to augment its capital faster than it would have augmented of its own accord had both capital and industry been left to find out their natural employments.

Though for want of such regulations the society should never acquire the proposed manufacture, it would not, upon that account, necessarily be the poorer in any one period of its duration. In every period of its duration its whole capital and industry might still have been employed, though upon different objects, in the manner that was most advantageous at the time. In every period its revenue might have been the greatest which its capital could afford, and both capital and revenue might have been augmented with the greatest possible rapidity.

The natural advantages which one country has over another in producing particular commodities are sometimes so great that it is acknowledged by all the world to be in vain to struggle with them. By means of glasses, hotbeds, and hot walls, very good grapes can be raised in Scotland, and very good wine too can be made of them at about thirty times the expense for which at least equally good can be brought from foreign countries. Would it be a reasonable law to prohibit the importation of all foreign wines merely to encourage the making of claret and burgundy in Scotland? But if there would be a manifest absurdity in turning towards any employment thirty times more of the capital and industry of the country than would be necessary to purchase from foreign countries an equal quantity of the commodities wanted, there must be an absurdity, though not altogether so glaring, yet exactly of the same kind, in turning towards any such employment a thirtieth, or even a three-hundredth part more of either. Whether the advantages which one country has over another be natural or acquired is in this respect of no consequence. As long as the one country has those advantages, and the other wants them, it will always be more advantageous for the latter rather to buy of the former than to make. It is an acquired advantage only, which one artificer has over his neighbour, who exercises another trade; and yet they both find it more advantageous to buy of one another than to make what does not belong to their particular trades.

Source: Adam Smith. *The Wealth of Nations.* Originally published in 1776.

Rights of Man

Thomas Paine

THOMAS PAINE *(1737-1809), an Englishman, travelled to America at the age of 37, where he soon became familiar with the instability of the pre-revolutionary years. Later in 1790, while in France, he began writing a defence of the fundamental ideas of revolution. This culminated in an attack upon Edmund Burke's* Reflections on the French Revolution, *in his own* The Rights of Man.

The error of those who reason by precedents drawn from antiquity, respecting the rights of man, is, that they do not go far enough into antiquity. They do not go the whole way. They stop in some of the intermediate stages of an hundred or a thousand years, and produce what was then done, as a rule for the present day. This is no authority at all. If we travel still farther into antiquity, we shall find a direct contrary opinion and practice prevailing; and if antiquity is to be authority, a thousand such authorities may be produced, successively contradicting each other. But if we proceed on, we shall at last come out right; we shall come to the time when man came from the hand of his Maker. What was he then? Man. Man was his high and only title, and a higher cannot be given him.—But of titles I shall speak hereafter.

We are now got at the origin of man, and at the origin of his rights. As to the manner in which the world has been governed from that day to this, it is no further any concern of ours than to make a proper use of the errors or the improvements which the history of it presents. Those who lived a hundred or a thousand years ago, were then moderns, as we are now. They had *their* ancients, and those ancients had others, and we also shall be ancients in our turn. If the mere name of antiquity is to govern in the affairs of life, the people who are to live an hundred or a thousand years hence, may as well take us for a precedent, as we make a precedent of those who lived an hundred or a thousand years ago. The fact is, that portions of antiquity, by proving everything, establish nothing. It is authority against authority all the way, till we come to the divine origin of the rights of man at the creation. Here our inquiries find a resting-place, and our reason finds a home. If a dispute about the rights of man had arisen at the distance of an hundred years from the creation, it is to this source

of authority they must have referred, and it is to the same source of authority that we must now refer.

Though I mean not to touch upon any sectarian principle of religion, yet it may be worth observing, that the genealogy of Christ is traced to Adam. Why then not trace the rights of man to the creation of man? I will answer the question. Because there have been upstart governments, thrusting themselves between, and presumptuously working to *un-make* man.

If any generation of men ever possessed the right of dictating the mode by which the world should be governed for ever, it was the first generation that existed; and if that generation did it not, no succeeding generation can show any authority for doing it, nor can set any up. The illuminating and divine principle of the equal rights of man, (for it has its origin from the Maker of man) relates, not only to the living individuals, but to generations of men succeeding each other. Every generation is equal in rights to the generation which preceded it, by the same rule that every individual is born equal in rights with his contemporary.

Every history of the creation, and every traditionary account, whether from the lettered or unlettered world, however they may vary in their opinion or belief of certain particulars, all agree in establishing one point, *the unity of man*; by which I mean, that men are all of *one degree*, and consequently that all men are born equal, and with equal natural right, in the same manner as if posterity had been continued by *creation* instead of *generation*, the latter being only the mode by which the former is carried forward; and consequently, every child born into the world must be considered as deriving its existence from God. The world is as new to him as it was to the first man that existed, and his natural right in it is of the same kind.

The Mosaic account of the creation, whether taken as divine authority, or merely historical, is full to this point, *the unity or equality of man*. The expressions admit of no controversy. "And God said, Let us make man in our own image. In the image of God created he him; male and female created he them." The distinction of sexes is pointed out, but no other distinc-

THOMAS PAINE (1737–1809)

Although THOMAS PAINE was born in England, he is best known today as one of the key ideologists of the American Revolution. His pamphlet, *Common Sense* (1776) contains his famous assertion that "government even in its best state is a necessary evil; in its worst state, an intolerable one."

In Paine's time, many people believed that a complicated system of government was the ideal one, since a multi-faceted political structure would necessarily contain enough checks and balances within it to prevent abuses by any one person or institution. Looking at England, which was usually held up as an ideal example of this type of government, Paine saw a system that had become too complicated and unable to contain enough internal controls against abuse. "The more simple anything is," said Paine, "the less liable it is to be disordered, and the easier repaired when disordered."

Upon its publication, *Common Sense* came under heavy fire from critics who disagreed with Paine's interpretation of human nature, society, and the English constitution. Historians have pointed out that this constitution was the last formal link between the colonies and England, and Paine's criticism of it enraged American and British Tories alike. In the end, though, Paine's thought became undoubtedly the major ideological inspiration for the American Revolution.

Paine also wrote *The Rights of Man* (1791), in response to Edmund Burke's 1790 commentary on the French Revolution. He believed in the doctrine of natural rights and therefore held that societal privilege should be abolished in favour of a spirit of egalitarianism. Paine viewed the newly-created United States as an ideal proving-ground for his theories about liberty and equality.

---

tion is even implied. If this be not divine authority, it is at least historical authority, and shows that the equality of man, so far from being a modern doctrine, is the oldest upon record.

It is also to be observed, that all the religions known in the world are founded, so far as they relate to man, on the *unity of man*, as being all of one degree. Whether in heaven or in hell, or in whatever state man may be supposed to exist hereafter, the good and the bad are the only distinctions. Nay, even the laws of governments are obliged to slide into this principle, by making degrees to consist in crimes, and not in persons.

It is one of the greatest of all truths, and of the highest advantage to cultivate. By considering man in this light, and by instructing him to consider himself in this light, it places him in a close connexion with all his duties, whether to his Creator, or to the creation, of which he is a part; and it is only when he forgets his origin, or, to use a more fashionable phrase, his *birth and family*, that he becomes dissolute. It is not among the least of the evils of the present existing governments in all parts of Europe, that man, considered as man, is thrown back to a vast distance from his Maker, and the artificial chasm filled up by a succession of barriers, or sort of turnpike gates, through which he has to pass. I will quote Mr Burke's catalogue of barriers that he has set up between man and his Maker. Putting himself in the character of a herald, he says—"We fear God—we look with *awe* to kings—with affection to parliaments—with duty to magistrates—with reverence to priests, and with respect to nobility." Mr Burke has forgotten to put in "*chivalry.*" He has also forgotten to put in Peter.

The duty of man is not a wilderness of turnpike gates, through which he is to pass by tickets from one to the other. It is plain and simple, and consists but of two points. His duty to God, which every man must feel; and with respect to his neighbour, to do as he would be done by. If those to whom power is delegated do well, they will be respected; if not, they will be despised: and with regard to those to whom no power is delegated, but who assume it, the rational world can know nothing of them.

Hitherto we have spoken only (and that but in part) of the natural rights of man. We have now to consider the civil rights of man, and to show how the one originates from the other. Man did not enter into society to become *worse* than he was before, nor to have fewer rights than he had before, but to have those rights better secured. His natural rights are the foundation of all his civil rights. But in order to pursue this distinction with more precision, it will be necessary to mark the different qualities of natural and civil rights.

A few words will explain this. Natural rights are those which appertain to man in right of his existence. Of this kind are all the intellectual rights, or rights of the mind, and also all those rights of acting as an individual for his own comfort and happiness, which are not injurious to the natural rights of others. Civil rights are those which appertain to man in right of his being a member of society. Every civil right has for its foundation, some natural right pre-existing in the individual, but to the enjoyment of which his individual power is not, in all cases, sufficiently competent. Of this kind are all those which relate to security and protection.

From this short review, it will be easy to distinguish between that class of natural rights which man retains after entering into society, and those which he throws into the common stock as a member of society.

The natural rights which he retains, are all those in which the *power* to execute is as perfect in the individual as the right itself. Among this class, as is before mentioned, are all the intellectual rights, or rights of the mind: consequently, religion is one of those rights. The natural rights which are not retained, are all those in which, though the right is perfect in the individual, the power to execute them is defective. They answer not his purpose. A man, by natural right, has a right to judge in his own cause; and so far as the right of mind is concerned, he never surrenders it: But what availeth it him to judge, if he has not power to redress? He therefore deposits this right in the common stock of society, and takes the arm of society, of which he is a part, in preference and in addition to his own. Society *grants* him nothing. Every man is a proprietor in society, and draws on the capital as a matter of right.

From these premises, two or three certain conclusions will follow.

First, That every civil right grows out of a natural right; or, in other words, is a natural right exchanged.

Secondly, That civil power, properly considered as such, is made up of the aggregate of that class of the natural rights of man, which becomes defective in the individual in point of power, and answers not his purpose; but when collected to a focus, becomes competent to the purpose of every one.

Thirdly, That the power produced from the aggregate of natural rights, imperfect in power in the individual, cannot be applied to invade the natural rights which are retained in the individual, and in which the power to execute is as perfect as the right itself.

We have now, in a few words, traced man from a natural individual to a member of society, and shown, or endeavoured to show, the quality of the natural rights retained, and of those which are exchanged for civil rights.

Source: Thomas Paine. *The Rights of Man.* Originally published in 1791/2.

On Liberty

John Stuart Mill

JOHN STUART MILL *(1806-1873), a British utilitarian philosopher, wrote several important philosophical works, notably* On Liberty, Utilitarianism, *and* Systems of Logic. *The first of these has had a lasting impression upon western political thought and proved to be one of the original analytical treatments of the subject of social freedom.*

The object of this essay is to assert one very simple principle, as entitled to govern absolutely the dealings of society with the individual in the way of compulsion and control, whether the means used be physical force in the form of legal penalties or the moral coercion of public opinion. That principle is that the sole end for which mankind are warranted, individually or collectively, in interfering with the liberty of action of any of their number is self-protection. That the only purpose for which power can be rightfully exercised over any member of a civilized community, against his will, is to prevent harm to others. His own good, either physical or moral, is not a sufficient warrant. He cannot rightfully be compelled to do or forbear because it will be better for him to do so, because it will make him happier, because, in the opinions of others, to do so would be wise or even right. Theses are good reasons for remonstrating with him, or reasoning with him, or persuading him, or entreating him, but not for compelling him or visiting him with any evil in case he do otherwise. To justify that, the conduct from which it is desired to deter him must be calculated to produce evil to someone else. The only part of the conduct of anyone for which he is amenable to society is that which concerns others. In the part which merely concerns himself, his independence is, of right, absolute. Over himself, over his own body and mind, the individual is sovereign.

It is, perhaps, hardly necessary to say that this doctrine is meant to apply only to human beings in the maturity of their faculties. We are not speaking of children or of young persons below the age which the law may fix as that of manhood or womanhood. Those who are still in a state to require being taken care of by others must be protected against their own actions as well as against external injury. For the same reason we may leave out of consideration those backward states of society in which the race itself may be considered as in its nonage. The early difficulties in the way of spontaneous progress are so great that there is seldom any choice of means for overcoming them; and a ruler full of the spirit of improvement is warranted in the use of any expedients that will attain an end perhaps otherwise unattainable. Despotism is a legitimate mode of government in dealing with barbarians, provided the end be their improvement and the means justified by actually effecting that end. Liberty, as a principle, has no application to any state of things anterior to the time when mankind have become capable of being improved by free and equal discussion. Until then, there is nothing to them but implicit obedience to an Akbar or a Charlemagne if they are so fortunate as to find one. But as soon as mankind have attained the capacity of being guided to their own improvement by conviction or persuasion (a period long since reached in all nations with whom we need here concern ourselves), compulsion, either in the direct form or in that of pains and penalties for noncompliance, is no longer admissible as a means to their own good, and justifiable only for the security of others.

It is proper to state that I forego any advantage which could be derived to my argument from the idea of abstract right as a thing independent of utility. I regard utility as the ultimate appeal on all ethical questions; but it must be utility in the largest sense, grounded on the permanent interests of man as a progressive being. Those interests, I contend, authorize the subjection of individual spontaneity to external control only in respect to those actions of each which concern the interest of other people. If anyone does an act hurtful to others, there is a *prima facie* case for punishing him by law or, where legal penalties are not safely applicable, by general disapprobation. There are also many positive acts for the benefit of others which he may rightfully be compelled to perform, such as to give evidence in a court of justice, to bear his fair share in the common defense or in any other joint work necessary to the interest of the society of which he enjoys the protection, and to perform certain acts of individual beneficence, such as saving a fellow creature's life or interposing to protect the defenseless against ill usage—things

JOHN STUART MILL (1806-1873)

JOHN STUART MILL was an English philosopher and political economist who is best remembered today as the leading nineteenth-century exponent of utilitarianism. Mill was educated by his father James and by the utilitarian philosopher Jeremy Bentham. Popular accounts hold that the younger Mill had mastered classical Greek by the age of three, and Latin at age eight. While his tutors were prominent utilitarian philosophers in their own rights, it was John Stuart Mill who truly defined this school of thought for successive generations.

In its simplest form, utilitarianism advocates acting in ways that produce the greatest amount of pleasure or happiness in the greatest number of people. It is easy to see how this way of thinking is tied directly to the most basic kind of democracy, wherein a numerical majority in a given population gains the right to decide on an issue of common concern. Al-

though his father and Bentham advocated this type of "strict" utilitarianism, Mill's version was somewhat less rigid.

Although utilitarianism appears to be the guiding principle for the ideal liberal democratic state, Mill warned of what he called the "tyranny of the majority," situations in which undue pressure is brought to bear upon people who are not in agreement with the popular will. Hypothetically, a majority of

51% of a population, if aligned ideologically on a number of issues, could possess a "tyrannical" decision-making authority over the rest of their fellow citizens in a given democracy. In his famous essay *On Liberty* (1859) Mill advocated the principles of freedom of thought and expression as counter-balances to the "greatest happiness" ideal. Mill believed that the threat of majority tyranny could be seriously undermined if a diverse exchange of ideas was promoted within society.

In the end, Mill occupied a middle ground—some commentators have called it the "best of both worlds"—between his support for social cohesion and individual liberty. He further expounded his philosophical and political theories in *Considerations on Representative Government* (1861), *Utilitarianism* (1863), and *The Subjection of Women* (1869).

which whenever it is obviously a man's duty to do he may rightfully be made responsible to society for not doing. A person may cause evil to others not only by his actions but by his inaction, and in either case he is justly accountable to them for the injury. The latter case, it is true, requires a much more cautious exercise of compulsion than the former. To make anyone answerable for doing evil to others is the rule; to make him answerable for not preventing evil is, comparatively speaking, the exception. Yet there are many cases clear enough and grave enough to justify that exception. In all things which regard the external relations of the individual, he is *de jure* amenable to those whose interests are concerned, and, if need be, to society as their protector. There are often good reasons for not holding him to the responsibility; but these reasons must arise from the special expedien-

cies of the case; either because it is a kind of case in which he is on the whole likely to act better when left to his own discretion than when controlled in any way in which society have it in their power to control him; or because the attempt to exercise control would produce other evils, greater than those which it would prevent. When such reasons as these preclude the enforcement of responsibility, the conscience of the agent himself should step into the vacant judgement seat and protect those interests of others which have no external protection; judging himself all the more rigidly, because the case does not admit of this being made accountable to the judgement of his fellow creatures.

But there is a sphere of action in which society, as distinguished from the individual, has, if any, only an indirect interest: comprehending all that portion of a person's life and conduct which affects only himself or, if it also affects others, only with their free, voluntary, and undeceived consent and participation. When I say only himself, I mean directly and in the first instance; for whatever affects himself may affect others through himself: and the objection which may be grounded on this contingency will receive consideration in the sequel. This, then, is the appropriate region of human liberty. It comprises, first, the inward domain of consciousness, demanding liberty of conscience in the most comprehensive sense, liberty of thought and feeling, absolute freedom of opinion and sentiment on all subjects, practical or speculative, scientific, moral, or theological. The liberty of expressing and publishing opinions may seem to fall under a different principle, since it belongs to that part of the conduct of an individual which concerns other people, but, being almost of as much importance as the liberty of thought itself and resting in great part on the same reasons, is practically inseparable from it. Secondly, the principle requires liberty of tastes and pursuits, of framing the plan of our life to suit our own character, of doing as we like, subject to such consequences as may follow, without impediment from our fellow creatures, so long as what we do does not harm them, even though they should think our conduct foolish, perverse, or wrong. Thirdly, from this liberty of each individual follows the liberty, within the same limits, of combination among individuals; freedom to untie for any purpose not involving harm to others: the persons combining being supposed to be of full age and not forced or deceived.

No society in which these liberties are not, on the whole, respected is free, whatever may be its form of government; and none is completely free in which they do no exist absolute and unqualified. The only freedom which deserves the name is that of pursuing our own good in our own way, so long as we do not attempt to deprive others of theirs or impede their efforts to obtain it. Each is the proper guardian of his own health, whether bodily *or* mental and spiritual. Mankind are greater gainers by suffering each other to live as seems good to themselves than by compelling each to live as seems good to the rest.

Source: John Stuart Mill. *On Liberty.* Originally published in 1859.

The Lockean Solution

Deborah Baumgold

DEBORAH BAUMGOLD *is Associate Professor of Political Science at the University of Oregon. She is the author of* Hobbe's Political Theory *(Cambridge University Press) and is currently working on a book on the treatment of violence in democratic thought.*

> Force, or a declared design of force upon the Person of another, where there is no common Superior on Earth to appeal to for relief, *is the State of War.* Locke, *Second Treatise of Government,* 3.19

Starting with the very suppositions about violence, civil society, and governmental accountability that underpinned Grotian and Hobbesian absolutism, Locke produced the definitive, modern brief for the right of resistance, popular sovereignty, and the accountability of government to the people. To stand late medieval absolutism on its head, we will see, he conceptualized the right of rebellion in a way that defused and tamed the resistance question. But the lineaments of modern, pacified politics are only incompletely sketched in the *Second Treatise.* Locke, like Hobbes, is a transitional figure, who envisions pacified society, yet by and large continues to associate governmental accountability with violent political conflict.

Two root assumptions that Locke held in common with Grotius and Hobbes were that the use of force by private individuals is inimical to civil society and that the principle of governmental accountability licenses violent conflict and rebellion. As I noted at the outset, his definition of political or civil society echoes Hobbes's in making renunciation by private individuals of the right to use force the defining feature of civil society:

> There, and there only is *Political Society*, where every one of the Members hath quitted this natural Power, resign'd it up into the hands of the Community in all cases that exclude him not from appealing for Protection to the Law established by it.[1]

Locke's account of the state of nature differs from Hobbes's, of course, in placing natural law limits on the right of the private sword, which may legitimately be used only for the purposes of preserving property, broadly defined, and punishing violations of the law of nature.[2] But he does not imagine that these natural law limits spawn a peaceful society. In the absence of a common authority to decide disputes among people, according to one vein of Lockean argument, any outbreak of aggressive violence is likely to escalate into continuous conflict and this would make the state of nature an ongoing state of war: "In the State of Nature, for want of positive Laws, and Judges with Authority to appeal to, *the State of War once begun, continues,* with a right to the innocent Party, to destroy the other whenever he can."[3] The argument casts as right what Hobbes had observed as fact about the state of nature. So long as some are aggressive in that state, the latter had argued: "If others, that otherwise would be glad to be at ease within modest bounds, should not by invasion increase their power, they would not be able, long time, by standing only on their defence, to subsist."[4] From the insecurity of the state of nature, if follows for Locke that renunciation of the right of punishment and creation of a state monopoly on that right are the foundation of civil society and government:

> 'Tis this makes them so willingly give up every one his single power of punishing to be exercised by such alone as shall be appointed to it amongst them; and by such Rules as the Community, or those authorised by them to that purpose, shall agree on. And in this we have the original *right and rise* of both *the Legislative and Executive Power,* as well as the Governments and Societies themselves.[5]

Yet Locke also, famously, defends the right of the people to remove a tyrannous government that violates the trust of the people. Where Hobbes translated the Grotian "absolutist" contract from a contingent into a necessary proposition, Locke universalizes the Grotian "accountability" contract: rulers are always, not merely sometimes, responsible to the people. "The Legislative being only a Fiduciary Power to act for certain ends, there remains still *in the People a Supream Power* to remove or *alter the Legislative,* when they find the *Legislative* act contrary to the trust reposed in them."[6] The Grotian-Hobbesian absolutist contract is untenable for two reasons. As God's creatures, we are not at liberty to consent to slavery or to absolute subjection, and self-preservation is, therefore, a "Fundamental, Sacred, and unalterable Law."[7] To arrive at the conclusion that tyrannous governments may be forcibly resisted, Locke only needs to add (following Grotius but contra Hobbes) the private law principle that the inalienable right of self-preservation applies to societies as well as to individuals.[8]

Nonetheless, he agrees with Grotius and with Hobbes that the right of rebellion is *antithetical* to political society: "this Power of the People" to defend themselves against tyrannous government "can never take place till the Government be dissolved."[9] At this crucial point in the argument, Locke reverses and advances on the arguments of his absolutist predecessors by conceptualizing the right of rebellion as an extraordinary right, which comes into force only in the special circumstances of a "state of war:"[10]

Whenever the Legislators endeavour to take away, and destroy the Property of the People, or to reduce them to Slavery under Arbitrary Power, they put themselves into a state of War with the People, who are thereupon absolved from any farther Obedience, and are left to the common Refuge, which God hath provided for all Men against Force and Violence.[11]

The introduction of the technical concept of a "state of war," as a juridical condition distinct from civil society and from the state of nature, was a simple and brilliant conceptual move. It effectively defused the resistance issue by distinguishing the right of rebellion from private warfare. The right of rebellion does not violate the ban on private warfare that defines civil society because it is an extraordinary right that obtains only when tyrannous rulers have themselves subverted civil society.[12]

The idea of a "state of war" was a natural extension of "private law" resistance doctrine and, in effect, renders that doctrine compatible with the absolutists' position that resistance is inconsistent with civil society. Before Locke, other "private law" thinkers had described tyrants as rebelling against the people,[13] and this was a stock argument of radical Whigs in the early 1680s.[14] From this point it was a short step to define the resistance situation as a special juridical circumstance. Nor was Locke alone in using the idea of a "state of war."[15] In a 1657 diatribe against Cromwell, *Killing Noe Murder*, for example, Edward Sexby had characterized a usurper as being in a "state of war with every man"; "therefore everything is lawful against him that is lawful against an open enemy, whom every private man has a right to kill."[16]

Does the concept of a state of war provide anything more than a conceptual solution to the problem of reconciling resistance with the idea of a pacified society? The supporting Lockean argument parallels Grotius's defense of the private law proposition that private warfare is legitimate in circumstances of extreme and imminent peril. He defines a "state of war" by the use of "force, or a declared design of force upon the Person of another, where there is no common Superior on Earth to appeal to for relief."[17] Just so, Grotius had said that private warfare is licensed within organized society when the "judicial procedure ceases to be available."[18] Locke then draws the traditional analogy between individual self-defense against immediate attack and collective defense against tyranny. Both are circumstances in which judicial relief is unavailable: "where [the law] cannot interpose to secure my Life from present force," a person is permitted the "liberty to kill the aggressor, because the aggressor allows not time to appeal to our common Judge, nor the decision of the Law."[19] Similarly, rebellion is legitimate when, in the face of tyranny, "the Appeal lies only to Heaven."[20] So far in the argument, there would appear to be little substantive difference between the Lockean concept of an extraordinary right of rebellion and the Grotian Private law stipulation that imminent peril licenses private warfare.

To be more than a novel conceptualization, the distinction between civil society and a state of war needed to be accompanied by a distinction between violent resistance and the principle of governmental accountability. Only when, in practice and in theory, the latter principle came to be firmly separated from the specter of violent conflict would the resistance issue finally be tamed. This development is but sketchily anticipated by Locke, whose principal concern lay with justifying the right of rebellion rather than with elaborating various dimensions of accountability.

Let us turn, then, to his discussions of the political conditions of civil society. Having defined rebellion as an *un*civil action, Locke could controvert the absolutists' position that conditional authority is antithetical to civil society. To the contrary, he argues on both formal and empirical grounds, it is unconditional authority that violates the terms of civil society. In principle, absolute monarchy is inconsistent with civil society because an absolute prince remains, in effect, in a state of nature with respect to his subjects: there is no common authority to adjudicate conflicts between them.[21] An absolutist state is actually worse than the state of nature because in it subjects have renounced the right of punishment: "By supposing they have given up themselves to the *absolute Arbitrary Power* and will of a Legislator, they have disarmed themselves, and armed him, to make prey of them when he pleases."[22] Second, Locke calls into question empirically the (Hobbesian) contention that conditional authority fosters civil war.[23] Granted, the ambition of private men has sometimes been the cause of great disorder:

But whether the *mischief* hath *oftner* begun *in the Peoples Wantonness*, and a Desire to cast off the lawful Authority of their Rulers; or *in the Rulers Insolence*, and

Endeavours to get, and exercise an Arbitrary Power over their People; whether Oppression, or Disobedience gave the first rise to the Disorder, I leave it to impartial History to determine.[24]

If violence is inimical to civil society and if civil society requires conditional political authority, it follows that there needs to be an ordinary, institutionalized, and *nonviolent* process of holding governments to account: in short, civil society requires peaceful electoral politics. This final step in the development of the idea of pacified politics is only intimated in the *Second Treatise*. It is suggested by the statement that parliamentary sovereignty is the one form of government consistent with civil society: "the People…could never be safe nor at rest, *nor think themselves in Civil Society*, till the Legislature was placed in collective Bodies of Men, call them Senate, Parliament, or what you please.[25] Yet Locke expressly grants that popular consent may underwrite hereditary monarchy as well as "elective" monarchy in which authority is held for life.[26] Rebellion being the sole mechanism of governmental accountability in these latter forms of government, it cannot be said to be a Lockean principle that a legitimate political society *must* have an electoral political system (and a peaceful electoral system at that).[27]

At the most, what can be said is that Locke preferred parliamentary sovereignty,[28] that he counted it among the tyrannous acts that dissolve government for a prince to interfere with parliamentary elections,[29] and, arguably, that he conceived of electoral politics and violent rebellion as alternative mechanisms of holding government to account. Richard Ashcraft has made the case that radical Whigs in the period, including Locke, presupposed the electoral alternative and came to espouse rebellion only after the failure of parliamentary efforts to exclude the Duke of York from the Throne.[30] Perhaps this is Locke's meaning in an elusive remark at the conclusion of the *Second Treatise*: "If any Men find themselves aggrieved who so proper to *Judge* as the Body of the *People*? But if the Prince, or whoever they be in the Administration, decline that way of Determination, the Appeal then lies no where but to Heaven."[31] To view elections as an alternative to the "appeal to Heaven" is not quite the same, however, as identifying a nonviolent electoral process as a necessary feature of civil society. Locke pointed the way to that conclusion by conceptualizing the right of rebellion as a extraordinary right, but the complementary principle that civil society requires ordinary, peaceful means of holding government to account eluded him. Like Grotius and Hobbes, his attention remained fixed on violent political conflict.

Source: Deborah Baumgold. " Pacifying Politics: Resistance, Violence, and Accountability in Seventeenth-Century Contract Theory." *Political Theory* 21, No.1 (1993): 6-27. Reprinted by permission of Sage Publications, Inc.

Notes

[1] *Second Treatise*, 7.87, in *Two Treatises of Government*, edited by Peter Laslett (Cambridge University Press, 1960) p.367. See also 7.89, pp.368-69, and 15.171, p.428.

[2] Ibid., 15.171, p.428. The idea that individuals in the state of nature possess the right to use the sword to enforce natural law was developed by Jacques Almain in an early sixteenth-century conciliarist tract: see Quentin Skinner, *The Foundations of Modern Political Thought*, Volume 2 (Cambridge University Press, 1978) vol. 2, pp.118-19.

[3] *Second Treatise*, 3.20, edited by C.B. McPherson (Harmondsworth: Penguin/Pelican, 1968) p.322.

[4] *Leviathan*, 13, pp.184-85.

[5] *Second Treatise*, 3.127, p.397.

[6] Ibid., 13.149, p.413.

[7] Ibid.; see also 4.23, p.325.

[8] Ibid., 19.220, p.459: "the *Society* can never lose the Native and original Right it has to preserve it self."

[9] Ibid., 13.149, p.413. Locke distinguishes the dissolution of government, which tyranny produces, from the dissolution of society through foreign conquest (19.211-12, pp.454-56; see also 19.243, p.477). Regarding the distinction, see Ashcraft, *Revolutionary Politics* and Locke's *Two Treatises of Government* (Princeton: Princeton University Press, 1986, 575-77. Julian H. Franklin argues that George Lawson, in *Politica sacra et civilis* (1660), originated the argument that power reverts to the people upon the dissolution of government. Franklin, *John Locke and the Theory of Sovereignty* (Cambridge: Cambridge University Press, paperback ed., 1981), chaps. 3-4.

[10] *Second Treatise*, 19.212, pp.455-56: "Civil Society being a State of Peace, amongst those who are of it, from whom the State of War is excluded by the Umpirage. When any one, or more, shall take upon them to make Laws, whom the People have not appointed so to do, they make Laws without Authority, which the People are not therefore bound to obey; by which means they come again to be out of subjection, and may constitute to themselves a *new Legislative*, as they think best, being in full liberty to resist the force of those, who without Authority would impose any thing upon them."

[11] Ibid., 19.222, pp.460-61; see also 18.205, p.450, and 11 19.226-227, p.464.

[12] Ibid., 19.226, p.464: "For when Men by entering into Society and Civil Government, have excluded force, and introduced Laws for the preservation of Property, Peace, and Unity amongst themselves; those who set up force in opposition to the Laws, do *Rebellare*, that is, bring back again the state of War, and are properly Rebels." See also.227, p.464, and 19.212, pp.455-56.

[13] Skinner, *Foundations*, vol. 2, pp.201-2, discusses Luther's use of the argument in a *Warning to His Dear German People* (1531): tyrants "are the real rebels, since they are nothing but 'assassins and traitors', refusing to 'submit to government and law', and are thus ' much closer to the name and quality which is termed rebellion' than those whom they accuse of being in rebellion against their supposed authority."

[14] Ashcraft, *Revolutionary Politics*, pp.195-97, 392-405; and "Revolutionary Politics and Locke's *Two Treatises of Government*," *Political Theory* 8 (1980): 469-74.

[15] Ashcraft ("Revolutionary Politics," 444; see also *Revolutionary Politics*, 236) claims the concept, along with other key Lockean terms, first appears in James Tyrell's *Patriarcha non monarcha* (1681). He also quotes the use of the phrase in a 1682 tract by Robert Ferguson: "whensoever laws cease to be a security unto men, they will be sorely tempted to apprehend themselves cast into a state of war, and justified in having recourse to the best means they can for their shelter and defense" (*Revolutionary Politics*, 322).

[16] William Allen [Edward Sexby], *Killing Noe Murder: Briefly Discourst in Three Quaestions* (1657), in Wootton, ed., *Divine Right*, 374-75. My thanks to Alan Houston for bringing this point to my attention.

[17] *Second Treatise*, 3.19, p.321.

[18] *De Jure Belli*, 1.3.2, p.92.

[19] *Second Treatise*, 3.19, p.321.

[20] Ibid., 19.242, p.477; see also 14.168, p.426, and 18.207, p.451.

[21] Ibid., 7.90, p.369; see also.94, pp.372-74, and 15.174, p.421. Cf. Hobbes, who argues from the absence of an authority to adjudicate conflicts between ruler and ruled to the absurdity of *conditional* sovereignty: "there is in this case, no Judge to decide the controversie: it returns therefore to the Sword again; and every man recovereth the right of Protecting himselfe by his own strength, contrary to the designe they had in the Institution" (*Leviathan*, 18, pp.230-31).

[22] *Second Treatise*, 11.137, p.405; see also 7.93, p.372.

[23] Ibid., 19.228, p.465.

[24] Ibid., 19.230, pp.466-67.

[25] Ibid., 7.94, p.373. It is worth noticing, however, that Locke bases the statement on the principle that rulers must be subject to law, rather than on the requirements of civil society: "By [this] means every single person became subject, equally with other the meanest Men, to those Laws, which he himself, as part of the Legislative had established."

[26] Ibid., 10.132, pp.399-400.

[27] Cf. John Plamenatz, *Man and Society*, vol. 1 (New York: McGraw-Hill, 1963), 231: "Locke nowhere makes it a *condition* of there being government by consent that authority to make laws should belong to an elected assembly. Where he condemns absolute monarchy as inconsistent with civil society and says that the absolute prince is in a state of nature in relation to his subjects, he is only attacking the doctrine that the prince is above the law and his subjects owe him unconditional obedience; he is not suggesting that, except where legislative power belongs to an elected assembly, there is not government by consent." See also 228-29, 237, 241.

[28] *Second Treaties*, 12.143, p.410. Locke's reasoning here echoes that discussed in note 75 above: parliamentary sovereignty serves the principle that rulers must themselves be subject to law. "Therefore in well order'd Commonwealths … the Legislative Power is put into the hands of divers Persons who dully Assembled, have by themselves, or jointly with others, a Power to make Laws, which when they have done, being separated again, they are themselves subject to the Laws, they have made; which is a new and near tie upon them, to take care, that they make them for the publick good." See also 11.138, pp.406-7

[29] Ibid., 19.216, p.457.

[30] Ashcraft, *Revolutionary Politics*, chaps. 5-7, 11 throughout.

[31] *Second Treatise*, 19.242, pp.476-77. John Dunn interprets the passage in this vein in *The Political Thought of John Locke: An Historical Account of the Argument of the 'Two Treatises of Government'* (Cambridge: Cambridge University Press, 1969), 182.

2

Reform Liberalism

The Ideals of Tempered Individualism and Toleration

In the nineteenth century, philosophers such as Robert Owen and T.H. Green perceived defects in the ideals of classical liberalism. Consequently, they developed two independent political schools of thought—democratic socialism (Owen) and reform liberalism (Green). The latter school of thought becomes more fully articulated in the twentieth century when the vulnerability of the individual to the forces of industry, economy and war are reappreciated. John Dewey is certainly among the first to raise the banner of reform liberalism that Green had so nobly elevated.

Dewey recognizes the importance of radical though non-violent measures to change the repressive institutions affecting the latent abilities of persons. In this respect, he sees room for state action to correct injustices which inhibit individual growth. By rejecting the *laissez faire* mentality of classical liberals, John Maynard Keynes ends up sharing Dewey's belief that state action is sometimes called for, especially in the economic arena. What emerges in Keynes' notion of semi-autonomous bodies within the state is neither rugged individualism nor pristine socialism, but rather a kind of tempered individualism. This same kind of individualism is found clearly in the writings of John Rawls, especially in his phrase "justice as fairness", which functions as a notion covering an amalgam of other concepts including rights, liberties, opportunities and equality.

All of these ideas—when converted into appropriate principles—yield, together with the recognition that there is no agreed conception of the good, what logicians would call a higher-ordered principle of toleration. It is this principle which complements the view of tempered individualism. William Galston attempts to flesh out the details of this tempered indi-

vidualism by talking in terms of liberal virtues, including those which are general and those that are specific to society, economics and politics. In Galston's view, these virtues are necessary to sustain the liberal state.

Christine Sypnowich's analysis takes us back in part to the classical statement of reform liberalism, namely the writings of John Rawls. She suggests that a feminist theory requires a new conceptual apparatus which would pull together the strengths of Rawls' liberalism and the strengths of his main critics, the communitarians. The new conceptual apparatus that Sypnowich presents would involve an innovative reworking of Marxist political theory.

In tracing the Kantian lineage of Rawls' thinking, Annette Baier criticizes it as fatally flawed. It is Baier's conclusion that the Kantian approach fails in two important ways. First, it does not deal appropriately with the important notion of shared responsibility, and secondly, it fails to provide for the basis of a democratic society. Finally, Susan Okin points out not only the pervasive gender bias in both the Kantian and Rawlsian scheme of things, but also the specific tendency of the latter to banish a large part of women's lives from the scope of a theory on justice. The effect of her analysis is to raise fundamental questions about the adequacy of the reform liberal theory of justice.

The tension between an ideal of liberty and an ideal of equality forces reform liberals to allow for the emergence of an individual much more tempered than the one envisioned by John Locke and Adam Smith. This same tension produces in reform liberals a recognition that one purchases peace by acknowledging a principle of toleration. Although tempered individualism and toleration thus emerge as ideals of reform liberals, they seem to rest upon more deeply embedded ideals of liberty and equality. These ideals do not turn out to be the happiest of partners.

Renascent Liberalism

John Dewey

JOHN DEWEY *(1859-1952) was an influential American philosopher who wrote widely in the field of education and social philosophy. Studying at Johns Hopkins University, he went on to positions at the University of Michigan and University of Chicago where he established a reputation for his educational ideas. His most important writings are* Experience and Nature, Logic: the Theory of Inquiry, *and* Liberalism and Social Action.

When, then, I say that the first object of a renascent liberalism is education, I mean that its task is to aid in producing the habits of mind and character, the intellectual and moral patterns, that are somewhere near even with the actual movements of events. It is, I repeat, the split between the latter as they have externally occurred and the ways of desiring, thinking, and of putting emotion and purpose into execution that is the basic cause of present confusion in mind and paralysis in action. The educational task cannot be accomplished merely by working upon men's minds, without action that effects actual change in institutions. The idea that dispositions and attitudes can be altered by merely "moral" means conceived of as something that goes on wholly inside of persons is itself one of the old patterns that has to be changed. Thought, desire and purpose exist in a constant give and take of interaction with environing conditions. But resolute thought is the first step in that change of action that will itself carry further the needed change in patterns of mind and character.

In short, liberalism must now become radical, meaning by "radical" perception of the necessity of thorough-going changes in the set-up of institutions and corresponding activity to bring the changes to pass. For the gulf between what the actual situation makes possible and the actual state itself is so great that it cannot be bridged by piecemeal policies undertaken *ad hoc*. The process of producing the changes will be, in any case, a gradual one. But "reforms" that deal now with this abuse and now with that without having a social goal based upon an inclusive plan, differ entirely from effort at re-forming, in its literal sense, the institutional scheme of things. The liberals of more than a century ago were denounced in their time as subversive radicals, and only when the new economic order was established did they become apologists for the *status quo* or else content with social patchwork. If radicalism be defined as perception of need for radical change, then today any liberalism which is not also radicalism is irrelevant and doomed.

But radicalism also means, in the minds of many, both supporters and opponents, dependence upon use of violence as the main method of effecting drastic changes. Here the liberal parts company. For he is committed to the organization of intelligent action as the chief method. Any frank discussion of the issue must recognize the extent to which those who decry the use of any violence are themselves willing to resort to violence and are ready to put their will into operation. Their fundamental objection is to change in the economic institution that now exists, and for its maintenance they resort to the use of the force that is placed in their hands by this very institution. They do not need to advocate the use of force; their only need is to employ it. Force, rather than intelligence, is built into the procedures of the existing social system, regularly as coercion, in times of crisis as overt violence. The legal system, conspicuously in its penal aspect, more subtly in civil practice, rests upon coercion. Wars are the methods recurrently used in settlement of disputes between nations. One school of radicals dwells upon the fact that in the past the transfer of power in one society has either been accomplished by or attended with violence. But what we need to realize is that physical force is used, at least in the form of coercion, in the very set-up of our society. That the competitive system, which was thought of by early liberals as the means by which the latent abilities of individuals were to be evoked and directed into socially useful channels, is now in fact a state of scarcely disguised battle hardly needs to be dwelt upon. That the control of the means of production by the few in legal possession operates as a standing agency of coercion of the many, may need emphasis in statement, but is surely evident to one who is willing to observe and honestly report the existing scene. It is foolish to regard the political state as the only agency now endowed with coercive power. Its exercise of this power is pale in contrast

JOHN DEWEY (1859-1952)

John Dewey was an American pragmatist philosopher who had a profound impact on educational theory in the US in the early part of the 20th century. He wrote an enormous number of books and articles, the best-known of which were *Experience and Nature* (1925), *Liberalism and Social Action* (1935), and *Logic: The Theory of Inquiry* (1938). Dewey taught and developed his ideas about education and political theory at the University of Michigan, the University of Chicago, and Columbia University.

Dewey acquired his undergraduate degree at the University of Vermont and his doctorate at Johns Hopkins University. He was heavily influenced by psychologist Stanley Hall and the idealist philosopher George S. Morris. Prior to completing his doctorate, Dewey taught high school for several years. His experience in the classroom later inspired much of

his writing on educational problems. While at the University of Chicago he originated the University Elementary School, the first experimental school of education, known popularly as the "Laboratory School."

Dewey's political thought was based on his conviction that a democratic society is impossible to achieve without the fullest possible education of its citizens. His pragmatic view also

maintained that it was impossible for people, and by extension societies, to progress without the creation of social conditions that encourage free inquiry and unobstructed access to knowledge. Dewey's thoughts on education were not pursued abstractly. "The educational task cannot be accomplished merely by working upon men's minds," he wrote, " without action that effects actual change in institutions." For Dewey, it was impossible to regard thoughts and the actions that follow them as having their origins entirely within a person; the environment in which a person exists is also partly responsible for what they think and do. Education, however, still has a crucial role in shaping that environment: "Resolute thought is the first step in that change of action that will itself carry further the needed patterns of mind and character."

with that exercised by concentrated and organized property interests.

It is not surprising in view of our standing dependence upon the use of coercive force that at every time of crisis coercion breaks out into open violence. In this country, with its tradition of violence fostered by frontier conditions and by the conditions under which immigration went on during the greater part of our history, resort to violence is especially recurrent on the part of those who are in power. In times of imminent change, our verbal and sentimental worship of the Constitution, with its guarantees of civil liberties of expression, publication and assemblage, readily goes overboard. Often the officials of the law are the worst offenders, acting as agents of some power that rules the economic life of a community. What is said about the value of free speech as a safety valve is then forgotten with the utmost of ease: a comment,

perhaps, upon the weakness of the defense of freedom of expression that values it simply as a means of blowing-off steam.

It is not pleasant to face the extent to which, as matter of fact, coercive and violent force is relied upon in the present social system as a means of social control. It is much more agreeable to evade the fact. But unless the fact is acknowledged as a fact in its full depth and breadth, the meaning of dependence upon intelligence as the alternative method of social direction will not be grasped. Failure in acknowledgment signifies, among other things, failure to realize that those who propagate the dogma of dependence upon force have the sanction of much that is already entrenched in the existing system. They would but turn the use of it to opposite ends. The assumption that the method of intelligence already rules and that those who urge the use of violence are introducing a new element into the social picture may not be hypo-critical but it is unintelligently unaware of what is actually involved in intelligence as an alternative method of social action.

I begin with an example of what is really involved in the issue. Why is it, apart from our tradition of violence, that liberty of expression is tolerated and even lauded when social affairs seem to be going in a quiet fashion, and yet is so readily destroyed whenever matters grow critical? The general answer, of course, is that at bottom social institutions have habituated us to the use of force in some veiled form. But a part of the answer is found in our ingrained habit of regarding intelligence as an individual possession and its exercise as an individual right. It is false that freedom of inquiry and of expression are not modes of action. They are exceedingly potent modes of action. The reactionary grasps this fact, in practice if not in express idea, more quickly than the liberal, who is too much given to holding that this freedom is innocent of consequences, as well as being a merely individual right. The result is that this liberty is tolerated as long as it does not seem to menace in any way the *status quo* of society. When it does, every effort is put forth to identify the established order with the public good. When this identification is established, it follows that any merely individual right must yield to the general welfare. As long as freedom of thought and speech is claimed as a merely individual right, it will give way, as do other merely personal claims, when it is, or is successfully represented to be, in opposition to the general welfare.

I would not in the least disparage the noble fight waged by early liberals in behalf of individual freedom of thought and expression. We owe more to them than it is possible to record in words. No more eloquent words have ever come from any one than those of Justice Brandeis in the case of a legislative act that in fact restrained freedom of political expression. He said:

> Those who won our independence believed that the final end of the State was to make men free to develop their faculties, and that in its government the deliberative faculties should prevail over the arbitrary. They valued liberty both as an end and as a means. They believed liberty to be the secret of happiness and courage to be the secret of liberty. They believed that freedom to think as you will and to speak as you think are means indispensable to the discovery and spread of political truth; that without free speech and assembly discussion would be futile; that with them, discussion affords ordinarily adequate protection against the dissemination of noxious doctrines; that the greatest menace to freedom is an inert people; that public discussion is a political duty; and that this should be a fundamental principle of the American government.

This is the creed of a fighting liberalism. But the issue I am raising is connected with the fact that these words are found in a dissenting, a minority opinion of the Supreme Court of the United States. The public function of free individual thought and speech is clearly recognized in the words quoted. But the reception of the truth of the words is met by an obstacle: the old habit of defending liberty of thought and expression as something inhering in individuals apart from and even in opposition to social claims.

Source: John Dewey. *Liberalism and Social Action.* New York: Capricorn Books, G.P. Putnam's Sons, 1963. Reprinted by permission of The Putnam Publishing Group from *Liberalism and Social Action* by John Dewey. Copyright © 1935 Renewed copyright by Roberta L. Dewey.

Laissez-Faire and Communism

John Maynard Keynes

JOHN MAYNARD KEYNES *(1883-1946) was one of the most influential economists of the twentieth century. His best known works are* A Treatise on Money; The General Theory of Employment, Interest and Money; *and* A Treatise on Probability.

The Assumptions of Economic Individualism

The principles of *laissez-faire* have had other allies besides economic text-books. They have been reinforced by the poor quality of the opponent proposals—Protectionism on one hand, and Marxian Socialism on the other. Yet these doctrines are both characterized, not only or chiefly by their infringing the general presumption in favour of *laissez-faire*, but by mere logical fallacy. Both are examples of poor thinking, of inability to analyse a process and follow it out to its conclusion. The arguments against them, though reinforced by the principle of *laissez-faire*, do not strictly require it. Of the two, Protectionism is at least plausible, and the forces making for its popularity are nothing to wonder at. But Marxian Socialism must always remain a portent to the historians of Opinion—how a doctrine so illogical and so dull can have exercised so powerful and enduring an influence over the minds of men, and, through them, the events of history. At any rate, the obvious scientific deficiencies of these two schools greatly contributed to the prestige and authority of nineteenth-century *laissez-faire*.

Nor has the most notable divergence into centralised social action on a great scale—the conduct of the late war—encouraged reformers or dispelled old-fashioned prejudices. There is much to be said on both sides. War experience in the organisation of socialised production has left some observers anxious to repeat it in peace conditions. War socialism unquestionably achieved a production of wealth on a scale far greater than we ever knew in Peace, for though the goods and services delivered were destined for immediate and fruitless extinction, none the less they were wealth. Nevertheless the dissipation of effort was also prodigious, and the atmosphere of waste and not counting the cost was disgusting to any thrifty or provident spirit.

Finally, Individualism and *laissez-faire* could not, in spite of their deep roots in the political and moral philosophies of the late eighteenth and early nineteenth centuries, have secured their lasting hold over the conduct of public affairs, if it had not been for their conformity with the needs and wishes of the business world of the day. They gave full scope to our erstwhile heroes, the great business men. "At least one-half of the best ability in the Western world," Marshall used to say, "is engaged in business." A great part of "the higher imagination" of the age was thus employed. It was on the activities of these men that our hopes of Progress were centred. "Men of this class," Marshall wrote,

> live in constantly shifting visions, fashioned in their own brains, of various routes to their desired end; of the difficulties which Nature will oppose to them on each route, and of the contrivances by which they hope to get the better of her opposition. This imagination gains little credit with the people, because it is not allowed to run riot; its strength is disciplined by a stronger will; and its highest glory is to have attained great ends by means so simple that no one will know, and none but experts will even guess, how a dozen other expedients, each suggesting as much brilliancy to the hasty observer, were set aside in favour of it. The imagination of such a man is employed, like that of the master chess-player, in forecasting the obstacles which may be opposed to the successful issue of his far-reaching projects, and constantly rejecting brilliant suggestions because he has pictured to himself the counter-strokes to them. His strong nervous force is at the opposite extreme of human nature from that nervous irresponsibility which conceives hasty Utopian schemes, and which is rather to be compared to the bold facility of a weak player, who will speedily solve the most difficult chess problem by taking on himself to move the black men as well as the white.[1]

This is a fine picture of the great Captain of Industry, the Master-Individualist, who serves us in serving himself, just as any other artist does. Yet this one, in his turn, is becoming a tarnished idol. We grow more doubtful whether it is he who will lead us into Paradise by the hand.

These many elements have contributed to the current intellectual bias, the mental make-up, the orthodoxy of the day. The compelling force of many of the original reasons has disappeared, but, as usual, the vitality of the conclusions outlasts them. To suggest social action for the public good to the City of London is like discussing the *Origin of Species* with a Bishop sixty years ago. The first reaction is not intellectual, but moral. An orthodoxy is in question, and the more persuasive the arguments the graver the offence. Nevertheless, venturing into the den of the lethargic monster, at any rate I have traced his claims

JOHN MAYNARD KEYNES (1883-1946)

John Maynard Keynes was the author of *The General Theory Of Employment, Interest, and Money* (1936) which is regarded today as the most important book on economics of the twentieth century.

Keynes was born into an upper-class English family and showed academic promise at an early age. His father was a well-known economist, and the younger Keynes distinguished himself at Eton and Cambridge. However, he was unable to attain a position in the British Treasury due to his low scores on the civil service examinations. Noting that his worst mark was on the economics section of the test, Keynes is rumoured to have remarked that "the examiners presumably knew less than I did." During World War I, Keynes did find employment with the Treasury and represented it during the 1919 peace conference at Versailles.

Keynes' background in economics led him to be concerned with the problem of unemployment in capitalist nations, especially during the pre-war Depression of the 1930s. Prior economic theory maintained that unemployment could be alleviated through a reduction in wages, thereby allowing companies to

realize greater profits and stimulate outside investment.

Keynes argued that an overall cut in wages would actually cause unemployment to increase, since demand would be reduced as workers had less money to spend. Keynes advocated the implementation of government-sponsored, large-scale labour projects, or "public works" that would provide sufficient wages to stimulate demand. This in turn would increase investment and production.

Keynes' theories convinced many of the need for governments to become directly involved in their economies. The most notable application of Keynes' approach to the problem of employment was seen during the "New Deal" era of Franklin D. Roosevelt in the US during the 1930s.

and pedigree so as to show that he has ruled over us rather by hereditary right than by personal merit.

The Future Organisation of Society

Let us clear from the ground the metaphysical or general principles upon which, from time to time, *laissez-faire* has been founded. It is *not* true that individuals possess a prescriptive "natural liberty" in their economic activities. There is *no* "compact" conferring perpetual rights on those who Have or on those who Acquire. The world is *not* so governed from above that private and social interest always coincide. It is *not* so managed here below that in practice they coincide. It is *not* a correct deduction from the Principles of Economics that enlightened self-interest always operates in the public interest. Nor is it true that self-interest generally *is* enlightened; more often individuals acting separately to promote their own ends are too ignorant or too weak to attain even these. Experience does *not* show that individuals, when they make up a social unit, are always less clear-sighted than when they act separately.

We cannot therefore settle on abstract grounds, but

must handle on its merits in detail what Burke termed "one of the finest problems in legislation, namely, to determine what the State ought to take upon itself to direct by the public wisdom, and what it ought to leave, with as little interference as possible, to individual exertion."[2] We have to discriminate between what Bentham, in his forgotten but useful nomenclature, used to term *Agenda* and *Non-Agenda*, and to do this without Bentham's prior presumption that interference is, at the same time, "generally needless" and "generally pernicious."[3] Perhaps the chief task of Economists at this hour is to distinguish afresh the *Agenda* of Government from the *Non-Agenda*; and the companion task of Politics is to devise forms of Government within a Democracy which shall be capable of accomplishing the *Agenda*. I will illustrate what I have in mind by two examples.

(1) I believe that in many cases the ideal size for the unit of control and organisation lies somewhere between the individual and the modern State. I suggest, therefore, that progress lies in the growth and the recognition of semi-autonomous bodies within the State—bodies whose criterion of action within their

own fields is solely the public good as they understand it, and from whose deliberations motives of private advantage are excluded, though some place it may still be necessary to leave, until the ambit of men's altruism grows wider, to the separate advantage of particular groups, classes, or faculties—bodies which in the ordinary course of affairs are mainly autonomous within their prescribed limitations, but are subject in the last resort to the sovereignty of the democracy expressed through Parliament.

I propose a return, it may be said, towards mediæval conceptions of separate autonomies. But, in England at any rate, corporations are a mode of government which has never ceased to be important and is sympathetic to our institutions. It is easy to give examples, from what already exists, of separate autonomies which have attained or are approaching the mode I designate—the Universities, the Bank of England, the Port of London Authority, even perhaps the Railway Companies. In the United States there are doubtless analogous instances.

But more interesting than these is the trend of Joint Stock Institutions, when they have reached a certain age and size, to approximate to the status of public corporations rather than that of individualistic private enterprise. One of the most interesting and unnoticed developments of recent decades has been the tendency of big enterprise to socialise itself. A point arrives in the growth of a big institution—particularly a big railway or big public utility enterprise, but also a big bank or a big insurance company—at which the owners of the capital, i.e., the shareholders, are almost entirely dissociated from the management, with the result that the direct personal interest of the latter in the making of great profit becomes quite secondary. When this stage is reached, the general stability and reputation of the institution are more considered by the management than the maximum of profit for the shareholders. The shareholders must be satisfied by conventionally adequate dividends; but once this is secured, the direct interest of the management often consists in avoiding criticism from the public and from the customers of the concern. This is particularly the case if their great size or semi-monopolistic position renders them conspicuous in the public eye and vulnerable to public attack. The extreme instance, perhaps, of this tendency in the case of an institution, theoretically the unrestricted property of private persons, is the Bank of England. It is almost true to say that there is no class of persons in the Kingdom of whom the Governor of the Bank of England thinks less when he decides on his policy than of his shareholders. Their rights, in excess of their conventional dividend, have already sunk to the neighborhood of zero. But the same thing is partly true of many other big institutions. They are, as time goes on, socialising themselves.

Not that this is unmixed gain. The same causes promote conservatism and a waning of enterprise. In fact, we already have in these cases many of the faults as well as the advantages of State Socialism. Nevertheless we see here, I think, a natural line of evolution. The battle of Socialism against unlimited private profit is being won in detail hour by hour. In these particular fields—it remains acute elsewhere—this is no longer the pressing problem. There is, for instance, no so-called important political question so really unimportant, so irrelevant to the re-organisation of the economic life of Great Britain, as the Nationalisation of the Railways.

It is true that many big undertakings, particularly Public Utility enterprises and other business requiring a large fixed capital, still need to be semi-socialised. But we must keep our minds flexible regarding the forms of this semi-socialism. We must take full advantage of the natural tendencies of the day, and we must probably prefer semi-autonomous corporations to organs of the Central Government for which Ministers of State are directly responsible.

I criticise doctrinaire State Socialism, not because it seeks to engage men's altruistic impulses in the service of Society, or because it departs from *laissez-faire*, or because it takes away from man's natural liberty to make a million, or because it has courage for bold experiments. All these things I applaud. I criticise it because it misses the significance of what is actually happening; because it is, in fact, little better than a dusty survival of a plan to meet the problems of fifty years ago, based on a misunderstanding of what someone said a hundred years ago. Nineteenth-century State Socialism sprang from Bentham, free competition, etc., and is in some respects a clearer, in some respects a more muddled version of just the same philosophy as underlies nineteenth-century individualism. Both equally laid all their stress on freedom, the one negatively to avoid limitations on existing freedom, the other positively to destroy natural or acquired monopolies. They are different reactions to the same intellectual atmosphere.

Source: John Maynard Keynes. *Laissez-Faire and Communism.* New York: New Republic, 1926.

Notes

[1] "The Social Possibilities of Economic Chivalry," *Economic Journal* (1907), xvii, p.9.

[2] Quoted by M'Culloch in his *Principles of Political Economy.*

[3] Bentham's *Manual of Political Economy*, published posthumously, in Bowring's edition (1843).

Justice as Fairness: Political not Metaphysical

John Rawls

JOHN RAWLS *is Professor of Philosophy at Harvard University. He is the author of* A Theory of Justice*, one of the most widely read books in political philosophy.*

There are, of course, many ways in which political philosophy may be understood, and writers at different times, faced with different political and social circumstances, understand their work differently. Justice as fairness I would now understand as a reasonably systematic and practicable conception of justice for a constitutional democracy, a conception that offers an alternative to the dominant utilitarianism of our tradition of political thought. Its first task is to provide a more secure and acceptable basis for constitutional principles and basic rights and liberties than utilitarianism seems to allow.[1] The need for such a political conception arises in the following way.

There are periods, sometimes long periods, in the history of any society during which certain fundamental questions give rise to sharp and divisive political controversy, and it seems difficult, if not impossible, to find any shared basis of political agreement. Indeed, certain questions may prove intractable and may never be fully settled. One task of political philosophy in a democratic society is to focus on such questions and to examine whether some underlying basis of agreement can be uncovered and a mutually acceptable way of resolving these questions publicly established. Or if these questions cannot be fully settled, as may well be the case, perhaps the divergence of opinion can be narrowed sufficiently so that political cooperation on a basis of mutual respect can still be maintained.[2]

The course of democratic thought over the past two centuries or so makes plain that there is no agreement on the way basic institutions of a constitutional democracy should be arranged if they are to specify and secure the basic rights and liberties of citizens and answer to the claims of democratic equality when citizens are conceived as free and equal persons. A deep disagreement exists as to how the values of liberty and equality are best realized in the basic structure of society. To simplify, we may think of this disagreement as a conflict within the tradition of democratic thought itself, between the tradition associated with Locke, which gives greater weight to what Constant called "the liberties of the moderns," freedom of thought and conscience, certain basic rights of the person and of property, and the rule of law, and the tradition associated with Rousseau, which gives greater weight to what Constant called "the liberties of the ancients," the equal political liberties and the values of public life. This is a stylized contrast and historically inaccurate, but it serves to fix ideas.

Justice as fairness tries to adjudicate between these contending traditions first, by proposing two principles of justice to serve as guidelines for how basic institutions are to realize the values of liberty and equality, and second, by specifying a point of view from which these principles can be seen as more appropriate than other familiar principles of justice to the nature of democratic citizens viewed as free and equal persons. What it means to view citizens as free and equal persons is, of course, a fundamental question and is discussed in the following sections. What must be shown is that a certain arrangement of the basic structure, certain institutional forms, are more appropriate for realizing the values of liberty and equality when citizens are conceived as such persons, that is (very briefly), as having the requisite powers of moral personality that enable them to participate in society viewed as a system of fair cooperation for mutual advantage. So to continue, the two principles of justice (mentioned above) read as follows:

1. Each person has an equal right to a fully adequate scheme of equal basic rights and liberties, which scheme is compatible with a similar scheme for all.

2. Social and economic inequalities are to satisfy two conditions: first, they must be attached to offices and positions open to all under conditions of fair equality of opportunity; and second, they must be to the greatest benefit of the least advantaged members of society.

Each of these principles applies to a different part of the basic structure; and both are concerned not only with basic rights, liberties, and opportunities, but also with the claims of equality; while the second part of the second principle underwrites the worth of these institutional guarantees.[3] The two principles together, when the first is given priority over the second, regulate the basic institutions which realize these values.[4] But these details, although important, are not our concern here.

We must now ask: how might political philosophy find a shared basis for settling such a fundamental question as that of the most appropriate institutional forms for liberty and equality? Of course, it is likely that the most that can be done is to narrow the range of public disagreement. Yet even firmly held convictions gradually change: religious toleration is now accepted, and arguments for persecution are no longer openly professed; similarly, slavery is rejected as inherently unjust, and however much the aftermath of slavery may persist in social practices and unavowed attitudes, no one is willing to defend it. We collect such settled convictions as the belief in religious toleration and the rejection of slavery and try to organize the basic ideas and principles implicit in these convictions into a coherent conception of justice. We can regard these convictions as provisional fixed points which any conception of justice must account for if it is to be reasonable for us. We look, then, to our public political culture itself, including its main institutions and the historical traditions of their interpretation, as the shared fund of implicitly recognized basic ideas and principles. The hope is that these ideas and principles can be formulated clearly enough to be combined into a conception of political justice congenial to our most firmly held convictions. We express this by saying that a political conception of justice, to be acceptable, must be in accordance with our considered convictions, at all levels of generality, on due reflection (or in what I have called "reflective equilibrium").[5]

The public political culture may be of two minds even at a very deep level. Indeed, this must be so with such an enduring controversy as that concerning the most appropriate institutional forms to realize the values of liberty and equality. This suggests that if we are to succeed in finding a basis of public agreement, we must find a new way of organizing familiar ideas and principles into a conception of political justice so that the claims in conflict, as previously understood, are seen in another light. A political conception need not be an original creation but may only articulate familiar intuitive ideas and principles so that they can be recognized as fitting together in somewhat different way than before. Such a conception may, however, go further than this: it may organize these familiar ideas and principles by means of a more fundamental intuitive idea within the complex structure of which the other familiar intuitive ideas are then systematically connected and related. In justice as fairness, as we shall see in the next section, this more fundamental idea is that of society as a system of fair social cooperation between free and equal persons. The concern of this section is how we might find a public basis of political agreement. The point is that a conception of justice will only be able to achieve this aim if it provides a reasonable way of shaping into one coherent view the deeper bases of agreement embedded in the public political culture of a constitutional regime and acceptable to its most firmly held considered convictions.

Now suppose justice as fairness were to achieve its aim and a publicly acceptable political conception of justice is found. Then this conception provides a publicly recognized point of view from which all citizens can examine before one another whether or not their political and social institutions are just. It enables them to do this by citing what are recognized among them as valid and sufficient reasons singled out by that conception itself. Society's main institutions and how they fit together into one scheme of social cooperation can be examined on the same basis by each citizen, whatever that citizen's social position or more particular interests. It should be observed that, on this view, justification is not regarded simply as valid argument from listed premises, even should these premises be true. Rather, justification is addressed to others who disagree with us, and therefore it must always proceed from some consensus, that is, from premises that we and others publicly recognize as true; or better, publicly recognize as acceptable to us for the purpose of establishing a working agreement on the fundamental questions of political justice. It goes without saying that this agreement must be informed and uncoerced, and reached by citizens in ways consistent with their being viewed as free and equal persons.[6]

Thus, the aim of justice as fairness as a political conception is practical, and not metaphysical or epistemological. That is, it presents itself not as a conception of justice that is true, but one that can serve as a basis of informed and willing political agreement between citizens viewed as free and equal persons. This agreement when securely founded in public political and social attitudes sustains the goods of all persons and associations within a just democratic regime. To secure this agreement we try, so far as we can, to avoid disputed philosophical, as well as disputed moral and religious, questions. We do this not because these questions are unimportant or regarded with indifference,[7] but because we think them too important and recognize that there is no way to resolve them politically. The only alternative to a principle of toleration is the autocratic use of state power. Thus, justice as fairness deliberately stays on the surface, philosophically speaking. Given the profound differences in belief and conceptions of the good at least since the Reformation, we must recognize that, just as on questions of religious and moral doctrine, public agreement on the basic questions of philosophy cannot be obtained without the state's infringement of basic liberties. Philosophy as the search for truth about an independent metaphysical and moral order cannot, I believe, provide a workable and shared basis for a political conception of justice in a democratic society.

We try, then to leave aside philosophical controversies whenever possible, and look for ways to avoid philosophy's longstanding problems. Thus, in what I have called "Kantian constructivism," we try to avoid the problem of truth and the controversy between realism and subjectivism about the status of moral and political values. This form of constructivism neither asserts nor denies these doctrines.[8] Rather, it recasts ideas from the tradition of the social contract to achieve a practicable conception of objectivity of justification founded on public agreement in judgement on due reflection. The aim is free agreement, reconciliation through public reason. And similarly, as we shall see (in Section V), a conception of the person in a political view, for example, the conception of citizens as free and equal persons, need not involve, so I believe, questions of philosophical psychology or a metaphysical doctrine of the nature of the self. No political view that depends on these deep and unresolved matters can serve as a public conception of justice in a constitutional democratic state. As I have said, we must apply the principle of toleration to philosophy itself. The hope is that, by this method of avoidance, as we might call it, existing differences between contending political views can at least be moderated, even if not entirely removed, so that social cooperation on the basis of mutual respect can be maintained. Or if this is expecting too much, this method may enable us to conceive how, given a desire for free and uncoerced agreement, a public understanding could arise consistent with the historical conditions and constraints of our social world. Until we bring ourselves to conceive how this could happen, it can't happen....

I now take up a point essential to thinking of justice as fairness as a liberal view. Although this conception is a moral conception, it is not, as I have said, intended as a comprehensive moral doctrine. The conception of the citizen as a free and equal person is not a moral ideal to govern all of life, but is rather an ideal belonging to a conception of political justice which is to apply to the basic structure. I emphasize this point because to think otherwise would be incompatible with liberalism as a political doctrine. Recall that as such a doctrine, liberalism assumes that in a constitutional democratic state under modern conditions there are bound to exist conflicting and incommensurable conceptions of the good. This feature characterizes modern culture since the Reformation. Any viable political conception of justice that is not to rely on the autocratic use of state power must recognize this fundamental social fact. This does not mean, of course, that such a conception cannot impose constraints on individuals and associations, but that when it does so, these constraints are accounted for, directly or indirectly, by the requirements of political justice for the basic structure.[9]

Given this fact, we adopt a conception of the person framed as part of, and restricted to, an explicitly political conception of justice. In this sense, the conception of the person is a political one. As I stressed in the previous section, persons can accept this conception of themselves as citizens and use it when discussing questions of political justice without being committed in other parts of their life to comprehensive moral ideals often associated with liberalism, for example, the ideals of autonomy and individuality. The absence of commitment to these ideals, and indeed to any particular comprehensive ideal, is essential to liberalism as a political doctrine. The reason is that any such ideal, when pursued as a comprehensive ideal, is incompatible with other conceptions of the good, with forms of personal, moral, and religious life consistent with justice and which, therefore, have a proper place in a democratic society. As comprehensive moral ideals, autonomy and individuality are unsuited for political conception of justice. As found in Kant and J.S. Mill, these comprehensive ideals, despite their very great importance in liberal thought, are extended too far when presented as the only appropriate foundation for a constitutional regime.[10] So understood, liberalism becomes but another sectarian doctrine.

This conclusion requires comment: it does not mean, of course, that the liberalisms of Kant and Mill are not appropriate moral conceptions from which we can be lead to affirm democratic institutions. But they are only two such conceptions among others, and so but two of the philosophical doctrines likely to persist and gain adherents in a reasonable just democratic regime. In such a regime the comprehensive moral views which support its basic institutions may include the liberalisms of individuality and autonomy; and

possibly these liberalisms are among the more prominent doctrines in an overlapping consensus, that is, in
a consensus in which, as noted earlier, different and
even conflicting doctrines affirm the publicly shared
basis of political arrangements. The liberalisms of
Kant and Mill have a certain historical preeminence as
among the first and most important philosophical
views to espouse modern constitutional democracy
and to develop its underlying ideas in a influential
way; and it may even turn out that societies in which
the ideals of autonomy and individuality are widely
accepted are among the most well-governed and harmonious.[11]

By contrast with liberalism as a comprehensive
moral doctrine, justice as fairness tries to present a
conception of political justice rooted in the basic intuitive ideas found in the public culture of a constitutional democracy. We conjecture that these ideas are
likely to be affirmed by each of the opposing comprehensive moral doctrines influential in a reasonably
just democratic society. Thus justice as fairness seeks
to identify the kernel of an overlapping consensus,
that is, the shared intuitive ideas which when worked
up into a political conception of justice turn out to be
sufficient to underwrite a just constitutional regime.
This is the most we can expect, nor do we need
more.[12] We must note, however, that when justice as
fairness is fully realized in a well-ordered society, the
value of full autonomy is likewise realized. In this
way justice as fairness is indeed similar to the liberalisms of Kant and Mill; but in contrast with them, the
value of full autonomy is here specified by a political
conception of justice, and not by a comprehensive
moral doctrine.

Source: John Rawls. "Justice as Fairness: Political not Metaphysical."
Philosophy & Public Affairs 14, No.3 (1985): 223-251. Reprinted with
permission. Copyright © 1985 by Princeton University Press.

Notes

[1] *Theory of Justice* (Cambridge: MA: Harvard University Press,1971)
Preface, p.viii.

[2] Ibid., pp.582f. On the role of a conception of justice in reducing the
divergence of opinion, see pp.44f., 53, 314, and 564. At various
places the limited aims in developing a conception of justice are
noted: see p.364 on not expecting too much of an account of civil
disobedience; pp.200f. on the inevitable indeterminacy of a conception of justice in specifying a series of points of view from which
questions of justice can be resolved; pp.8ff. on the social wisdom of
recognizing that perhaps only a few moral problems (it would have
been better to say; problems of political justice) can be satisfactorily
settled, and thus of framing institutions so that intractable questions
do not arise; on pp.53, 87ff., 320f. the need to accept simplifications
is emphasized. Regarding the last point, see also "Kantian Constructivism," *Journal of Philosophy* 77 (1980) pp.560-64.

[3] The statement of these principles differs from that given in *Theory*
and follows the statement in "The Basic Liberties and Their Priority,"
Tanner Lectures on Human Values, Vol. III (Salt Lake City: University
of Utah Press, 1982), p.5. The reasons for the changes are discussed at pp.46-55 of that lecture. They are important for the revi-
sions made in the account of the basic liberties found in *Theory* in the
attempt to answer the objections of H.L.A. Hart; but they need not
concern us here.

[4] The idea of the worth of these guarantees is discussed ibid., pp.40f.

[5] *Theory*, pp.2ff., 48-51 and 120f.

[6] Ibid., pp.580-83.

[7] Ibid., pp.214f.

[8] On Kantian constructivism, see especially the third lecture referred to
above.

[9] For example, churches are constrained by the principle of equal
liberty of conscience and must conform to the principle of toleration,
universities by what may be required to maintain fair equality of
opportunity, and the rights of parents by what is necessary to maintain their childrens' physical well-being and to assure the adequate
development of their intellectual and moral powers. Because
churches, universities, and parents exercise their authority within the
basic structure, they are to recognize the requirements this structure
imposes to maintain background justice.

[10] For Kant, see *The Foundations of the Metaphysics of Morals* and
The Critique of Practical Reason. For Mill, see *On Liberty*, particularly
Ch. 3 where the ideal of individuality is most fully discussed.

[11] This point has been made with respect to the liberalisms of Kant and
Mill, but for American culture one should mention the important conceptions of democratic individuality expressed in the works of Emerson, Thoreau, and Whitman. These are instructively discussed by
George Kateb in his "Democratic Individuality and the Claims of Politics," *Political Theory* 12 (August 1984).

[12] For the idea of the kernel of an overlapping consensus (mentioned
above), see *Theory*, last part of Sec. 35, pp.220f. For the idea of full
autonomy, see "Kantian Constructivism," pp.528ff.

Justice and Gender

Susan Moller Okin

SUSAN MOLLER OKIN *is Professor of Political Science and Director of the Program in Ethics in Society at Stanford University. She is the author of* Women in Western Political Thought (1979) *and* Justice, Gender and the Family (1989). *Currently she is doing research on gender and cultural relativism.*

An ambiguity runs throughout John Rawls's *A Theory of Justice*, continually noticeable to anyone reading it from a feminist perspective. On the one hand, as I shall argue below, a consistent and wholehearted application of Rawls's liberal principles can lead us to challenge fundamentally the gender system of our society. On the other hand, in his own account of his theory, this challenge is barely hinted at, much less developed. The major reason is that throughout most of the argument, it is assumed (as throughout almost the entire liberal tradition) that the appropriate subjects of political theories are heads of families. As a result, although Rawls indicates on several occasions that a person's sex is a morally arbitrary and contingent characteristic, and although he states explicitly that the family itself is one of those basic social institutions to which the principles of justice must apply, his theory of justice fails to develop either of these convictions.

Rawls, like almost all political theorists until very recent years, employs supposedly generic male terms of reference. "Men," "mankind," "he" and "his" are interspersed with nonsexist terms of reference such as "individual" and "moral person." Examples of intergenerational concern are worded in terms of "fathers" and "sons," and the difference principle is said to correspond to "the principle of fraternity."[1] This linguistic usage would perhaps be less significant if it were not for the fact that Rawls is self-consciously a member of a long tradition of moral and political philosophy that has used in its arguments either such supposedly generic masculine terms, or even more inclusive terms of reference ("human beings," "persons," "all rational beings as such"), only to exclude women from the scope of the conclusions reached. Kant is a clear example.[2] But when Rawls refers to the generality and universality of Kant's ethics, and when he compares the principles chosen in his own original position to those regulative of Kant's kingdom of ends, "acting from [which] expresses our nature as free and equal rational persons,"[3] he does not mention the fact that women were not included in that category of "free and equal rational persons," to which Kant meant his moral theory to apply. Again, in a brief discussion of Freud's account of moral development, Rawls presents Freud's theory of the formation of the male superego in largely gender-neutral terms, without mentioning that Freud considered women's moral development to be sadly deficient, on account of their incomplete resolution of the Oedipus complex.[4] Thus there is a certain blindness to the sexism of the tradition in which Rawls is a participant, which tends to render his terms of reference even more ambiguous than they might otherwise be. A feminist reader finds it difficult not to keep asking: "Does this theory of justice apply to women, or not?"

This question is not answered in the important passages that list the characteristics that persons in the original position are not to know about themselves, in order to formulate impartial principles of justice. In a subsequent article, Rawls has made it clear that sex is one of those morally irrelevant contingencies that is to be hidden by the veil of ignorance.[5] But throughout *A Theory of Justice*, while the list of things unknown by a person in the original position includes

> his place in society, his class position or social status, his fortune in the distribution of natural assets and abilities, his intelligence and strength, and the like, his conception of the good, the particulars of his rational plan of life, [and] even the special features of his psychology...[6]

"his" sex is not mentioned. Since the parties also "know the general facts about human society,"[7] presumably including the fact that it is structured along the lines of gender both by custom and by law, one might think that whether or not they knew their sex might matter enough to be mentioned. Perhaps Rawls means to cover it by his phrase "and the like," but it is also possible that he did not consider it significant.

The ambiguity is exacerbated by Rawls's statement that those free and equal moral persons in the original position who formulate the principles of justice are to be thought of not as "single individuals" but as "heads of families" or "representatives of families."[8] He says that it is not necessary to think of the parties as heads of families, but that he will generally do so.

The reason he does this, he explains, is to ensure that each person in the original position cares about the well-being of some persons in the next generation. These "ties of sentiment" between generations, which Rawls regards as important in the establishment of his just savings principle, would otherwise constitute a problem, because of the general assumption that the parties in the original position are mutually disinterested. In spite of the ties of sentiment *within* families, then, "as representatives of families their interests are opposed as the circumstances of justice imply."[9]

The head of a family need not necessarily, of course, be a man. The very fact, however, that in common usage the term "female-headed households" is used *only* in reference to households without resident adult males, tends to suggest that it is assumed that any present male adult takes precedence over a female as the household or family head. Rawls does nothing to dispel this impression when he says of those in the original position that "imagining themselves to be fathers, say, they are to ascertain how much they should set aside for their sons by noting what they would believe themselves entitled to claim of their fathers."[10] He makes the "heads of families" assumption only in order to address the problem of savings between generations, and presumably does not intend it to be a sexist assumption. Nevertheless, Rawls, is effectively trapped by this assumption into the traditional mode of thinking that life within the family and relations between the sexes are not properly to be regarded as part of the subject matter of a theory of social justice.

Before I go on to argue this, I must first point out that Rawls states at the outset of his theory that the family is part of the subject matter of social justice. "For us" he says,

> the primary subject of justice is the basic structure of society, or more exactly, the way in which the major social institutions distribute fundamental rights and duties and determine the division of advantages from a social cooperation.[11]

He goes on to specify "the monogamous family" as an example of such major social institutions, together with the political constitution, the legal protection of essential freedoms, competitive markets, and private property. The reason that Rawls makes such institutions the primary subject of his theory of social justice is that they have such profound effects on people's lives from the start, depending on where they find themselves placed in relation to them. He explicitly distinguishes between these major institutions and other "private associations," "less comprehensive social groups," and "various informal conventions and customs of everyday life,"[12] for which the principles of justice satisfactory for the basic structure might be less

appropriate or relevant. There is no doubt, then, that in his initial definition of the sphere of social justice, the family is included.[13] The two principles of justice that Rawls defends in Part I, the principle of equal basic liberty, and the difference principle combined with the requirement of fair equality of opportunity, are intended to apply to the basic structure of society. They are "to govern the assignment of rights and duties and to regulate the distribution of social and economic advantages."[14] Whenever in these basic institutions there are differences in authority, in responsibility, in the distribution of resources such as wealth or leisure, these differences must be both to the greatest benefit of the least advantaged, and attached to positions accessible to all under conditions of fair equality of opportunity.

In Part II, Rawls discusses at some length the application of his principles of justice to almost all of the major social institutions listed at the beginning of the book. The legal protection of freedom of thought and liberty of conscience is defended, as are just democratic constitutional institutions and procedures; competitive markets feature prominently in the discussion of the just distribution of income; the issue of the private or public ownership of the means of production is explicitly left open, since Rawls argues that justice as fairness might be compatible with certain versions of either. But throughout these discussions, the question of whether the monogamous family, in either its traditional or any other form, is a just social institution, is never raised. When Rawls announces that "the sketch of the system of institutions that satisfy the two principles of justice is now complete,"[15] he has still paid not attention at all to the internal justice of the family. The family, in fact, apart from passing references, appears in *A Theory of Justice* in only three contexts: as the link between generations necessary for the savings principle, as a possible obstacle to fair equality of opportunity—on account of inequalities amongst families—and as the first school of moral development. It is in the third of these contexts that Rawls first specifically mentions the family as a just institution. He mentions it, however, not to *consider* whether or not the family "in some form" is a just institution, but to *assume* it. Clearly regarding it as important, Rawls states as part of his first psychological law of moral development: "given that family institutions are just...[16]

Clearly, however, by Rawls's own reasoning about the social justice of major institutions, this assumption is unwarranted. For the central tenet of the theory is that justice characterizes institutions whose members could hypothetically have agreed to their structure and rules from a position in which they did not know which place in the structure they were to occupy. The argument of the book is designed to show that the two principles of justice as fairness are those that individuals in such a hypothetical situation would indeed agree upon. But since those in the original position are the heads or representatives of families, *they are not in a position to determine questions of justice within families.*[17] As far as children are concerned, Rawls makes a convincing argument from paternalism for their temporary inequality. But wives (or whichever adult member[s] of a family are not its "head") go completely unrepresented in the original positions. If families are just, as Rawls assumes, then they must get to be just in some different way (unspecified by Rawls) than other institutions, for it is impossible to see how the viewpoint of their less advantaged members ever gets to be heard.

There are two occasions where Rawls seems either to depart from his assumption that those in the original position are "family heads" or to assume that a "head of a family" is equally likely to be a woman as a man. In the assumption of the basic rights of citizenship, Rawls argues, favouring men over women is "justified by the difference principle only if it is to the advantage of women and acceptable from their standpoint."[18] Later, he seems to imply that the injustice and irrationality of racist doctrines are also characteristic of sexist ones.[19] But in spite of these passages, which appear to challenge formal sex discrimination, the discussions of institutions in Part II implicitly rely, in a number of respects, on the assumption that the parties formulating just institutions are (male) heads of (fairly traditional) families, and are therefore not concerned with issues of just distribution within the family. Thus the "head of family" assumption, far from being neutral or innocent, has the effect of banishing a large sphere of human life—and a particularly large sphere of most women's lives—from the scope of the theory.

First, Rawls's discussion of the distribution of wealth seems to assume that all the parties in the original position expect to be, once the veil of ignorance is removed, participants in the paid labor market. Distributive shares are discussed in terms of household income, but reference to "individuals" is interspersed into this discussion as if there were no difference between the advantage or welfare of a household and that of an individual.[20] This confusion obscures the fact that wages are paid to those in the labor force but that in societies characterized by a gender system (all current societies) a much larger proportion of women's than men's labor is unpaid, and is often not even acknowledged to be labor. It obscures the fact that such resulting disparities and the economic dependence of women on men are likely to affect power relations within the household, as well as access to leisure, prestige, political office, and so on amongst its adult members. Any discussion

of justice *within* the family would have to address these issues.

Later, too, in his discussion of the obligations of citizens, Rawls's assumption that justice is the result of agreement amongst heads of families in the original position seems to prevent him from considering an issue of crucial importance to women as citizens—their exemption from the draft. He concludes that military conscription is justifiable in the case of defense against an unjust attack on liberty, so long as institutions "try to make sure that the risks of suffering from these imposed misfortunes are more or less evenly shared by all members of society over the course of their life, and that there is no avoidable *class* bias in selecting those who are called for duty."[21] However, the issue of the exemption of women from this major interference with the basic liberties of equal citizenship is not even mentioned.

Source: Susan Moller Okin. "Justice and Gender." *Philosophy and Public Affairs* 16, No.1 (1987): 42-72. Reprinted with Permission. Copyright © 1987 by Princeton University Press.

Notes

[1] *A Theory of Justice* (Cambridge, MA: Harvard University Press).

[2] See Okin, "Women and the Making of the Sentimental Family," *Philosophy and Public Affairs* 11, No. 1 (winter 1982): 65-88

[3] *Theory*, pp.251, 256.

[4] Ibid., p.459.

[5] "Fairness to goodness," *Philosophical Review* 84 (1975): 537. He says: "That we have one conception of the good rather than another is not relevant from a moral standpoint. In acquiring it we are influenced by the same sort of contingencies that lead us to rule out a knowledge of our sex and class."

[6] *Theory*, p.137; see also p.12.

[7] Ibid., p.137.

[8] Ibid., pp.128, 146.

[9] Ibid., p.128; see also p.292.

[10] Ibid., p.289.

[11] Ibid., p.7.

[12] Ibid., p.8.

[13] It is interesting to note that in a subsequent paper on the question why the basic structure of society is the primary subject of justice, Rawls does not mention the family as part of the basic structure. "The Basic Structure as Subject," *American Philosophical Quarterly* 14, No. 2 (April 1977): 159.

[14] *Theory*, p.61.

[15] Ibid., p.303.

[16] *Theory*, p.490. See Deborah Kearns, "A Theory of Justice—and love; Rawls on the Family," *Politics* (Australian Political Studies Association Journal) 18, No. 2 (November 1983): 39-40 for an interesting discussion of the significance of Rawls's failure to address the justice of the family for his theory of moral development.

[17] As Jane English says, in a paper that is more centrally concerned with the problems of establishing Rawls's savings principle than with justice within the family *per se*: "By making the parties in the original position heads of families rather than individuals, Rawls makes the family opaque to claims of justice." "Justice between Generations," *Philosophical Studies* 31 (1977): 95.

[18] *Theory*, p.99.

[19] Ibid., p.149.

[20] Ibid., pp.270-74, 304-309.

[21] Ibid., pp.380-81 (emphasis added).

Justice, Community, and the Antinomies of Feminist Theory

Christine Sypnowich

CHRISTINE SYPNOWICH *is Associate Professor of Philosophy at Queen's University. She has published* The Concept of Socialist Law (1990) *and a number of articles in the areas of jurisprudence and socialism.*

The Liberal-Communitarian Debate

John Rawls has provided the most influential statement of contemporary liberalism, and his theory has been the main target of the communitarians' critique. By this time the terms of the debate are known. Rawls employs a hypothetical contract made in an original position under a veil of ignorance to reach political principles that protect liberty and ameliorate inequality.[1] For their part, communitarians such as Michael Sandel, Alasdair MacIntyre, and Charles Taylor question the very project of elaborating a formal theory of justice from which to build political membership. Rawls's theory is attacked on moral grounds for reducing social life to the neutral observance of rights and contracts, which places liberal society in constant danger of disintegration and breakdown.[2] The communitarians also make a methodological critique which invokes the age-old complaint that liberalism employs an "atomistic" conception of the person. It is argued that only this "unencumbered" individual can, as Rawls requires, first, participate in a decision procedure under the veil of ignorance and, second, forego any title to the "accidental" attributes of talent and industry that produce social wealth.[3] According to Rawls's critics, either this robs one of the very basis for choice or it begs the question in Rawls's favor—for what could one choose but a liberal society that maximizes "free choice," a society in which whatever kind of person you turned out to be, it allowed you to be it? Communitarians urge an alternative philosophical anthropology, which sees the human being as socially constituted, living a life in a context of shared meanings and understandings, in reference to a culture, or as MacIntyre puts it, a tradition or narrative. For Sandel, only this "intersubjective" conception of the self can ward off attacks from libertarians such as Robert Nozick, who finds Rawls's attempt to redistribute wealth an illegitimate infringement of liberty.[4]

Phenomena ranging from mass murders in America to the demise of the British welfare state, Canada's wrenching crisis over region and language, or the poor record of economic restructuring in Russia: all can be put down as symptoms of an apparent lack of community that Rawlsian liberalism is unable to restore.[5] On the other hand, the political import of community is difficult to assess, particularly since nostalgia seems to be the communitarians' main posture, be it for the fragile communities of the Canadian Maritimes as invoked by Taylor,[6] Sandel's Jeffersonian town council,[7] or the Aristotelian polis of MacIntyre.[8] In the absence of a more substantive political theory, the communitarians cannot rise to Rawls's challenge that it is political philosophy, not metaphysics, that is his ultimate project and to which he demands a response in kind.[9] ...

A Return to Rawls?

Some have sought to use the liberal emphasis on impartiality and freedom for feminist ends. Okin, for instance, makes an interesting and important argument for the feminist potential of Rawls's work. In *A Theory of Justice*, Rawls does not include sex or gender in the catalogue of those characteristics, knowledge of which is forbidden to the parties of the original position.[10] But Okin argues that there is no logical reason why he could not add it to his list, on the supposition that if we do not know what sex we might have in the polity which we are designing we are less likely to choose sexist arrangements. Indeed, Okin argues that any theory of justice worthy of the name must consider the injustice of a gender-structured society, and she makes a compelling case for the pursuit of justice in the neglected domain of the family. For Okin, a just family is worthwhile both for its own sake and to instill in citizens the sense of justice necessary for the adoption of Rawls's egalitarian ideals. To achieve this broader conception of justice, Okin contends that Rawls's original position should be understood not as removed from the needs and concerns of particular persons but, rather, as wholly inclusive of them. For this to be possible,

Okin concludes, the original position requires partici-pants with a strong sense of empathy, a "prepared-ness to listen carefully to the very different points of views of others."[11]

It seems doubtful, however, that Rawls can be "feminized" in this way. First, the idea that feminist concerns need only be inserted into a theory and tradition that takes the abstract, universal "man" of the public sphere as its unit of analysis may be conten-tious. More particularly, even if the empathy that Okin calls for were possible (which many cultural feminists, insisting on the essential differences be-tween female and male experience, would deny), Rawls himself would doubtless object to its inclusion. The veil of ignorance denies us the information about ourselves or others that would enable us to step in other people's shoes in the empathetic way that Okin commends. Moreover, the point of the veil of igno-rance is precisely to avoid appeal to such motives as empathy or altruism. So long as we live in a society characterized by inequality, prejudice, and moral un-certainty, we will either fail to empathize or if we succeed, the results may reflect the very failings that empathy is supposed to overcome. What am I sup-posed to do when called upon to empathize with the sexist? And what may I expect of the sexist when it is his or her turn to empathize with me? Rawls's point is not to require empathy of us or of the sexist but, rather, to ask each of us to consider what we would countenance if we did not know our lot. It is part of the attraction of Rawls's theory that he drives us to take account of the needs of some hypothetical, worst-off person without demanding any skills of em-pathy on our part.

In any case, Okin herself indicates that there may be some difficulty achieving empathy across sexual boundaries. For Okin, the empathy needed for Rawls's theory can only be fostered in the thus far elusive ideal of the justly ordered, ungendered family. Moreover, the possibility that Rawls could contribute to gender justice is cast into doubt; Okin fatalistically concludes that in a gender-structured society there will be a distinct standpoint of women that "cannot be adequately taken into account by male philoso-phers," however intent on neutrality.[12] It turns out, then, that the empathy required by the original posi-tion (as Okin understands it) can only be achieved once gender differences have been eliminated in real-ity.[13] By incorporating empathy in Rawls's theory, Okin renders the theory irrelevant, for on her view the successful application of his method presupposes the prior solution of some of the very problems that caused us to turn to Rawls in the first place. Present injustice limits the extent to which empathy is possi-ble, and yet empathy is required to combat injustice: we are left, on Okin's account, with the unhappy conclusion that the union between the care perspec-tive of cultural feminists and the justice perspective of liberals, while essential, is unattainable.

An Alternative Solution

I want to suggest another way of achieving a syn-thesis of community and justice, which focuses on the historical process of remedying injustice as the basis for community rather than installing community as the precondition of justice. This, I shall argue, involves a reconstitution of Marxist political theory. Marxism has historically been associated with an emphasis on community to the exclusion of liberal ideas such as impartial justice, freedom, and rights. But socialist thinkers have begun seeking a reconciliation between the socialist ideal of equality with the liberal ideal of freedom, calling for social justice, market socialism, and socialist rights.[14] Can the debates in feminism profit form these efforts by socialists? Feminists have long looked to Marxism for theoretical inspiration, and recent feminist writings continue to employ Marx-ist frameworks. Like Shulamith Firestone before her, Catharine MacKinnon appeals to the idea of women as a sex class, whose sexuality, like the proletariat's labor, is exploited. Mary O'Brien expands Marx's con-cept of alienation to portray men's dominance as con-sisting in the appropriation of the reproductive labor power of women. Nancy Hartsock and Alison Jaggar suggest that a "feminist standpoint" emerges in the sexual division of labor just as a proletarian stand-point is constituted in the division of labor in the productive sphere.[15]

It is far from obvious, however, that this focus on sexuality can be incorporated into a Marxist analysis. As Wendy Brown has argued against MacKinnon, concepts like patriarchy or misogyny sit ill with the concept of exploitation because whereas the idea of misogyny supposes that men's control of women's sexuality is its own reward, capitalist exploitation is aimed not simply at access to labor but at the conver-sion of labor into surplus value. Babies are not much like commodities, and the sexual self is even less so; moreover, MacKinnon's idea of the expropriation of sex suggests that sexuality and reproduction have an existence "prior to and innocent of" its social con-struction. Thus what Brown calls the "mimicry of Marxist moves to map a political economy of sex" defies the recognition of either sex or Marx.[16]

On the other hand, being faithful to the tenets of Marxism may seem an unlikely solution. Feminists have long complained that classical Marxism's empha-sis on class has made for a "sex blind" analysis, with the upshot that women take their place at the rear of the proletariat's march through history.[17] But although sexism and capitalism may be linked in important ways, the removal of capitalism is no guarantee for a feminist agenda; women have not been the equal of men in either feudalism or the former Soviet Union. Marxism offers poor prospects for feminist theory as either a biblical canon of pronouncements on the women's movement and its connection to workers' struggles or a vocabulary to be resituated in the arena of reproduction after its tenure in the realm of production.

Source: Christine Sypnowich. "Justice, Community, and the Antinomies of Feminist Theory." *Political Theory* 21, No.3 (1993): 484-506. Reprinted by permission of Sage Publications, Inc.

Notes

1 Rawls, *A Theory of Justice* (Cambridge, MS: Harvard University Press, 1971).

2 See Sandel, *Liberalism and the Limits of Justice* (Cambridge: Cambridge University Press, 1982), 33; MacIntyre, *After Virtue: A Study in Moral Theory* (London: Duckworth, 1981), 236-37; *Whose Justice? Which Rationality?* (Notre Dame: University of Notre Dame Press, 1988), chap. 17; and Taylor, "The Nature and Scope of Distributive Justice," *Philosophy and the Human Sciences: Philosophical Papers*, Volume 2 (Cambridge: Cambridge University Press, 1985), esp. 314-17, and "Alternative Futures: Legitimacy, Identity and Alienation in Late Twentieth Century Canada," in A. Cairns and C. Williams, eds., *Constitutionalism, Citizenship and Society in Canada* (Toronto: University of Toronto Press, 1985).

3 *Liberalism and the Limits of Justice*, chaps., 1-3.

4 Ibid., 92-103.

5 An especially influential sociological treatment of this theme is Robert Bellah, Richard Madsen, William Sullivan, Ann Swidler, and Steven Tipton, *Habits of the Heart: Individualism and Commitment in American Life* (New York: Harper & Row, 1985).

6 "Distributive Justice," 295.

7 Sandel, "The Procedural Republic and the Unencumbered Self," *Political Theory*, February 1984. See also Bellah et al., *Habits of the*

Heart; and William Sullivan, *Reconstructing Public Philosophy* (Berkeley and Los Angeles: University of California Press, 1982).

8 *After Virtue*, chap. 11 and throughout.

9 Rawls, "Justice as Fairness: Political Not Metaphysical," *Philosophy and Public Affairs* 14, No. 3 (Summer 1985). See J. Wallach, "Liberals, Communitarians and the Tasks of Political Theory," *Political Theory* 15 (1987).

10 Rawls does include sex, however, in the version of the original position outlined in his subsequent article, "Fairness to Goodness," *Philosophical Review* 84 (1975), which raises some of the difficulties I outline here.

11 S. Okin, *Justice, Gender and the Family* (New York: Basic Books, 1989) 101-9.

12 Ibid., 106-7.

13 It is as if we were to argue that Rawls's original position could be used to eliminate racism, interpreting it as encouraging the parties to empathize with the situations of others, only then to argue that for this empathy to be operable racial prejudice would have to be eliminated.

14 C.B. Macpherson's pioneering work sought a radical "retrieval" of liberal ideals. See also A. Nove, *The Economics of Feasible Socialism* (London: Allen & Unwin, 1983); W. Brus, *The Economics and Politics of Socialism* (London: Routledge & Kegan Paul, 1973); J. Elster and K. O. Moene, eds., *Alternatives to Capitalism* (Cambridge: Cambridge University Press, 1989); F. Feher and A. Heller, *Eastern Left Western Left* (Cambridge: Polity, 1987); J. Keane, *Public Life and Late Capitalism* (Cambridge: Cambridge University Press, 1984); A. Buchanan, *Marx and Justice* (London: Methuen, 1982); T. Campbell, *The Left and Rights* (London: Routledge & Kegan Paul, 1983); T. O'Hagan, *The End of Law?* (Oxford: Blackwell, 1984); and my *Concept of Socialist Law* (Oxford: Clarendon, 1990).

15 Firestone, *Dialectic of Sex* (New York: Morrow, 1970); MacKinnon, "Feminism, Marxism and the State," pts. 1 and 2, *Signs*, Spring 1982 and Summer 1983; MacKinnon, *Feminism Unmodified*; O'Brien, *The Politics of Reproduction*; Hartsock, "The Feminist Standpoint," in S. Harding, ed., *Feminism and Methodology* (Bloomington: Indiana University Press and Open University Press, 1987); and Jaggar, *Feminist Politics and Human Nature*.

16 Review of MacKinnon, *Feminism Unmodified*, in *Political Theory*, August 1989.

17 H. Hartmann, "The Unhappy Marriage of Marxism and Feminism," and I. Young, "Beyond the Unhappy Marriage," in L. Sargent, *Women and Revolution* (Boston: South End Press, 1981); and L. Nicholson, "Feminism and Marx: Integrating Kinship with the Economic," in Benhabib and Cornell, eds., *Feminism as Critique*.

How Can Individualists Share Responsibility?

Annette C. Baier

ANNETTE C. BAIER *is Professor of Philosophy at the University of Pittsburgh. She has published many articles in the philosophy of mind, ethics, and the history of philosophy. Her books include* Postures of the Mind *and* A Progress of Sentiments: Reflections on Hume's Treatise.

The noun "individual" is a relative latecomer in the English language, not occurring until the seventeenth century. The earlier adjectival form has the sense of "indivisible." Individualism, as de Tocqueville defines it (and as its coiner, he cannot be defining it wrongly), is not so much a determination to be one unified self, not to divide oneself up into plural *personae*, as a disposition of "each member of a community to sever himself from the mass of his fellow creatures and draw apart with his family and friends."[1] The OED gives as its first sense of "individualism" the sense that de Tocqueville gives it, then moves to more recent senses: "self-centered feeling or conduct as a principle, a mode of life in which the individual pursues his own ends or follows his own ideas, free and independent individual action or thought, egoism." Here we have included both the near egoism that de Tocqueville intends the word to convey plus the independence of thought and action that gives us our concept of sturdy individualism as a virtue.

Egotism, de Tocqueville thinks, originates in blind instinct, but he finds individualism to be more reflective, a product of judgment, even if erroneous judgment: "Egotism blights the germ of all virtue; individualism, at first, only saps the virtues of public life; but in the long run it attacks and destroys all others, and is at last absorbed in downright egotism. Egotism is a vice as old as the world, which does not belong to one form of society more than to another: individualism is of democratic origin."[2] He contrasts the close but limited ties binding people together in aristocracies with democracies, where "the bond of human affection is extended, but relaxed." American ties are theoretically to all fellow Americans, but in fact "the interest of man is confined to those in close propinquity to himself." And even that interest has narrow bounds: "not only does democracy make every man forget his ancestors, but it hides his descendants, and separates his contemporaries from him; it throws him back for ever on himself alone, and threatens in the end to confine him entirely within the solitude of his own heart."

What prevents this threatened solipsism, on de Tocqueville's analysis, is voluntary association of individualists, with the press as communicative vehicle. White male Americans struck this aristocratic French observer as constantly ready to form a new association, be it to provide entertainment, to enforce temperance, or to send missionaries to the antipodes. He writes, "The first time I heard in the United States that a hundred thousand men had bound themselves publicly to abstain from spirituous liquors it appeared to me more like a joke than a serious engagement,"[3] but then he saw it was no joke but a manifestation of special need in democracies, an "artificial" creation of mutual ties, through voluntary association of like-minded people: "In democratic countries the science of association is the mother of science; the progress of all the rest depends on the progress it has made."[4] So voluntary association compensates for individualism, and the press facilitates communication between far-flung individuals united in various common causes, including political causes.

So where is the deficiency of the mind and perversity of the heart? Why should this "individualism," when combined with an eagerness for voluntary association and the cultivation of a free press, lead to egotism and to the sapping of the virtues of public life? Why should it lead to a forgetting of ancestors and an ignoring of the interests of our descendants? Among the voluntary associations eventually formed will be the Daughters of the American Revolution and various organizations formed to protect parks, wilderness areas, and other goods for our descendants. What public virtues are threatened by replacing inherited ties with voluntary loyalties, by replacing fixed rank with equality of opportunity for advancement, deferential with independent thinking, especially once slavery is abolished and once women get the vote? Public life will surely be different in a democratic republic, peopled by geographically and socially mobile individualists, than in a republic where the domiciles and ranks of persons are more fixed, where association is less voluntary and more hierarchical, but why should it not have its own virtues? In particular, why should democratic individualists lose the memory of what they owe their ancestors who forged the democracy, or be less concerned than others to preserve what they value for their descendants?

If recent historians of this nation such as Gordon S. Wood[5] are right, some of the framers of the U.S. Constitution were themselves appalled at what it appeared, by the end of their lives, that they had wrought. They had intended to institute a republic that would foster the traditional republican virtues of public service in the gentry and appreciative docility in the lower classes, leaving traditional hierarchical ties between master and slave or servant (not to mention man and woman) largely untouched. Wood, in *The Radicalism of the American Revolution*, quotes Thomas Jefferson's lament in 1825: "All, all dead, and ourselves left alone amid a new generation whom we know not, and who knows not us." Instead of the classical republican virtues, the new republic was spawning the new commercial and capitalist virtues of individual market enterprise, conspicuous consumption in the working class as well as among their "betters," a radical egalitarianism that threatened traditional class structure, and all too little public spiritness. So within one generation there was that "forgetting of ancestors," or at least of their aspirations, that de Tocqueville found striking.

Rather than look only at de Tocqueville's own answers to these questions, which plausibly enough point to the risks of leaving the protection of public values to voluntary support for them, support which may wax and wane, and to the dangers of majority despotism and the fickleness of the mass of voters, I shall return to Kant and to the version of republicanism that he erected on his individualist foundations. As I have indicated, I do this because of the recent appeal to Kant by John Rawls, one of the ablest and most influential defenders of this republic's liberal tradition, and because of the general enthusiasm among moral, social, and political philosophers for Kant's views,[6] or at least for those of them that are most familiar, through regular teaching of Kant's *Groundwork of the Metaphysics* of Morals, along with the sparse attention given to his *Doctrine of Right* (only recently available in unabridged translation).[7] If Rawls sees Kant, rather than Mill, Locke, Hume, or Burke, as giving us a moral and social philosophy that best articulates the basic principles of this nation's scheme of cooperation, then we detached ob-

servers (since I speak as a U.S. resident who is not a U.S. but a New Zealand citizen and who did not imbibe the ideology of American democracy with my mother's milk nor with by school lessons in history and social studies) presumably may without irrelevance turn there to understand what relationship there is, and is believed to be, between individual autonomous persons and the life that they live together under one constitution and one set of laws and between individual and collective responsibility.[8] I shall ignore the complication brought in by the fact that this nation is a federal union of states, so that we all live under both state and federal law, as this by no means unimportant aspect of American political life is not one that Rawls has emphasized nor one whose relationship to individualism de Tocqueville had views about.[9] Kant's remarks about federations of republics, in *Perpetual Peace*,[10] while they build on his earlier views about cooperation between fellow citizens within a republic, do no have much to say about the way that such federation affects or is affected by the sort of autonomy that belongs to individual citizens, nor about the way the individual responsibility of persons for their own choices somehow sums, in a democratic republic, to the states' and the nation's responsibility for its choice, say, the choice to fight the Gulf war and to inflict the massive casualties that the Iraqi people suffered in that war, or to return the Haitian refugees to Haiti, or to cut down Oregon's forests to supply timber, or to fail to get aid to the starving in East Africa, or to have no women candidates for the presidency, for that is the issue that my title promises and that I now begin to approach. ...

If we insist on clinging to the idea that moral responsibility must divide without remainder into the bit that is mine and not yours, and the other bits that belong exclusively to specific individuals, then not only will we limit the sort of shared action we engage in but we will drastically limit our ability to reform our inherited schemes of cooperation for the better. We will bog down on endless disputes about just who should get what portion of the blame for past evils, about just who deserves what compensatory advantages now. In *Metaphysics of Morals*, Kant writes that ownership is a concept correlative with that of a noumenal self—a property right is *possessio noumenon*.[11] Kant is speaking here of rights to external things, and, like John Locke, he believes that such things, particularly land, were originally possessed in common (*communio fundi originaria*), private ownership being consequent on a general will to allow individual claims by occupation. What Kant believes with respect to which tasks are a given person's own tasks, and whether originally there was a common task from which private tasks were divided out by agreement, is less clear. Rawls, who invokes the idea of a common fund of human talents,[12] may be adapting not just a Lockean but a Kantian concept of common fund of at least some crucial components of life, human work, and human responsibility. (Did Kant believe that there was a common fund of reason from which you reason and mine derive? Can a Kantian take a social view of reason? Did Kant believe that the respect-worthy humanity in each person is a derivate of some species-being that commands respect? The answer is not clear.) But it is, in any case, hard to see how essentially *individual* responsibility for action can be geared to essentially *collective* rights to goods and to essentially shared responsibility for the "general will" that divvies out the individual tasks and goods that particular persons get as their individual allotments. If the noumenal self is an individualist, he will insist on dividing up what was common, blurring the traces of the act of division, and disowning responsibility for this crucial action, as well as for maintaining what is brought about.

The Kantian form of individualism that has been and still is being appropriated in the American tradition has two fatal and connected flaws. It has no account of really shared responsibility but only pooled or passed-along individual autonomy and responsibility. Its version of the way the realm of ends legislates for itself, far from providing the basis for a democratic society, in fact degenerates, in Kant's own version of it, into law-giving by some elite, accompanied by willing subjection of the rest. When we look in Kant's writings and in most of the tradition that honors him to see just how this legislating elite is to be constituted, we find there the fairly undisguised "integrity" of a patriarchal and sexist tradition. If we are to avoid the deficiencies of the mind and the perversity of the heart that this Kantian tradition incorporates, then it is time we stopped paying deferential lip service to Immanuel Kant or, indeed, to any other preachers of the piety that consists in reverence to the faith of our patriarchal fathers.[13] If we do turn to continental Europe for our social theorists, we should turn not just to the Prussian who glorified individualism but to the Frenchman who criticized it

and to those who rejected the sexism of which both of them were guilty. We must mine our multifarious traditions for worthier versions of equality, of mutual respect, and of how responsibility is to be shared than the versions we find in Kant. If we cannot find them in any of our inherited traditions, we should be willing to be called revolutionaries. In the American tradition, that surely is not a dishonorable label.

Source: Annette C. Baier. "How Can Individualists Share Responsibility?" *Political Theory* 21, No.2 (1993): 228-248. Reprinted by permission of Sage Publications, Inc.

Notes

[1] Alexis de Tocqueville, *Democracy in America*, translated by Henry Reeve, in 2 vols. with a critical appraisal of each by John Stuart Mill (New York: Schocken, 1967), vol. 2, 118.

[2] Ibid.

[3] *Democracy in America,* 2:132.

[4] Ibid., p.133.

[5] Gordon S. Wood, *The Radicalism of the American Revolution* (New York: Alfred A. Knopf, 1992).

[6] Even those who have fairly fundamental disagreements with Kant, such as David Gauthier, appear to feel obliged to offer "subversive reinterpretations" and to appropriate the Kantian terminology, as if to give a borrowed authority to their own views. See "The Unity of Reason: A Subversive Reinterpretation of Kant," in David Gauthier, *Moral Dealing* (Ithaca, NY: Cornell University Press, 1990), 110-26.

[7] The Library of Liberal Arts translation by John Ladd, *The Metaphysical Elements of Justice* (Indianapolis, New York, Kansas City: Bobbs Merrill, 1965), which was all we had before Gregor's translation, omitted large sections of Kant's text.

[8] I have argued for the moral centrality of the concept of responsibility over that of individual rights in "Claims, Rights, Responsibilities," in *Prospects for a Common Morality*, edited by Gene Outka and J.P. Reeder, Jr. (Princeton University Press, forthcoming).

[9] He does of course discuss at length the advantages and disadvantages of a union or federation of republics and marvels at the "surprising facility" of the plain American citizen in distinguishing the jurisdictions of state and federal law. See *Democracy in America*, vol. 1, 185.

[10] Immanuel Kant, *Perpetual Peace*, in *Kant's Political Writings*, translated by H. B. Nisbet and edited by Hans Reiss (New York: Cambridge University Press, 1970).

[11] *Immanuel Kant, Metaphysics of Morals*, translated by Mary Gregor (New York: Cambridge University Press, 1991), pt. 1, §5.

[12] See John Rawls, *A Theory of Justice* (Cambridge, MA: Belknap Press of Harvard University Press, 1971), 100ff.

[13] I do not, of course, want to deny that many who saw and see themselves as Kantians or neo-Kantians have had a welcome liberalizing influence on political and social developments. The idea of equal respect for all persons continues to be a liberating and inspiring one.

Liberal Virtues

William Galston

WILLIAM A. GALSTON *is Professor in the School of Public Affairs and Institute for Philosophy and Public Policy, University of Maryland at College Park.*

General Virtues

Some of the virtues needed to sustain the liberal state are requisites of every political community. From time to time, each community must call upon its members to risk their lives in its defense. Courage—the willingness to fight and even die on behalf of one's country is thus very widely honoured even though there may be occasions on which the refusal to fight is fully justified.

In addition, every community creates a complex structure of law and regulations in the expectation that they will be accepted as legitimate, hence binding, without recourse to direct threats or sanctions. The net social value of a law is equal to the social benefits it engenders minus the social costs of enforcing it. As the individual propensity to obey the law diminishes, so does a society's ability to pursue collective goals through the law. Law-abidingness is therefore a core social virtue, in liberal communities and elsewhere. (This does not mean that disobedience is never justified, but only that a heavy burden of proof must be discharged by those who propose to violate the law.)

Finally, every society is constituted by certain core principles and sustained by its members' active belief in them. Conversely, every society is weakened by the diminution of its members' belief in its legitimacy. Loyalty—the developed capacity to understand, to accept and to act on the core principles of one's society—is thus a fundamental virtue. And it is particularly important in liberal communities, which tend to be organized around abstract principles rather than shared ethnicity, nationality or history.

Beyond the virtues needed to sustain all political communities are virtues specific to liberal communities—those required by the liberal spheres of society, economy, and polity.

Virtues of Liberal Society

A liberal society is characterized by two key features: individualism and diversity. To individualism corresponds the liberal virtue of independence—the disposition to care for, and take responsibility for, oneself and to avoid becoming needlessly dependent on others. Human beings are not born independent, nor do they attain independence through biological maturation alone. A growing body of evidence suggests that in a liberal society, the family is the critical arena in which independence and a host of other virtues must be engendered. The weakening of families is thus fraught with danger for liberal societies. In turn, strong families rest on specific virtues. Without fidelity, stable families cannot be maintained. Without a concern for children that extends well beyond the boundaries of adult self-regard, parents cannot effectively discharge their responsibility to help form secure, self-reliant young people. In short, the independence required for liberal social life rests on self-restraint and self-transcendence—the virtues of family solidarity.

I turn now from individualism to diversity, the second defining feature of liberal society. The maintenance of social diversity requires the virtue of tolerance. This virtue is widely thought to rest on the relativistic belief that every personal choice, every "life plan," is equally good, hence beyond rational scrutiny and cynicism. Nothing could be further from the truth. Tolerance is fully compatible with the proposition that some ways of life can be known to be superior to others. It rests rather on the conviction that the pursuit of the better course should be (and in many cases has to be) a consequence of education or persuasion rather than of coercion. Indeed, tolerance may be defined as the ability to make this conviction effective as a maxim of personal conduct.

Virtues of the Liberal Economy

The liberal market economy relies on two kinds of virtues: those required by different economic roles and those required by liberal economic life taken as a whole. In a modern market economy, the basic roles are those of the entrepreneur and the organization employee. The entrepreneurial virtues form a familiar litany: imagination, initiative, drive, determination. The organizational virtues are very different from (and in some respects the reverse of) the entrepreneurial. They include such traits as punctuality, reliability, civility toward co-workers, and a willingness to work within established frameworks and tasks. As economic units evolve, one of the great management challenges is to adjust the mix of entrepreneurial and organizational practices. Sometimes this takes the form of an organizational displacement (or routinization) of entrepreneurial charisma, as in the ouster of Steven Jobs as head of Apple Computer. Sometimes it requires just the opposite as when a large, stodgy organization replaces a centralized structure with semi-autonomous units and loosens individual task and role definitions in an effort to encourage more entrepreneurial practices on the part of its employees.

There are three generic (as distinct from role-specific) virtues required by modern market economies. The first is the work ethic, which combines the sense of obligation to support personal independence through gainful effort with the determination to do one's job thoroughly and well. The second is the achievement of a mean between ascetic self-denial and untrammelled self-indulgence; call it a capacity for moderate delay of gratification. For although market economies rely on the liberation and multiplication of consumer desires, they cannot prosper in the long run without a certain level of saving, which rests on the ability to subordinate immediate gratification to longer-run self-interest.

The third generic economic virtue is adaptability. Modern market economies are characterized by rapid, sweeping changes that reconfigure organizations and occupations. Patterns of life long employment within a single task or organization, common for much of this century are being displaced. Most individuals will change jobs several times during their working lives moving into new occupations, new organizations and even new sectors of the economy. To be sure, collective political action can help regulate the pace of change, ameliorate its consequences, and share its costs. Still, domestic and international pressures combine to make the fact and basic direction of economic change irresistible. Thus, the disposition to accept new tasks as challenges rather than threats and the ability to avoid defining personal identity and worth in reference to specific, fixed occupations are essential attributes of individuals and economies able to cope successful with the demands of change.[1]

Virtues of Liberal Politics

I come finally to the sphere of politics which calls for virtues of both citizens and leaders.

1. *Virtues of citizenship.* Some generic citizen virtues have already been identified: courage, law-abidingness, loyalty. In addition to these are the citizen virtues specific to the liberal polity. Because a liberal

order rests on individual rights, the liberal citizen must have the capacity to discern and the restraint to respect the rights of others. (Invasion of the rights of others is the form of *pleonexia* specific to liberal political life.) Because liberalism incorporates representative government, the liberal citizen must have the capacity to discern the talent and character of candidates vying for office, and to evaluate the performance of individuals who have attained office. Liberalism also envisions popular government, responsive to the demands of its citizens. The greatest vices of popular governments are the propensity to gratify short-term desires at the expense of long-term interests and the inability to act on unpleasant truths about what must be done. To check these vices, liberal citizens must be moderate in their demands and self-disciplined enough to accept painful measures when they are necessary. From this standpoint the willingness of liberal citizens to demand no more public services than their country can afford and to pay for all the benefits they demand is not just a technical economic issue but a moral issue as well. Consistently unbalanced budgets—the systematic displacement of social costs to future generations—are signs of a citizenry unwilling to moderate its desires or to discharge its duties.

The liberal citizen is not the same as the civic-republican citizen. In a liberal polity there is no duty to participate actively in politics, no requirement to place the public above the private and to systematically subordinate personal interest to the common good, no commitment to accept collective determination of personal choices. But neither is liberal citizenship simply the pursuit of self-interest individually or in factional collusion with others of like mind. Liberal citizenship has its own distinctive restraints—virtues that circumscribe and check without wholly nullifying, the promptings of self-aggrandizement.

2. *Virtues of leadership:* The need for virtue and excellence in political leaders is perhaps more immediately evident than is the corresponding requirement in the case of citizens. The U.S. Founding Fathers saw popular elections as the best vehicle for discerning and selecting good leaders. Thomas Jefferson spoke for them when he wrote to John Adams:

> There is a natural aristocracy among men. The grounds of this are virtue and talents ... The natural aristocracy I consider as the most precious gift of nature, for the instruction, trusts, and government of society ... May we not even say, that that form of government is the best, which provides the most effectively for a pure selection of these natural *aristoi* into the offices of government? ... I think the best remedy is exactly that provided by all our constitutions, to leave to the citizens the free election and separation of the *aristoi* from the *pseudo-aristoi.*[2]

The leadership virtues specific to liberal polities include patience—the ability to accept, and work within, the constraints on action imposed by social diversity and constitutional institutions. Second, liberal leaders must have the capacity to forge a sense of common purpose against the centrifugal tendencies of an individualistic and fragmented society. Third liberal leaders must be able to resist the temptation to earn popularity by pandering to immoderate public demands. Against desire liberal leaders must counterpose restraints; against the fantasy of the free lunch they must insist on the reality of the hard choice; against the lure of the immediate they must insist on the requirements of the long term. Finally, while liberal leaders derive authority from popular consent, they cannot derive policy from public opinion. Rather, they must have the capacity to narrow—insofar as public opinion permits—the gap between popular preference and wise action. The liberal leader who disregards public sentiment will quickly come to grief, but so will the leader who simply takes that sentiment as the polestar of public policy. Through persuasion, the liberal leader tries to move the citizenry toward sound views. But the limits of persuasion must constitute the boundaries of public action, or else leadership becomes usurpation.

As the authors of the *Federalist* insisted, and as experience confirms, there are also specific virtues required for the successful conduct of the different offices in a liberal-constitutional order: optimism and energy in the executive, deliberative excellence and civility in the legislator, impartiality and interpretive skill in the judge.[3] And, as Jefferson suggested, the ultimate test of systems of election or appointment is their tendency to select office holders with the appropriate virtues. For that reason, it is appropriate and necessary to inquire whether particular systems of selection (e.g. presidential nominating primaries) tend on balance to reward the kinds of personal traits that their corresponding offices require.

3. General political virtues: There are two other political virtues required of liberal citizens and leaders alike. While not all public policies need be made in the full light of day, liberal politics rests on a presumption of publicity, that is, on a commitment to resolve disputes through open discussion unless compelling reasons can be adduced for restricting or concealing the policy process. Thus, a general liberal political virtue is the disposition, and the developed capacity, to engage in public discourse. This virtue includes the willingness to listen seriously to a range of views which, given the diversity of liberal societies, will include ideas the listener is bound to find strange and even obnoxious. The virtue of political discourse also includes the willingness to set forth one's own views intelligibly and candidly as the basis of a politics of persuasion rather than manipulation or coercion.

A second general political virtue is the disposition to narrow the gap (insofar as it is in one's power) between principles and practices in liberal society. For leaders, this means admitting and confronting social imperfections through a public appeal to collective convictions. For citizens it can mean either such a public appeal, or quiet acts that reduce the reach of hypocrisy in one's immediate community. For both, it can lead to a tension between social transformation and law-abidingness, which can be resolved prudentially only with reference to the facts of specific cases. (This is a tension rather than a contradiction between two liberal virtues, because the virtue of law-abidingness embodies not the absolute priority of law but rather a presumption in favour of the law that can be rebutted in a narrow range of instances.)

Source: William A. Galston. *Liberal Purposes: Goods, Virtues, and Diversity in the Liberal State.* Cambridge: Cambridge University Press, 1991. Reprinted by permission of Cambridge University Press.

Notes

[1] This virtue should not be confused with Roberto Unger's much broader strictures against identifying personality with external structure.

[2] Thomas Jefferson, Letter to John Adams, October 28,62 1813, in Alpheus T. Mason, ed., *Free Government in the Making.* (New York: Oxford University Press, 1965), p.385.

[3] For a parallel account, see Harvey Mansfield "Constitutional Government," *The Public Interest* 86 (1987): 60.

3

Conservatism

The Ideal of Tradition

Shocked by the developments of the French Revolution, Edmund Burke wrote what has become the classic work about conservatism and its ideal of tradition. None of Burke's words resound more loudly on this issue than those which address the intricacies of human nature and the complexity of the objects of society, motifs to which Madison gives a Hobbesian interpretation in the *Federalist Papers*. From this philosophical position, it is a short step to establishing the concept of the preservation of the status quo. In his discussion of rationalism in politics, Michael Oakeshott criticizes the tendency of philosophers like John Locke to stress abstract principle rather than tradition in guiding the proper organization of society. Here one finds a definite echo of Burke. Eric Voegelin also stresses the necessity of tradition. He sees contemporary Western society as having within it both elements of modernity and elements of the classic and Christian tradition, but with gnosticism favouring the classical tradition. In his writings, Voegelin warns of the dangers of modern gnosticism with its rejection of some of the touchstones of tradition as found in philosophy and religion.

Aldous Huxley focuses attention upon a single aspect of Western tradition, namely religion. For Huxley, religion takes the form of perennial philosophy. He is pessimistic about the direction of liberal thinking and stresses the importance of the spiritual welfare of mankind as it has been traditionally defined.

In a similar vein, Donald Livingston brings to the fore some of the subtle and often hidden comments of David Hume on religion. Livingston makes a persuasive exegetical case for claiming that Hume believed that the effect of true philosophy and true religion is to endorse a conservative and traditional view of social and political order. Livingston's explication of Hume's writings concludes that the primary mandate of religion and philosophy should be the preservation of the sacredness of the common life. According to this thesis, any religion or philosophy that advocates anything else is false.

What one sees in conservative thought is a repudiation of *hubris* or pride in human reasoning that carries one beyond the empirical evidence available. At the same time there is a recognition that there are other constraints operating on persons and these include, but do not exhaust, the following: human intricacy, the complexity of the objects of society, and the ritualistic and passionate needs of humankind. Anchored firmly in all conservative thought is the defence of common sense afforded by Hume and the recognition that tradition gains sustenance from this common sense.

Reflections on the Revolution in France

Edmund Burke

EDMUND BURKE *(1729-1797) was an Irish political philosopher perhaps most famous for* Reflections on the Revolution in France (1790). *He placed considerable faith in the wisdom of the species as personified in the major institutions in society.*

Far am I from denying in theory, full as far is my heart from withholding in practice (if I were of power to give or to withhold), the *real* rights of men. In denying their false claims of right, I do not mean to injure those which are real, and are such as their pretended rights would totally destroy. If civil society be made for the advantage of man, all the advantages for which it is made become his right. It is an institution of beneficence; and law itself is only beneficence acting by a rule. Men have a right to live by that rule; they have a right to do justice, as between their fellows, whether their fellows are in public function or in ordinary occupation. They have a right to the fruits of their industry; and to the means of making their industry fruitful. They have a right to the acquisitions of their parents; to the nourishment and improvement of their offspring; to instruction in life, and to consolation in death. Whatever each man can separately do, without trespassing upon others, he has a right to do for himself; and he has a right to a fair portion of all which society, with all its combinations of skill and force, can do in his favour. In this partnership all men have equal rights; but not to equal things. He that has but five shillings in the partnership, has as good a right to it, as he that has five hundred pounds has to his larger proportion. But he has not a right to an equal dividend in the product of the joint stock; and as to the share of power, authority, and direction which each individual ought to have in the management of the state, that I must deny to be amongst the direct original rights of man in civil society; for I have in my contemplation the civil social man, and no other. It is a thing to be settled by convention.

If civil society be the offspring of convention, that convention must be its law. That convention must limit and modify all the descriptions of constitution which are formed under it. Every sort of legislative, judicial, or executory power are its creatures. They can have no being in any other state of things; and how can any man claim under the conventions of civil society, rights which do not so much as suppose its existence? rights which are absolutely repugnant to it? One of the first motives to civil society, and which becomes one of its fundamental rules, is, *that no man should be judge in his own cause*. By this each person has at once divested himself of the first fundamental right of uncovenanted man, that is, to judge for himself, and to assert his own cause. He abdicates all right to be his own governor. He inclusively, in a great measure, abandons the right of self-defence, the first law of nature. Men cannot enjoy the rights of an uncivil and of a civil state together. That he may obtain justice, he gives up his right of determining what it is in points the most essential to him. That he may secure some liberty, he makes a surrender in trust of the whole of it.

Government is not made in virtue of natural rights, which may and do exist in total independence of it; and exist in much greater clearness, and in a much greater degree of abstract perfection: but their abstract perfection is their practical defect. By having a right to everything they want everything. Government is a contrivance of human wisdom to provide for human *wants*. Men have a right that these wants should be provided for by this wisdom. Among these wants is to be reckoned the want, out of civil society, of a sufficient restraint upon their passions. Society requires not only that the passions of individuals should be subjected, but that even in the mass and body, as well as in the individuals, the inclinations of men should frequently be thwarted, their will controlled, and their passions brought into subjection. This can only be done *by a power out of themselves*; and not, in the exercise of its function, subject to that will and to those passions which it is its office to bridle and subdue. In this sense the restraints on men, as well as their liberties, are to be reckoned among their rights. But as the liberties and the restrictions vary with times and circumstances, and admit of infinite modifica-

EDMUND BURKE (1729-1797)

EDMUND BURKE was a Whig member of the British Parliament and a native of Ireland. He was the author of *Reflections on the Revolution in France* (1790) which is widely held to be the earliest formal enunciation of modern conservatism.

In this work, Burke outlined his theory that social change should occur slowly, with the inherent intention of "conserving" the best elements of a society over time. Burke was also a critic of British attempts to deny the autonomy of the North American colonists. He based this criticism on the grounds that the colonists were being ruled by an absentee government that was denying their right of effective representation. Burke expressed his views on this matter in *Thoughts on the Causes of the Present Discontents* (1770).

Commentators on Burke's political thought have interpreted his views on the state as almost "mysterious." He believed that it could not be manufactured or taken apart by its citizens but rather "ought ... to be looked upon with ... reverence," and its existence should be accepted without attempting to assign the responsibility of a "social contract" to it, an interpretation that today represents the classic conservatist thought.

---

tions, they cannot be settled upon any abstract rule; and nothing is so foolish as to discuss them upon that principle.

The moment you abate anything from the full rights of men, each to govern himself, and suffer any artificial, positive limitation upon those rights, from that moment the whole organization of government becomes a consideration of convenience. This it is which makes the constitution of a state, and the due distribution of its powers, a matter of the most delicate and complicated skill. It requires a deep knowledge of human nature and human necessities, and of the things which facilitate or obstruct the various ends, which are to be pursued by the mechanism of civil institutions. The state is to have recruits to its strength, and remedies to its distempers. What is the use of discussing a man's abstract right to food or medicine? The question is upon the method of procuring and administering them. In that deliberation I shall always advise to call in the aid of the farmer and the physician, rather than the professor of metaphysics.

The science of constructing a commonwealth, or renovating it, or reforming it, is, like every other experimental science, not to be taught *a priori*. Nor is it a short experience that can instruct us in that practical science; because the real effects of moral causes are not always immediate; but that which in the first instance is prejudicial may be excellent in its remoter operation; and its excellence may arise even from the ill effects it produces in the beginning. The reverse also happens: and very plausible schemes, with very pleasing commencements, have often shameful and lamentable conclusions. In states there are often some obscure and almost latent causes, things which appear at first view of little moment, on which a very great part of its prosperity or adversity may most essentially depend. The science of government being therefore so practical in itself, and intended for such practical purposes, a matter which requires experience, and even more experience than any person can gain in his whole life, however sagacious and observing he may be, it is with infinite caution that any man ought to venture upon pulling down an edifice, which has answered in any tolerable degree for ages the common purposes of society, or on building it up again, without having models and patterns of approved utility before his eyes.

These metaphysic rights entering into common life, like rays of light which pierce into a dense medium, are, by the laws of nature, refracted from their straight line. Indeed in the gross and complicated mass of human passions and concerns, the primitive rights of men undergo such a variety of refractions and reflections, that it becomes absurd to talk of them as if they continued in the simplicity of their original direction. The nature of man is intricate; the objects of society are of the greatest possible complexity: and therefore no simple disposition or direction of power can be suitable either to man's nature, or to the quality of his affairs. When I hear the simplicity of contrivance aimed at and boasted of in any new political constitutions, I am at no loss to decide that the artificers are grossly ignorant of their trade, or totally negligent of their duty. The simple governments are fundamentally defective, to say no worse of them. If you were to contemplate society in but one point of view, all these simple modes of polity are infinitely captivating. In effect each would answer its single end much more perfectly than the more complex is able to attain all its complex purposes. But it is better that the whole should be imperfectly and anomalously answered, than that, while some parts are provided for with great exactness, others might be totally neglected, or perhaps materially injured, by the overcare of a favourite member.

The pretended rights of these theorists are all extremes: and in proportion as they are metaphysically true, they are morally and politically false. The rights of men are in a sort of *middle*, incapable of definition, but not impossible to be discerned. The rights of men in governments are their advantages; and these are often in balances between differences of good; in compromises sometimes between good and evil, and sometimes between evil and evil. Political reason is a computing principle; adding, subtracting, multiplying, and dividing, morally and not metaphysically, or mathematically, true moral denominations.

Source: Edmund Burke. *Reflections on the Revolution in France.* Originally published in 1790.

Hume's Philosophy of Common Life

Donald W. Livingston

DONALD W. LIVINGSTON *is Associate Professor of Philosophy at Emory University.*

True Religion

Most conservatives have rejected misplaced philosophy in politics not by a searching philosophical criticism but by an appeal to a sacred ordering of things. The revolutionary is in rebellion not only against the established order of things but against God. Samuel Johnson could say that "the Devil was the first Whig."[1] De Maistre interpreted the entrance of philosophic reason into politics as an instance of the "fierce and rebellious pride" of the "intellectuals" whose "insolent doctrines… unceremoniously judge God."[2] Burke believed in a providential order and interpreted the norms of historical society (especially the British constitution) as the work of a "mysterious wisdom." Coleridge viewed the Bible as a statesman's manual and held that the first duty of the state is to make men "soberly and steadily religious."[3] That established social and political order is, in some way, grounded in a divine ordering of things has been vigorously taught by twentieth-century conservatives such as T.S. Eliot, Jacques Maritain, Leo Strauss, and Eric Voegelin. We may call these thinkers metaphysical conservatives because they seek to rebut metaphysical rebellion by appealing to an alternative metaphysical theory.

Metaphysical conservatives and metaphysical revolutionaries operate on the same logical level; their positions are logical contraries. Consider Marx's description of his own revolutionary thinking: "Thus the criticism of heaven is transformed into the criticism of earth, the *criticism of religion* into the *criticism of law*, and the *criticism of theology* into the *criticism of politics*."[4] Marx's metaphysical total criticism of the established order is logically tied to the falsity of certain theological propositions. Should those propositions be true, the criticism would be unjustified. Because their criticism is of the same logical type, metaphysical conservatives may become as totally alienated from the historical norms of common life as any revolutionary, depending on what the divine ordering is supposed to be and whether or not historical society conforms to it. But since the principle of correct order is a metaphysical thesis structured by the autonomy principle, there will always be, as we have repeatedly observed, a logical gap between the metaphysical principle and the historical norms it is supposed to certify or reject. Failing an original, unprincipled affirmation of these norms, no nonarbitray criticism of them is possible. Thus a metaphysical conservative may, if he likes, remain in total alienation from the established order no matter what changes are made.

Again, the familiar Humean point is that the proper way to criticize the goings-on in the world is to affirm the legitimacy of the work as a whole, abstract out the norms implicit in it, render them as coherent as possible, and them critically apply them to the practice. Always the movement is from the concrete to the abstract. Ideas follow impressions. We cannot begin with a theistic vision of the world (as metaphysical conservatives do) or an atheistic vision (as metaphysical rebels such as Marx do) and use these as standards to criticize the world. We could justify a choice between these metaphysical alternatives, but, even if one of them were preferable, criticism of the world would still be impossible since anything could appear to satisfy the alternative or not to satisfy it. The actual goods and evils which are lived out in common life cannot be distinguished by such standards. Whatever legitimate content theism, atheism, or any other metaphysical theory may have as a ground for criticizing the doings of common life must be determined by an original affirmation and involvement in the order of common life itself.

Although we may not class Hume among the metaphysical conservatives, he does, in his own way, share with them the conviction that established order has a sacred character and that this sacred character constitutes part of the authority of that order. To appreciate this, we must examine more closely Hume's conception of the relation between religion and philosophy.

In an earlier section, we observed that Hume's attack on religion is not against religion per se but against the modern notion of religion which, since the emergence of Christianity, has had philosophy analytically, built into it. Hume is not opposed to those pre-Christian civic religions consisting of "traditional tales and fictions" where "every one adheres to the tradition of his own sect without much reasoning or disputation" (E, 61). Likewise, the Epicurean (who may be taken to speak for Hume) in the first *Enquiry*, defending himself before the Athenians, attacks "The religious philosophers," not "the tradition of your forefathers and doctrine of your priests (in which I willingly acquiesce)" (EU, 135). Nor would Hume have any objection to Christianity purged, if it could be purged, of its philosophic structure.

What would religion be like for Hume if purged of philosophy? Pre-Christian religion would, of course, be one example, but Hume did not think it possible in the modern world to return to a completely non-philosophic practice of religion. He viewed his own age as one determined to establish science, morals, politics, and religion on the basis of something called *reason*, that is, on principles determined by autonomous philosophy. He called it, sarcastically, "this philosophic age," by which he meant an age governed by false philosophy (EM, 197n). In such an age, any reformed conception of religion must have a critical philosophic base. So we can only consider religion purged of false philosophy, not of philosophy as such. The result is what Hume calls "true religion," a concept mentioned often in his works but not systematically discussed. Piecing together his scattered remarks, we can discern the main features of this concept.

True religion, epistemologically, presupposes the critical work of "true philosophy" (post-Pyrrhonian philosophy) and is what Hume calls "philosophical theism." Theistic belief under this conception is neither caused nor justified by inductive or a-priori arguments, and so is not supported by reason as traditionally understood. Its justification, rather, follows the line of Hume's justification of the popular system in the *Treatise*: there is a psychological and a logical justification. Once we have consciously formed a policy of guiding our thought and action by empirical regularities, we are led by virtue of a propensity of our nature to view these regularities as a system produced by a single intelligence. This propensity to philosophical theism, though more variable by custom than the propensity to believe that our perceptions are continuously and independently existing objects, is, nevertheless, a universal propensity of human nature. The logical justification consists in the fact that the convention of scientific inquiry presupposes the belief: "astronomers often, *without thinking of it*, lay this strong foundation of piety and religion" and "all the sciences almost lead us *insensibly* to acknowledge a first intelligent Author; and their authority is often so much the greater, as they do not

directly profess that intention" (D, 214-15, emphasis mine).

God as conceived by "true religion" is "*mind or intelligence*" but is not a person and therefore has no moral relations to the world: the supreme being issues no commands, imposes no sanctions, and responds to no invocations. The moral world is no more than a set of social relations framed by men for men. Yet morality, for Hume, is not entirely independent of true religion: "The proper office of religion is to regulate the heart of men, humanize their conduct, infuse the spirit of temperance, order, and obedience; and as its operation is silent and only enforces the motives of morality and justice, it is in danger of being overlooked, and confounded with these other motives. When it distinguishes itself, and acts as a separate principle over men, it has departed from its proper sphere, and has become only a cover to faction and ambition" (D,220). True religion is perverted when it becomes "a separate principle over men." But this is precisely the error of false philosophy structured by the autonomy principle, which leads to the alienated philosopher caught within and without the world of common life and for whom "no one can answer for what will please or displease [him]" (EM, 343). Again, the "errors of religion" are just those of philosophy and true religion, like true philosophy, must abandon the autonomy principle. Both must accept common life not as an object of critical reflection but as a categories of their own activity. Just as the task of true philosophy is to methodize and correct the historically established maxims of common life, so true religion works within the order of common life to "humanize" conduct by giving men a pious regard for the sacredness of their common order.[5]

In this way, true philosophy and true religion are internally connected. True religion is of "the philosophical and rational kind" and presupposes the critical work of true philosophy as a condition (D,220). But the permanent temptation of philosophy is to slip back into the impious arrogance of the autonomy principle. To this, true religion sets up a barrier of *passion*, in the form of a feeling of the sacredness of common life which provides a motive for keeping philosophy within its proper sphere. Since, for Hume, false philosophy in politics is the greatest threat to morality under modern conditions, true religion and the reverence for common life that it inspires may be viewed as an essential support for morality. The "profound adoration" which Philo has for the "divine Being" issues in a total acceptance of and reverence for the order of common life as it is. The effect of philosophical theism is to endorse a deeply traditionalistic and conservative view of social and political order.

But it is conservative only in the sense of protecting the order against the revolutionary intrusion of the autonomy principle which has the conceptual effect of transforming the world of common life as a whole into an order of illusion, having no authority.

I would now like to sketch briefly how Hume understands the content of the sacredness of common life which is an essential part of true religion. One of his most original discoveries is that of the performative use of language. Language used in ritual acts constitutes essential realities of common life such as property, contracts, courtesy, marriage, political authority, and the entire hierarchy of status and rank among men, the whole of which, for Hume, is the moral world. So conceived, the moral world is an order of nonnatural relations held together by the ritualistic use of language, which is, Hume says, "one of the most mysterious and incomprehensible operations that can possibly be imagined, and may even be compared to *transubstantiation,* or *holy orders,* where a certain form of words, along with a certain intention, changes entirely the nature of an external object" (T, 524). Hume's criticism of popular religious ritual is not that it is merely "ritualistic; " it is, rather, that it purports to be cognitive and causal: a power is invoked by a sacred use of words to transform a natural object.[6] For Hume, the power of the ritual lies not in supernaturally changing the natural order but in constituting some part of the moral order: "Had I worn this apparel an hour ago, I had merited the severest punishment; but a man, by pronouncing a few magical syllables, has now rendered it fit for my use and service" (EM, 199). True religion, unlike popular religion, has no special set of sacred rituals for which reverence is due, precisely because the whole of the moral order is the set of rituals to which reverence is due.

The rationale behind the word-magic that constitutes the moral world is social utility. That is why the system of ritual acts in common life is more flexible, less systematic, and less consistent than that of popular religion which acts as "a separate principle over men" and is not guided by social utility (T, 524-25). But though utility is the origin of the ritualistic order of common life, its reality is not directly experienced or appreciated as utilitarian. It is a world of its own whose symbolic acts and the status they generate have intrinsic value; indeed, it is the distinctively human world. But it is not possible at all without an established social and political order, which is why Hume had to rework the concepts of philosophy and reason to include a broadly conservative view of common life as a category of philosophical thinking. It is against the background of this ritualistic conception of the moral world that we are to appreciate Hume's lifelong effort to promote literature, manners, and eloquence, and his dismay that philosophical and religious fanaticism were threatening to tear apart the constitutional system of liberty and the emerging commercial and industrial society in Britain that would enable the cultivation of letters (and all that that meant) to flourish.

The moral world emerges as a delicate structure held together by the narrative imagination and by the ritualistic use of language. It is especially vulnerable to the autonomy principle of false philosophy which under modern intellectual conditions informs both religion and philosophy. When false philosophy takes on ritualistic form, it spawns a world of *its* own. This is the world of superstition and of metaphysical politics which is logically and psychologically parasitic upon, yet destructive of, the world of common life. In Hume's own special way, it is conceived as a desecration of the sacredness of the secular order.

Source: Donald W. Livingston. *Hume's Philosophy of Common Life.* Chicago: University of Chicago Press, 1984. Reprinted by permission.

Notes

[1] James Boswell, *Boswell's Life of Johnson,* ed. George Birkbeck Hill, 2nd ed., 6 vol. (Oxford: Clarendon Press, 1964), 3:326.

[2] Joseph de Maistre, *The Saint Petersburg Dialogues,* in *The Works of Joseph de Maistre,* trans. Jack Lively (New York: Macmillan, 1965).

[3] Samuel T. Coleridge, *On the Constitution of the Church and State* (London: J. M. Dent, 1972), p.53.

[4] Karl Marx, *Marx and Engels, Basic Writings on Politics and Philosophy,* ed. Lewis S. Feuer (Garden City: Anchor, 1959), p.263.

[5] David Norton has discussed in some depth Hume's view that philosophy, if done properly, "softens and humanizes the temper" and "insensibly refines the temper," pointing out "those dispositions which we should endeavour to attain, by a constant *bent* of mind, and by repeated *habit.*" Quoted in Norton's *David Hume, Common-Sense Moralist.* Princeton University Press, 1982, p.219. See also chapter 5 above. That the reflections of true philosophy have ethical implications provides additional support for the thesis advanced here that true philosophy and true religion are internally connected, as are false philosophy and false religion. Consider also Hume's remark in "Of Essay Writing" that "sound understanding and delicate affections" are "characters, it is to be presumed, we shall always find *inseparable*" (E, 570, emphasis mine), and Pàll Àrdal's thesis that Hume treats reason (the reason of true philosophy) as a virtue, "The Virtue of Reasonableness in Hume's *Treatise,*" in *Hume: A Re-Evaluation.* Edited by Donald Livingston and James King. New York: Fordham University Press, 1976. pp.91-106.

[6] For a brief but interesting discussion of the role of ritual in Hume's thought, see Karl Britton, "Hume on some Non-Natural Distinctions," in *David Hume, Bicentenary Papers,* ed. by G.P. Morice (Edinburgh University Press, 1977), pp.205-09.

Abbreviations for Hume's Works

A *An Abstract of A Treatise of Human Nature,* ed. J. M. Keynes and P. Sraffa. Hamden: Archon Books, 1965.

D *Dialogues Concerning Natural Religion*, ed. Norman
   Kemp Smith. Indianapolis: Bobbs-Merrill, 1947.

E *Essays, Moral, Political, and Literary*. Oxford: Clarendon
   Press, 1966.

EM *Concerning the Principles of Morals* [EM], ed. L.A. Selby-
   Bigge. 3d ed. revised P.H. Nidditch. Oxford: Clarendon
   Press, 1975.

EU *David Hume's Enquries Concerning Human Understanding* [EU]

T *A Treatise of Human Nature*, ed. L. A. Selby-Bigge. 2nd
   edition with text revised and variant readings by P.H. Nidditch. Oxford: Clarendon Press, 1978.

Bibliography

Àrdal, Pàll. "Convention and Value." In *David Hume: Bicentenary Papers*. Edited by G.P. Morice. Edinburgh: Edinburgh University Press,
   1977.

————. "Some Implications of the Virtue of Reasonableness in *Hume's
   Treatise*." In *Hume: A Re-Evaluation*. Edited by Donald Livingston
   and James King. New York: Fordham University Press, 1976.

Boswell, James. *Boswell's Life of Johnson*. 6 vols. 2nd edition. Edited
   by George Birbeck Hill. Oxford: Clarendon Press, 1964.

Coleridge, Samuel T. *On the Constitution of the Church and State*.
   London: J. M. Dent, 1972.

De Maistre, Joseph. *The Saint Petersburg Dialogues*. In *The Works of
   Joseph de Maistre*. Translated by Jack Lively. New York: Macmillan,
   1965.

Livingston, D. W. "Hume's Historical Theory of Meaning." In *Hume: A
   Re-Evaluation*. Edited by D. W. Livingston and James King. New
   York: Fordham University Press. 1976.

Marx, Karl. *Marx and Engels Basic Writings on Politics and Philosophy*.
   Edited by Lewis S. Feuer. Garden City: Anchor, 1959.

Morice, G. P., ed. *David Hume: Bicentenary Papers*. Edinburgh: Edinburgh University Press, 1977.

Norton, David Fate. *David Hume: Common-Sense Moralist, Sceptical
   Metaphysican*. Princeton: Princeton University Press, 1982.

The Federalist Papers

James Madison (*Publius*)

JAMES MADISON *(1751-1836) shared the authorship of* The Federalist Papers *with Alexander Hamilton and John Jay. In addition to having a long and distinguished political career, he argued successfully for a political theory upon which the constitution of the USA was based. He wrote* The Federalist Paper No. 10 *under the pseudonym of "Publius."*

Among the numerous advantages promised by a well constructed Union, none deserves to be more accurately developed than its tendency to break and control the violence of faction. The friend of popular governments never finds himself so much alarmed for their character and fate as when he contemplates their propensity to this dangerous vice. He will not fail, therefore, to set a due value on any plan which, without violating the principles to which he is attached, provides a proper cure for it. The instability, injustice, and confusion introduced into the public councils have, in truth, been the mortal diseases under which popular governments have everywhere perished, as they continue to be the favorite and fruitful topics from which the adversaries to liberty derive their most specious declamations. The valuable improvements made by the American constitutions on the popular models, both ancient and modern, cannot certainly be too much admired; but it would be an unwarrantable partiality to contend that they have as effectually obviated the danger on this side, as was wished and expected. Complaints are everywhere heard from our most considerate and virtuous citizens, equally the friends of public and private faith and of public and personal liberty, that our governments are too unstable, that the public good is disregarded in the conflicts of rival parties, and that measures are too often decided, not according to the rules of justice and the rights of the minor party, but by the superior force of an interested and overbearing majority. However anxiously we may wish that these complaints had no foundation, the evidence of known facts will not permit us to deny that they are in some degree true. It will be found, indeed, on a candid review of our situation, that some of the distresses under which we labor have been erroneously charged on the operation of our governments; but it will be found, at the same time, that other causes will not alone account for many of our heaviest misfortunes; and, particularly, for that prevailing and increasing distrust of public engagements and alarm for private rights which are echoed from one end of the continent to the other. These must be chiefly, if not wholly, effects of the unsteadiness and injustice with which factious spirit has tainted our public administration.

By a faction I understand a number of citizens, whether amounting to a majority or minority of the whole, who are united and actuated by some common impulse of passion, or of interest, adverse to the rights of other citizens, or to the permanent and aggregate interests of the community.

There are two methods of curing the mischiefs of faction: the one, by removing its causes; the other, by controlling its effects.

There are again two methods of removing the causes of faction: the one, by destroying the liberty which is essential to its existence; the other, by giving to every citizen the same opinions, the same passions, and the same interests.

It could never be more truly said than of the first remedy that it was worse than the disease. Liberty is to faction what air is to fire, an aliment without which it instantly expires. But it could not be less folly to abolish liberty, which is essential to political life, because it nourishes faction than it would be to wish the annihilation of air, which is essential to animal life, because it imparts to fire its destructive agency.

The second expedient is as impracticable as the first would be unwise. As long as the reason of man continues fallible, and he is at liberty to exercise it, different opinions will be formed. As long as the connection subsists between his reason and his self-love, his opinions and his passions will have a reciprocal influence on each other; and the former will be objects to which the latter will attach themselves. The diversity in the faculties of men, from which the rights of property originate, is not less an insuperable obstacle to a uniformity of interests. The protection of these faculties is the first object of government. From the protection of different and unequal faculties of acquiring property, the possession of different degrees and kinds of property immediately results; and from the influence of these on the sentiments and views of the respective proprietors ensues a division of the society into different interests and parties.

The latent causes of faction are thus sown in the nature of man; and we see them everywhere brought into different degrees of activity, according to the different circumstances of civil society. A zeal for dif-

JAMES MADISON (1751–1836)

JAMES MADISON of Virginia was a member of the U.S. Congress, Secretary of State from 1801 to 1809, and President of the United States (1809–1817).

Among political theorists, Madison is best known, along with Alexander Hamilton and John Jay, as the author of the *Federalist Papers*. At the time they were written, the *Federalist Papers* were the most definitive commentary on the newly-formed United States Constitution, and they remain so today in the opinion of most scholars of American politics. Madison was heavily influenced by Enlightenment philosophers like Voltaire, David Hume, John Locke and Isaac Newton.

Madison's greatest fear was that the Articles of Confederation, which eventually formed the Constitution, would not have sufficient legislative force to bind the various states into a permanent union. It was possible that the rights of the individual states

to pass laws, carry on commerce and elect their own governments would create a situation in which central governmental authority would become irrelevant and eventually disappear. In writing the *Federalist Papers*, Madison articulated his ideas about how a strong central government was the surest path to safety and happiness for the citizens of the new Republic.

Madison and the other "Founding Fathers" of the U.S. Constitution were also aware of the possibility that one of the states that comprised the Union could become disenchanted with the rule of central government and attempt to remove itself from the authority of federal power. But one of the benefits of such a government, as Alexander Hamilton declared, was that "should a popular insurrection happen in one of the confederate states, the others are able to quell it." In less than a century, this idea was put to the test by the American Civil War.

During the first session of the new Congress, Madison was successful in ensuring the passage of the so-called "Bill of Rights," the first ten amendments to the Constitution.

Along with Thomas Jefferson, Madison was one of the founders of what became today's Democratic party in the United States.

---

ferent opinions concerning religion, concerning government, and many other points, as well of speculation as of practice; an attachment to different leaders ambitiously contending for pre-eminence and power; or to persons of other descriptions whose fortunes have been interesting to the human passions, have, in turn, divided mankind into parties, inflamed them with mutual animosity, and rendered them much more disposed to vex and oppress each other than to co-operate for their common good. So strong is this propensity of mankind to fall into mutual animosities that where no substantial occasion presents itself the most frivolous and fanciful distinctions have been sufficient to kindle their unfriendly passions and excite their most violent conflicts. But the most common and durable source of factions has been the various and unequal distribution of property. Those who hold and those who are without property have ever formed distinct interests in society. Those who are creditors, and those who are debtors, fall under a like discrimi-

nation. A landed interest, a manufacturing interest, a mercantile interest, a moneyed interest, with many lesser interests, grow up of necessity in civilized nations, and divide them into different classes, actuated by different sentiments and views. The regulation of these various and interfering interests forms the principal task of modern legislation and involves the spirit of party and faction in the necessary and ordinary operations of government.

No man is allowed to be a judge in his own cause, because his interest would certainly bias his judgment, and, not improbably, corrupt his integrity. With equal, nay with greater reason, a body of men are unfit to be both judges and parties at the same time; yet what are many of the most important acts of legislation but so many judicial determinations, not indeed concerning the rights of single persons, but concerning the rights of large bodies of citizens? And what are the different classes of legislators but advocates and parties to the causes which they determine?

Is a law proposed concerning private debts? It is a question to which the creditors are parties on one side and the debtors on the other. Justice ought to hold the balance between them. Yet the parties are, and must be, themselves the judges; and the most numerous party, or in other words, the most powerful faction must be expected to prevail. Shall domestic manufacturers be encouraged, and in what degree, by restrictions on foreign manufacturers? are questions which would be differently decided by the landed and the manufacturing classes, and probably by neither with a sole regard to justice and the public good. The apportionment of taxes on the various descriptions of property is an act which seems to require the most exact impartiality; yet there is, perhaps, no legislative act in which greater opportunity and temptation are given to a predominant party to trample on the rules of justice. Every shilling with which they overburden the inferior number is a shilling saved to their own pockets.

It is in vain to say that enlightened statesmen will be able to adjust these clashing interests and render them all subservient to the public good. Enlightened statesmen will not always be at the helm. Nor, in many cases, can such an adjustment be made at all without taking into view indirect and remote considerations, which will rarely prevail over the immediate interest which one party may find in disregarding the rights of another or the good of the whole.

The inference to which we are brought is that the *causes* of faction cannot be removed and that relief is only to be sought in the means of controlling its *effects*.

If a faction consists of less than a majority, relief is supplied by the republican principle, which enables the majority to defeat its sinister views by regular vote. It may clog the administration, it may convulse the society; but it will be unable to execute and mask its violence under the forms of the Constitution. When a majority is included in a faction, the form of popular government, on the other hand, enables it to sacrifice to its ruling passion or interest both the public good and the rights of other citizens. To secure the public good and private rights against the danger of such a faction, and at the same time to preserve the spirit and the form of popular government, is then the great object to which our inquiries are directed. Let me add that it is the great desideratum by which alone this form of government can be rescued from the opprobrium under which it has so long labored and be recommended to the esteem and adoption of mankind.

By what means is this object attainable? Evidently by one of two only. Either the existence of the same passion or interest in a majority at the same time must be prevented, or the majority, having such coexistent passion or interest, must be rendered, by their number and local situation, unable to concert and carry into effect schemes of oppression. If the impulse and the opportunity be suffered to coincide, we well know that neither moral nor religious motives can be relied on as an adequate control. They are not found to be such on the injustice and violence of individuals, and lose their efficacy in proportion to the number combined together, that is, in proportion as their efficacy becomes needful.

From this view of the subject it may be concluded that a pure democracy, by which I mean a society consisting of a small number of citizens, who assemble and administer the government in person, can admit of no cure for the mischiefs of faction. A common passion or interest will, in almost every case, be felt by a majority of the whole; a communication and concert results from the form of government itself; and there is nothing to check the inducements to sacrifice the weaker party or an obnoxious individual. Hence it is that such democracies have ever been spectacles of turbulence and contention; have ever been found incompatible with personal security or the rights of property; and have in general been as short in their lives as they have been violent in their deaths. Theoretic politicians, who have patronized this species of government, have erroneously supposed that by reducing mankind to a perfect equality in their political rights, they would at the same time be perfectly equalized and assimilated in their possessions, their opinions, and their passions.

A republic, by which I mean a government in which the scheme of representation takes place, opens a different prospect and promises the cure for which we are seeking. Let us examine the points in which it varies from pure democracy, and we shall comprehend both the nature of the cure and the efficacy which it must derive from the Union.

The two great points of difference between a democracy and a republic are: first, the delegation of the government, in the latter, to a small number of citizens elected by the rest; secondly, the greater number of citizens and greater sphere of country over which the latter may be extended.

The effect of the first difference is, on the one hand, to refine and enlarge the public views by passing them through the medium of a chosen body of citizens, whose wisdom may best discern the true interest of their country and whose patriotism and love of justice will be least likely to sacrifice it to temporary or partial considerations. Under such a regulation it may well happen that the public voice, pronounced by the representatives of the people, will be more consonant to the public good than if pronounced by the people themselves, convened for the purpose. On the other hand, the effect may be inverted. Men of factious tempers, of local prejudices, or of sinister designs, may, by intrigue, by corruption, or by other means, first obtain the suffrages, and then betray the interests of the people. The question resulting is, whether small or extensive republics are most favorable to the election of proper guardians of the public weal; and it is clearly decided in favor of the latter by two obvious considerations.

In the first place it is to be remarked that however small the republic may be the representatives must be raised to a certain number in order to guard against the cabals of a few; and that however large it may be they must be limited to a certain number in order to guard against the confusion of a multitude. Hence, the number of representatives in the two cases not being in proportion to that of the constituents, and being proportionally greatest in the small republic, it follows that if the proportion of fit characters be not less in the large than in the small republic, the former will present a greater option, and consequently a greater probability of a fit choice.

In the next place, as each representative will be chosen by a greater number of citizens in the large than in the small republic, it will be more difficult for unworthy candidates to practise with success the vicious arts by which elections are too often carried; and the suffrages of the people being more free, will be more likely to center on men who possess the most attractive merit and the most diffusive and established characters.

It must be confessed that in this, as in most other cases, there is a mean, on both sides of which inconveniences will be found to lie. By enlarging too much the number of electors, you render the representative too little acquainted with all their local circumstances and lesser interests; as by reducing it too much, you render him unduly attached to these, and too little fit to comprehend and pursue great and national objects. The federal Constitution forms a happy combination in this respect; the great and aggregate interests being referred to the national, the local and particular to the State legislatures.

The other point of difference is the greater number of citizens and extent of territory which may be brought within the compass of republican than of democratic government; and it is this circumstance principally which renders factious combinations less to be dreaded in the former than in the latter. The smaller the society, the fewer probably will be the distinct parties and interests composing it; the fewer the distinct parties and interests, the more frequently will a majority be found of the same party; and the smaller the number of individuals composing a majority, and the smaller the compass within which they are placed, the more easily will they concert and execute their plans of oppression. Extend the sphere and you take in a greater variety of parties and interests; you make it less probable that a majority of the whole will have a common motive to invade the rights of other citizens; or if such a common motive exists, it will be more difficult for all who feel it to discover their own strength and to act in unison with each other. Besides other impediments, it may be remarked that, where there is a consciousness of unjust or dishonorable purposes, communication is always checked by distrust in proportion to the number whose concurrence is necessary.

Hence, it clearly appears that the same advantage which a republic has over a democracy in controlling the effects of faction is enjoyed by a large over a small republic—is enjoyed by the Union over the States composing it. Does this advantage consist in the substitution of representatives whose enlightened views and virtuous sentiments render them superior to local prejudices and to schemes of injustice? It will not be denied that the representation of the Union will be most likely to possess these requisite endowments. Does it consist in the greater security afforded by a greater variety of parties, against the event of any one party being able to outnumber and oppress the rest? In an equal degree does the increased variety of parties comprised within the Union increase this security. Does it, in fine, consist in the greater obstacles opposed to the concert and accomplishment of the secret wishes of an unjust and interested majority? Here again the extent of the Union gives it the most palpable advantage.

The influence of factious leaders may kindle a flame within their particular States but will be unable to spread a general conflagration through the other States. A religious sect may degenerate into a political faction in a part of the Confederacy; but the variety of sects dispersed over the entire face of it must secure the national councils against any danger from that source. A rage for paper money, for an abolition of debts, for an equal division of property, or for any other improper or wicked project, will be less apt to pervade the whole body of the Union than a particular county or district than an entire State.

In the extent and proper structure of the Union, therefore, we behold a republican remedy for the diseases most incident to republican government. And according to the degree of pleasure and pride we feel in being republicans ought to be our zeal in cherishing the spirit and supporting the character of federalists.

Source: Alexander Hamilton, James Madison, and John Jay. *The Federalist Papers* Originally published in 1788.

The Perennial Philosophy

Aldous Huxley

ALDOUS HUXLEY *(1894-1963) was a prolific writer made famous by a number of his writings including* Brave New World *(1932). Being a moralist rather than a fictionalist, he wrote to inform and moved from nihilism to religion and mysticism in the latter years of his life.*

The Greeks believed that *hubris* was always followed by *nemesis*, that if you went too far you would get a knock on the head to remind you that the gods will not tolerate insolence on the part of mortal men. In the sphere of human relations, the modern mind understands the doctrine of *hubris* and regards it as mainly true. We wish pride to have a fall, and we see that very often it does fall.

To have too much power over one's fellows, to be too rich, too violent, too ambitious—all this invites punishment, and in the long run, we notice, punishment of one sort or another duly comes. But the Greeks did not stop there. Because they regarded Nature as in some way divine, they felt that it had to be respected and they were convinced that a hubristic lack of respect for Nature would be punished by avenging *nemesis*. In "The Persians," Aeschylus gives the reasons—the ultimate, metaphysical reasons—for the barbarians' defeat. Xerxes was punished for two offences—overweening imperialism directed against the Athenians, and overweening imperialism directed against Nature. He tried to enslave his fellow men, and he tried to enslave the sea, by building a bridge across the Hellespont. ...

Today we recognize and condemn the first kind of imperialism; but most of us ignore the existence and even the very possibility of the second. And yet the author of *Erewhon* was certainly not a fool, and now that we are paying the appalling price for our much touted "conquest of Nature" his book seems more than ever topical. And Butler was not the only nineteenth-century sceptic in regard to Inevitable Progress. A generation or more before him, Alfred de Vigny was writing about the new technological marvel of his days, the steam engine—writing in a tone very different from the enthusiastic roarings and trumpetings of his great contemporary, Victor Hugo. ...

Looking backwards across the carnage and the devastation, we can see that Vigny was perfectly right. None of those gay travellers, of whom Victor Hugo was the most vociferously eloquent, had the faintest notion where that first, funny little Puffing Billy was taking them. Or rather they had a very clear notion, but it happened to be entirely false. For they were convinced that Puffing Billy was hauling them at full speed towards universal peace and the brotherhood of man; while the newspapers which they were so proud of being able to read, as the train rumbled along towards its Utopian destination not more than fifty years or so away, were the guarantee that liberty and reason would soon be everywhere triumphant. Puffing Billy has now turned into a four-motored bomber loaded with white phosphorus and high explosives, and the free press is everywhere the servant of its advertisers, of a pressure group, or of the government. And yet, for some inexplicable reason, the travellers (now far from gay) still hold fast to the religion of Inevitable Progress—which is, in the last analysis, the hope and faith (in the teeth of all human experience) that one can get something for nothing. How much saner and more realistic is the Greek view that every victory has to be paid for, and that, for some victories, the price exacted is so high that it outweighs any advantage that may be obtained! Modern man no longer regards Nature as being in any sense divine and feels perfectly free to behave towards her as an overweening conqueror and tyrant. The spoils of recent technological imperialism have been enormous; but meanwhile *nemesis* has seen to it that we get our kicks as well as halfpence. For example, has the ability to travel in twelve hours from New York to Los Angeles given more pleasure to the human race than the dropping of bombs and fire has given pain? There is no known method of computing the amount of felicity or goodness in the world at large. What is obvious, however, is that the advantages accruing from recent technological advances—or, in Greek phraseology, from recent acts of *hubris* directed against Nature—are generally accompanied by corresponding disadvantages, that gains in one direction entail losses in other directions, and that we never get something except for something. Whether the net result of these elaborate credit and debit operations is a genuine Progress in virtue, happiness, charity and intelligence is something we can never definitely determine. It is because the reality of Progress can never be determined that the nineteenth and twentieth centuries have had to treat it as an article of religious faith. To the exponents of the Perennial Philosophy, the question whether Progress is inevitable or even real is not a matter of primary importance. For them, the important thing is that individual men and women should come to the unitive knowledge of the divine Ground, and what interests them in regard to the social environment is not its progressiveness or non-progressiveness (whatever those terms may mean), but the degree to which it helps or hinders individuals in their advance towards man's final end.

Source: Aldous Huxley. *The Perennial Philosophy* New York: Harper & Brothers, 1945. Copyright © 1944, 1945 by Aldous Huxley. Copyright © renewed 1973, 1974 by Laura A. Huxley. Reprinted by permission of HarperColins Publishers, Inc.

The Dangers of Gnosticism

Eric Voegelin

ERIC VOEGELIN *(1901-1985) was born in Cologne and taught law at the University of Vienna, government at Louisiana State University, and most recently political science at the University of Munich. He is famous as an interpreter of the conservative streams of European thought. His writings include* Order and History *and* The New Science of Politics.

This exposition of the dangers of gnosticism as a civil theology of Western society will probably have aroused some misgivings. The analysis did fully pertain only to the progressive and idealistic varieties which prevail in Western democracies; it would not equally well apply to the activist varieties which prevail in totalitarian empires. Whatever share of responsibility for the present plight may be laid on the doorsteps of progressivists and idealists, the most formidable source of imminent danger seems to be the activists. The intimate connection between the two dangers, therefore, requires clarification—all the more so because the representatives of the two Gnostic varieties are antagonists in battle on the world scene. The analysis of this further question can appropriately use as a preface the pronouncements of a famous liberal intellectual on the problem of communism:

> Lenin was surely right when the end he sought for was to build his heaven on earth and write the precepts of his faith into the inner fabric of a universal humanity. He was surely right, too, when he recognized that the prelude to peace is a war, and that it is futile to suppose that the tradition of countless generations can be changed, as it were, overnight.[1]

> The power of any supernatural religion to build that tradition has gone; the deposit of scientific inquiry since Descartes has been fatal to its authority. It is therefore difficult to see upon what basis the civilized tradition can be rebuilt save that upon which the idea of the Russian Revolution is founded. It corresponds, its supernatural basis apart, pretty exactly to the mental climate in which Christianity became the official religion of the West.[2]

> It is, indeed, true in a sense to argue that the Russian principle cuts deeper than the Christian since it seeks salvation for the masses by fulfilment in this life, and, thereby, orders anew the actual world we know.[3]

Few passages could be more revealing for the plight of the liberal intellectual in our time. Philosophy and Christianity are beyond his range of experience. Science, besides being an instrument for power over nature, is something that makes you sophisti-cated enough not to believe in God. Heaven will be built on earth. Self-salvation, the tragedy of gnosticism which Nietzsche experienced to the full until it broke his soul, is a fulfilment of life that will come to every man with the feeling that he is making his contribution to society according to his ability, compensated by a weekly paycheck. There are no problems of human existence in society except the immanent satisfaction of the masses. Political analysis tells you who will be the winner, so that the intellectual can advance in proper time to the position of a court theologian of the Communist empire. And, if you are bright, you will follow him in his expert surf-riding on the wave of the future. The case is too well known today to need further comment. It is the case of the petty paracletes in whom the spirit is stirring, who feel the duty to play a public role and be teachers of mankind, who with good faith substitute their convictions for critical knowledge, and with a perfectly good conscience express their opinions on problems beyond their reach. Moreover, one should not deny the immanent consistency and honesty of this transition from liberalism to communism; if liberalism is understood as the immanent salvation of man and society, communism certainly is its most radical expression; it is an evolution that was already anticipated by John Stuart Mill's faith in the ultimate advent of communism for mankind.

In more technical language one can formulate the problem in the following manner. The three possible varieties of immanentization—teleological, axiological, and activist—are not merely three co-ordinated types but are related to one another dynamically. In every wave of the Gnostic movement the progressivist and utopian varieties will tend to form a political right wing, leaving a good deal of the ultimate perfection to gradual evolution and compromising on a tension between achievement and ideal, while the activist variety will tend to form a political left wing, taking violent action toward the complete realization of the perfect realm. The distribution of the faithful from right to left will in part be determined by such personal equations as enthusiasm, temperament, and consistency; to another, and perhaps the more important part, however, it will be determined by their relation to the civilizational environment in which the Gnostic revolution takes place. For it must never be forgotten that Western society is not all modern but that modernity is a growth within it, in opposition to the classic and Christian tradition. If there were nothing in Western society but gnosticism, the movement toward the left would be irresistible because it lies in the logic of immanentization, and it would have been consummated long ago. In fact, however, the great Western revolutions of the past, after their logical swing to the left, settled down to a public order which reflected the balance of the social forces of the moment, together with their economic interests and civilizational traditions. The apprehension or hope, as the case may be, that the "partial" revolutions of the past will be followed by the "radical" revolution and the establishment of the final realm rests on the assumption that the traditions of Western society are now sufficiently ruined and that the famous masses are ready for the kill.[4]

The dynamics of gnosticism, thus, moves along two lines. In the dimension of historical depth, gnosticism moves from the partial immanentization of the high Middle Ages to the radical immanentization of the present. And with every wave and revolutionary outburst it moves in the amplitude of right and left. The thesis, however, that these two lines of dynamics must now meet according to their inner logic, that Western society is ripe to fall for communism, that the course of Western history is determined by the logic of its modernity and nothing else, is an impertinent piece of Gnostic propaganda at both its silliest and most vicious and certainly has nothing to do with a critical study of politics. Against this thesis must be held a number of facts which today are obscured because the public debate is dominated by the liberal clichés. In the first place, the Communist movement in Western society itself, wherever it had to rely on its own mass appeal without aid from the Soviet government, has got exactly nowhere at all. The only Gnostic activist movement that achieved a noteworthy measure of success was the National Socialist movement on a limited national basis; and the suicidal nature of such an activist success is amply testified by the atrocious internal corruption of the regime while it lasted as well as by the ruins of the German cities. Second, the present Western plight in the face of the Soviet danger, in so far as it is due to the creation of the previously described power vacuum, is not of Communist making. The power vacuum was created by the Western democratic governments freely, on the height of a military victory, without pressure from anybody. Third, that the Soviet Union is an expanding great power on the Continent has nothing to do with communism. The present extension of the Soviet empire over the satellite nations corresponds substantially to the program of a Slavic empire under Russian hegemony as it was submitted, for instance, by Bakunin to Nicolai I. It is quite conceivable that a non-Communist Russian hegemonic empire would today have the same expanse as the Soviet empire and be a greater danger because it might be better consolidated. Fourth, the Soviet empire, while it is a formidable power, is no danger to Western Europe on the level of material force. Elementary statistics shows that Western manpower, natural resources, and industrial potential are a match to any strength the Soviet empire can muster—not counting our own power in the background. The danger strictly arises from national particularism and the paralyzing intellectual and moral confusion.

The problem of Communist danger, thus, is thrown back on the problem of Western paralysis and self-destructive politics through the Gnostic dream. The previously quoted passages show the source of the trouble. The danger of a sliding from right to left is inherent in the nature of the dream; in so far as communism is a more radical and consistent type of immanentization than progressivism or social utopianism, it has the *logique du coeur* on its side. The Western Gnostic societies are in a state of intellectual and emotional paralysis because no fundamental critique of left-wing gnosticism is possible without blowing up right-wing gnosticism in its course. Such major experiential and intellectual revolutions, however, take their time and the change of at least one generation. One can do no more than formulate the conditions of the problem. There will be a latent Communist danger under the most favorable external circumstances as long as the public debate in Western societies is dominated by the Gnostic clichés. That is to say: as long as the recognition of the structure of reality, the cultivation of the virtues of *sophia* and *prudentia*, the discipline of the intellect, and the development of theoretical culture and the life of the spirit are stigmatized in public as "reactionary," while disregard for the structure of reality, ignorance of facts, fallacious misconstruction and falsification of history, irresponsible opining on the basis of sincere conviction, philosophical illiteracy, spiritual dulness, and agnostic sophistication are considered the virtues of man and their possession opens the road to public success. In brief: as long as civilization is reaction, and moral insanity is progress.

Source: Eric Voegelin. *The New Science of Politics.* Chicago: University of Chicago Press, 1966. Reprinted with permission.

Notes

[1] Harold J Laski, *Faith, Reason and Civilization: An Essay in Historical Analysis* (New York: Viking Press, 1944), p.184.

[2] *Ibid.,* p.51.

[3] *Ibid.,* p.143.

[4] The concepts of "partial" and "radical" revolution were developed by Karl Marx in *Kritik der Hegelschen Rechtsphilosophie, Einleitung* (1843), Vol. I: Gesamtausgabe, p.617.

Rationalism in Politics

Michael Oakeshott

MICHAEL OAKESHOTT *(1901-1990) was one of Britain's leading political philosophers in the twentieth century and Professor Emeritus at the London School of Economics and Political Science and Fellow of the British Academy. His books included* On Human Conduct (1975).

The new and politically inexperienced social classes which, during the last four centuries, have risen to the exercise of political initiative and authority, have been provided for in the same sort of way as Machiavelli provided for the new prince of the sixteenth century. None of these classes had time to acquire a political education before it came to power; each needed a crib, a political doctrine, to take the place of a habit of political behaviour. Some of these writings are genuine works of political vulgarization; they do not altogether deny the existence or worth of a political tradition (they are written by men of real political education), but they are abridgements of a tradition, rationalizations purporting to elicit the "truth" of a tradition and to exhibit it in a set of abstract principles, but from which, nevertheless, the full significance of the tradition inevitably escapes. This is pre-eminently so of Locke's *Second Treatise of Civil Government*, which was as popular, as long-lived and as valuable a political crib as that greatest of all cribs to a religion, Paley's *Evidences of Christianity*. But there are other writers, like Bentham or Godwin, who, pursuing the common project of providing for the political inexperience of succeeding generations, cover up all trace of the political habit and tradition of their society with a purely speculative idea: these belong to the strictest sect of Rationalism. But, so far as authority is concerned, nothing in this field can compare with the work of Marx and Engels. European politics without these writers would still have been deeply involved in Rationalism, but beyond question they are the authors of the most stupendous of our political rationalisms— as well they might be, for it was composed for the instruction of a less politically educated class than any other that has ever come to have the illusion of exercising political power. And no fault can be found with the mechanical manner in which this greatest of all political cribs has been learned and used by those for whom it was written. No other technique has so imposed itself upon the world as if it were concrete knowledge; none has created so vast an intellectual proletariat, with nothing but its technique to lose.[1]

The early history of the United States of America is an instructive chapter in the history of the politics of Rationalism. The situation of a society called upon without much notice to exercise political initiative on its own account is similar to that of an individual or a social class rising not fully prepared to the exercise of political power; in general, its needs are the same as theirs. And the similarity is even closer when the independence of the society concerned begins with an admitted illegality, a specific and express rejection of a tradition, which consequently can be defended only by an appeal to something which is itself thought not to depend upon tradition. Nor, in the case of the American colonists, was this the whole of the pressure which forced their revolution in to the pattern of Rationalism. The founders of American independence had both a tradition of European thought and a native political habit and experience to draw upon. But, as it happened, the intellectual gifts of Europe to America (both in philosophy and religion) had, from the beginning, been predominantly rationalistic: and the native political habit, the product of the circumstances of colonisation, was what may be called a kind of natural and unsophisticated rationalism. A plain and unpretending people, not given over-much to reflection upon the habits of behaviour they had in fact inherited, who, in frontier communities, had constantly the experience of setting up law and order for themselves by mutual agreement, were not likely to think of their arrangements except as the creation of their own unaided initiative; they seemed to begin with nothing, and to owe to themselves all that they had come to possess. A civilization of pioneers is, almost unavoidably, a civilization of self-consciously self-made men, nationalists by circumstance and not by reflection, who need no persuasion that knowledge begins with a *tabula rasa* and who regard the free mind, not even as the result of some artificial Cartesian purge, but as the gift of Almighty God, as Jefferson said.

Long before the Revolution, then, the disposition of mind of the American colonists, the prevailing intellectual character and habit of politics, were rationalistic. And this is clearly reflected in the constitutional documents and history of the individual colonies. And when these colonies came "to dissolve the political bands which had connected them with one another", and to declare their independence, the only fresh inspiration that this habit of politics received from the outside was one which confirmed its native character in every particular. For the inspiration of Jefferson and the other founders of American independence was the ideology which Locke had distilled from the English political tradition. They were disposed to believe, and they believed more fully than was possible for an inhabitant of the Old World, that the proper organization of a society and the conduct of its affairs were based upon abstract principles, and not upon a tradition which, as Hamilton said, had "to be rummaged for among old parchments and musty records". These principles were not the product of civilization; they were natural, "written in the whole volume of Human nature".[2] They were to be discovered in nature by human reason, by a technique of inquiry available alike to all men and requiring no extraordinary intelligence in its use. Moreover, the age had the advantage of all earlier ages because, by the application of this technique of inquiry, these abstract principles had, for the most part recently, been discovered and written down in books. And by using these books, a newly made political society was not only not handicapped by the lack of a tradition, but had a positive superiority over older societies not yet fully emancipated from the chains of custom. What Descartes had already perceived, "que souvent il n'y a pas tant de perfection dans les ouvrages composés de plusieurs pièces et faits de la main de divers maitres qu'en ceux auxquels un seul a travaillé", was freshly observed in 1777 by John Jay—"The Americans are the first people whom Heaven has favoured with an opportunity of deliberating upon, and choosing the forms of government under which they should live. All other constitutions have derived their existence from violence or accidental circumstances, and are therefore probably more distant from their perfection ... "[3] The Declaration of Independence is a characteristic product of *saeculum rationalisticum*. It represents the politics of the felt need interpreted with the aid of an ideology. And it is not surprising that it should have become one of the sacred documents of the politics of Rationalism, and, together with the similar documents of the French Revolution, the inspiration and pattern of many later adventures in the rationalist reconstruction of society. ...

To this brief sketch of the character, and the social and intellectual context of the emergence of Rationalism in politics, may be added a few reflections. The generation of rationalist politics is by political inexperience out of political opportunity. These conditions have often existed together in European societies; they did so in the ancient world, and that world at times suffered the effects of their union. But the particular quality of Rationalism in modern politics derives from the circumstance that the modern world succeeded in inventing so plausible a method of covering up lack of political education that even those who suffered from that lack were often left ignorant that they lacked anything. Of course, this inexperience was never, in any society, universal; and it was never absolute. There has always been men of genuine political education immune from the infection of Rationalism (and this is particularly so of England, where a political education of some sort has been much more widely spread than in some other societies); and sometimes a dim reminder of the limitations of his technique has penetrated even the mind of the Rationalist. Indeed, so impractical is a *purely* rationalist politics, that the new man, lately risen to power, will often be found throwing away his book and relying upon his general experience of the world as, for example, a business man or a trade union official. This experience is certainly a more trustworthy guide than the book—at least it is real knowledge and not a shadow—but still, it is not a knowledge of the political traditions of his society, which, in the most favourable circumstances, takes two or three generations to acquire.

Nevertheless, when he is not arrogant or sanctimonious, the Rationalist can appear a not unsympathetic character. He wants so much to be right. But unfortunately he will never quite succeed. He began too late and on the wrong foot. His knowledge will never be more than half-knowledge, and consequently he will never be more than half-right.[4] Like a foreigner or a man out of his social class, he is bewildered by a tradition and a habit of behaviour of which he knows only the surface; a butler or an observant house-maid has the advantage of him. And he conceives a contempt for what he does not understand; habit and custom appear bad in themselves, a kind of nescience of behaviour. And by some strange self-deception, he attributes to tradition (which, of course, is pre-eminently fluid) the rigidity and fixity of character which in fact belongs to ideological politics. Consequently, the Rationalist is a dangerous and expensive character to have in control of affairs, and he does most damage, not when he fails to master the situation (his politics, of course, are always in terms of mastering situations and surmounting crises), but when he appears to be successful; for the price we pay for each of his apparent successes is a firmer hold of the intellectual fashion of Rationalism upon the whole life of society.

Without alarming ourselves with imaginary evils, it may, I think, be said that there are two characteristics, in particular, of political Rationalism which make it exceptionally dangerous to a society. No sensible man will worry greatly because he cannot at once hit upon a cure for what he believes to be a crippling complaint; but if he sees the complaint to be of a kind which the passage of time must make more rather than less severe, he will have a more sustainable cause for anxiety. And this unfortunately appears to be so with the disease of Rationalism.

First, Rationalism in politics, as I have interpreted it, involves an identifiable error, a misconception with regard to the nature of human knowledge, which amounts to a corruption of the mind. And consequently it is without the power to correct its own short-comings; it has no homeopathic quality; you cannot escape its errors by becoming more sincerely or more profoundly rationalistic. This, it may be observed, is one of the penalties of living by the book; it leads not only to specific mistakes, but it also dries up the mind itself: living by precept in the end generates intellectual dishonesty. And further, the Rationalist has rejected in advance the only external inspiration capable of correcting his error; he does not merely neglect the kind of knowledge which would save him, he begins by destroying it. First he turns out the light and then complains that he cannot see, that he is "comme un homme qui marche seul et dans les ténèbres". In short, the Rationalist is essentially ineducable; and he could be educated out of his Rationalism only by an inspiration which he regards as the great enemy of mankind. All the Rationalist can do when left to himself is to replace one rationalist project in which he has failed by another in which he hopes to succeed. Indeed, this is what contemporary politics are fast degenerating into: the political habit and tradition, which, not long ago, was the common possession of even extreme opponents in English politics, has been replaced by merely a common rationalist disposition of mind.

But, secondly, a society which has embraced a rationalist idiom of politics will soon find itself either being steered or drifting towards an exclusively rationalist form of education. I do not mean the crude purpose of National Socialism or Communism of allowing no education except a training in the dominant rationalist doctrine, I mean the more plausible project of offering no place to any form of education which is not generally rationalistic in character.[5] And when an exclusively rationalist form of education is fully established, the only hope of deliverance lies in the discovery by some neglected pedant, "rummaging among old parchments and musty records", of what the world was like before the millennium overtook it.

Source: Michael Oakeshott. *Rationalism in Politics and Other Essays.* London: Methuen, 1962. Reprinted with permission.

Notes

[1] By casting his technique in the form of a view of the course of events (past, present and future), and not of "human nature", Marx thought he had escaped from Rationalism; but since he had taken the precaution of first turning the course of events into a doctrine, the escape was an illusion. Like Midas, the Rationalist is always in the unfortunate position of not being able to touch anything, without transforming it into an abstraction; he can never get a square meal of experience.

[2] There is no space here to elucidate the exceedingly complicated connections between the politics of "reason" and the politics of "nature". But it may be observed that, since both reason and nature were opposed to civilization, they began with a common ground; and the 'rational' man, the man freed from the idols and prejudices of a tradition, could, alternatively, be called the "natural" man. Modern Rationalism and modern Naturalism in politics, in religion and in education, are all alike expressions of a general presumption against all human achievement more than about a generation old.

[3] Of course both "violence" and "accidental circumstances" were there, but being present in an unfamiliar form they were unrecognized.

[4] There is a reminiscence here of a passage in Henry Jarnes, whose study of Mrs Headway in *The Siege London* is the best I know of a person in this position.

[5] Something of this sort happened in France after the Revolution; but it was not long before sanity began to break in.

4

Neo-Conservatism

The Ideal of Economic Liberty

In neo-conservatism one sees the re-emergence of some of the spirit of classical liberalism; in fact, when referring to the uncompromising capitalist systems that have emerged in Chile and during the regimes of Reagan and Thatcher in the USA and UK respectively, this ideology is sometimes referred to as "neo-liberalism". The subtle difference between these two ideologies, if such there be, lies in the emphasis that neo-conservatives place on economic liberty in contrast to the more general emphasis that classical liberals such as Locke place on rights such as life, liberty and property. The difference between these two could be pushed too far. Neo-conservatives share much with libertarians, and this is captured very nicely in the comments of Ayn Rand when she says that freedom in the political context has only one meaning: the absence of physical coercion.

This preoccupation with negative liberty is given a sharper focus by Madsen Pirie, the head of the Adam Smith Institute, when he emphasizes such economic policies as monetarism and privatization. There is a sense in which Pirie and, to a lesser extent Rand, are simply developing some of the notions put forward much earlier by the Austrian economist, Friedrich Hayek, who attacked as fallacious the Keynsian diagnosis that unemployment could be explained in terms of the inadequacy of total demand. Without a doubt, Hayek's repudiation of Keynes is expressed accurately in the writing of Milton Friedman who, consistent with his earlier work, maintains that inflation is everywhere a monetary phenomenon. Friedman's thesis that government is the culprit implies that negative liberty, especially in the field of economics, is a virtue.

The beginnings of a philosophical defence of the neo-conservatism inherent in the foregoing writers is offered by Robert Nozick, who argues in favour of the minimal state which in turn is linked to justice and entitlements viewed, not in terms of end-result principles, but in terms of historical principles. Not surprisingly this premise takes one back to Locke. But, as Peter Self correctly points out, it also brings one to the present day fashions including the trend in much of economics to accept the public-choice school of thought. The nub of this philosophy is that political failures are greater than market failures and that the greatest threat to individual liberty is the state.

Whatever its weaknesses, neo-conservatism has forced a breath of fresh air into ideological and philosophical discussions. While advocates of this ideology may be too confident of the truth and applicability of their ideas, there can be no disputing the fact that they have drawn attention to the stark realities of human life so often ably defended by those in the realist school of thinking. At the very least, the neo-conservatives have provided a hard standard against which reform liberals and democratic socialists can test their own ideas and arguments. One of the interesting questions is whether these latter ideologies and philosophies can rise to the challenge by engaging in something other than simple rhetoric and sloganeering.

America's Persecuted Minority: Big Business

Ayn Rand

AYN RAND *(1905-1982) was born in St. Petersburg, Russia, and moved to the USA in 1926. She wrote several best-selling novels including* The Fountainhead *and* Atlas Shrugged. *The virtue of rational self-interest and its connection with laissez-faire economics is a frequent theme in her writings. She would vigorously object to the classification "neo-conservative" and her estate permits the use of this excerpt only because this text does not have the categories "Capitalism" or "Objectivism."*

If a small group of men were always regarded as guilty, in any clash with any other group, regardless of the issues or circumstances involved, would you call it persecution? If this group were always made to pay for the sins, errors, or failures of any other group, would you call *that* persecution? If this group had to live under a silent reign of terror, under special laws, from which all other people were immune, laws which the accused could not grasp or define in advance and which the accuser could interpret in any way he pleased—would you call *that* persecution? If this group were penalized, not for its faults, but for its virtues, not for its incompetence,but for its ability, not for its failures, but for its achievements, and the greater the achievement, the greater the penalty—would you call *that* persecution?

If your answer is "yes"—then ask yourself what sort of monstrous injustice you are condoning, supporting, or perpetrating. That group is the American businessmen.

The defense of minority rights is acclaimed today, virtually by everyone, as a moral principle of a high order. But this principle, which forbids discrimination, is applied by most of the "liberal" intellectuals in a *discriminatory* manner: it is applied only to racial or religious minorities. It is not applied to that small, exploited, denounced, defenseless minority which consists of businessmen.

Yet every ugly, brutal aspect of injustice toward racial or religious minorities is being practised toward businessmen. For instance, consider the evil of condemning some men and absolving others, without a hearing, regardless of the facts. Today's "liberals" con-

sider a businessman guilty in any conflict with a labor union, regardless of the facts or issues involved, and boast that they will not cross a picket line "right or wrong." Consider the evil of judging people by a double standard and of denying to some the rights granted to others. Today's "liberals" recognize the workers' (the majority's) right to their livelihood (their wages), but deny the businessmen's (the minority's) right to *their* livelihood (their profits). If workers struggle for higher wages, this is hailed as "social gains"; if businessmen struggle for higher profits, this is damned as "selfish greed." If the workers' standard of living is low, the "liberals" blame it on the businessmen; but if the businessmen attempt to improve their economic efficacy, to expand their markets, and to enlarge the financial returns of their enterprises, thus making higher wages and lower prices possible, the same "liberals" denounce it as "commercialism." If a non-commercial foundation—i.e., a group which did not have to *earn* its funds—sponsors a television show, advocating its particular views, the "liberals" hail it as "enlightenment," "education," "art," and "public service"; if a businessman sponsors a television show and wants it to reflect *his* views, the "liberals" scream, calling it "censorship," "pressure," and "dictatorial rule." When three locals of the International Brotherhood of Teamsters deprived New York City of its milk supply for fifteen days—no moral indignation or condemnation was heard from the "liberal" quarters; but just imagine what would happen if businessmen stopped that milk supply for one hour—and how swiftly they would be struck down by that legalized lynching or pogrom known as "trust-busting."

Whenever, in any era, culture, or society, you encounter the phenomenon of prejudice, injustice, persecution, and blind, unreasoning hatred directed at some minority group—look for the gang that has something to gain from that persecution, look for those who have a vested interest in the destruction of these particular sacrificial victims. Invariably, you will find that the persecuted minority serves as a scapegoat for some movement that does not want the nature of its own goals to be known. Every movement that seeks to enslave a country, every dictatorship or potential dictatorship, needs some minority group as a scapegoat which it can blame for the nation's troubles and use as a justification of its own demands for dictatorial powers. In Soviet Russia, the scapegoat was the bourgeoisie; in Nazi Germany, it was the Jewish people; in America, it is the businessmen.

America has not yet reached the stage of a dictatorship. But, paving the way to it, for many decades past, the businessmen have served as the scapegoat for *statist* movements of all kinds: communist, fascist, or welfare. For whose sins and evils did the businessmen take the blame? For the sins and evils of the bureaucrats.

A disastrous intellectual package-deal, put over on us by the theoreticians of statism, is the equation of *economic* power with *political* power. You have heard it expressed in such bromides as: "A hungry man is not free," or "It makes no difference to a worker whether he takes orders from a businessman or from a bureaucrat." Most people accept these equivocations—and yet they know that the poorest laborer in America is freer and more secure than the richest commissar in Soviet Russia. What is the basic, the essential, the crucial principle that differentiates freedom from slavery? It is the principle of voluntary action *versus* physical coercion or compulsion.

The difference between political power and any other kind of social "power," between a government and any private organization, is the fact that a *government holds a legal monopoly on the use of physical force*. This distinction is so important and so seldom recognized today that I must urge you to keep it in mind. Let me repeat it: *a government holds a legal monopoly on the use of physical force*.

No individual or private group or private organization has the legal power to initiate the use of physical force against other individuals or groups and to compel them to act against their own voluntary choice. Only a government holds that power. The nature of governmental action is: *coercive* action. The nature of political power is: the power to force obedience under threat of physical injury—the threat of property expropriation, imprisonment, or death.

Foggy metaphors, sloppy images, unfocused poetry, and equivocations—such as "A hungry man is not free"—do not alter the fact that *only* political power is the power of physical coercion and that freedom, in a political context, has only one meaning: *the absence of physical coercion*.

The only proper function of the government of a free country is to act as an agency which protects the individual's rights, *i.e.*, which protects the individual from physical violence. Such a government does not have the right to *initiate* the use of physical force against anyone—a right which the individual does not possess and, therefore, cannot delegate to any agency. But the individual does possess the right of self-defense and *that* is the right which he delegates to the government, for the purpose of an orderly, legally defined enforcement. A proper government has the right to use physical force *only* in retaliation and *only* against those who initiate its use. The proper functions of a government are: the police, to protect men from criminals; the military forces, to protect men from foreign invaders; and the law courts, to protect men's property and contracts from breach by force or fraud, and to settle disputes among men according to objectively defined laws.

These, implicitly, were the political principles on which the Constitution of the United States was based; implicitly, but not explicitly. There were contradictions in the Constitution, which allowed the statists to gain an entering wedge, to enlarge the breach, and, gradually, to wreck the structure.

A statist is a man who believes that some men have the right to force, coerce, enslave, rob, and murder others. To be put into practice, this belief has to be implemented by the political doctrine that the government—the state—has the right to *initiate* the use of physical force against its citizens. How often force is to be used, against whom, to what extent, for what purpose and for whose benefit, are irrelevant questions. The basic principle and the ultimate results of all statist doctrines are the same: dictatorship and destruction. The rest is only a matter of time.

Now let us consider the question of economic power.

What is economic power? It is the power to produce and to trade what one has produced. In a free economy, where no man or group of men can use physical coercion against anyone, economic power can be achieved only by *voluntary* means: by the voluntary choice and agreement of all those who participate in the process of production and trade. In a free market, all prices, wages, and profits are determined—not by the arbitrary whim of the rich or of the poor, not by anyone's "greed" or by anyone's need—but by the law of supply and demand. The mechanism of a free market reflects and sums up all the economic choices and decisions made by all the participants. Men trade their goods or services by mutual consent to mutual advantage, according to their own independent, uncoerced judgment. A man can grow rich only if he is able to offer better *values*—better products or services, at a lower price—than others are able to offer.

Wealth, in a free market, is achieved by a free, general, "democratic" vote—by the sales and the purchases of every individual who takes part in the economic life of the country. Whenever you buy one product rather than another, you are voting for the success of some manufacturer. And, in this type of voting, every man votes only on those matters which he is qualified to judge: on his own preferences, interests, and needs. No one has the power to decide for others or to substitute *his* judgment for theirs; no one has the power to appoint himself "the voice of the public" and to leave the public voiceless and disfranchised.

Now let me define the difference between economic power and political power: economic power is exercised by means of a *positive*, by offering men a reward, an incentive, a payment, a value; political power is exercised by means of a *negative*, by the threat of punishment, injury, imprisonment, destruction. The businessman's tool is *values*; the bureaucrat's tool is *fear*.

America's industrial progress, in the short span of a century and a half, has acquired the character of a legend: it has never been equalled anywhere on earth, in any period of history. The American businessmen, as a class, have demonstrated the greatest productive genius and the most spectacular achievements ever recorded in the economic history of mankind. What reward did they receive from our culture and its intellectuals? The position of a hated, persecuted minority. The position of a scapegoat for the evils of the bureaucrats.

A system of pure, unregulated laissez-faire capitalism has never yet existed anywhere. What did exist were only so-called mixed economies, which means: a mixture, in varying degrees, of freedom and controls, of voluntary choice and government coercion, of capitalism and statism. America was the freest country on earth, but elements of statism were present in her economy from the start. These elements kept growing, under the influence of her intellectuals who were predominantly committed to the philosophy of statism. The intellectuals—the ideologists, the interpreters, the assessors of public events—were tempted by the opportunity to seize political power, relinquished by all other social groups, and to establish their own versions of a "good" society at the point of a gun, i.e., by means of legalized physical coercion. They denounced the free businessmen as exponents of "selfish greed" and glorified the bureaucrats as "public servants." In evaluating social problems, they kept damning "economic power" and exonerating political power, thus switching the burden of guilt from the politicians to the businessmen.

All the evils, abuses, and iniquities, popularly ascribed to businessmen and to capitalism, were not caused by an unregulated economy or by a free market, but by government intervention into the economy. The giants of American industry—such as James Jerome Hill or Commodore Vanderbilt or Andrew Carnegie or J.P. Morgan—were self-made men who earned their fortunes by personal ability, by free trade on a free market. But there existed another kind of businessmen, the products of a mixed economy, the men with political pull, who make fortunes by means of special privileges granted to them by the government, such men as the Big Four of the Central Pacific Railroad. It was the political power behind their activities—the power of forced, unearned, economically unjustified privileges—that caused dislocations in the country's economy, hardships, depressions, and mounting public protests. But it was the free market and the free businessmen that took the blame. Every calamitous consequence of government controls was used as a justification for the extension of the controls and of the government's power over the economy.

Source: Ayn Rand. *Capitalism: The Unknown Ideal.* New York: Signet, Signet Classics, Mentor and Plume, 1967. The extract is part of a lecture given at The Ford Hall Forum, Boston, on December 17, 1961, and at Columbia University on February 15, 1962. Reprinted by permission of The Estate of Ayn Rand.

The Principles and Practice of Privatization: The British Experience

Madsen Pirie

MADSEN PIRIE *is a British economist and advocate of privatization, as well as the head of the Adam Smith Institute. He was one of Prime Minister Margaret Thatcher's close advisers on economic reform inside the UK.*

Let me start by sharing with you a report from last month's *Financial Times*. Very significant—it described a story in which Britain's largest union of public sector workers had employed a public opinion poll agency to guide them in spending $2 million in a campaign against privatization. And they had asked the independent polling agency how they could spend it most effectively. And the story in the *Financial Times* was that the agency had told them not to waste their money, for there was nothing on earth that they could do to change the British public's opinion on privatization and, furthermore, there was a deeply ingrained attitude in British public opinion which thought of public sector workers as "People who sat on their backsides all day and did nothing." The report said that the union had decided not to make public the results of their survey. But they are going to spend the $2 million anyway so ... it'll be interesting to see if that was correct.

What an astonishing change—that that should happen in 1987. Consider, if you will, Britain as she was in the Stone Age. By that I mean 1979! The economy was dominated entirely by the public sector. The government ran the airplanes, it ran the ships and the buses. It actually made the airplanes, the ships and the buses. It ran the telephone service, it ran the gas system, it extracted oil from the North Sea and sold it, it ran hotels and the Hovercraft service, it made radiochemicals and microchips, it made trucks and motorcars, it ran the freight services, it cleared the garbage, it swept the streets and it even rented out the deck chairs at Margate.

What was Britain like in the Stone Age? Very difficult to remember now. It was characterized by extremely poor services, which were grossly overpriced, which required massive public subsidies, which took high taxation. It was a nation characterized by astronomical inflation, it was strike-ridden, it was uncompetitive and it was on the skids. It was referred to as the Sick Man of Europe, and had a living standard which was heading pretty close to that of Bulgaria. People spoke of the British Disease, and tourists, if they came at all, attempted to leave in a hurry in case they caught it.

Emerging from the Stone Age

And it was into that Stone Age climate in 1979 that the New Breed appeared. Homothaturius or Thatcherite Man will be readily identified by future archaeologists because of the subtle physical differences—the slightly domed skull to accommodate visions of a prosperous and a free society. The creature walks a little more upright with its eyes fixed firmly on the future, one of choice and enterprise, and takes longer and longer strides as it gains confidence in its ability to set loose the forces of innovation and productivity.

I might add that the most remarkable characteristic of the New Breed, is that it's led by a woman. Archaeologists will be amazed that the New Breed under such leadership accomplished so much in so short a time. I'm amazed, I was there to see it.

In eight years, for that is all it has been, we have privatized the ports and the docks. We have privatized the tele-communications industry, the radionics industry, the petroleum industry and North Sea oil extraction. We've privatized the state bus companies and the state shipping lines. We've privatized shipbuilding in Britain, Jaguar cars, Leyland buses, Leyland trucks, freight haulage, the telephone service, the state airline, the aerospace industry, the state gas service, to name but a few.

We have sold over one million state houses to the people who live in them, and we are well on our way to the next million. In July, this year, we will be privatizing the airports and later in the summer we'll be privatizing Rolls Royce.

And what has been the effect of all this in eight years? When I was in Toronto, in the Fall, I said then that Britain had acquired the lowest inflation rate for twenty years. It's now lower, it is 3.5 percent. I said then that Britain had the lowest level of strikes in forty years, it's now lower. I said then, that Britain had achieved the lowest income tax it has had in fifty years, it is now two points lower still. Mrs. Thatcher, at the time I spoke, was down in the opinion polls but I said not to worry it will all work out. British people like to keep her humble so they keep her low in the polls between elections. She only surges ahead very briefly when we take the real poll. She's now well ahead in the opinion polls which probably means that the election is not far away. All is set for a third term of the Thatcher Administration.

What is going to happen in that third term? Well, last October our Finance Minister said, "We have privatized 20 percent of public sector, in the next year we will privatize another 20 percent, and then in our next term of office we'll privatize whatever is left."

Privatization: Two Key Questions

There are two questions I want to ask before I turn the subject over to Canada. And the first question is "Why was this done in Britain" and the second is "How was it done?"

Why? is the first question. We did it because the public sector is no good. Now there are 114 reasons why it is no good. I shall deal with the first four and then give the remainder in answers to questions, if anyone expresses interest.

The first reason we found is that the public sector is always under-capitalized. The Crown corporations need money to modernize, to update their equipment, to expand their services but alas, because they are in the public sector they are facing competing claims for hospitals, for education, for the care of the sick. The money they do get goes overwhelmingly to the payment of wages because the unions in the public sector have this extraordinary power that they know that no matter how big their demands, the firm they work for, that is the government, is not going to go bankrupt. And so there is no limit to the claims they make, or the measures they take to pursue them. They are restrained in the private sector by the knowledge that their firm might go bankrupt and they'd lose their jobs. There is no such threat in the public sector so they can always command more of the resources. The result is that the public sector is chronically under-capitalized, and you look at its equipment in Britain and you find it's out of date, it's shoddy, it needed replacing long ago, but the money hasn't been available for it. There were always too many competing claims.

Secondly, the public sector is always too expensive. It doesn't have to compete. It's normally protected by a monopoly. It always has the bottom-less purse of taxpayers waiting to support it, it's always got customers, it doesn't need to streamline its act and always you pay more for your public services than you would for the private equivalent. We reckon it's always somewhere between 20 and 40 percent more expensive in the public sector than for the equivalent private service.

Thirdly, don't forget I'm not doing the 114, I'm only doing the four. So, thirdly, the public sector is always inefficient, there's absolutely no incentive to keep it lean and streamlined, there are no gains to be had by doing so. In the private sector you would gain extra profits, you'd become more competitive, you'd gain a wider share of the market. All of those incentives are absent in the public sector, there are no pressures on it to be efficient so it is characterized by a chronic inefficiency.

And fourthly, the public sector is unresponsive. It doesn't need to provide what consumers want. It is fundamentally dominated by these two words. Producer capture. They don't have to attract consumers. Since you've got a guarantee of money from taxpayers, why should the service be responsive to the needs of consumers? It might just as well serve the needs of the producers, because they are, in fact, more powerful. And so you have state railways whose function is not to carry passengers, it's to provide jobs for railway workers. You have state mines, whose function is not to dig coal out of the ground. It's to give a comfortable living to those employed in the industry. You actually examine, one by one, your public sector operations and you find out that overwhelmingly they serve the needs of the producers. And look at something like, for example, the post office. Over the years the quality of its service to the public has declined almost as rapidly as the price of that service has gone up. The second deliveries on Saturday are gone as is the Sunday collection. It's increasingly orienting its activities towards what the producers want to do rather than what the consumers want to buy.

I gave you four reasons why we had to begin to privatize the public sector in Britain. Now it's quite possible that it is totally different here. It is quite possible that in Canada your public sector is cheap, efficient, streamlined, anxious to please. But then again it's possible that it isn't.

The effect of all this in Britain was to give us an inflated and over extensive public sector. It was producing inadequate goods and services and we paid too much for their product. And what that meant for British industry was that it was paying more than it should for its freight, for its transport, for its telecommunications, for its mail services. In other words, all of the costs of British industry were put up and on top of all those increased costs and the extra costs which delays and inefficiencies brought, was the added injury that all of this had to be paid for by a monstrous rate of taxation.

This was Britain in the Stone Age, in 1979. The nation was uncompetitive, it took so much money to sustain all of these public sector activities, that there was not enough left for private enterprise, for private investment, and the wealth creating private sector.

Right, so much for why we did it. The second question—how did we do it? And the answer is—systematically. There are two approaches you can take here, you take your choice.

The first, we call the hair-shirt politics method. This operates in the belief that you must do this stuff as fast as possible and as soon as you get into office. It is so terribly unpleasant that you must do it now so that the inevitable chaos and unpopularity which follows will have time to recede by the time the election comes. It will all work out in the long run so you'd better do it in your first year to allow as long as possible to recover from it. Well that's approach number one, the notion that you should strike while your mandate's hot. We rejected that because it had been tried before and it always takes much longer to do unpopular things than you suppose possible, and there are always more groups coming along to slow the process down and you end up four and a half years later having done half of one thing, incurred vast odium of unpopularity without sufficient time to recover before the next election.

So, we opted for the systematic method. Its basis is, do it a little at a time and follow three golden rules.

The first is you must do it in such a way as to make friends out of enemies. What this means is that you identify all of the people who could oppose you, whose interests, whose livelihood, whose benefits and advantages are tied up in the public sector and you make sure they have more advantage from your privatized version.

So, for example, when we sold British Gas, (this was last December) the management of British Gas became the new Board of Directors of the private company, and they liked that. They liked it particularly because they thought they'd have more independence once they were free from government. And it's possible they also saw that private sector salaries for top management tended to be twice as high as those limited by civil service guidelines. So, that was the management.

The work-force were given two hundred shares each and allowed to buy special allocation of shares for which they didn't have to compete in the general

draw. And the 98 percent of the work-force of British Gas chose to invest in their own company and pool their savings into buying British Gas shares. So that was the workers gaining more benefit.

The general public and gas consumers were given reductions on their gas bills if they bought shares in British Gas. The shares were priced in such a way that you only had to pay one-third of the cost at the time of purchase and you could pay the balance over a period of a year, sort of a credit sale, designed to encourage as many people as possible to buy the shares. They were so attractively priced that everyone who did buy them was pretty confident of making money on the deal, so that was the public taken care of.

Of course, that left the fourth significant group—the legislators. Well, it turned out that what helped them most was the success of the operation. Once British Gas was privatized successfully everyone applauded the legislators who did it. Instead of gaining the unpopularity that needs four years to recover from, they found themselves with a political success coming right on the verge of a general election.

In February, we privatized British Airways. This summer we're privatizing British Airports and Rolls Royce. You see we're continuing the program right into the election itself, because it doesn't bring unpopularity which has to be recovered from. It makes the government very popular if it's done right so that all the different groups gain the advantages.

Look at some of the other things we did in Britain. When we privatized National Freight Corporation, for example, we faced a report (in 1979) from the Secretary of the company who said, "I see no prospect of National Freight Corporation being privatized until there are substantial and long-term changes in the attitude of the work-force." Two years later it was a profitable, private company owned by its work-force.

That was the magic formula for National Freight. The workers pooled their savings, some of them mortgaged their houses. They bought shares in their own company, and the company immediately became profitable. So profitable has it been since that for every dollar they put in then, they are now worth $41 today. Forty-one times increased in value, and how is that brought about? Because when they are working for their own firm, they work a lot harder, a lot more efficiently. They are a lot less bothered about who does what and more concerned about how much trade they can bring their way to increase the profits of their company. That's the performance of a management-work-force collective set up.

Look at the way this was done in British Airways, which we sold in February. Five years ago that company was losing a lot of money. By the time we sold it, it was making a lot of money. The work-force was trimmed down from 60,000 to 39,000, and not one of them was fired. Very generous terms were offered to encourage voluntary retirement and enough people took it to bring the work-force down to efficient operating levels. The index-linked public sector pensions were brought out by cash funds and turned into conventional pensions and what had been an airline requiring horrendous subsidies became a very profitable, private company which got a good price when it was sold.

The unsung story in some ways is the state houses in Britain. Up until last September, the government had taken more money from the sale of its state houses than from all other privatizations added together—including big firms like Telecom. It was only the sale of British Gas in December that changed the relative balance.

People enjoyed living in subsidized council housing owned by the state. They like having subsidized rents. They liked even more the substantial cash discounts which were offered starting at 20 percent off going up to 50 percent off. It's now by the way, under the latest act, 70 percent off market value to those who buy their own houses. It depends on how long you've lived in them. But it is very much more effective to many people to get that substantial capital asset. More attractive, indeed, than the subsidized rents which they were enjoying before. Trade one benefit for a better one.

We learned three rules, I said. The first was make friends of enemies. The second was privatize the process of privatization. Government doesn't have to learn how to sell companies, how to float them on the stock exchange, how to sell them to their management and work-force. There are firms which know how to do that already. There are firms in the City of London Financial Sector that buy and sell companies every day. Since they have that expertise it's folly for government to try to acquire it. So we learned early on, that you must buy in the expertise and government began hiring merchant banks and stockbrokers to handle its privatization. This keeps government at quite an attractive distance. It doesn't get as much criticism over the technical details if this is contracted out to experts who are assumed to know how it's done. And we learned very rapidly that privatizing the process is a very efficient message of getting the thing done properly.

We learned the third rule which is disarm the objections. Anticipate in advance every single objection which will be raised against you when you privatize, and deal with it. We're going to privatize British Tele-

com, we said. What are people going to say? They are going to say, "Will a private company push up prices to gain exploitation profits?" So we wrote in a clause that says for ten years they cannot increase their prices. They have to keep them 3 percent below increases in the cost of living. Three percent below the increases in the cost of living ... that is written into the act. And lo and behold that dealt with that objection.

People said, "When we privatize our aerospace industry are we not open to foreign takeover?" Would not a foreign company perhaps buy it out and then we would be without this vital strategic industry in British hands. So we built in a Golden Share, and if foreign ownership ever amounts to over half the company, that Golden Share is activated giving the British government voting control. So that one was dealt with.

When we privatized Telecom—"Would they still maintain the remote services to rural areas, very scattered, where it can't pay very much?" We wrote it into the act that they have to do so. You see one by one we identify every possible source of objection and write it into the bill. We deal with it in advance. And, when you then introduce the bill to privatize Telecom, as the objectors stand up one by one they discover to their horror that you've already dealt with every single conceivable possible objection. So British Telecom was privatized, a great political success. So, point three was disarm the objectors.

A few more case histories. Again, the figures for privatization that make the news over here tend to be the ones involving the big public flotations like Telecom and British Gas. But there are unsung stories in the use of local contractors throughout Britain's cities now. Privatization of the garbage collection, the street sweeping, the deck chairs at Margate, and various other activities saves us money. The Institute of Fiscal Studies calculated the average savings so far as 26 percent, but significantly you don't only get the savings, you get better service. When you are controlling and monitoring work done by a private contractor you can have more control over it than over your own rather recalcitrant work-force which has a long history of getting its own way and resents attempts to make it do things in the way you want. You have actually, paradoxically, more control over an outside firm than you used to have over your own force-work.

How do you deal with the objections of the trade unions? The answer is again, remorselessly. First of all, we found the golden formula is to outflank them, go over their heads directly to their members. The union activists told their workers to go on strike to oppose the privatization of Telecom. What does the management do? It offers shares, and it offers shares at very attractive rates. And, given a straight choice between loyalty to the union leadership or enrichment via the shares well, you can guess the outcome. You know, the average take up in Britain has exceeded 90 percent whenever we have made that offer to a work-force. On average, 90 percent of them have taken the government line rather than that of the union leadership.

Reiterating the other points, if there has to be job reductions make sure nobody is fired against their will. If benefits have to be altered make sure it's done voluntarily. Once those are done you find that you've basically dealt with the unions by dealing with their members.

We now look at Canada briefly. We see Crown corporations waiting to be privatized. Some small ones have gone and the world is waiting to see the big ones. Wherever else this has been done in the world, it's been successful. The moral of the story is don't be timid. Look at the example of the rest of the world, learn from any mistakes they've made and then do something which is uniquely suited to your own situation here. You've got to produce a Canadian policy to achieve a Canadian success. But there's no reason why you have to learn from scratch. The rest of the world has been doing this for eight years and there is plenty of experience to be learned from.

We look here at transport services, these are privatized all over the world. We look at city services which are being contracted out. We wonder why private sector disciplines aren't introduced into some of the big public services like education, because this is being done elsewhere in the world. So basically Canada does not stand alone. There are one hundred countries in the world privatizing. I can do a quick sort of two minute world tour. Starting as I'm sure they would like, with the French whose five-year campaign aims to privatize $130 billion worth of the public sector. The French might have come to privatization a bit late but they certainly make up in passion what they lack in punctuality—as they do in other fields too, I am told. Spain has just privatized its car manufacturer. There we had the spectacle of Phillippe Gonzales, a so-called socialist, talking about the public sector as a "white elephant graveyard" and expressing his determination to privatize.

We have privatization taking place across Europe. Really the cases are coming thick and fast: Germany, Denmark, nominally socialist Sweden, Italy. Astonishingly the big success story outside Britain is to be found probably in Asia. In countries like Bangladesh, really a very poor country, which has gained huge success in privatizing its shoes and textile mills. You've got the Pacific Rim countries Singapore, Malaysia, privatizing their telephone services and their state airlines. You have your banana farms being privatized in Belize, you have sugar refineries in Jamaica. They just privatized their national bank in Jamaica. It amounted to 5 percent of the total available capital in Jamaica and yet it was done. We have the Bosphorous bridge in Turkey that was privatized. Japan is privatizing its telephone system and its railway—by the way the single biggest piece of privatization in the world. In India, it's textile cooperatives.

Then we look and find with astonishment that privatization is overtaking the communist world. Cuba is selling their houses to their tenants on the Thatcher model. In China, private businesses are starting up restaurants and shops at four times the rate of the state ones. In the Soviet Union they're allowing private firms of taxi drivers in Riga to compete with the state sector and what do they find everywhere? When they do it, it's more efficient, the service goes up, the prices go down. There is less subsidy and less taxation to support.

So Britain, to sum up, was indeed an example to avoid in 1979. Don't be naughty or you'll end up like Britain was what mothers used to frighten their children with in other countries. Well, Britain, is now the example, but the example to follow. So my advice in Canada is step in, the water is warm. The rest of the world is already bathing and you'll find once you've been into that little dip in privatization you'll come out a lot cleaner, your economy will come out fitter, and you'll feel a lot healthier too.

So, let me close by, of course giving you the stock market tip. I always like to do this, it's great fun. Buy British Airport Society when it comes on sale in July. The last time I did that I was telling people to buy British Gas, and those who took my advice would have done very well, and the time before that it was Telecom. But now my current hot tip is British Airport Society. I take no liability, by the way, I simply give it as a recommendation. Do it for three reasons. One, of course, you'll make money which is always very nice. The other is so that you'll get a piece of Britain to put up on your wall and you can show your grandchildren—see, when they dismantled Britain I got a piece. The third reason, though, is fundamentally because the writing is on the wall for the public sector in Britain and that writing comes to three words: Everything Must Go.

Source: Madsen Pirie. *Vital Speeches of the Day* 53, No. 21 (August 15, 1987): 655-658. This speech was delivered to the Fraser Institute, Vancouver, British Columbia, Canada, March 30, 1987. Reprinted by permission of the *Fraser Forum* and *Vital Speeches of the Day.*

Distributive Justice

Robert Nozick

ROBERT NOZICK *(1938-) is currently a professor of philosophy at Harvard University. His* Anarchy, State, and Utopia *made him one of the most influential figures in recent years in political philosophy in the English-speaking philosophical world. Another of his works is* Philosophical Explanations.

The minimal state is the most extensive state that can be justified. Any state more extensive violates people's rights. Yet many persons have put forth reasons purporting to justify a more extensive state. It is impossible within the compass of this book to examine all the reasons that have been put forth. Therefore, I shall focus upon those generally acknowledged to be most weighty and influential, to see precisely wherein they fail. In this chapter we consider the claim that a more extensive state is justified, because necessary (or the best instrument) to achieve distributive justice; in the next chapter we shall take up diverse other claims.

The term "distributive justice" is not a neutral one. Hearing the term "distribution," most people presume that some thing or mechanism uses some principle or criterion to give out a supply of things. Into this process of distributing shares some error may have crept. So it is an open question, at least, whether redistribution should take place; whether we should do again what has already been done once, though poorly. However, we are not in the position of children who have been given portions of pie by someone who now makes last minute adjustments to rectify careless cutting. There is no *central* distribution, no person or group entitled to control all the resources, jointly deciding how they are to be doled out. What each person gets, he gets from others who give to him in exchange for something, or as a gift. In a free society, diverse persons control different resources, and new holdings arise out of the voluntary exchanges and actions of persons. There is no more a distributing or distribution of shares than there is a distributing of mates in a society in which persons choose whom they shall marry. The total result is the product of many individual decisions which the different individuals involved are entitled to make. Some uses of the term "distribution," it is true, do not imply a previous distributing appropriately judged by some criterion (for example, "probability distribution"); nevertheless, despite the title of this chapter, it would be best to use a terminology that clearly is neutral. We shall speak of people's holdings; a principle of justice in holdings describes (part of) what justice tells us (requires) about holdings. I shall state first what I take to be the correct view about justice in holdings, and then turn to the discussion of alternate views.[1]

The Entitlement Theory

The subject of justice in holdings consists of three major topics. The first is the *original acquisition of holdings*, the appropriation of unheld things. This includes the issues of how unheld things may come to be held, the process, or processes, by which unheld things may come to be held, the things that may come to be held by these processes, the extent of what comes to be held by a particular process, and so on. We shall refer to the complicated truth about this topic, which we shall not formulate here, as the principle of justice in acquisition. The second topic concerns the *transfer of holdings* from one person to another. By what processes may a person transfer holdings to another? How may a person acquire a holding from another who holds it? Under this topic come general descriptions of voluntary exchange, and gift and (on the other hand) fraud, as well as reference to particular conventional details fixed upon in a given society. The complicated truth about this subject (with placeholders for conventional details) we shall call the principle of justice in transfer. (And we shall suppose it also includes principles governing how a person may divest himself of a holding, passing it into an unheld state.)

If the world were wholly just, the following inductive definition would exhaustively cover the subject of justice in holdings.

1. A person who acquires a holding in accordance with the principle of justice in acquisition is entitled to that holding.

2. A person who acquires a holding in accordance with the principle of justice in transfer, from someone else entitled to the holding, is entitled to the holding.

3. No one is entitled to a holding except by (repeated) applications of 1 and 2.

The complete principle of distributive justice would say simply that a distribution is just if everyone is entitled to the holdings they possess under the distribution.

A distribution is just if it arises from another just distribution by legitimate means. The legitimate means of moving from one distribution to another are specified by the principle of justice in transfer. The legitimate first "moves" are specified by the principle of justice in acquisition.[2] Whatever arises from a just situation by just steps is itself just. The means of change specified by the principle of justice in transfer preserve justice. As correct rules of inference are truth-preserving, and any conclusion deduced via repeated application of such rules from only true premises is itself true, so the means of transition from one situation to another specified by the principle of justice in transfer are justice-preserving, and any situation actually arising from repeated transitions in accordance with the principle from a just situation is itself just. The parallel between justice-preserving transformations and truth-preserving transformations illuminates where it fails as well as where it holds. That a conclusion could have been deduced by truth-preserving means from premises that are true suffices to show its truth. That from a just situation a situation *could* have arisen via justice preserving means *does not* suffice to show its justice. The fact that a thief's victims voluntarily *could* have presented him with gifts does not entitle the thief to his ill-gotten gains. Justice in holdings is historical; it depends upon what actually has happened. We shall return to this point later.

Not all actual situations are generated in accordance with the two principles of justice in holdings: the principle of justice in acquisition and the principle of justice in transfer. Some people steal from others, or defraud them, or enslave them, seizing their product and preventing them from living as they choose, or forcibly exclude others from competing in exchanges. None of these are permissible modes of transition from one situation to another. And some persons acquire holdings by means not sanctioned by the principle of justice in acquisition. The existence of past injustice (previous violations of the first two principles of justice in holdings) raises the third major topic under justice in holdings: the rectification of injustice in holdings. If past justice has shaped present holdings in various ways, some identifiable and some not, what now, if anything, ought to be done to rectify these injustices? What obligations do the performers of injustice have toward those whose position

is worse than it would have been had the injustice not been done? Or, than it would have been had compensation been paid promptly? How, if at all, do things change if the beneficiaries and those made worse off are not the direct parties in the act of injustice, but, for example, their descendants? Is an injustice done to someone whose holding was itself based upon an unrectified injustice? How far back must one go in wiping clean the historical slate of injustices? What may victims of injustice permissibly do in order to rectify the injustices being done to them, including the many injustices done by persons acting through their government? I do not know of a thorough or theoretically sophisticated treatment of such issues.[3] Idealizing greatly, let us suppose theoretical investigation will produce a principle of rectification. This principle uses historical information about previous situations and injustices done in them (as defined by the first two principles of justice and rights against interference), and information about the actual course of events that flowed from these injustices, until the present, and it yields a description (or descriptions) of holdings in the society. The principle of rectification presumably will make use of its best estimate of subjunctive information about what would have occurred (or a probability distribution over what might have occurred, using the expected value) if the injustice had not taken place. If the actual description of holdings turns out not to be one of the descriptions yielded by the principle, then one of the descriptions yielded must be realized.[4]

The general outlines of the theory of justice in holdings are that the holdings of a person are just if he is entitled to them by the principles of justice in acquisition and transfer, or by the principle of rectification of injustice (as specified by the first two principles). If each person's holdings are just, then the total set (distribution) of holdings is just. To turn these general outlines into a specific theory we would have to specify the details of each of the three principles of justice in holdings: the principle of acquisition of holdings, the principle of transfer of holdings, and the principle of rectification of violations of the first two principles. I shall not attempt that task here. (Locke's principle of justice in acquisition is discussed below.)

Historical Principles and End-Result Principles

The general outlines of the entitlement theory illuminate the nature and defects of other conceptions of distributive justice. The entitlement theory of justice in distribution is *historical*; whether a distribution is just depends upon how it came about. In contrast, current *time-slice principles of justice* hold that the justice of a distribution is determined by how things are distributed (who has what) as judged by some *structural* principle(s) of just distribution. A utilitarian who judges between any two distributions by seeing which has the greater sum of utility and, if the sums tie, applies some fixed equality criterion to choose the more equal distribution, would hold a current time-slice principle of justice. As would someone who had a fixed schedule of trade-offs between the sum of happiness and equality. According to a current time-slice principle, all that needs to be looked at, in judging the justice of a distribution, is who ends up with what; in comparing any two distributions one need look only at the matrix presenting the distributions. No further information need be fed into a principle of justice. It is a consequence of such principles of justice that any two structurally identical distributions are equally just. (Two distributions are structurally identical if they present the same profile, but perhaps have different persons occupying the particular slots. My having ten and your having five, and my having five and your having ten are structurally identical distributions.) Welfare economics is the theory of current time-slice principles of justice. The subject is conceived as operating on matrices representing only current information about distribution. This, as well as some of the usual conditions (for example, the choice of distribution is invariant under relabelling of columns), guarantees that welfare economics will be a current time-slice theory, with all of its inadequacies.

Most persons do not accept current time-slice principles as constituting the whole story about distributive shares. They think it relevant in assessing the justice of a situation to consider not only the distribution it embodies, but also how that distribution came about. If some persons are in prison for murder or war crimes, we do not say that to assess the justice of the distribution in the society we must look only at what this person has, and that person has, and that person has, … at the current time. We think it relevant to ask whether someone did something so that he *deserved* to be punished, deserved to have a lower share. Most will agree to the relevance of further information with regard to punishments and penalties. Consider also desired things. One traditional socialist view is that workers are entitled to the product and full fruits of their labour; they have earned it; a distribution is unjust if it does not give the workers what they are entitled to. Such entitlements are based upon some past history. No socialist holding this view would find it comforting to be told that because the actual distribution *A* happens to coincide structurally with the one he desires *D*, *A* therefore is no less just than *D*; it differs only in that the "parasitic" owners of capital receive under *A* what the workers are entitled to under *D*, and the workers receive under *A* what the owners are entitled to under *D*, namely very little.

This socialist rightly, in my view, holds onto the notions of earning, producing, entitlement, desert, and so forth, and he rejects current time-slice principles that look only to the structure of the resulting set of holdings. (The set of holdings resulting from what? Isn't it implausible that how holdings are produced and come to exist has no effect at all on who should hold what?) His mistake lies in his view of what entitlements arise out of what sorts of productive processes.

We construe the position we discuss too narrowly by speaking of *current* time-slice principles. Nothing is changed if structural principles operate upon a time sequence of current time-slice profiles and, for example, give someone more now to counterbalance the less he has had earlier. A utilitarian or an egalitarian or any mixture of the two over time will inherit the difficulties of his more myopic comrades. He is not helped by the fact that *some* of the information others consider relevant in assessing a distribution is reflected, unrecoverable, in past matrices. Henceforth, we shall refer to such unhistorical principles of distributive justice, including the current time-slice principles, as *end-result principles* or *end-state principles*.

In contrast to end-result principles of justice, *historical principles* of justice, hold that past circumstances or actions of people can create differential entitlements or differential deserts to things. An injustice can be worked by moving from one distribution to another structurally identical one, for the second, in profile the same, may violate people's entitlements or deserts; it may not fit the actual history.

Notes

[1] The reader who has looked ahead and seen that the second part of this chapter discusses Rawls' theory mistakenly may think that every remark or argument in the first part against alternative theories of justice is meant to apply to, or anticipate, a criticism of Rawls' theory. This is not so; there are other theories also worth criticizing.

[2] Applications of the principle of justice in acquisition may also occur as part of the move from one distribution to another. You may find an unheld thing now and appropriate it. Acquisitions also are to be understood as included when, to simplify, I speak only of transitions by transfers.

[3] See, however, the useful book by Boris Bittker, *The Case for Black Reparations* (New York: Random House, 1973).

[4] If the principle of rectification of violations of the first two principles yields more than one description of holdings, then some choice must be made as to which of these is to be realized. Perhaps the sort of considerations about distributive justice and equality that I argue against play a legitimate role in *this* subsidiary choice. Similarly, there may be room for such considerations in deciding which otherwise arbitrary features a statute will embody, when such features are unavoidable because other considerations do not specify a precise line; yet a line must be drawn.

The Cause and Cure of Inflation

Milton Friedman

MILTON FRIEDMAN *(1912-) was Professor of Economics at the University of Chicago and currently is Senior Research Fellow at The Hoover Institution. He is noted for adopting a strong monetarist position, a position which he sees as the logical extension of laissez-faire capitalism.*

> There is no subtler, no surer means of overturning the existing basis of society than to debauch the currency. The process engages all the hidden forces of economic law on the side of destruction, and does it in a manner which not one man in a million is able to diagnose.
> John Maynard Keynes (*The Economic Conferences of the Peace* (New York: Harcourt and Brace, 1920, p.236)

The Chinese hyperinflation is a striking example of Keynes's dictum. If the Chiang Kai-shek regime had been able to avoid inflation or keep it to single- or even low double-digit rates, whether by better management of its finances and its monetary policy or because of a different silver policy of the United States in the 1930s, the odds are high that China today would be a wholly different society.

War and revolution have been the progenitors of most hyperinflations. The earliest episodes in the West are the U.S. Revolution, with its Continental currency, and the French Revolution, with its *assignats*—both paper currencies that ultimately became nearly worthless.

The many earlier inflations included no hyperinflations for one simple reason. So long as money consisted of specie (whether gold, silver, copper, iron, or tin) inflation was produced either by new discoveries or technological innovations that reduced the cost of extraction or by debasement of the currency—the substitution of "base" metals for "precious" metals. New discoveries or innovations necessarily led to modest rates of growth in the quantity of money—producing nothing like the double-digit rates of inflation *per month* that are characteristic of hyperinflations. In the case of debasement, no matter how "base" the metal, it still cost something to produce, and that cost set a limit to the quantity of money. As Forrest Capie points out in a fascinating paper (1986, p.117), it took a century for the inflation in Rome, which contributed to the decline and fall of the empire, to raise the price level "from a base of 100 in 200 AD to 5000 …—in other words a rate of between 3 and 4 percent per annum compound." The

limit was set by the relative price of silver, the initial money metal, and copper, the ultimate money metal. The implications is that the silver-copper price ratio was of the order of 50 to 1—roughly the same market ratio as in 1960. (Since then, silver has risen sharply in price relative to copper, so the ratio is now much higher.)

Inflation in the range to which we have become accustomed, let alone in the hyperinflationary range, became feasible only after paper money came into wide use. The nominal quantity of paper money can be multiplied indefinitely at a negligible cost; it is necessary only to print higher numbers on the same pieces of paper.

The first recorded "true currency," according to Lien-sheng Yang, author of *Money and Credit in China*—which is subtitled *A Short History* and covers more than two millennia—"appeared in Szechuan [China] … during the early part of the eleventh century" (1952, p.52). It lasted for more than a century but eventually succumbed to the fatal temptation of inflationary overissue, "primarily," writes Yang, "to meet military expenditures." He records a number of additional paper money issues during the next five centuries in different parts of China and under various dynasties, each going through the same cycle of a period of initial stability, moderate and then substantial overissue, and eventual abandonment. There is not further record of extensive paper money issues in China until the nineteenth century.

Paper money came into wide use in the West only in the eighteenth century. It began, so I believe, with John Law's "Mississippi Bubble" of 1719-20, when as the *Encyclopedia Britannica* (1970) puts it, "the excessive issue of bank notes stimulated galloping inflation with commodity prices more than doubled" (see also Hamilton 1936)—a pale precursor of the million-, billion-, and trillionfold multiplication of prices in subsequent true hyperinflations.

Until recent decades, all the hyperinflations that I know of were the product of war or revolution. But that is no longer the case. Bolivia, Brazil, Argentina, Israel have all had hyperinflations in peacetime—hyperinflations that are still continuing, as I write, in Brazil and Argentina. And there may well be others

MILTON FRIEDMAN (1912-   )

The world's best-known advocate of the so-called "libertarian" school of political economy, Milton Friedman was born in Brooklyn, New York. Other than perhaps John Maynard Keynes, Friedman is considered to be the foremost economist of the twentieth century.

Although he grew up in a poor immigrant family, Friedman distinguished himself early in the field of economics. After obtaining a BA from Rutgers University in 1932 and an MA from Chicago in 1933, Friedman worked as a research assistant and as an analyst for various government-sponsored economic projects. Friedman also taught at the Universities of Minnesota and Chicago before completing his PhD at Columbia University in 1946. During this period, Friedman developed an impressive reputation in the field of statistical economics, a reputation he has enhanced in subsequent years with the publication of *Essays in Positive Economics* (1953), *A Theory of the Consumption Function* (1957), *A Monetary History of the United States, 1867–1960* (1963), and *Milton Friedman's Monetary Framework* (1974). In 1977, Friedman received a long-overdue Nobel Prize for economics.

Friedman's career as a formal economist is an impressive one. He has attained considerably more fame, or perhaps notoriety, however, as a tireless spokesperson for libertarian economic theory. Friedman has gained a broad forum for his ideas through countless magazine and newspaper articles. This view essentially holds that competitive and unrestricted capitalism is the ideal economic system for promoting political freedom. Governments must occasionally intervene to uphold laws, but according to Friedman this should be the limit of their responsibility to citizens and businesses.

Milton Friedman is currently retired from teaching at the University of Chicago and is a resident scholar at the Hoover Institute, an economic and political "think-tank" at Stanford University in California.

that I am not aware of. The reason, as we shall see, is because war and revolution are no longer the only, or even the primary, reasons why governments resort to the printing press to finance their activities.

Whatever its proximate source, inflation is a disease, a dangerous and sometimes fatal disease, a disease that, if not checked in time, can destroy a society, as it did in China. The hyperinflations in Russia and Germany after World War I prepared the ground for communism in the one country and Nazism in the other. When inflation in Brazil reached 100 percent a year in 1954, it brought military government. More extreme inflations also brought military government to Chile and Argentina by contributing to the overthrow of Salvador Allende in Chile in 1973 and of Isabel Peron in Argentina in 1976. Repeated inflations in Brazil and Argentina in the 1980s have led to repeated unsuccessful "reforms," the replacement of governments, flights of capital, and heightened economic instability.

No government willingly accepts the responsibility for producing inflation even in moderate degree, let alone at hyperinflationary rates. Government officials always find some excuse—greedy businessmen, grasping trade unions, spendthrift consumers, Arab sheikhs, bad weather, or anything else that seems remotely plausible. No doubt businessmen are greedy, trade unions are grasping, consumers are spendthrifts, Arab sheikhs have raised the price of oil, and the weather is often bad. Any of these can produce high prices for individual items; they cannot produce rising prices for goods in general. They can cause temporary ups and downs in the rate of inflation. But they cannot produce continuing inflation, for a very simple reason: not one of the alleged culprits possesses a printing press on which it can legally turn out those pieces of paper we carry in our pockets and call money; none can legally authorize a bookkeeper to make entries on ledgers that are the equivalent of those pieces of paper.

Inflation is not a capitalist phenomenon. Yugoslavia, a communist country, has experienced one of the most rapid rates of inflation of any country in Europe; Switzerland, a bastion of capitalism, one of the lowest. Neither is inflation a communist phenomenon. China had little inflation under Mao; the Soviet Union had little for decades, though it is now (1991) in the midst of rapid inflation; Italy, the United Kingdom,

Japan, the United States—all largely capitalist—have experienced substantial inflation, most recently in the 1970s. In the modern world, inflation is a printing-press phenomenon.

The recognition that *substantial inflation is always and everywhere a monetary phenomenon* is only the beginning of an understanding of the cause and cure of inflation. The more basic questions are: Why do governments increase the quantity of money too rapidly? Why do they produce inflation when they understand its potential for harm? ...

Conclusions

Five simple truths embody most of why we know about inflation:

1. Inflation is a monetary phenomenon arising from a more rapid increase in the quantity of money than in output (though, of course, the reasons for the increase in money may be various).

2. In today's world, government determines—or can determine—the quantity of money.

3. There is only one cure for inflation, a slower rate of increase in the quantity of money.

4. It takes time (measured in years, not months) for inflation to develop; it takes time for inflation to be cured.

5. Unpleasant side effects of the cure are unavoidable.

The United States has embarked on raising its monetary growth five times between 1960 and 1990. Each time the higher monetary growth has been followed first by economic expansion and later by inflation. Each time the authorities have slowed monetary growth in order to stem inflation. Lower monetary growth has been followed inflationary recession. Later still, inflation has declined and the economy has improved. So far, the sequence is identical with Japan's experience from 1971 to 1975. Unfortunately, until the 1980s the United States did not display the patience Japan did in continuing the monetary restraint long enough. Instead, our government overreacted to the recession by accelerating monetary growth, setting off on another round of inflation, and condemning the country to higher inflation plus higher unemployment. Finally, in the 1980s, the United States began to display some persistence. When more rapid monetary growth in late 1982 was followed by economic expansion, the Fed exercised monetary restraint in 1987,

well before inflation could reach its prior peak, though not before it had risen appreciably above the low point reached in the mid-1980s. Once again the Fed is seeking to exercise the restraint required to reduce inflation permanently to low levels—and again we have experienced, as I write (July 1991), an inflationary recession, which seems to have ended, or to be on the verge of ending, though inflation has not yet come down appreciably.

We have been misled by a false dichotomy: inflation or unemployment. That option is an illusion. The real option is whether we have higher unemployment as a result of higher inflation or as a temporary side effect of a cure for inflation.

Notes

[1.] Capie, Forrest. "Conditions in Which Very Rapid Inflation Has Appeared." In *The National Bureau Method, International Capital Mobility and Other Essays,* edited by Karl Brunner and Allan H. Meltzer. Carnegie-Rochester Conference Series on Public Policy, vol. 24. Amsterdam: North-Holland, 1986.

[2.] *Encyclopaedia Britannica,* 1970 ed. S.V. "Panic."

[3.] Hamilton, Earl J. "Prices and Wages at Paris under John Law's System." *Quarterly Journal of Economics* 51 (November 1936): 42-70.

[4.] Keynes, John Maynard. *The Economic Consequences of the Peace.* New York: Harcourt, Brace & Howe, 1920.

[5.] Yang, Lien-sheng. *Money and Credit in China* Cambridge: Harvard University Press, 1952.

References

Capie, Forrest, "Conditions in Which Very Rapid Inflation Has Appeared." In *The National Bureau Method, International Capital Mobility and Other Essays,* edited by Karl Brunner and Allan H. Meltzer. Carnegie-Rochester Conference Series on Public Policy, vol. 24. Amsterdam: North-Holland, 1986.

Feavearyear, Albert, *The Pound Sterling,* 2d ed., revised by E. Victor Morgan (Oxford: The Clarendon Press, 1963).

Hamilton, Earl J., "Prices and Wages at Paris under John Law's System." *Quarterly Journal of Economics* 51 (November 1936): 42–70.

Keynes, John Maynard, *The Economic Consequences of the Peace* (New York: Harcourt, Brace & Howe, 1920).

Yang, Lien-sheng, *Money and Credit in China* (Cambridge: Harvard University Press, 1952).

What's Wrong with Government?

Peter Self

PETER SELF, *currently located in the Urban Research Unit, Research School of Social Sciences, The Australian National University, is Profesor Emeritus of Public Administration, London School of Economics and Political Science.*

For a group of academic scribblers, the public choice school of political economists appear to have had a large impact upon the actual world of politics. They or their disciples are to be found in numerous well-endowed right-wing think tanks around the world, or acting as advisers to right-wing governments. They are an academic success story, exemplifying perhaps their own belief in rational egoism. They have certainly influenced and tried to justify the policies of the Thatcher Government.

I will first set out briefly some leading ideas of this school of thought, necessarily simplifying greatly. I will consider how far these theories have been utilised and applied by the Thatcher Government. I will then offer a critique of the public choice concept of politics and suggest an alternative analysis with quite different normative conclusions.

The public choice school are methodological individualists of a special kind. They explain all social behaviour as the product of the free choices of individuals, and they argue that the public good is a meaningless concept except as the sum total of individual choices. More specifically they view individual motivation as being the same in economic and political settings, and they model political behaviour on the assumption of the neoclassical economists that the individual will on the whole act rationally to pursue her personal advantage. This idea of "rational egoism" was once used to explain how competitive markets maximise individual satisfactions, but its psychological assumptions have largely been dropped by modern descriptive economics. Ironically some economists have carted the same assumptions wholesale into the more intractable sphere of politics.

Armed with these very slender and generalised assumptions, public choice theorists have ventured to make numerous predictions about political behaviour, backing them with any convenient supporting evidence. This approach works best when their deductions are purely logical and no empirical evidence is needed, as in the famous (or infamous) "prisoner's dilemma", the theory of games, or strategic voting in committees. In all these cases an unambiguous personal goal or preference can be posited and its interpersonal consequences worked through, but in most actual political settings the nature of the individual's goal is much less certain, however egoistic s/he may be.

For example, much has been written by public choice thinkers about the ways in which individual self-interest fuels bureaucratic expansion. A departmental head, argues Niskanen,[1] will always seek to maximise staff and income and status. However, the bureaucrat may place more weight upon having a quiet life or a cautious security (surely the best choice in some institutional settings), or, as Dunleavy has shown, he may maximise his personal gains by controlling or dismantling other parts of government.[2] Also relevant would be the nature of his career structure, peer influence and opinion, institutional and group rivalries, and even perhaps the bureaucrat's own sense of public service. What these demonstrations have mainly done is to remind us that the public service is not driven principally by public duty, but when did we suppose that it was?

There is space here only to record the main conclusions often drawn from a public choice approach, recognising that its academic exponents actually differ appreciably.[3]

(a) Government is an inefficient transmitter of individual preferences for particular goods and services when compared with a competitive economic market—in other words, it is weak on "allocative efficiency." While the housewife can balance her budget between apples and pears, the voter cannot specify her preferences between health, education and defence, save in crude terms of party voting.

(b) Politics, of course, proceeds through other channels than voting, such as membership of political parties, interest groups, etc. However Olson's, "free rider" hypothesis is a barrier to participation, because the individual will get any benefits going from group efforts without incurring its cost (given that one person makes an insignificant difference to the outcome).[4] This theory has been applied to show the silliness of voting. In the same way the cost of information about complex public policy issues is a barrier to participation—which led Downs to conclude that it was rational to leave such issues to an elected representative if he reflected the voter's general position along a single political cleavage (a condition only sometimes partially met).[5]

(c) Governments have a strong bias towards continuous expansion and wasteful expenditure. On one view this comes about through the capacity of politicians and bureaucrats to extract a surplus for their own uses from ignorant or apathetic voters.[6] On another view the cause is the ability of interest groups (including bureaucratic ones) to extract benefits for themselves from taxpayers and consumers generally.[7] On a third view, the "free rider" tendency leads to an oversupply of free or subsidised public goods since there is no connection between their cost and benefit to the individual.[8] (Downs,however, disagrees, arguing that individuals lack the motivation to get together and demand all the public goods they would like to have.)[9]

To the extent that these arguments are thought to be true, certain normative conclusions seem to follow. First it would be efficient where possible to transfer functions from government to market—subject to the important qualification (often lost sight of) that there are no other relevant considerations.

Secondly, the political system should be made to resemble the market system more closely through greater use of economic incentives within bureaucracy, closer linkages between the costs and benefits of public services to the individual, and a more effective transmission of individual preferences within the political system.

Finally, some public choice writers, notably their doyen James Buchanan, emphasize the desirability of constitutional reform so as to place some restrictions upon the growth of government, which (he supposes) the individual upon calm deliberation will see as desirable for the protection of his own freedom and property, but which get obscured under the pressure of transient political majorities.[10]

Public Choice and Thatcherism

The *Mein Kampf* of Thatcherism is surely the book *Micropolitics* by Madsen Pirie, President of the Adam Smith Institute, which explains clearly and quite closely the strategy actually pursued by the Conservative Government.[11] Pirie claims that public choice theories have demonstrated the inevitability of government expansion in a democratic system under the pressure of interest groups, including especially public employees and state-run or subsidised industries, who are able to extract profits at the general expense of taxpayers and consumers. The result, claims Pirie, has been a grossly inflated and distorted public sector.

The basic goal is to move as much of the public sector as possible into the private sector, thus widening individual freedom of choice. The necessary tactics, however, are not a frontal attack upon the system (which would be doomed to failure because of the political accumulation of vested interests), but piecemeal changes which offer transitional or new political benefits to groups disadvantaged by each step of the process. These tactics have been duly followed in such measures as the large discounts given to purchasers of council houses; the generous redundancy payments and discounted shares offered to employees (and consumers) of privatised industries; the higher salaries payable in the market to their management boards; and so on. The next step will be to widen choice within the heartland public services of health and education through offering tax and other incentives for private provision, thereby freeing more resources for those who still depend upon the public service.

It would be impossible to deny some truth in Pirie's contention about greedy interest groups within and without the public sector. Their influence is not, however, a necessary deduction of public choice methodology, which emphasizes individual egoism and barriers to successful group action, but represents one conclusion of a pessimistic version of pluralism, which shows the potential leverage of a well-organized group in situations where the benefits of group action are concentrated but the consequent costs are widely diffused. There are other political distributions of costs and which favour different results. The direction of the political process is not one-dimensionally upwards.

Indeed, the Thatcherite strategy clearly shows that it is just as possible (and a lot quicker) to provide private profits out of running down the state as out of building it up. The beneficiaries of this strategy include not only those groups, such as public industry management and employees, who, as Pirie says, must be bribed into compliance, but City institutions making a fortune from the privatisation boom, and the top quintile of households who are the main gainers from the tax reliefs financed by the sale of public assets. The Thatcher strategy also represents a self-fulfilling prophecy of an alleged defect of the political process—namely its shortsightedness. The eventual losers will include all those consumers of public services whose financing will necessarily become more difficult. While Pirie makes no mention of the class of owner-occupiers who will increase their tax benefits further through the abolition of rates, the queues of the ill-housed and homeless grow ever longer through the strict curtailment of expenditure imposed upon local authorities (despite the large revenues from the sale of council houses which had to be surrendered to the Treasury).[12] Such developments give the lie to the hypothesis that a smaller state will be more even-handed and less open to group pressures.

The basic public choice criterion, it must be remembered, is the maximum possible satisfaction of individual wants or preferences. This produces a certain bias, as has been said, towards market rather than government provision of goods and services; but the bias is not absolute or unconditional. One point is that it is competitive markets which are supposed to yield consumer satisfaction, whereas most of the Thatcher privatizations have resulted in at least partial private monopolies. The defence is that *any* system of private ownership is more efficient than public ownership. History shows that defence as empirically false. There are many examples of public monopolies performing better in an overall sense than private ones—indeed, this was a recognised reason for nationalisation even if the results were somewhat disappointing (as they will certainly prove to be in some of the privatised utilities), while the rapid improvements of productivity in steel and coal while in public hands itself refutes the argument about the inevitability of public enterprise inefficiency.

More fundamental, however, is the question of how extensive are the private wants which can only be reasonably met by public action. In my view that list of such wants has been growing, not primarily (as public choice theory would have it) through egoistic political action but as a consequence of changes in the economic and social environment. The obsession of public choice thinkers, and still more of Thatcherites, with issues of allocative inefficiency have blinded them to other forms of consumer interest. Consumers do not only want the cheapest possible market goods; they also want safe drugs, wholesome foods, clean air and water, quiet and safe streets, unpolluted beaches, a beautiful countryside. Can economic markets provide or ensure these many and other decencies and amenities of existence?

The fashionable cry is for deregulation, but there are enormous pressures pointing in the opposite direction. Even the much lauded deregulation of the airlines in the USA, which produced drastic fare cuts for consumers, can now be seen to have increased the problems of air safety—not to mention those of

noise blight and oil consumption. One wonders most anxiously about the effects of water privatisation in the UK upon health standards and river pollution, not to mention upon fisheries and access to recreation. The environmental catastrophes of oil spills, acid rain, atmospheric pollution, deforestation, noxious wastes, etc, provide a large and very urgent agenda for strong and effective public measures to be taken in the interests of today's and tomorrow's individual citizens. Popular concern is rising; for example, half of more of the questions in European Parliament concern deficiencies of public regulation. These wants fly in the face of the argument for a minimum state, or for policies which would channel the brightest brains into profit-making activities such as the money markets, rather than into tackling urgent social and environmental issues.

There is plenty of evidence too that citizens' ideas of a satisfactory life cannot be met through market processes. A recent survey to find the most livable British cities covered such factors as the cost of living, the quality of housing, access to facilities, the local environment, etc. The most livable cities turned out to be Edinburgh, Aberdeen, Cardiff and Plymouth, with towns in the South East of England ranking low and London near the bottom.[13] Other regional surveys have shown similar results. The idea that measured economic wealth is the index to individual satisfaction takes a hard knock from such surveys. Many valued qualities of life seem to turn upon good local services and amenities, and upon the avoidance of urban congestion and sprawl—a case for effective public planning. Possibly the good showing of Scotland in the above survey owes something to the lesser rundown of public planning and investment there (out of political necessity) as compared with England.

The most glaring contradiction between Thatcherism and public choice thinking lies in the Government's highly repressive treatment of elected local councils. Public choice stresses the virtues of maximum political decentralisation so as to widen the expression of individual preferences over the volume and quality of public services, to control bureaucracy more closely and to improve the linkage between the perceived costs and benefits of collective action. Some thinkers in this school push this policy to extremes, as in Ostrom's proposal for the dismantling of central bureaucracy in favour of systems of client and localised political control.[14] The Conservative Government is trying to import some small degree of parental control into the administration of schools, but the preferences of local electorates have been given very short shift. Public choice, it seems, is only to be expressed through the 43 percent of voters who supported the Conservative Government, not through any other channels of free election. This is a flat contradiction of the public choice gospel, as well as a repudiation of more soundly-based traditional arguments for local democracy. Even so strong a protagonist of market systems as Hayek is a supporter of local government, believing that many public services like town planning are better controlled locally than centrally.[15]

How is this contradiction to be explained? It is sometimes suggested that there need be no incongruity between a mixture of market philosophy and social authoritarianism because they concern different spheres of behaviour (economic and moral); but the phenomenon here is one of political not moral authoritarianism. The explanation, I believe, is a sort of dictatorship of the proletariat in reverse, whereby a supreme end of rolling back the state is held to justify a temporary authoritarianism. Once this is well under way the public is expected, as Pirie explains, to rejoice and to carry on the process with enthusiasm. And if they do not rejoice? A more sinister but more plausible outcome could be that authoritarian government becomes still more necessary to maintain an enlarged but inegalitarian and unstable market system. Political authoritarianism is a dangerous companion for what is supposed to be liberal individualism.

The Nature of Politics

Let me return to public choice theory itself. *Is* political behaviour similar to market behaviour? Does the individual have the same motivations within the two systems? The short answer is no—or anyhow only to a limited extent, just as a man does not behave the same way in his office and his home.

The neoclassical economic man of public choice is not "natural man," but an ideal type actor within a historically specialised and rare institutional framework. The functioning and maintenance of this system depends crucially upon public laws (about property, contract, taxation, etc) which have become increasingly complex and which cannot be socially and ethically neutral—hence the market cannot be detached from politics.

The actual organisation of the market system does not comply at all closely with the neoclassical model. The growth of giant firms and conglomerates, and the ever-widening complexities of the money market, together with the consequential necessities for public regulation (a necessity which even the Thatcher Government is beginning to recognise in the case of the City)[16] mean that economic behaviour has become more like politics than vice versa. Takeover bids, for example, typically revolve around coalitions of inter-

ests. The public choice economists by-pass these facts by focusing upon the rational, self-regarding choices of market consumers; but insofar as the neoclassical paradigm does apply, it represents a socially legitimated form of rational egoism which is acceptable ethically so long as market rules and outcomes are themselves acceptable; and these depend on politics.

Politics occupies a different institutional terrain and social relationships and norms from Adam Smith's self-regarding and atomistic market order (supposing that existed). Politics involves multiple and often contradictory goals which cannot be effectively reconciled and "traded off" even in one individual's mind, let alone expressed in some common measuring rod like money. Politics involves emotional preferences (frequently irrational ones in terms of rational egoism) as well as highly uncertain and speculative outcomes. Politics necessarily involves the individual in subsuming her own private interest within some view of group interest, whether that group be an occupation or profession, an ethnic group, a socio-economic class, the nation, or some still broader reference group such as humanity. Dogmatic politics involves the attempted imposition of some single group interest, democratic politics revolves around the unceasing adjustments of differing group interests (including the nation as a reference group); and, of course, the nature of group interest is always contestable.

I am not here saying by any means that market behaviour is selfish and political behaviour altruistic, but that the terms of such behaviour differ. Rational egoism in consumer purchases is quite consistent with giving one's goods to the poor. Conversely, group loyalties in politics can be and frequently are exploited by self-seeking leaders—hence the easy transition from political idealism to cynicism. Nonetheless an ambitious politician can only climb to personal success and patronage on the backs of his party, and resignations—whether due to principle or ambition—are rarely the key to personal advantage. The point is that politics necessarily involves the disciplines, norms and loyalties of group behaviour in ways that the behaviour of a market consumer or investor need not.

The great moral problem of politics is group selfishness or aggression, whether this be shown in the protective rationalism of established material interests, the assertive emotionalism of ethnic majorities, or the distorted ideologies of military or party elites. Politics after all is the key to harnessing or exploiting the enormous material and coercive resources of government. Within any of these contexts political leaders can ether intensify group assertiveness (sometimes to a pathological degree) or modify and balance interests, and often they will combine rational and emotional appeals (as is the familiar mixture of class economic interest with nationalism). The raw material is always the shifting collective identifications of individual interests and emotions.

Responsible individual judgment is the only possible basis for checking the pathologies of politics and maintaining a decent political order. This blinding platitude only seems such because it is deeply embedded in the Western liberal tradition of respect for individual rights, political tolerance, and concern for the social effects of one's political choices. In this sense I share the methodological individualism of the public choice school, but with the differences that they (or many of them) assume that rational egoism is a sufficient basis for political action. This approach cancels out any but a self-regarding attention to social effects, hence too any necessary regard for more than very limited formal rights for others. As with the early Utilitarians, enlightened self-interest can be said to require a broader range of concerns, but the logical foundation for such an attitude is lacking in public choice theory. That foundation can only be provided by a principle which states that, just as self-regarding behaviour is (within limits) an acceptable norm of the market, so is other-regarding behaviour (within wider limits) a necessary norm of politics—or, at the very least, in Kantian terms, a significant regulative ideal. Put simply, I ought not to vote against the education budget on the egoistic grounds that I have no children, or against environmental laws on the grounds that I am too old to suffer from environmental degradation.

Thus put these points may seem obvious, yet they are only illustrations of the older belief—now ridiculed by public choice thinkers as a myth—that politics is concerned with the general welfare. Much in politics could not be so described—I have emphasized this point already—and yet the belief is a necessary regulative ideal of politics without which it would dissolve into barbaric conflict. In breaking with the traditions of responsible liberal individualism, these "new individualists" are reverting to the world of Hobbes, not Locke, a world whose nasty, short and brutish features would destroy individual liberty alike in politics and the market; for physical coercion not free exchange is the ultimate fate of such a world.

Markets and Government

Let me now turn to the normative conclusions of the public choice theorists. They often claim that "political failures" are greater than "market failures', but a comparison in these terms is hard to sustain because goals are different and the two systems (market and government) are today so closely entangled. Political performance is also extremely variable.

Thus it may be plausibly claimed that government makes less efficient use of resources where the outputs of the two systems are comparable; but often they are not comparable. Market failures consist not only in internal inefficiencies, but in social effects such as a high degree of inequality of wealth, instability of employment, and adverse "externalities" such as pollution etc. These forms of market failure are certainly not declining. Political failures might also be evaluated by the degree to which governments achieve economic stability and equity, protect the environment and human resources of society, and overcome poverty, squalor and destitution. These were the aims of the post-war Keynesian welfare state, except that environmental goals have now taken on a much more urgent salience.

The fashionable "public choice" viewpoint is that governments have rather little capacity to pursue such goals effectively, and that welfare goals should largely be left to the trickle-down effects of market incentives and economic growth. The performance of some democracies, such as the Scandinavian countries, shows, however, that these goals of government are not in fact unattainable even in adverse economic circumstances. Large welfare states such as Sweden seem to combine the results of high quality public services, far-sighted environmental measures, and economic growth—and to end up with a more contented and less divisive society than the English-speaking democracies. There is even a growing body of evidence that high levels of public expenditure and taxation are positively not negatively correlated with economic growth—at any rate to the extent that public expenditure is geared towards welfare rather than military goals.[17]

The basic value assumption of public choice theory is individual liberty. Libertarians generally perceive the state as the great threat to liberty, and in some situations they are right. Hayek's famous argument against Socialism or any comprehensive form of public planning was that it would destroy the spontaneous market order on which individual liberty depends. (Hayek was not, however, opposed to an extensive system of public social services or even nationalised industries where there were clear economies of scale.)[18] Hayek was right in seeing a close connection between pluralism and individual freedom—but his idealised model does not correspond with the present concentration of power within the market system, nor need one look to that system as the only possible counter to political tyranny. Moreover, because market power can be, and increasingly is, deployed for political ends, political liberty is clearly reduced and undermined by large inequalities of market power and wealth.

Once happy pluralists such as Dahl and Lindblom have been disillusioned by the inequality of resources between political groups. Dahl's answer would be to extend the basic value of democracy into large business enterprises through the gradual introduction of worker's ownership along lines already being pioneered in Sweden, Denmark and Spain (the Mondragon Co-operatives).[19]

Buchanan's theories of constitutionalism likewise reflect the idealised order of Jeffersonian America—one where a rough degree of economic equality among farmers and small businessmen and an open frontier could be seen as the essential foundations of political liberty. Today when 1.3 percent of the population are said to own over 50 percent of the wealth,[20] and managerial oligarchies have largely taken over control from stockholders (with little connection either between salaries and profit rates), this connection has been snapped. There seems little reason why a majority of rational egoists (let alone the unanimous agreement which Buchanan favours) should support constitutional constraints upon government expenditure which could be directed against redistribution. But, in any case, if constitutional constraints are desirable, they might take a quite different direction. The short-sightedness of transient majorities which Buchanan cites could today be an argument for entrenched environmental laws which governments must implement.

Political Reform

There can be no single criterion of a good political system. The public choice recipe of maximum attention to individual wants or preferences, while a vital input into such a system, is limited by factors which these theorists themselves emphasize, such as voters' ignorance and apathy and manipulation by the media. Certainly political reform turns, as I have said, upon a more responsible exercise of political choice, and possible reforms—such as greater economic equality, the breaking of media monopolies and some old-fashioned civic education—would serve this goal. However, much will also turn upon those cause and professional groups which at least partly and sometimes wholly contradict the assumption of egoistic behaviour. Environmental groups, for example, are slowly changing the political agenda, despite the disadvantages which a public choice approach would emphasize such as lack of direct material incentives and resources. Equally important are professional groups, both inside and outside government, who can contribute the "authority of knowledge" (for knowledge can never be neutral) towards redefining and implementing the tasks of government.

Certainly the decentralisation of the state has an important part to play over promoting the responsible exercise of political choice, just as market power needs to be decentralised. In most European democracies except Britain, where the process is reversed, political decentralisation has gathered pace. However, it is possible to doubt whether in Europe national states should for much longer be regarded as the optimum political units. A European federation seems to be the only entity capable of managing the forms of public regulation that will be required to deal with a high volume of economic, social and environmental interdependencies; but this development could also go with much more decentralisation of power to the regional authorities which (except in the UK) are increasingly making their presence felt upon the European scene, often with the benefit of historical, cultural or ethnic roots. A "Europe of the regions" can have no attraction for the Thatcherites, yet ironically their policies of economic deregulation may be paving the way for just this result as their social and environmental consequences become apparent.

Public choice theory represents a one dimensional view of the relations between the individual and society. It provides some insights into the logic of interpersonal conflict under specified rules, and it is plausible enough to capture one significant dimension of human and political behaviour. It cannot map the rich complexity of political life, and, indeed, its loose assumptions lead themselves to conflicting conclusions. (Much depends, for example, upon whether one uses the language of individual egoism or individual preferences.)

The theory has lent itself to a narrow political ideology and agenda, which greatly exaggerates the spontaneous and beneficent character of the market system (although public choice theorists have themselves pointed out the mistake),[21] and which underplays the significance of government action for the satisfaction of its own criterion of private wants. Its normative criterion of individual liberty is narrowly and artificially conceived through abstraction from the accumulated cultural and institutional environment. Its recipes often misplace the nature of the problem—for example, the project of modelling government upon the market overlooks that government is there to control the market and needs an appropriate bureaucratic independence and integrity for this purpose. Its lack of any but a negative concept of "public philosophy" blocks understanding of the broader role which governments must today accept, and the moral and intellectual resources essential to this task.

Postscript on Political Culture

David Marquand has said that British political culture is rooted in a reductionist individualism linked to faith in the market economy, and understands only two modes of social change—the economic exchange mode and the political command one.[22] Mrs Thatcher has certainly successfully appealed to both modes of achieving change, but I believe that Marquand's analysis is mistaken.

The Thatcher appeal reverts (in theory) to the nineteenth century tradition of laissez-faire liberalism linked with social Darwinism, as propounded by Herbert Spencer. The public choice concept of rational egoism offers a useful modern substitute for the ancient belief in original sin, which can be used to explain the inevitability of inequality and the necessity for any social improvement to come about through individual effort and competition unaided by the state—ideas which seem more persuasive under conditions of economic depression and disillusion with government planning.

However, this negative individual tradition was countered by the views of the welfare liberals such as L.T. Hobhouse[23] and T.H. Green.[24] Green's view of the proper role of the state as "removing obstacles to the good life" for all its citizens has had and continues to have a considerable impact upon political culture. T.H. Marshall developed the doctrine into an argument for the complementarity of political, economic and social rights which is akin to the views of neo-pluralists such as Dahl.[25] Not only did the old Liberal Party divide long ago on this issue, but the same ideas have had a deep impact upon both Fabian Socialism and the "welfare Tories" such as Macmillan or Heath.

Far from the present Government representing the dominant British culture, it represents a throwback to an ideology which seemed until recently to have had its day. The unreality of the ideology, in terms of the actual functioning and distribution of power within both state and market system must make its survival for long improbable. The present success of Conservatism in Britain can be seen in various lights—as a marginal shift in the perspective of the median voter, as a protest against irresponsible unionism, or (more intellectually) as a shift to simple dogmatic rule in reaction from the inevitable complexities of governmental policy-making in a rapidly changing world. There is also the strong penalty inflicted by the British electoral system upon a divided Opposition.

Mainspring British political culture still runs, I believe, in a different direction from any vulgarised interpretation of public choice theories—theories which, I have endeavoured to point out, by no means support many measures which are politically justified in their name.

Source: Peter Self. "What's Wrong with Government?: The Problem of Public Choice." *Canberra Journal of Public Administration* 60, (1990): 17-22. Reprinted with the permission of the author and *Canberra Journal of Public Administration.*

Notes

1. W.A. Niskanen. *Bureaucracy and Representative Government.* Chicago: Aldine-Altherton, 1971.

2. P. Dunleavy. "Bureaucrats, Budgets and the Growth of the State," *British Journal of Political Science* 15 (1985): 299–328.

3. For a triple classification of public choice theorists see ch 2 in Peter Self. *Political Theories of Modern Government.* London: Allen and Unwin, 1985.

4. M. Olson. *The Logic of Collective Action.* Cambridge, Mass: Harvard University Press, 1965.

5. A. Downs. *An Economic Theory of Democracy.* New York: Harper Press, 1957.

6. A. Breton. *The Economic Theory of Representative Government.* Chicago: Aidine, 1974.

7. M. Olson. *The Rise and Decline of Nations.* New Haven: Yale University Press, 1982.

8. J.M. Buchanan. *The Demand and Supply of Public Goods.* Chicago: Rand McNally, 1968.

9. A. Downs. "Why the Government Budget Is Too Small in a Democracy." *World Politics* 12 (1960): 541–563.

10. G. Brennan and J.M. Buchanan. *The Reason of Rules: Constitutional Political Economy.* Cambridge: Cambridge University Press, 1985.

11. M. Pirie. *Micropolitics.* London: Wildwood House, 1988.

12. See, for example, *The Municipal Review.* Jan/Feb, 1989. p.230.

13. R. Rogerson et al. "The Best Cities to Live In." *Town and Country Planning.* Oct. 1988: 270-273.

14. V. Ostrom. *The Intellectual Crisis in American Public Administration.* Tuscaloosa, Ala: University of Alabama Press, 1973.

15. F.A. Hayek. *The Constitution of Liberty.* London: Routledge & Kegan Paul, 1960.

16. See M. Wright. "City Rules OK?" *Public Administration* 64, No. 4, 389–410.

17. See for example, F.G. Castles and S. Dowrick. *The Impact of Government Spending Levels on Medium Term Economic Growth in the OECD, 1960-1985.* Centre for Economic Research, The Australian National University, Canberra.

18. F.A. Hayek. *The Road to Serfdom.* London: Routledge & Kegan Paul, 1944. See pp.27–29, 37–38.

19. R.A. Dahl. *A Preface to Economic Theory.* Berkeley: University of California Press, 1985.

20. Op cit, p.103.

21. See the review in P.M. Jackson. *The Political Economy of Bureaucracy.* Dedington, Oxon: Philip Allan, 1982.

22. D. Marquand. "Beyond Social Democracy." *Political Quarterly.* July-Sept, 1987.

23. L.T. Hobhouse. *Liberalism.* London: Oxford University Press, 1944.

24. T.H. Green. *Lectures on the Principles of Political Obligation.* London: Longmans Green, 1931.

25. T.H. Marshall. *Citizenship and Social Class.* Cambridge: Cambridge University Press, 1950.

5

Marxism

The Ideal of Proletarian Liberty

There is little doubt that Karl Marx, Charles Darwin and Sigmund Freud were among the intellectual giants of the nineteenth century. Concentrating on Marx alone, one can see in his writings a deep and abiding concern for the inhumanity of people to one another.

Marx's historical materialism leads to an unqualified humanism quite unlike anything found in classical or reform liberalism or in various versions, old and new, of conservatism. Regrettably, Marx's philosophical humanism is somewhat obscured owing to the emphasis he and his successors, such as Lenin and Trotsky, place upon notions such as modes of production, class struggle, imperialism, freedom of criticism, collectivism, internationalism and permanent revolution. But Marx's real interest lies in revealing to the masses the importance of our humanity. By continuing the process of demythologizing social structures and institutions which Feuerbach and Strauss began before him, Marx seeks to reveal to us that our humanity is attainable.

While Lenin and Trotsky develop Marx's theoretical ideas and add strategic ones of their own, Freud, never lacking in intellectual courage, attacks Marx's thinking at its foundations by challenging the latter's presupposed psychological theory of aggression. Additional instructive points concerning Marxism are made by David Held, who argues that, notwithstanding the radically different views of liberalism and Marxism, the two ideologies share a common view of reducing arbitrary power and regulatory capacity to their lowest possible extent. The fact that Held does not distinguish between liberals as varied as Locke, Mill and Nozick only slightly diminishes the force of his remarks.

Marxists share a concern for redistributive justice based upon, as Nozick would say, ends principles. The redistribution sought is for the masses, the sea of humanity, crystallized in the working or labouring class and the *lumpenproletariat* existing at its margins. Accordingly, the key to this new found justice is the liberty of the proletariat. It is this liberty which, presumably, will triumph in humankind's realization of its humanity.

Bourgeois and Proletarians

Karl Marx and Friedrich Engels

KARL MARX *(1818-1883) was born in Trier, Germany, and became a renowned economic and social thinker. His most famous early work, written in collaboration with Fredrich Engels, was the pamphlet and classic statement of communist theory,* The Communist Manifesto. *Much of his life was spent in London where he wrote* Das Kapital.

FRIEDRICH ENGELS *(1820-1895) was born in Germany and was both a socialist intellectual and a textile manufacturer. He is best known as the collaborator and intellectual companion of Karl Marx. He was the co-author with Marx of* The Communist Manifesto, *and he edited and completed the manuscript for Volumes II and III of Marx's* Das Kapital.

A spectre is haunting Europe—the spectre of Communism. All the Powers of old Europe have entered into a holy alliance to exorcize this spectre: Pope and Czar, Metternich and Guizot, French Radicals and German police spies.

Where is the party in opposition that has not been decried as Communistic by its opponents in power? Where the Opposition that has not hurled back the branding reproach of Communism, against the more advanced opposition parties, as well as against its reactionary adversaries?

Two things result from this fact:

I. Communism is already acknowledged by all European Powers to be itself a Power.

II. It is high time that Communists should openly, in the face of the whole world, publish their views, their aims, their tendencies, and meet this nursery tale of the Spectre of Communism with a Manifesto of the party itself.

To this end, Communists of various nationalities have assembled in London, and sketched the following Manifesto, to be published in the English, French, German, Italian, Flemish and Danish languages.

Bourgeois and Proletarians[1]

The history of all hitherto existing society[2] is the history of class struggles.

Freeman and slave, patrician and plebeian, lord and serf, guild-master[3] and journeyman, in a word, oppressor and oppressed, stood in constant opposition to one another, carried on an uninterrupted, now hidden, now open fight, a fight that each time ended, either in a revolutionary reconstitution of society at large, or in the common ruin of the contending classes.

In the earlier epochs of history, we find almost everywhere a complicated arrangement of society into various orders, a manifold gradation of social rank. In ancient Rome we have patricians, knights, plebeians, slaves; in the Middle Ages, feudal lords, vassals, guild-masters, journeymen, apprentices, serfs; in almost all of these classes, again, subordinate gradations.

The modern bourgeois society that has sprouted from the ruins of feudal society has not done away with class antagonisms. It has but established new classes, new conditions of oppression, new forms of struggle in place of the old ones.

Our epoch, the epoch of the bourgeoisie, possesses, however, this distinctive feature: it has simplified the class antagonisms. Society as a whole is more and more splitting up into two great hostile camps, into two great classes directly facing each other: Bourgeoisie and Proletariat.

From the serfs of the Middle Ages sprang the chartered burghers of the earliest towns. From these burgesses the first elements of the bourgeoisie were developed.

The discovery of America, the rounding of the Cape, opened up fresh ground for the rising bourgeoisie. The East-Indian and Chinese markets, the colonization of America, trade with the colonies, the increase in the means of exchange and in commodities generally, gave to commerce, to navigation, to industry, an impulse never before known, and thereby, to the revolutionary element in the tottering feudal society, a rapid development.

The feudal system of industry, under which industrial production was monopolized by closed guilds, now no longer sufficed for the growing wants of the new markets. The manufacturing system took its place. The guild-masters were pushed on one side by the manufacturing middle class; division of labour between the different corporate guilds vanished in the face of division of labour in each single workshop.

Meantime the markets kept ever growing, the demand ever rising. Even manufacture no longer suf-

KARL MARX (1818-1883)

KARL MARX was born into a middle-class family in Trier, a town in the Rhineland region of Germany. His father was a lawyer and civil servant, a fact that is perhaps surprising to those who, due to the nature of Marx's economic and political theories, might have imagined him to have grown up in a working-class household. Marx first attended the University of Bonn and later the University of Berlin, where he came under the influence of the so-called "Young Hegelians," a group of students and professors dedicated to furthering the work of the renowned German philosopher Georg Wilhelm Friedrich Hegel.

After a stint as the editor of a newspaper in Cologne, Marx left Germany for France with his wife and children in 1843. In Paris he was to meet several prominent socialist and revolutionary thinkers of the day, one of whom, Friedrich Engels, was later to co-author the *Communist Manifesto* (1848) with Marx. Engels was the son of a wealthy textile manufacturer. As the manager of one of his father's mills in England, Engels had written a tract entitled *The Condition Of The Working Class In England* (1844) which drew heavily upon a controversial parliamentary report on the same subject.

Marx moved to Belgium in 1845, then returned to Germany in 1848. He was expelled from Germany in 1849, and after spending a short time in France, departed for England where he would live for the rest of his life under fairly dire financial circumstances.

Regarded by many as the most influential social critic and revolutionary of all time, Marx's best known work, aside from the *Communist Manifesto*, was *Das Kapital* (*Capital*) which he published in 1867. The entire body of Marx's thought is complex and varied. Many terms and phrases that are commonplace today within the language of politics and political science are attributable to Marx, such as "surplus value," "exploitation," the "lumpenproletariat" and the "alienation" of the working class.

Marx's basic political/economic theory held that the capitalist ruling class within a given society was doomed to failure, and its weakening would encourage the workers to take over not only the means of industrial production but the political realm as well. Marx viewed economic and material conditions as responsible for every aspect of human life in an industrial society. People's governments, as well as their morals, attitudes and values were all shaped by their relationship to property and labour. It was the exploitation, Marx claimed, of those who did not own property and the means of their production by those who did that constituted the core of capitalism. And although class-based revolution could and often did take violent forms, Marx saw conflict between workers and capitalists as a necessary and inevitable stage in the economic history of the industrialized world.

ficed. Thereupon, steam and machinery revolutionized industrial production. The place of manufacture was taken by the giant, Modern Industry, the place of the industrial middle class, by industrial millionaires, the leaders of whole industrial armies, the modern bourgeois.

Modern industry has established the world market, for which the discovery of America paved the way. This market has given an immense development to commerce, to navigation, to communication by land. This development has, in its turn, reacted on the extension of industry; and in proportion as industry, commerce, navigation, railways extended, in the same proportion the bourgeoisie developed, increased its capital, and pushed into the background every class handed down from the Middle Ages.

We see, therefore, how the modern bourgeoisie is itself the product of a long course of development, of a series of revolutions in the modes of production and of exchange.

Each step in the development of the bourgeoisie was accompanied by a corresponding political advance of that class. An oppressed class under the sway of the feudal nobility, an armed and self-governing association in the medieval commune;[4] here independent urban republic (as in Italy and Germany), there taxable "third estate" of the Monarchy (as in France), afterwards, in the period of manufacture proper, serving either the semi-feudal or the absolute monarchy as a counterpoise against the nobility, and, in fact, corner-stone of the great monarchies in general, the bourgeoisie has at last, since the establishment of Modern Industry and of the world market, conquered for itself, in the modern representative State, exclusive political sway. The executive of the modern State is but a committee for managing the common affairs of the whole bourgeoisie.

The bourgeoisie, historically, has played a most revolutionary part.

The bourgeoisie, wherever it has got the upper hand, has put an end to all feudal, patriarchal, idyllic relations. It has pitilessly torn asunder the motley feudal ties that bound man to his "natural superiors," and has left remaining no other nexus between man and man than naked self-interest, than callous "cash payment." It has drowned the most heavenly ecstasies of religious fervour, of chivalrous enthusiasm, of philistine sentimentalism, in the icy water of egotistical calculation. It has resolved personal worth into exchange value, and in place of the numberless indefeasible chartered freedoms, has set up that single, unconscionable freedom—Free Trade. In one word, for exploitation, veiled by religious and political illusions, it has substituted naked, shameless, direct, brutal exploitation.

The bourgeoisie has stripped of its halo every occupation hitherto honoured and looked up to with reverent awe. It has converted the physician, the lawyer, the priest, the poet, the man of science, into its paid wage-labourers.

The bourgeoisie has torn away from the family its sentimental veil, and has reduced the family relation to a mere money relation.

The bourgeoisie has disclosed how it came to pass that the brutal display of vigour in the Middle Ages, which Reactionists so much admire, found its fitting complement in the most slothful indolence. It has been the first to show what man's activity can bring about. It has accomplished wonders far surpassing Egyptian pyramids, Roman aqueducts, and Gothic cathedrals; it has conducted expeditions that put in the shade all former Exoduses of nations and crusades.

The bourgeoisie cannot exist without constantly revolutionizing the instruments of production, and thereby the relations of production, and with them the whole relations of society. Conservation of the old modes of production in unaltered form, was, on the contrary, the first condition of existence for all earlier industrial classes. Constant revolutionizing of production, uninterrupted disturbance of all social conditions, everlasting uncertainty and agitation distinguish the bourgeois epoch from all earlier ones. All fixed, fast-frozen relations, with their train of ancient and venerable prejudices and opinions are swept away, all new-formed ones become antiquated before they can ossify. All that is solid melts into air, all that is holy is profaned, and man is at last compelled to face with sober senses, his real conditions of life, and his relations with his kind.

The need of a constantly expanding market for its products chases the bourgeoisie over the whole surface of the globe. It must nestle everywhere, settle everywhere, establish connexions everywhere …

Hitherto, every form of society has been based, as we have already seen, on the antagonism of oppressing and oppressed classes. But in order to oppress a class, certain conditions must be assured to it under which it can, at least, continue its slavish existence. The serf, in the period of serfdom, raised himself to membership in the commune, just as the petty bourgeois, under the yoke of feudal absolutism managed to develop into a bourgeois. The modern labourer, on the contrary, instead of rising with the progress of industry, sinks deeper and deeper below the conditions of existence of his own class. He becomes a pauper, and pauperism develops more rapidly than population and wealth. And here it becomes evident, that the bourgeoisie is unfit any longer to be the ruling class in society, and to impose its conditions of existence upon society as an overriding law. It is unfit to rule because it is incompetent to assure an existence to its slave within his slavery, because it cannot help letting him sink into such a state, that it has to feed him, instead of being fed by him. Society can no longer live under this bourgeoisie, in other words, its existence is no longer compatible with society.

The essential condition for the existence, and for the sway of the bourgeois class, is the formation and augmentation of capital; the condition for capital is wage labour. Wage labour rests exclusively on competition between the labourers. The advance of industry, whose involuntary promoter is the bourgeoisie, replaces the isolation of the labourers, due to competition, by their revolutionary combination, due to association. The development of Modern Industry, therefore, cuts from under its feet the very foundation on which the bourgeoisie produces and appropriates products. What the bourgeoisie, therefore, produces, above all, is its own grave-diggers. Its fall and the victory of the proletariat are equally inevitable.

Source: Karl Marx and Friedrich Engels. *The Communist Manifesto.* Originally published in 1849. Reprinted with the permission of International Publishers Co., Inc.

Notes

[1] By bourgeoisie is meant the class of modern Capitalists, owners of the means of social production and employers of wage labour. By proletariat, the class of modern wage-labourers who, having no means of production of their own, are reduced to selling their labour power in order to live. [*Added by Engels to the English edition, 1888.*]

[2] That is, all *written* history. In 1847, the pre-history of society, the social organization existing previous to recorded history, was all but unknown. Since then, Haxthausen discovered common ownership of land in Russia, Maurer proved it to be the social foundation from which all Teutonic races started in history, and by and by village communities were found to be, or to have been the primitive form of society everywhere from India to Ireland. The inner organization of this primitive Communistic society was laid bare, in its typical form, by Morgan's crowning discovery of the true nature of the *gens* and its relation to the *tribe.* With the dissolution of these primeval communities society begins to be differentiated into separate and finally antagonistic classes. I have attempted to retrace this process of dissolution in: *Der Ursprung der Familie, des Privateigenthums und des Staats (The Origin of the Family, Private Property and the State),* 2nd edition, Stuttgart 1886. [*Added by Engels to the English edition, 1888.*]

[3] Guild-master, that is, a full member of a guild, a master within, not a head of a guild. [*Added by Engels to the English edition, 1888.*]

[4] "Commune" was the name taken, in France, by the nascent towns even before they had conquered from their feudal lords and masters local self-government and political rights as the "Third Estate." Generally speaking, for the economical development of the bourgeoisie, England is here taken as the typical country; for its political development, France. [*Added by Engels to the English edition, 1888.*] This was the name given their urban communities by the townsmen of Italy and France, after they had purchased or wrested their initial rights of self-government from their feudal lords. [*Added by Engels to the German edition, 1890.*]

Toward a Critique of Hegel's Philosophy of Right: Introduction

Karl Marx

For Germany the *criticism of religion* has been essentially completed, and criticism of religion is the premise of all criticism.

The *profane* existence of error is comprised when its *heavenly oratio pro aris et focis* [defense of altar and hearth] has been refuted. Man, who has found only the *reflection* of himself in the fantastic reality of heaven where he sought a supernatural being, will no longer be inclined to find the *semblance* of himself, only the non-human being, where he seeks and must seek his true reality.

The basis of irreligious criticism is: *Man makes religion*, religion does not make man. And indeed religion is the self-consciousness and self-regard of man who has either not yet found or has already lost himself. But *man* is not an abstract being squatting outside the world. Man is the *world of men*, the state, society. This state and this society produce religion, which is an *inverted consciousness of the world* because they are an *inverted world*. Religion is the generalized theory of this world, its encyclopedic compendium, its logic in popular form, its spiritualistic point d'honneur, its enthusiasm, its moral sanction, its solemn complement, its general ground of consolation and justification. It is the *fantastic realization* of the human essence inasmuch as the *human essence* possesses no true reality. The struggle against religion is therefore indirectly the struggle against *that world* whose spiritual *aroma* is religion.

Religious suffering is the *expression* of real suffering and at the same time the *protest* against real suffering.

Religion is the sigh of the oppressed creature, the heart of a heartless world, as it is the spirit of spiritless conditions. It is the *opium* of the people.

The abolition of religion as people's illusory happiness is the demand for their *real* happiness. The demand to abandon illusions about their condition *is a demand to abandon a condition which requires illusions*. The criticism of religion is thus in *embryo* a *criticism of the vale of tears* whose *halo* is religion.

Criticism has plucked imaginary flowers from the chain, not so that man will wear the chain that is without fantasy or consolation but so that he will throw it off and pluck the living flower. The criticism of religion disillusions man so that he thinks, acts, and shapes his reality like a disillusioned man who has come to his senses, so that he revolves around himself and thus around his true sun. Religion is only the illusory sun that revolves around man so long as he does not revolve about himself.

Thus it is the *task of history*, once the *otherworldly truth* has disappeared, to establish the *truth of this world*. The immediate *task of philosophy* which is in the service of history is to unmask human self-alienation in its *unholy forms* now that it has been unmasked in its *holy form*. Thus the criticism of heaven turns into the criticism of the earth, the criticism of religion, into the criticism of law, and the *criticism of theology* into the *criticism of politics*.

Source: Karl Marx. *Toward a Critique of Hegel's Philosophy of Right.* Originally published in 1843.

Toward a Critique of Political Economy: Preface

Karl Marx

I examine the system of bourgeois economy in the following order: *capital, landed property, wage-labour; the State, foreign trade, world market.* The economic conditions of existence of the three great classes into which modern bourgeois society is divided are analysed under the first three headings; the interconnection of the other three headings is self-evident. The first part of the first book, dealing with Capital, comprises the following chapters: 1. The commodity; 2. Money or simple circulation; 3. Capital in general. The present part consists of the first two chapters. The entire material lies before me in the form of monographs, which were written not for publication but for self-clarification at widely separated periods; their remoulding into an integrated whole according to the plan I have indicated will depend upon circumstances.

A general introduction,[1] which I had drafted, is omitted, since on further consideration it seems to me confusing to anticipate results which still have to be substantiated, and the reader who really wishes to follow me will have to decide to advance from the particular to the general. A few brief remarks regarding the course of my study of political economy may, however, be appropriate here.

Although I studied jurisprudence, I pursued it as a subject subordinated to philosophy and history. In the year 1842-43, as editor of the *Rheinische Zeitung*, I first found myself in the embarrassing position of having to discuss what is known as material interests. The deliberations of the Rhenish Landtag on forest thefts and the division of landed property; the official polemic started by Herr von Schaper, then Oberpräsident of the Rhine Province, against the *Rheinische Zeitung* about the condition of the Moselle peasantry, and finally the debates on free trade and protective tariffs caused me in the first instance to turn my attention to economic questions. On the other hand, at that time when good intentions "to push forward" often took the place of factual knowledge, an echo of French socialism and communism, slightly tinged by philosophy, was noticeable in the *Rheinische Zeitung*. I objected to this dilettantism, but at the same time

frankly admitted in a controversy with the *Allgemeine Augsburger Zeitung* that my previous studies did not allow me to express any opinion on the content of the French theories. When the publishers of the *Rheinische Zeitung* conceived the illusion that by a more compliant policy on the part of the paper it might be possible to secure the abrogation of the death sentence passed upon it, I eagerly grasped the opportunity to withdraw from the public stage to my study.[2]

The first work which I undertook to dispel the doubts assailing me was a critical re-examination of the Hegelian philosophy of law; the introduction to this work being published in the *Deutsch-Französische Jahrbücher* issued in Paris in 1844.[3] My inquiry led me to the conclusion that neither legal relations nor political forms could be comprehended whether by themselves or on the basis of a so-called general development of the human mind, but that on the contrary they originate in the material conditions of life, the totality of which Hegel, following the example of English and French thinkers of the eighteenth century, embraces within the term "civil society"; that the anatomy of this civil society, however, has to be sought in political economy. The study of this, which I began in Paris, I continued in Brussels, where I moved owing to an expulsion order issued by M. Guizot.[4] The general conclusion at which I arrived and which, once reached, became the guiding principle of my studies can be summarised as follows. In the social production of their existence, men inevitably enter into definite relations, which are independent of their will, namely relations of production appropriate to a given stage in the development of their material forces of production. The totality of these relations of production constitutes the economic structure of society, the real foundation, on which arises a legal and political superstructure and to which correspond definite forms of social consciousness. The mode of production of material life conditions the general process of social, political and intellectual life. It is not the consciousness of men that determines their existence, but their social existence that determines their consciousness. At a certain stage of development, the material productive forces of society come into conflict with the existing relations of production or—this merely expresses the same thing in legal terms—with the property relations within the framework of which they have operated hitherto. From forms of development of the productive forces these relations turn into their fetters. Then begins an era of social revolution. The changes in the economic foundation lead sooner or later to the transformation of the whole immense superstructure. In studying such transformations it is always necessary to distinguish between the material transformation of the economic conditions of production, which can be determined with the precision of natural science, and the legal, political, religious, artistic or philosophic—in short, ideological forms in which men become conscious of this conflict and fight it out. Just as one does not judge an individual by what he thinks about himself, so one cannot judge such a period of transformation by its consciousness, but, on the contrary, this consciousness must be explained from the contradictions of material life, from the conflict existing between the social forces of production and the relations of production. No social order is ever destroyed before all the productive forces for which it is sufficient have been developed, and new superior relations of production never replace older ones before the material conditions for their existence have matured within the framework of the old society. Mankind thus inevitably sets itself only such tasks as it is able to solve, since closer examination will always show that the problem itself arises only when the material conditions for its solution are already present or at least in the course of formation. In broad outline, the Asiatic, ancient, feudal and modern bourgeois modes of production may be designated as epochs marking progress in the economic development of society. The bourgeois mode of production is the last antagonistic form of the social process of production—antagonistic not in the sense of individual antagonism but of an antagonism that emanates from the individuals' social conditions of existence—but the productive forces developing within bourgeois society create also the material conditions for a solution of this antagonism. The prehistory of human society accordingly closes with this social formation.

Frederick Engels, with whom I maintained a constant exchange of ideas by correspondence since the publication of his brilliant essay on the critique of economic categories[5] (printed in the *Deutsch-Französische Jahrbücher*), arrived by another road (compare his *Lage der arbeitenden Klasse in England*)[6] at the same result as I, and when in the spring of 1845 he too came to live in Brussels, we decided to set forth together our conception as opposed to the ideo-

logical one of German philosophy, in fact to settle accounts with our former philosophical conscience. The intention was carried out in the form of a critique of post-Hegelian philosophy.[7] The manuscript, two large octavo volumes, had long ago reached the publishers in Westphalia when we were informed that owing to changed circumstances it could not be printed. We abandoned the manuscript to the gnawing criticism of the mice all the more willingly since we had achieved our main purpose—self clarification. Of the scattered works in which at that time we presented one or another aspect of our views to the public, I shall mention only the *Manifesto of the Communist Party*, jointly written by Engels and myself, and a *Discours sur le libre échange*, which I myself published. The salient points of our conception were first outlined in an academic, although polemical, form in my *Misère de la philosophie...*, this book which was aimed at Proudhon appeared in 1847. The publication of an essay on *Wage-Labour*[8] written in German in which I combined the lectures I had held on this subject at the German Workers' Association in Brussels, was interrupted by the February Revolution and my forcible removal from Belgium in consequence.

The publication of the *Neue Rheinische Zeitung*[9] in 1848 and 1849 and subsequent events cut short my economic studies, which I could only resume in London in 1850. The enormous amount of material relating to the history of political economy assembled in the British Museum, the fact that London is a convenient vantage point for the observation of bourgeois society, and finally the new stage of development which this society seemed to have entered with the discovery of gold in California and Australia, induced me to start again from the very beginning and to work carefully through the new material. These studies led partly of their own accord to apparently quite remote subjects on which I had to spend a certain amount of time. But it was in particular the imperative necessity of earning my living which reduced the time at my disposal. My collaboration, continued now for eight years, with the *New York Tribune*,[10] the leading Anglo-American newspaper, necessitated an excessive fragmentation of my studies, for I wrote only exceptionally newspaper correspondence in the strict sense. Since a considerable part of my contributions consisted of articles dealing with important economic events in Britain and on the Continent I was compelled to become conversant with practical detail which, strictly speaking, lie outside the sphere of political economy.

This sketch of the course of my studies in the domain of political economy is intended merely to show that my views—no matter how they may be judged and how little they conform to the interested prejudices of the ruling classes—are the outcome of conscientious research carried on over many years. At the entrance to science, as at the entrance to hell, the demand must be made:

Qui si convien lasciare ogni sospetto
Ogni viltà convien che qui sia morta.[11]

Source: Karl Marx. *Toward a Critique of Political Economy.* Originally published in 1859. Reprinted with the permission of International Publishers Co., Inc.

Notes

[1] This introduction is included in the *Grundrisse.*

[2] Marx edited the *Rheinische Zeitung* from April, 1842 March, 1843. The *Augsburger Allgemeine Zeitung* was a reactionary newspapers to whose criticisms of French utopian communism Marx replied in an 1843 article.

[3] The article referred to is "Toward a Critique of Hegel's *Philosophy of Right.* Introduction." [*Ed. note:* see p.96.]

[4] Francois Pierre Guizot (1787-1874), French historian and statesman, active in the Second Republic, precursor of Marx's view that the key to modern political history is the struggle of economic classes.

[5] Friedrich Engels, "Outlines of a Critique of Political Economy," *German-French Annals* (1844).

[6] Friedrich Engels, *The Condition of the Working Class in England* (1845).

[7] Marx and Engels, *The German Ideology* (1845-1846).

[8] Marx, *Wage Labor and Capital* (1847).

[9] The *Neue Rheinische Zeitung* was the radical newspaper Marx edited in Cologne during the revolution of 1848-49.

[10] Marx served as European correspondent for Horace Greeley's *New York Tribune* throughout the 1850s, writing articles for £1 apiece. The *Neue Rheinische Zeitung* was the radical newspaper Marx edited in Cologne during the revolution of 1848-1849.

[11] "Here must be abandoned all distrust,
All cowardice must here be dead.
Dante, *The Divine Comedy.* Inferno 3:13

Imperialism, as a Special Stage of Capitalism

V. I. Lenin

V.I. LENIN *(1870-1924) was born in Simbirsk, Russia. At an early age and following the hanging of his brother, Lenin became a revolutionary. He soon became the driving force behind the Bolshevik movement in its struggle with the Mensheviks and ultimately with the Tsarist authorities. Two of his famous works were* What Is to Be Done? *(1905) and* Imperialism, the Highest Stage of Capitalism (1917).

We must now try to sum up, put together what has been said above on the subject of imperialism. Imperialism emerged as the development and direct continuation of the fundamental characteristics of capitalism in general. But capitalism only became capitalist imperialism at a definite and very high stage of its development, when certain of its fundamental characteristics began to change into their opposites, when the features of the epoch of transition from capitalism to a higher social and economic system had taken shape and revealed themselves all along the line. Economically, the main thing in this process is the displacement of capitalist free competition by capitalist monopoly. Free competition is the fundamental characteristic of capitalism, and of commodity production generally; monopoly is the exact opposite of free competition, but we have seen the latter being transformed into monopoly before our eyes, creating large-scale by still larger-scale industry, and carrying concentration of production and capital to the point where out of it has grown and is growing monopoly: cartels, syndicates and trusts, and merging with them, the capital of a dozen or so banks, which manipulate thousands of millions. At the same time the monopolies, which have grown out of free competition, do not eliminate the latter, but exist over it and alongside of it, and thereby give rise to a number of very acute, intense antagonisms, frictions and conflicts. Monopoly is the transition from capitalism to a higher system.

If it were necessary to give the briefest possible definition of imperialism we should have to say that imperialism is the monopoly stage of capitalism. Such a definition would include what is most important, for, on the one hand, finance capital is the bank capital of a few very big monopolist banks, merged with the capital of the monopolist combines of industrialists; and, on the other hand, the division of the world is the transition from a colonial policy which has extended without hindrance to territories unseized by any capitalist power, to a colonial policy of monopolistic possession of the territory of the world which has been completely divided up.

But very brief definitions, although convenient, for they sum up the main points, are nevertheless inadequate, since very important features of the phenomenon that has to be defined have to be especially deduced. And so, without forgetting the conditional and relative value of all definitions in general, which can never embrace all the concatenations of a phenomenon in its complete development, we must give a definition of imperialism that will include the following five of its basic features: 1) the concentration of production and capital has developed to such a high stage that it has created monopolies which play a decisive role in economic life; 2) the merging of bank capital with industrial capital, and the creation, on the basis of this "finance capital," of a financial oligarchy; 3) the export of capital as distinguished from the export of commodities acquires exceptional importance; 4) the formation of international monopolist capitalist combines which share the world among themselves; and 5) the territorial division of the whole world among the biggest capitalist powers is completed. Imperialism is capitalism in that stage of development in which the dominance of monopolies and finance capital has established itself; in which the export of capital has acquired pronounced importance; in which the division of the world among the international trusts has begun; in which the division of all territories of the globe among the biggest capitalist powers has been completed.

We shall see later that imperialism can and must be defined differently if we bear in mind, not only the basic, purely economic concepts—to which the above definition is limited—but also the historical place of this stage of capitalism in relation to capitalism in general, or the relation between imperialism and the two main trends in the working-class movement. The

V.I. LENIN (1870-1924)

V.I. LENIN was the son of a school and civil service official. When he was 16 his brother was executed for involvement in a plot to kill the Tsar. He was drawn early to the revolutionary cause. He studied Marx and began directing propaganda at the workers, especially in St. Petersburg. In 1887 he was exiled to Siberia. During this exile he completed his studies in law as an external student at the University of St. Petersburg. In 1900 he left Russia for Germany and later spent time in Brussels, Paris and London, always as part of the fluctuating group of expatriate Russian revolutionaries in Europe.

Through his pamphlets and his newspaper (*The Spark*), Lenin established himself as the leader of the most extreme members of the Russian Social Democrats: the Bolsheviks ("majority" faction). Returning to

Russia in 1905 he organized the resistance of workers in St. Petersburg but after three months he was forced abroad again. In 1914 he settled in Switzerland. Following the revolution of March 1917 he returned to Russia via Germany. With the help of the Germans, who hoped that Lenin and his followers would spread dissent amongst Russian troops now facing Germany

in war, the Bolsheviks attempted a coup d'état but its failure forced Lenin to flee to Finland. In October of 1917 he returned to Russia and this time lead the uprising that captured the Government offices on November 6. The Council of Peoples' Commissars made Lenin its leader and from this position he carried out extensive land distribution and nationalized the banks and property. Lenin then extricated Russia from the war by authorizing signature of an armistice between Russia and the Central Powers. By the end of 1920, the Russian economy was in ruins, and in response Lenin espoused the New Economic Policy for Russia.

In 1923, following an attempt on his life, Lenin's health went into decline and he died in January 1924.

point to be noted just now is that imperialism as interpreted above, undoubtedly represents a special stage in the development of capitalism. To enable the reader to obtain the most well-grounded idea of imperialism possible, we deliberately tried to quote as largely as possible bourgeois economists who are obliged to admit the particularly incontrovertible facts concerning the latest stage of capitalist economy. With the same object in view, we have quoted detailed statistics which enable one to see to what degree bank capital, etc., has grown, in what precisely the transformation of quantity into quality, of developed capitalism into imperialism, was expressed. Needless to say, of course, all boundaries in nature and in society are conditional and changeable, that it would be absurd to argue, for example, about the particular year or decade in which imperialism "definitely" became established.

Source: V.I. Lenin. *Imperialism, the Highest State of Capitalism.* Originally published in 1912.

Dogmatism and "Freedom of Criticism"

V. I. Lenin

A. What Is "Freedom of Criticism?"

Freedom of criticism is undoubtedly the most fashionable slogan at the present time, and the one most frequently employed in the controversies between the socialists and democrats of all countries. At first sight, nothing would appear to be more strange than the solemn appeals by one of the parties to the dispute to freedom of criticism. Have voices been raised in the advanced parties against the constitutional law of the majority of European countries which guarantees freedom to science and scientific investigation? "Something must be wrong here," will be the comment of the onlooker, who has not yet fully grasped the essence of the disagreements among the disputants, but has heard this fashionable slogan repeated at every crossroad. "Evidently this slogan is one of the conventional phrases which, like a nickname, becomes legitimatized by use, and becomes almost an appellative," he will conclude.

In fact, it is no secret that two trends have taken shape in the present-day international[1] Social Democracy. The fight between these trends now flares up in a bright flame, and now dies down and smoulders under the ashes of imposing "truce resolutions." What this "new" trend, which adopts a "critical" attitude towards "obsolete dogmatic" Marxism, represents has with sufficient precision been *stated* by Bernstein, and *demonstrated* by Millerand.

Social-Democracy must change from a party of the social revolution into a democratic party of social reforms. Bernstein has surrounded this political demand with a whole battery of symmetrically arranged "new" arguments and reasonings. The possibility of putting Socialism on a scientific basis and of proving from the point of view of the materialist conception of history that it is necessary and inevitable was denied, as was also the growing impoverishment, proletarianization and the intensification of capitalist contradictions. The very *conception, "ultimate aim,"* was declared to be unsound, and the idea of the dictatorship of the proletariat was absolutely rejected. It was denied that there is any counterdistinction in principle between liberalism and Socialism. *The theory of the class struggle* was rejected on the grounds that it could not be applied to a strictly democratic society, governed according to the will of the majority, etc.

Thus, the demand for a resolute turn from revolutionary Social-Democracy to bourgeois social-reformism was accompanied by a no less resolute turn towards bourgeois criticism of all the fundamental ideas of Marxism. As this criticism of Marxism has been going on for a long time now, from the political platform, from university chairs, in numerous pamphlets and in a number of learned treatises, as the entire younger generation of the educated classes has been systematically trained for decades on this criticism, it is not surprising that the "new, critical" trend in Social-Democracy should spring up, all complete, like Minerva from the head of Jupiter. The content of this new trend did not have to grow and take shape, it was transferred bodily from bourgeois literature to socialist literature.

To proceed. If Bernstein's theoretical criticism and political yearnings are still unclear to anyone, the French have taken the trouble graphically to demonstrate the "new method." In this instance, too, France has justified its old reputation of being the country in which "more than anywhere else, the historical class struggles were each time fought out to a decision ..." (Engels, in his introduction to Marx's *The Eighteenth Brumaire*). The French Socialists have begun, not to theorize, but to act. The democratically more highly developed political conditions in France have permitted them to put "Bernsteinism into practice" immediately, with all its consequences. Millerand has provided an excellent example of practical Bernsteinism; not without reason did Bernstein and Vollmar rush so zealously to defend and praise him! Indeed, if Social-Democracy, in essence, is merely a party of reform, and must be bold enough to admit this openly, then not only has a Socialist the right to join a bourgeois cabinet, but must always strive to do so. If democracy, in essence, means the abolition of class domination, then why should not a Socialist minister charm the whole bourgeois world by orations on class collaboration? Why should he not remain in the cabinet even after the shooting down of workers by gendarmes has exposed, for the hundredth and thousandth time, the real nature of the democratic collaboration of classes? Why should he not personally take part in greeting the tsar, for whom the French Socialists now have no other name than hero of the gallows, knout and exile (knouteur, pendeur et déportateur)? And the reward for this utter humiliation and self-degradation of Socialism in the face of the whole world, for the corruption of the socialist consciousness of the worker masses—the only basis that can guarantee our victory—the reward for this is pompous *plans* for niggardly reforms, so niggardly in fact that much more has been obtained from bourgeois governments!

He who does not deliberately close his eyes cannot fail to see that the new "critical" trend in Socialism is nothing more nor less than a new variety of *opportunism*. And if we judge people not by the brilliant uniforms they don, not by the high-sounding appellations they give themselves, but by their actions, and by what they actually advocate, it will be clear that "freedom of criticism" means freedom for an opportunistic trend in Social-Democracy, the freedom to convert Social-Democracy into a democratic party of reform, the freedom to introduce bourgeois ideas and bourgeois elements into Socialism.

"Freedom" is a grand word, but under the banner of free trade the most predatory wars were conducted; under the banner of free labour, the toilers were robbed. The modern use of the term "freedom of criticism" contains the same inherent falsehood. Those who are really convinced that they have advanced science would demand, not freedom for the new views to continue side by side with the old, but the substitution of the new views for the old. The cry "long live freedom of criticism," that is heard today, too strongly calls to mind the fable of the empty barrel.

We are marching in a compact group along a precipitous and difficult path, firmly holding each other by the hand. We are surrounded on all sides by enemies, and we have to advance under their almost constant fire. We have combined voluntarily, precisely for the purpose of fighting the enemy, and not to retreat into the adjacent marsh, the inhabitants of which, from the very outset, have reproached us with having separated ourselves into an exclusive group and with having chosen the path of struggle instead of the path of conciliation. And now several among us begin to cry out: let us go into this marsh! And when we begin to shame them, they retort: how conservative you are! Are you not ashamed to deny us the liberty to invite you to take a better road! Oh, yes, gentlemen! You are free not only to invite us, but to go yourselves wherever you will, even into the marsh. In fact, we think that the marsh is your proper place, and we are prepared to render *you* every assistance to get there. Only let go of our hands, don't clutch at us and don't besmirch the grand word "freedom," for we too are "free" to go where we please, free to fight not only against the marsh, but also against those who are turning towards the marsh!

Source: V.I. Lenin. *What Is to Be Done?* Originally published in 1912.

Notes

[1] Incidentally, this perhaps is the only occasion in the history of modern Socialism in which controversies between various trends within the socialist movement have grown from national into international controversies; and this, in its own way, is extremely encouraging. Formerly, the disputes between the Lassalleans and the Eisenachers, between the Guesdites and the Possibilists, between the Fabians and the Social-Democrats, and between the Narodnaya Volya-ites and Social-Democrats, remained purely national disputes, reflected purely national features and proceeded, as it were, on different planes. At the present time (this is quite evident now), the English Fabians, the French Ministerialists, the German Bernsteinians and the Russian critics—all belong to the same family, all extol each other, learn from each other, and together come out against "dogmatic" Marxism. Perhaps in this first really international battle with socialist opportunism, international revolutionary Social-Democracy will become sufficiently strengthened to put an end to the political reaction that has long reigned in Europe?

Proletarian Rule

Leon Trotsky

LEON TROTSKY *(1879-1940) played a central role in the revolutionary movement in Russia, was Chairman of Petersburg Soviet in 1905, and author of the theory of permanent revolution. In 1940 he was assassinated in Mexico by agents acting on behalf of Stalin.*

The proletariat can get into power only at a moment of national upheaval, of sweeping national enthusiasm. The proletariat assumes power as a revolutionary representative of the people, as a recognized leader in the fight against absolutism and barbaric feudalism. Having assumed power, however, the proletariat will open a new era, an era of positive legislation, of revolutionary politics, and this is the point where its political supremacy as an avowed spokesman of the nation may become endangered.

The first measures of the proletariat—the cleansing of the Augean stables of the old régime and the driving away of their inhabitants—will find active support of the entire nation whatever the liberal casttraters may tell us of the power of some prejudices among the masses. The work of political cleansing will be accompanied by democratic reorganization of all social and political relations. The labor government, impelled by immediate needs and requirements, will have to look into all kinds of relations and activities among the people. It will have to throw out of the army and the administration all those who had stained their hands with the blood of the people; it will have to disband all the regiments that had polluted themselves with crimes against the people. This work will have to be done immediately, long before the establishment of an elective responsible administration and before the organization of a popular militia. This, however, will be only a beginning. Labor democracy will soon be confronted by the problems of a normal workday, the agrarian relations and unemployment. The legislative solution of those problems will show the *class character* of the labor government. It will tend to weaken the revolutionary bond between the proletariat and the nation; it will give the economic differentiation among the peasants a political expression. Antagonism between the component parts of the nation will grow step by step as the policies of the labor government become more outspoken, lose their general democratic character and become *class policies.*

The lack of individualistic bourgeois traditions and anti-proletarian prejudices among the peasants and the intelligentsia will help the proletariat assume power. It must not be forgotten, however, that this lack of prejudices is based not on political understanding, but on political barbarism, on social shapelessness, primitiveness, and lack of character. These are all qualities which can hardly guarantee support for an active, consistent proletarian rule.

The abolition of the remnants of feudalism in agrarian relations will be supported by all the peasants who are now oppressed by the landlords. A progressive income tax will be supported by an overwhelming majority of the peasants. Yet, legislative measures in defense of the rural proletariat (farm hands) will find no active support among the majority, and will meet with active opposition on the part of a minority of the peasants.

The proletariat will be compelled to introduce class struggle into the village and thus to destroy that slight community of interests which undoubtedly unites the peasants as a whole. In its next steps, the proletariat will have to seek for support by helping the poor villagers against the rich, the rural proletariat against the agrarian bourgeoisie. This will alienate the majority of the peasants from labor democracy. Relations between village and city will become strained. The peasantry as a whole will become politically indifferent. The peasant minority will actively oppose proletarian rule. This will influence part of the intellectuals and the lower middle class of the cities.

Two features of proletarian politics are bound particularly to meet with the opposition of labor's allies: *Collectivism* and *Internationalism.* The strong adherence of the peasants to private ownership, the primitiveness of their political conceptions, the limitations of the village horizon, its distance from world-wide political connections and interdependencies, are terrific obstacles in the way of revolutionary proletarian rule.

To imagine that Social-Democracy participates in the provisional government, playing a leading rôle in

LEON TROTSKY (1879–1940)

The Russian Marxist and revolutionary LEON TROTSKY was born Lev Davidovich Bronstein in Kherson Province, Ukraine. After embracing Marxism in the late 1890s, Trotksy attempted to organize the Southern Russian Workers Union in 1897 and was exiled to Siberia for his role in this affair. He escaped in 1902 and went to Europe. It was at this time that he adopted his pseudonym and allied himself with Lenin and other Russian social democrats who were publishing the revolutionary newspaper, *The Spark*. In 1903, Trotsky opposed Lenin and the Bolsheviks; in 1905 he returned to Russia to participate in the Revolution of that year. He was jailed and again sent to Siberia where he wrote two books, *1905* and *Results and Prospects*.

When the 1917 Revolution erupted, Trotsky assumed leadership of the Social-Democratic

Interdistrict Group, joined the Bolshevik Party's Central Committee, and allied with Lenin in the Politburo. But when Lenin suffered a stroke in 1922, Trotsky was unable to gain control of the Party. Ultimately, he was expelled from Russia in 1929 by Josef Stalin. In 1940, he was assassinated by one of Stalin's agents in Mexico. During his final exile, Trotsky wrote *My Life*

(1930), *History of the Russian Revolution* (1931–33), and *The Revolution Betrayed* (1937).

Ideologically, Trotsky differed from Marx in that he supported the theory of "permanent revolution." This doctrine holds that all countries do not necessarily follow the same pattern of social evolution, as Marx had claimed, from feudalism to capitalism to socialism. According to Trotsky, it is possible for one or more stages to be skipped, or for societies to possess characteristics of several stages at once. Once revolution is waged successfully by the proletariat, this class must go beyond the borders of its own society and aid like-minded revolutionaries in other countries. In this way, Trotsky was also directly opposed to the ideology of Stalin, who advocated the doctrine of "socialism in one country."

---

the period of revolutionary democratic reconstruction, insisting on the most radical reforms and all the time enjoying the aid and support of the organized proletariat,—only to step aside when the democratic program is put into operation, to leave the completed building at the disposal of the bourgeois parties and thus to open an era of parliamentary politics where Social-Democracy forms only a party of opposition,—to imagine this would mean to compromise the very idea of a labor government. It is impossible to imagine anything of the kind, not because it is "against principles"—such abstract reasoning is devoid of any substance—but because it is *not real*, it is the worst kind of Utopianism, it is the revolutionary Utopianism of Philistines. ...

Social-Democracy can never assume power under a double obligation: to put the *entire* minimum program into operation for the sake of the proletariat, and to keep strictly *within the limits* of this program,

for the sake of the bourgeoisie. Such a double obligation could never be fulfilled. Participating in the government, not as powerless hostages, but as a leading force, the representatives of labor *eo ipso* break the line between the minimum and maximum program. *Collectivism becomes the order of the day.* At which point the proletariat will be stopped on its march in this direction, depends upon the constellation of forces, not upon the original purpose of the proletarian Party.

It is, therefore, absurd to speak of a *specific* character of proletarian dictatorship (or a dictatorship of the proletariat *and* the peasantry) within a bourgeois revolution, viz., a *purely democratic* dictatorship. The working class can never secure the democratic character of its dictatorship without overstepping the limits of its democratic program. Illusions to the contrary may become a handicap. They would compromise Social-Democracy from the start.

Once the proletariat assumes power, it will fight for it to the end. One of the means to secure and solidify its power will be propaganda and organization, particularly in the village; another means will be a *policy of Collectivism.* Collectivism is not only dictated by the very position of the Social-Democratic Party as the party in power, but it becomes imperative as a means to secure this position through the active support of the working class.

When our Socialist press first formulated the idea of a *Permanent Revolution* which should lead from the liquidation of absolutism and civic bondage to a Socialist order through a series of ever growing social conflicts, uprisings of ever new masses, unremitting attacks of the proletariat on the political and economic privileges of the governing classes, our "progressive" press started a unanimous indignant uproar. Oh, they had suffered enough, those gentlemen of the "progressive" press; this nuisance, however, was too much. Revolution, they said, is not a thing that can be made "legal!" Extraordinary measures are allowable only on extraordinary occasions. The aim of the revolutionary movement, they asserted, was not to make the revolution go on forever, but to bring it as soon as possible into the channels of *law*, etc., etc. The more radical representatives of the same democratic bourgeoisie do not attempt to oppose the revo-

lution from the standpoint of completed constitutional "achievements:" tame as they are, they understand how hopeless it is to fight the proletariat revolution with the weapon of parliamentary cretinism *in advance* of the establishment of parliamentarism itself. They, therefore, choose another way. They forsake the standpoint of law, but take the standpoint of what they deem to be facts—the standpoint of historic "possibilities," the standpoint of political "realism,"— even the standpoint of "Marxism." It was Antonio, the pious Venetian bourgeois, who made the striking observation:

> Mark you this, Bassanio,
> The devil can cite scriptures for his purpose.

Those gentlemen not only consider the idea of labor government in Russia fantastic, but they repudiate the very probability of a Social revolution in Europe in the near historic epoch. The necessary "prerequisites" are not yet in existence, is their assertion.

Is it so? It is, of course, not our purpose to set a time for a Social revolution. What we attempt here is to put the Social revolution into a proper historic perspective.

Source: Leon Trotsky. *Our Revolution: Essays on Working-Class and International Revolution, 1904-1917.* Originally published in 1918.

Civilization and Its Discontents

Sigmund Freud

SIGMUND FREUD *(1856-1939) was the founder of psychoanalysis. His more important writings include* The Interpretation of Dreams, Introductory Lectures in Psychoanalysis, Beyond the Pleasure Principle, *and* The Ego and the Id. *Freud also examined the connection between psychoanalysis and social organization in works such as* Civilization and Its Discontents (1930) *from which this excerpt is taken.*

The communists believe that they have found the path to deliverance from our evils. According to them, man is wholly good and is well-disposed to his neighbour; but the institution of private property has corrupted his nature. The ownership of private wealth gives the individual power, and with it the temptation to ill-treat his neighbour; while the man who is excluded from possession is bound to rebel in hostility against his oppressor. If private property were abolished, all wealth held in common, and everyone allowed to share in the enjoyment of it, ill-will and hostility would disappear among men. Since everyone's needs would be satisfied, no one would have any reason to regard another as his enemy; all would willingly undertake the work that was necessary. I have no concern with any economic criticisms of the communist system; I cannot enquire into whether the abolition of private property is expedient or advantageous.[1] But I am able to recognize that the psychological premises on which the system is based are an untenable illusion. In abolishing private property we deprive the human love of aggression of one of its instruments, certainly a strong one, though certainly not the strongest; but we have in no way altered the differences in power and influence which are misused by aggressiveness, nor have we altered anything in its nature. Aggressiveness was not created by property. It reigned almost without limit in primitive times, when property was still very scanty, and it already shows itself in the nursery almost before property has given up its primal, anal form; it forms the basis of every relation of affection and love among people (with the single exception, perhaps, of the mother's relation to her male child). If we do away with personal rights over material wealth, there still remains prerogative in the field of sexual relation-

Sigmund Freud

ships, which is bound to become the source of the strongest dislike and the most violent hostility among men who in other respects are on an equal footing. If we were to remove this factor, too, by allowing complete freedom of sexual life and thus abolishing the family, the germ-cell of civilization, we cannot, it is true, easily foresee what new paths the development of civilization could take; but one thing we can expect, and that is that this indestructible feature of human nature will follow it there.

Source: Sigmund Freud. *Civilization and Its Discontents.* Trans. and ed. by James Strachey. New York: Norton and Co., 1961. Originally published in 1930. Reprinted from *Civilization and Its Discontents,* translated and edited by James Strachey, with the permission of W.W. Norton & Company, Inc. Copyright © 1961 by James Strachey, renewed in 1989 by Alix Strachey.

Notes

[1] Anyone who has tasted the miseries of poverty in his own youth and has experienced the indifference and arrogance of the well-to-do, should be safe from the suspicion of having no understanding or good will towards endeavours to fight against the inequality of wealth among men and all that it leads to. To be sure, if an attempt is made to base this fight upon an abstract demand, in the name of justice, for equality for all men, there is a very obvious objection to be made— that nature, by endowing individuals with extremely unequal physical attributes and mental capacities, has introduced injustices against which there is no remedy.

Liberalism and Marxism

David Held

DAVID HELD *is Senior Lecturer in Social Sciences at the Open University. He is the author of several books including* Models of Democracy.

Liberal thinkers have in general tied the goals of liberty and equality to individualist political, economic and ethical doctrines.[1] The individual is, in essence, sacrosanct, and is free and equal only to the extent that he or she can pursue and attempt to realize, with minimum political impediment, self-chosen ends and personal interests. Equal justice can be sustained between individuals if, above all, individuals' entitlement to certain rights or liberties is respected and all citizens are treated equally before the law. Liberalism is preoccupied with the creation and defence of a world in which "free and equal" individuals can flourish; this is a position maintained alike by, for example, Locke, J.S. Mill and Nozick. By contrast, the thinkers in the Marxist tradition (and in most strands of socialism) defended the desirability of certain social or collective goals. For Marx and Engels to take equality and liberty seriously is to challenge the view that these values can be realized by individuals through essentially private enterprise and the liberal-democratic state. Equality, liberty and justice—recognized by them as "the great universal ideals"—cannot be achieved in a world dominated by private ownership of property and the capitalist economy. These values, according to them, can be realized only through class struggle, the dictatorship of the proletariat and eventually through the complete democratization of society and the "withering away of the state". Only the latter conditions can ultimately guarantee the reduction of all forms of coercive power so that human beings can develop—as free and equal.

The views of liberals and Marxists are, of course, radically different. The key elements of their theories are fundamentally at odds. It is therefore somewhat paradoxical to note that they share a vision of reducing arbitrary power and regulatory capacity to its lowest possible extent. Both liberals and Marxists fear the extension of networks of intrusive power into society, "choking", to borrow a phrase from Marx, "all its pores". They both have traditions of criticizing the bureaucratic, inequitable and often repressive character of much state action. In addition, they are both concerned with the political, social and economic conditions for the development of people's capacities, desires and interests. Put in this general and abstract way, there appears to be a convergence of emphasis on ascertaining the circumstances under which people can develop as "free and equal".

To put the point another way, the aspiration of the liberal and Marxist traditions to a world characterized by free and equal relations among mature adults reflects, above all, a concern to ensure the following:

1. The creation of the best circumstances for all humans to develop their nature and express their diverse qualities (involving an assumption of respect for individuals' diverse capacities, their ability to learn and enhance their potentialities).

2. Protection from the arbitrary use of political authority and coercive power (involving an assumption of respect for privacy in all matters which are not the basis of potential and demonstrable "harm" to others).[2]

3. The involvement of citizens in the regulation of public life (involving an assumption of respect for the dignity and equal worth of human lives).[3]

4. Provision for the consent of individuals in the maintenance, justification and legitimation of regulative institutions (involving an assumption of respect for the authentic and reasoned nature of individuals' judgements);

5. The expansion of economic opportunity to maximize the availability of resources (involving an assumption that when individuals are free from the burdens of unmet physical need they are best able to develop themselves).

There is, in other words, a set of aspirations which liberalism and Marxism have in common. These aspirations can be linked together and stated in the form of a central principle—what I call the "principle of autonomy".[4] The principle can be stated as follows:

Individuals should be free and equal in the determination of the rules by which they live; that is, they should enjoy equal rights (and, accordingly, equal obligations) in the specification of the framework which generates and limits the opportunities available to them throughout their lives.

Both liberalism and Marxism give priority to the development of "autonomy" or "independence". But to state this—and to try and articulate its meaning in a fundamental but highly abstract principle—is not yet to say very much. For the full meaning of a principle cannot be specified independently of the conditions of its enactment. Liberalism and Marxism may prioritize "autonomy", but they differ radically over how to secure it and, hence, over how to interpret it.

The specification of a principle's conditions of enactment is a vital matter; for if a perspective on the most desirable form of the state and civil society is to be at all plausible, it must be concerned with both theoretical and practical issues, with philosophical as well as organizational and institutional questions. In this regard I shall contend that both liberalism and Marxism are mistaken about the conditions under which the principle of autonomy can be enacted. It is, therefore, important to identify and examine these conditions—conditions which cannot, of course, be specified independently of historical and political circumstances. I should like to stress from the outset that the discussion maintains as its backdrop Western capitalist countries and, in particular, Britain. My argument is that the conditions of enactment of the principle of autonomy can be specified adequately only if one draws upon aspects of both liberalism and Marxism, and appreciates the limitations of both overall positions.

The principle of autonomy can only be realized adequately if we take seriously some of the central prescriptions, and thus some of the central arguments, of both liberalism and Marxism. Equality and liberty—the interconnections of which the principle tries to specify—can only be advanced if one appreciates the complementarity of liberalism's scepticism about political power and Marxism's scepticism about economic power. Liberalism's thrust to create a sovereign democratic state, a diversity of power centres and a world marked by openness, controversy and plurality is radically compromised by the reality of the so-called "free market"—the imperatives of the system of corporate power and multinational corporations, the logic of commercial and banking houses and the economic and political rivalry of the power blocs. If liberalism's central failure is to see markets as "powerless" mechanisms of coordination and, thus, to neglect the distorting nature of economic power in relation to democracy, Marxism's central failure is the reduction of political power to economic power and, thus, the neglect of the dangers of centralized political power and the problems of political accountability. Marxism's embodiment in East European societies today is marked by the growth of the centralized bureaucratic state; its claim to represent the forces of progressive politics is tarnished by socialism's relations in practice, in the East and also in the West, with bureaucracy, surveillance, hierarchy and state control. Accordingly, liberalism's account of the nature of markets and economic power must be doubted while Marxism's account of the nature of democracy must be questioned.

It is important to take note also of some of the limitations shared by liberalism and Marxism. Generally, these two political perspectives have failed to explore the impediments to full participation in democratic life other than those imposed—however important these may be—by state and economic power. The roots of the difficulty lie in narrow conceptions of "the political". In the liberal tradition the political is equated with the world of government or governments alone. Where this equation is made and where politics is regarded as a sphere apart from economy or culture—that is, as governmental activity and institutions—a vast domain of politics is excluded form view: above all, the spheres of productive and reproductive relations. A similar thing can be said about the Marxist conception of politics. Although the Marxist critique of liberalism is of great significance—showing as it does that the organization of the economy cannot be regarded as non-political, and that the relations of production are central to the nature and distribution of power—it is ultimately limited because of the direct connection it draws (even when the state is conceived as "relatively autonomous") between political and economic life. By reducing political to economic and class power—and by calling for "the end of politics"—Marxism itself tends to marginalize or exclude certain types of issues from politics. This is true of all those issues which cannot, in the last analysis, be reduced to class-related matters. Classic examples of this are the domination of nature by industry (which raises ecological questions), of women by men, and of certain racial and ethnic groups by others. Other central concerns include the power of public administrators or bureaucrats over their "clients" and the role of "authoritative resources" (the capacity to coordinate and control the activities of human beings) which build up in most social organizations.

The narrow conception of "the political" in both liberalism and Marxism has meant that key conditions for the realization of the principle of autonomy have been eclipsed from view—conditions concerning, for instance, equal rights and obligations in the organization of economic life (essentially unexamined by liberalism) and equal rights and obligations with respect to the household, child-rearing and many aspects of human reproduction (essentially unexamined by liberalism and Marxism). (I am not saying, of course, that no liberal or Marxist has been concerned with these things; rather I am arguing that their perspectives or frameworks of analysis cannot adequately encompass them.) In order to grasp the diverse conditions necessary for the adequate institutionalization of the principle of autonomy, we need a broader conception of "the political" than is found in either of these perspectives—a conception which emphasizes that politics is about power; that is to say, about the "transformative capacity" of social agents, agencies and institutions, about the forces which influence and reflect its distribution and use, and about the effect of this on resource use and distribution.

If politics is understood in this broad way, then the specification of the conditions of enactment of the principle of autonomy amounts to the specification of the conditions for the participation of citizens in decisions about the use and distribution of resources in relation to affairs that are important to them (that is, us). Thus, rather than striving toward a world in which there is an "end of politics", we should strive toward a state of affairs in which political life—democratically organized—is an essential part of all people's lives. Can we specify the nature of this state of affairs more precisely? How can "the state" and "civil society" be combined to promote equality and liberty, that is, the principle of autonomy?

Source: David Held. *Political Theory and the Modern State: Essays on State, Power and Democracy.* Cambridge: Polity, 1989. Reprinted with permission of Basil Blackwell.

Notes

[1] Unless I indicate to the contrary, I shall use "liberalism" here to connote both liberalism since Locke and liberal democracy. See my "Central perspectives on the modern state" (pp.12-28) for a discussion of these terms; but cf. Dunn (1979, ch. 2).

[2] This is, of course, subject to all the same problems as Mill's principle of harm.

[3] Mill and Marx (in characteristic nineteenth-century and ethnocentric style) held this to be true for humans in "advanced stages" of social development: Mill sought to justify at some length the British rule of India and Marx was convinced of the "progressive" impact of capitalism on countries with less "advanced" social and economic systems.

[4] I have developed and refined my conception of this principle, and its place in modern democratic theory, in *Models of Democracy* (1987), especially ch. 9. In addition, see Beetham (1981) and Cohen and Rogers (1983) whose writings have directly informed the argument set out below.

References

Beetham, D. 1981: Beyond liberal democracy. *Socialist Register.*

Cohen, J., and Rogers, J. 1983: *On Democracy.* New York: Penguin.

Dunn, J., 1979: *Western Political Theory in the Face of the Future.* Cambridge University Press.

Held, D., 1987: *Models of Democracy.* Cambridge: Polity Press.

6

Democratic Socialism

The Ideal of Equality

In contradistinction to reactionary and bourgeois socialism, Marx defined Robert Owen's brand as critical-utopian socialism. What the founder of communism realized was that Owen in 1812 recognized class antagonisms as well as the decomposing elements in the prevailing form of society, but did not recognize a class with any historical initiative. What Marx did not anticipate exactly was the direction in which socialism would develop after Owen. Perhaps one can best understand its development by first seeing what Owen thought and advocated.

Most surprising in Owen's case is to discover what a Benthamite he is. In other words, he believes that the best government is the one which produces the greatest happiness for the greatest number. But perhaps almost as surprising is to discover that Owen is a curious kind of gnostic, for he seems to wish to lay the blame for the great and leading evils of Britain squarely on the shoulders of ignorance, the chief error of which is the belief that individuals form their own characters. According to Owen, one needs only to apply intelligence in tracing the origin of evil and then administer the appropriate remedies.

In much the same spirit as Owen, Sir William Beveridge, writing at the end of World War II, speaks of the five giant evils: want, disease, ignorance, squalor and idleness. He singles out idleness for special consideration, owing to the essential role it plays in bringing about the other giants. Contrary to present day public-choice theorists, Beveridge urges action by the state to whatever extent necessary. It is Beveridge's contention, however, that state action would be subject to the preservation of essential liberties. Although neither Owen nor Beveridge talk of the ideal of equality, it remains their implicit measuring rod in attempting to landscape a field of justice.

The comments of C.B. Macpherson represent an uncompromising attack upon classical or free-market liberalism. Whether these comments are intended to establish a beachhead for reform liberalism in the Dewey tradition, or to establish the primacy of democratic socialism, is not easy to tell. Macpherson is able to challenge the proposition that economic freedom is a necessary condition of political freedom. The actual outcome of this challenge depends upon further analysis of such notions as freedom and power, and upon this depends the success of his attempted refutation of Milton Friedman's claim that socialism is inconsistent with political freedom.

Stuart Hampshire, with customary clarity, maintains that socialists would do better to view their disputes with conservatives and liberals as disputes of justice rather than equality. More argument is required by Hampshire on this point, especially in light of his acknowledgement that socialist parties in Europe have grounded their moral appeals on the ideal of equality. Nonetheless, it would be foolish to dismiss his comments as uninstructive. Both the novice and the initiated political philosopher would do well to consider whether there is a way of engaging in revisionary political philosophy by re-categorizing ideologies, and marking different ideals that separate one ideology from another.

Perhaps the thought of Peter Burns, S.J. is evidence that Hampshire is on the correct path, for justice his focus as he analyzes liberation theology in Latin America. But it is striking how easily one can construe in terms of *equality* most of the substantive issues Burns raises, including the prevalence of hunger, slums, infant mortality, illiteracy, unemployment, and low wages. One should not lose sight of the fact that Burns is maintaining that liberation theology characterizes the system responsible for these evils as capitalist, and as remediable only by socialist replacement. Many issues raised earlier by Robert Owen, and subsequently by Sir William Beveridge in particular, are raised again today in a different era and different ethnic and geographic domains.

The Principles of the Former Essays Applied to Government

Robert Owen

ROBERT OWEN *(1771-1858) was a reformer, philanthropist and socialist theorist and was born in Newtown, Montgomeryshire. He became one of the great cotton manufacturers of his time and, encouraged by his partners, Jeremy Bentham and William Allen, established a model factory village in which he diminished children's hours of employment and created an educational system for them.*

The end of government is to make the governed and the governors happy. That government then is the best, which in practice produces the greatest happiness to the greatest number; including those who govern, and those who obey.

In a former Essay we said, and it admits of practical demonstration, that by adopting the proper means, man may, by degrees, be trained to live in any part of the world without poverty, without crime, and without punishment; for all these are the effects of error in the various systems of training and governing; error, proceeding from very gross ignorance of human nature.

It is of primary importance to make this ignorance manifest, and to show what are the means which are endowed with that transcendent efficacy.

We have also said that man may be trained to acquire any sentiments and habits, or any character; and no one now, possessing pretensions to the knowledge of human nature, will deny that the government of any independent community may form the individuals of that community into the best, or into the worst characters.

If there be one duty therefore more imperative than another, on the government of every country, it is, that it should adopt, without delay, the proper means to form those sentiments and habits in the people, which shall give the most permanent and substantial advantages to the individuals and to the community.

Survey the acquirements of the earliest ages; trace the progress of those acquirements, through all the subsequent periods, to the present hour; and say if there be anything of real value in them, except that which contributes in practice to increase the happiness of the world.

And yet, with all the parade of learning contained in the myriads of volumes which have been written, and which still daily pour from the press, the knowledge of the first step of the progress which leads to human happiness remains yet unknown, or disregarded by the mass of mankind.

The important knowledge to which we allude is, "That the old collectively may train the young collectively, to be ignorant and miserable, or to be intelligent and happy". And, on investigation, this will be found to be one of those simple yet grand laws of the universe which experience discovers and confirms, and which, as soon as men become familiar with it, will no longer admit of denial or dispute. Fortunate will be that government which shall first acquire this knowledge in theory, and adopt it in practice.

To obtain its introduction into our own country first, a mode of procedure is now submitted to the immediate governing powers of the British Empire; and it is so submitted with an ardent desire that it may undergo the most full and ample discussion; that if it shall, as on investigation it will, be found to be the only consistent, and therefore rational, system of conducting human beings, it may be temperately and progressively introduced, instead of those defective national practices by which the state is now governed.

We therefore proceed to explain how this principle may now be introduced into practice, without injury to any part of society. For it is the time and manner of introducing this principle, and its consequent practice, which alone constitute any difficulty.

This will appear evident, when it is considered that, although, from a plain statement of the most simple facts, the truth of the principle cannot fail to prove so obvious that no one will ever attempt openly to attack it; and although its adoption into practice will speedily accumulate benefits of which the world can now form no adequate conception: yet both theory and practice are to be introduced into a society,

ROBERT OWEN (1771–1858)

Although he was one of thirteen children and began work at the age of nine, ROBERT OWEN started his own business at eighteen and became a wealthy factory owner. Unlike most early British industrialists, however, Owen was deeply concerned with the working conditions faced by his employees, many of whom were very young. He devoted considerable time and energy to improving their work environment. His cotton mills at New Lanark, Scotland, became famous as "model" work sites, as Owen reduced work hours, improved housing and schooling, forbade alcohol, and organized pensions and a sick-pay system. Owen eventually discovered that this "lenient" approach actually improved production, contrary to the popular opinion that workers had to be disciplined strictly to maximize their output.

Owen recognized that the social life of his workers could not be separated from their work life, and believed that the means of production in a capitalist society should be privately owned in a nation of "small independent producers." Because of his views on labour and production, Owen has been termed a "Utopian" socialist. He also attempted to popularize an unusual "rational religion" but his efforts in this area did not match his highly progressive thinking about labour and society.

---

trained and matured under principles that have impressed upon the individuals who compose it the most opposite habits and sentiments; which have been so entwined from infancy in their bodily and mental growth, that the simplicity and irresistible power of truth alone can disentangle them, and expose their fallacy. It becomes then necessary, to prevent the evils of a too sudden change, that those who have been thus nursed in ignorance may be progressively removed from the abodes of mental darkness, to the intellectual light which this principle cannot fail to produce. The light of true knowledge therefore must be first made to dawn on those dwellings of darkness, and afterwards gradually to increase, as it can be borne by the opening faculties of their inhabitants.

To proceed on this plan, it becomes necessary to direct our attention to the actual state of the British population; to disclose the cause of those great and leading evils of which all now complain.

It will then be seen that the foundation on which these evils have been erected is ignorance, proceeding from the errors which have been impressed on the minds of the present generation by its predecessors; and chiefly by that greatest of all errors, the notion, that individuals form their *own characters*. For while this most inconsistent and therefore most absurd of all human conceptions shall continue to be forced upon the young mind, there will remain no foundation whatever on which to build a sincere love and extended charity from man to his fellow-creatures.

But destroy this hydra of human calamity, this immolator of every principle of rationality; this monster, which hitherto has effectually guarded every avenue that can lead to true benevolence and active kindness, and human happiness will be speedily established on a rock from whence it shall never more be removed.

This enemy of humanity may now be most easily destroyed. Let it be dragged forth from beneath the dark mysterious veil by which, till now, it has been hid from the eyes of the world; expose it but for an instant to the clear light of intellectual day; and, as though conscious of its own deformity, it will instantaneously vanish, never to reappear.

As a ground-work then of a rational system, let this absurd doctrine, and all the chain of consequences which follow from it, be withdrawn, and let that only be taught as sacred, which can be demonstrated by its never-failing consistency to be true.

This essential object being accomplished, and accomplished it must be before another step can be taken to form man into a rational being, the next is to withdraw those national laws which chiefly emanate from that erroneous doctrine, and now exist in full vigour; training the population to almost every kind of crime. For these laws are, without chance of failure, adapted to produce a long train of crimes, which crimes are accordingly produced.

Some of the most prominent to which allusion is made are such as encourage the consumption of ardent spirits, by fostering and extending those receptacles to seduce the ignorant and wretched, called gin-shops and pot-houses;—those which sanction and legalize gambling among the poor, under the name of a state lottery;—those which are insidiously destroying the real strength of the country under the name of providing for the poor;—and those of punishment, which, under the present irrational system of legislation, are supposed to be absolutely necessary to hold society together.

To prove the accuracy of this deduction, millions of facts exist around us, speaking in a language so clearly connected and audible, that it is scarcely credible any man can misunderstand it.

These facts proclaim aloud to the universe, that ignorance generates, fosters, and multiplies sentiments and actions which must produce private and public misery; and that when evils are experienced, instead of withdrawing the *cause* which created them, it invents and applies punishments, which, to a super-ficial observer, may appear to lessen the evils which afflict society, while, in reality, they greatly increase them.

Intelligence, on the contrary, traces to its source the cause of every evil which exists; adopts the proper measures to remove the *cause;* and then, with the most unerring confidence, tests satisfied that its object will be accomplished.

Thus then intelligence, or, in other words, plain unsophisticated reason, will consider the various sentiments and actions which now create misery in society, will patiently trace the cause whence those sentiments and actions proceed, and immediately apply the proper remedies to remove them.

Source: Robert Owen. *A New View of Society.* Originally published in 1813-14.

Maintenance of Employment

Sir William H. Beveridge

WILLIAM BEVERIDGE *(1879-1963) helped shape the welfare state policies in Great Britain after World War II. An economist by training, Beveridge was Director of the London School of Economics and Political Science before becoming master of University College, Oxford.*

At the present stage of this savage and critical war, how much time and thought ought we to spend in discussing what may happen after the war, in planning for reconstruction? Obviously, not many of us ought to spend much of our time upon that subject. The war, if we are going to get through it with success, must be total war: it is taxing and is going still more to tax all our strength. One of the faults which I, with others, find in the design of our central Government is that somehow it has not brought home to everybody sufficiently the urgency of total war and the difference between what is suitable for war and what is suitable for peace. It has not done so, I think, because in the central Government of the country, as we have had it since the beginning of this war and up to this moment, we have kept too much of peace-time methods, of the old forms of Cabinet and Ministerial responsibility, of party politics.

That is a question on which I've said a good deal in the past. With a different form of central Government, I believe that we should now be further on towards winning the war. Today I'm concerned with a different question. Is it a help or a hindrance to winning the war to concern ourselves with what is to happen after the war is won? My answer to this question is that it is a help.

There are three ways of winning a war: by relying on speed and efficiency to deal a knock-out blow, by the mistakes of the enemy, by one's own staying power. Whatever we may hope from the first two ways we cannot afford in this war to neglect the third way. There is no reason to doubt the natural staying power of our people, but there is every reason to strengthen that staying power. The Government can strengthen staying power by convincing the people that it is taking reconstruction seriously.

Whatever the nature of other peoples, I am certain that it is correct of any nation, like our own, in which freedom is not a surface veneer, but an inveterate habit, that we will refuse even in the worst of wars to give up thinking about peace; we are waging war not for its own sake, not for dominion, but for peace. Our staying power will be increased, in proportion as we can be given confidence that the peace which will come at the end of this war will be better than peace as we have known it before. That is why thinking about reconstruction is one of the ways of ensuring victory, and something worth doing even today. That is why you, who are all busy people, engaged on vital war production, have come to discuss with me some of the problems of reconstruction.

The Five Giants

Reconstruction has many sides, international and domestic. On the domestic side one can define its aims best by naming five giant evils to be destroyed—Want, Disease, Ignorance, Squalor and Idleness. Today I am going to say little or nothing about any of the first four giants. Destruction of Want means ensuring that every citizen, in return for service, has income sufficient for his subsistence and that of his dependents both when he is working and when he cannot work. Want is really the subject of the enquiry which I have been making as Chairman of the Inter-Departmental Committee on Social Insurance and the Allied Services. That is, in effect, an enquiry as to how far we can go by development of social insurance and other services to ensure that no one in this country lacks the actual means of subsistence, even when unemployed or sick, or injured or old, or having lost a breadwinner.

The second giant—Disease—is one against which I am glad there is now a general move and a growing and, I hope, an effective demand for putting the health service of the country—preventive, curative, palliative—upon an altogether better and larger basis.

The attack on Ignorance is a matter of education. It means having more scholars and better schools. But it is not just a question of raising the school age: it is a question of the kind of education that we give at school, and it is even more a question of adult education.

By the giant Squalor I mean all those evils which come through the unplanned, disorderly growth of cities, bearing in its train congestion, bad housing, waste of energy of wage-earners in travelling and of housewives in struggling with needless dirt and difficulties at home, needless destruction of natural and historic beauty. Attack on Squalor means better location of industry and population and a revolution in housing.

Each of these four giants—Want, Disease, Ignorance, Squalor—would be a more than ample subject for discussion today and over many days. This afternoon I shall speak only of the fifth giant—Idleness. Can we hope to destroy Idleness after the war and, if so, by what methods? Destruction of Idleness means ensuring for every citizen a reasonable opportunity of productive service and of earning according to his service. It means maintenance of employment of labour and our other resources. Idleness is the largest and fiercest of the five giants and the most important to attack. If the giant Idleness can be destroyed, all the other aims of reconstruction come within reach. If not, they are out of reach in any serious sense and their formal achievement is futile. To hold out hopes, to announce a determination that at all costs we will prevent mass unemployment, is the most important of all reconstruction aims. The people of Britain today do not look back to the time before the war, as in the last war the people of Britain looked back upon the time before that war, as something to which they wish to return. This difference of attitude has its source in memories of the mass unemployment which ruined so many lives between the two wars from 1920 to 1939. In regard to that, British people today have only one sentiment: "Never again."

What are the conditions of successful attack upon the giant Idleness, of preventing mass unemployment in the aftermath of the present way?

War Solution of Unemployment

One way of trying to answer that question is to look at the conditions under which unemployment is reduced to insignificance today. Unemployment has been practically abolished twice in the lives of most of us—in the last war and in this war. Why does war solve the problem of unemployment which is so insoluble in peace? The main conditions of the war solution of unemployment are twofold:

(i) The Government on behalf of the nation prepares a schedule of vital needs to be met (men to fight, arms, ships, food, raw materials), makes a plan for the use of all productive resources to meet those needs, and secures that use either directly by regulations and instructions or indirectly by control of purchasing power.

(ii) The Government has one need for men without effective limit of numbers and with no restrictions in the choice of men to meet it. No one physically fit to be a sailor, soldier or air-man can refuse to be one if called on or be prevented from becoming one by the opposition of those who are sailors, soldiers or airmen already. There are no craft barriers in regard to the Armed Forces: no right of an individual to refuse to enter them on the ground that he belongs to a different trade: nothing to keep out those who wish to enter if they will be useful there. Moreover, in civilian industry, craft barriers, though not wholly abolished, as in the Armed Forces, are greatly reduced.

The two conditions on which in war-time unemployment gets abolished are comprehensive planning by the State of the use of all important resources and the making of those resources, including labour, completely fluid. Can we hope to accomplish the same full use of resources in the aftermath of war, except on something like the same conditions?

Maintenance of productive employment means adjustment of productive resources to real needs. In time of peace, in all countries other than Russia, this adjustment has been carried out in the main by price mechanism. In so far as the price mechanism has failed to do what was desired, most States have limited themselves to seeking remedies of a general financial nature, that is to say, they have still worked through the price mechanism, endeavouring to manipulate the volume of purchasing power in general, but not to direct it down particular channels. In times of total war adjustment of resources to needs is carried out by complete State planning. Shall the aftermath of this war be treated by the former methods of peace or by the methods of war? On the face of it, the experience of 1920-1939 suggests that the former methods of peace are unlikely to accomplish the object in view with even tolerable success, and that there are probably two unavoidable conditions for the maintenance of productive employment after the present war, namely (a) continuance of fluidity of labour and resources, and (b) continuance of national planning.

Essential Liberties

National planning does not mean surrender of any essential citizen liberties; whatever may suit other countries, a plan for Britain must preserve freedom of opinion and its expression, in public or private, in speech or writing; freedom of association for political and other purposes; freedom of movement and choice of useful occupations; personal property and an income of one's own, with freedom to save or spend it. These are essential liberties. They must be preserved. They can be preserved.

What about private enterprise—the right to manage one's own business? Private enterprise at private risk is a good ship and a ship that has brought us far on the journey to higher standards of living and of leisure. No one with any regard to facts will deny the merits of this system or part from it lightly. But private enterprise at private risk is a ship for fair weather and open seas. For the ice-bound straits of war we find in practice that we need a vessel of a different build, sturdier if less speedy, a Fram like Nansen's, not a China clipper. To find our way out of war into peace again we may need such a sturdier vessel still.

In any case, private control of means of production, with the right to employ others at a wage in using those means, whatever may be said for it or against it on other grounds, cannot be described as an essential liberty of the British people. Not more than a tiny fraction of British people have ever enjoyed that right. I myself have never owned any means of production except a fountain pen and an occasional garden tool.

The question of how to carry out a national plan after the war is a question not of essential liberties but of machinery: it is a question to which at the moment I do not feel that I know the answer.

Need for a Declaration of Policy

We want our Government now to declare and to make us believe:

(a) That, subject to leaving untouched the essential British liberties, it will be prepared to use the powers of the State to whatever extent may prove to be necessary, in order to maintain employment after the war;

(b) That it has set up an Economic General Staff (a body that doesn't exist today) to prepare a plan or plans for that purpose and to show just what will need to be done.

That must be said by our Government and believed. I do not know what chance there is of such a declaration or what sort of Government could make it and be believed. I am sure only that that is what we would like to see. The people of this country aren't looking for easy good times for all. Maintenance of employment doesn't mean easy times for all. It means opportunity for all: it is the chance for all of productive work and release of energy from paralysing fear.

We want our Government now to declare and to make us believe that it will be prepared to use the powers of the State to whatever extent may prove to be necessary, subject only to the preservation of essential citizen liberties, in order to maintain employment after the war. When that has, been said, and believed, we shall be, as we are not now, past the corner which hides victory from our eyes. We shall have, if not a second front in Europe, what is at least as important for winning the war—a second wind. We shall by that belief and purpose have energies beyond estimate released for war. We shall be united in combined attack on tyranny and savagery abroad and on Want, Disease, Ignorance, Squalor and Idleness at home. Let us become united now for total war and for a peace different from the last peace abroad and at home.

Source: Sir William H. Beveridge. *The Pillars of Security.* New York: MacMillan, 1943.

Elegant Tombstones: A Note on Friedman's Freedom

C. B. Macpherson

C. B. MACPHERSON (1911-1987) *was a distinguished Canadian political philosopher whose best-known works are* The Political Theory of Possessive Individualism: Hobbes to Locke, The Real World of Democracy, *and* The Life and Times of Liberal Democracy.

Academic political scientists who want their students to think about the problem of liberty in the modern state are properly anxious to have them confront at first hand various contemporary theoretical positions on the relation between freedom and capitalism. The range of positions is wide: at one extreme freedom is held to be incompatible with capitalism; at the other freedom is held to be impossible except in a capitalist society; in between, all sorts of necessary or possible relations are asserted. Different concepts of freedom are involved in some of these positions, similar concepts in others; and different models of capitalism (and of socialism) are sometimes being used. It is clearly important to sort them out. But there is some difficulty in finding adequate theoretical expositions of the second extreme position, which might be called the pure market theory of liberalism. There are very few of them. Probably the most effective, and the one most often cast in this role, is Milton Friedman's *Capitalism and Freedom* (Chicago, 1962), which is now apt to be treated by political scientists as the classic defence of free-market liberalism. As such it deserves more notice from the political theorists' standpoint than it got on publication, when its technical arguments about the possibility of returning to *laissez-faire* attracted most attention. Whether or not *Capitalism and Freedom* is now properly treated as the classic defence of the pure market theory of liberalism, it is at least a classic example of the difficulty of moving from the level of controversy about *laissez-faire to* the level of fundamental concepts of freedom and the market.

The first thing that strikes the political scientist about *Capitalism and Freedom* is the uncanny resemblance between Friedman's approach and Herbert Spencer's. Eighty years ago Spencer opened his *The Man versus the State* by drawing attention to a reversal which he believed had taken place recently in the meaning of liberalism: it had, he said, originally meant individual market freedom as opposed to state coercion, but it had come to mean more state coercion in the supposed interest of individual welfare. Spencer assigned a reason: earlier liberalism had in fact abolished grievances or mitigated evils suffered by the many, and so had contributed to their welfare; the welfare of the many then easily came to be taken by liberals not as a by-product of the real end, the relaxation of restraints, but as the end itself. Spencer regretted this, without offering any evidence that market freedom ever was more basic, or more desired, than the maximization of wealth or of individual welfare. Professor Friedman does the same. *Capitalism and Freedom* opens by drawing attention to the same reversal of meaning, and rejecting it out of hand. "Freedom of the individual, or perhaps of the family" is for him the liberal's "ultimate goal in judging social arrangements" (p.12). His case is that "a free private enterprise exchange economy", or "competitive capitalism" (p.13), is both a direct component of freedom, and a necessary though not a sufficient condition of political freedom, which he defines as "the absence of coercion of a man by his fellow men" (p.15).

To maximize this freedom, he argues, governments should be allowed to handle only those matters "which cannot be handled through the market at all, or can be handled only at so great a cost that the use of political channels may be preferable" (p.25). This would mean government moving out of almost all its welfare and regulatory functions. Controls on, or support of, any prices, wages, interest rates, rents, exports, imports, and amounts produced, would all have to go; so would present social security programmes, housing subsidy programmes, and the like. The functions properly left to governments because the market cannot perform them at all, or perform them well, are summarized:

> A government which maintained law and order, defined property rights, served as a means whereby we could modify property rights and other rules of the economic game, adjudicated disputes about the interpretation of the rules, enforced contracts, promoted competition, provided a monetary framework, engaged

in activities to counter technical monopolies and to overcome neighborhood effects widely regarded as sufficiently important to justify government intervention, and which supplemented private charity and the private family in protecting the irresponsible, whether madman or child—such a government would clearly have important functions to perform. The consistent liberal is not an anarchist (p.34).

No one ever thought that *laissez-faire* was anarchism; Spencer would scarcely have objected to this list of allowable government functions. But what is this economic game which is supposed to maximize individual freedom? The argument is that competitive capitalism can resolve "the basic problem of social organization", which is "how to coordinate the economic activities of large numbers of people" (p.12), by voluntary co-operation of individuals as opposed to central direction by state coercion.

In addition to arguing that competitive capitalism is a system of economic freedom and so an important component of freedom broadly understood, Professor Friedman argues that capitalism is a necessary condition of political freedom (and that socialism is incompatible with political freedom). And although he is more concerned with freedom than with equity, he does argue also that the capitalist principle of distribution of the whole product is not only preferable to a socialist principle but is in fact accepted by socialists.

This essay deals with (I) an error which vitiates Friedman's demonstration that competitive capitalism co-ordinates men's economic activities without coercion; (II) the inadequacy of his arguments that capitalism is a necessary condition of political freedom and that socialism is inconsistent with political freedom; and (III) the fallacy of his case for the ethical adequacy of the capitalist principle of distribution.

I

Professor Friedman's demonstration that the capitalist market economy can co-ordinate economic activities without coercion rests on an elementary conceptual error. His argument runs as follows. He shows first that in a simple market model, where each individual or household controls resources enabling it to produce goods and services either directly for itself or for exchange, there will be production for exchange because of the increased product made possible by specialization. But "since the household always has the alternative of producing directly for itself, it need not enter into any exchange unless it benefits from it. Hence no exchange will take place unless both parties do benefit from it. Co-operation is thereby achieved without coercion" (p.13). So far, so

good. It is indeed clear that in this simple exchange model, assuming rational maximizing behaviour by all hands, every exchange will benefit both parties, and hence that no coercion is involved in the decision to produce for exchange or in any act of exchange.

Professor Friedman then moves on to our actual complex economy, or rather to his own curious model of it:

> As in [the] simple model, so in the complex enterprise and money-exchange economy, co-operation is strictly individual and voluntary *provided:* (a) that enterprises are private, so that the ultimate contracting parties are individuals and (b) that individuals are effectively free to enter or not to enter into any particular exchange, so that every transaction is strictly voluntary (p.14).

One cannot take exception to proviso (a): it is clearly required in the model to produce a co-operation that is "strictly individual". One might, of course, suggest that a model containing this stipulation is far from corresponding to our actual complex economy, since in the latter the ultimate contracting parties who have the most effect on the market are not individuals but corporations, and moreover, corporations which in one way or another manage to opt out of the fully competitive market. This criticism, however, would not be accepted by all economists as self-evident: some would say that the question who has most effect on the market is still an open question (or is a wrongly posed question). More investigation and analysis of this aspect of the economy would be valuable. But political scientists need not await its results before passing judgement on Friedman's position, nor should they be tempted to concentrate their attention on proviso (a). If they do so they are apt to miss the fault in proviso (b), which is more fundamental, and of a different kind. It is not a question of the correspondence of the model to the actual: it is a matter of the inadequacy of the proviso to produce the model.

Proviso (b) is "that individuals are effectively free to enter or not to enter into any particular exchange", and it is held that with this proviso "every transaction is strictly voluntary." A moment's thought will show that this is not so. The proviso that is required to make every transaction strictly voluntary is *not* freedom not to enter into any *particular* exchange, but freedom not to enter into any exchange *at all*. This, and only this, was the proviso that proved the simple model to be voluntary and non-coercive; and nothing less than this would prove the complex model to be voluntary and non-coercive. But Professor Friedman is clearly claiming that freedom not to enter into *any particular* exchange is enough: "The consumer is protected from coercion by the seller because of the presence of other sellers with whom he can deal … The employee is protected from coercion by the employer because of other employers for whom he can work ... " (pp.14-15).

One almost despairs of logic, and of the use of models. It is easy to see what Professor Friedman has done, but it is less easy to excuse it. He has moved from the simple economy of exchange between independent producers, to the capitalist economy, without mentioning the most important thing that distinguishes them. He mentions money instead of barter, and "enterprises which are intermediaries between individuals in their capacities as suppliers of services and as purchasers of goods" (pp.13-14), as if money and merchants were what distinguished a capitalist economy from an economy of independent producers. What distinguishes the capitalist economy from the simple exchange economy is the separation of labour and capital, that is, the existence of a labour force without its own sufficient capital and therefore without a choice as to whether to put its labour in the market or not. Professor Friedman would agree that where there is no choice there is coercion. His attempted demonstration that capitalism co-ordinates without coercion therefore fails.

Since all his specific arguments against the welfare and regulatory state depend on his case that the market economy is not coercive, the reader may spare himself the pains (or, if an economist, the pleasure) of attending to the careful and persuasive reasoning by which he seeks to establish the minimum to which coercion could be reduced by reducing or discarding each of the main regulatory and welfare activities of the state. None of this takes into account the coercion involved in the separation of capital from labour, or the possible mitigation of this coercion by the regulatory and welfare state. Yet it is because this coercion can in principle be reduced by the regulatory and welfare state, and thereby the amount of effective individual liberty be increased, that liberals have been justified in pressing, in the name of liberty, for infringements on the pure operation of competitive capitalism.

II

While the bulk of *Capitalism and Freedom* is concerned with the regulatory and welfare state, Friedman's deepest concern is with socialism. He undertakes to demonstrate that socialism is inconsistent with political freedom. He argues this in two ways: (1) that competitive capitalism, which is of course negated by socialism, is a necessary (although not a sufficient) condition of political freedom; (2) that a socialist society is so constructed that it cannot guarantee political freedom. Let us look at the two

arguments in turn. [*Editor's note: The second part of the argument has been omitted from this extract.*]

I. The argument that competitive capitalism is necessary to political freedom is itself conducted on two levels, neither of which shows a necessary relation.

(a) The first, on which Friedman properly does not place very much weight, is a historical correlation. No society that has had a large measure of political freedom "has not also used something comparable to a free market to organize the bulk of economic activity" (p.9). Professor Friedman rightly emphasizes "how limited is the span of time and the part of the globe for which there has ever been anything like political freedom" (p.9); he believes that the exceptions to the general rule of "tyranny, servitude and misery" are so few that the relation between them and certain economic arrangements can easily be spotted. "The nineteenth century and early twentieth century in the Western world stand out as striking exceptions to the general trend of historical development. Political freedom in this instance clearly came along with the free market and the development of capitalist institutions" (pp.9-10). Thus, for Professor Friedman, "history suggests ... that capitalism is a necessary condition for political freedom" (p.10).

The broad historical correlation is fairly clear, though in cutting off the period of substantial political freedom in the West at the "early twentieth century" Friedman seems to be slipping into thinking of economic freedom and begging the question of the relation of political freedom to economic freedom. But granting the correlation between the emergence of capitalism and the emergence of political freedom, what it may suggest to the student of history is the converse of what it suggests to Professor Friedman: i.e., it may suggest that political freedom was a necessary condition for the development of capitalism. Capitalist institutions could not be fully established until political freedom (ensured by a competitive party system with effective civil liberties) had been won by those who wanted capitalism to have a clear run: a liberal state (political freedom) was needed to permit and facilitate a capitalist market society.

If this is the direction in which the causal relation runs, what follows (assuming the same relation to continue to hold) is that freedom, or rather specific kinds and degrees of freedom, will be or not be maintained according as those who have a stake in the maintenance of capitalism think them useful or necessary. In fact, there has been a complication in this relation. The liberal state which had, by the mid-nineteenth century in England, established the political freedoms needed to facilitate capitalism, was not democratic: that is, it had not extended political freedom to the bulk of the people. When, later, it did so, it began to abridge market freedom. The more extensive the political freedom, the less extensive the economic freedom became. At any rate, the historical correlation scarcely suggests that capitalism is a necessary condition for political freedom.

(b) Passing from historical correlation, which "by itself can never be convincing", Professor Friedman looks for "logical links between economic and political freedom" (pp.11-12). The link he finds is that "the kind of economic organization that provides economic freedom directly, namely, competitive capitalism, also promotes political freedom because it separates economic power from political power and in this way enables the one to offset the other" (p. 9). The point is developed a few pages later. The greater the concentration of coercive power in the same hands, the greater the threat to political freedom (defined as "the absence of coercion of a man by his fellow men"). The market removes the organization of economic activity from the control of the political authority. It thus reduces the concentration of power and "enables economic strength to be a check to political power rather than a reinforcement" (p. 15).

Granted the validity of these generalizations, they tell us only that the market *enables* economic power to offset rather than reinforce political power. They do not show any necessity or inherent probability that the market *leads to* the offsetting of political power by economic power. We may doubt that there is any such inherent probability. What can be shown is an inherent probability in the other direction, i.e., that the market leads to political power being used not to offset but to reinforce economic power. For the more completely the market takes over the organization of economic activity, that is, the more nearly the society approximates Friedman's ideal of a competitive capitalist market society, where the state establishes and enforces the individual right of appropriation and the rules of the market but does not interfere in the operation of the market, the more completely is political power being used to reinforce economic power.

Professor Friedman does not see this as any threat to political freedom because he does not see that the capitalist market necessarily gives coercive power to those who succeed in amassing capital. He knows that the coercion whose absence he equates with political freedom is not just the physical coercion of police and prisons, but extends to many forms of economic coercion, e.g. the power some men may have over others' terms of employment. He sees the coercion possible (he thinks probable) in a socialist society where the political authority can enforce certain terms of employment. He does not see the coercion in a capitalist society where the holders of capital can enforce certain terms of employment. He does not see this because of his error about freedom not to enter into any particular exchange being enough to prove the uncoercive nature of entering into exchange at all.

The placing of economic coercive power and political coercive power in the hands of different sets of people, as in the fully competitive capitalist economy, does not lead to the first checking the second but to the second reinforcing the first. It is only in the welfare-state variety of capitalism, which Friedman would like to have dismantled, that there is a certain amount of checking of economic power by political power.

The logical link between competitive capitalism and political freedom has not been established.

Source: C.B. Macpherson. *Democratic Theory: Essays in Retrieval.* Oxford: Oxford University Press, 1973. © Oxford University Press 1973. Reprinted from Democratic Theory: Essays in Retrieval by C.B. Macpherson (1973) by permission of Oxford University Press.

The Problem of Socialism in Liberation Theology

Peter Burns, S.J.

PETER BURNS, S.J. *holds an M.Div. from the Jesuit School of Theology in Berkley, California, and is pursuing a Ph.D. at the University of Southern California in Los Angeles.*

From its inception in the late 1960s Latin American liberation theology has been the subject of much controversy. Unquestionably one major factor in generating the heat surrounding the liberation debate has been the tendency, common to both its proponents and critics, to regard liberation theology as bound up with an unmistakeably left-wing political stance. Some have gone as far as to pronounce it Marxism pure and simple. This latter claim is one I reject. Nor do I accept that liberation theology is reducible to left-wing politics, even if conceived more broadly than Marxism as such. But there is a strong case to be made that a left-wing political posture, though somewhat indeterminate, has been a marked feature of liberation theology. In particular, many liberation theologians have at various times and in various ways made explicit a preference for socialism over capitalism. In this article I will explore the possible meanings of this preference, the reasons adduced for it, and some of the criticisms made of it.

I will confine my discussion to the issue of what might be called "the socialist option," and will not examine the related but separable issues of the use in liberation theology of Marxism and of dependency theory. At first sight this might appear an unwise or unworkable separation, since Marxism is obviously a major source of inspiration for much socialist thinking, and has had some influence on liberation theology; and dependency theory played an important role in the "break" with traditional Catholic approaches to social ethics which made liberation theology stand out as a novel and distinct theological movement. I would defend the separation on several grounds: that the acceptance of socialism does not depend on a prior evaluation of the core theory in Marxism, namely historical materialism; that few if any liberation theologians appear to subscribe to that core theory in any case, at least in anything like its classical form; and that analogous remarks can be made substituting dependency theory for Marxism.

Reasons for the Option for Socialism

I mentioned above that liberation theology represented a break from a traditional Catholic approach to social problems. This break was due in part to the utterly inhuman situation of massive poverty that continues to scar Latin America. Hunger, slums, high infant mortality, illiteracy, high unemployment, and low wages were typical throughout the continent when liberation theology was born. There was a strong sense that these problems were not simply due to misfortune or mere circumstance, but were the result of structural forms of exploitation and oppression. It was deeply felt that it was the *system,* in some sense, that was to blame. Given this understanding of the cause of socioeconomic misery, many Latin Americans found the standard social teaching of the Church insufficient because it seemed to call for reforms within the system, rather than a radical transformation of the political, social, and economic structures that constituted the system. Whether or not this was a fair assessment of the Church's teaching is arguable, but for the moment we may simply note that for liberation theologians the present reality cried out for profound change.

This urgent sense of the need for radical change was expressed in three characteristic ways. The first was an explicit acceptance that an authentic Christian faith would necessarily require a definite, concrete sociopolitical option for a more just society. This position was given official support at Medellin and was confirmed at Puebla: "The fact is that the need for the church's presence in the political arena flows from the very core of the Christian faith."[1]

What was a little more noticeable among liberation theologians, however, was their recognition that this connection between faith and politics had to be mediated by particular, historical, sociopolitical programs and ideologies which were part of the secular world. This was due to the fact, as the International Theological Commission recognized in its 1977 Declaration on Human Development and Christian Salvation, that "theology ... cannot deduce concrete political norms sheerly from theological principles."[2] But such norms were urgently required to address and remedy the enormous deprivation being experienced in Latin

America. In other words, if Christians were going to engage effectively in the quest for social justice, secular political options would have to mediate their praxis. Among liberation theologians this point has been elaborated most fully by Juan Luis Segundo.[3]

The second characteristic of liberation theology's new approach to the social problems of Latin America was its clear identification of the system, whose unjust character it saw as the source of these problems, as capitalist. In this way capitalism practically became equated with injustice. As McGovern writes, "When Pope Leo XIII wrote his encyclical *Rerum novarum* (1891) he criticized the abuses of capitalism, but rejected socialism as false in principle. Many liberation theologians would reverse this judgment."[4] Among the liberation writers who were most openly opposed to capitalism were Jose Miguez Bonino, Jose Porfirio Miranda, Franz Hinkelammert, and of course the Christians for Socialism group based in Chile.[5] Indeed the very word "capitalism" tended to have negative connotations—suggesting foreign domination, exploitation, and concentration of wealth—not just for liberation theologians, but for many Latin Americans generally.[6] Antipathy towards capitalism was evident even among members of the hierarchy as early as 1967.[7]

Identification of the system as unjust *and* capitalist was obviously fraught with major political implications. For it is important to recognize that if the injustices had been cited simply as such without the accompanying claim that the system producing them was capitalist, then much of the unease and criticism aimed at liberation theology would probably not have arisen.

Description of the Latin American political-economic system as capitalist is found quite clearly, even bluntly, in the writings of liberation theology's founding father, Gustavo Gutierrez: "[Capitalism is] the only system that really exists in Latin America, save for Cuba."[8] In his classic text, *A Theology of Liberation*, Gutierrez calls for a radical transformation of the socioeconomic structure and not simply for reforms that leave capitalism in place.[9] In the same book Gutierrez claims that Latin American development is not viable given the existing structures of international capitalism,[10] and that a truly liberated society cannot be reached by capitalist means.[11] This opposition to the capitalist order is reiterated in Gutierrez's *The Power of the Poor in History*.[12] Again, his view is stated quite bluntly: "Capitalist development is of its very nature detrimental to the masses.[13]

A similar view is taken by Enrique Dussel, who blames capitalism for the exploitation and alienation of workers and for the domination of poor countries by rich ones.[14] Strong opposition to capitalism is found even in some liberation theologians who are not usually noted for their treatment of specifically socioeconomic matters. Thus Leonardo and Clodovis Boff criticized the U.S. Bishops' Pastoral Letter on the Economy, *Economic Justice For All*, because it failed in their view to call into question capitalism as such:

> Capitalism can be more or less *immoral*; it can never be more or less *moral*. You do not eliminate the ferocity of the wolf by filing down its teeth … It is just as impossible to create a moral market system as it is to build a Christian brothel.[15]

This criticism is all the more significant coming as it does from theologians who have distanced themselves from dependency theory.[16] Even noted conservative opponents of liberation theology in Latin America have had little good to say about capitalism. Archbishop Lopez Trujillo has said, "We are convinced that capitalism is a human failure." And Roger Vekemans, S.J. has advocated a "Christian socialism" as preferable to either capitalism or Marxism.[17] Hence McGovern is surely right when he says that

> One reason liberation theologians opt for socialism stands out above all others: their abhorrence of the prevailing capitalist system. If, as many liberation theologians stress, capitalism cannot be reformed to meet the basic needs of the poor or to give them true participation in society, then socialism would seem to be the only real option.[18]

Liberation theologians spend little time arguing that Latin America is capitalist; they simply assume that it is, and that it is unjust. In this they appear to reflect an attitude that is pervasive in Latin America generally.[19]

The third characteristic expression of liberation theology's new and distinctive approach to the socioethical evaluation of Latin American problems was its eschewal of *tercerismo* or Third Way strategies. It had not been uncommon among Catholic social ethicists before the middle 1960s to interpret the social doctrine of the Church as pointing to a middle approach to socioeconomic matters which would retain the benefits and shed the defects of both capitalism and socialism. But as the 1960s progressed many in the Latin American Church (and not only there) became disenchanted with the practical results of this approach. This was especially true in Chile where the Christian Democratic government failed to meet the expectations of many Christians committed to social justice. The example of the Cuban revolution also inspired many Latin Americans to believe that a far more radical (i.e. more socialist) strategy was required to bring about the fundamental changes they regarded as necessary. Liberation theology reflected and contributed to this shift of perspective.

As military dictatorships came to power in several Latin countries, and repressive measures became more widespread and systematic, for example in Brazil after the 1964 coup and in Chile after its 1973 coup, the adoption of a middle-of-the-road position seemed to many to be a form of appeasement of evil, and therefore totally unacceptable. Meanwhile, economic growth was apparently failing to benefit the majority of poor Latin Americans. Reformism seemed not only a failure as far as social justice was concerned, but an ideological weapon of the ruling classes to keep the oppressed in a quiescent state politically. Thus Gutierrez called for socialism, and not simply "the modernization of the existing system."[20] He criticized the "socio-Christian" search for a middle way between capitalism and socialism, which he saw as based on an outmoded and anti-historical "distinction of planes" approach to the relation between faith and social action.[21] Segundo judged the search for Third Ways as fundamentally misconceived:

> I think that the whole phenomenon of adopting "third ways" presents a profound methodological challenge to liberation, and represents the ultimate consequence of an erroneous way of formulating the whole problem of the relationship between theology and politics.[22]

Dussel simply avers that "a concrete, positive Christian economico-political project does not exist."[23]

It now seems that the official magisterium of the Church does not regard or invite others to regard its social teaching as a Third Way either, given John Paul II's disclaimer to this effect in his encyclical *Sollicitudo rei socialis*.[24] By this disclaimer I think is meant above all that Catholic social doctrine is a moral theological guide that must be applied to, but cannot substitute for, specific political options and proposals. In this light Catholics should not disdain entering into the secular arena and making definite, albeit provisional commitments to particular political programs. There seems to be no reason in principle why such a commitment should not extend to embrace programs that customarily are identified as socialist in a broad sense (notwithstanding verbal injunctions to the contrary, especially in the early social encyclicals).[25]

We have seen, then, three reasons why liberation theology was led to embrace a broadly left-wing political agenda. First, there was a strongly felt need to concretize the faith-inspired quest for social justice in specific political options. Since revelation and theology were incapable by themselves of selecting one such option, the use of a mediating political ideology drawn from the secular realm was deemed both legitimate and inescapable. Second, confronted with the facts of systemic injustice, an almost unanimous identification was made that characterized the system in question as capitalist, and so justified a desire not merely to see changes within capitalism, but to replace it with a different kind of socioeconomic system altogether. Third, since traditional Third Way approaches were judged to be accommodating of the capitalist system, and therefore incapable of the radical transformation that was thought to be necessary, the only real alternative appeared to be an unabashed

option for socialism. The clearest example of such a position was that of the Christians for Socialism movement in Chile. But, with perhaps less emphasis on the use of Marxist language, most liberation theologians adopted a similar stance.

Source: Peter Burns, S.J. "The Problem of Socialism in Liberation Theology." *Theological Studies* 53 (1992):493-516. Reprinted by permission.

Notes

[1] Quoted in E.L. Cleary, *Crisis and Change* (Maryknoll, N.Y.: Orbis, 1985) 165. Similar statements were made in the document *Justice in the World* from the 1971 Bishops' Synod, and in Paul VI's encyclical *Euangelii nuntiandi* (1975).

[2] Quoted in A. T. Hennelly, ed., *Liberation Theology: A Documentary History* (Maryknoll, N.Y.: Orbis, 1990) 208.

[3] See esp. his books, *The Liberation of Theology* (Maryknoll, N.Y.: Orbis, 1976), and *Faith and Ideologies* (Maryknoll, N.Y.: Orbis, 1984).

[4] A. F. McGovern, *Liberation Theology and Its Critics* (Maryknoll, N.Y.: Orbis, 1989) 139.

[5] J. M. Bonino, *Christians and Marxists: The Mutual Challenge to Revolution* (Grand Rapids: Eerdmans, 1976); J.P. Miranda, *Marx and the Bible: A Critique of the Philosophy of Oppression* (Maryknoll, N.Y.: Orbis, 1974); F.J. Hinkelammert, *The Ideological Weapons of Death: A Theological Critique of Capitalism* (Maryknoll, N.Y.: Orbis, 1986) and the "Final Document" of the Christians for Socialism 1972 Convention, printed i Hennelly, ed., *A Documentary History* 147.

[6] See McGovern, *Liberation Theology*, xviii-xix and 180.

[7] See Third World Bishops, "A Letter to the Peoples of the Third World," in Hennelly ed., *A Documentary History* 52; see also the Bishops of Peru, "Justice in the World," ibid., p.129.

[8] G. Gutierrez, *The Power of the Poor in History* (Maryknoll, N.Y.: Orbis, 1983) 113 (Gutierrez traces capitalism in Latin America back to the 16th century, but Otto Madur sees it arising only in the latter part of the 19th century; see his *Religion and Social Conflicts* (Maryknoll, N.Y.: Orbis, 1982) 60.

[9] G. Gutierrez, *A Theology of Liberation* (Maryknoll, N.Y.: Orbis, 1988; originally published 1971) 65.

[10] Ibid., p.88.

[11] Ibid., p.127.

[12] Gutierrez, *Power of the Poor* 133.

[13] Ibid., p.85.

[14] E. Dussel, *Ethics and Community* (Maryknoll, N.Y.: Orbis, 1988) chaps. 12-13.

[15] Quoted in McGovern, *Liberation Theology* 139.

[16] Ibid., p.136-37.

[17] Ibid., p.xix.

[18] Ibid., p.178.

[19] See M. Falcoff, "Political Systems and Economic Growth: The Case of Latin America," in M. Novak, ed., *Liberation Theology and the Liberal Society* (Washington D.C.: American Enterprise Institute, 1987) 195.

[20] Gutierrez, *Power of the Poor* 45.

[21] Ibid., pp.40, 198.

[22] Segundo, *The Liberation of Theology* 91.

[23] Dussel, *Ethics and Community* 193.

[24] See *Sollicitudo rei socialis* (Washington D.C.: U.S. Catholic Conference, 1987) No. 41.

[25] In *Centesimus annus* John Paul II seems more or less to equate "socialism" with the Stalinist regimes of the erstwhile Soviet bloc (though he also calls it "state capitalism"); and he gives a qualified verbal approval of "capitalism; " see *Centesimus annus*, Nos. 35 and 42 (printed in *National Catholic Reporter*, 24 May 1991, 17-30). Western socialists will recall, however, that in his earlier social encyclicals the pope distinguishes between authentic and inauthentic forms of socialized property, which seems to chime well with their calls for the radical democratization of the ownership and control of capital; see *Laborem exercens*, No. 14; printed in G. Baum, *The Priority of Labor* (New York: Paulist, 1982); and *Sollicitudo rei socialis*, Nos. 15 and 21.

Justice and the Dispossessed

Stuart Hampshire

STUART HAMPSHIRE (1914-) was Professor of Philosophy at Princeton University and University of London before taking on a similar post at the University of California. His works display a broad outlook in the fields of theory of knowledge, metaphysics, philosophy of mind, and ethics.

In successive periods of history the demands of the dispossessed for recognition and for redress have often been expressed as appeals for substantial justice. But the demands of the dispossessed have also often been expressed, particularly in the last two centuries, as demands for greater freedom or for greater equality. This has been the Jacobin tradition, set in motion by Rousseau and passing to Robespierre, the tradition of revolution that came to life again in the Paris Commune of 1870. Socialist parties in Europe have later drawn on the Jacobin concept of equality when prescribing the moral goal of a socialist transformation of society. They have sometimes also invoked the Jacobin conception of freedom, which entails that every citizen feels that he or she is an equal member of a self-governing community which pursues the common good. Both the ideal of social equality, and the ideal of the Rousseauesque community of free citizens, are elements in an imaginative conception of the good. There is no compelling reason to be found in the universal practices of mankind to claim that citizenship in a genuine community is always to be preferred, and is always intrinsically better, than citizenship in some looser and larger and more atomistic society. Rousseau, and many socialists after him, have legitimately and successfully evoked the emotions that are associated with a communitarian way of life. As moralists they have argued for the superiority of this way of life, and their cause is certain to be divisive and to have enemies.

If socialists argued their case by appeals to substantial justice, rather than in terms of equality and freedom, their cause would still be divisive and have enemies, because a substantial conception of distributive justice is being invoked; therefore some conception of the good is also being invoked. Is it unjust and unfair that so much wealth should accrue to financiers, landowners, entrepreneurs, and managers and so little should be earned by labourers engaged in arduous and tedious work? Is the contrast in a single place between great wealth and abject poverty less of an evil than the methods which would be necessary to eliminate it? Conservatives, liberals, and socialists will derive different answers to these two questions from their different conceptions of the human good, and therefore of what is just and right. But all three groups, including the socialists, will think more clearly about the issues of poverty, property, and property rights, if they see their disagreements as disagreements about substantial justice. The concept of justice provides a common framework within which the points of divergence can be clearly marked, and traced to their sources in different psychological, historical, metaphysical, and religious beliefs, beliefs which support different conceptions of the good.

If the conflict over conceptions of justice supplies the framework within which the political conflict is fought out, there will be some congruity between the means used to impose any temporary settlement that emerges and the settlement itself. There will not be that incongruity between means and ends which was evident in Robespierre's Jacobinism and which descended to Lenin's "democratic centralism" and thereafter to the domination of the Communist Party in communist countries.

Socialist parties in European democracies have been misguided when they ground their moral appeals in the ideal of equality rather than of justice, following the thought and rhetoric of the French revolutionary tradition. The implicit moral appeal of *Das Kapital* is to the in-built unfairness of the distribution of property under capitalism, which ensures, according to Marx, that the labourer can never receive the just rewards of his labour, which will be skimmed off as surplus value and distributed to the owners and controllers of the means of production. That is the core of the moral argument, without its pseudo-scientific clothing. This argument links the nineteenth-century factory worker and agricultural labourer as victims of injustice to the dispossessed of previous ages: to slaves in the ancient world and in the American South and elsewhere; to conquered populations everywhere, untouchables, ethnic minorities without citizen's rights; to landless peasants, and to all those who have nothing themselves and who depend on the will of others for their survival and for the survival of their children. Such persons have no alternatives: they must organise themselves as strongly as they can in order to present an effective demand for justice, which entails that their substantial claims should become a cause of conflict leading sooner or later to serious negotiation. If they achieve no access to fair considerations of their claims, and if they have a reasonable chance of success through violence, they will fight for justice, as they perceive it, until their substantial claims are fairly considered. This has always been the way, the justifiable way, of the dispossessed who have come to feel strongly enough the injustice of which they are the victims and who have been denied the minimum decencies of procedural justice.

There are always open possibilities of improving human life in indefinitely many ways, and among the possibilities is the elimination of gross poverty and of at least some of the risks of war. But practical possibilities exist as such only as long as they are vividly imagined and actively explored. They disappear as practical possibilities when we are deceived by old arguments which represent customary practices as the only natural ones, with the implication that there are no other possible worlds—which would be as natural as the actual one, if we combined to create them.

Source: Stuart Hampshire. *Innocence and Experience*. Cambridge, MA: Harvard University Press, 1989. Reprinted by permission of the publishers from *Innocence and Experience* by Stuart Hampshire, Cambridge, Mass.: Harvard University Press. Copyright © by Stuart Hampshire.

7

Fascism

The Ideals of Tyrannical Power and Racial Purity

The Social Darwinism implied in the writings of the Englishmen Karl Pearson and Houston Chamberlain reveals, manifestly, the roots of racism in Germany during the Third Reich. These English writers merely pick up where the nineteenth century thinker Arthur Gobineau, and Herbert Spencer before him, leave off. The ink is barely dry on the Treaty of Versailles when Adolph Hitler in his notorious *Twenty-Five Points* exploits the Chamberlain-Pearson notion of racial purity by speaking in terms of German blood as a primary condition of citizenship. The consequence of this Nazi line of thinking is that Jews are excluded both from membership in the nation and participation in citizenship.

It would be misleading to cast Hitler's *Twenty-Five Points* as a speech based solely on racial purity, for other dangerous and ominous ideas are also mentioned. Notable among these is a barely concealed *lebensraum* doctrine, press censorship and an uncompromising approach in dealing with usury, profiteering and unpatriotic art and literature. The hidden *motif* in most of this rhetoric is power and its consolidation.

The *motif* of power and the doctrine of racial purity come together in Hannah Arendt's comments on the banality of evil as evidenced in Eichmann's participation in the *Final Solution (Endlösing)*. Her analysis reveals the destructive effect of the Nazi machinery and its corresponding methods of killing. In her discussion of the events surrounding Treblinka and Auschwitz and Eichmann's connection with these events, Arendt does an effective job of exposing the logical consequences of the Nazi ideas of political power and racial purity.

But it remains for Benito Mussolini under fascism to outline clearly the elements of tyrannical power. These elements include a denunciation of socialism and the democratic ideals of the majority: universalism, liberalism and egalitarianism. From Mussolini's perspective all of these philosophical positions are spent forces or deserted temples—they have no relevant application to the real world. With these ideals abandoned, the fascist state becomes the embodiment of the Nietzschian will-to-power.

But what is the psychological profile of someone attracted to these new Nietzschian ideals? Roger Griffin offers some tantalizing suggestions that tie together historical, literary, philosophical and psychological observations. Although his position of attributing Eichmann-like atrocities to perversions of self-transcendent emotions is arguable, the premise is worthy of serious consideration.

Foundations of the Nineteenth Century

Houston Stewart Chamberlain

HOUSTON STEWART CHAMBERLAIN *(1855-1926) was an Englishman who developed the notion of the genetically superior folk-nation. He made use of Darwinian ideas and applied them to the Aryan race. Most of his thoughts on racial traits are discussed in* Foundations of the Nineteenth Century.

The Jews

At a later time, indeed, a Semitic flood swept once more across the European, Asiatic and African world, a flood such as, but for the destruction of Carthage by Rome, would have swept over Europe a thousand years before, with results which would have been decisive and permanent. But here, too, the Semitic idea—"faith wide, narrow the thought"—proved itself more powerful than its bearers; the Arabs were gradually thrown back and, in contrast to the Jews, not one of them remained on European soil; but where their abstract idolatry had obtained a foothold all possibility of a culture disappeared; the Semitic dogma of materialism, which in this case and in contrast to Christianity had kept itself free of all Aryan admixtures, deprived noble human races of all soul, and excluded them for ever from the "race that strives to reach the light."—Of the Semites only the Jews, as we see, have positively furthered our culture and also shared, as far as their extremely assimilative nature permitted them, in the legacy of antiquity.

The Teutonic Races

The entrance of the Teutonic races into the history of the world forms the counterpart to the spread of this diminutive and yet so influential people. There, too, we see what pure race signifies, at the same time, however, what variety of races is—that great natural principle of many-sidedness, and of dissimilarity of mental gifts, which shallow, venal, ignorant babblers of the present day would fain deny, slavish souls sprung from the chaos of peoples, who feel at ease only in a confused atmosphere of characterlessness and absence of individuality. To this day these two powers—Jews and Teutonic races—stand, wherever the recent spread of the Chaos has not blurred their features, now as friendly, now as hostile, but always as alien forces face to face.

In this book I understand by "Teutonic peoples" the different North-European races, which appear in history as Celts, Teutons (Germanen) and Slavs, and from whom—mostly by indeterminable mingling—the peoples of modern Europe are descended. It is certain that they belonged originally to a single family, as I shall prove in the sixth chapter; but the Teuton in the narrower Tacitean sense of the word has proved himself so intellectually, morally and physically pre-eminent among his kinsmen, that we are entitled to make his name summarily represent the whole family. The Teuton is the soul of our culture. Europe of to-day, with its many branches over the whole world, represents the chequered result of an infinitely manifold mingling of races: what binds us all together and makes an organic unity of us is "Teutonic" blood. If we look around, we see that the importance of each nation as a living power to-day is dependent upon the proportion of genuinely Teutonic blood in its population. Only Teutons sit on the thrones of Europe.—What preceded in the history of the world we may regard as Prolegomena; true history, the history which still controls the rhythm of our hearts and circulates in our veins, inspiring us to new hope and new creation, begins at the moment when the Teuton with his masterful hand lays his grip upon the legacy of antiquity.

Importance of Race

Nothing is so convincing as the consciousness of the possession of Race. The man who belongs to a distinct, pure race, never loses the sense of it. The guardian angel of his lineage is ever at his side, supporting him where he loses his foothold, warning him like the Socratic Daemon where he is in danger of going astray, compelling obedience, and forcing him to undertakings which, deeming them impossible, he would never have dared to attempt. Weak and erring like all that is human, a man of this stamp recognizes himself, as others recognise him, by the sureness of his character, and by the fact that his actions are marked by a certain simple and peculiar greatness, which finds its explanation in his distinctly typical and super-personal qualities. Race lifts a man above himself: it endows him with extraordinary—I might almost say supernatural—powers, so entirely does it distinguish him from the individual who springs from the chaotic jumble of peoples drawn from all parts of the world: and should this man of pure origin be perchance gifted above his fellows, then the fact of Race strengthens and elevates him on every hand, and he becomes a genius towering over the rest of mankind, not because he has been thrown upon the earth like a flaming meteor by a freak of nature, but because he soars heavenward like some strong and stately tree, nourished by thousands and thousands of roots—no solitary individual, but the living sum of untold striving for the same goal. He who has eyes to see at once detects Race in animals. It shows itself in the whole habit of the beast, and proclaims itself in a hundred peculiarities which defy analysis: nay more, it proves itself by achievements, for its possession invariably leads to something excessive and out of the common—even to that which is exaggerated and not free from bias. Goethe's dictum, "only that which is extravagant (*überschwänglich*) makes greatness," is well known.[1] That is the very quality which a thoroughbred race reared from superior materials bestows upon its individual descendants—something "extravagant"—and, indeed, what we learn from every racehorse, every thoroughbred fox-terrier, every Cochin China fowl, is the very lesson which the history of mankind so eloquently teaches us! Is not the Greek in the fullness of his glory an unparalleled example of this "extravagance?" And do we not see this "extravagance" first make its appearance when immigration from the North has ceased, and the various strong breeds of men, isolated on the peninsula once for all, begin to fuse into a new race, brighter and more brilliant, where, as in Athens, the racial blood flows from many sources—simpler and more resisting where, as in Lacedemon, even this mixture of blood had been barred out. Is the race not as it were extinguished, as soon as fate wrests the land from its proud exclusiveness and incorporates it in a greater whole?[2] Does not Rome teach us the same lesson? Has not in this case also a special mixture of blood produced an absolutely new race, similar in qualities and capacities to no later one, endowed with exuberant power? And does not victory in this case effect what disaster did in that, but only much more quickly? Like a cataract the stream of strange blood overflooded the almost depopulated Rome and at once the Romans ceased to be. Would one small tribe

from among all the Semites have become a world-embracing power had it not made "purity of race" its inflexible fundamental law? In days when so much nonsense is talked concerning this question, let Disraeli teach us that the whole significance of judaism lies in its purity of race, that this alone gives it power and duration, and just as it has outlived the people of antiquity, so, thanks to its knowledge of this law of nature, will it outlive the constantly mingling races of to-day.[3]

What is the use of detailed scientific investigations as to whether there are distinguishable races? whether race has a worth? how this is possible? and so on. We turn the tables and say: it is evident that there are such races: it is a fact of direct experience that the quality of the race is of vital importance; your province is only to find out the how and the wherefore, not to deny the facts themselves in order to indulge your ignorance. One of the greatest ethnologists of the present day, Adolf Bastian, testifies that, "what we see in history is not a transformation, a passing of one race into another, but entirely new and perfect creations, which the ever-youthful productivity of nature sends forth from the invisible realm of Hades."[4] Whoever travels the short distance between Calais and Dover, feels almost as if he had reached a different planet, so great is the difference between the English and French, despite their many points of relationship. The observer can also see from this instance the value of purer "inbreeding." England is practically cut off by its insular position: the last (not very extensive) invasion took place 800 years ago; since then only a few thousands from the Netherlands, and later a few thousand Huguenots have crossed over (all of the same origin), and thus has been reared that race which at the present moment is unquestionably the strongest in Europe.[5]

Direct experience, however, offers us a series of quite different observations on race, all of which may gradually contribute to the extension of our knowledge as well as to its definiteness. In contrast to the new, growing, Anglo-Saxon race, look, for instance, at the Sephardim, the so-called "Spanish Jews;" here we find how a genuine race can by purity keep itself noble for centuries and tens of centuries, but at the same time how very necessary it is to distinguish between the nobly reared portions of a nation and the rest. In England, Holland and Italy there are still genuine Sephardim but very few, since they can scarcely any longer avoid crossing with the Ashkenazim (the so-called "German Jews"). Thus, for example, the Montefiores of the present generation have all without exception married German Jewesses. But every one who has travelled in the East of

Europe, where the genuine Sephardim still as far as possible avoid all intercourse with German Jews, for whom they have an almost comical repugnance, will agree with me when I say that it is only when one sees these men and has intercourse with them that one begins to comprehend the significance of Judaism in the history of the world. This is nobility in the fullest sense of the world, genuine nobility of race! Beautiful figures, noble heads, dignity in speech and bearing.

Source: Houston Stewart Chamberlain. *Foundations of the Nineteenth Century.* New York: John Lane, London: The Bodley Head, 1912.

Notes

[1] *Materialien zur Geschichte der Farbenlehre*, the part dealing with Newton's personality.

[2] It is well known that it was but gradually extinguished, and that in spite of a political situation, which must assuredly have brought speedy destruction on everything Hellenic, had not race qualities here had a decisive influence. Till late in the Christian era Athens remained the centre of intellectual life for mankind; Alexandria was more talked of, the strong Semitic contingent saw to that; but any one who wished to study in earnest travelled to Athens, till Christian narrow-mindedness for ever closed the schools there in the year 529, and we learn that as late as this even the man of the people was distinguished in Athens "by the liveliness of his intellect, the correctness of his language and the sureness of his taste" (Gibbon, chap. xl.). There is in George Finlay's book, *Medieval Greece*, chap. i., a complete and very interesting and clear account of the gradual destruction of the Hellenic race by reign immigration. One after the other colonies of Roman soldiers from all parts of the Empire, then Celts, Teutonic peoples, Slavonians, Bulgarians. Wallachians, Albanesians, etc., had moved into the country and mixed with the original population. The Zaconians, who were numerous even in the fifteenth century, but have now almost died out, are said to be the only pure Hellenes.

[3] See the novels *Tancred* and *Coningsby.* In the latter Sidonia says: "Race is everything; there is no other truth. And every race must fall which carelessly suffers its blood to become mixed."

[4] *Das Beständige in den Menschenrassen und die Spielweite ihrer Veränderlichkeit*, 1868, p.26.

[5] Mention should also be made of Japan, where likewise a felicitous crossing and afterwards insular isolation have contributed to the production of a very remarkable race, much stronger and (within the Mongoloid sphere of possibility) much more profoundly endowed than most Europeans imagine. Perhaps the only books in which one gets to know the Japanese soul are those of Lafcadio Hearn: *Kokoro, Hints and Echoes of Japanese Inner Life; Gleanings in Buddha Fields*, and others.

National Life from the Standpoint of Science

Karl Pearson

KARL PEARSON *(1857-1936) was Professor of Applied Mathematics and Mechanics and later Galton Professor of National Eugenics, both at the University of London. He applied mathematics to general biology and national character traits, among many other subjects. He laid special emphasis upon the idea of the tribe rather than the individual and attempted to relate this idea to that of bad stock and lower races. His popular works include* National Life *and* The Grammar of Science.

Now, if we once realize that this law of inheritance is as inevitable as the law of gravity, we shall cease to struggle against it. This does not mean a fatal resignation to the presence of bad stock, but a conscious attempt to modify the percentage of it in our own community and in the world at large. Let me illustrate what I mean. A showman takes a wolf and, by aid of training and nurture, a more or less judicious administration of food and whip, makes it apparently docile and friendly as a dog. But one day, when the whip is not there, it is quite possible that the wolf will turn upon its keeper, or upon somebody else. Even if it does not, its offspring will not benefit by the parental education. I don't believe that the showman's way can be a permanent success; I believe, however, that you might completely domesticate the wolf, as the dog has been domesticated, by steadily selecting the more docile members of the community through several generations, and breeding only from these, rejecting the remainder. Now, if you have once realized the force of heredity, you will see in natural selection—the choice of the physically and mentally fitter to be the parents of the next generation—a most munificent provision for the progress of all forms of life. Nurture and education may immensely aid the social machine, but they must be repeated generation by generation; they will not in themselves reduce the tendency to the production of bad stock. Conscious or unconscious selection can alone bring that about.

What I have said about bad stock seems to me to hold for the lower races of man. How many centuries, how many thousand of years, have the Kaffir or the negro held large districts in Africa undisturbed by the white man? Yet their intertribal struggles have not yet produced a civilization in the least comparable with the Aryan. Educate and nurture them as you will, I do not believe that you will succeed in modifying the stock. History shows me one way, and one way only, in which a high state of civilization has been produced, namely, the struggle of race with race, and the survival of the physically and mentally fitter race. If you want to know whether the lower races of man can evolve a higher type, I fear the only course is to leave them to fight it out among themselves, and even then the struggle for existence between individual and individual, between tribe and tribe, may not be supported by that physical selection due to a particular climate on which probably so much of the Aryan's success depended.

If you bring the white man into contact with the black, you too often suspend the very process of natural selection on which the evolution of a higher type depends. You get superior and inferior races living on the same soil, and that coexistence is demoralizing for both. They naturally sink into the position of master and servant, if not admittedly or covertly into that of slave-owner and slave. Frequently they intercross, and if the bad stock be raised the good is lowered. Even in the case of Eurasians, of whom I have met mentally and physically fine specimens, I have felt how much better they would have been had they been pure Asiatics or pure Europeans. Thus it comes about that when the struggle for existence between races is suspended, the solution of great problems may be unnaturally postponed; instead of the slow, stern processes of evolution, cataclysmal solutions are prepared for the future. Such problems in suspense, it appears to me, are to be found in the negro population of the Southern States of America, in the large admixture of Indian blood in some of the South American races, but, above all, in the Kaffir factor in South Africa.

You may possibly think that I am straying from my subject, but I want to justify natural selection to you. I want you to see selection as something which renders the inexorable law of heredity a source of progress which produces the good through suffering, an infinitely greater good which far outbalances the very obvious pain and evil. Let us suppose the alternative were possible. Let us suppose we could prevent the white man, if we liked, from going to lands of which the agriculture and mineral resources are not worked to the full; then I should say a thousand times better for him that he should not go than that he should settle down and live alongside the inferior race. The only healthy alternative is that he should go and completely drive out the inferior race. That is practically what the white man has done in North America. We sometimes forget the light that chapter of history throws on more recent experiences. Some 250 years ago there was a man who fought in our country against taxation without representation, and another man who did not mind going to prison for the sake of his religious opinions. As Englishmen we are proud of them both, but we sometimes forget that they were both considerable capitalists for their age, and started chartered companies in another continent. Well, a good deal went on in the plantations they founded, if not with their knowledge, with that at least of their servants and of their successors, which would shock us all at the present day. But I venture to say that no man calmly judging will wish either that the whites had never gone to America, or would desire the whites and Red Indians were today living alongside each other as negro and white in Southern States, as Kaffir and European in South Africa, still less that they had mixed their blood as Spaniard and Indian in South America. The civilization of the white man is a civilization dependent upon free white labour, and when that element of stability is removed it will collapse like those of Greece and Rome. I venture to assert, then, that the struggle for existence between white and red man, painful and even terrible as it was in its details, has given us a good far outbalancing its immediate evil. In place of the red man, contributing practically nothing to the work and thought of the world, we have a great nation, mistress of many arts, and able, with its youthful imagination and fresh, untrammelled impulses, to contribute much to the common stock of civilized man. Against that we have only to put the romantic sympathy for the Red Indian generated by the novels of Cooper and the poems of Longfellow, and then—see how little it weights in the balance!

But America is but one case in which we have to mark a masterful human progress following an interracial struggle. The Australian nation is another case of great civilization supplanting a lower race unable to work to the full the land and its resources. Further back in history you find the same tale with almost every European nation. Sometimes when the conquering race is not too diverse in civilization and in type of energy there is an amalgamation of races, as when Norman and Anglo-Saxon ultimately blended; at other times the inferior race is driven out before the superior, as the Celt drove out the Iberian. The struggle means suffering, intense suffering, while it is in progress; but that struggle and that suffering have been the stages by which the white man has reached his present stage of development, and they account for the fact that he no longer lives in caves and feeds on roots and nuts. This dependence of progress on the survival of the fitter race, terribly black as it may seem to some of you, gives the struggle for existence its redeeming features; it is the fiery crucible out of which comes the finer metal. You may hope for a time when the sword shall be turned into the ploughshare, when American and German and English traders shall no longer compete in the markets of the world for their raw material and for their food supply, when the white man and the dark shall share the soil between them, and each till it as he lists. But, believe me, when that day comes mankind will no longer progress; there will be nothing to check the fertility of inferior stock; the relentless law of heredity will not be controlled and guided by natural selection. Man will stagnate; and unless he ceases to multiply, the catastrophe will come again; famine and pestilence, as we see them in the East, physical selection instead of the struggle of race against race, will do the work more relentlessly, and, to judge from India and China, far less efficiently than of old.

Source: Karl Pearson. National Life from the Standpoint of Science. Originally published in 1901.

The Political and Social Doctrine of Fascism

Benito Mussolini

BENITO MUSSOLINI *(1883-1945) was born in central Italy and was leader of that country from 1922 until 1943. His political views are best summed up in* The Political and Social Doctrine of Fascism.

Fascism is now a completely individual thing, not only as a regime but as a doctrine. And this means that to-day Fascism, exercising its critical sense upon itself and upon others, has formed its own distinct and peculiar point of view, to which it can refer and upon which, therefore, it can act in the face of all problems, practical or intellectual, which confront the world.

And above all, Fascism, the more it considers and observes the future and the development of humanity quite apart from political considerations of the moment, believes neither in the possibility nor the utility of perpetual peace. It thus repudiates the doctrine of Pacifism—born of a renunciation of the struggle and an act of cowardice in the face of sacrifice. War alone brings up to its highest tension all human energy and puts the stamp of nobility upon the peoples who have the courage to meet it. All other trials are substitutes, which never really put men into the position where they have to make the great decision—the alternative of life or death. Thus a doctrine which is founded upon this harmful postulate of peace is hostile to Fascism. And thus hostile to the spirit of Fascism, though accepted for what use they can be in dealing with particular political situations, are all the international leagues and societies which, as history will show, can be scattered to the winds when once strong national feeling is aroused by any motive—sentimental, ideal, or practical. This anti-Pacifist spirit is carried by Fascism even into the life of the individual; the proud motto of the *Squadrista*, "Me ne frego," written on the bandage of the wound, is an act of philosophy not only stoic, the summary of a doctrine not only political—it is the education to combat, the acceptation of the risks which combat implies, and a new way of life for Italy. Thus the Fascist accepts life and loves it, knowing nothing of and despising suicide: he rather conceives of life as duty and struggle and conquest, life which should be high and full, lived for oneself, but above all for others—those who are at hand and those who are far distant, contemporaries, and those who will come after.

This "demographic" policy of the regime is the result of the above premise. Thus the Fascist loves in actual fact his neighbour, but this "neighbour" is not merely a vague and undefined concept, this love for one's neighbour puts no obstacle in the way of necessary educational severity, and still less to differentiation of status and to physical distance. Fascism repudiates any universal embrace, and in order to live worthily in the community of civilized peoples watches its contemporaries with vigilant eyes, takes good note of their state of mind and, in the changing trend of their interests, does not allow itself to be deceived by temporary and fallacious appearances.

Such a conception of life makes Fascism the complete opposite of that doctrine, the base of so-called scientific and Marxian Socialism, the materialist conception of history; according to which the history of human civilization can be explained simply through the conflict of interests among the various social groups and by the change and development in the means and instruments of production. That the changes in the economic field—new discoveries of raw materials, new methods of working them, and the inventions of science—have their importance no one can deny; but that these factors are sufficient to explain the history of humanity excluding all others is an absurd delusion. Fascism, now and always, believes in holiness and in heroism; that is to say, in actions influenced by no economic motive, direct or indirect. And if the economic conception of history be denied, according to which theory men are no more than puppets, carried to and fro by the waves of chance, while the real directing forces are quite out of their control, it follows that the existence of an unchangeable and unchanging class-war is also denied—the natural progeny of the economic conception of history. And above all Fascism denies

BENITO MUSSOLINI (1883–1945)

BENITO MUSSOLINI was the fascist dictator of Italy from 1922 until 1945, leading Italy through World War Two. His father was a blacksmith who had spent time in jail for his socialist beliefs. Mussolini spent a brief period as a teacher but soon went to Switzerland where he studied socialism. After returning to Italy in 1904, Mussolini was jailed for political agitation in 1908, joined the Milan socialist newspaper *Avvenire* in 1909 and was imprisoned again in 1911 for denouncing Italy's imperialist efforts in Libya. In 1914, Mussolini spoke in favour of Italian entry into World War One on the Allied side. By 1917, Mussolini's *Il Popolo d'Italia* newspaper had become the main organ of discontent for Italians who were disappointed in their country's conduct during the war.

In 1919, Mussolini founded the first *fascio di combattimento*, introducing his early version of political fascism to discontented war veterans and taking the *fasces*, an early Roman symbol of power and authority, as the movement's emblem. By 1922, Mussolini had secured a man-

date from King Victor Emannuel II to form a coalition government after his "black shirts" had marched on Rome. The Fascists soon declared that they were the only legal party in Italy. In the mid-thirties, Mussolini (or *Il Duce* as he had come to be known) decided to pursue an aggressive imperialist policy. He invaded Ethiopia in 1935, assisted Franco in the Spanish Civil War in 1936–39 and annexed Albania in 1939. Italy entered World War Two after the fall of France in 1940, but after heavy defeats in Africa and the Balkans and the loss of Sicily, Mussolini was forced to resign by the fascist Grand Council. He attempted to flee to Switzerland in 1945 but was apprehended and shot by Italian partisans.

---

that class-war can be the preponderant force in the transformation of society. These two fundamental concepts of Socialism being thus refuted, nothing is left of it but the sentimental aspiration—as old as humanity itself—towards a social convention in which the sorrows and sufferings of the humblest shall be alleviated. But here again Fascism repudiates the conception of "economic" happiness, to be realized by Socialism and, as it were, at a given moment in economic evolution to assure to everyone the maximum of well-being. Fascism denies the materialist conception of happiness as a possibility, and abandons it to its inventors, the economists of the first half of the nineteenth century: that is to say, Fascism denies the validity of the equation, well-being-happiness, which would reduce men to the level of animals, caring for one thing only—to be fat and well-fed—and would thus degrade humanity to a purely physical existence.

After Socialism, Fascism combats the whole complex system of democratic ideology, and repudiates it, whether in its theoretical premises or in its practical application. Fascism denies that the majority, by the simple fact that it is a majority, can direct human

society; it denies that numbers alone can govern by means of a periodical consultation, and it affirms the immutable, beneficial and fruitful inequality of mankind, which can never be permanently levelled through the mere operation of a mechanical process such as universal suffrage. The democratic regime may be defined as from time to time giving the people the illusion of sovereignty, while the real effective sovereignty lies in the hands of other concealed and irresponsible forces. Democracy is a regime nominally without a king, but it is rules by many kings—more absolute, tyrannical and ruinous than one sole king, even though a tyrant. This explains why Fascism, having first in 1922 (for reasons of expediency) assumed an attitude tending towards republicanism, renounced this point of view before the march to Rome; being convinced that the question of political form is not to-day of prime importance, and after having studied the examples of monarchies and republics past and present reached the conclusion that monarchy or republicanism are not to be judged, as it were, by an absolute standard; but that they represent forms in which the evolution—political, historical, traditional or psychological—of a particular country had expressed itself. Fascism supersedes the antithesis monarchy or republicanism, while democracy still tarries beneath the domination of this idea, for ever pointing out the insufficiency of the first and for ever the praising of the second as the perfect regime. To-day, it can be seen that there are republics innately reactionary and absolutist, and also monarchies which incorporate the most ardent social and political hopes of the future.

"Reason and science," says Renan (one of the inspired pre-Fascists) in his philosophical meditations, "are products of humanity, but to expect reason as a direct product of the people and a direct result of their action is to deceive oneself by a chimera. It is not necessary for the existence of reason that everybody should understand it. And in any case, if such a decimation of truth were necessary, it could not be achieved in a low-class democracy, which seems as though it must of its very nature extinguish any kind of noble training. The principle that society exists solely through the well-being and the personal liberty of all the individuals of which it is composed does not appear to be conformable to the plans of nature, in whose workings the race alone seems to be taken into consideration, and the individual sacrificed to it. It is greatly to be feared that the last stage of such a conception of democracy (though I must hasten to point out that the term "democracy" may be interpreted in various ways) would end in a condition of society in which a degenerate herd would have no other preoccupation but the satisfaction of the lowest desires of common men." Thus Renan. Fascism denies, in democracy, the absurd conventional untruth of political equality dressed out in the garb of collective irresponsibility, and the myth of "happiness" and indefinite progress. But, if democracy may be conceived in diverse forms—that is to say, taking democracy to mean a state of society in which the populace are not reduced to impotence in the State—Fascism may write itself down as "an organized, centralized and authoritative democracy."

Fascism has taken up an attitude of complete opposition to the doctrines of Liberalism, both in the political field and the field of economics. There should be no undue exaggeration (simply with the object of immediate success in controversy) of the importance of Liberalism in the last century, nor should what was but one among many theories which appeared in that period be put forward as a religion for humanity for all time, present and to come. Liberalism only flourished for half a century …

The era of Liberalism, after having accumulated an infinity of Gordian knots, tried to untie them in the slaughter of the World War—and never has any religion demanded of its votaries such a monstrous sacrifice. Perhaps the Liberal Gods were athirst for blood? But now, to-day, the Liberal faith must shut the doors of its deserted temples, deserted because the peoples of the world realize that its worship—agnostic in the field of economics and indifferent in the field of politics and morals—will lead, as it has already led, to certain ruin. In addition to this, let it be pointed out that all the political hopes of the present day are anti-Liberal, and it is therefore supremely ridiculous to try to classify this sole creed as outside the judgment of history, as though history were a hunting ground reserved for the professors of Liberalism alone—as though Liberalism were the final unalterable verdict of civilization.

But the Fascist negation of Socialism, Democracy and Liberalism must not be taken to mean that Fascism desires to lead the world back to the state of affairs before 1789, the date which seems to be indicated as the opening years of the succeeding semi-Liberal century: we do not desire to turn back; Fascism has not chosen De Maistre for its high-priest. Absolute monarchy has been and can never return, any more than blind acceptance of ecclesiastical authority …

The foundation of Fascism is the conception of the State, its character, its duty, and its aim. Fascism conceives of the State as an absolute, in comparison with which all individuals or groups are relative, only to be conceived of in their relation to the State. The conception of the Liberal State is not that of a directing force, guiding the play and development, both material and spiritual, of a collective body, but merely a force limited to the function of recording results: on the other hand, the Fascist State is itself conscious, and has itself a will and a personality—thus it may be called the "ethic" State. In 1929, at the first five-yearly assembly of the Fascist regime, I said:

> For us Fascists, the State is not merely a guardian, preoccupied solely with the duty of assuring the personal safety of the citizens; nor is it an organization with purely material aims, such as to guarantee a certain level of well-being and peaceful conditions of life; for a mere council of administration would be sufficient to realize such objects. Nor is it a purely political creation, divorced from all contact with the complex material reality which makes up the life of the individual and the life of the people as a whole. The State, as conceived of and as created by Fascism, is a spiritual and moral fact in itself, since its political, juridical and economic organization of the nation is a concrete thing: and such an organization must be in its origins and development a manifestation of the spirit. The State is the guarantor of security both internal and external, but it is also the custodian and transmitter of the spirit of the people, as it has grown up through the

centuries in language, in customs and in faith. And the State is not only a living reality of the present, it is also linked with the past and above all with the future, and thus transcending the brief limits of individual life, it represents the immanent spirit of the nation. The forms in which States express themselves may change, but the necessity for such forms is eternal. It is the State which educated its citizens in civic virtue, gives them a consciousness of their mission and welds them into unity; harmonizing their various interests through justice, and transmitting to future generations the mental conquests of science, of art, of law and the solidarity of humanity. It leads men from primitive tribal life to that highest expression of human power which is Empire: it links up through the centuries the names of those of its members who have died for its existence and in obedience to its laws, it holds up the memory of the leaders who have increased its territory and the geniuses who have illumined it with glory as an example to be followed by future generations. When the conception of the State declines, and disunifying and centrifugal tendencies prevail, whether of individuals or of particular groups, the nations where such phenomena appear are in their decline …

The Fascist State is not indifferent to the fact of religion in general, or to that particular and positive faith which is Italian Catholicism. The State professes no theology, but a morality, and in the Fascist State religion is considered as one of the deepest manifestations of the spirit of man, thus it is not only respected but defended and protected. The Fascist State has never tried to create its own God, as at one moment Robespierre and the wildest extremists of the Convention tried to do; nor does it vainly seek to obliterate religion from the hearts of men as does Bolshevism: Fascism respects the God of the ascetics, the saints and heroes, and equally, God as He is perceived and worshipped by simple people.

The Fascist State is an embodied will to power and government: The Roman tradition is here an ideal of force in action. According to Fascism, government is not so much a thing to be expressed in territorial or military terms as in terms of morality and the spirit. It

must be thought of as an Empire—that is to say, a nation which directly or indirectly rules other nations, without the need for conquering a single square yard of territory. For Fascism, the growth of Empire, that is to say the expansion of the nation, is an essential manifestation of vitality, and its opposite a sign of decadence. Peoples which are rising, or rising again after a period of decadence, are always imperialist; any renunciation is a sign of decay and of death. Fascism is the doctrine best adapted to represent the tendencies and the aspirations of a people, like the people of Italy, who are rising again after many centuries of abasement and foreign servitude. But Empire demands discipline, the co-ordination of all forces and a deeply-felt sense of duty and sacrifice; this fact explains many aspects of the practical working of the regime, the character of many forces in the State, and the necessarily severe measures which must be taken against those who would oppose this spontaneous and inevitable movement of Italy in the twentieth century, and would oppose it by recalling the outworn ideology of the nineteenth century—repudiated wheresoever there has been the courage to undertake great experiments of social and political transformation: for never before has the nation stood more in need of authority, of direction and of order. If every age has its own characteristic doctrine, there are a thousand signs which point to Fascism as the characteristic doctrine of our time. For if a doctrine must be a living thing, this is proved by the fact that Fascism has created a living faith; and that this faith is very powerful in the minds of men, is demonstrated by those who have suffered and died for it.

Fascism has henceforth in the world the universality of all those doctrines which, in realizing themselves, have represented a stage in the history of the human spirit.

Source: Benito Mussolini. *The Political and Social Doctrines of Fascism.* Translated by J. Soames. London: Hogarth Press, 1933. Reprinted with the permission of the estate of Benito Mussolini and the Hogarth Press.

The Twenty-Five Points

Adolf Hitler

ADOLF HITLER *(1889-1945) was the leader of Germany during the Third Reich (1933-1945). He was a skillful orator. He wrote* Mein Kampf *while in prison for his attempting to overthrow the Government of Germany in 1923.*

The Twenty-Five Points of the German Workers' Party, 1920[1]

The program of the German Workers' Party is limited as to period. The leaders have no intention, once the aims announced in it have been achieved, of setting up fresh ones, merely in order to increase the discontent of the masses artificially, and so ensure the continued existence of the party.

1. We demand the union of all Germans to form a Great Germany on the basis of the right of self-determination enjoyed by nations.

2. We demand equality of rights for the German people in its dealings with other nations, and abolition of the peace treaties of Versailles and Saint-Germain.

3. We demand land and territory (colonies) for the nourishment of our people and for settling our excess population.

4. None but members of the nation may be citizens of the state. None but those of German blood, whatever their creed, may be members of the nation. No Jew, therefore, may be a member of the nation.

5. Anyone who is not a citizen of the state may live in Germany only as a guest and must be regarded as being subject to foreign laws.

6. The right of voting on the leadership and legislation is to be enjoyed by the state alone. We demand therefore that all official appointments, of whatever kind, whether in the Reich, in the country, or in the smaller localities, shall be granted to citizens of the state alone. We oppose the corrupting custom of Parliament of filling posts merely with a view to party considerations, and without reference to character or capacity.

7. We demand that the state shall make it its first duty to promote the industry and livelihood of citizens of the state. If it is not possible to nourish the entire population of the state, foreign nationals (non-citizens of the state) must be excluded from the Reich.

8. All non-German immigration must be prevented …

9. All citizens of the state shall be equal as regards rights and duties.

10. It must be the first duty of each citizen of the state to work with his mind or with his body. The activities of the individual may not clash with the interests of the whole, but must proceed within the frame of the community and be for the general good.

We demand therefore:

11. Abolition of incomes unearned by work.

12. In view of the enormous sacrifice of life and property demanded of a nation by every war, personal enrichment due to a war must be regarded as a crime against the nation. We demand therefore ruthless confiscation of all war gains.

13. We demand nationalization of all businesses (trusts) …

14. We demand that the profits from wholesale trade shall be shared.

15. We demand extensive development of provision for old age.

16. We demand creation and maintenance of a healthy middle class, immediate communalization of wholesale business premises, and their lease at a cheap rate to small traders, and that extreme consideration shall be shown to all small purveyors to the state, district authorities, and smaller localities.

17. We demand land reform suitable to our national requirements …

18. We demand ruthless prosecution of those whose activities are injurious to the common interest. Sordid criminals against the nation, usurers, profiteers, etc., must be punished with death, whatever their creed or race.

19. We demand that the Roman Law, which serves the materialistic world order, shall be replaced by a legal system for all Germany.

20. With the aim of opening to every capable and industrious German the possibility of higher education and of thus obtaining advancement, the state must consider a thorough reconstruction of our national system of education …

ADOLF HITLER (1889–1945)

ADOLF HITLER is indelibly stamped into history as the founder and leader of German Nazism, but he was in fact born in Austria. His early ambitions to become a painter were frustrated when he failed to gain admission to the Vienna Academy in 1907 and 1908. Some historians have argued that the leadership and rank and file of the National Socialist German Workers' Party (NSDAP), commonly known in English as the "Nazi" party tended to be frustrated, self-taught, pseudo-intellectuals who found their main ambitions in life somehow thwarted. After his rejection from painting school, Hitler lived an impoverished existence in Vienna, during which time he read extensively in the anti-semitic and racist literature that was beginning to become popular in Austria.

After serving in World War One and attaining the rank of corporal, Hitler joined and eventually took control of the German Workers' Party, which he renamed the *Nationalsozialistiche Deutsche Arbeiterpartei*. After an unsuccessful attempt to take

control of the German government in Munich in 1923, Hitler was imprisoned and began writing *Mein Kampf*, which became a virtual guidebook of Nazism. This book expanded Hitler's racial theories which at their core stressed the superiority of the "Aryan" race while denigrating the supposedly conspiratorial and exploitive Jews. Re-establishment of German purity was, according to Hitler, necessary to rebuild a nation that was still reeling from the effects of the First World War.

By 1932, the NSDAP had become the largest party in Ger-

many due mainly to the appeal that Hitler's ideology had on a people hit hard by economic depression. His appeal to a national myth of superiority combined with the creation of a ready-made racial scapegoat allowed Hitler to gain 37% of the popular vote in the 1932 presidential election. In 1933, he became Chancellor of Germany. During his reign as Chancellor, the *Führer* combined brutal repression at home with a systematic program of imperial aggression that eventually led to the outbreak of World War Two. Extermination of Jews and other "undesirables" within Germany while invading first parts of Eastern and Central Europe and later Western Europe were the beginnings of Hitler's plan to strengthen the racial purity and the territorial holdings of the "Third Reich." The eventual defeat of the Nazis by the Allied forces, however, thwarted Hitler's ambition of a thousand-year reign for the Aryan race, and led ultimately to his suicide in Berlin in 1945.

---

21. The state must see to raising the standard of health in the nation by protecting mothers and infants, prohibiting child labor, increasing bodily efficiency by obligatory gymnastics and sports laid down by law, and by extensive support of clubs engaged in the bodily development of the young.

22. We demand abolition of a paid army and formation of a national army.

23. We demand legal warfare against conscious political lying and its dissemination in the press. In order to facilitate creation of a German national press we demand: a) that all editors of newspapers and their

assistants, employing the German language, must be members of the nation; b) that special permission from the state shall be necessary before non-German newspapers may appear. These are not necessarily printed in the German language; c) that non-Germans shall be prohibited by law from participation financially in or influencing German newspapers …

It must be forbidden to publish papers which do not conduce to the national welfare. We demand legal prosecution of all tendencies in art and literature of a kind likely to disintegrate our life as a nation, and the suppression of institutions which militate against the requirements above-mentioned.

24. We demand liberty for all religious denominations in the state, so far as they are not a danger to it and do not militate against the moral feelings of the German race.

The party, as such, stands for positive Christianity, but does not bind itself in the matter of creed to any particular confession. It combats the Jewish-materialist spirit within us and without us …

25. That all the foregoing may be realized we demand the creation of a strong central power of the state. Unquestioned authority of the politically centralized Parliament over the entire Reich and its organizations; and formation of chambers for classes and occupations for the purpose of carrying out the general laws promulgated by the Reich in the various states of the confederation.

The leaders of the party swear to go straight forward—if necessary to sacrifice their lives—in securing fulfillment of the foregoing points.

Source: Adolf Hitler. *The Twenty-Five Points.* Originally published in 1920.

Notes

[1] Ed. note: the content of this speech was prepared by Anton Drexler, Gottfried Eckart, and Adolf Hitler. The speech was delivered February 24, 1920, and proclaimed the following day. In August of the same year the name of the party was changed to the National Socialist German Workers' Party.

The Final Solution: Killing

Hannah Arendt

HANNAH ARENDT *(1906-) was a political scientist and philosopher who was born in Germany and studied under Karl Jaspers in Switzerland. In 1941 she emigrated to the USA and became a citizen of that country in 1951. She was a visiting professor at several universities in the USA and wrote extensively in opposition to facism. Her works include* Origins of Totalitarianism (1951) *and* The Human Condition (1958).

Hannah Arendt

On June 22, 1941, Hitler launched his attack on the Soviet Union, and six or eight weeks later Eichmann was summoned to Heydrich's office in Berlin. On July 31, Heydrich had received a letter from Reichsmarschall Hermann Göring, Commander-in-Chief of the Air Force, Prime Minister of Prussia, Plenipotentiary for the Four-Year-Plan, and, last but not least, Hitler's Deputy in the State (as distinguished from the Party) hierarchy. The letter commissioned Heydrich to prepare "the general solution *[Gesamtlösung]* of the Jewish question within the area of German influence in Europe," and to submit "a general proposal ... for the implementation of the desired final solution *[Endlösung]* of the Jewish question." At the time Heydrich received these instructions, he had already been—as he was to explain to the High Command of the Army in a letter dated November 6, 1941—"entrusted for years with the task of preparing the final solution of the Jewish problem" (Reitlinger), and since the beginning of the war with Russia, he had been in charge of the mass killings by the *Einsatzgruppen* in the East.

Heydrich opened his interview with Eichmann with "a little speech about emigration" (which had practically ceased, though Himmler's formal order prohibiting all Jewish emigration except in special cases, to be passed upon by him personally, was not issued until a few months later), and then said: *"The Führer has ordered the physical extermination of the Jews."* After which, "very much against his habits, he remained silent for a long while, as though he wanted to test the impact of his words. I remember it even today. In the first moment, I was unable to grasp the significance of what he had said, because he was so careful in choosing his words, and then I understood, and didn't say anything, because there was nothing to say any more. For I had never thought of such a

thing, such a solution through violence. I now lost everything, all joy in my work, all initiative, all interest; I was, so to speak, blown out. And then he told me: 'Eichmann, you go and see Globocnik [one of Himmler's Higher S.S. and Police Leaders in the General Government] in Lublin, the Reichsführer [Himmler] has already given him the necessary orders, have a look at what he has accomplished in the meantime. I think he uses the Russian tank trenches for the liquidation of the Jews.' I still remember that, for I'll never forget it no matter how long I live, those sentences he said during that interview, which was already at an end." Actually—as Eichmann still remembered in Argentina but had forgotten in Jerusalem, much to his disadvantage, since it had bearing on the question of his own authority in the actual killing process—Heydrich had said a little more: he had told Eichmann that the whole enterprise had been "put under the authority of the S.S. Head Office for Economy and Administration"—that is, not of his own R.S.H.A.—and also that the official code name for extermination was to be "Final Solution."

Eichmann was by no means among the first to be informed of Hitler's intention. We have seen that Heydrich had been working in this direction for years, presumably since the beginning of the war, and Himmler claimed to have been told (and to have protested against) this "solution" immediately after the defeat of France in the summer of 1940. By March,

1941, about six months before Eichmann had his interview with Heydrich, "it was no secret in higher Party circles that the Jews were to be exterminated," as Viktor Brack, of the Führer's Chancellery, testified at Nuremberg. But Eichmann, as he vainly tried to explain in Jerusalem, had never belonged to the higher Party circles; he had never been told more than he needed to know in order to do a specific, limited job. It is true that he was one of the first men in the lower echelons to be informed of this "top secret" matter, which remained top secret even after the news had spread throughout all the Party and State offices, all business enterprises connected with slave labor, and the entire officer corps (at the very least) of the Armed Forces. Still, the secrecy did have a practical purpose. Those, who were told explicitly of the Führer's order were no longer mere "bearers of orders," but were advanced to "bearers of secrets," and a special oath was administered to them. (The members of the Security Service, to which Eichmann had belonged since 1934, had in any case taken an oath of secrecy.)

Furthermore, all correspondence referring to the matter was subject to rigid "language rules," and, except in the reports from the *Einsatzgruppen,* it is rare to find documents in which such bald words as "extermination," "liquidation," or "killing" occur. The prescribed code names for killing were "final solution," "evacuation" *(Aussiedlung),* and "special treatment" *(Sonderbehandlung);* deportation—unless it involved Jews directed to Theresienstadt, the "old people's ghetto" for privileged Jews, in which case it was called "change of residence"—received the names of "resettlement" *(Umsiedlung)* and "labor in the East" *(Arbeitseinsatz im Osten),* the point of these latter names being that Jews were indeed often temporarily resettled in ghettos and that a certain percentage of them were temporarily used for labor. Under special circumstances, slight changes in the language rules became necessary. Thus, for instance, a high official in the Foreign Office once proposed that in all correspondence with the Vatican the killing of Jews be called the "radical solution;" this was ingenious, because the Catholic puppet government of Slovakia, with which the Vatican had intervened, had not been, in the view of the Nazis, "radical enough" in its anti-Jewish legislation, having committed the "basic error" of excluding baptized Jews. Only among themselves could the "bearers of secrets" talk in uncoded language, and it is very unlikely that they did so in the ordinary pursuit of their murderous duties—certainly not in the presence of their stenographers and other office personnel. For whatever other reasons the language rules may have been devised, they proved of enormous help in the maintenance of order and sanity in the various widely diversified services whose cooperation was essential in this matter. Moreover, the very term "language rule" *(Sprachregelung)* was itself a code name; it meant what in ordinary language would be called a lie. For when a "bearer of secrets" was sent to meet someone from the outside world—as when Eichmann was sent to show the Theresienstadt ghetto to International Red Cross representatives from Switzerland—he received, together with his orders, his "language rule," which in this instance consisted of a lie about a nonexistent typhus epidemic in the concentration camp of Bergen-Belsen, which the gentlemen also wished to visit. The net effect of this language system was not to keep these people ignorant of what they were doing, but to prevent them from equating it with their old, "normal" knowledge of murder and lies. Eichmann's great susceptibility to catch words and stock phrases, combined with his incapacity for ordinary speech, made him, of course, an ideal subject for "language rules."

The system, however, was not a foolproof shield against reality, as Eichmann was soon to find out. He went to Lublin to see Brigadeführer Odilo Globocnik, former Gauleiter of Vienna—though not, of course, despite what the prosecution maintained, "to convey to him personally the secret order for the physical extermination of the Jews," which Globocnik certainly knew of before Eichmann did—and he used the phrase "Final Solution" as a kind of password by which to identify himself. (A similar assertion by the prosecution, which showed to what degree it had got lost in the bureaucratic labyrinth of the Third Reich, referred to Rudolf Höss, Commander of Auschwitz, who it believed had also received the Führer's order through Eichmann. This error was at least mentioned by the defense as being "without corroborative evidence." Actually, Höss himself testified at his own trial that he had received his orders directly from Himmler, in June, 1941, and added that Himmler had told him Eichmann would discuss with him certain "details." These details, Höss claimed in his memoirs, concerned the use of gas—something Eichmann strenuously denied. And he was probably right, for all other sources contradict Höss's story and maintain that written or oral extermination orders in the camps always went through the W.V.H.A. and were given either by its chief, Obergruppenführer [lieutenant general] Oswald Pohl, or by Brigadeführer Richard Glöcks, who was Höss's direct superior. And with the use of gas Eichmann had nothing whatever to do. The "details" that he went to discuss with Höss at regular intervals concerned the killing capacity of the camp—how many shipments per week it could absorb and also, perhaps, plans for expansion.) Globocnik, when Eichmann arrived at Lublin, was very obliging, and showed him around with a subordinate. They came to a road through a forest, to the right of which there was an ordinary house where workers lived. A captain of the Order Police (perhaps Kriminalkommissar Christian Wirth himself, who had been in charge of the technical side of the gassing of "incurably sick people" in Germany, under the auspices of the Führer's Chancellery) came to greet them, led them to a few small wooden bungalows, and began, "in a vulgar uneducated harsh voice," his explanations: "how he had everything nicely insulated, for the engine of a Russian submarine will be set to work and the gases will enter this building and the Jews will be poisoned. For me, too, this was monstrous. I am not so tough as to be able to endure something of this sort without any reaction … If today I am shown a gaping wound, I can't possibly look at it. I am that type of person, so that very often I was told that I couldn't have become a doctor. I still remember how I pictured the thing to myself, and then I became physically weak, as though I had lived through some great agitation. Such things happen to everybody, and it left behind a certain inner trembling."

Well, he had been lucky, for he had still seen only the preparations for the future carbon-monoxide chambers at Treblinka, one of the six death camps in the East, in which several hundred thousand people were to die. Shortly after this, in the autumn of the same year, he was sent by his direct superior Müller to inspect the killing center in the Western Regions of Poland that had been incorporated into the Reich, called the Warthegau. The death camp was at Kulm (or, in Polish, Chelmno), where, in 1944, over three hundred thousand Jews from all over Europe, who had first been "resettled" in the Lódz ghetto, were killed. Here things were already in full swing, but the method was different; instead of gas chambers, mobile gas vans were used. This is what Eichmann saw: The Jews were in a large room; they were told to strip; then a truck arrived, stopping directly before the entrance to the room, and the naked Jews were told to enter it. The doors were closed and the truck started off. "I cannot tell [how many Jews entered], I hardly looked. I could not; I could not; I had had enough. The shrieking, and … I was much too upset, and so on, as I later told Müller when I reported to him; he did not get much profit out of my report. I then drove along after the van, and then I saw the most horrible sight I had thus far seen in my life. The truck was making for an open ditch, the doors were opened, and the corpses were thrown out, as though they were still alive, so smooth were their limbs. They were hurled into the ditch, and I can still see a civilian extracting the teeth with tooth plyers. And then I was off—jumped into my car and did not open my mouth any more. After that time, I could sit for hours beside my driver without exchanging a word with him. There I got enough. I was finished. I only remember that a physician in white overalls told me to look through a hole into the truck while they were still in it. I refused to do that. I could not. I had to disappear."

Very soon after that, he was to see something more horrible. This happened when he was sent to Minsk, in White Russia, again by Müller, who told him: "In Minsk, they are killing Jews by shooting. I want you to report on how it is being done." So he went, and at first it seemed as though he would be lucky, for by the time he arrived, as it happened, "the affair had almost been finished," which pleased him very much. "There were only a few young marksmen who took aim at the skulls of dead people in a large ditch." Still, he saw, "and that was quite enough for me, a woman with her arms stretched backward, and then my knees went weak and off I went." While driving back, he had the notion of stopping at Lwów; this seemed a good idea, for Lwów (or Lemberg) had been an Austrian city, and when he arrived there he "saw the first friendly picture after the horrors. That was the railway station built in honor of the sixtieth year of Franz Josef's reign"—a period Eichmann had always "adored," since he had heard so many nice things about it in his parents' home, and had also been told how the relatives of his stepmother (we are made to understand that he meant the Jewish ones) had enjoyed a comfortable social status and had made good money. This sight of the railway station drove away all the horrible thoughts, and he remembered it down to its last detail—the engraved year of the anniversary, for instance. But then, right there in lovely Lwów, he made a big mistake. He went to see the local S.S. commander, and told him: "Well, it is horrible what is being done around here; I said young people are being made into sadists. How can one do that? Simply bang away at women and children? That is impossible. Our people will go mad or become insane, our own people." The trouble was that in Lwów they were doing the same thing they had been doing in Minsk, and his host was delighted to show him the sights, although Eichmann tried politely to excuse himself. Thus, he saw another "horrible sight. A ditch had been there, which was already filled in. And there was, gushing from the earth, a spiling of blood like a fountain. Such a thing I had never seen before. I had had enough of my commission, and I went back to Berlin and reported to Gruppenführer Müller."

This was not yet the end. Although Eichmann told him that he was not "tough enough" for these sights, that he had never been a soldier, had never been to the front, had never seen action, that he could not sleep and had nightmares, Müller, some nine months later, sent him back to the Lublin region, where the very enthusiastic Globocnik had meanwhile finished his preparations. Eichmann said that this now was the most horrible thing he had ever seen in his life. When he first arrived, he could not recognize the place, with its few wooden bungalows. Instead, guided by the same man with the vulgar voice, he came to a railway station, with the sign "Treblinka" on it, that looked exactly like an ordinary station anywhere in Germany—the same buildings, signs, clocks, installations; it was a perfect imitation. "I kept myself back, as far as I could, I did not draw near to see all that. Still, I saw how a column of naked Jews filed into a large hall to be gassed. There they were killed, as I was told, by something called cyanic acid."

The fact is that Eichmann did not see much. It is true, he repeatedly visited Auschwitz, the largest and most famous of the death camps, but Auschwitz, covering an area of eighteen square miles, in Upper Silesia, was by no means only an extermination camp; it was a huge enterprise with up to a hundred thousand inmates, and all kinds of prisoners were held there, including non-Jews and slave laborers, who were not subject to gassing. It was easy to avoid the killing installations, and Höss, with whom he had a very friendly relationship, spared him the gruesome sights. He never actually attended a mass execution by shooting, he never actually watched the gassing process, or the selection of those fit for work—about twenty-five per cent, of each shipment, on the average—that preceded it at Auschwitz. He saw just enough to be fully informed of how the destruction machinery worked: that there were two different methods of killing, shooting and gassing; that the shooting was done by the *Einsatzgruppen* and the gassing at the camps, either in chambers or in mobile vans; and that in the camps elaborate precautions were taken to fool the victims right up to the end.

The police tapes from which I have quoted were played in court during the tenth of the trial's hundred and twenty-one sessions, on the ninth day of the almost nine months it lasted. Nothing the accused said, in the curiously disembodied voice that came out of the tape-recorder—doubly disembodied, because the body that owned the voice was present but itself also appeared strangely disembodied through the thick glass walls surrounding it—was denied either by him or by the defense. Dr. Servatius did not object, he only mentioned that "later, when the defense will rise to speak," he, too, would submit to the court some of the evidence given by the accused to the police; he never did. The defense, one felt, could rise right away, for the criminal proceedings against the accused in this "historic trial" seemed complete, the case for the prosecution established. The facts of the case, of what Eichmann had done—though not of everything the prosecution wished he had done— were never in dispute; they had been established long before the trial started, and had been confessed to by him over and over again. There was more than enough, as he occasionally pointed out, to hang him. ("Don't you have enough on me?" he objected, when the police examiner tried to ascribe to him powers he never possessed.) But since he had been employed in transportation and not in killing, the question remained, legally, formally, at least, of whether he had known what he was doing; and there was the additional question of whether he had been in a position to judge the enormity of his deeds—whether he was legally responsible, apart from the fact that he was medically sane. Both questions now were answered in the affirmative: he had seen the places to which the shipments were directed, and he had been shocked out of his wits. One last question, the most disturbing of all, was asked by the judges, and especially by the presiding judge, over and over again: Had the killing of Jews gone against his conscience? But this was a moral question, and the answer to it may not have been legally relevant.

Source: Hannah Arendt. *Eichmann in Jerusalem: A Report on the Banality of Evil.* New York: Viking, 1963. Copyright © 1963, 1964 by Hanna Arendt. Used by permission of Viking Penguin, a division of Penguin Books USA Inc.

The Psychological Basis of Fascism

Roger Griffin

ROGER GRIFFIN *is Senior Lecturer in the History of Ideas at Oxford Brookes University.*

The Human Need for Self-Transcendence

To simplify crudely Koestler's subtly argued and extensively documented contention, human beings are endowed with two basic drives, that of self-assertiveness and the opposite one of self-transcendence, which enable them to be both autonomous individuals and members of a social hierarchy such as the family or the tribe. A healthy relationship with the world in all its aspects, that is one based on harmony and creative symbiosis with it rather than possessive or destructive urges towards it, depends on a delicate balance of the two drives which allows people to experience themselves simultaneously as unique, independent personalities and as integral parts of larger social entities, both equally vital for the continued dynamism and cohesion of all human societies. However, because of the "paranoid", "delusional" streak in the human make-up, both the self-assertive and self-transcendent drives can assume a pathological aspect when they take on an obsessive, nihilistic form inconsistent with the demands of survival and irrespective of the damage they inflict on fellow creatures. Ironically, it is the perversion of self-transcendent emotions, not self-assertive ones, which has been largely responsible for the chronicle of atrocities which human beings have inflicted on each other down through the ages because they allow the perpetrators of "inhuman" deeds to act not on their own behalf but as subordinate parts of a hierarchy, whether human or metaphysical, which absolves them of personal responsibility and invests their actions with sense of fulfilling a "higher" purpose or mission. ...

The Psychological Dynamics of Fascism

What this rampant syncretism boils down to in relation to the psychological foundations of fascism is that the affective basis of all ideologies can be located in a perennial neuro-psychological human drive to find a sense of belonging. This drive is fulfilled through the medium of myths capable of providing a powerful experience of self-transcendence which immunizes people from the sense of isolation, impotence and absurdity which might otherwise engulf them. It is this drive which underlies the complex cosmologies which have been a defining feature of the countless cultures created by human communities since time immemorial, as well as the elaborate metaphysical legends and rituals which have always underpinned them. In modern (that is partially secularized and pluralistic) culture there is no longer any central all-pervasive source of transcendent myth. Since, as T.S. Eliot observed, "human beings cannot bear too much reality", the need for transcendence has come to express itself in contemporary society through myriad personal and communal forms of cultic behaviour, including the conversion to one of the scores of belief systems, religious and nonreligious, now on offer.

In *Equus* Peter Shaffer explored the way individuals can even be driven by the need for self-transcendence to create a personal religion. In it he dramatized the story of a psychologist, Dysart, who is called upon to "cure" Alan Strang of the private horse cult he has evolved. Dysart comes to recognize its psychic source to be the same mythic energy that had created the Greek legend of the centaurs and permeated the civilization whose greatness he vainly attempts to recapture through the experiences of the tourist on summer holiday in the Aegean. The sessions with Strang leave him tormented by the impoverishment of his own experience of the numinous and anguished at the ambiguity of the bland, magic-less (or to use Weber's term, "disenchanted") normality into which his professional skill is meant to seduce those living in a painful but intensely real delusional world of their own. The implication is that the countless idiosyncratic complexes and fixations known to abnormal psychology as forms of madness are fuelled by the same archaic psychic energy that, channelled through a communal cosmology and ritual, guarantees the cohesion of all so-called "primitive" societies. At the same time the play suggests that a rational existence bereft of the direct experience of that energy is the world of greatness punctuated by the *Angst* explored by existentialist philosophers and artists.

In modem anomic or "centre-less" society the communal aspect of myth is by its very nature more conspicuous, though not necessarily more prevalent than the private one, providing the raw material of a mass culture and a media age dominated by fashion, consumerism, spectator sports, and soap operas, and susceptible to the latest equivalents of the seventeenth century tulip craze in Holland such as skateboarding, aerobics or Madonna-mania. The continuous "manufacture of myth" is as important to the cohesion and stability of modern society as the "manufacture of consensus". With mythic energies no longer securely invested in a cohesive religious or ethnic culture, they move freely around social space like petrodollars, available to fund new sub-cultures such as the student and Hippy movements of the sixties, and the "skinhead" or "new age" movements of the eighties. It is in political ideologies, however, that mythic energies have the greatest power for effecting social and historical change, and where the distinction between integration and identification with the community of fellow-believers becomes crucial in the potential for inhumanity and destruction they unleash.

It follows from this analysis that the psychological precondition for the ideology of fascism to be espoused with a degree of genuine affective commitment is *an individual's need for self-transcendent myth which, in the "right" historical circumstances, is satisfied by one centred on the reborn nation.* We will consider more closely what constitutes such circumstances in the next chapter. For now it is enough to say that this particular form of identification can only take place in a society where secularization, populist nationalism and a plurality of values and ideologies are already well established and where the life of the nation can be subjectively perceived as undergoing a profound crisis. In a minority of cases the individual's sense of external social or historical crisis may be practically autogenic (self-induced), the externalization of a defective capacity for individuation and integration with few apparent objective triggers. But clearly for the experience of dysfunction to trigger the rise of a mass movement it needs to be concretized in major upheavals in contemporary history which affect society as a whole (for example a power vacuum, civil war, economic breakdown). This then constitutes the "situationally produced chaos" (Platt, 1980, p.83) which may undermine a person's material and psychological security, and hence sense of self, to a point where he (for it is a predominantly masculine syndrome: see Milfull, 1990) becomes inwardly available to an ideology of national regeneration which offers "both an explanation of the failure and a reason for hope" and hence "a renewed sense of meaning in the world" (Platt, 1980, p.83). This cannot occur if he is already "booked by", or predisposed to take refuge in, another mythic scheme, whether this is a religious or ethical value-system or a competing ideology, or if he is sufficiently tough-minded (integrated, individuated, in existentialist terms "authentic") to cope with the nomic crisis and the distress it causes without resorting to such a mythic panacea.

The committed fascist is thus someone who has resolved his "sense-making crisis", whether objective or subjective, by projecting the experience of chaos and longing for a feeling of wholeness and meaning on to external reality so that it is the nation which he experiences as sick and the nation which is to be healed. Were he psychically healthy he would surmount the crisis by creating a new *psychological* order for himself in which he would become the hero of his inner life and achieve spiritual self control, self-knowledge and freedom, whatever the physical and material privations he is exposed to. Instead, he wants to play a heroic role in public life by participating in the foundation of a new *social and political order* under the aegis of a national leader-figure, one who has total certainty of the mission history has assigned "his" people. In this way he seeks to be fully relieved of the burden of individualism and freedom altogether (that is he does not, like Mussolini and Hitler, arrogate the historic role of leader to himself and thus find an even more radical solution to his crisis of identity). Rather than search for a new level of consciousness, for mystic reawakening, for a personal "Buddha experience" (in Sanskrit Buddha connotes being "awoken") to rise above the vicissitudes of material and temporal existence, the fascist craves for "the people" to be stirred from "their" sleeping sickness, a hope embodied in the Nazi slogan *Deutschland erwache,* Germany Awake!

The psycho-historical dynamics of this situation as it manifested itself in the early Weimar Republic were explored with remarkable lucidity by Broch in his novel, *The Sleepwalkers.* Published in 1932 this trilogy portrays the life of three contrasting characters, the romantic Pasenow, the anarchist Esch and the realist Hugenau, each one emblematic of the reactions of a different generation to the progressive "decay of values" which, as Broch argues in a lengthy excursus of that name interpolated into the narrative, set in with the Renaissance but which reached crisis point (in Europe) between 1888 and 1918. Broch's central theme is the way the inexorable breakdown of the absolute system of meaning, the erosion of the mythopoeic centre, once provided by the Christian church, has produced in the mass of ordinary citizens of the modern age a profound sense of isolation, "for the speech of the old community life has failed them".

The acute personal disorientation which this causes makes them strive continually "to find a haven in some partial system" of values, each one of which fuses its own logical premises with irrational energies and aspires to become a total, absolute truth to provide a bulwark against the definitive disintegration of nomic principles. The distressing experience of the "icy breath sweeping over the world, freezing it to rigidity and withering all meaning out of the things of the world", has turned the individual into a sleep-walker groping his way through a reality which is becoming increasingly unintelligible, and has made him "defenceless before the invasion of the irrational", or the "irruption from below" in the form of spontaneous conversion to one of these partial (mythic) systems. It was this peculiar cultural climate of nomic crisis, radicalized by the cataclysm of the First World War, which bred in Weimar Germany the conditions for revolution, revolution which represents "that act of self-elimination and self-renewal, the last and greatest ethical achievement of the old disintegrating system and the first achievement of the new, the moment when time is annulled and history radically formed in the heightened emotional climate of absolute zero!" (Broch, 1964, pp.631-48).

These conditions of acute psychological and epistemological crisis arouse in the man "who becomes aware of his isolation" a "doubly strong yearning for a Leader to take him tenderly and lightly by the hand, to set things in order and show him the way ... the Leader who will build the house anew that the dead may come to life again ... the Healer who by his actions will give meaning to the incomprehensible events of the Age, so that Time can begin again" (ibid., p.647). With the subtlety and emotional intensity that can only be communicated in art, Broch thus suggests that the psychological bases of Nazism (and hence of generic fascism) lie in an intense longing for rebirth projected on to a revolutionary nationalist movement.

The same conclusion has been arrived at on the basis of entirely different methodological premises and in a quite different register by Theweleit's case study of several individuals who played an active part in German protofascism (1987, 1989). Theweleit documents his highly individual investigation of the fascist mentality with the *memoirs,* diaries and letters of several members of the *Freikorps* (one of whom, Höss, later became commandant of Auschwitz) and supplements these with the literary expressions of "soldierly nationalism" bequeathed by Ernst Jünger, Franz Schauwecker and Ernst von Salomon, as well as with Goebbels' novel *Michael*. Using a highly syncretic psychoanalytical model of the mechanisms which allow individuals to form a dynamic relationship with external reality, Theweleit explores the inner compulsions which motivated his sample of proto-fascist and future fascist activists to volunteer in the aftermath of 1918, thereby taking the nationalists' battle against communism into their own hands. He argues that in each case there is evidence that a particular syndrome was at work: the process of "separation-individuation" had been disrupted in childhood, leaving the person trapped in a state of consciousness which precluded a healthy relationship between a "whole ego and a whole other", so that,

psychologically speaking, they were "not-yet-fully-born". This induced not only an urge to turn their body into a (military) machine so as to tame the chaotic inner world of instincts and emotions but a radical misogyny or flight from the feminine, manifesting itself in a pathological fear of being engulfed by anything in external reality associated with softness, with dissolution, with the uncontrollable.

The result of this syndrome is the "soldier-male", driven by a longing to transcend the hell of his private self in a collective struggle against an inner chaos which has been projected on to society. At this point the mainstream of the fascist's affective energy becomes channelled into the fight for victory over the perceived agents of the nation's dissolution which would represent the final completion of his birth into the world:

> The texts of the soldier males perpetually revolve around the same axes: the communality of the male society, non-female creation, rebirth, the rise upward to hardness and tension ... The man is released from a world that is rotten and sinking (from the morass of femaleness): he finally dissolves in battle. (Theweleit, 1989, p.361)

According to Theweleit it is this drive which promoted the violent reaction of *Freikorps* members to the undisciplined masses, to communists, to Jews, to any forces which could be perceived as enemies of the national community, for it is with this mythic entity that the craving for wholeness had led them to identify. Obsessed by a permanent sense of the imminent decomposition of inner and outer reality, the aim of all those who are "not-yet-fully-born" is to "annihilate what they perceive as absolute falsity and evil, in order to regenerate their ego in a better world" (ibid., p.253), in fact to become "new men" (ibid., pp.161-2). This leads Theweleit to conclude that "fascism's most significant achievement was to organize the resurrection and rebirth of dead life in the masses", by assembling it "into blocks of human totality-machines, knitted into interlocking networks of order" (ibid., p.189). Nazism's success as an ideology can thus be ascribed to its capacity to transmute the repressed drives and fantasies of thousands of "not-yet-fully-born" males into fanatical commitment to a political programme of national rebirth. (Interestingly enough, the most articulate representatives of the minority of women who became Nazi activists before 1933 saw in a Third Reich based on Aryan principles the chance, not to return to the passive roles imposed by the "bourgeois" Second Reich, but to be reborn as a *"new woman"*. Not only would she be emancipated from emancipation, that is from the "perversions" of her natural and biological functions advocated by feminists under Weimar, but through her maternal qualities and ethical integrity play a key role in the racial and social regeneration of the Germans. See Kaplan and Adams, 1990.)

Thus whether we approach the question from the point of view of comparative religion, the history of ideas, sociology, political science or psychoanalysis, there is no shortage of theories which can be adduced to suggest that the convinced fascist is to be seen as someone whose flight from inner chaos has found expression in a powerful elective affinity with an intensely mythic ideology of national regeneration. This ideology, though objectively representing just one partial system of values among so many others he (and even on occasions she) experiences affectively as an absolute vehicle of personal salvation. By promising to redeem the nation from the quagmire of "demo-liberalism," fascism offers its converts the prospect of a renewed sense of meaning, of transcendence, of ritual time, of imminent rebirth in a world otherwise threatened with inexorable decadence, a decadence which, however real the objective factors of social dysfunction at the time, at bottom was no more than their inner world of anxiety and chaos projected on to contemporary history.

Having made this pronouncement, though, we must never lose sight of the fact that only a small percentage of the population, and then only in special historical circumstances, will fall prey to this particular elective affinity, and that, no matter how much they share the same structural core in terms of psychological predisposition, even they will have their own idiosyncratic motivations and rationalizations for investing their yearning for rebirth in an actual fascist movement. This point, though made powerfully by Platt (1980) and Weinstein (1980), is blurred by several others among the more psychoanalytically inclined theorists we have cited, including Fromm, Jung and Theweleit (for example, the *Freikorps* cannot stand for *all* fascists, let alone all males, even if they certainly provide a valuable case study of one way the predisposition to one current within one form of fascism could manifest itself). Ultimately the mechanisms of the psyche and its interactions with external reality are simply too complex to be comprehensively modelled or fully unravelled. As Theweleit's study confirms, writers provide the psycho-historian in their novels and poems unusually articulate guides to the labyrinth of their personality. Yet it is still impossible to establish precisely why Barrès, Drieu la Rochelle, Pound, Johst and Hamsun succumbed to the lure of ultra-nationalist and fascist political myth, while figures such as Gide, Hesse, Huxley, Wyndham Lewis and Yeats, who shared so many of their preoccupations with the crisis and decadence of modern culture, remained (the latter two only just) within the fold of a relativist humanism (see for example Soucy, 1972, p.92; Leal, 1985; Cadwallader, 1981). Definitive answers to such questions are simply beyond the explanatory powers of the human sciences. In this respect the theoretician who sets out to lay bare the

psychological dynamics of fascism is in the same dilemma as Dysart when he tries to get to the bottom of Strang's "case". Left alone to wrestle with Equus he muses:

I can hear the creature's voice. It's calling me out of the black cave of the Psyche. I shove in my dim little torch, and there he stands—waiting for me. He raises his matted head. He opens his great square teeth, and says *(Mocking)Why?* ... Why me? ... Why—ultimately—*Me?* ... do you really think you can account for Me? Totally, infallibly, inevitably account for Me? ... Poor Doctor Dysart!" ... A child is born into the world of phenomena all equal in the power to enslave. It sniffs—it sucks—it strokes its eyes over the whole uncountable range. Suddenly one strikes. *Why?* Moments snap together like magnets, forging a chain of shackles. *Why?* I can trace them. I can even, with time, pull them apart again. But why at the start they were ever magnetized at all—just those particular moments of experience and no others—I don't know. *And nor does anyone else.* (Shaffer, 1973, p.44)

The psychological dynamics of fascism are thus destined to remain in the last analysis shrouded in mystery and speculation. Nevertheless, using the psycho-historical model we have devised it is possible to identify some of *the external* factors that are conducive to the establishment of the particular ideological structure it represents, the objective situation in which it is likely to attract a mass following as a refuge from the pervasive *anomie of* modern society or the sensation of being overtaken by the collapse of society. In doing so we will be addressing the problem of answering our second question concerning the dynamics of fascism—why it first surfaced as a new form of "total identification" myth in the early twentieth century, and then only in certain areas of Western and Central Europe.

References

Broch, H., 1964. *The Sleepwalkers,* Grosset and Dunlap, New York.
Cadwallader, B., 1981. *Crisis of European Mind: A Study of Andre Malraux and Drieu la Rochelle,* University of Wales Press, Cardiff.
Kaplan, G. T. and Adams, C. E., 1990. Early women supporters of national socialism, in J. Milfull (ed.), *The Attractions of Fascism,* Berg, New York.
Koestler, A., 1970. *The Ghost in the Machine,* Pan, London.
Leal, R. B., 1985 Drieu la Rochelle and Huxley: cross channel perspectives on decadence, *Journal of European Studies,* Vol. 15.
Milfull, J., 1990. 'My Sex the Revolver': fascism as a theatre for the compensation of male inadequacies, in J. Milfull (ed.), *The attractions of Fascism,* Berg, New York.
Platt, G.M., 1980. Thoughts in a theory of collective action: language, affect, and ideology in revolution, in M. Albin (ed.), *New Directions in Psychohistory,* Lexington Books, Lexington, Massachusetts.
Shaffer, P., 1973. *Equus,* Samuel French, London.
Soucy, R., 1972. *Fascism in France. The Case of Maurice Barrès,* University of Los Angeles Press, Berkeley and Los Angeles.
Theweleit, K., 1989. *Male Fantasies.* Vol. 1(1987): Women, Floods, Bodies, History; Vol. 2 (1989); Male Bodeis: Psychoanalysing the White Terror, Polity Press, Cambridge.
Weinstein, F., 1980. *The Dynamics of Nazism: Leadership, Ideology and the Holocaust,* Academic Press, New York.

8

Anarchism

The Ideal of Freedom from Authority

Emma Goldman offers a lucid definition of anarchism as a new social order based on unrestricted liberty and an absence of government. William Godwin's research into the subject of justice leads him in Goldman's direction. He carefully distinguishes property as being one of three kinds: that to which no one is permanently entitled, that to which one is entitled by virtue of one's labour, and that which one gains as a result of dispossessing others of it. It is the third of these which Godwin attacks in the name of justice. Careful not to suggest that property should be removed by regulation, still less by violence, Godwin stresses that people should rely upon the investigations of reason and the well-informed community to correct such injustices. Compulsion should be avoided, except in the case of indispensable urgency. He also contends that government should be limited, that its primary mandate should be to guard the right of private judgment.

Peter Kropotkin is more unrelenting in his condemnation of law. In his view, property, criminal and constitutional laws protect the privileged classes and ought to be flung into the fire. Perhaps Kropotkin here is lacking in analytical insight, but the story of his life as a brilliant student who abandoned a promising military career only to turn to anarchism is sufficient to transform all but the most ardent sceptic into one prepared to hear him out when he says that the solution to people's cruelty lies in liberty, equality and practical human sympathy.

The position of revolutionary anarchism is defended by Michael Bakunin in his attack upon Marx's *Theory of the State*. Bakunin assails the dialectical materialism of Marx on account of its metaphysical and scientific traits and because, importantly, of its naive faith in the dictatorship of the proletariat. Bakunin concludes that this type of dictatorship is still government and ought to be denounced. It is Bakunin's position that this educated minority is indistinguishable from statism and equally reactionary.

Bakunin's indictment of Marxism is indeed a punishing one. His main argument against Marx is rooted in his thesis that the natural and social life of the people precedes science and the state. According to Bakunin, it is people in the basic natural and social forms of existence who should be educated, since this education would result in the widest possible expansion of social life. Here Bakunin engages Marx in his own game and comes out on top.

Goldman takes aim at those pernicious forces which impede a blending of individuals and society. According to Goldman, these forces include ownership of property, adherence to religion, and commitment to government. In part she echoes the lessons of Godwin and Kropotkin: anarchism is the liberation from the phantoms that have held people captive.

Finally Richard Falk raises three difficult questions for anarchists. Suffice it to say they are indeed complex ones, and they move Falk to come up with resourceful answers. The answers he provides cover much fertile ground. In his other writings, Falk has been prescient and he does not disappoint in this respect in the present extract. Several other demanding questions, though, which he does not ask would have added to the scope of the paper; for example, is the anarchical society anything more than a state of nature? If the anarchical society is more than a state of nature, what equilibrium does it have? Would not Nozick-like protective associations naturally arise all over again, thereby disrupting the state of nature or the state of anarchy? And would these associations not be constituents of a proto-state?

Of Property

William Godwin

WILLIAM GODWIN *(1756-1836) was born in England and was both a libertarian and anarchist who argued against the tyranny of tradition and authority. Central to his ideas was his attack upon the institution of property. His ideas are most clearly expressed in* Enquiry Concerning Political Justice.

Having considered at large the question of the person entitled to the use of the means of benefit or pleasure, it is time that we proceed to the second question, of the person, in whose hands the preservation and distribution of any of these means, will be most justly and beneficially vested ...

Of property there are three degrees.

The first and simplest degree, is that of my permanent right in those things, the use of which being attributed to me, a greater sum of benefit or pleasure will result, than could have arisen from their being otherwise appropriated. It is of no consequence, in this case, how I came into possession of them, the only necessary conditions being, their superior usefulness to me, and that my title to them is such as is generally acquiesced in, by the community in which I live. Every man is unjust, who conducts himself in such a manner respecting these things, as to infringe, in any degree, upon my power of using them, at the time when the using them will be of real importance to me.

It has already appeared[1] that one of the most essential of the rights of man, is my right to the forbearance of others; not merely that they shall refrain from everything that may, by direct consequence, affect my life, or the possession of my powers, but that they shall refrain from usurping upon my understanding, and shall leave me a certain equal sphere for the exercise of my private judgement. This is necessary, because it is possible for them to be wrong, as well as for me to be so, because the exercise of the understanding is essential to the improvement of man, and because the pain and interruption I suffer, are as real, when they infringe, in my conception only, upon what is of importance to me, as if the infringement had been, in the utmost degree, palpable. Hence it follows, that no man may, in ordinary cases, make use of my apartment, furniture or garments, or of my food, in the way of barter or loan, without having first obtained my consent.

The second degree of property, is the empire to which every man is entitled, over the produce of his own industry, even that part of it the use of which ought not to be appropriated to himself. It has been repeatedly shown that all the rights of man which are of this description, are passive.[2] He has no right of option in the disposal of anything which may fall into his hands. Every shilling of his property, and even every, the minutest, exertion of his powers, have received their destination from the decrees of justice. He is only the steward. But still he is the steward. These things must be trusted to his award, checked only by the censorial power that is vested, in the general sense, and favourable or unfavourable opinion, of that portion of mankind among whom he resides. Man is changed, from the capable subject of illimitable excellence, into the vilest and most despicable thing that imagination can conceive, when he is restrained from acting upon the dictates of his understanding. All men cannot individually be entitled to exercise compulsion on each other, for this would produce universal anarchy. All men cannot collectively be entitled to exercise unbounded compulsion, for this would produce universal slavery: the interference of government, however impartially vested, is, no doubt, only to be resorted to, upon occasions of rare occurrence, and indispensable urgency.

It will readily be perceived, that this second species of property, is in a less rigorous sense fundamental, than the first. It is, in one point of view, a sort of usurpation. It vests in me the preservation and dispensing of that, which in point of complete and absolute right belongs to you.

The third degree of property, is that which occupies the most vigilant attention in the civilized states of Europe. It is a system, in whatever manner established, by which one man enters into the faculty of disposing of the produce of another man's industry. There is scarcely any species of wealth, expenditure or splendour, existing in any civilized country, that is not, in some way, produced, by the express manual labour, and corporeal industry, of the inhabitants of that country. The spontaneous productions of the earth are few, and contribute little to wealth, expenditure or splendour. Every man may calculate, in every glass of wine he drinks, and every ornament he annexes to his person, how many individuals have been condemned to slavery and sweat, incessant drudgery, unwholesome food, continual hardships, deplorable ignorance, and brutal insensibility, that he may be supplied with these luxuries. It is a gross imposition, that men are accustomed to put upon themselves, when they talk of the property bequeathed to them by their ancestors. The property is produced by the daily labour of men who are now in existence. All that their ancestors bequeathed to them, was a mouldy patent, which they show, as a title to extort from their neighbours what the labour of those neighbours has produced.

It is clear therefore that the third species of property, is in direct contradiction to the second.

The most desirable state of human society would require, that the quantity of manual labour and corporeal industry to be exerted, and particularly that part of it which is not the uninfluenced choice of our own judgement, but is imposed upon each individual by the necessity of his affairs, should be reduced within as narrow limits as possible. For any man to enjoy the most trivial accommodation, while, at the same time, a similar accommodation is not accessible to every other member of the community, is, absolutely speaking, wrong. All refinements of luxury, all inventions that tend to give employment to a great number of labouring hands, are directly adverse to the propagation of happiness. Every additional tax that is laid on, every new channel that is opened for the expenditure of the public money, unless it be compensated (which is scarcely ever the case) by an equivalent deduction from the luxuries of the rich, is so much added to the general stock of ignorance, drudgery and hardship. The country gentleman who, by levelling an eminence, or introducing a sheet of water into his park, finds work for hundreds of industrious poor, is the enemy, and not, as has commonly been imagined, the friend, of his species. Let us suppose that, in any country, there is now ten times as much industry and manual labour, as there was three centuries ago. Except so far as this is applied to maintain an increased population, it is expended in the more costly indulgences of the rich. Very little indeed is employed to increase the happiness or conveniences of the poor. They barely subsist at present, and they did as much at the remoter period of which we speak. Those who, by fraud or force, have usurped the power of buying and selling the labour of the great mass of the community, are sufficiently disposed to take care that they should never do more than subsist. An object of industry added to or taken from the

general stock, produces a momentary difference, but things speedily fall back into their former state. If every labouring inhabitant of Great Britain were able and willing today to double the quantity of his industry, for a short time he would derive some advantage from the increased stock of commodities produced. But the rich would speedily discover the means of monopolizing this produce, as they had done the former. A small part of it only, could consist in commodities essential to the subsistence of man, or be fairly distributed through the community. All that is luxury and superfluity, would increase the accommodations of the rich, and perhaps, by reducing the price of luxuries, augment the number of those to whom such accommodations were accessible. But it would afford no alleviation to the great mass of the community. Its more favoured members would give their inferiors no greater wages for twenty hours' labour, suppose, than they now do for ten.

What reason is there then that this species of property should be respected? Because, ill as the system is, it will perhaps be found, that it is better than any other, which, by any means, except those of reason, the love of distinction, or the love of justice, can be substituted in its place. It is not easy to say whether misery or absurdity would be most conspicuous, in a plan which should invite every man to seize, upon everything he conceived himself to want. If, by positive institution, the property of every man were equalized today, without a contemporary change in men's dispositions and sentiments, it would become unequal tomorrow. The same evils would spring up with a rapid growth; and we should have gained nothing, by a project, which, while it violated every man's habits, and many men's inclinations, would render thousands miserable. We have already shown,[3] and shall have occasion to show more at large,[4] how pernicious the consequences would be, if government were to take the whole permanently into their hands, and dispense to every man his daily bread. It may even be suspected that agrarian laws, and others of a similar tendency, which have been invented for the purpose of keeping down the spirit of accumulation, deserve to be regarded, as remedies, more pernicious, than the disease they are intended to cure.[5]

An interesting question suggests itself in this stage of the discussion. How far is the idea of property to be considered as the offspring of positive institution? The decision of this question may prove extremely essential to the point upon which we are engaged. The regulation of property by positive laws may be a very exceptionable means of reforming its present inequality, at the same time that an equal objection may by no means lie, against a proceeding, the object of which shall be merely to supersede positive laws, or such positive laws as are peculiarly exceptionable.

In pursuing this enquiry, it is necessary to institute a distinction, between such positive laws, or established practices (which are often found little less efficacious than laws), as are peculiar to certain ages and countries, and such laws or practices, as are common to all civilized communities, and may therefore be perhaps interwoven with the existence of society.

The idea of property, or permanent empire, in those things which ought to be applied to our personal use, and still more in the produce of our industry, unavoidably suggests the idea of some species of law or practice by which it is guaranteed. Without this, property could not exist. Yet we have endeavoured to show that the maintenance of these two kinds of property is highly beneficial. Let us consider the consequences that grow out of this position.

Every man should be urged to the performance of his duty, as much as possible, by the instigations of reason alone.[6] Compulsion to be exercised by one human being over another, whether individually, or in the name of the community, if in any case to be resorted to, is at least to be resorted to only in cases of indispensable urgency. It is not therefore to be called in, for the purpose of causing one individual to exert a little more, or another a little less, of productive industry. Neither is it to be called in, for the purpose of causing the industrious individual to make the precise distribution of his produce which he ought to make. Hence it follows that, while the present erroneous opinions and prejudices respecting accumulation continue, actual accumulation will, in some degree, take place.

For, let it be observed that, not only no well-informed community will interfere with the quantity of any man's industry, or the disposal of its produce, but the members of every such well-informed community will exert themselves, to turn aside the purpose of any man who shall be inclined, to dictate to, or restrain, his neighbour in this respect.

The most destructive of all excesses, is that, where one man shall dictate to another, or undertake to compel him to do, or refrain from doing, anything (except, as was before stated, in cases of the most indispensable urgency), otherwise than with his own consent. Hence it follows that the distribution of wealth in every community, must be left to depend upon the sentiments of the individuals of that community. If, in any society, wealth be estimated at its true value, and accumulation and monopoly be regarded as the seals of mischief, injustice and dishonour, instead of being treated as titles to attention and deference, in that society the accommodations of human life will tend to their level, and the inequality of conditions will be destroyed.[7] A revolution of opinions is the only means of attaining to this inestimable benefit. Every attempt to effect this purpose by means of regulation, will probably be found ill conceived and abortive. Be this as it will, every attempt to correct the distribution of wealth by individual violence, is certainly to be regarded as hostile to the first principles of public security ...

There is another circumstance necessary to be stated, by way of qualification to the preceding conclusion. Evils often exist in a community, which, though mere excrescences at first, at length become so incorporated with the principle of social existence, that they cannot suddenly be separated, without the risk of involving the most dreadful calamities ... The inequalities of property perhaps constituted a state, through which it was at least necessary for us to pass, and which constituted the true original excitement to the unfolding the powers of the human mind ... Yet, were they to be suddenly and instantly abolished, two evils would necessarily follow. First, the abrupt reduction of thousands to a condition, the reverse of that to which they had hitherto been accustomed, a condition, perhaps the most auspicious to human talent and felicity, but for which habit had wholly unfitted them, and which would be to them a continual source of dejection and suffering. It may be doubted, whether the genuine cause of reform ever demands, that, in its name, we should sentence whole classes of men to wretchedness. Secondly, an attempt abruptly to abolish practices, which had originally no apology to plead for their introduction, would be attended with as dreadful convulsions, and as melancholy a series of public calamities, as an attack upon the first principles of society itself. All the reasonings therefore, which were formerly adduced under the head of revolutions,[8] are applicable to the present case.

Having now accomplished what was last proposed,[9] and endeavoured to ascertain in what particulars the present system of property is to be considered as the capricious offspring of positive institution, let us return to the point which led us to that enquiry, the question concerning the degree of respect to which property in general is entitled. And here it is only necessary that we should recollect the principle in which the doctrine of property is founded, the sacred and indefeasible right of private judgement. There are but two objects for which government can rationally be conceived to have been originated: first, as a treasury of public wisdom, by which individuals might, in all cases, with advantage be directed, and which might actively lead us, with greater certainty, in the path of happiness: or, secondly, instead of being forward to act itself as an umpire, that the community might fill the humbler office of guardian of the rights of private judgement, and never interpose, but when one man appeared, in this respect, alarmingly to encroach upon another. All the arguments of this work have tended to that the latter, and not the former, is the true end of civil institution. The first idea of property then, is a deduction from the right of private judgement; the first object of government, is the preservation of this right. Without permitting to every man, to a considerable degree, the exercise of his own discretion, there can be no independence, no improvement, no virtue and no happiness. This is a privilege in the highest degree sacred; for its maintenance, no exertions and sacrifices can be too great. Thus deep is the foundation of the doctrine of property. It is, in the last resort, the palladium of all that ought to be dear to us, and must never be approached but with awe and veneration. He that seeks to loosen the hold of this principle upon our minds, and that would lead us to sanction any exceptions to it without the most deliberate and impartial consideration, however right may be his intentions, is, in that instance, an enemy to the whole. A condition indispensably necessary to every species of excellence, is security. Unless I can foresee, in a considerable degree, the treatment I shall receive from my species,

and am able to predict, to a certain extent, what will be the limits of their irregularity and caprice, I can engage in no valuable undertaking. Civil society maintains a greater proportion of security among men, than can be found in the savage state: this is one of the reasons why, under the shade of civil society, arts have been invented, sciences perfected, and the nature of man, in his individual and relative capacity, gradually developed.

Source: William Godwin. *Of Property.* Originally published in 1793.

Notes

[1] II. v and vi. [Ed. note: Godwin refers here to Book II, Chapters V and VI wherein he discusses rights and the right of private judgement.]

[2] II. v.

[3] VI, viii, p.237. [Ed. note: Book VI deals with Opinion As A Subject, and c. viii with National Education.]

[4] Ch. viii.

[5] VI. i, p.224. [Ed. note: the subject of this is the Political Superintendence of Opinion.]

[6] II. vi; Book VII, *passim.* [Ed. note: Book VII deals with Crimes and Punishments.]

[7] Ch. i, [Ed. note: Here Godwin refers to c.i in Book VIII, which deals with Property.]

[8] IV. ii, [Ed. note: Book IV deals with The Operation of Opinion in Societies and Individuals, and c. ii with Revolutions.]

[9] [Ed. note: Godwin refers here to Book VIII which covers the Subject Property, and c. ii which touches the Principles of Property.]

Law and Authority

Peter Kropotkin

PETER KROPOTKIN *(1840-1921) was born into an aristocratic family in Russia. He eventually turned his back upon a promising military and academic career to explore his developing anarchistic ideas and attempt to put them into practice. His most famous writing was* Mutual Aid.

The protection of the person, which is put forward as the true mission of law, occupies an imperceptible space among them, for, in existing society, assaults upon the person directly dictated by hatred and brutality tend to disappear. Nowadays, if anyone is murdered, it is generally for the sake of robbing him; rarely because of personal vengeance. But if this class of crimes and misdemeanors is continually diminishing, we certainly do not owe the change to legislation. It is due to the growth of humanitarianism in our societies, to our increasingly social habits rather than to the prescriptions of our laws. Repeal tomorrow every law dealing with the protection of the person, and tomorrow stop all proceedings for assault, and the number of attempts dictated by personal vengeance and by brutality would not be augmented by one single instance.

It will perhaps be objected that during the last fifty years, a good many liberal laws have been enacted. But, if these laws are analyzed, it will be discovered that this liberal legislation consists in the repeal of the laws bequeathed to us by the barbarism of preceding centuries. Every liberal law, every radical program, may be summed up in these words,—abolition of laws grown irksome to the middle-class itself, and return and extension to all citizens of liberties enjoyed by the townships of the twelfth century. The abolition of capital punishment, trial by jury of all "crimes" (there was a more liberal jury in the twelfth century), the election of magistrates, the right of bringing public officials to trial, the abolition of standing armies, free instruction, etc., everything that is pointed out as an invention of modern liberalism, is but a return to the freedom which existed before church and king had laid hands upon every manifestation of human life.

Thus the protection of exploitation directly by laws on property, and indirectly by the maintenance of the State is both the spirit and the substance of our modern codes, and the one function of our costly legislative machinery. But it is time we gave up being satisfied with mere phrases, and learned to appreciate their real significance. The law, which on its first appearance presented itself as a compendium of customs useful for the preservation of society, is now perceived to be nothing but an instrument for the maintenance of exploitation and the domination of the toiling masses by rich idlers. At the present day its civilizing mission is *nil*; it has but one object,—to bolster up exploitation.

This is what is told us by history as to the development of law. Is it in virtue of this history that we are called upon to respect it? Certainly not. It has no more title to respect than capital, the fruit of pillage. And the first duty of the revolution will be to make a bonfire of all existing laws as it will of all titles to property.

...

The millions of laws which exist for the regulation of humanity appear upon investigation to be divided into three principal categories: protection of property, protection of persons, protection of government. And by analyzing each of these three categories, we arrive at the same logical and necessary conclusion: *the uselessness and hurtfulness of law.*

Socialists know what is meant by protection of property. Laws on property are not made to guarantee either to the individual or to society the enjoyment of the produce of their own labor. On the contrary, they are made to rob the producer of a part of what he has created, and to secure to certain other people that portion of the produce which they have stolen either from the producer or from society as a whole. When, for example, the law establishes Mr. So-and-So's right to a house, it is not establishing his right to a cottage he has built for himself, or to a house he has erected with the help of some of his friends. In that case no one would have disputed his right. On the contrary, the law is establishing his right to a house which is not the product of his labor; first of all because he has had it built for him by others to whom he has not paid the full value of their work, and next because that house represents a social value which he could not have produced for himself. The

PETER KROPOTKIN (1842–1921)

Prince PETER ALEK-SEIEVITCH KROPOTKIN was the founder and leading advocate of anarchist communism, an ideology known to modern students of political theory as "anarcho-communism." Kropotkin argued that in social relations, the competitive Darwinian ideal of "survival of the fittest" was far less practical than cooperation, or what he termed the principle of "mutual aid." Kropotkin outlined his political theories in two major works, *Law and Authority, an Anarchist Essay* (1886) and *Mutual Aid, a Factor of Evolution* (1890–6).

Kropotkin believed that despite the popular idea that society was held together by laws and the authorities that enforce them, it was common customs and voluntary agreements between people that really created social cohesion. In *Mutual Aid*, Kropotkin contended that the

natural instinct of people is to join together to form social bonds and that governments or states were unnecessary. This rejection of authority while simultaneously accepting collective and "natural" social cohesion among people formed the basis of Kropotkin's ideological alliance between communism and anarchism.

Many people associate anarchism with terrorism. The model put forward by Kropotkin, however, suggests a completely different approach. Rather than encouraging political and social chaos, collective action was to be preferred. Kropotkin was part of a nineteenth-century tradition of anarchist thought that was closely allied with socialist principles. The ownership of private property was discouraged in favour of property held by voluntary associations. The liberty of the individual could only be assured when the property-holding class was destroyed. But as the contrast between Kropotkin and the more violent anarchists illustrates, this destruction could take on varied forms.

Although he maintained an anti-war stance in theory, Kropotkin nevertheless vigorously supported Russia's participation in the First World War.

law is establishing his right to what belongs to everybody in general and to nobody in particular. The same house built in the midst of Siberia would not have the value it possesses in a large town, and, as we know, that value arises from the labor of something like fifty generations of men who have built the town, beautified it, supplied it with water and gas, fine promenades, colleges, theatres, shops, railways, and roads leading in all directions. Thus, by recognizing the right of Mr. So-and-So to a particular house in Paris, London, or Rouen, the law is unjustly appropriating to him a certain portion of the produce of the labor of mankind in general. And it is precisely because this appropriation and all other forms of property bearing the same character are a crying injustice, that a whole arsenal of laws and a whole army of soldiers, policemen, and judges are needed to maintain it against the good sense and just feeling inherent in humanity.

Half our laws,—the civil code in each country,—serves no other purpose than to maintain this appropriation, this monopoly for the benefit of certain individuals against the whole of mankind. Three-fourths of the causes decided by the tribunals are nothing but quarrels between monopolists—two robbers disputing over their booty. And a great many of our criminal laws have the same object in view, their end being to keep the workman in a subordinate position towards his employer, and thus afford security for exploitation.

As for guaranteeing the product of his labor to the producer, there are no laws which even attempt such a thing. It is so simple and natural, so much a part of the manners and customs of mankind, that law has not given it so much as a thought. Open brigandage, sword in hand, is no feature of our age. Neither does one workman ever come and dispute the produce of his labor with another. If they have a misunderstanding they settle it by calling in a third person, without having recourse to law. The only person who exacts from another what that other has produced, is the proprietor, who comes in and deducts the lion's share. As for humanity in general, it everywhere respects the right of each to what he has created, without the interposition of any special laws.

As all the laws about property which make up thick volumes of codes and are the delight of our lawyers have no other object than to protect the unjust appropriation of human labor by certain monopolists, there is no reason for their existence, and, on the day of the revolution, social revolutionists are thoroughly determined to put an end to them. Indeed, a bonfire might be made with perfect justice of all laws bearing upon the so-called "rights of property." All title-deeds, all registers, in a word, of all that is in any way connected with an institution which will soon be looked upon as a blot in the history of humanity, as humiliating as the slavery and serfdom of past ages.

The remarks just made upon laws concerning property are quite as applicable to the second category of laws; those for the maintenance of government, i.e., constitutional law.

It again is a complete arsenal of laws, decrees, ordinances, orders in council, and what not, all serving to protect the diverse forms of representative government, delegated or usurped, beneath which humanity is writhing. We know very well—anarchists have often enough pointed out in their perpetual criticism of the various forms of government—that the mission of all governments, monarchical, constitutional, or republican, is to protect and maintain by force the privileges of the classes in possession, the aristocracy, clergy, and traders. A good third of our laws—and each country possesses some tens of thousands of them—the fundamental laws on taxes, excise duties, the organization of ministerial departments and their offices, of the army, the police, the church, etc., have no other end than to maintain, patch up, and develop the administrative machine. And this machine in its turn serves almost entirely to protect the privileges of the possessing classes. Analyze all these laws, observe them in action day by day, and you will discover that not one is worth preserving.

About such laws there can be no two opinions. Not only anarchists, but more or less revolutionary radicals also, are agreed that the only use to be made of laws concerning the organization of government is to fling them into the fire.

The third category of law still remains to be considered; that relating to the protection of the person and the detection and prevention of "crime." This is the most important because most prejudices attach to it;

because, if law enjoys a certain amount of consideration, it is in consequence of the belief that this species of law is absolutely indispensable to the maintenance of security in our societies. These are laws developed from the nucleus of customs useful to human communities, which have been turned to account by rulers to sanctify their own domination. The authority of the chiefs of tribes, of rich families in towns, and of the king, depended upon their judicial functions, and even down to the present day, whenever the necessity of government is spoken of, its function as supreme judge is the thing implied. "Without a government men would tear one another to pieces," argues the village orator. "The ultimate end of all government is to secure twelve honest jurymen to every accused person," said Burke.

Well, in spite of all the prejudices existing on this subject, it is quite time that anarchists should boldly declare this category of laws as useless and injurious as the preceding ones.

First of all, as to so-called "crimes"—assaults upon persons—it is well known that two-thirds, and often as many as three-fourths, of such "crimes" are instigated by the desire to obtain possession of someone's wealth. This immense class of so-called "crimes and misdemeanors" will disappear on the day on which private property ceases to exist. "But," it will be said, "there will always be brutes who will attempt the lives of their fellow citizens, who will lay their hands to a knife in every quarrel, and revenge the slightest offense by murder, if there are no laws to restrain and punishments to withhold them." This refrain is repeated every time the right of society to *punish* is called in question.

Yet there is one fact concerning this head which at the present time is thoroughly established; the severity of punishment does not diminish the amount of crime. Hang, and, if you like, quarter murderers, and the number of murders will not decrease by one. On the other hand, abolish the penalty of death, and there will not be one murder more; there will be fewer. Statistics prove it. But if the harvest is good, and bread cheap, and the weather fine, the number of murders immediately decreases. This again is proved by statistics. The amount of crime always augments and diminishes in proportion to the price of provisions and the state of the weather. Not that all murderers are actuated by hunger. That is not the case. But when the harvest is good, and provisions are at an obtainable price, and when the sun shines, men, lighter-hearted and less miserable than usual, do not give way to gloomy passions, do not from trivial motives plunge a knife into the bosom of a fellow creature.

Moreover, it is also a well known fact that the fear of punishment has never stopped a single murderer. He who kills his neighbor from revenge or misery does not reason much about consequences; and there have been few murderers who were not firmly convinced that they should escape prosecution.

Without speaking of a society in which a man will receive a better education, in which the development of all his faculties, and the possibility of exercising them, will procure him so many enjoyments that he will not seek to poison them by remorse—even in our society, even with those sad products of misery whom we see today in the public houses of great cities—on the day when no punishment is inflicted upon murderers, the number of murders will not be augmented by a single case. And it is extremely probable that it will be, on the contrary, diminished by all those cases which are due at present to habitual criminals, who have been brutalized in prisons.

We are continually being told of the benefits conferred by law, and the beneficial effect of penalties, but have the speakers ever attempted to strike a balance between the benefits attributed to laws and penalties, and the degrading effect of these penalties upon humanity? Only calculate all the evil passions awakened in mankind by the atrocious punishments formerly inflicted in our streets! Man is the cruelest animal upon earth. And who has pampered and developed the cruel instincts unknown, even among monkeys, if it is not the king, the judge, and the priests, armed with law, who caused flesh to be torn off in strips, boiling pitch to be poured into wounds, limbs to be dislocated, bones to be crushed, men to be sawn asunder to maintain their authority? Only estimate the torrent of depravity let loose in human society by the "informing" which is countenanced by judges, and paid in hard cash by governments, under pretext of assisting in the discovery of "crime." Only go into the jails and study what man becomes when he is deprived of freedom and shut up with other depraved beings, steeped in the vice and corruption which oozes from the very walls of our existing prisons. Only remember that the more these prisons are reformed, the more detestable they become. Our model modern penitentiaries are a hundred-fold more abominable than the dungeons of the middle ages. Finally, consider what corruption, what depravity of mind is kept up among men by the idea of obedience, the very essence of law; of chastisement; of authority having the right to punish, to judge irrespective of our conscience and the esteem of our friends; of the necessity for executioners, jailers, and informers—in a word, by all the attributes of law and authority. Consider all this, and you will assuredly agree with us in saying that a law inflicting penalties is an abomination which should cease to exist.

Peoples without political organization, and therefore less depraved than ourselves, have perfectly understood that the man who is called "criminal" is simply unfortunate; that the remedy is not to flog him, to chain him up, or to kill him on the scaffold or in prison, but to help him by the most brotherly care, by treatment based on equality, by the usages of life among honest men. In the next revolution we hope that this cry will go forth:

> Burn the guillotines; demolish the prisons; drive away the judges, policemen and informers—the impurest race upon the face of the earth; treat as a brother the man who has been led by passion to do ill to his fellow; above all, take from the ignoble products of middle-class idleness the possibility of displaying their vices in attractive colors; and be sure that but few crimes will mar our society.

The main supports of crime are idleness, law and authority; laws about property, laws about government, laws about penalties and misdemeanors: and authority, which takes upon itself to manufacture these laws and to apply them.

No more laws! No more judges! Liberty, equality, and practical human sympathy are the only effectual barriers we can oppose to the anti-social instincts of certain among us.

Source: Peter Kropotkin. "Law and Authority." Originally published in 1886.

Critique of the Marxist Theory of the State

Michael Bakunin

MICHAEL BAKUNIN *(1814-1876) was a Russian revolutionary anarchist who talked about creating the workers' revolution. He was a prolific writer and antagonist of Karl Marx.*

Liberty without socialism is privilege, injustice; socialism without liberty is slavery and brutality.
                                                    Michael Bakunin

There is no road leading from metaphysics to the realities of life. Theory and fact are separated by an abyss. It is impossible to leap across this abyss by what Hegel called a "qualitative jump" from the world of logic to the world of nature and of real life.

The road leading from concrete fact to theory and vice versa is the method of science and is the true road. In the practical world, it is the movement of society toward forms of organization that will to the greatest possible extent reflect life itself in all its aspects and complexity.

Such is the people's way to complete emancipation, accessible to all—the way of the anarchist social revolution, which will come from the people themselves, an elemental force sweeping away all obstacles. Later, from the depths of the popular soul, there will spontaneously emerge the new creative forms of social life.

The way of the gentlemen metaphysicians is completely different. Metaphysician is the term we use for the disciples of Hegel and for the positivists, and in general, for all the worshippers of science as a goddess, all those modern Procrusteans who, in one way or another, have created an ideal of social organization, a narrow mold into which they would force future generations, all those who, instead of seeing science as only one of the essential manifestations of natural and social life, insist that all of life is encompassed in their necessarily tentative scientific theories. Metaphysicians and positivists, all these gentlemen who consider it their mission to prescribe the laws of life in the name of science, are consciously or unconsciously reactionaries.

This is very easy to demonstrate.

Science in the true sense of that word, real science, is at this time within reach of only an insignificant minority. For example, among us in Russia, how many accomplished savants are there in a population of eighty million? Probably a thousand are engaged in science, but hardly more than a few hundred could be considered first-rate, serious scientists. If science were to dictate the laws, the overwhelming majority, many millions of men, would be ruled by one or two hundred experts. Actually it would be even fewer than that, because not all of science is concerned with the administration of society. This would be the task of sociology—the science of sciences—which presupposes in the case of a well-trained sociologist that he have an adequate knowledge of all the other sciences. How many such people are there in Russia—in all Europe? Twenty or thirty—and these twenty or thirty would rule the world? Can anyone imagine a more absurd and abject despotism?

It is almost certain that these twenty or thirty experts would quarrel among themselves, and if they did agree on common policies, it would be at the expense of mankind. The principal vice of the average specialist is his inclination to exaggerate his own knowledge and deprecate everyone else's. Give him control and he will become an insufferable tyrant. To be the slave of pedants—what a destiny for humanity! Give them full power and they will begin by performing on human beings the same experiments that the scientists are now performing on rabbits and dogs.

We must respect the scientists for their merits and achievements, but in order to prevent them from corrupting their own high moral and intellectual standards, they should be granted no special privileges and no rights other than those possessed by everyone—for example, the liberty to express their convictions, thought, and knowledge. Neither they nor any other special group should be given power over others. He who is given power will inevitably become an oppressor and exploiter of society.

But we are told: "Science will not always be the patrimony of a few. There will come a time when it will be accessible to all." Such a time is still far away and there will be many social upheavals before this dream will come true, and even then, who would want to put his fate in the hands of the priests of science?

It seems to us that anyone who thinks that after a social revolution everybody will be equally educated is very much mistaken. Science, then as now, will remain one of the many specialized fields, though it will cease to be accessible only to a very few of the privileged class. With the elimination of class distinctions, education will be within the reach of all those who will have the ability and the desire to pursue it, but not to the detriment of manual labor, which will be compulsory for all.

Available to everyone will be a general scientific education, especially the learning of the scientific method, the habit of correct thinking, the ability to generalize from facts and make more or less correct deductions. But of encyclopedic minds and advanced sociologists[1] there will be very few. It would be sad for mankind if at any time theoretical speculation became the only source of guidance for society, if science alone were in charge of all social administration. Life would wither, and human society would turn into a voiceless and servile herd. The domination of life by science can have no other result than the brutalization of mankind.

We, the revolutionary anarchists, are the advocates of education for all the people, of the emancipation and the widest possible expansion of social life. Therefore we are the enemies of the State and all forms of the statist principle. In opposition to the metaphysicians, the positivists, and all the worshippers of science, we declare that natural and social life always comes before theory, which is only one of its manifestations but never its creator. From out of its own inexhaustible depths, society develops through a series of events, but not by thought alone. Theory is always created by life, but never creates it; like mileposts and road signs, it only indicates the direction and the different stages of life's independent and unique development.

In accordance with this belief, we neither intend nor desire to thrust upon our own or any other people any scheme of social organization taken from books or concocted by ourselves. We are convinced that the masses of the people carry in themselves, in their instincts (more or less developed by history), in their daily necessities, and in their conscious or unconscious aspirations, all the elements of the future social organization. We seek this ideal in the people themselves. Every state power, every government, by its very nature places itself outside and over the people and inevitably subordinates them to an organization and to aims which are foreign to and opposed to the real needs and aspirations of the people. We declare ourselves the enemies of every government and every state power, and of governmental organization in general. We think that people can be free and happy only when organized from the bottom up in completely free and independent associations, without governmental paternalism though not without the influence of a variety of free individuals and parties.

Such are our ideas as social revolutionaries, and we

are therefore call anarchists. We do not protest this name, for we are indeed the enemies of any governmental power, since we know that such a power depraves those who wear its mantle equally with those who are forced to submit to it. Under its pernicious influence the former become ambitious and greedy despots, exploiters of society in favor of their personal or class interests, while the latter become slaves.

Idealists of all kinds—metaphysicians, positivists, those who support the rule of science over life, doctrinaire revolutionists—all defend the idea of state and state power with equal eloquence, because they see in it, as a consequence of their own systems, the only salvation for society. Quite logically, since they have accepted the basic premise (which we consider completely mistaken) that thought precedes life, that theory is prior to social experience, and, therefore, that social science has to be the starting point for all social upheavals and reconstructions. They then arrive unavoidably at the conclusion that because thought, theory, and science, at least in our times, are in the possession of very few, these few ought to be the leaders of social life, not only the initiators, but also the leaders of all popular movements. On the day following the revolution the new social order should not be organized by the free association of people's organizations or unions, local and regional, from the bottom up, in accordance with the demands and instincts of the people, but only by the dictatorial power of this learned minority, which presumes to express the will of the people.

This fiction of a pseudorepresentative government serves to conceal the domination of the masses by a handful of privileged elite; an elite elected by hordes of people who are rounded up and who do not know for whom or for what they vote. Upon this artificial and abstract expression of what they falsely imagine to be the will of the people and of which the real living people have not the least idea, they construct both the theory of statism as well as the theory of so-called revolutionary dictatorship.

The differences between revolutionary dictatorship and statism are superficial. Fundamentally they both represent the same principle of minority rule over the majority in the name of the alleged "stupidity" of the latter and the alleged "intelligence" of the former. Therefore they are both equally reactionary since both directly and inevitably must preserve and perpetuate the political and economic privileges of the ruling minority and the political and economic subjugation of the masses of the people.

Source: Michael Bakunin. *Statism and Anarchy.* Originally published in 1873.

Notes

[1] Ed. note: By sociologists Bakunin means those we nowadays call generalists, people who know enough of all special fields to deal with the entire range of intellectual endeavor.

Anarchism: What It Really Stands For

Emma Goldman

EMMA GOLDMAN *(1869-1940) was known as 'Red Emma' owing to her support for anarchism and militant labour movements as well as for her radical views on women and sexuality.*

The history of human growth and development is at the same time the history of the terrible struggle of every new idea heralding the approach of a brighter dawn. In its tenacious hold on tradition, the Old has never hesitated to make use of the foulest and cruelest means to stay the advent of the New, in whatever form or period the latter may have asserted itself. Nor need we retrace our steps into the distant past to realize the enormity of opposition, difficulties, and hardships placed in the path of every progressive idea. The rack, the thumbscrew, and the knout are still with us; so are the convict's garb and the social wrath, all conspiring against the spirit that is serenely marching on.

Anarchism could not hope to escape the fate of all other ideas of innovation. Indeed, as the most revolutionary and uncompromising innovator, Anarchism must needs meet with the combined ignorance and venom of the world it aims to reconstruct.

To deal even remotely with all that is being said and done against Anarchism would necessitate the writing of a whole volume. I shall therefore meet only two of the principal objections. In so doing, I shall attempt to elucidate what Anarchism really stands for.

The strange phenomenon of the opposition to Anarchism is that it brings to light the relation between so-called intelligence and ignorance. And yet this is not so very strange when we consider the relativity of all things. The ignorant mass has in its favor that it makes no pretence of knowledge or tolerance. Acting, as it always does, by mere impulse, its reasons are like those of a child. "Why?" "Because." Yet the opposition of the uneducated to Anarchism deserves the same consideration as that of the intelligent man.

What, then, are the objections? First, Anarchism is impractical, though a beautiful ideal. Second, Anarchism stands for violence and destruction, hence it must be repudiated as vile and dangerous. Both the intelligent man and the ignorant mass judge not from a thorough knowledge of the subject, but either from hearsay or false interpretation.

A practical scheme, says Oscar Wilde, is either one already in existence, or a scheme that could be carried out under the existing conditions; but it is exactly the existing conditions that one objects to, and any scheme that could accept these conditions is wrong and foolish. The true criterion of the practical, therefore, is not whether the latter can keep intact the wrong or foolish; rather is it whether the scheme has vitality enough to leave the stagnant waters of the old, and build, as well as sustain, new life. In the light of this conception, Anarchism is indeed practical. More than any other idea, it is helping to do away with the wrong and foolish; more than any other idea, it is building and sustaining new life.

The emotions of the ignorant man are continuously kept at a pitch by the most blood-curdling stories about Anarchism. Not a thing is too outrageous to be employed against this philosophy and its exponents. Therefore Anarchism represents to the unthinking what the proverbial bad man does to the child—a black monster bent on swallowing everything; in short, destruction and violence.

Destruction and violence! How is the ordinary man to know that the most violent element in society is ignorance; that its power of destruction is the very thing Anarchism is combating? Nor is he aware that Anarchism, whose roots, as it were, are part of nature's forces, destroys, not healthful tissue, but parasitic growths that feed on the life's essence of society. It is merely clearing the soil from weeds and sagebrush, that it may eventually bear healthy fruit.

Someone has said that it requires less mental effort to think. The widespread mental indolence, so prevalent in society, proves this to be only too true. Rather than to go to the bottom of any given idea, to examine into its origin and meaning, most people will either condemn it altogether, or rely on some superficial or prejudicial definition of non-essentials.

Anarchism urges man to think, to investigate, to analyze every proposition; but that the brain capacity of the average reader be not taxed too much, I also shall begin with a definition, and then elaborate on the latter.

EMMA GOLDMAN (1869–1940)

Best known today for her advocacy of "perfect, unrestrained freedom for everyone," EMMA GOLDMAN was born in Lithuania and died in Toronto. Known in North America as "Red Emma" because of her anarchist views, Goldman came to the United States in 1886 and became an anarchist in 1889. In 1893 she was imprisoned for her role in a workers' riot. In 1901 she was accused (without proof) of assisting in the plot to assassinate U.S. President William McKinley.

From 1906 to 1917, Goldman was the co-publisher of the anarchist magazine, *Mother Earth*. She again spent time in jail during World War One, this time for her opposition to the draft. In 1919 during the anti-communist "Red Scare" she was deported to Russia. Goldman briefly returned to the U.S. in 1934 for a lecture tour. The year 1936 saw her in Spain, assisting anarchists there in the Civil War against Franco.

The term "anarchist" or "anarchism" comes from the Greek *anarkhia*, meaning "absence of rule." Anarchists are often portrayed in the popular media as "bomb-throwers" or people committed to the assassination of heads of state. Although certain anarchists are also terrorists, it is not necessary that one advocate violence in order to be an anarchist. In the strictest sense, anarchists like Emma Goldman simply reject the authority of states or governments and support instead voluntary co-operation between people and institutions. Goldman's opposition to U.S. military conscription in World War One, for example, is an illustration of an anarchist's refusal to comply with state coercion of individual citizens. Goldman's political career and philosophy are detailed in her autobiography, *Living My Life*, published in 1931.

ANARCHISM: The philosophy of a new social order based on liberty unrestricted by man-made law; the theory that all forms of government rest on violence, and are therefore wrong and harmful, as well as unnecessary.

The new social order rests, of course, on the materialistic basis of life; but while all Anarchists agree that the main evil today is an economic one, they maintain that the solution of that evil can be brought about only through the consideration of *every phase* of life—individual, as well as the collective; the internal, as well as the external phases.

A thorough perusal of the history of human development will disclose two elements in bitter conflict with each other; elements that are only now beginning to be understood, not as foreign to each other, but as closely related and truly harmonious, if only placed in proper environment: the individual and social instincts. The individual and society have waged a relentless and bloody battle for ages, each striving for supremacy, because each was blind to the value and importance of the other. The individual and social instincts—the one a most potent factor for individual endeavor, for growth, aspiration, self-realization; the other an equally potent factor for mutual helpfulness and social well-being.

The explanation of the storm raging within the individual, and between him and his surroundings, is not far to seek. The primitive man, unable to understand his being, much less the unity of all life, felt himself absolutely dependent on blind, hidden forces ever ready to mock and taunt him. Out of that attitude grew the religious concepts of man as a mere speck of dust dependent on superior powers on high, who can only be appeased by complete surrender. All the early sagas rest on that idea, which continues to be the *Leitmotiv* of the biblical tales dealing with the relation of man to God, to the State, to society. Again and again the same motif, *man is nothing, the powers are everything*. Thus Jehovah would only endure man on condition of complete surrender. Man can have all the glories of the earth, but he must not become conscious of himself. The State, society, and moral laws all sing the refrain: Man can have all the glories of the earth, but must not become conscious of himself.

Anarchism is the only philosophy which brings to man the consciousness of himself; which maintains that God, the State, and society are non-existent, that their promises are null and void, since they can be fulfilled only through man's subordination. Anarchism is therefore the teacher of the unity of life; not merely in nature, but in man. There is no conflict between the individual and the social instincts, any more than there is between the heart and the lungs: the one the receptacle of a precious life essence, the other the repository of the element that keeps the essence pure and strong. The individual is the heart of society, conserving the essence of social life; society is the lungs which are distributing the element to keep the life essence—that is, the individual—pure and strong.

"The one thing of value in the world," says Emerson, "is the active soul; this every man contains within him. The soul active sees absolute truth and utters truth and creates." In other words, the individual instinct is the thing of value in the world. It is the true soul that sees and creates the truth alive, out of which is to come a still greater truth, the re-born social soul.

Anarchism is the great liberator of man from the phantoms that have held him captive; it is the arbiter and pacifier of the two forces for individual and social harmony. To accomplish that unity, Anarchism has declared war on the pernicious influences which have so far prevented the harmonious blending of individual and social instincts, the individual and society.

Religion, the dominion of the human mind; Property, the dominion of human needs; and Government, the dominion of human conduct, represent the stronghold of man's enslavement and all the horrors it entails. Religion! How it dominates man's mind, how it humiliates and degrades his soul. God is everything, man is nothing, says religion. But out of that nothing God has created a kingdom so despotic, so tyrannical, so cruel, so terribly exacting that naught but gloom and tears and blood have ruled the world since gods began. Anarchism rouses man to rebellion against this black monster. Break your mental fetters, says Anarchism to man, for not until you think and judge for yourself will you get rid of the dominion of darkness, the greatest obstacle to all progress.

Property, the dominion of man's needs, the denial of the right to satisfy his needs. Time was when property claimed a divine right, when it came to man with the same refrain, even as religion, "Sacrifice! Abnegate! Submit!" The spirit of Anarchism has lifted man from his prostrate position. He now stands erect, with his face toward the light. He has learned to see the insatiable, devouring, devastating nature of property, and he is preparing to strike the monster dead.

Source: Emma Goldman. "Anarchy: What It Really Stands For." In *Red Emma Speaks: Selected Writings and Speeches by Emma Goldman.* Edited by Alix Kates Shulman. New York: Random House, 1972.

Anarchism and World Order

Richard A. Falk

RICHARD A. FALK *is Albert G. Milbank Professor of International Law and Practice, Center of International Studies, Princeton University.*

Three Hard Questions For Anarchists

1. *Are not the preconditions for anarchist success insurmountable?* The great anarchist success stories have been episodic, short-lived (e.g., the Paris Commune of 1871, the anarchist collectives in parts of Spain during the 1939s, the May uprising in Paris in 1968). Nowhere have anarchists enjoyed a period of sustained success. Generally, anarchist success has generated an overpowering reaction of repression, as when the mercenary soldiery of Versailles crushed and massacred the Paris Communards in May 1871 only weeks after their extraordinary triumph. Anarchists view such failures as inevitable "first attempts." Kropotkin calls "the Commune of Paris, the child of a period of transition … doomed to perish" but "the forerunner of social revolution."[1] Murray Bookchin and Daniel Guérin make a similar assessment of the Paris uprising of 1968, regarding its occurrence as proof of the anarchist critique, its collapse as evidence that "the molecular movement below that prepares the condition for revolution" had not yet carried far enough.[2]

On a deeper level, anarchists understand that the prerequisite for anarchist success anywhere is its success *everywhere*. It is this vital precondition that is at once so convincing and so formidable as to call into question whether the anarchist position can in fact be taken seriously as a progressive alternative to state socialism.

Bakunin expressed the anarchist demand and rationale with clarity:

> A federalist in the internal affairs of the country, he desires an international confederation, first of all in the spirit of justice, and second because he is convinced that the economic and social revolution, transcending all the artificial and pernicious barriers between states, can only be brought about, in part at least, by the solidarity in action, if not of all, then at least of the majority of the nations constituting the civilized world today, so that sooner or later all nations must join together.[3]

Or, as Daniel Guérin expressed it: "An isolated national revolution cannot succeed. The social revolution inevitably becomes a world revolution."[4]

In essence, not only is it difficult for anarchists to attain power, but once they manage to do so their "organic institutions" seem incapable of holding it. Their movements will be liquidated ruthlessly by statists of "the left" of "the right."[5] Given such vulnerability, it may even be a betrayal of one's followers to expose them to slaughter by mounting a challenge against the entrenched forces of statism in the absence of either the will or the capabilities to protect the challengers.[6]

There is a report of a fascinating conversation between Lenin and Kropotkin in May 1919 in which Lenin mounts such an argument in two ways. First, he makes his familiar point that "You can't make a revolution wearing white gloves. We know perfectly well that we have made and will make a great many mistakes … But it is impossible not to make mistakes during a revolution. Not to make them means to renounce life entirely and do nothing at all. But we have preferred to make errors and thus to act … We want to act and we will, despite all the mistakes, and will bring our socialist revolution to the final and inevitably victorious end."[7] Lenin here in effect acknowledges the errors that flow from using state power to secure the revolutionary victory from external and internal enemies, and he rebuffs the anarchist view that state power can be dissolved. Lenin's second rebuff of the anarchist position is his condescending view of its revolutionary power: "Do you really think that the capitalist world will submit to the path of the cooperative movement? … You will pardon me, but this is all nonsense! We need direct action of the masses, revolutionary action of the masses, that activity which seizes the capitalist world by the throat and brings it down."[8] Of anarchist concepts of "social revolution," Lenin says "these are children's playthings, idle chatter, having no realist soil underneath, no force, no means, and almost nothing approaching our socialist goals … We don't need the struggle and violent acts of separate persons. It is high time that the anarchists understood this and stopped scattering their revolutionary energy on utterly useless affairs."[9] In sum, Lenin is arguing that the ends of anarchists must be pursued by mass violent revolution and secured through state power. The anarchist response is, of course, that the choice of such means perverts and dooms the ends. The antagonism of anarchists toward the Bolshevik Revolution has been vindicated many times over.[10] On the level of their discussion, it seems that both Lenin and Kropotkin are correct,[11]—Lenin in saying that there is no other way to succeed, the anarchists by contending that such success is as bad, if not worse than, defeat.

But, in my view, the strongest case for the feasibility of the anarchist position still remains to be argued. It is implicit, perhaps, in Kropotkin's own work on the origins of the modern state and on its feudal antecedents in the European cities of the eleventh and twelfth centuries.[12] Kropotkin's argument rests on the historical claim that a vital society of communes and free cities created by brotherhoods, guilds, and individual initiative existed earlier: " ... it is shown by an immense documentation from many sources, that never, either before or since, has mankind known a period of relative well-being for all as in the cities of the Middle Ages. The poverty, insecurity, and physical exploitation of labor that exist in our times were then unknown."[13] Drawing on non-Western experience as well, Kropotkin argues in effect that societal well-being and security based on anarchist conceptions of organic institutions (of a cooperative character) were immensely successful over a wide geographical and cultural expanse until crushed by the emergent states of the fifteenth and sixteenth centuries. Thus, there is a kind of *prima facie* case for plausibility of the anarchist model, although in a prestatal context.

But evidence of the anarchist potential for "success" does not end with medieval Europe. The direction of contemporary China, especially its antiparty, populist phase that culminated in the Cultural Revolution, contains strong anarchist elements.[14] Indeed, it was precisely on these grounds of repudiating "organization" and "bureaucracy" as a basis for communist discipline that China made itself so offensive to communist ideologues in the Kremlin.[15] China is, of course, a mixed case. In its foreign policy it places great stress on statist prerogatives. Nevertheless, in its domestic patterns the Chinese example lends some credibility to Bakunin's and Kropotkin's claim that there are nonbureaucratic roads to socialism, and gives the anarchist orientation renewed plausibility as a serious political alternative.[16]

Such plausibility can, it seems to me, be extrapolated in a poststatal context. Here, my argument, sustained by sources as dissimilar as Saul Mendlovitz and Henry Kissinger, is that we are undergoing a profound historical transformation that is destroying the organizational matrix of a global system based on territorial states.[17] That is, we are entering a poststatal period, although its character remains highly conjectural. Whatever the outcome, however, the anarchist stress on nonterritorial associations and communal consciousness seems highly relevant because of its basic compatibility with the inevitable shift in the relation of forces.

In sum, the anarchist case for radical reform (i.e., for social revolution) was *chimerical within* the confines of the state system. However, the state system is now being superseded. In this context, one set of plausible possibilities is the globalization of societal life in a way that allows cooperative organizational forms to flourish. That is, the anarchist vision (as epitomized in Bakunin's writings) of a fusion between a universal confederation and organic societal forms of a communal character lies at the very center of the *only* hopeful prospect for the future of world order.[18] Needless to say, such a prospect has slim chances for success, but at least the possibility is no longer chimerical, given the change of objective circumstances. The state system is not an implacable foe, for many economic, political, technological, and sociological forces are everywhere undermining its bases of potency, if unevenly and at an uncertain rate. Therefore, although the political precondition of scale imposed by anarchism still remains formidable, it may yet prove historically surmountable. It may be surmountable because the preparatory processes going on throughout the world during this historical period are creating more favorable global conditions for the anarchist cause than have hitherto existed for several centuries. This assessment arises from several distinct developments. Perhaps the most significant is the growing disenchantment with the values, goals, and methods of industrial society. This sense of disenchantment is coming to be shared by increasing numbers of citizens, particularly in the developed nations of the West, and is finding various forms of expression that reflect revised notions of necessity based on "limits to growth," notions of well-being based on intermediate technology and small-scale institutions, and notions of personal transcendence based on a new spiritual energy that repudiates both conventional religion and secular humanism. In this setting, the quest for an appropriate politics converges rather dramatically with the central tenets of anarchist belief. This modern sensibility realizes, at last, that the state is simultaneously *too large* to satisfy human needs and *too small* to cope with the requirements of guidance for an increasingly interdependent planet. This realization is temporarily offset by a rising tide of statism in many other parts of the world, where political independence is a forbidden fruit only recently tasted, but where the fruit will be poisoned, as every-where else, by a world of nuclear weapons, ecological decay, and mass economic privation. The main *problematique* of our age is whether an appropriate politics of global reform, combining a centralized form of functional guidance with decentralized economic, social, and political structures, can be shaped by voluntary action, or whether it must be formed in a crucible of tragedy and catastrophe. Attentiveness to the anarchist tradition can be one part of an effort to achieve an appropriate politics *this* side of catastrophe. Obviously, the objective conditions which require such a reassessment of political forms are not by themselves sufficient to effect a transformation. Indeed, the very relevance of these ideas may lead their powerful opponents to regard them as even more dangerous now than in the past. Prudence and patience are essential in these circumstances. The crises of the state system may yet require several decades to develop to the point where eruptions of spontaneous anarchistic energies would not unleash a variety of devastating backlashes.

2. *Given the urgency of global reform, isn't the anarchist prospect too remote in time?* Even accepting the optimistic assessment of the preceding section, namely, that the hour of anarchism may coincide with the collapse of statism, restructuring of the world system would still appear to be developed for an unnecessarily and dangerously long period of several decades or more. Just as the emergence of the state system was a matter of centuries, so might the consolidation of a new system of political order require hundreds of years.[19] Two sets of questions call for judgment based on imponderables. First, how serious and pressing is the crisis? Is the fire close at hand, or still barely visible on a distant horizon? How can we know? Second, are any alternative means available through which the principal goals of global reform could be attained more reliably and rapidly than through anarchism? Do we have any responsible basis for selecting or rejecting these alternatives? In part, we are forced here to confront the most fundamental issues of politics, knowledge, and action. In the abstract, we do not know enough to choose or to act. Of course this same limitation bears on every school of political thought, including those that defend the status quo or incline toward gradualism. But it has even greater bearing on a political position that proposes radical tactics and goals, especially if large-scale violence is likely to ensue. On the other hand, this line of reasoning may be deceptive. In a moment of crisis, to do nothing may be the most risky of all postures toward the future. It is generally better to jump from a sinking ship than it is to stay on board, even if one knows nothing about the prospects of

rescue from the waters below. The collective situation of human society cannot be cast in such deceptive simplicity. The veil of ignorance is thick indeed when it comes to assessing policy alternatives for the future of world society.

But the argument from ignorance cuts the other way as well. We have no real way to assess the degrees of progress along the transition path. Perhaps the collapse of statism is closer than we think. As Paul Goodman wrote:

> It will be said that there is no time. Yes, probably. But let me cite a remark of Tocqueville. In his last work, *L'Ancien Régime*, he notes "with terror," as he says, how throughout the eighteenth century writer after writer and expert after expert pointed out that this and that detail of the Old Regime was unviable and could not possibly survive; added up, they proved that the entire Old Regime was doomed and must soon collapse; and yet *there was not a single man who foretold that there would be a mighty revolution.*[20]

In the face of such uncertainty, compounded by the many evidences of pressure on the state system, it makes political as well as moral sense to pursue a *principled set of conclusions* even if their realization cannot be immediately foreseen. In one sense Herbert Read is correct in saying that "the task of the anarchist philosopher is not to prove the imminence of a Golden Age, but to justify the value of believing in its possibility."[21]

Such a value depends on some degree of plausibility, but also on whether or not there are any preferable alternatives. Given the established bankruptcy of statist solutions on the right and left, given the vulnerability of the state system as a whole to catastrophic and, quite possibly, irreversible damage, and given the insufficiency of gradualist strategies of amelioration, the case for some variant of radical anarchism seems strong despite the inability of the anarchist to provide skeptics with a credible timetable.

In essence, the issue of urgency reinforces the anarchist case. The primary world order need is to find an alternative to statism. Anarchism, despite its limited political success during the statist era, provides the most coherent, widespread, and persistent tradition of antistatist thought. It is also a tradition that has generally been inclined toward world-order values: peace, economic equity, civil liberties, ecological defense. As such, it represents the most normatively acceptable sequel to the state system. Other sequels include imperial consolidation; world state; regional federation; intergovernmental functionalism.[22]

To affirm the relevance of the anarchist tradition is not to accept the adequacy of its current formulations but only of its general orientation. Advocates of an anarchist approach need to formulate the globalist implications of anarchism in a manner responsive to the current world-order crisis. As far as I know, this has not yet been done. Indeed, anarchism suffers from the tendency of other traditions of philosophical speculation generated during the statist era, namely, to concentrate upon the national question and to assume that the global question will disappear when all nations have correctly resolved their own domestic problems. As I have suggested, anarchists are more dependent than other reformers on supportive transnational developments; but their analysis of international events is usually identical to that of Marxists, on the level of critique, and highly impressionistic when it comes to making specific proposals. Thus, the claims of anarchism are not weakened by the urgency of the world crisis, but the need for a more historically sensitive interpretation and for a globally oriented formulation of anarchist response is essential.

3. *Does the receptivity of anarchism to violence undermine the moral basis of its claim to provide an ideology for global reform?* I am not discussing here the anarchist as "bomb-thrower," but neither do I identify anarchism with pacifist ethics. As a philosophical position anarchism adopts an equivocal view of violence as an agent of change. Although anarchists tend to rely on spontaneous militancy of a nonviolent character—most typically, the general strike or other forms of unarmed struggle and resistance—there is no prevailing anarchist view on the role of violence.

I think Howard Zinn has sympathetically, but reliably, presented the anarchist position on violence in this assessment:

> Some anarchists—like other revolutionaries throughout history … have emphasized violent uprising. Some have advocated, and tried, assassination and terror … What makes anarchists unique among revolutionaries, however, is that most of them see revolution as a cultural, ideological, creative process, in which violence would be as incidental as the outcries of mother and baby in childbirth. It might be unavoidable—given the natural resistance to change—but something to be kept at a minimum while more important things happen.[23]

The question is whether, given the technology of destruction and the ruthlessness of statist leadership, this view of violence is adequate. It can be attacked from either side, as underestimating the role of violence for any serious revolutionary position, or as too willing to accept the moral Trojan Horse of political violence.

Mainstream Marxists and neo-Marxists generally contend that revolution depends upon mass-based armed struggle. A recent formulation is "the political statement of the Weather Underground" released under the title *Prairie Fire*:

> It's an illusion that imperialism will decay peacefully. Imperialism has meant constant war. Imperialists defend their control of the means of life with terrible force. There is no reason to believe they will become humane or relinquish power … To not prepare the people for this struggle is to disarm them ideologically and physically and to perpetrate a cruel hoax.[24]

The cruel hoax is, of course, the illusion that revolution can occur without armed struggle, that a revolution can be made with white gloves. But as Kropotkin soon perceived, once the white gloves have been thrown away, it becomes all too easy to adopt terror and torture.[25] In my view, the abuse of state power by socialism has reversed the presumption that violence is a necessary concomitant of revolution. On the contrary, it now seems a cruel hoax to promise humane outcomes from any revolutionary process that embraces violence with anything other than the utmost reluctance. Any genuinely radical position that purports moral (as well as political) credibility must, above all else, reject a cult of violence, and justify the use of specific forms of violence in the most careful and conditional manner.

Source: Richard A. Falk. "Anarchism and World Order." In *Anarchism: Nomos XIX.* Edited by J. Roland Pennock and John W. Chapman. New York: New York University Press, 1978. Reprinted with permission.

Notes

[1] *Kropotkin*, p.127. [Ed. note: Falk cites here Kropotkin, "The Commons of Paris" in Martin A. Miller, ed. *Selected Writings on Anarchism and Revolution* by P.A. Kropotkin (Cambridge, Mass.: MIT Press, 1970).]

[2] Bookchin, *Post-Scarcity Anarchism*, p.258. [Ed. note: Falk cites here M. Bookchin, *Post-Scarcity Anarchism* (Berkeley, Calif.: Ramport Press, 1971).]

[3] *Bakunin*. p.118. [Ed. note: Falk's reference is to Sam Dolgoff, ed. *Bakunin on Anarchy* (New York: Anchor, 1973).]

[4] Guérin, *Anarchism: From Theory to Practice* (New York: Monthly Review Press, 1970), p.69.

[5] George Woodcock, *Anarchism* (New York: World Publishing Co., 1962), pp.275-424.

[6] Such allegations have been made with respect to Salvador Allende's efforts in the early 1970s to transform the societal base of Chile without dismantling the state apparatus with its strong links to the vested interests of the older order.

[7] *Kropotkin*, p.328.

[8] *Kropotkin*. pp.329-30.

[9] *Kropotkin*. p.330.

[10] One of the earliest and most eloquent anarchist critics of the Soviet experience was Emma Goldman. See her *My Disillusionment with Russia* (Garden City, New York: Doubleday, 1923).

[11] Kropotkin's position can be extrapolated from his general anarchist writings; he did not state the anarchist case in his conversations with Lenin.

[12] See Kropotkin's excellent essay, "The State: Its Historic Rule," in *Kropotkin*, pp.211-64.

[13] *Kropotkin* p.231.

[14] See perceptive discussion, in Schurmann, *Logic of World Power* (New York: Pantheon, 1974), pp.369-80.

[15] Schurmann, *Logic of World Power*. p.380.

[16] For a skeptical interpretation of China's domestic experience see Donald Zagoria, "China by Daylight," *Dissent* (Spring 1975), pp.135-47.

[17] For opposing interpretations on the durability of the state and the state system see Saul H. Mendlovitz, Introduction, in Saul H. Mendlovitz, ed., *On the Creation of a Just World Order* (New York: Free Press, 1975), pp.vii-xvii, and Stanley Hoffmann, "Obstinate or Obsolete? The Fate of the Nation-State and the Case of Western Europe," *Daedalus* (Summer 1966), pp.862-915.

[18] A general interpretation can be found in Robert Heilbroner, *An Inquiry into the Human Prospect* (New York: Norton, 1974); see also Falk, *A Study of Future Worlds* (New York: Free Press, 1975), pp.417-37; Richard A. Falk, "A New Paradigm for International Legal Studies: Prospects and Proposals," *Yale Law Journal 84:* 969-1021 (1975).

[19] See Joseph R. Strayer, *On the Medieval Origins of the Modern State* (Princeton University Press, 1970).

[20] Goodman, "Ambiguities of Pacifist Politics," in Leonard I. Krimerman and Lewis Perry, eds. *Patterns of Anarchy* (New York: Anchor, 1966), p.136; see also *Kropotkin*, pp.121-24.

[21] Read, *Anarchy and Order* (Boston: Beacon Press, 1971), p.14.

[22] For consideration of world order option see Falk, *Future Worlds*, pp.150-276; Falk, "A New Paradigm ... " pp.999-1017.

[23] Zinn, Introduction, Read, *Anarchy and Order*. p.xvii.

[24] *Prairie Fire*, Political Statement of the Weather Underground, 1974. p.3.

[25] See Kropotkin letter to Lenin date 21 December 1920, in *Kropotkin*. pp.338-39.

9

Nationalism

The Ideal of the Nation State

The last decade of the twentieth century has seen a surprising rejuvenation of nationalism. Thomas Eriksen claims that much of this phenomenon is attributable to recent changes in the global system—changes which cannot be understood in the idiom of the Cold War. Recent changes show a tendency for the modern nation state to be ethnically divided and for ethnic ideologies to be at odds with dominant nationalist ideologies. Eriksen does an effective job not only in drawing out the distinctions between nationalism and ethnicity, but also in stressing their importance as ideologies.

Unity is the law of the moral world according to Mazzini. In a few short sentences Mazzini carries the reader from his comment on unity to remarks on establishing a nation, and a people, in the name of republicanism. What he advocates is a religion of patriotism which blends humanism and nationality without sinking into the narrow spirit of nationalism. How one is to prevent the historic fact of nationality—which he advocates—from collapsing into nationalism—which he opposes—is far from clear.

Peter Alter discusses both the Greek nationalism of 1821, which resulted in Greece regaining its independence from Turkish rule, and the re-evaluation of nationalism which occurred in Europe after World War II. He offers a persuasive account of the past and present relevance of nationalism in determining domestic and foreign policies of countries.

In an analytical mood, Alexander Motyl breaks nationalism down into belief in the nation-state, in self-government, in national identity, in national well-being and in national superiority. He urges us to employ these terms in an even-handed way and then argues that nationalism so defined is alive and well even in the West. And in a last burst of insight, he presents some evidence against the claim that the market—with its punitive and competitive features—is the best solvent of nationalism.

The subject of national identity in the context of European unity is the subject of Anthony Smith's contribution. Recognizing the subtle tension between national identity and other loyalties, Smith attempts to establish a theoretical framework for national identities which a study of cultural identities facilitates. He concludes by predicting the persistence of strong ethnic sentiments as well as the periodic revival of national identities in Europe.

Paul Lendvai takes the discussion away from theoretical nationalism and into the Yugoslav world of the 1990s. Lendvai's contribution serves as a forceful reminder of the importance of tradition, history, and demographics in shaping national sentiment. His emphasis of these factors relates very nicely to John Pilger's passionate account of the tragedy of Bosnia and the culpability of the West. Its prevarication in doing anything to stop the suffering in Bosnia, preceded by its intervention in recognizing Croatia, lead Pilger to castigate it.

Eric Hobsbawm challenges the rationality of Mazzini's belief that every nation should form a state. Hobsbawm disagrees that there should only be one state for each nation, maintaining that this proposition has always been unworkable in ethnic and linguistic terms. Hobsbawm explains why nationalism along ethnic lines has surfaced in places as widespread as Kazakhstan, Québec, Croatia and Scotland. Finally, the author questions whether such nationalistic endeavours will lead to increased cultural and/or economic autonomy.

In a perceptive essay written twenty-five years ago, Pierre Eliott Trudeau reveals the connections and tensions between nationalism and federalism. Trudeau is quite happy to see federalism triumph over nationalism if the former is based—which he thinks is the case—on pragmatic and territorial considerations, rather than on raw emotions. He ends with a plea for internationalism that is driven by a spirited defence of international law.

Unity and Nationality

Giuseppe Mazzini

GIUSEPPE MAZZINI *(1805–72) was a revolutionary Italian thinker and writer who became involved in the movement for Italian unification. He hoped for the establishment of an Italian republic, and hence was disappointed with the creation of an Italian monarchy in 1861.*

Unity is the law of the physical as well as of the moral world … Where there exists no authority derived from a ruling national principle, to which all the accidents and occurrences of social life may be referred, a conflict of individual opinions is sure to arise, in which force will be of necessity become the sole arbitrator, and the path to despotism will thus be thrown open … The natural impulse of every social body is to harmonize the various forces of which it is composed. All strife or dissonance between these forces is an indication of disease.

Every revolution is an attempt to co-ordinate the springs of social progress, an attempt to obtain recognition for an hitherto neglected element, and to procure for that element its rightful place in the constitution of the power that governs the national edifice.

Now this impulse towards harmony, and the creation of a system, are one and the same thing.

A principle, its legitimate consequences, and their exact application to a given aim, are the component parts of a doctrine.

Merely to shout liberty, without reflecting what it is intended the word should imply, is the instinct of the oppressed slave—no more.

It is impossible to realize a great aim by confining ourselves to a vague sentiment of reaction, and an indefinite idea of war against every obstacle in our way. Liberty thus understood will lead us to martyrdom, not victory … (Works, vol. I)

My nature was profoundly subjective, and master of its own course. The I was even for me an active force called upon to modify the medium in which it lived, not to passively submit to it. Life radiated from the centre to the circumference, not from the circumference to the centre. Ours was not an undertaking of simple reaction, the movement of a sick man who changes sides to alleviate his pains. We did not reach towards liberty as the end, but as the means for attaining an end yet higher and more positive.

Upon the banners we had inscribed Republican Unity. We wished to found a Nation, to create a People. To men who had proposed to themselves an end so vast, what was a defeat? Was it not an appointed part of our educational work, this teaching of imperturbability amid adverse events? Could we teach without setting our example? And would not our abdication have subserved as an argument for those who held Unity to be impossible? The radical spoiler in Italy that condemned her to impotence was evidently not the lack of desire, but a distrust of her own strength, a facile tendency towards discouragement, a defect in that constancy without which no virtue can fructify, a fatal want of harmony between thought and action. The moral teaching which would remedy this evil was not possible in Italy, under the persecuting scourge of the police, in the way of writing or of speech on a large scale, proportionate to the need. A living Apostolate was necessary, a nucleus of Italians strong in their constancy, inaccessible to discouragement,—such as could show themselves, in the name of an Idea; capable of affronting with a smile of faith persecution and discomfiture; falling one day, rising upon the next, but ready always for the combat; and believing always, without calculation of time or circumstance, in the final victory. Ours was not a sect but a religion of patriotism. Sects may die under violence; religion may not. I shook off my doubts, and deliberated how to pursue my way.

In Italy the work was inevitably slackened. Time was needed for souls to recover, for masters to believe themselves conquerors, and to betake them again to sleep. But we might make up outside for the loss at home, and labour to rise again one day and fling out a second call to Italy, strong in alliance with foreign elements and with European opinion. We might in the effacing, which I saw was being slowly accomplished, of every regenerative principle initiative of European action, prepare the ground for the only idea which appeared to me called to remake the life of the peoples, that of Nationality, with the initiative influence of Italy in some future movement.

Nationality and the possibility of the Italian initiative: this was the programme and the dominating idea of all my labours.

There exists in Europe no alliance for Good, for the protection of national liberties, for the defence of the feeble, for the peaceful evolution of the progressive principle. There is absolutely nothing collective to represent the consolidation of the families of humanity ... Hate reigns, for it is only hate that acts; it has its armies, its treasures, its compacts. Its right is Force. The narrow spirit of Nationalism substituted for the spirit of Nationality; the stupid presumption on the part of each people that they are capable of solving the political, social, and economic problem alone; the forgetfulness of the great truths that cause of the peoples is one, that the cause of the Fatherland must lean upon Humanity, that the aim of our warfare is the Holy Alliance of the Nations.

Is it too much to hope that some day the nations will assemble as brethren gathered together round the twin altars of the Fatherland and Humanity? That men should have faith in things to come and labour un-ceasingly to hasten their coming, even though without hope of living to witness their triumph? Are these illusions? Do we presume too far in asking such faith in an age undermined by scepticism, among men still slaves of the ego, who love little, and forget early; who do not cherish courage in their hearts, and are earnest in nothing save in the calculations of egoism, and in the passing pleasures of the hour? No, we do not ask too much. It is necessary that these things should be, and they will be. We have faith in God, in the power of truth, and in the historic logic of things. The principle which was the soul of the old world is exhausted. It is our part to clear the way for the new principle. To-morrow the world now incredulous or indifferent will bow before it. For we know, like Galileo, that, in spite of the Inquisition, the world moves.

Source: Giuseppe Mazzini: Selected Writings, edited by N. Gangulee, Lindsay Drummond, London 1945.

Emancipation and Oppression: Towards a Typology of Nationalism

Peter Alter

PETER ALTER *is Deputy Director of the German Historical Institute, London, and Professor of Modern History in the University of Cologne.*

The Spectrum of Historical Experience

During its first flourishing in early nineteenth-century Europe, modern nationalism was seen as a force that would enable the peoples of the continent to cast off the fetters of their political and social bondage. As the ideology which inscribed self-determination upon the flags of the peoples, nationalism supplied the demand for independent statehood with its legitimation. It awakened hopes and expectations.

One of the leading personalities in the Greek independence movement—one of the first of its type—Prince Alexander Ypsilanti, who was in the service of the Russian Tsar, penned a stirring appeal to his compatriots in February 1821 at the beginning of the Greek revolt against Ottoman rule. He wrote:

> Just raise your eyes, comrades! Behold your pitiful condition, your desecrated temples, your daughters delivered up to the lust of barbarians, your plundered houses, your devastated fields, you yourselves living as wretched slaves! Has the time not come to throw off this unbearable yoke and free the fatherland? Cast aside all that is alien, wave the flag, make the sign of the cross and you will surely triumph and save the fatherland and our religion from the blasphemy of the pagans. Which of you, noble Greeks, will not with a glad heart seek to free the fatherland from its chains? ...
>
> Above all, however, your sense of community must prevail. The rich among you must contribute a part of their wealth, the priests must encourage the people by teaching and example, and those civilian and military personnel serving at foreign courts must resign their duties under whatever regime they find themselves. They must all strive together towards the great goal, and thereby pay off their old debt to the fatherland. As is fitting for men of noble race, they must all arm themselves without delay and I promise them victory in short order and with it the advent of all happiness. Stand up as a bold people against those decadent slaves, those hirelings, and show yourselves to be true descendants of the heroes of classical times.[1]

Like the other peoples of the Balkans, the Greeks had at that stage been under Turkish rule for centuries. As Christians, they suffered discrimination in the Sultan's empire and yet they occupied key positions in the economy and even in the administration. Their situation was insecure, but not unbearable. There were colonies of Greek merchants and traders in all the larger cities of the eastern Mediterranean under Ottoman rule. Although the Greeks drew significant economic advantage from their unhindered freedom of movement in the Ottoman Empire, aspirations towards greater political freedom stirred among them, as they did among their northern neighbours as Ottoman central government progressively declined. From the late eighteenth century onwards, under the influence of the French Revolution and its ideas, there had been outbreaks of guerilla warfare and revolt against the Turks, the first result of which had been the acquisition of a limited political autonomy by Serbia in 1815.

The Serbian success encouraged the Greeks to press forward their struggle for a change in the political status quo in the regions which they considered to be Greek territory. Ypsilanti's appeal is a typical example of these aspirations and the colourful rhetoric that accompanied them. The arguments presented in his appeal were repeated with only minor variations in the programmes of the other national movements in nineteenth-century Europe. Even later they appear with thoroughly tiresome monotony, right up to the anti-colonial liberation movements in Asia and Africa since the First World War. What were these arguments?

Ypsilanti's clarion call to struggle against alien Ottoman rule appealed to the solidarity of the people, the deeds of the mythical heroes of its history and the willingness of individuals to sacrifice themselves. Ypsilanti demanded unconditional service to the fatherland and urged a consciousness of "Greekness", whatever he might have understood by that. He promised victory over the Turks and "with it the advent of all happiness". In so doing, he was attempting quite openly to arouse hopes of a better life in an independent Greek state, which, however, as an economic unit (and this was already easy to see at the time) would offer the Greeks substantially less potential for development than the Ottoman empire, which stretched over three continents. Economics did not, however, enter into it at the time. The superordinate goal of Greek nationalism, a Greek nation-state, took precedence over all other considerations. In the 1820s, the Greeks seemed to have drawn palpably nearer their goal as their struggle for liberation had found sympathy and support in Europe. Above all, the liberal political public of Western and Central Europe saw in nationalism an effective means of transforming congealed political and social conditions in the years of Restoration after the Congress of Vienna.

Some 130 years after the inception of the movement for Greek independence from Turkish rule, nationalism was still being regarded as a revolutionary force by the peoples of Africa and Asia. In Europe, meanwhile, it had undergone a startling re-evaluation since the days of Prince Ypsilanti. There it was no longer seen as the overture and accompaniment to a "springtime of peoples" nor as a force that could lead Europe towards a better future and create a more peaceful order among nations. In the middle of the twentieth century, nationalism had become a destructive force with horrific associations. For the people of Europe, nationalism now signified as Huizinga put it, primarily "the powerful drive to dominate", the "urge to have one's own nation, one's own state assert itself above, over, and at the cost of others".[2] After the second World War, the vast majority of Europeans equated nationalism with bellicose aggression, the unbridled urge for expansions, and racism. They regarded it as the expression of blinkered mentality which had brought immeasurable calamity down upon Europe. In his autobiography of 1952, the British publisher and author Victor Gollancz wrote:

> Of all the evils I hate I think I hate nationalism most' wrote the British publisher and author Victor Gollancz in his autobiography of 1952. Nationalism—national egoism, thinking in terms of one's nation rather than in terms of humanity—nationalism is evil because it concentrates on comparative inessentials (where a man lives, what sort of language he speaks, the type of his culture, the character of his "blood") and ignores the essential, which is simply that he is a man ... It makes one set of people hate another set that they haven't the smallest real occasion for hating: it leads to jealously, expansionism, oppression, strife and eventually war.[3]

Gollancz lived at a time when nationalism had entirely shed its original emancipatory and liberal character and had turned out to be an extreme ideology with disastrous consequences for the co-existence of the European peoples. German and Italian nationalism, in particular, had advocated a programme of oppression, and even annihilation, of other peoples, and in the 1930s and 1940s had translated words into action. To Europeans, having experienced the perverted nationalism of Fascist Italy and National Socialist Germany, it represented a morally reprehensible phenomenon.

The negative evaluation of nationalism after 1945, so unmistakeable in Gollancz's writings, still largely determines current European opinion on nationalism. Even its earlier manifestations are in retrospect judged in these moral tones. The change in attitude is particularly evident among Germans, for whom nationalism was thoroughly discredited after the last war. They had seen the nationalism of Wilhelmine Germany culminate in the First World War, and knew how the excesses of Third Reich ultranationalism, with its radical *volkisch* and racial policies, had led to the destruction of the German national state, itself founded only in 1871. This complete reversal of attitude subsequently encouraged in the western part of Germany a tendency to underestimate the continuing significance of nationalism in other areas of the world. To consider nationalism and its history chiefly in terms of National Socialism and the self-emasculation of Europe through two world wars, however, prevents deeper understanding. As a political principle that is currently more crucial than ever in determining the foreign and domestic policies of many countries, and which has retained its power to mobilize the masses against internal and external opposition, nationalism, is still far from irrelevant.

Source: Peter Alter. *Nationalism.* London: Edward Arnold, 1989. Reprinted with permission.

Notes

[1] Quoted in R. Ruland (ed.), *Restauration und Fortschritt*, Munich 1963, p.46-46.

[2] Johan Huizinga, *Men and Ideas. Essays on History, the Middle Ages, the Renaissance*, New York 1959, p.97.

[3] Victor Gollancz, *My Dear Timothy. An autobiographical Letter to his Grandson*, Harmondsworth 1952, pp.294-5.

The Modernity of Nationalism: Nations, States and Nation-States in the Contemporary World

Alexander J. Motyl

A.J. MOTYL *is a professor of political science at Columbia University in New York City.*

Defining Nationalism

How should nationalism be defined? I shall not answer this question in this article, although I do, of course, have my own preferences.[1] The most important points to keep in mind when defining nationalism are: First, the definition should not rest on the erroneous view of concepts as being descriptive of a reality that is divorced from the conceptualization of it; second, it should not conflate defining characteristics with central or associated ones; and third, it should avoid creating megaphenomena that subvert attempts at explanation.

With these cautionary words, I suggest that nationalism, if it is to be a useful concept, should be endowed with only one of the possible meanings noted above; the others may then be demoted to the rank of central characteristics that generally appear to "go with" the defined phenomenon. That is, nationalism may be a political ideology or ideal that argues that nations should have their own states (or enjoy self-rule); it may be the belief that the world is divided into nations and that this division is both proper and natural; it may be love of one's nation; and, finally, it may be the belief that one's own nation should stand above all other nations. In simple terms, these views of nationalism boil down, respectively, to the following beliefs: in the nation-state, in self-government, in national identity, in national well-being and in national superiority[2] these or other beliefs are not forms of behavior, individuals or groups with such beliefs may attempt to translate them into reality, but the specific actions they undertake cannot, by definition, be nationalism—unless we make the absurd assumption that beliefs invariably translate automatically into behavior[3]

If and when we employ the above definitions, it is imperative that we do so in an even-handed manner that permits the term *nationalism* to be maximally applicable to a variety of situations, including one's own. Thus, if nationalism is belief in the nation-state, then it can be found only amongst those nations that lack their own states, and to speak of contemporary American or French nationalism would be illogical. If nationalism is belief in self-government, then the pool of potential candidates expands to include those individuals and movements that aspire to autonomy: In this sense, even the ostensibly quiescent Turkmen would have to be considered fervid nationalists. If nationalism is belief in nations and in national identity, then we are all nationalists. If nationalism is dedication to a nation's well-being, then, again, we are all nationalists. Finally, if nationalism is some form of chauvinism or supremacism, then we would have to admit that it is manifest in East and West, North and South—indeed, as I suggested above, no less in the United States than in Iraq, no less in Great Britain than in Romania.

A dispassionate application of the concept of nationalism leads us to the conclusion that nationalism, in all of the above five designations, is not only alive and well in the West, which claims to be everything but nationalist, but that it is also quite modern. True, fewer groups may be striving for the nation-state in the West than in other parts of the world (although this claim appears questionable in light of the Québecois, Basque, Puerto Rican, Corsican, Scottish, Welsh, Northern Irish and South Tyrolean independence movements), but only because nation-states already emerged in Europe and North America some one hundred years ago.[4] National identity, national well-being, chauvinism and the desire for self-government, however, remain fully enthroned in the United States, Canada and Western Europe. The desire of East European nations or of Third World nations to attain their own states or to be nationalist in the other four senses of the term are thus nothing but attempts to be like the modern world. That is to say, to be nationalist, in any or all of the senses of the term, is to be modern—naturally, if by modernity we mean that which the self-styled modern world is or claims to be.

Nationalism and Modernity

But there are also more substantive reasons for suspecting that nationalism is not about to leave the world stage and that West Europeans and Americans will, *volens nolens,* continue to be among the world's most important promoters of the idea. As I will argue below, the central elements of what generally passes for modernity promote all "forms" of nationalism. Democracy, the market and secularism strengthen the nation and reinforce its current hegemony. Contemporary values regarding social justice and the dynamics of the international system strengthen the state and, thus, willy-nilly its current incarnation, the nation-state. Education, urbanization and industrialization create national elites, who, together with nations and states, represent the necessary conditions of the actual striving for nation-states and selfgovernment. The discourse of human rights enormously facilitates this pursuit, while democracy acts as the sufficient condition of its emergence. Because the nation and the state are, respectively, the dominant social and political organizing principles of the contemporary world, the continued striving of national elites for their own states is inevitable in a world of democracy and human rights.

If, on the other hand, nationalism is defined as, say, a form of chauvinism, then the above division of factors into necessary, facilitating and sufficient ones would obviously be different. The existence of elites and states with national identities would only facilitate chauvinism; the ubiquity of the nation would be necessary to its emergence, while democracy and the market might suffice to produce it. Although the perception of others as "other" will be with us for a long time, national differentiation on its own does not produce chauvinism. For such attitudes to arise, nations must be brought into contact and competition, in which some lose and others win. Democracy and the market are two forces that compel individuals and groups to compete unremittingly, that produce winners and losers continually—it goes without saying that there will always be bad winners and sore losers—and that encourage groups to pursue their interests on the basis of their semiotic self-understanding, their cultural "groupness." Add to this combustible mixture the modern state, which acts as an arena within which struggles can be pursued, and another potent element contributes to conflict and competition. And if, as seems likely, the state becomes the preserve of some dominant group, we may expect ethnic animosities only to intensify.

The Modernity of Nations

Fundamental to my argument is the proposition that the nation and the nation-state are, as I stated above, the dominant forms of organization in the modern world. Of course, the claims that modern countries make are quite different: namely, that they are modern precisely because they are on the verge of abandoning the nation-state and demoting the nation. This self-perception, which I believe is both self-serving and fundamentally wrong, seems to be part and parcel of the discourse of human rights that has been appropriated by the elites of these countries and which functions to legitimize their rule internally, to preserve their hegemony externally and to isolate "Europe" from troubling developments in neighboring states. We need not take this self-perception too seriously as a practical program, except perhaps to ask, as I do at the end of this essay, what the subtext is of so unabashedly ideological a formulation.

Despite such rhetoric, neither the nation—as a self-conscious cultural community—nor the state—as a political organization with a monopoly of violence in some territory—appears to be on the verge of extinction. Ethnic groups in the United States and Canada are very much in the process of asserting their nationhood, even as Washington and Ottawa desperately struggle to foster pan-ethnic identities. The peoples of Western Europe, both the majority nations and the minorities, are all reclaiming their history, asserting their prerogatives and establishing themselves as bona fide corporate entities. To be sure, people are learning foreign languages, traveling and developing multiple identities, but none of these characteristics contravenes the fact that the background on which all of these trends are taking place is the nation. And if the emergence of a self-confident Japan, a reunified Germany and a beleaguered America is a portent of things to come, we may expect the sense of national identity and the feeling of belongingness to a nation to continue to grow. The trend may change, of course, but there seem to be few indications of why it should anytime in the near future.

Why and how nations emerged several centuries ago are questions that John Armstrong, Benedict Anderson, Ernest Gellner, Carlton Hayes, Eric Hobsbawm and many others have attempted to answer, but these issues do not concern us here.[5] Far more important is explaining why nations, which are regularly denounced for their supposedly atavistic qualities, still exist. Although a definitive answer is probably impossible, critically important to the nation's continued hold on humanity are, as I suggested above, secularism, democracy and the market. Thus Anthony D. Smith has argued that the crisis of the intelligentsia, a crisis that had much to do with the emergence of secularism in a religious world, was directly responsible for the emergence of national identity among nineteenth-century European elites.[6] Regardless of whether or not Smith is correct in his argument, it seems unquestionable that the growing absence of the divine from the world, its *Entzauberung,* to use Max Weber's term, at least facilitates the continued maintenance of national identity and national self-assertiveness in the modern world. God's presumed "death" has surely contributed to the growing emphasis on values that underline the human side of life. Human rights is in this sense an ersatz of sorts for the divine. Possibly even more powerful a substitute is the nation, or, until recently perhaps, the class. As many observers have noted, the fervor with which nationalists and communists have dedicated themselves to their groups has often resembled that of religious devotees in their common willingness to sacrifice their lives for the higher goal of an abstract ideal.

The connection between democracy and the nation is equally straightforward. Democratic regimes are self-styled popular regimes; they derive their legitimacy from the people and from their activity on behalf of the people. The American Declaration of Independence, in its insistence on government by, for and of the people is thus a classic nationalist document. Naturally, the people can be a multiethnic, indeed a multinational association. Yet it would appear to be highly likely, if not indeed inevitable, that in its appeals to the people, a democratic regime will either emphasize the national characteristics of that people if it is ethnically homogeneous, or will attempt to create more or less homogeneous characteristics if the people is ethnically heterogeneous. Legitimacy requires that a strong connection be established between government and "the" people: The logic of the situation demands that a people, or people in general, be transformed into a collectivity deserving of the definite article. The United States, with its constant emphasis on the American qualities of the people that inhabit the country, may serve as an example of the pressures faced by strongly democratic governments in multiethnic societies and of their tendency to adopt positions that lead to the creation of self-conscious cultural communities and an emphasis on national solidarity and national superiority.

The market, so goes the claim, is the best solvent of nationalism: It overcomes national differences, brings nations together, makes the state and, of course the nation-state superfluous. Contemporary Western Europe is supposed to be the prime example of the manner in which market relations overcome national narrowness, passions and emotionalism. Of course, one could point to just as many, if not far more, examples of how market relations also seem to have the radically opposite effect, leading to such phenomena as neo-Nazi attacks on racial minorities in Germany, Jean-Marie Le Pen's fulminations against immigrant threats in France, Jorg Haider's encouragement of *Ausländerfeindlichkeit* in Austria and Thatcherite economics in England. Theoretically, however, the important point is that markets place peoples into contact and competition. Nations that may have not known one another and thus, *ipso facto,* could not have been in conflict, are brought together under conditions that contribute little to peaceful resolutions of emergent problems.[7] What is more, the market has an inevitably differential impact on individuals and peoples. After all, it is in the very nature of market relations to reward efficient regions and to penalize inefficient ones. As Michael Hechter has argued, the market's accentuation of regional differences can create national differences, thereby not only leading to competition but also actually generating the drive toward independence as the only solution to the perceived inequities of capitalist relations.[8]

If these considerations are correct, we should expect "national liberation struggles" to multiply in Western Europe after 1992, with the creation of a unified market in a democratically ruled "Europe of regions." Not only will regionally based national minorities assert their right to self-determination, but the dominant nations will likely experience a renewal of national pride, perhaps even hatred, toward these minorities, toward other nations and toward other states.

Source: Alexander J. Motyl. "The Modernity of Nationalism: Nations, States and Nation-States in the Contemporary World." *Journal of International Afffairs* 45, No. 2 (1992): 307ff. Reprinted by permission of the *Journal of International Affairs* and the Trustees of Columbia University in the City of New York.

Notes

[1] See Alexander J. Motyl, *Sovietology, Rationality, Nationality: Coming to Grips with Nationalism in the USSR* (New York-Columbia University Press,1991) where I define nationalism as a "Political ideal that views statehood as-the optimal form of political organization for each nation," p.53.

[2] Classic views of nationalism as a thing of the mind are Hans Kohn, The *Idea of Nationalism* (New York: Macmillan, 1944) and Elie Kedourie, *Nationalism* (London: Hutchinson, 1966).

[3] See Motyl, *Sovietology, Rationality, Nationality,* pp.49-52.

[4] See Edward Tiryakian and Ronald Rogowski, eds., *New Nationalisms of the Developed West* (Boston: Allen & Unwin, 1985).

[5] John A. Armstrong, *Nations before Nationalism* (Chapel Hill, NC: University of North Carolina Press, 1982); Benedict Anderson, *Imagined Communities* (London: Verso, 1983); Ernest Gellner, *Nations and Nationalism* (Ithaca, NY: Cornell University Press, 1983); Carlton Hayes, *Essays on Nationalism* (New York.: Russell & Russell, 1966); Eric Hobsbawm, *Nations and Nationalism since 1780* (Cambridge, UK: Cambridge University Press, 1990).

[6] Anthony D. Smith, *Theories of Nationalism* (London: Duckworth, 1971).

[7] Karl Deutsch, *Nationalism and Social Communication* (Cambridge, MA: MIT Press, 1966).

[8] Michael Hechter, *Internal Colonialism* (Berkeley, CA: University of California Press, 1977).

Ethnicity Versus Nationalism

Thomas Hylland Eriksen

THOMAS HYLLAND ERIKSEN *(1962-) is a research fellow in the Department of Anthropology, University of Oslo. His publications include* Communicating Cultural Difference and Identity: Ethnicity and Nationalism in Mauritius.

Aims and Concepts

Virtually every modern nation-state is to a greater or lesser extent ethnically divided. This frequently implies a potential for various forms of conflict—from armed conflicts to autonomist movements and political segregation along ethnic lines.[1]

Two central aspects of the contemporary global situation indicate that ethnic conflicts may be of increasing relative importance. First, the East-West conflict is presently on the wane. The recent changes in the global political system call the attention of both scholars and policy-makers to conflicts which cannot be understood within the idiom of the Cold War, and further directly stimulate the growth of a wide range of new ideological movements in the former Eastern bloc, many of them drawing explicitly on nationalist and ethnic rhetoric. Secondly, processes of modernization in the Third World lead to ever more encompassing confrontations between dominant nationalisms and other ideologies in many countries.

Ethnic ideologies are at odds with dominant nationalist ideologies, since the latter tend to promote cultural similarity and wide-ranging integration of all the inhabitants of the nation-state, regardless of their ethnic membership. It can therefore be instructive to contrast ethnic ideologies with nationalism in contemporary nation-states. Through examples from ethnically complex nation-states, the variable content and social impact of such different ideologies are explored. The purpose is to identify some conditions under which *culturally justified conflicts* may arise within modern nation-states,[2] and to suggest conditions for their resolution or avoidance. The general perspective is from within; that is, ideologies and practices are considered largely from the point of view of their adherents. It will be argued, further, that the multi-ethnic nation-state is no contradiction in terms that it may indeed be a viable and stable political entity.

Ideology

The central concept of *ideology* is treated throughout as a double concept. On the one hand, ideology serves to legitimize a particular power structure and in this respect conforms to a conventional Marxist view. On the other hand, ideologies necessarily derive their popular, potentially mobilizing force from their ability to organize and make sense of the immediate experiences of their adherents; they cannot, therefore, be regarded simply as forms of false consciousness.[3] The term ideology can profitably be used in the plural insofar as people evaluate available ideologies critically and compare them through choosing their strategies and practices. The final outcome of a competitive situation involving two or several ideologies depends on their respective persuasive power among their frequently ambivalent audiences. It follows from this that an analysis of particular ideologies, in this case nationalist and ethnic ones, demands an understanding of the lives of *the followers* of the ideologies in question. An analysis of ideology cannot solely consider the properties of the political system and the ideational content of the ideologies themselves, since beliefs and other forms of knowledge contribute to the reproduction of society only to the extent that they are embedded in interaction.

Nationalism vs. Ethnicity

Viewed geopolitically, nationalism is an ambiguous type of ideology. It can be aggressive and expansionist—within and outside state boundaries; and it can serve as a truly peace-keeping and culturally integrating force in a nation-state or a region. Nationalism is frequently regarded by liberal theorists as a universalist kind of ideology emphasizing equality and human rights within its polity, but it can just as plausibly be seen as a kind of particularism denying non-citizens or culturally deviant citizens full human rights and, in extreme cases, even denying them membership in the community of humans (see Giddens, 1987, pp.177ff. for a critical discussion of these aspects of nationalism). Depending on the social context, then, nationalism may have socio-culturally integrating as well as disintegrating effects; it sometimes serves to identify a large number of people as *outsiders,* but it may also define an ever increasing number of people as *insiders* and thereby encourage social integration on a higher level than that which is current. There is nothing natural or historically inevitable in this. For the nation is an invention and a recent one at that; to paraphrase Anderson (1983), it is an *imagined community*; it is *not* a natural phenomenon, despite the fact that the object of every nationalism is to present a particular image of society as natural. Nationalism is ever emergent and must be defended and justified ideologically, perhaps particularly in new states, where alternative modes of social integration, usually on a lower systemic level, remain immediately relevant to a large number of people. The "multi-ethnic" or "plural" state is the rule rather than the exception (Smith, 1981); however, cultural plurality can evaporate historically, it can lead to the formation of new nation-states, it can lead to conflict between ethnics or between state and ethnic, or it can be reconciled with nationhood and nationalism.

The Emergence of Nationalism

Historically, an important part played by nationalist ideologies in many contemporary nation-states has been to integrate an ever larger number of people culturally, politically and economically. The French could not be meaningfully described as a "people" before the French revolution, which brought the Ile-de-France (Parisian) language, notions of liberal political rights, uniform primary education and, not least, the self-consciousness of being French, to remote areas—first to the local bourgeoisies, later to the bulk of the population. Similar large-scale processes took place in all European countries during the 19th century, and the modern state, as well as nationalist ideology, is historically and logically linked with the spread of literacy (Goody, 1986), the quantification of time and the growth of industrial capitalism. The model of the nation-state as the supreme political unit has spread throughout the 20th century. Not least due to the increasing importance of international relations (trade, warfare, etc.), the nation-state has played an extremely important part in the making of the contemporary world. Social integration on a large scale through the imposition of a uniform system of education, the introduction of universal contractual wage-work, standardization of language, etc., is accordingly the explicit aim of nationalists in, for example, contemporary Africa. It is, of course, possible to achieve this end through contrasting the nation with a different nation or a minority residing in the state, which is then depicted as inferior or threatening. This strategy for cohesion is extremely widespread and is not a peculiar characteristic of the nation-state as such: similar ideologies and practices are found in tribal

societies and among urban minorities alike. Insofar as enemy projections are dealt with in the present context, they are regarded as means to achieve internal. national cohesion, since international conflicts are not considered.

Nationalism as a mode of social organization represents a qualitative leap from earlier forms of integration. Within a national state, all men and women are *citizens*, and they participate in a system of relationships where they depend upon, and contribute to. the existence of a vast number of individuals whom they will never know personally. The main social distinction appears as that between insiders and outsiders; between citizens and non-citizens. The total system appears abstract and impenetrable to the citizen, who must nevertheless trust that it serves his needs. The seeming contradiction between the individual's *immediate* concerns and the large-scale machinations of the nation-state is bridged through nationalist ideology proposing to accord each individual citizen particular value. The ideology simultaneously depicts the nation metaphorically as an enormous system of blood relatives or as a religious community, and as a benefactor satisfying immediate needs (education jobs, health, security, etc.). Through these kinds of ideological technique, nationalism can serve to open and close former boundaries of social systems. Some become brothers metaphoricaly; others whose citizenship (and consequently, loyalty) is dubitable, become outsiders. ...

Nationalism is ideally based on abstract norms, not on personal loyalty. Viewed as a popular ideology, nationalism is inextricably intertwined with the destiny of the nation-state. Where the nation-state is ideologically successful, its inhabitants become nationalists; that is, their identities and ways of life gradually grow compatible with the demands of the nation-state and support its growth. Where nationalism fails to convince, the state may use violence or the threat of violence to prevent fission (that is, in the modern world, the potential formation of new nation-states on its former territory). The monopoly on the use of legitimate violence is, together with its monopoly of taxation, one of the most important characteristics of the modern state; however, violence is usually seen as a last resort. More common are ideological strategies aiming to integrate hitherto distinctive categories of people culturally. Since national boundaries change historically, and since nations can be seen as shifting collectivities of people conceiving of their culture and history as shared, this is an ongoing process. Ethnic groups can vanish through annihilation or, more commonly, through assimilation. They may also continue to exist, and may pose a threat to the dominant nationalism in two main ways, either as agents of subversion (they do, after all, represent alternative cultural idioms and values—this was how the Jews of Nazi Germany were depicted) or as agents of fission (which is evidently the case with Baltic nationalists).

Nationalist strategies are truly successful only when the state simultaneously increases its sphere of influence and responds credibly to popular demands. It is tautologically true that if the nation-state and its agencies can satisfy perceived needs in ways acknowledged by the citizens, then its inhabitants become nationalists. The main threats to national integration are therefore alternative social relationships which can also satisfy perceived needs. There are potential conflicts between the nation-state and non-state modes of organization which may follow normative principles incompatible with those represented by the state. This kind of conflict is evident in every country in the world, and it can be studied as ideological conflict provided ideology is not seen as a system of ideas but as *sets of ideological practices*. Typical examples are African countries, where "tribalism" or organization along ethnic lines is perceived as a threat (by the nation-state), or as an alternative (by the citizens), to the universalist rhetoric and practices of nationalism. From the citizen's point of view, nationalism may or may not be a viable alternative to kinship or ethnic ideology (or there may be two nationalisms to choose between, e.g., a Soviet and a Lithuanian one)—and she will choose the option best suited to satisfy her needs, be they of a metaphysical, economic or political nature. The success or failure of attempts at national integration must therefore be studied not only at the level of political strategies or systemic imperatives, it must equally be understood at the level of the everyday life-world. In a word, the ideological struggles and the intrastate conflicts, as well as the context-specific options for "the good life", shape and are simultaneously rooted in the immediate experiences of its citizens—and the analysis must begin there.

Source: Thomas Hylland Eriksen. "Ethnicity Versus Nationalism." *Journal of Peace Research* 28, No. 3 (1991): 263-278. Reprinted by permission of Sage Publications, Inc.

Notes

[1] See, e.g., Horowitz (1985) for a comprehensive overview of ethnic conflicts.

[2] Relationships of coercion and integration between and within states are not, of course, necessarily constituted on the principles of the sovereignty of the state. When, in 1968, the USSR invaded Czechoslovakia and when, a decade later, the Red Army invaded Afghanistan, the limits of the relevant polity were drawn outside of national boundaries. Conversely, to the extent that the USSR failed to use violence to suppress autonomists in the Baltic republics in 1989-90, the relevant limits of the polity were drawn *inside* the state. In neither case was the state unambiguously perceived as the relevant political unit.

[3] A good, topically relevant demonstration of this dual character of ideology, is Kapferer's (1988) analysis of the nationalisms of Sri Lanka and Australia.

References

Anderson, Benedict, *Imagined Communities (London: Verso, 1983).*

Giddens, Anthony, "Nation-States and Violence," in A. Giddens, *Social Theory and Modern Sociology* (Cambridge: Polity, 1987) pp.166-182.

Goody, Jack, *The Logic of Writing and the Organization of Society* (Cambridge: Cambridge University Press, 1986).

Horowitz, Donald C., *Ethnic Groups in Conflict* (Berkley, CA: University of California Press, 1985).

Kapferer, Bruce, *Legends of People; Myths of State* (Washington, DC: Smithsonian Institution Press, 1988).

Smith, Anthony D., *The Ethnic Revival* (Cambridge: Cambridge University Press, 1981).

Smith, Anthony D., *State and Nation in the Third World* (Brighton: Wheatsheaf, 1983).

National Identity and the Idea of European Unity

Anthony D. Smith

ANTHONY D. SMITH *is Editor of* Ethnic and Racial Studies *and Professor of Sociology at the London School of Economics. His books include* National Identity *(1991) and* The Ethnic Origins of Nations *(1986).*

There is nothing new about the idea of European unity. It can be traced back to Sully, Podiebrad, perhaps even Charlemagne and the Holy Roman Empire. Nor is there anything new about national identity. Even if not as old as nationalists would have us believe, national consciousness can be traced back to the later Middle Ages, to the wars of the Scots, English and French in the fourteenth century, to Joan of Arc, to Spanish unification under the Catholic monarchs, and certainly to the Elizabethans and the age of Shakespeare; though not until the next century, in the Puritan Netherlands and England, can one discern the first flowerings of popular (albeit religious) nationalism, and not until the American and French Revolutions does nationalism appear as a fully fledged secular ideology.[1]

So why should there be such interest now in the European idea and its relationship to national identities? Is it simply the fact that European unification, in whatever form, is for the first time a distinct possibility—that we can "make Europe" where previous generations could only dream about it? Or is it rather that the sheer pace of social and political change has forced us to reassess rooted structures like the nation-state, and hallowed values like national identity?[2]

Clearly, modern technologies and communications have led many people to question the old certainties. They grope in some confusion towards a new type of social order, yet are afraid to let go of the old. They wonder whether the new structures and identities that may be forged will answer to their needs and interests as well as the habitual and familiar ones. What exactly will a vast, overarching "Europe" mean for individuals and families? Will the seat of authority become still more impersonal and remote? Will it be less sensitive to local problems and needs? What does growing European unification mean for the values, heritages and cultures of Europe's many ethnic communities, regions and nations?

There is a more fundamental reason for the current interest in the cultural impact of European unification. It lies in the problem of "identity" itself, one that has played a major part in European debates over the past 30-40 years. At issue has been the possibility and the legitimacy of a "European identity", as opposed to the existing national identities. For nationalists, the nation is the sole criterion of legitimate government and of political community. Does this exclude the possibility of a European identity and political community? Or can, and must, a unified Europe be designated a "super-nation"? Alternatively, should we regard a United States of Europe as a new type of "supranational" identity and community? What exactly does that mean? These issues are central to the continuing debates between pro- and anti-Europeans, between federalists, Gaullists and today's Bruges Group. ...

Multiple Identities

A comparative method using case-studies of national identity and culture needs some kind of theoretical framework; and given the nature of our problem, a logical starting-point is the concept of collective cultural identity. This would refer not to some fixed pattern or uniformity of elements over time, but rather to a sense of shared continuity on the part of successive generations of a given unit of population, and to shared memories of earlier periods, events and personages in the history of the unit. From these two components we can derive a third: the collective belief in a common *destiny* of that unit and its culture. From a subjective standpoint, there can be no collective cultural identity without shared memories or a sense of continuity on the part of those who feel they belong to that collectivity. So the subjective perception and understanding of the communal past by each generation of a given cultural unit of population—the "ethno-history" of that collectivity, as opposed to a historian's judgement of that past—is a defining element in the concept of cultural identity, and hence of more specific national and European identities.[3]

From this starting-point we might go on to characterize the cultural history of humanity as a successive differentiation (but also enlargement) of processes of identification. In the simplest and earliest societies, the number and scale of such identities were relatively limited; but as populations organized themselves into more complex agrarian societies in a variety of political formations, the number and scale of such identifications multiplied. Where once gender, age, clan and tribe had provided the chief units of identity, now there were also village communities, regions, city-states, religious communities and even empires. With the growing stratification of such societies, classes and status groups (castes, estates, ethnic communities) also took on vital roles as focuses of identification in many societies.

In the modern era of industrial capitalism and bureaucracy, the number and in particular the scale of possible cultural identities have increased yet again. Gender and age retain their vitality; class and religious loyalties continue to exercise their influence; but today, professional, civic and ethnic allegiances have proliferated, involving ever larger populations across the globe. Above all, *national* identification has become the cultural and political norm, transcending other loyalties in scope and power.

Yet however dominant the nation and its national identification, human beings retain a multiplicity of allegiances in the contemporary world. They have multiple identities. These identifications may reinforce national identities or cross-cut them. The gendered perceptions of the male population may reinforce their sense of national identity, whereas those of the female part of the same collectivity may detract from it. The class allegiances of upper and middle classes may subjectively fuse with their sense of national identification, whereas the class solidarities of workers may conflict with their national loyalties. Similarly, some collective religious sentiments can reinforce a sense of national identity, as we witness today in Ireland, Poland and Israel; whereas some other kinds of religious loyalty transcend and thereby diminish purely national identities, as in the case of Roman Catholicism and Islam.[4]

Under normal circumstances, most human beings can live happily with multiple identifications and enjoy moving between them as the situation requires. Sometimes, however, one or other of these identities will come under pressure from external circumstances, or come into conflict with one of the individual's or family's other identities. Conflicts between loyalty to a national state and solidarity with an ethnic community, within or outside the boundaries of that state, may lead to accusations of "dual loyalties", and families may find themselves torn between the claims of competing communities and identities. There is in fact always the potential for such identity conflicts. That they occur less often than one might expect is the result of a certain fluidity in all processes of individual identification.

At this point it becomes important to observe the distinction between individual and collective identification. For the individual, or at any rate for most individuals, identity is usually "situational", if not always optional. That is to say, individuals identify themselves and are identified by others in different ways according to the situations in which they find themselves; as when one goes abroad, one tends to classify oneself (and be classified by others) differently from one's categorization at home.[5]

Collective identities, however, tend to be pervasive and persistent. They are less subject to rapid changes and tend to be more intense and durable, even when quite large numbers of individuals no longer feel their power. This is especially true of religious and ethnic identities, which even in pre-modern eras often became politicized. It is particularly true of national identities today, when the power of mass political fervour reinforces the technological instruments of mass political organization, so that national identities can outlast the defection or apathy of quite large numbers of individual members. So we need to bear this distinction between the collective and the individual levels of identity in mind and to exercise caution in making inferences about collective sentiments and communal identifications on the basis of individual attitudes and behaviour.[6]

National Identity: Some Bases and Legacies

This preliminary survey of the types and levels of *cultural* identity provides a general framework for analyzing specifically *national* identities. Here it may be useful to take together the first two areas of analysis—the impact of the premodern past and the nature and consequences of national identity—since in Europe at any rate it is mainly through such identities that these "pasts" have been retained and mediated.

The concept of national identity is both complex and highly abstract. Indeed the multiplicity of cultural identities, both now and in the past, is mirrored in the multiple dimensions of our conceptions of nationhood. To grasp this, we need only enumerate of few of these dimensions. They include:

- the territorial boundedness of separate cultural populations in their own "homelands";

- the shared nature of myths of origin and historical memories of the community;

- the common bond of a mass, standardized culture;

- a common territorial division of labour, with mobility for all members and ownership of resources by all members in the homeland;

- the possession by all members of a unified system of common legal rights and duties under common laws and institutions.

These are some of the main assumptions and beliefs common to all nationalists everywhere. Drawing on these, we may define a nation as a named human population sharing a historical territory, common memories and myths of origin, a mass, standardized public culture, a common economy and territorial mobility, and common legal rights and duties for all members of the collectivity.[7]

This definition is just one of many that have been proffered for the concept of the "nation". But, like most others, it reveals the highly complex and abstract nature of the concept, one which draws on dimensions of other types of cultural identity, and so permits it to become attached to many other kinds of collective identification—of class, gender, region and religion. National identifications are fundamentally multidimensional. But though they are composed of analytically separable components—ethnic, legal, territorial, economic and political—they are united by the nationalist ideology into a potent vision of human identity and community.

The ideology of nationalism which emerged in Western Europe and America in the late eighteenth century was premised on the belief in a world of exclusive nations. The basic goals of nationalists everywhere were identical: they sought to unify the nation, to endow it with a distinctive individuality, and to make it free and autonomous. For nationalists, the nation was the supreme object of loyalty and the sole criterion of government. There was no legitimate exercise of political power which did not emanate expressly from the nation, for this was the only source of political power and individual freedom.[8]

Yet there were also important differences between nationalists in their conceptions of the nation. In fact we can usefully distinguish two main models of the nation, which emerged out of different historical contexts and which retain a certain importance even in our era. The first, or "Western", model of the nation arose out of the Western absolutist states whose rulers inadvertently helped to create the conditions for a peculiarly territorial concept of the nation. The second, or "Eastern", model emerged out of the situation of incorporated ethnic communities or *ethnies* (from the French), whose intelligentsias sought to liberate them from the shackles of various empires.

The Western model of the nation tended to emphasize the centrality of a national territory or homeland, a common system of laws and institutions, the legal equality of citizens in a political community, and the importance of a mass, civic culture binding the citizens together. The Eastern model, by contrast, was more preoccupied with ethnic descent and cultural ties. Apart from genealogy, it emphasized the popular or folk element, the role of vernacular mobilization, and the activation of the people through a revival of their native folk culture—their languages, customs, religions and rituals, rediscovered by urban intellectuals such as philologists, historians, folklorists, ethnographers and lexicographers.[9]

The contrast between these two concepts of the nation should not be overdrawn, as we find elements of both at various times in several nationalisms in both Eastern and Western Europe. And it is perhaps more important for our purposes to underline the distinction between the concepts of the nation and of the state. The latter is a legal and institutional concept. It refers to autonomous public institutions which are differentiated from other, social institutions by their exercise of a monopoly of coercion and extraction within a given territory.[10] The idea of the nation, by contrast, is fundamentally cultural and social. It refers to a cultural and political bond which unites in a community of prestige all those who share the same myths, memories, symbols and traditions. Despite the obvious overlap between the concepts of state and nation in terms of common territory and citizenship, the idea of the nation defines and legitimates politics in cultural terms, because the nation is a political community only in so far as it embodies a common culture and a common social will. This is why today no state possesses legitimacy which does not also claim to represent the will of the "nation", even where there is as yet patently no nation for it to represent. Though the vast majority of contemporary states are "plural" in character—that is, why they have more than one ethnic community within their borders and so cannot claim to be true "nation-states" in the strict sense—they aspire to become at least "national states" with a common public culture open to all citizens. Their claim to legitimacy, in other words, is based on the aspiration of a heterogeneous population to unity in terms of public culture and political community, as well as popular sovereignty.[11]

The reiterated reference to a community of common public culture reveals the continuing influence of ethnicity and its common myths, symbols and memories in the life of modern European nations. On the one hand, these nations seek to transcend their ethnic origins, which are usually the myths and memories of the dominant ethnic community (the English, the northern French, the Castilians); on the other hand, in a world of growing interdependence, they very often feel the need to revert to them to sustain community as well as to justify their differences. The link with the distinctive pre-modern past serves to dignify the nation as well as to explain its mores and character. More important, it serves to "remake the collective personality" of the nation in each generation. Through rituals and ceremonies, political myths and symbols, the arts and history textbooks—through these the links with a community of origin, continually reshaped as popular "ethno-history", are reforged and disseminated.

In this respect, national identifications possess distinct advantages over the ideal of a unified European identity. They are vivid, accessible, well established, long popularized, and still widely believed, in broad outline at lest. In each of these respects, "Europe" is deficient both as idea and as process. Above all, it lack a pre-modern past—a "prehistory" which can provide it with emotional sustenance and historical depth. In these terms it singularly fails to combine, in the words of Daniel Bell à propos ethnicity, "affect with interest", resembling rather Shelley's bright reason, "like the sun from a wintry sky".[12]

Recently it has been suggested that nationalism's halcyon days are drawing to a close, and that the current spate of fissiparous ethnic nationalism runs counter to the "major trends" of world history, which are towards ever-larger economic and political units. In other words, that substance is belied by appearance—that today's ethnic nationalisms are divisive and have lost the breadth and power of the former mass democratic and civic nationalisms of Western Europe.[13]

Others take the view that the current renewal of ethnic nationalism represents the shape of the future "post-industrial" society, one whose economy is based increasingly on the service sector and on the social and cultural needs of consumers. They argue that in such societies the means of communication and information become much more important than mass production of commodities; that the mass media, telecommunications and computerized information spawn smaller but dense networks for those who share the same ethno-linguistic networks of language, symbols and culture. This, they argue, is the reason why we are witnessing the proliferation of ethnic nationalisms; they are intrinsic to a post-industrial "service society".[14]

There are in fact a number of reasons why we are witnessing an ethnic revival today, and why it is challenging the accepted frameworks of the national state.

For one thing, the state itself has become immensely more powerful, both as an international actor and vis à vis society within its boundaries. Its powers, scope and capacity for intervention in every sphere of social life—and will to do so—have increased profoundly since 1945 (helped, no doubt, by the powers conferred on it by the exigencies of two world wars). Second, the spread of literacy and the mass media to the remotest hinterlands of European and other states has raised the level of consciousness and expectations of minority peoples, who witness national protests and movements in neighbouring territories almost as soon as they occur. Third, the impact of public, mass education systems, while on the face of it uniting a given national population into a single civic culture, also creates divisions along pre-existing ethnic lines. By forcing all its different peoples to employ a single civic language and by preaching allegiance to national symbols and historical myths, the state's elites may actually stir up resentment and bitterness at the neglect of minority cultures and the suppression of minority peoples' histories. The latter have not been entirely forgotten among the relevant peoples themselves; they remain embedded in separate folklore, customs, myths and symbols. State intervention, literacy and civic culture, and mass education and the mass media tend to rekindle these memories and regenerate these ancient cultures in new forms.

So recent political developments in Western as well as Eastern Europe, not to mention the Third World, offer few grounds for hope of an early end to the proliferation of ethnic nationalisms, even if their intensity periodically diminishes. What we are currently witnessing is no more than the latest of the periodic waves of ethnic nationalism that have swept different parts of the world since the early nineteenth century, and such demotic ethnic nationalisms have always accompanied the more territorial state-based nationalisms of ethnic majorities since the first stirrings of Serb, Greek and Irish nationalisms. There is therefore little warrant for regarding recent ethnic nationalisms as inimical or irrelevant to the "major trends" of economic development or world history, as long as most of the world's trade, production and consumption is still organized in terms of relations between sovereign (if increasingly interdependent) national states.[15]

If we disregard the evolutionary undertones of these recent interpretations of nationalism, we are left with the problem of determining the relative strength and influence of European nations, their cultures and their myths from their ethnic pasts at the turn of the second millennium. Anthropologists have begun to explore some of the cultural aspects of the ethnic identity of such European nations as the Basque, the

Breton and the Greek, but much research still needs to be conducted into the continuing impact of ethno-histories, of ethnic myths and symbols, and of the different value systems embodied in various popular traditions, ceremonies and rituals. There is also much work to be done on the recent revival of cultural heritages and political traditions in the wake of new concepts of multiculturalism, which have gained ground following demographic shifts and population migrations.

Given the multiplicity of language groups and ethnic heritages in Europe, it is reasonable to expect the persistence of strong ethnic sentiments in many parts of the continent, as well as the continuity or periodic revival of national identities, fuelled by the quest for ethnic traditions and cultural heritages of distinctive myths, memories and symbols.

Source: Anthony D. Smith. "National Identity and the Idea of European Unity." *International Affairs* 68, (1992): 55-76. Reprinted with permission.

Notes

[1] On the forerunners of the idea of European unity, see Denis de Rougemont, *The Meaning of Europe* (London: Sidgwick & Jackson, 1965).

[2] This article was prepared for a seminar series on "Europe in the 1990s: forces for change", held at the RIIA in 1991 and funded by the Economic and Social Research Council.

[3] For studies of ethnic identity, see George de Vos and Lola Romanucci-Rossi, eds., *Ethnic identity: cultural continuities and change* (Chicago, Ill.: University of Chicago Press. 1975), and A. L. Epstein, *Ethos and identity* (London: Tavistock. 1978).

[4] On the relationships between religion and nationalism, see Donald E. Smith, eds., *Religion and political modernisation* (New Haven, Conn.: Yale University Press, 1974), and Pedro Ramet, ed., *Religion and nationalism in Soviet and East European politics* (Durham, NC.: Duke University Press, 1989). For some case-studies of the relationships between gender and nationality, see Flova Anthias and Nira Yuval-Davis. eds., *Woman-nation-state* (London: Macmillan, 1989).

[5] For the concept of 'situational ethnicity' see J. Y. Okamura, 'Situational ethnicity', *Ethnic and Racial Studies* 4: 4 (1981), pp.452-65.

[6] On the 'individualist fallacy' see E. K. Scheuch, 'Cross-national comparisons with aggregate data', in Richard L. Merritt and Stein Rokkan, eds., *Comparing nations: the use of qualitative data in cross-national research* (New Haven, Conn.: Yale University Press. 1956).

[7] This definition summarizes long and complex discussions of the many definitions of 'nation'. See, *inter alia,* Karl Deutsch, *Nationalism and social communication* (2nd edn, New York: MIT Press, 1966), ch. I; and Walker Connor, 'A nation is a nation, is a state, is an ethnic group, is ... " *Ethnic and Racial Studies 1:* 4 (1978), pp.377-400.

[8] For fuller discussions of nationalist ideologies, see Elie Kedourie, *Nationalism* (London: Hutchinson, 1960); Elie Kedourie, ed., *Nationalism in Asia and Africa* (London: Weidenfeld & Nicolson, l971); and A. D. Smith, *Theories of Nationalism* (2nd edn., London: Duckworth, 1983). On the multidimensionality of national identity, see A. D. Smith, *National identity* (London: Penguin, 1991), ch. 1.

[9] On the distinction between these types of nationalism, see Hans Kohn, *Tile idea of nationalism (2nd* edn, New York: Macmillan, 1967) and A. D. Smith, *The ethnic origins of nations* (Oxford: Blackwell, 1986), ch. 6.

[10] I have adapted the definitions given in the introductions to Charles Tilly, ed., *The formation of national states in Western Europe* (Princeton, NJ: Princeton University Press, 1975), and Leonard Tivey, ed., *The nation-state* (Oxford: Martin Robertson, 1980).

[11] See Walker Connor's seminal article, 'Nation-building or nation-destroying?'. *World Politics* 24 (1972), pp.119-55; and Ernest Gellner, *Nations and nationalism* (Oxford: Blackwell, 1983).

[12] See Daniel Bell, 'Ethnicity and social change', in Nathan Glazer and Daniel P. Moynihan, eds., *Ethnicity: theory and experience* (Cambridge, Mass.: Harvard University Press, 1975).

[13] This argument is presented in the last chapter of Eric Hobsbawm, *Nations and nationalism since 1780* (Cambridge: Cambridge University Press, 1990).

[14] This argument is presented with force and clarity by Anthony Richmond in 'Ethnic nationalism and post-industrialism', *Ethnic and Racial Studies 7:* 1 (I984), pp.4-18: it is also implicit in Benedict Anderson. *Imagined communities: reflections on the origins and spread of nationalism* (London: Verso, 1983).

[15] The ethnic revival in the West in the 1970s suggests the difficulty of 'reading' any 'major trends' of world history. Regions and ethnic communities are being revitalized *alongside* a strengthened national state and an over-arching European Community. On ethnic nationalisms in the West see Milton Esman, ed., *Ethnic conflict in the Western world* (Ithaca, NY: Cornell University Press, 1977), and A. D. Smith, *The Ethnic Revival in the Modern World* (Cambridge: Cambridge university Press, 1981).

Yugoslavia Without Yugoslavs: The Roots of the Crisis

Paul Lendvai

PAUL LENDVAI *is Editor of* Europäische Rundschau *in Vienna, and Director of Radio Austria International. His books include* Eagles in Cobwebs: Nationalism and Communism in the Balkans *(1970) and* Hungary: The Art of Survival *(1988).*

Yugoslavia is a front-rank example of the difficulty of penetrating what Norbert Elias termed "the veil of concepts".[1] The "unveiling" process began to gain momentum in the crisis decade of the 1990s. In the 1960s and 1970s, who could have predicted that Yugoslavia would undergo the worst crisis of its postwar history just at the point when the East-West divide was being overcome and against the background of the almost total disappearance of an external threat to its existence? In 1980, when Tito died but the expected collapse failed to materialize, who would have foreseen that the deceptive calm would be so short-lived, bringing the land of the south Slavs once again to the point of collapse?[2]

After the Second World War and up to the 1970s, Yugoslavia was regarded as an exception among the communist countries of the crisis-ridden Eastern bloc. There were several reasons for this. One was the split of 1948 between Tito and Stalin, which demonstrated widely and in a way which was ultimately very damaging to the unity of the Eastern bloc that it was possible to espouse communism and Leninism while simultaneously remaining independent of Moscow control. A second, more important factor underlying the prestige enjoyed by Tito's Yugoslavia, which many find so incomprehensible today, was the Non-Aligned Movement and the pioneering role played in it by Yugoslavia, and in particular by Tito alongside Nasser and Nehru. A third reason for the admiration expressed particularly in Left-wing circles in the West, and by many communist reformers in the East, was the fact that Yugoslavia symbolized a "third way" between state socialism run along orthodox Soviet lines and a Western free-market economy achieved through independent control of the economy and decentralized government.

But there was more to Yugoslavia's special status, both in practical political terms and, more importantly, in terms of ideology. There was also a special mythology surrounding Yugoslavia which can be traced back to the Second World War. Then and subsequently, Yugoslavia stood out as the only country to have liberated itself, the one whose strong partisan movement contributed more than any other occupied country to the defeat of Hitler's Germany. The fact that the victorious communist partisans not only assumed total power but also rewrote the history of this contradictory country in simplified terms played and still continues to play a major role, often overlooked in the West, in the misjudgements and misunderstandings surrounding Yugoslavia's development.[3]

Wishful thinking, prejudices and stigmatizations have always coloured perceptions of Yugoslavia. This is true not only of perceptions of Yugoslavia abroad, but also of those which the different national minorities living together within the framework of the state have nurtured of each other. If one supposes that the disintegration of Yugoslavia as a single state is only a matter of time and that the only issue for debate is now the extent to which this seemingly inevitable disintegration will be peaceful or bloody—in other words whether it will take the form of a civil war—then we need only look back into history to find the roots of the situation. Despite the smooth facade of the Tito period, the forces and traditions that marked the immediate postwar years have now re-emerged with a vengeance in Yugoslavia. The developments that have surprised so many by their dramatic violence can only make sense if the historical dimension is taken into account.[4] The starting point is the long and widely suppressed fact that Yugoslavia is a country without Yugoslavs. That is, it lacks people prepared to declare themselves as belonging to a Yugoslav entity as opposed to a specific nationality. According to the last census in 1981, only 1.2 million people out of a total population of 22.4 million described themselves as Yugoslavs.[5] Who were these people, these "Yugoslavs"? They were primarily partners in or children of so-called "mixed marriages" between, for example, Croats and Serbs or Slovenes and Macedonians. Others were army officers and

NCOs, civil servants and diplomats. The number of"Yugoslavs" had been somewhat higher, but the recognition of the Muslim population in Bosnia as a separate nation in 1971 led to a decrease. In 1981, 40% of the population of the republic of Bosnia-Herzegovina described themselves as "Muslim" in the sense of nationhood as opposed to religious affiliation.

The nationality problem of Yugoslavia centres on a fundamental conflict between federalism and centralization, a situation in which the largest nation's over-riding claims to power come up against the defence of the interests of the smaller nations and minorities. At the same time these conflicting tendencies, partly inherited from the interwar period and partly intensified indirectly during the Tito decades, have been aggravated to breaking-point by the bankruptcy of so-called "self-management socialism", by economic crisis and by the North-South divide within the state.

Source: Paul Lendvai. "Yugoslavia Without Yugoslavs: The Roots of the Crisis." *International Affairs* 67, No. 2 (1991): 251-261. Reprinted with permission.

Notes

[1] See Norbert Elias, *Uber sich selbst* (Frankfurt, 1990), pp.50-5.

[2] This article has been expanded from an original first published in German in *Europa-Archiv,* No. 18 (1990).

[3] See Paul Lendvai, *Eagles in cobwebs: nationalism and communism in the Balkans* (London, 1970), pp.23-172.

[4] For the continuation of the nationality problem see Lujo Toncic-Sorinj, 'Jugoslawien, das Land Der Widersprüche', *Europäische Rundschau 90:* 2, and Christopher Cviic, 'Ein geplagtes Land nüchtem gesehen: die Nationen Jugoslawiens', *Europäische Rundschau 90:* 3.

[5] In the 1981 census the Yugoslav population totalled 22,424,711, with ethnic groups making up the following proportions: Serbs 36%, Croats 20%, Muslims 9%, Slovenes 8%, ethnic Albanians 8%, Macedonians 6%, "Yugoslavs" (i.e. not professing any ethnic group) 5%, Montenegrins 3%, and ethnic Hungarians 2%. 1981 figures for the ethnic groups within the republics and autonomous provinces (some of these are now significantly changed) were as follows: Serbia (without Kosovo and Vojvodina): Serbs 85%; Croatia: Croats 75%, Serbs 12%; Bosnia-Herzegovina: Muslims 40%, Serbs 32%, Croats 18%; Vojvodina: Serbs 54%, Ethnic Hungarians 19%; Macedonia: Macedonians 67%, Ethnic Albanians 20%, Ethnic Turks 5%; Slovenia: Slovenes 91%; Kosovo: Ethnic Albanians 77%, Serbs 13%; Montenegro: Montenegrins 69%, Muslims 13%, Ethnic Albanians 6%.

The West is Guilty in Bosnia

John Pilger

JOHN PILGER *is a frequent contributor to the* New Statesman & Society.

If the Bosnian Serbs fail to implement the Vance-Owen "peace plan," the Americans are likely to bomb the Balkans, with the British in tow. The last time this alliance took to the air in strength, some 200,000 people were slaughtered, many of them the very ethnic minorities whom President Bush claimed he wished to "protect." The difference now is that even the turkey-shooting generals know they can't get away with this one. Yet President Clinton—fresh from giving the usual nod to the latest round of Israeli "ethnic cleansing"—believes that Caesar must make a gesture "to stop the killing."

"Political language," wrote George Orwell, "is designed to make lies sound truthful and murder respectable, and to give an appearance of solidity to pure wind." Regardless of what the "ethnic cleansers" have done to their neighbours in former Yugoslavia, western governments are also guilty; and the threat of American bombing adds a grotesque, if predictable, dimension to an often secret western policy of dividing Yugoslavia along ethnic lines, dismantling it and eventually recolonising it.

The Balkans have many tragic distinctions. Certainly, if ever a single issue has illuminated the difference between expressions of public morality in the west and the "pure wind" of *realpolitik,* it is the fate of Bosnia. The unctuous semantics of Douglas Hurd are now unacceptable to people watching the Balkan horrors unfold on television. Public opinion has become more than a fleeting force. Having been made witnesses to genocide, perhaps for the first time, people want it stopped. But it can only be stopped if its unstated causes, and the west's complicity, are understood.

Western governments are not the handwringing bystanders they pretend to be. From the beginning, the west has backed the ethnic warlords and neglected the non-sectarian and anti-war citizenry who represent the ideal of Yugoslavia; and for all its flaws, the old federation offered at least nominal constitutional respect to "separate identities" and minority rights. The west's support for the regime in Croatia and its encouragement of Croatia's historical fascism is hardly referred to these days; yet Croatia's president, the Hitler apologist Franjo Tudjman, has been openly courted by western governments, notably the German government, while his soldiers and surrogates have been murdering thousands of Serbs and "cleansing" their communities, mostly out of sight of the western media. It is only since the Croatians have begun to murder large numbers of Muslims in the vicinity of the British military that the full disastrous scale of western "clientism" has been revealed.

According to the *Guardian,* the Vance-Owen plan has been "accepted eagerly by Bosnia's Croats and reluctantly by the Muslims." This is hardly surprising. Even if it succeeds in a limited form, Vance-Owen will owe a great deal to its appeasement of Croatia. Dr Owen's ethnic map gives the Croats more of Bosnia than they can possibly have dreamed of; and, in doing so, it builds an entirely unnecessary obstacle to productive negotiations and provides the Bosnian Serbs with an excuse to get on with their own barbarism.

Tudjman's regime has been the beneficiary of European intervention, which has been forced by Germany's new expansionism. Once reunified, Germany began its economic drive east and to dominate *Mitteleuropa.* "It's our natural market," said the chairman of the East Committee, the German industrial group promoting German takeovers in the east. "In the end, this market will perhaps bring us to the same position we were in before the first world war. Why not?"

This "natural market" extended to the northern republics of Yugoslavia-Croatia and Slovenia. During the second world war, the Nazis installed a puppet fascist state in Croatia. After the war, half a million Croats moved to Germany, where their emigre organisations enjoy great influence. In 1989, Milovan Djilas warned that: "In some states [of Europe], for example Austria and Germany, there are influential groups that would like to see Yugoslavia disintegrate—from traditional hatred, from expansionist tendencies and vague, unrealistic desires for revenge."

In February 1991, the Council of Europe promoted Germany's separatist plans by linking economic advantage to the Yugoslav federal government's "restraint" in dealing with the secessionist movements in

Croatia and Slovenia. The Tudjman regime was ready for this; violent anti-Serb demonstrations were held in Split, giving a clear signal to Croat and Serb minorities elsewhere to begin fighting for land and their lives.

The EC then compounded this by openly threatening the federal government that future economic assistance would depend on "respect for minority rights." Interpreted in Yugoslavia, this meant that the secessions had tacit EC approval. Indeed, once the Yugoslav army had deployed units throughout the country, with the objective of holding the federation together, the EC secretly threatened to cut off $1 billion in promised aid.

In October 1991, the EC delivered the *coup de grace* at a special conference on Yugoslavia at The Hague. Behind a rhetorical veil of reasonableness, ministers gave *de facto* recognition to the secessions by effectively abolishing Yugoslavia. In its *Draft Convention on Yugoslavia,* the EC announced that the republics "are sovereign and independent with [an] international identity." As a former US ambassador to Yugoslavia, William Zimmerman, told the *New Yorker.* "We discovered later that [German foreign minister] Genscher had been in daily contact with the Croatian foreign minister. He was encouraging the Croats to leave the federation and declare independence, while we and our allies, including the Germans, were trying to fashion a joint approach."

Bosnia's leaders pleaded with the west not to recognise the secessionist states, knowing that both Croats and Serbs would then fall on multi-ethnic Bosnia. They argued that whatever had gone before, the worst could be contained without the eventuality of recognition. They were supported by the Macedonians who said that they, like the Bosnians, would have no choice but to seek independence; and that, in turn, would provoke Serbia. No EC minister sounded a warning or reminded his colleague of what was an open secret in western capitals: that in March of that year, Tudjiman and Slobadan Milosevic, the Serb leader, although despising each other, had conspired to carve up Bosnia between them as soon as the time was right. And international recognition would be that time.

The momentum in Germany for recognition was now well under way. Most of the German media concentrated on Serb atrocities. By the time the European leaders met at Maastricht in December 1991, a deal had been done in all but name.

The deal was that Germany would submerge its most exalted postwar achievement, the Deutschmark, into a common European currency if the German Croatia lobby was given its way on recognition. This was never publicly linked to the Maastricht treaty itself, however, brokered by the French, it was a major factor. To put a decent interval between Maastricht and the recognition of Croatia and Slovenia, 15 January 1992 was the date set for the announcement. Two days after the Maastricht conference broke up, on 18 December, Germany broke ranks and recognised Croatia.

No EC government publicly objected to this opportunism. Neither Hurd nor Major said anything. Yet, at a stroke, it made mockery of European strictures to the developing world on human rights and civilised behaviour. Set against what has happened since in Bosnia, and is likely to happen elsewhere as a result, recognition was an act of breathtaking irresponsibility. The Europeans, wrote Sean Gervasi, "turned a manageable internal conflict into appalling fratricide."

The west's role in Yugoslavia's suffering is not confined to Germany's *fait accompli.* The fact that the Bush administration waged economic warfare against Yugoslavia has received little attention, yet the effect on ethnic tensions has been devastating. In 1989, when the Berlin Wall fell, pressure was applied by Washington to all the former communist states to follow the "market" model. The usual "market reforms" were demanded, notably privatisation and conditions amenable to western "investment."

Having embraced something of a "mixed economy" and dependent on western capital transfers, trade and tourism, Yugoslavia had already fallen victim to a "market" recession long before the rest of Europe. Throughout the 1980s, discontent had risen among working people, while those willing to exploit ethnic tensions waited for their opportunity. In 1989, the new federal prime minister, Ante Marcovic, went to Washington and requested $1 billion in loans from the US and $3 billion from the World Bank. When told of the scale of austerity his country would have to accept, he warned that unemployment would increase to 20 per cent and "there is the threat of increased ethnic and political tensions … " The moment the Marcovic government devalued the currency and began to close "unprofitable" state enterprises and cut public services, 650,000 Serbian workers went on strike and the plan collapsed. Yugoslavia was now on its own, denied a fraction of the aid Washington gave to ideologically friendly Poland.

However, "economic reforms" had begun to take hold in separatist republics, as the Germans encouraged Croatia and Slovenia to join the great "European market" and to "disassociate themselves from Yugoslavia. The federation, noted Gervasi, had "walked a tightrope through the 1980s until economic and political crisis, particularly the fall in the standard of living, broke its balance. As rival ethnic groups shook the rope and the state teetered, EC intervention helped push [it] into the abyss ... ”

When the western allies recognised Bosnia last year, the date chosen was the anniversary of the Nazi bombing of Serbia—a day when Serbs renew their cherished self-image of heroic resistance against impossible odds. In Serb nationalist eyes, here was the west partitioning their homeland, having not long celebrated the end of the partition of Germany. And now here was the German airforce choosing the skies over Bosnia for its first military operation since the second world war. With such disregard for national sensitivity, the west has smoothed the way for rabid nationalism to exploit a past shared by decent people and for the Serbian peace movement to be condemned as “unpatriotic.”

In Russia, with its close ties to Serbia, the spectacle of Nato forces, with German participation, bombing Serbian targets, killing and maiming Serbian women and children, might well have the kind of reaction that not even Boris Yeltsin, the west's man, could stop. The first world war began, after all, in Sarajevo.

Even belated attempts by the EC to deter the medievalists and fascists now promoting “Greater Serbia” have been botched. True sanctions of the kind that were imposed on Iraq have only recently come into force. They must now be tightened if Serbia's isolation is to lead to the kind of popular disaffection and opposition to fascism of which the Serbs, contrary to myth, have shown they are capable. But sanctions should also be applied to Croatia—ask any British soldier who has to carry the incinerated corpses of the victims of Croatian fascism. That the multi-ethnic Bosnians, especially those in the towns who have demonstrated no desire to attack anybody, should have been denied the means of defending themselves is absurd, and wrong. They stand defenceless not only against Serbs, whose arms supplies are assured; but against Croats, who through extensive emigre connections and powerful foreign friends, continue to move large shipments of weapons from Austria, Slovenia and Hungary.

Just as I believe the Cambodian people should be armed in order to resist the Khmer Rouge, so the Bosnians should be armed to resist those who would visit a version of “Year Zero” on them. Until they are armed, “we”—the west—are firmly on the side of their killers. Moreover, they are up against fascism on two fronts, and I always understood that fascism had to be resisted.

Meanwhile, the people of Bosnia have a right to be protected. Armies are not required, the 40,000 troops envisaged by Vance-Owen are unnecessary overkill. The 150 Canadians in Srebrenica and the British battalion around Vitez, by their very presence have already provided “havens” and stopped the kind of atrocities that have happened wherever the “cleansers” have been allowed to go about their murderous ways unobserved. What is needed is a careful strategy that makes more use of these troops, and their reinforcements, as both monitors and defenders.

The Germans ought to have nothing to do with this, because of their complicity; and the Americans, too. This is not Iraq, or Panama, or Grenada, or Indochina, where American actions have brought only the ruthlessness of a conqueror. One turkey-shooter could ignite the rest of the Balkan tinderbox. As for the Vance-Owen plan, it is as provocative as it is collusive; it disregards those Croats and Serbs who have remained loyal to the pluralism of Bosnia, and it ignores all those Bosnians of mixed marriages. Vance-Owen ought to be scrapped and replaced by a genuine treaty and ceasefire that covers all the Balkans, from Croatia to Macedonia.

None of this ought to minimise the painful moral and practical dilemmas faced in a region bearing the legacies and scars of competing empires. Neither is it in any way an advocacy of moral policing, but merely as recompense for the actions of so-called western statesmen, most of whom never see in person the nightmarish result of their culpability.

Source: John Pilger. “The West is Guilty in Bosnia.” *New Statesman & Society* (May 7, 1993) 14-15. Copyright © John Pilger. Reprinted with the permission of Guardian News Service Ltd.

Dangerous Exit from a Stormy World

Eric Hobsbawm

ERIC HOBSBAWM *is Professor Emeritus at the University of London and teaches at the New School for Social Research.*

A t a time when the Marshall Islands have just been admitted to the United Nations, nearly 20 of whose members have a population of less than 250,000, the argument that a territory is too small to constitute a state can no longer be convincingly maintained. Of course such states—even much larger ones—are not independent in any meaningful sense. Politically and militarily they are helpless without outside protection, as Kuwait and Croatia show. Economically they are even more dependent. Few separatist movements hope to go it alone. They want to exchange dependence on a single-state economy for dependence on the European Community or some other larger unit that limits its members' economic sovereignty just as much.

Still, if a territory wishes to run up its flag outside the UN building in New York and acquire all the other fringe benefits of statehood—a national anthem, a national airline and a few embassies—the chances today seem better than ever.

But why should anyone wish to set up such a state, mostly by breaking up existing political units in Eurasia and Africa? The usual reason given by would-be state-builders is that the people of the territory concerned have constituted a "nation" from the beginning of time, a special ethnic group, usually with its own language, which cannot live under the rule of strangers. The right of self-determination, they argue, implies states that coincide with nations.

Almost everything about this argument is historically wrong, but, as Ernest Renan noted more than a century ago, "Forgetting history, and even historical error, are an essential factor in the formation of a nation." However, we are concerned not with history or with rationality, but with politics. The nationalist belief, first expressed in the 19th century by Giuseppe Mazzini, that every nation should form a state, and that there should be only one state for each nation, is, and always was, quite unworkable in ethnic-linguistic terms.

There are, with the exception of some island ministates, probably not more than a dozen ethnically and linguistically homogeneous states, and probably none that includes anything like the totality of the "nation" they claim to embody. The territorial distribution of the human race is older than the idea of ethnic-linguistic nation-states and therefore does not correspond to it. Development in the modern world economy, because it generates vast population movements, constantly undermines ethnic-linguistic homogeneity. Multi-ethnicity and pluralism of language are unavoidable, except temporarily by mass exclusion, forcible assimilation, mass expulsion or genocide in short, by coercion. There is only a dark future for a world of nation-states such as a Georgia, which has a government that wants to deny citizenship rights to any inhabitant who cannot prove that his or her ancestors were Georgian speakers and lived in the territory before 1801.

There are today four reasons that such sentiments, and their political expression in separatism, are widely supported. The first is that the collapse of the communist system, which imposed political stability over a large part of Europe, has reopened the wounds of the first world war, or, more precisely, of the misconceived and unrealistic peace settlements after it. The explosive nationalist issues in central and eastern Europe today are not ancient ethnic conflicts but those created during the formation of the successor states to the collapsing multi-ethnic Habsburg, Ottoman and Tsarist Russian empires. Baltic and Caucasian separatism, and conflicts between Serbs and Croats, and Czechs and Slovaks, were not serious problems in 1917, or could not have existed before the establishment of Yugoslavia and Czechoslovakia. What has made those problems acute is not the strength of national feeling, which was no greater than in countries like Britain and Spain, but the disintegration of central power, for this forced even Soviet or Yugoslav republics that did not dream of separation, like Kazakhstan and Macedonia, to assert independence as a means of self-preservation.

The breakdown of communist systems has given separatist agitations elsewhere enormous encouragement. But the prospects of independence for, say, Scotland, Quebec or Corsica remain the same as before. The second reason for the rise of separatism is more general, though probably more important in the west than in the east. The massive population movements of the past 40 years have made xenophobia a major political phenomenon, as the earlier mass migrations of 1880-1920 did to a lesser extent. Xenophobia encourages ethnic nationalism, since the essence of both is hostility to other groups. United States nationalism is by origin nonlinguistic. It is only because of mass Hispanic immigration that demands are now made, for the first time, that English should be the official language of the US. But ethnic hatred does not necessarily produce separatism, as the US also proves.

The third reason is that the politics of group identity are easier to understand than any others, especially for peoples who, after decades of dictatorship, lack political education and experience. In central Europe, argues Miroslav Hroch, a leading Czech historian, language is again replacing complicated concepts such as constitutions, and civil rights. Nationalism is among the simple, intuitively comprehensible beliefs that substitute for less understandable political programmes.

The fourth reason is perhaps the most fundamental. To quote Hroch: "Where an old regime disintegrates, where old social relations have become unstable, amid the rise of general insecurity, belonging to a common language and culture may become the only certainty in society, the only value beyond ambiguity and doubt." In former communist countries, this insecurity and disorientation may derive from the collapse of the planned economy and the social security that went with it. In the west, other forms of disorientation and insecurity have built up over recent decades, when life changed more rapidly and profoundly than ever before.

Is it an accident that Quebec separatism emerged as a serious political factor at the end of a decade when a traditional, Catholic, pious and clerical community suddenly gave way to a society in which people no longer went to church and the birthrate fell almost vertically? After two generations, when continents of peasants have become continents of city-dwellers, when, the relations between the generations, and increasingly between the sexes, have been transformed, and past wisdom seems irrelevant to present problems, the world is full of people who long for something that still looks like an unchallengeable certainty. It is not surprising that they turn to group identity or that the demand for a political unit exclusively for the members of the group, in the form of ethnic-linguistic nation-states, once again comes to the fore.

However, if we can understand the forces that lead to a revival of the politics of national consciousness, and even sympathize with the feelings that inspire it, let us have no illusions. Adding another few dozen member-states of the UN will not give any of them any more control over their affairs than they had before they became independent. It will not solve or diminish the problems of cultural or any other autonomy in the world, any more than it did in 1919. Establishing nation-states on the post-first world war model is not necessarily a recipe for disaster. Among the potential new nation states there may well be one or two future Netherlands and Switzerlands, bastions of tolerance and democracy. But who, looking at Serbia and Croatia, at Slovakia and Lithuania, at Georgia and Quebec, would expect many of the newly separated nation-states to go that way? And who would expect a Europe of such new states to be a zone of peace?

Source: Eric Hobsbawm. "Dangerous Exit From a Stormy World." *New Statesman & Society* (November 8, 1991) 16-17. Copyright © *New Statesman & Society.* Reprinted with the permission of Guardian News Service Ltd.

Nationalism and Federalism

Pierre Elliott Trudeau

PIERRE ELLIOTT TRUDEAU (1919-) *was a graduate of the University of Montreal and Harvard where he studied law and political economy. Later he played an active role in establishing the quarterly,* Cité Libre *in Quebec, a publication that became an adversary of the Duplessis regime in that province. He became Minister of Justice for the Government of Canada in 1967 and Prime Minister in 1968. He remained in this position until 1979 and was re-elected in 1980 until 1984.*

Many of the nations which were formed into states over the past century or two included peoples who were set apart geographically (like East and West Pakistan, or Great Britain and Northern Ireland), historically (like the United States or Czechoslovakia), linguistically (like Switzerland or Belgium), racially (like Soviet Union or Algeria). Half of the aforesaid countries undertook to form the national consensus within the framework of a unitary state; the other half found it expedient to develop a system of government called federalism. The process of consensus-formation is not the same in both cases.

It is obviously impossible, as well as undesirable, to reach unanimity on all things. Even unitary states find it wise to respect elements of diversity, for instance by administrative decentralization as in Great Britain,[1] or by language guarantees as in Belgium; but such limited securities having been given, a consensus is obtained which recognizes the state as the sole source of coercive authority within the national boundaries. The federal state proceeds differently; it deliberately reduces the national consensus to the greatest common denominator between the various groups composing the nation. Coercive authority over the entire territory remains a monopoly of the (central) state, but this authority is limited to certain subjects of jurisdiction; on other subjects, and within well-defined territorial regions, other coercive authorities exist. In other words, the exercise of sovereignty is divided between a central government and regional ones.

Federalism is by its very essence a compromise and a pact. It is a compromise in the sense that when national consensus on all things is not desirable or cannot readily obtain, the area of consensus is reduced in order that consensus on *some* things be reached. It is a pact or quasi-treaty in the sense that the terms of that compromise cannot be changed unilaterally. That is not to say that the terms are fixed forever; but only that in changing them, every effort must be made not to destroy the consensus on which the federated nation rests. For what Ernest Renan said about the nation is even truer about the federated nation: "L'existence d'une nation est...un plebiscite de tous les jours."[2] This obviously did not mean that such a plebiscite could or should be held every day, the result of which could only be total anarchy; the real implication is clear: the nation is based on a social contract, the terms of which each new generation of citizens is free to accept tacitly, or to reject openly.

Federalism was an inescapable product of an age which recognized the principle of self-determination. For on the one hand, a sense of national identity and singularity was bound to be generated in a great many groups of people, who would insist on their right to distinct statehood. But on the other hand, the insuperable difficulties of living alone and the practical necessity of sharing the state with neighbouring groups were in many cases such as to make distinct statehood unattractive or unattainable. For those who recognized that the first law of politics is to start from the facts rather than from historical "might-have-been's", the federal compromise thus became imperative.

But by a paradox I have already noted in regard to the nation-state, the principle of self-determination which makes federalism necessary makes it also rather unstable. If the heavy paste of nationalism is relied upon to keep a unitary nation state together, much more nationalism would appear to be required in the case of a federal nation-state. Yet if nationalism is encouraged as a rightful doctrine and noble passion, what is to prevent it from being used by some group, region, or province within the nation? If "nation algerienne" was a valid battle cry against France, how can the Algerian Arabs object to the cry of "nation kabyle" now being used against them?

The answer, of course, is that no amount of logic can prevent such an escalation. The only way out of the dilemma is to render what is logically defensible actually undesirable. The advantages *to the minority group* of staying integrated in the whole must on balance be greater than the gain to be reaped from separating. This can easily be the case when there is no real alternative for the separatists, either because they are met with force (as in the case of the U.S. Civil War), or because they are met with laughter (as in the case of the *Bretons bretonnisants*). But when there is a real alternative, it is not so easy. And the greater the advantages and possibilities of separatism, the more difficult it is to maintain an unwavering consensus within the whole state.

One way of offsetting the appeal of separatism is by investing tremendous amounts of time, energy, and money in nationalism, *at the federal level*. A national image must be created that will have such an appeal as to make any image of a separatist group unattractive. Resources must be diverted into such things as national flags, anthems, education, arts councils, broadcasting corporations, film boards; the territory must be bound together by a network of railways, highways, airlines; the national culture and the national economy must be protected by taxes and tariffs; ownership of resources and industry by nationals must be made a matter of policy. In short, the whole of the citizenry must be made to feel that it is only within the framework of the federal state that their language, culture, institutions, sacred traditions, and standard of living can be protected from external attack and internal strife.

It is, of course, obvious that a national consensus will be developed in this way only if the nationalism is emotionally acceptable to all important groups within the nation. Only blind men could expect a consensus to be lasting if the national flag or the national image is merely the reflection of one part of the nation, if the sum of values to be protected is not defined so as to include the language or the cultural heritage of some very large and tightly knit minority, if the identity to be arrived at is shattered by a colour-bar. The advantage as well as the peril of federalism is that it permits the development of a regional consensus based on regional values; so federalism is ultimately bound to fail if the nationalism it cultivates is unable to generate a national image which has immensely more appeal than the regional ones.

Moreover, this national consensus—to be lasting—must be a living thing. There is no greater pitfall for federal nations than to take the consensus for granted, as though it were reached once and for all. The compromise of federalism is generally reached under a very particular set of circumstances. As time goes by these circumstances change; the external menace recedes, the economy flourishes, mobility increases, industrialization and urbanization proceed; and also the federated groups grow, sometimes at

uneven paces, their cultures mature, sometimes in divergent directions. To meet these changes, the terms of the federative pact must be altered, and this is done as smoothly as possible by administrative practice, by judicial decision, and by constitutional amendment, giving a little more regional autonomy here, a bit more centralization there, but at all times taking great care to preserve the delicate balance upon which the national consensus rests.

Such care must increase in direct proportion to the strength of the alternatives which present themselves to the federated groups. Thus, when a large cohesive minority believes it can transfer its allegiance to a neighbouring state, or make a go of total independence, it will be inclined to dissociate itself from a consensus the terms of which have been altered in its disfavour. On the other hand, such a minority may be tempted to use its bargaining strength to obtain advantages which are so costly to the majority as to reduce to naught the advantages to the latter of remaining federated. Thus, a critical point can be reached in either direction beyond which separatism takes place, or a civil war is fought.

When such a critical point has been reached or is in sight, no amount, however great, of nationalism can save the federation. Any expenditure of emotional appeal (flags, professions of faith, calls to dignity, expressions of brotherly love) at the national level will only serve to justify similar appeals at the regional level, where they are just as likely to be effective. Thus the great moment of truth arrives when it is realized that *in the last resort* the mainspring of federalism cannot be emotion but must be reason.

To be sure, federalism found its greatest development in the time of the nation-states, founded on the principle of self-determination, and cemented together by the emotion of nationalism. Federal states have themselves made use of this nationalism over periods long enough to make its inner contradictions go unnoticed. Thus, in a neighbouring country, Manifest Destiny, the Monroe Doctrine, the Hun, the Red Scourge, the Yellow Peril, and Senator McCarthy have all provided glue for the American Way of Life; but it is apparent that the Cuban "menace" has not been able to prevent the American Negro from obtaining a renegotiation of the terms of the American national consensus. The Black Muslims were the answer to the argument of the Cuban menace; the only answer to both is the voice of reason.

It is now becoming obvious that federalism has all along been a product of reason in politics. It was born of a decision by pragmatic politicians to face facts as they are, particularly the fact of the heterogeneity of the world's population. It is an attempt to find a rational compromise between the divergent interest-groups which history has thrown together; but it is a compromise based on the will of the people.

Looking at events in retrospect, it would seem that the French Revolution attempted to delineate national territories according to the will of the people, without reference to rationality; the Congress of Vienna claimed to draw state boundaries according to reason, without reference to the will of the people; and federalism arose as an empirical effort to base a country's frontiers on both reason and the will of the people.

I am not heralding the impending advent of reason as the prime mover in politics, for nationalism is too cheap and too powerful a tool to be soon discarded by politicians of all countries; the rising *bourgeoisies* in particular have too large a vested interest in nationalism to let it die out unattended.[3] Nor am I arguing that as important an area of human conduct as politics could or should be governed without any reference to human emotions. But I would like to see emotionalism channelled into a less sterile direction than nationalism. And I am saying that within sufficiently advanced federal countries, the auto-destructiveness of nationalism is bound to become more and more apparent, and reason may yet reveal itself even to ambitious politicians as the more assured road to success. This may also be the trend in unitary states, since they all have to deal with some kind of regionalism or other. Simultaneously in the world of international relations, it is becoming more obvious that the Austinian concept of sovereignty could only be thoroughly applied in a world crippled by the ideology of the nation-state and sustained by the heady stimulant of nationalism. In the world of today, when whole groups of so-called sovereign states are experimenting with rational forms of integration, the exercise of sovereignty will not only be divided within federal states; it will have to be further divided between the states and the communities of states. If this tendency is accentuated the very idea of national sovereignty will recede and, with it, the need for an emotional justification such as nationalism. International law will no longer be explained away as so much "positive international morality", it will be recognized as true law, a "coercive order...for the promotion of peace".[4]

Thus there is some hope that in advanced societies, the glue of nationalism will become as obsolete as the divine right of kings; the title of the state to govern and the extent of its authority will be conditional upon rational justification; a people's consensus based on reason will supply the cohesive force that societies require; and politics both within and without the state will follow a much more functional approach to the problems of government. If politicians must bring emotions into the act, let them get emotional about functionalism!

The rise of reason in politics is an advance of law; for is not law an attempt to regulate the conduct of men in society rationally rather than emotionally? It appears then that a political order based on federalism is an order based on law. And there will flow more good than evil from the present tribulations of federalism if they serve to equip lawyers, social scientists, and politicians with the tools required to build societies of men ordered by reason.

Who knows? humanity may yet be spared the ignominy of seeing its destinies guided by some new and broader emotion based, for example, on continentalism.

Source: Pierre Elliot Trudeau. *Federalism and the French Canadians.* Toronto: MacMillan, 1968. Reprinted with the permission of the author.

Notes

[1] Since the Government of Ireland Act, 1920, it might be more exact to think of Great Britain and Northern Ireland as forming a quasi-unitary state.

[2] Ernest Renan, *Discours et conferences* (Paris, 1887), p.307; also p.299.

[3] On the use of nationalism by the middle classes, see Cobban, *Dictatorship,* p.140. And for a striking and original approach, see Albert Breton, "The Economics of Nationalism," *Journal of Political Economy,* August 1964.

[4] Hans Kelsen, *Law and Peace* (Cambridge, 1948), pp.1, 7.

10

Fundamentalism

The Ideal of Faith

The twentieth century has witnessed a re-birth of fundamentalism, of strict adherence to the social and moral codes of revealed religion and the promise it holds for a life lived by faith. This phenomenon, seemingly more evident in the West than in the East, is as true of Islam as it is of Judaism and Christianity. In Judaism, devotion to the life of faith manifests itself in Hasidism and Orthodoxy and their struggle with Zionism and secularism. In Islam, fundamentalism manifests itself not only in Shi'ism and the emergence of politically powerful leaders like Ayatollah Khomeini, but also occasionally in Sunnism and the rise of charismatic leaders such as Malcolm X. In Christianity, fundamentalism manifests itself in movements such as the Moral Majority in its struggle against legalized abortion, humanistic textbooks, and the failed Equal Rights Amendment.

In all three movements, as Joseph Piscatori suggests, the struggle is with modernity and the spiritual dislocation it has caused. This having been said, the real scholarly work remains to be done. In particular, comparative analyses of the perceived ills of modernity as determined by these versions of fundamentalism should be undertaken. This research would have a two-fold advantage. First, it would facilitate the construction of a better psychological explanation of the reasons that people choose what many post-modern thinkers regard to be cognitively dissonant positions. Secondly, this research would perhaps assist members of each of these movements to understand each other, thereby contributing to the growth of tolerance.

Although it is fashionable to be disdainful of fundamentalism and its ideal of a life of faith, a dismissal of it should proceed by examining the philosophical alternatives. At this stage in metaphysical thinking one seems left with three possibilities: perennial naturalism with its linkage to humanism, critical anti-realism with its linkage to pluralism and relativism, and theism with its perceived cognitive dissonance. While it is too soon to say how each of these positions will fare in the storms ahead, the evidence in hand for the practical credibility of perennial naturalism and critical anti-realism no longer looks as promising as it once did. So while fundamentalism may seem to many post-modern thinkers an unsatisfactory paradigm, these scholars need to show how their political philosophy allows them to deal effectively with emerging social and political problems without appealing to the life of faith.

The Nature of the Islamic Revival

James P. Piscatori

JAMES P. PISCATORI *is a Research Fellow at the Royal Institute of International Affairs in London.*

Reasons for the Revival

In looking for an explanation of the [Islamic] revival, therefore, we must take a somewhat longer view. Four broad reasons come into sight.

First, the defeat of Egypt, Syria, and Jordan in the 1967 war with Israel shattered the morale not only of the Arabs, who lost in a head-to-head fight with the enemy, but also of most Muslims, who lost the holy city of Jerusalem. This was not just a defeat or a loss, it was *al-nakba, "the* disaster"—the culmination of a long series of setbacks and humiliations which stretched back in modern times to the first militarily unsuccessful encounters that the Ottoman Muslims had with the Europeans. These defeats had given rise to a sense of inferiority, which at first was based on an appreciation of technological, though not theological, inadequacy. But now, in the mid-twentieth century, the loss of sacred territory led many Muslims to conclude either one of two things—either that Islam was an inferior religion, or that they were inadequate believers who had not lived up to the ideals of Islam and therefore deserved their fate.

Most Muslims seem to have concluded that they—or at least their governments—had gone astray, although by and large they did not work out the implication of their failure: that the other side, the enemy, had done something right. This inability or unwillingness to grasp the nettle was the despair of many intellectuals, but, probably because of its simplicity, the popular conclusion concentrated the emotions: Muslims needed to be better Muslims, and their governments more Islamic, if God was to spare them further calamity, or if they were ever to have a chance of recapturing Jerusalem. At the very least the Israeli occupation outraged them, and in the common outrage Muslims everywhere found a stronger identification with each other than had existed previously in the modern era. Some Arab Muslims, in particular, came to see a certain hollowness in Nasirism, the ideology that had seemed the panacea for the Arabs' problems, and were prompted to search for an ideol-

ogy and programme that could be both coherent and effective. Even before the war, some had come to regard 'Abd al-Nasir as an impious and incompetent tyrant, and as such a greater enemy than the Israelis.[1] But, when it came, the catastrophe of 1967 forced many others to reconsider basic principles and to look for an Islamic ideology.

It is all the more ironic, then, that in 1985, less than twenty years after the 1967 war, many Muslim—mainly Shi'i—activists in Lebanon came to see the Palestinians as an obstacle to their own Islamic revolution. They reached this conclusion as a consequence of disputes, over power and territorial control in Lebanon, and these disputes, along with the generally heightened awareness of Islam since the Iranian revolution, led them to de-emphasize the Palestinian struggle *per se* while putting more stress on liberating Jerusalem, the third holiest city of Islam. For whatever reason, then—the defeat of the Arabs by Israel or the conflict between Palestinians and Shi'i groups in Lebanon—a new sense of Islamic commitment has emerged out of the general Arab-Israeli imbroglio.

Second, the process of development has been a contributing factor. It has stimulated the revival in two main ways: (a) it has often strained the social and political fabric, thereby leading people to turn to traditional symbols and rites as a way of comforting and orienting themselves; and (b) it has provided the means of speedy communication and easy dissemination of both domestic and international information.

(a) The most important dimension to the first point is the unsettling and unrelieved exodus of people from the countryside to the cities. For example, between 1960 and 1975 the rate of increase in the urban population exceeded the growth of the industrial labour force in Egypt by 2 per cent, Iran by 3 per cent, Iraq by 8 per cent, Jordan by 18 per cent, Kuwait by 14 percent, Lebanon by 3 per cent, Morocco by 10 per cent, Saudi Arabia by 11 per cent, Syria by 3 per cent, and South Yemen by 13 per cent.[2] More recent data would undoubtedly show this trend continuing. Most rural migrants quickly become the urban poor, victims of their own hope, swallowed by the very process which they believed would liberate them. Unscrupulous contractors exploit the members of this seemingly inexhaustible labour pool in order to build as cheaply as possible the new buildings that dot the urban landscape, and government is often unwilling or unable to protect them and to give them basic shelter. In countries such as India and Nigeria, they are also subjected to ethnic or racial discrimination and made to feel that they do not belong and that they probably never will. Many of their children are likely to be forgotten, escaping the educational net and remaining largely unprotected against serious disease.

I must not leave the simplistic impression that these rural migrants have the same destiny or produce the same effect everywhere that they settle. These obviously differ with the culture, the state of the economy, and the size of the city. With regard to the last point, for example, migrants are able to spread rural attitudes more widely in small provincial towns than in the large cities, and not simply because of the difference in size. As Serif Mardin shows in the case of Turkey, the provincial towns provide fertile ground for Islamic sentiment because the petty-bourgeois merchants and the small-scale farmers feel exploited by the large capitalists and alienated from their Europeanized culture.[3] But there does seem to be a general connection between the sense of not belonging and the turn to religion. In places where Sufi *tariqas*, or brotherhoods, are present, such as Morocco or Senegal, the mystical assimilation of a local saint's grace (*baraka*) is a powerful antidote to the joylessness of everyday life. In some societies, such as Iran, where well-established religious institutions provide some degree of financial assistance, or at least cushion the move from the countryside, migrants naturally come into close contact with the religious officials. In Lebanon the Shi'a who have migrated from the south or the Beqaa Valley to Beirut do not seem to lose their sectarian identification. If anything, they become more aware of it. In the city and suburbs, as outsiders needing the patronage of families to which they do not belong, they feel that they have incurred dishonour and lowered the status that they had in the countryside. In such an alien environment, the political point of reference is no longer family, as it was in the village, but sect.[4] In other societies, such as Nigeria, where extreme economic imbalance and a climate of religious tension prevail, the migrants become natural recruits of millenarian movements. The official report on the Kano disturbances in December 1980, in which the followers of the self-proclaimed prophet known as Maitatsine wreaked horrendous devastation, explained this phenomenon well:

> We have earlier made mention of his [Maitatsine's] application for a piece of land to erect temporary structures. His intention, we believe, was to provide accommodation for these men coming from the rural areas since he knew very well that the first problem they would face on arrival at Kano was accommodation ... These fanatics who have been brought up in extreme poverty, generally had a grudge against privileged people in the society, whose alleged ostentatious way of living often annoyed them. Because of the very wide gap between the rich and the poor in our society and coupled with the teaching of Muhammad Marwa [Maitatsine], they were more than prepared to rise against the society at the slightest opportunity. After all they did not have much to lose ... They did not own more than the clothes they wore. They had nothing to fall back to.[5]

In every case, the migration from the countryside has helped to spread rural attitudes in the cities, particularly a pronounced emphasis on Islamic tradition. It has thus given impetus to the urban Islamic revival.

The effects are less dramatic among the middle classes, but many of these, too, are unhappy with the process of development. As sophisticated education has become increasingly available, technicians, lawyers, engineers, and teachers have become the new "productive" middle class in place of the old bazaaris and landowners. These latter resent the loss of status and influence and are suspicious of the Western advisers, suddenly indiscreetly visible, who are purportedly exemplars of a different lifestyle and set of values, and are supposed to show the local people the way to a more efficient and prosperous future. The former, the members of the "new" middle class, are impatient with the old ideology and anxious to better their position socially and politically.

Poverty and deprivation affect the attitudes of the rural migrants and, equally true, greater wealth and an improved social position affect the attitudes of the middle classes. It is precisely because the middle classes are better off that they are dissatisfied; their appetite has been whetted and they want more. This is particularly true of the lower middle class. According to Saad Eddin Ibrahim's profile of Egyptian Islamic militants, over 70 per cent were from modest, not poor, backgrounds and were first-generation city-dwellers.[6] Nazih Ayubi shows further that there is a difference in social background between those who attend al-Azhar and those who attend the secular universities, and that it is this latter, upwardly mobile and largely non-peasant, group that yields more of the new activists than we might have guessed. In fact, there is nothing new in this pattern: for example, of the 1,950 members of the main assembly of the Egyptian Muslim Brotherhood (al-Ikhwan al-Muslimun) in 1953, only 22 were not of the educated urban middle classes.[7]

For many urban Muslims, however, the sense of not

belonging, of being neither fully modern nor suitably traditional, has been the price of success. A 1971 study of middle-class Egyptians indicated that a high proportion did not feel integrated into society and in fact regarded their relations with other people in terms of hostility and even conflict.[8] Religion may not hold the answer for these people, but they are automatically attracted to it because the religious instinct runs deep and because such secular ideologies as Nasirism and Ba'thism have seemed so obviously wanting—both materially and spiritually. Most members of the middle classes will express their religious feeling through the state-controlled religious establishment and will oppose a radical challenge to it.[9] Yet some will turn to more radical alternatives as they sense that the religious establishment is indistinguishable from a regime whose policies appear to close doors to them, even as they open doors to foreign political and business elites. (President al-Sadat's economic policy of attracting outside investment was called *infitah*, or "opening.") These Muslims will take to radical and often violent activity as they shout "Allahu Akhbar!" ("God is most great!"), but they have something in common with those others who feel at sea. Islam, not clearly defined but keenly felt, is their mooring. The metaphor is different in a short story by the Egyptian writer Alifa Rifaat, but the point is the same: for the middle-class woman trying to come to terms with her new sexual assertiveness, "the five daily prayers were like punctuation marks that divided up and gave meaning to her life."[10]

(b) The other way in which the process of development has stimulated a sense of renewal is by advancing the dissemination of information throughout the developing world. Despite the static plight of the sub-proletariat or *lumpenproletariat*,[11] there have been substantial improvements in literacy among the rest of the population; moreover, radios have become a common possession. As a result, people are now more in touch with what is going on in the rest of the world, and are anxious to formulate Islamic positions on current political, economic, and social issues—or, in other words, to think of the world's problems in Islamic terms. At the same time, Muslims come to know how dissatisfaction and protest against injustices can be and have been, in other places, framed by reference to Islam.

The fast and efficient distribution within Iran of Ayatullah Khumayni's sermons, delivered in exile and recorded on cassettes—"revolution-by-cassette"—demonstrates further how modern information technology can help people focus their discontent and build their identity around one set of ideas, even though the exponent of those ideas is far removed.

To put it the other way around, it shows how religious leaders can use popular feelings by appealing to traditional values, even when they are not physically present: this projection is the powerful extension of the mosque sermon (*khutba*).

Khumayni provides the most celebrated example, but there are others. Cassettes of the sermons of Shaykh 'Abd al-Hamid Kishk, an Egyptian *'alim*, are played throughout the Middle East. Young people are particularly attracted by them, as young people throughout Malaysia are attracted by recordings of the *khutbas* of Haji Hadi Awang, who, from his base in rural Trengganu, rails—impartially—against infidels and half-hearted Muslims alike. Because of the emphasis on community, the importance of the mosque as a central meeting-place, the gathering together of Muslims from all over the world during the Pilgrimage, and the respect given to such official interpreters as the *'ulama*, Islam constitutes a vigorous communication system of its own and is what Marshal Lyautey called "a sounding board."[12] Modern technology has dramatically enhanced this capability.

The third general reason for the present revival, in addition to the intellectual and spiritual malaise since the 1967 war and the effects of the development process, is that Muslim societies have been caught up in the universal crisis of modernity. Most Muslims, like virtually everyone else in the developed and developing world, are feeling ill at ease with a way of life that places less and less emphasis on loyalties to the family and seems to find religious institutions increasingly irrelevant. In the past century a discernible shift towards the individual has taken place within societies—i.e., towards lessening the individual's dependence on the extended family (even in such socially conservative Gulf shaykhdoms as Qatar),[13] weakening parental authority, liberating women, and questioning the authority of the clergy. No direct causal relationship exists of course, but this period has also seen an alarming increase in divorce, alcohol and drug addiction, nerve disorders, and crime. It is not surprising, therefore, that "dropping-out," or "evaporation" (*johatsu*) as the Japanese say, has come to seem attractive to many. At the very least, modernism has led to a diminution of belief: "After the dizzying history of the last fifty years, the world has grown strange, and people floated."[14] Iranian writers, for example, are now beginning to talk about modernity, not modernization, as the problem, and the notion that something is missing in one's life seems to have generated a time of "secular discontents,"[15] leading many to wonder whether the age has lost its way and to ask, "What is it, after all, to be modern?"

Modernity gives rise to a basic search for identity, in which many people accept that knowing oneself comes through associating with the crowd rather than seeking to rise above it. This search is in fact an individual act of self-discovery, but because of Islam's intense association of the individual believer with the whole community of believers, it seems as if it is an act of self-abnegation. Muslims in a sense are looking for what Daniel Bell called "new rites of incorporation," which link today's deracinated individual to a community and a history.[16] And yet, in another sense, this is wrong: they are looking, rather, for *old* rites of incorporation that appear to be new even as they are familiar. Religion, precisely because in the past it answered questions on life and death and provided its followers with moral links to each other, becomes the means by which individuals hope to answer the new question of what it is to be modern, and, in so doing, to gain perhaps a reassuring, common world-view. In this respect, born-again Christians and veiled-again Muslims are responding to the same broad phenomenon.

Islam supplies a particularly powerful rite of incorporation because it puts great emphasis on the idea of community and on the Prophet's time as the model for the organization of society. Prior to the revelation that Muhammad received, the people of the Arabian peninsula had worshipped several gods and organized themselves according to tribal, blood ties. But it was the radical innovation of Islam to insist that each person is to be subservient to the one true God and to look upon every other person as brother. This community is based on the bonds of morality, not blood or tribal custom or expediency, and involves the acceptance of responsibilities towards God and men. Although the *umma* incorporates all the believers, it will eventually become universal and include all mankind. In the meantime, Muslims are to follow the example of the Prophet and, in the case of the Sunnis, his four immediate successors, "the rightly guided Caliphs," or, in the case of the Shi'a, the Imams. It is this perception of fraternity, and of a glorious past, that gives all Muslims—Sunnis and Shi'a—a powerful sense of belonging.

Finally, the fourth general reason for the revival is that the conditions of political development in these societies have tended to heighten the importance of Islam as a political ideology. Because most of these societies are poor in institutions and dominated by unelected rulers, it is natural for those in power to look for a way of legitimating themselves. Legitimation may perhaps be too grand a word to convey what I mean: rulers seek evidence of approval from the ruled or, at least, evidence of acquiescence or the

absence of outright opposition. Several monarchies are especially adept at using Islamic symbols for this purpose: the Moroccan king makes much of his traditional title, Commander of the Faithful (*amir al-mu'minin*); the Saudi king finds a naturally sympathetic response when he speaks of his role as protector of Mecca and Medina; and the Jordanian king is careful to emphasize his descent from the Prophet. Monarchs probably always need reassurance, but the need in the case of these leaders has certainly become greater and more definite since the unleashing by the Iranian revolution of a violent ideological storm whose avowed purpose has been to overcome all the remaining shahs of the Muslim world. The fact that development schemes seem to be losing momentum or running into trouble has further contributed to the uneasy climate.

This defensiveness on the part of the existing leaders has been apparent not only in the traditional monarchies, but also in the republics, where such leaders as al-Sadat and Mubarak of Egypt and al-Numayri of the Sudan have faced considerable opposition to their rule and have found it expedient to put Islam to their service. Al-Sadat, for example, found it useful—although it was extremely controversial—to have a *fatwa* from al-Azhar supporting his peace treaty with Israel; Mubarak has created an official Islamic publication, *al-Liwa al-Islami* (*The Islamic Standard*), to rival the popular and often censorious Muslim Brotherhood publication *al-Da'wa* (*The Call*); and al-Numayri courted Sufi leaders and made concessions to the Muslim Brothers, such as the introduction of Islamic law. In Malaysia as well, the government, although keenly aware of the multi-ethnic composition of the population, has increasingly affirmed its Islamic credentials, and the ruling party, the United Malays' National Organization (UMNO), has claimed that it is the largest Islamic party in the country.

In all these countries governments have been able to use Islam with such ease because, as an ideology, it is vague in content yet highly charged: people instinctively respond to it as a general symbol but also as a guide to their loyalties. Its vocabulary, too, is thoroughly familiar to everyone, thereby guaranteeing that the government's message cannot be missed. Napoleon recognized the value and ease—of using Islamic symbolism at the time of this invasion of Egypt in 1798. His proclamation to the people of Egypt began with the standard Muslim invocation of "God, the Merciful, the Compassionate" (*bismallah*), and went on to say "I worship God (may He be exalted) far more than the Mamlukes do, and respect His

Prophet and Glorious Quran … [T]he French also are sincere Muslims."[17]

Governments have also been able to use Islam to their own ends because it lends itself readily to nationalization; or, to express it differently, they have been able to make it part of the bureaucracy. Even the Malaysian federal government, which is sensitive to states' rights, pre-eminently including the right to regulate religion, has moved to bureaucratize Islam. It has not only created such coordinating bodies as the National Council for Islamic Affairs, the National Fatwa Council, and the Religious Affairs Division of the Prime Minister's office, but has also taken over a number of religious schools in the states. In effect, then, governments have recognized the power of Islam and sought to harness it to their own ends.

But just as Islam can be used to legitimate, so can it be used to express opposition. And there are signs that this use has been increasing too. The increase has come about partly as a result of the Shah's overthrow, but also because in many countries in which there are no regular outlets for political expression Islam has been found to be an effective and relatively safe way of making a political stand. Governments have been hesitant to suppress groups speaking in the name of Islam because of the need to appear orthodox themselves, in order either to forestall domestic opposition or to attract aid from Muslim "patrons" such as Saudi Arabia. As a result, many Muslim groups have been relatively free to criticize their governments, albeit in a circumspect way. The Muslim Brotherhood has been doing this in Jordan, where it has been tolerated as long as it remains a loyal opposition; this pattern was also true of the Brotherhood in the Sudan for most of the al-Numayri regime. Furthermore, it has happened in Algeria and Tunisia, where Muslim groups have acted as a kind of pressure group that tries to influence policies rather than to replace the regime.

In regimes so repressive that they brook no dissent and regard Muslim criticism of any sort as a threat to their survival, the "Islamic alternative" almost invariably has become more radical. It has become a kind of party, whose aim is to replace the regime, rather than a pressure group. This radicalization of a political alternative of course happens in any repressive society, as it did in Poland, where Solidarity may be thought of as the opposition party. It even happens in societies perceived by only a small minority to be repressive, such as West Germany, which is totalitarian in the eyes of the Baader-Meinhoff gang. My point is not to demonstrate the uniqueness of Muslim societies but merely to indicate that in the Muslim case, too, ostensibly ideological—or religious—groups may become politically radicalized in certain circumstances.

Islam might acquire an even more contentious political centrality, a revolutionary character, if social and economic conditions were dire. This would be the case if there were a marked division between the haves and have-nots, or, to use the terminology at once Qur'anic and secular of the Iranian revolution, between the "oppressors" (*mustakburun*) (16:22-3) and the "oppressed" (*mustad'afun*)(4:97). The rural poor and new urban immigrants would constitute the "oppressed" (or the "disinherited," as is said in Lebanon),[18] and the large landowners and urban middle-class professionals would constitute the "oppressors." In this situation, as was the case in Iran, politics would become increasingly polarized and vicious as all were caught up in a double revolution of expectations: peasants expecting the good life in the dazzling capitals; professionals and intellectuals expecting greater influence, status, and political participation. Both sides would be destined for disappointment, and would inevitably see each other as obstacles. The professionals and intellectuals would come to regard the urban immigrants as a drain on scarce resources; and, more importantly, given the role played by street politics in the increasingly city-dominated developing countries, the "disinherited" would come to regard members of the new professional middle class as new oppressors, who used Islam as a tactic to gain mass support but who really cared only about advancing their own narrow self-interest. Moreover, those who said they wanted to make Islam relevant to the conditions of the modern world would be seen as having sold out to, or at least compromised with, the Westernized, secularizing leadership. It is in this way that "modernist" groups, such as the Masyumi party in Indonesia, lose ground to more "traditionalist" ones, such as the Nahdatul Ulama.

In effect, then, a revolution of *falling* expectations would take place, particularly among the rural poor and urban immigrants. Seeing a prosperous future recede on the horizon, they would naturally cling to the only comfort of the present, the pillar of traditional faith, and, in doing so, would give political expression to the frustration and indignities of living on the margin of the society. It is a phenomenon that Soviet writers have come to regard as inevitable: "It is natural for them, therefore, to express their socio-political aspirations and protest against colonial and imperialist oppression in religious form."[19]

Notes

[1] See, for example, 'Ali Jirisha, '*Indama yakhuma al-tughah* (Cairo, Dar al-I'tisam, 1975), pp.48-50.

[2] Lewis W. Snider, "Political Instability and Social Change in the Middle East," *Korea and World Affairs*, 8 (Summer, 1984), 288.

[3] Serif Mardin, "Religion and Politics in Modern Turkey," in Piscatori (ed.), *Islam in the Political Process*, p.154.

[4] Fuad I. Khuri, "Sectarian Loyalty Among Rural Migrants in Two Lebanese Suburbs: A Stage Between Family and National Allegiance," in Richard Antoun and Iliya Harik (eds), *Rural Politics and Social Change in the Middle East* (Bloomington and London, Indiana University Press, 1972), pp.204-10.

[5] Federal Republic of Nigeria, *Report of Tribunal of Inquiry on Kano Disturbances* (Lagos, Federal Government Press, 1981), p.79.

[6] Saad Eddin Ibrahim, "Anatomy of Egypt's Militant Islamic Groups: Methodological Note and Preliminary Findings," *International Journal of Middle East Studies*, 12 (December 1980), 438-9; "Militant Islam Joins and Mainstream," *Arabia: the Islamic World Review* (April 1984), p.68.

[7] In 1966, for example, 5.8 per cent of the students at Cairo University were *fallahin*, or of rural background, whereas 45.5 per cent of al-Azhar University's students were *fallahin*: Nazih Nasif al-Ayubi, *Siyasat al-ta'lim fi misr: dirasa siyasiyya wa idariyya* (Cairo, Markaz al-Dirasat al-Siyasiyya wa'l-Istratijiyya [al-Ahram], May 1978), p.72. Also see his "The Political Revival of Islam: The Case of Egypt," *International Journal of Middle East Studies*, 12 (December 1980), 493.

[8] Study by Fu'ad al-Bahi al-Sayyid in L.K. Malika (ed.), *Qira' at fi'ilm al-nafs al-ijtima'i fi'l-watan al-'arabi*, vol. 3 (Cairo, Al-Hay'a al-Misriyya al-'Amma li'l-Kitab, 1979).

[9] Dale F. Eickelman shows how the Moroccan bourgeoisie benefited from French encouragement of non-Sherqawi brotherhoods and, later, the Sultan's encouragement of "scripturalist" Muslim authorities. Accordingly, its religious attitudes were accommodating to those of the official establishment: *Moroccan Islam: Tradition and Society in a Pilgrimage Center* (Austin and London, University of Texas Press, 1976), pp.222-32.

[10] Alifa Rifaat, *Distant View of a Minaret*, trans. by Denys Johnson-Davies (London, Quartet Books, 1983), p.3.

[11] Marxists make a distinction between the two. For example, the Iranian Bizhan Jazani speaks of the sub-proletariat as the shanty-town urban poor who are potential revolutionaries, whereas the *lumpen-proletariat* are thieves, hooligans, and prostitutes who are inevitably "depraved," "classless," and reactionary: *Capitalism and Revolution in Iran* (London, Zed Press, 1980), pp.141-3.

[12] Quoted in Charles-André Julien, "Crisis and Reform in French North Africa," *Foreign Affairs*, 29 (April 1951), 455.

[13] In Qatar, by 1975, only 37 per cent of families living close to each other were related, and since then the trend towards the nuclear family as the primary social unit has continued: Levon H. Melikian and Juhaina S. El-Easa, "Oil and Social Change in the Gulf," *Journal of Arab Affairs*, I (October 1981), 83.

[14] V.S. Naipaul, *Among the Believers: An Islamic Journey*, (London, Deutsch, 1981), p.285.

[15] James Finn, "Secular Discontents," *Worldview*, 24 (March 1981), 5-8.

[16] Daniel Bell, *The Cultural Contradictions of Capitalism* (London, Heinemann, 2nd edn. 1979), p.170.

[17] Quoted in Albert Hourani, *Arabic Thought in the Liberal Age, 1798-1939* (London, Oxford University Press, 1970), p.30.

[18] In 1974 Shi'i authorities, particularly Musa al-Sadr, established Harakat al-Mahrumin (Movement of the Disinherited) in Lebanon in order to advance Shi'i rights. A military wing, Amal (an acronym meaning "hope"), was set up the following year.

[19] A. Vasilyev, "Islam in the Present-Day World," *International Affairs* (Moscow), No. II (November 1981), p.53.

We Shall Confront the World with Our Ideology

Ayatollah Khomeini

AYATOLLAH KHOMEINI (1900-1989) took on his surname in 1930 in honour of his birthplace, Khomein, Iran. He assumed the title "ayatollah" when he had gained enough of a following to merit the designation. After fourteen years in exile he returned to Iran after the fall of the Shah, replacing the monarchy with a theocracy.

In the name of God, the compassionate, the merciful, let me congratulate all oppressed people and the noble Iranian nation on the occasion of the new year, whose present is the consolidation of the foundation of the Islamic Republic. The will of almighty God, may He be praised, decreed the release of this oppressed nation from the yoke of the tyranny and crimes of the satanical regime and from the yoke of the domination of oppressive powers, especially the government of the world-devouring America, and to unfurl the banner of Islamic justice over our beloved country. It is our duty to stand up to the superpowers and we have the ability to stand up against them, provided that our intellectuals give up their fascination with Westernization or Easternization and follow the straight path of Islam and nationalism.

We are fighting against international communism to the same degree that we are fighting against the Western world—devourers led by America, Israel and Zionism. My dear friends, you should know that the danger from the communist powers is not less than America and the danger of America is such that if we show the slightest negligence we shall be destroyed. Both superpowers have risen for the obliteration of the oppressed nations and we should support the oppressed people of the world. [shouts of "God is great"]

We should try hard to export our revolution to the world, and should set aside the thought that we do not export our revolution, because Islam does not regard various Islamic countries differently and is the supporter of all the oppressed people of the world. On the other hand, all the superpowers and all the powers have risen to destroy us. If we remain in an enclosed environment we shall definitely face defeat. We should clearly settle our accounts with the powers and superpowers and should demonstrate to them that, despite all the grave difficulties that we have, we shall confront the world with our ideology.

My dear youth, who are the object of my attention, take the Koran in one hand and the weapon in the other and so defend your dignity and honor that you can deprive them of the power of thinking and plotting against you. [shouts of approval]

Be so merciful to your friends that you do not cease from bestowing upon them all that you possess. Be aware that today's world is the world of oppressed people and that, sooner or later, theirs is the victory. [shouts of approval] The oppressed are the ones who shall inherit the earth and shall govern by God's decree.

Once again, I announce my support for all movements, fronts, and groups which are fighting in order to escape from the claws of the Eastern or Western superpowers. I announce my support for beloved Palestine and beloved Lebanon. Once again, I strongly condemn the dastardly occupation of Afghanistan by the plunderers and occupiers of the aggressive East. [shouts of "God is great"] I hope that the Muslim and noble people of Afghanistan will as soon as possible achieve true victory and independence and be released from the grip of these so-called supporters of the working classes. [shouts of "God is great"]

The noble nation should know that the entire victory was achieved through the will of almighty God and by means of transformation which came about throughout the country, and through the spirit of faith and a spirit of self-sacrifice, which was manifested in the decisive majority of the nation. Turning toward God and the unity of expression was the basis of our victory. If we forget the secret of victory and we turn away from great Islam and its holy teachings and if we follow the path of disunity and dissension, there is the danger that the bounty of God almighty may cease and the path may be laid open for the oppressors, and that the deceits and plots of the satanical powers may put our beloved nation in bondage and waste the pure blood which has been shed on the path of independence and freedom and spoil the

IMAM KHOMEINI (1900–1989)

AYATOLLAH RUHOLLAH KHOMEINI (1900–1989) adopted his surname in 1930 in honour of his birthplace, Khomein, Iran. The term "Ayatollah" means "reflection of God." Eventually Khomeini attained the status of Grand Ayatollah.

Khomeini's political career in Iran was initially marked by his opposition to Shah Reza Pahlavi who ruled the country from 1954–1979. In 1962, Khomeini was arrested and placed under house arrest; in 1964, he was exiled to Turkey and in 1965 to Iraq. In 1978 he was expelled from Iraq and went to France where he remained until his return to Iran in 1979.

Khomeini vowed to free Iran from the secular, western-influenced rule of the Shah. Under the Pahlavi dynasty rule, the

muslim clergy had been persecuted and western industry and commerce had flourished. Khomeini advocated the reconstruction of an Islamic republic with the Ayatollahs in command. His message appealed to Iranians who had become disenchanted with western factory owners and employers; in addi-

tion, the *mullahs* (clergy) spread Khomeini's fundamentalist message to vast numbers of Iranians. In a widespread purge, thousands were executed for failing to follow the dictates of Islamic fundamentalist law.

Khomeini's brand of Islamic fundamentalism holds that society is best governed by strict adherence to the Koran, which is in turn interpreted by the clergy as the supreme religious, social and political authority. It is not surprising that Iran under Khomeini was constantly at odds with more secular muslim nations such as Iraq, Syria and Egypt.

hardships which our dear young and old have endured, and that our Islamic country may forever endure that which passed during the satanical regime, and that those who were defeated as a result of the Islamic revolution may do to us that which they did and continue to do to the deprived and oppressed people of the world.

Therefore, being conscious of my divine and religious duty, I remind you of certain points. And his excellency the president and the Revolutionary Council and the government and the security forces are emphatically entrusted with the execution of these points. [shouts of support] I ask the entire nation, with all its power and with its strong allegiance to beloved Islam, to seriously support them throughout the country.

I see that the plots of the anti-revolutionary satans aimed at providing opportunities for the East or the West are increasing. It is the divine, human and na-

tional duty of our government and nation to prevent these plots, with all of our ability.

Now I point out certain issues: [shouts of "God is great"]

1. This year is a year in which security should return to Iran [shouts of "God is great"] and the noble people live in utmost comfort. Once again, I announce my support for the noble Iranian Armed Forces. [shouts of "God is great"] However, the Armed Forces of the Islamic Republic should fully observe all laws and regulations. His excellency, the president, who has been appointed commander in chief of the Armed Forces on my behalf, is duty-bound to severely punish anyone, regardless of his position and grade, who wishes to create disruption in the army or organize strikes or indulge in slowdowns or violate army discipline and regulations or rebel against army regulations. As soon as an offense has been determined, the president should immediately expel the

guilty individual from the Armed Forces and begin legal proceedings against him. I shall no longer tolerate disorder within the army in any form. Whoever causes disruption in the work of the Armed Forces will be presented to the nation as a counterrevolutionary, so that the dear nation may settle its account with the remnants of the criminal Shah's army. [shouts of "God is great"]

My dear military brothers, O you who turned your backs on the vile Shah and his plundering agents and joined the ranks of the nation. Today is the day of service to the nation and to beloved Iran. You should try to save this country from the enemies of Islam and Iran through hard work and endeavor.

2. Once again, I announce my support for the Guards Corps, and I remind them and their commanders that the lightest violation will lead to prosecution. If, God forbid, you do something which may cause disruption in the discipline of the corps, you will be immediately expelled. All that I said about the army will also be carried out concerning them. My revolutionary children, be sure that you deal with all people with kindness and with Islamic manners. [shouts of "God is great"]

3. The police and the gendarmerie of the country should observe order. As I have been informed, there are a great number of slowdowns at police stations. Those who do not have good records should strive to show greater harmony with the people and in order to establish order throughout Iran. They should regard themselves as part of the nation. I hope that in the future a fundamental reorganization be carried out in the gendarmerie and the police. The security forces should regard themselves as belonging to Islam and the Muslims. The explosions in the south have greatly aggrieved me; why do not the corps and the police and gendarmerie clearly identify and punish a group of ungodly persons dependent on the former regime, corrupt, foreign and dependent on America? These people are guilty of sowing corruption on earth, both those who directly take part in such actions and those who guide the affairs from afar. Their conviction as those who are guilty of sowing corruption on earth is clear. The Revolution Courts should show greater decisiveness, so that they may uproot them. [shouts of "God is great"]

4. Revolution Courts throughout the country should be perfect examples of the implementation of God's religion. They should try not to be diverted from the teachings of God almighty, even by one step. They should observe complete care. They should sit in justice with revolutionary patience. The courts have no right to have armed forces of their own. They should act according to the constitution and gradually

the Islamic judicial system should take over the responsibilities of the courts. Therefore, they should prevent wrongdoings with utmost decisiveness and if, God forbid, a person has violated God's teachings, this should immediately be made known to the nation and he should be punished. [shouts of "God is great"]

5. The government is duty-bound to provide the means of labor and production for workers, farmers and laborers. However, they too should know that strikes and slowdowns will not only strengthen the superpowers, but also cause the hope of the oppressed people in the Islamic and non-Islamic countries who have risen to be turned into despair. The people of each city, as soon as they learn of a strike at a factory, should go to that place and see what they want. You should identify the counterrevolutionaries and make them known to the people. The noble people of Iran can no longer pay unearned salaries to a number of ungodly people. [shouts of approval]

My dear workers, you should know that those who every day create tumult in a corner of the country and who basically come to the field with the logic of force are your headstrong enemies and wish to turn you away from the path of the revolution. They are dictators, who if they ever come to power will not allow anyone to breathe. You should fight against them in all fields and identify them to the public as your number one enemy and reveal their connection and dependence upon the aggressive East or the colonial West. The government is duty-bound to severely punish those who are involved in such actions. [shouts of approval]

6. I do not understand why the government is not reactivating the wheels of industry, which have stopped and are in the interest of the public. The government should, as soon as possible, implement the projects which have been stopped and are in the interest of the nation, as well as some new projects, so that the economic situation of our country may be set right. [shouts of "God is great"]

7. In government departments, all government employees must obey the government elected by the people; otherwise, harsh actions are needed. Anybody who wishes to disrupt a government department should be expelled immediately and should be made known to the nation. I am amazed at how the responsible officials are not making use of the strength of the people. The people themselves will settle their accounts with the counterrevolutionaries and expose them. [shouts of "God is great"]

8. The confiscation of the property of the oppressors by unauthorized individuals or unqualified courts is strongly condemned. All confiscations should be carried out according to religious regulations, with the

verdict of the prosecutor or the court judges. No one else has any right to interfere in such actions. The violators should be severely punished. [shouts of "God is great"]

9. The distribution of land should be carried out according to religious regulations; and when it is proved that somebody's land should be distributed, only the qualified courts have the right to seize the land. No one else has any right to trespass on anybody's land, place of residence or orchard and, basically, unqualified individuals have no right to interfere in such actions. However, they can pass to responsible officials information concerning the land, house or orchards of members of the satanical regime who have wrongfully usurped other people's property. If anybody commits an action contrary to Islamic principles and regulations, he will be vigorously prosecuted. [shouts of "God is great"]

10. The Housing Foundation and the Foundation of the Oppressed should produce as soon as possible the balance sheets of their actions so that the people may be informed of the activities of these two revolutionary organs. The Housing Foundation should clarify how much work it has performed; and the Foundation of the Oppressed should clearly publish the list of movable and real property of the satanical people, especially the Shah, his family and his filthy lackeys throughout Iran and should announce what they have carried out so far. They should say to whom they have given the property of the traitorous Shah.

Is it true that the foundation of the Oppressed has been turned into the foundation of the oppressors? If this is so, purging is necessary and to neglect this important matter is forbidden. These two foundations should clearly explain to the people why they have not been able to carry out their duties faster. If some people are committing evil deeds in the name of the oppressed, it is the duty of all the courts throughout Iran to act with speed. [shouts of "God is great"]

11. Revolution should come about in all the universities throughout Iran, so that the professors who are in contact with the East or the West will be purged, and so that the universities may become healthy places for the study of higher Islamic teachings. The false teachings of the former regime should be abruptly stopped in universities throughout Iran because all the misery of the Iranian society during the reign of this father and son was due to these false teachings. If we had a proper set-up in our universities, we would have never had a university-educated intelligentsia who during Iran's most critical period are engaged in conflict and schism among themselves and are cut off from the people and are so negligent

of what happens to the people, as though they do not live in Iran. [shouts of "God is great"] All of our backwardness is due to the lack of proper understanding by most of the university intellectuals of the Islamic society of Iran. Unfortunately, the same thing is still true. Most of the deadly blows which have been delivered to this society have been due to the majority of these university-educated intellectuals who have always regarded—and still regard—themselves as being great and have always said things—and still continue to say things—which only their other intellectual friends can understand, regardless of whether the people understand them or not. Because the public is of no significance to them and all that is important to them is themselves. This is due to the fact that false university education during the reign of the Shah so trained university-educated intellectuals that they attached no value whatsoever to the oppressed masses. Unfortunately, even now it is the same.

Committed and responsible intellectuals, you should set aside dissension and schism and should think of the people and you should free yourselves from the evil of the "isms" and "ists" of the East or the West, for the sake of the salvation of the people, who have given martyrs. You should stand on your own feet and should refrain from relying on foreigners. The students of religious teaching and university students should carefully study Islamic principles and should set aside the slogans of deviant groups and should replace all deviationist thinking with beloved and genuine Islam. Religion students and university students should know that Islam is itself a rich school, which is never in need of grafting any other ideologies to it. All you should know that mixed thinking is a betrayal of Islam and the Muslims [shouts of "God is great"] and the bitter results of such thinking will become apparent in future years.

Most regrettably, at times it can be seen that due to the lack of the proper and precise understanding of Islamic issues, some people have mixed Islamic ideas with Marxist ideas and have created a concoction which is in no way in accordance with the progressive teachings of Islam. Dear students, do not follow the wrong path of the uncommitted university intellectuals and do not separate yourselves from the people.

12. Another issue is the press and the mass media. Once again, I ask all the press throughout Iran to come and join hands and freely write about the issues, but not to engage in plots. I have repeatedly said that the press should be independent and free.

But unfortunately and with great amazement I have seen a number of them engaged in implementing the evil designs of the right or the left, most unjustly, in Iran; and they are still doing it. In every country the press plays an essential role in the creation of a healthy or unhealthy atmosphere. I hope that they will engage in service to God and the people. Also, radio and television should be independent and free and should broadcast every kind of criticism with complete impartiality, so that once again we will not see the radio and television from the time of the deposed Shah. Radio and television should be purged of its pro-Shah or deviant elements. [shouts of "God is great"]

13. These days, through the agents of the Shah and his lackeys, attacks have increased on the true clergy, who in fact, both at the time of the Shah and at the time of his father, were among the most distinguished strata of the nation, who through their numerous uprisings against the corruption of the regime engaged in struggle and divulged the crimes of the regime. Throughout the rightful struggles of the noble nation against the Shah and America, the clergy led the struggles that led to victory. Exactly at the time when the clergy started its irrepressible struggle against the traitorous Shah in the years 1962 and 1963, the Shah called the committed and responsible clergy black reactionaries, because the only serious threat to him and to his rule came from the struggling clergy, who had roots in the depth of the souls of the people and stood up against him and against his oppression. Now, the agents of the Shah have again put the word reaction into the mouths of my children who are unaware of the depth of the issues, in order to crush the clergy, who are the foundation of independence and freedom of this country. My beloved and revolutionary children: Today the insulting and the weakening of the role of the clergy is a blow against independence, freedom and Islam. Today, it is treason to follow the path of the traitorous Shah and use the word treason concerning this respected class, who are among the most distinguished strata, not accepting either the yoke of the East or that of the West.

My dear sisters and brothers, you should know that those people who regard the clergy as reactionary are, ultimately, following the path of the Shah and America. [shouts of "God is great"] The noble Iranian nation, by supporting the genuine and committed Iranian clergy, who have always been the guardians and protectors of this country, will remit their debts to Islam and will cut off the hands of all of history's oppressors of their country.

On the other hand, I announce to the respected clergy, wherever they are, that it is possible that the satans and their agents may engage in hostile propaganda against the dear youth, especially the university students. The clergy should know that today all strata of the nation especially these two respected strata, who are the intellectual power of the nation, should join hands and fight against satanic forces and the oppressors and advance the Islamic movement in united ranks and protect independence and freedom as they would their own dear lives. It was the plan of the world-devourers and their agents to separate these two effective and thinking strata from one another during the satanic regime; and, unfortunately, they were successful and they ruined the country. This plan is once again being implemented and with the slightest negligence we shall be ruined.

I hope that all strata of the nation, especially these two respected strata, will not be negligent of plots and conspiracies in the new year and will nullify the evil plans through their unity of expression. [shouts of "God is great"]

Finally, after praying for forgiveness for the martyrs of the Islamic Revolution and expressing gratitude for their self-sacrifice, it is necessary on this new year to express my congratulations to their relatives, to their mothers and fathers and congratulate them on their being able to train such lions and lionesses. Also, I wish to congratulate the injured and the crippled of the revolution, who were pioneers in the advancement of the movement of the nation and the establishment of the Islamic Republic. Verily, our Islamic revolution is indebted to the self-sacrifice of these two beloved groups. I and the nation will not forget their brave deeds and will honor their memory.

I beseech almighty God for the greatness of Islam and the Muslims. God's greetings and blessings be upon you.

Source: Ayatollah Khomeini. "We Shall Confront the World with Our Ideology." *Middle East Research and Information Project Reports.* 88 (1980): 22–25. Reprinted with the permission of *MERIP/Middle East Report*, 1500 Massachusetts Ave. NW, #119, Washington DC 20005.

Islamic Aspects of the Legacy of Malcolm X

Samory Rashid

SAMORY RASHID *is Assistant Professor in the Department of Political Science at Indiana State University, Terre Haute, Indiana.*

Spike Lee's 1992 film, "Malcolm X," is the most recent evidence of the increased popularity of Malcolm X (El Hajj Malik El Shabazz). The film, based on a screenplay by James Baldwin and Arnold Perl, sparked controversy over "X" memorabilia and also a debate over the appropriate interpretation of Malcolm X's legacy. For example, black nationalist Amiri Baraka opposed Lee's portrayal and criticized the film as an attempt to "make middle class Negroes sleep easier."[1] Yet when the current controversy and debate end, the Islamic aspects will remain, as before, the most significant and least recognized elements of Malcolm X's legacy. This paper briefly examines this phenomenon in order to offer a more accurate and meaningful analysis of the significance of Malcolm X. ...

Since his murder on February 21, 1965, during a speech at the Audubon Ballroom in New York, just three months before his forty-ninth birthday, analyses of Malcolm X have focused on one or more of the following questions: (a) Did he advocate violence; (b) Did his assassins work alone; (c) In addition to the Nation of Islam, did the American government play a role in his assassination; (d) Which period of his life more closely reflects "the real Malcolm X"; and (e) What might he have evolved into politically had he not been assassinated?

The speculative character of these questions has produced a variety of erroneous accounts of his legacy. For example, one assessment argues that Malcolm X evolved from an "impoverished child" to a "powerful humanist."[2] Another states that during the final months of his life, he became increasingly anti-capitalist, although he is also known to have stated: "I still would be hard-pressed to give a specific definition of the overall philosophy which I think is necessary for the liberation of the black people in this country."[3] A *New York Times* book review by Michael Eric Dyson on Bruce Perry's *Malcolm X: The Life of a Man Who Changed Black America* makes reference to his alleged "hatred of women."

Malcolm X espoused many strong views during his life, among them support for human rights, opposition to capitalist exploitation and imperialism, rejection of public "welfare" for blacks, and black separatist nationalism. Yet it is erroneous to conclude, as many have done, that his advocacy of these view makes him a humanist, a socialist, a neoconservative, or a black nationalist. One view even suggests that Malcolm X's discussions with the Ku Klux Klan and association with the "black supremacist" Nation of Islam made him a racist. The erroneous and speculative nature of such views intensifies the need for a serious examination of the Islamic aspects of his legacy.

An analysis of the Islamic aspects of his life is essential to understanding Malcolm X. These center around several points: (a) Islam's consistency and centrality in his message; (b) Its role as a method of analysis and instrument of change; (c) Its significance as a vehicle for political mobilization; (d) The influence of Makkah; and (e) Islam's role as a facilitator of alliances with Muslims and others engaged in the struggle for freedom, justice, and equality.

In life and in death, Malcolm X remained a Muslim. Attempts to understand him through the lens of America's perennial racial debate trivialize his message and the universality of his significance. While his Detroit Red, demagogic, and El Hajj Malik El Shabbaz images are essential to understanding his evolution from street hustler to black nationalist to Muslim, his entire life and message provide a more enduring reflection of his legacy. In light of this, the choice of some youths to emulate only one or another aspect of his complex and evolving life seems misguided.

Although often overlooked, it was Islam that stimulated Malcolm X to educate and discipline himself in prison. Islamic principles, such as the right of self-defense, provided the moral basis for Malcolm X's most controversial message. As it says in the Qur'an:

Fight in the cause of Allah those who fight you. But do not transgress Limits; for Allah loveth not transgressors;

MALCOLM X

Malcolm X was born Malcolm Little in Omaha, Nebraska. He was assassinated in 1965. His life has recently been portrayed in the film *Malcolm X*.

While in prison, Malcolm X joined the Nation of Islam. He took on the surname "X" to signify that, like most descendants of the slaves forcibly brought to the United States from Africa, he had lost his ancestral name. He joined the Nation of Islam in prison and became a devoted follower of the Islamic religion.

The Nation of Islam maintained that the solution for black people in the United States was complete separation for blacks.

However, Malcolm X's views underwent a radical change in 1964. During a series of religious trips to Mecca and the

newly independent African states, he encountered good people of all races. His views began to change accordingly. He came to the conclusion that he had yet to discover true Islam. He came to regard not all whites as racists, and saw the struggle of black people as part of a wider freedom struggle. He established his own religious group and a political organization, the Organization for Afro-American Unity.

Along with Martin Luther King, Malcolm X symbolized the civil rights movement in the United States during the 1960s.

And slay them wherever ye catch them, And turn them out from where they have turned you out; For persecution is worse than slaughter; But fight them not at the Sacred Mosque unless they (first) fight you there; But if they fight you, slay them. Such is the reward of those who reject faith. But if they cease, Allah is Oft Forgiving, Most Merciful. And fight them on until there is no more persecution and the religion becomes Allah's. But if they cease, let there be no hostility except to those who practice oppression. (2:190-93)

Malcolm X's wife and children were Muslims. It was his brothers Philbert, Wesley, Wilfred, and Reginald, rather than the fictional character "Baines" in Lee's film, who introduced him to Islam.[4] They, along with their sister Ella (who financed Malcolm X's hajj[5]), were members of the Nation of Islam. And it was his hajj that inspired him to change his antiwhite racial attitudes and to form the Muslim Mosque Inc. upon his return to the United States.

Those analyses of Malcolm X that ignore the Islamic legacy of his message reflect a rejection by some of the authenticity of American-based Islamic movements. Despite his adoption of Sunni Islam following his hajj, many writers continue to associate him exclusively with the Nation of Islam. Another reflection of cynicism toward the authenticity of the Islamic identity of American blacks is the media term "Black Muslim," which ironically is only used to refer to Muslims in America of ex-slave ancestry and never to those Muslims from abroad who are also black.

Moreover, blacks in America are frequently challenged by white Americans to distinguish between "Muslim" and "Moslem" and ultimately between "Black Muslim" and "Moslem." Arabic speakers know that "Moslem" is an incorrect transliteration of the Arabic "Muslim," although it is significant to note that other Muslims often provide quite different explanations of this phenomenon. However, from the point of view of American blacks, when whites ask them to distinguish "Muslim" from "Moslem," what they are actually asking is: are you really a Moslem, and if you are, then why are people abroad who presumably follow the same religion often called Moslems, while American blacks (whether they are Sunni, Shi'a, or other) are called Black Muslims? What's the difference?

American blacks who are Muslims, not unlike other Muslims, display varying degrees of Islamic awareness and practice. Their Islamic sophistication before the mid-1960s was severely constrained by limited opportunities to maintain contact with overseas Muslims. Most were further constrained by the limited socioeconomic and educational opportunities that curtailed their ability to acquire a more thorough knowledge and understanding of Islam. For example, while Muslims of the Nation of Islam, the Moorish Science Movement, and other groups display only elements of Islam, other Muslim groups in America, such as the

Sunni communities in New York, Washington, D.C., and the Midwest, and organizations led by Warith Deen Muhammad in Chicago and California, display a greater affinity with the Sunnah of the Prophet and therefore with traditional Islam.

The first Muslim organizations among free black Americans consisted of blacks introduced to Islam either in prison or in the ghetto—a community stripped of its language, history, culture, and religion, and faced with the constant challenge of racism. Relatively few were introduced to Islam through other avenues. Thus the quality, sophistication, and practice of true Islam among black Americans was often adversely affected. Despite this, however, their lack of sophistication and purity had no visible impact on their strength of belief or quality of commitment. For example, the demonstrated success of such Islamic organizations as the Nation of Islam in positively transforming these circumstances has been frequently praised.

Malcolm X's own words capture this phenomenon clearly. Following his hajj, he visited Senegal, where a Senegalese revealed that: "Our people can't speak Arabic, but we have Islam in our hearts." Malcolm X's response was: "I told them that exactly described their fellow Afro-American Muslims."[6]

The more general question of Islamic authenticity among American blacks is a matter of historical record rather than one of political debate. For example, Lincoln notes that despite stern measures to discourage such practices, "accounts persist of Muslim slaves who committed the entire Qur'an to memory in an effort to keep the faith alive and to pass it on to others."[7] He concludes: "The memory of Islam however tenuous, was never completely lost to the slave experience."[8]

In fact, it was the "Moors" among the Spanish conquistadors who introduced Islam to the New World.[9] Several writers, including Carter G. Woodson and (more recently) Emily Kalled Lovell, have written that the first Muslim in America was a black Spanish conquistador named Estevanico (or Little Stephen), who arrived in Arizona during 1539. Woodson credits him with being the first non-native to "discover" what is now the American southwest.[10] The second recorded Muslim to reach America was Hajj Ali-Hi Jolly, who worked in Arizona and California as an experimental camel breeder.[11]

The authenticity of the Islam practised by Africans and their descendants in America is given credence by: (a) Important black figures in Islamic history such as Bilal, the first muezzin in Islam; (b) African centers of learning such as Timbuktu, Gao, and Jene; (c) Famous African Islamic leaders like Mansa Musa, Uth-man dan Fodio, Sundiata, and Samoty ibn Lafia as well as black scholars like "Luqman the Wise" (mentioned in the Qur'an); and (d) Great Islamic empires in Africa: Mali, Guinea, and Songhay. While the evolutionary history of Muslim organizations in the United States makes it clear that reeducation is required for blacks in order to adopt a more accurate knowledge of themselves and their practice of Islam, the average white American displays an even greater ignorance of the roots of Islam in America.

Even among Islamic scholars, the awareness of the history of Islam among blacks in Africa and the United States is often minuscule or rudimentary at best. Thus there is little wonder why the Islamic aspects of Malcolm X's legacy, as well as the legacy of Islam itself, are so often ignored or dismissed as fantasy. In the final analysis, though, questions concerning the Islamic authenticity of blacks in America are best resolved by the Qur'anic reminder that Allah is the best knower.

The role of Islam as a method of analysis and an instrument of change is well documented among American blacks. Timothy Drew, known among his followers as Noble Drew Ali, established the "Moorish Science Temple" in Newark, New Jersey, during 1913. Lincoln describes this movement as a "melange of Black nationalism and Christian revivalism with an awkward, confused admixture of the teaching of the Prophet Muhammad." Although the Moorish Science Temple movement did not practice pure Islam, it was a "significant recovery of the awareness of Islam."[12]

Ali died mysteriously in 1929 following a "violent eruption" with the Moorish Science Movement. His movement is generally recognized as the first in the postslavery era to promote aspects of Islam as a method of analysis and a vehicle for change and social consciousness among blacks. It was succeeded by the Nation of Islam in the early 1930s. The Nation, as it is often called by American blacks, was led by Elijah Muhammad, who recruited Malcolm X as national spokesman shortly after the latter's release from prison and rise within the organization.

Islam's role as a vehicle for political mobilization among American blacks has been an important factor in Islam's emergence in this country. As Lovell asserts: "Probably the most spectacular phase in the history of Islam in the U.S. was the conversion of Black Muslims to true Islam after pilgrimages to Mecca and other Muslim countries by such leaders as Malcolm X.[13] However, analyses of religious movements, such as the one provided by Lovell, typically evaluate religious movements by the strength of their numbers rather than the quality of their beliefs. Thus Lovell's interpretation of the post-Makkah phase of Malcolm X's Islamic experience as the "most spectacular phase in the history of Islam in the U.S." due to the "conversion of Black Muslims to 'true Islam," reflects a Christian missionary perspective rather than an Islamic one.

Although Lovell's attention is to quality of belief, as illustrated by her reference to the conversion of blacks to "true Islam," her statement, like most of the literature, emphasizes the weaknesses while ignoring the strengths of Islamic belief among American blacks. Such statements create divisiveness among Muslims by conveying an erroneous image of American blacks to Muslims around the world. They also trivialize the historical role of Islam among blacks in the United States through (a) their use of the word "conversion" rather than "reversion," and (b) their practice of failing to acknowledge that Islamic revival movements among American blacks appeared at least two decades before similar movements emerged elsewhere in the Islamic world during this century.

Unfortunately, details regarding the character of early Islam in the United States, especially among American blacks, remains largely absent from the literature. A number of factors account for this condition. First, a hostile climate toward minorities forced Muslim organizations to remain underground. In this regard, it is important to note that most of the major Islamic movements among American blacks prior to the 1980s were secret and separatist in nature. Thus the reply of Malcolm X and other "Black Muslims" in the Nation of Islam to the question of how many "Black Muslims" there were in America was: "Those who say do not know, and those who know do not say." An amazing consequence of this phenomenon has been the number of young writers who, in recent years, have attempted to examine Islam among American blacks without ever directly witnessing or experiencing the phenomenon. The status of secret societies of "Black Muslims," especially during the 1950s to the 1970s, was not unlike the Muslim Brotherhood in the Islamic world. Indeed, Malcolm X's legacy of political mobilization of American blacks under the banner of Islam was not unlike that of Hasan al Bannà, founder of the Muslim Brotherhood in Egypt.

As public knowledge of black American Muslim organizations is lacking due to their clandestine character, limitations exist in the quality and quantity of published material. Yvonne Haddad's work is a major exception. Nonpublic sources of information, such as the FBI's files on the "Black Muslims," are no doubt abundant. The Nation of Islam was so thoroughly infiltrated during the 1960s and the 1970s that Malcolm X's personal bodyguard is alleged to have been a police informant. In the only detailed study of the Nation of Islam, E. U. Essien Udom found it "under police surveillance in every city where there is a Temple" and under FBI surveillance for "possible subversive tendencies."[14] Malcolm X, who assisted Essien Udom with his book on black nationalism, was later received by this man during his post-Makkah visit to Nigeria.[15]

Malcolm X's impact on the turbulent politics of the 1960s was both deep and extensive. While his recent growth in popularity, especially among young blacks, is in part a recognition of this impact, the sentimental character of his recent popularity often obscures his legacy's organizational and institutional impact. Malcolm X not only set the tone of political activism and debate for black Americans during the 1960s and 1970s; he provided an ideological core for that debate emanating from a highly organized and nationwide base (the Nation of Islam) in its early stage, and from a diffuse set of black nationalist organizations (i.e., the OAAU, the Black Power Movement, and the Black Panther Party) in its later stage. The force of his ideas and leadership skills created an Islamic legacy of "Black Muslim"-inspired political themes such as the need for a new self-image, black pride, economic self-sufficiency, black community control, independent schools, and an uncompromising demand for equality, all of which continue to defy analyses relying exclusively on Islamicist or race politics perspectives.

Essien Udom's study recognizes the Nation of Islam's vast influence on a generation of black American leaders, many of whom were former members or were directly influenced by one or more of its articulate and dynamic ministries. Eldridge Cleaver, a founder of the Black Panther Party, was a former member of the Nation of Islam. In addition, such prominent black politicians, writers, activists, and entrepreneurs as Rev. Jesse Jackson, Amiri Baraka, Dick Gregory, and Spike Lee have incorporated significant features of Malcolm X and the Nation of Islam into their own activities with varying degrees of success.

The influence of Malcolm X's hajj represents a turning point not only in his own life but in the evolution of Islam in America, for it allowed him to acquire a more thorough understanding of Islam and its universal and therefore far-reaching appeal. In spite of his contribution to the evolution of Islam in America, his post-Makkah message proved too much for some, and he was assassinated. While his courage and determination caused him to become a martyr, to many of his fellow Muslims his legacy reinforced their commitment to the Islamic ideals for which he fought and died. The martyrdom of Malcolm X was therefore an important milestone in the evolution of "true Islam" in America.

After his hajj, Malcolm X visited Egypt, Lebanon, Sudan, Nigeria, Ghana, Liberia, Senegal, Morocco, and Algeria. He returned to the United States on May 21, 1964. His successful trip and efforts to forge international links represent perhaps the first deliberate bid by a black American leader to internationalize the struggle for civil and human rights. His international travel, hajj, and visits with prominent Islamic leaders provided legitimacy to black American Muslims. While it is true that Malcolm X's hajj was among the first to be made by a black American Muslim, it is important to remember that this as well as his other achievements were driven by Islamic beliefs, values, and principles: the unity and oneness of Allah *(tawhid),* the value of historical analysis and observation, the centrality of struggle (jihad), and the merits of emigration *(hijrah)* and of change in the search for knowledge and meaning.

In conclusion, the Islamic aspects of Malcolm X's legacy provide a compelling though long-ignored perspective on his life. The American preoccupation with racial politics obscures his more central contributions to Islamic life in the United States: his introduction of distinctly Muslim values and beliefs to black social consciousness, the development of "true Islam," and the forging of international alliances between American blacks' and other oppressed peoples' struggles. Such a perspective provides a more accurate and a more meaningful interpretation not only of Malcolm X and his legacy, but also of the struggle for freedom, justice, and equality undertaken by American Muslims and the evolution of a domestic and international consciousness among black Americans.

Source: Samory Rashid. "Islamic Aspects of the Legacy of Malcolm X." *American Journal of Islamic Social Sciences* 10, No. 1 (1993) 60-155. Reprinted with the permission of the *American Journal of Islamic Social Sciences.*

Notes

[1] New York Times, 15 November 1992.

[2] Ibid., 15 November 1992

[3] Ibid., 29 November 1992.

[4] Ibid., 3 December 1992.

[5] Haley, Autobiography, 324

[6] Ibid., p.366.

[7] C. Eric Lincoln, "The American Muslim Mission in the Context of American Social History" in *The Muslim Community in North America.* eds. Earle H. Waugh, Baha Abu-Laban, and Regula B. Qureshi (Edmonton, Alberta: Univ. of Alberta Press, 1983), 218.

[8] Ibid., p.219.

[9] Ibid.

[10] Lovell, Emily Kalled, "Islam in the United States: Past and Present," in *The Muslim Community in North America.* eds. Earle H. Waugh, Baha Abu-Laban, and Regula B, Qureshi (Edmonton, Alberta: Univ. of Alberta Press, 1983), 94.

[11] Ibid.

[12] Lincoln, "The American Muslim Mission," 221.

[13] Lovell, "Islam in the United States," 95.

[14] Essien Udom, E. U. *Black Nationalism* (Chicago: Univ. of Chicago Press, 1962), 5.

[15] Haley *Autobiography*, 355.

References

Essien Udom, E. U. *Black Nationalism.* Chicago: University of Chicago Press, 1962.

Haley, Alex. *The Autobiography of Malcolm X.* New York: Grove Press, 1964.

Lincoln, C. Eric. "The American Muslim Mission in the Context of American Social History." In *The Muslim Community in North America,* edited by Earle H. Waugh, Baha Abu-Laban, and Regula B. Qureshi. Edmonton, Alberta: Univ. of Alberta Press, 1983.

Lovell, Emily Kalled. "Islam in the United States: Past and Present." In *The Muslim Community in North America,* edited by Earle H. Waugh, Baha Abu-Laban, and Regula B. Qureshi. Edmonton, Alberta: Univ. of Alberta Press, 1983.

"Malcolm X: As Complex as Its Subject," *New York Times,* 18 November, 1992.

"Malcolm X: The Facts, the Fictions, the Film," *New York Times,* 15 November, 1992.

"Reflections on the Lessons of Malcolm," *New York Times,* 15 November, 1992.

"The Search Continues for the Real Malcolm X," *New York Times,* 3 December, 1992.

"27 Years Later, the Young Clearly Hear Malcolm X," *New York Times,* 12 November, 1992.

"Who Speaks for Malcolm X?" *New York Times,* 29 November, 1992.

Fundamentalists in Defence of the Jewish Collectivity

Bruce B. Lawrence

BRUCE B. LAWRENCE *is Professor of Religion at Duke University in Durham, North Carolina. He has written extensively in the fields of comparative religion and the history of religion.*

The relationship of Judaism to fundamentalism is crucial for both Judaism and fundamentalism. For Judaism it provides the lens through which one can glimpse the struggle to assert the sharpest profile of Jewish identity in the modern world. For fundamentalism it offers the necessary third dimension of a religious protest against modernism conceived and sustained with reference to monotheistic loyalties. How do Jewish zealots relate to Muslim and Christian counterparts? The presumption is that Judaism, Islam, and Christianity can be correlated at the level of monotheistic belief, as we indicated in the previous chapter. Beyond that apparent convergence, one must draw attention to the fact that Judaism is more intensely related to practice, right practice, or orthopraxis, while Christianity stresses the notion of right belief or orthodoxy. If Jews are more prone to ask one another: "what do you do?" Christians are more likely to demand: "what do you believe?" The contrast between the two outlooks makes it even more difficult to comprehend what the term "ultraorthodox" means in a Jewish context, as we will see below. Preliminarily, however, one can cite Islam as straddling the polar dispositions of Judaism and Christianity. While some observers are fond of pointing out that Islam, like Judaism, stresses orthopraxis, the concept of orthodoxy also looms large in the discourses of modernist as well as fundamentalist Muslims: for those engaged by Islamic symbols and rites, it is not only what you do but why you do it that matters.

Jewish zealots relate to both their Muslim and Christian counterparts. All three are inescapably shaped by their response to that global pattern of change that we, following Marshall Hodgson, identify as the Great Western Transmutation. To the extent that there is a distinctly Jewish reaction to modernity traceable through some segments of European Jewry during the past century, its complex elaboration within present day Israel may be appropriately termed fundamentalist.

Every expression of fundamentalism, whether it be Jewish, Christian, or Muslim, whether it originates in the first or third world, has a double emphasis: the collective good above individual choice, and advocacy of one interpretation of the collective good against all others, especially all inside others. To the recurring question, Are there any absolutes in a changing world? fundamentalists respond with a triumphant "Yes!" Their "yes" always pits believers against believers. The level of bitterest conflict focuses on the authority, which is also the responsibility, for actualizing the collective good of the community.

The clearest initial contrast is between Muslim and Jewish fundamentalists, since in the case of Protestant Christianity, as we will see, a public ethos that requires collective assent did not emerge till the late Agrarianate Age, concomitant with the Reformation. Judaism and Islam contrast precisely because representatives for both have long asserted, and continue to assert, the priority of communitarian goals over individual rights. Among both Sunni and Shi'i Muslims, the battle is waged in the political arena. Fundamentalists require an Islamic state since the collective good of Muslims can only be realized through conformity to the *shari'a*, and only an Islamic state can fulfill the demands of a religious society by upholding the high standard of *shari'a* loyalty. Jewish fundamentalists, on the other hand, do not idealize the state. Unlike their Muslim counterparts, they are at best ambivalent, at worst hostile to the Zionist state. They challenge the government of Israel because of its pretensions: after centuries of Diaspora existence, it claims to be a polity representing Jewish aspirations for return to the Holy Land. The claim is as extraordinary as it is threatening to Jewish fundamentalists. While most attach importance to the notion of a Jewish state, such a state, in their view, can function only as a messianic reality. What is most required to prepare for and hasten the coming of the Messiah is strict adherence to Jewish laws, the cherished *mitzvoth*. If the state of Israel claims to be, even implicitly, the longed for Jewish Commonwealth, it preempts the messianic timetable. The *mitzvoth* would have to be suspended, their performance rendered nugatory. Such a perceptual dilemma cloys the imagination of

Jewish fundamentalists. Their opposition to the implicit messianic function of the state of Israel makes it unlikely that Israelis will ever achieve consensus on the meaning of the Third Commonwealth as a *Jewish* state. While tacitly accepting the state's instrumental function, to maintain public order and to ward off external aggression, the most observant Jews publicly contend with others about the appropriate strategies for promoting that collectivity known as the people of Israel.

The oft told story of Judaism in the twentieth century pits the Jewish people against a host of inimical forces: European anti-Semitism leading up to but not exhausted by the Holocaust, the Palestinian resistance to the Zionist movement and since 1948, the further isolation of Israel from its hostile Arab neighbors. Those are the headline stories. They ignore the other story of Jewish resistance to assimilation and secularization. That resistance has issued in conflict. It has become an internal struggle. It does not pit Jews against the outside world but Jews against other Jews. It is a fight for the soul of Judaism. It is a fight to prove that Jews are not merely a special race with a piece of territory but a divine instrument with a universal mission.

The chasm is invisible to most because non-Israelis, even non-Israeli Jews, do not readily identify with this struggle as their struggle. It is an ideological struggle between those who defend the right of Israel to exist as a modern-day nation-state and those others who question the meaning of its existence. So much has been at stake in the former issue during that last forty years that the latter issue has seemed to pale in comparison. Those groups labeled extremist, or better, fundamentalists, focus exclusively on the question of Jewish identity and its consequences: Who is a Jew? What does it mean to be a Jew? What should a Jew do as a Jew? Others may raise the same questions but relate them to cultural, ethnic, or social concerns. For fundamentalists, the questions demand repeated asking on their own terms. They demand to be raised not for the existential well-being of the individual but of the long range good of the collectivity.

Were a political *modus vivendi* to be struck between Zion and its neighbors, public interest, stoked by fundamentalist passion, might move these questions of identity from offstage to center stage. Even in the absence of a diplomatic truce reducing external tensions, they may dominate the next phase of Israel's history as much as the right to exist as a state has dominated its first phase.

And those who can best be described as Jewish fundamentalists have already staked out their claim on one criterion. It is a single, encompassing canon of Jewish identity. To be a Jew means three things:

(1) living by the commandments of the Torah [the *mitzvoth*], but also

(2) obeying the directives of the sages who have been ordained to determine the *halakha*, and

(3) believing in the truth of everything that the Torah teaches according to the interpretation of scholars whose greatness in *halakha* also invests them with superiority in this area.[1]

Many would argue that it is possible to cast off the yoke of Jewish law and still be Jewish. After all, there is patriotic identity as part of a Jewish nation-state, modern Israel; outside Israel, there is cultural identity as part of a Jewish community wherever one happens to be in the Diaspora, no matter what the dominant culture. Yet for those who maintain that Jewishness is defined not by genetic code of familial memory but rather by observance of canonical commandments, all nonobservant Jews become apostates. One Jewish fundamentalist has gone as far as to declare there is "no difference between red apostasy and blue apostasy, between apostasy with a cross (converting to Christianity) and apostasy without a cross (becoming a secular Jew)."[2]

Almost all Jews living outside of Israel, and the majority within Israel, would be offended by such a narrow definition of Jewish Identity. It is for this reason that groups advocating such views have been called "extremists" or "ultraorthodox" or, even occasionally before now, "fundamentalists."[3] The difficulty of evaluating them by hurling invectives or heaping up defamatory stereotypes becomes clear when one examines the linchpin of the system, that is, the personal force of the exemplars who embody the *mitzvoth* and withstand the challenges of the Enlightenment. At stake is the larger issue: who will ultimately succeed? Will it be those Jews who have survived the adversity of the contemporary world by adopting the Enlightenment mentality in general and the nation-state in particular, forging new institutions while also accommodating to new values? Or will it be those other claimants to Jewish authenticity who embrace the premodern concept of collectivity, who locate it in adherence to all the *mitzvoth* without compromise, even to the point of disallowing secular education and secular vocations, while also challenging other Jews either to follow that discipline or else forfeit their claim to participate in the mellennia-old drama known as Judaism?

It is at base a battle of absolutes, universals couched as ideological appeals to particular interest groups. On the one hand is the modern crusade of openness, experimentation, and adaptation to the new or untried and opposition to closedness, perpetuation of norms, and compliance with the old and familiar. On the other hand is the definition of dark and light, bad and good, nonobservant Jew and observant Jew as ironclad equivalencies. It is then a choice between myth and reality, or is it a choice between two ideologies each of which is partly myth-making, partly reality-defining? However that question is answered will depend on the influence of leaders who shape policies and inspire followers to specific ideological ends. All fundamentalists, whether they be Christian, Islamic, or Jewish, agree that the leadership of certain extraordinary individuals is decisive for the collective good. Since the values expressive of the collective good are abstract and universal, they must be actualized by specific human agents, almost always male, who represent values for which the group as a whole is striving at any moment in its history. In Judaism, even more than in Islam or Christianity, one finds spiritual luminaries who defend a notion of collectivity. To preserve and also refine the *kehilla* (which is at once the political-legal structure of a local Jewish community and also the essence of that community) is the core value in traditional Judaism. Its staunchest preservers have become authoritative figures in all aspects of life for their followers. Some are rabbis of such personal piety and scholarly renown that groups of the devout nucleate around them. Others are not "mere" rabbis; they are *zaddikim* or *rebbes*, masters in that distinctly Jewish movement for spiritual renewal known as Hasidism.

It was Hasidism that provided the spiritual model for what has emerged as Jewish fundamentalism. Historically the Hasidim have been the exemplary group defending Jewish collective existence against foreign challenges. It was they who spearheaded the first Jewish resistance to Greek acculturation, culminating in the Maccabean revolt of 165 B.C. (or at least that is the claim of contemporary Hasidim in their reading of the Jewish past). It was also Hasidim who spurred outbursts against acculturation during the late Middle Ages, in twelfth-thirteenth century Germany, just as they have, from the eighteenth century on, sparked a widespread reaction to the Technical Age. In its latest manifestation, the Hasidic movement has had two phases: it first emerged among East European Jewry from the early eighteenth till about the mid-nineteenth century; then it began to attract followers amid the larger Ashkenazi community. It did not affect the Sephardic or so-called Oriental Jewish community.

What has distinguished Hasidism throughout the modern period, setting it apart from both its prior history and also form all forms of non-Hasidism, is its doctrine of the *zaddik*, or righteous man.[4] Indeed, the history of the Hasidim since the eighteenth century can be encapsulated in the colorful biographical profiles of those pious sages knows as *rebbes* or *zaddiks*. Not only did they respond to the gradual impoverishment of the Ashkenazi community beyond Germany, they also showed a way to cope with brutal pogroms, like those waged against the Jews of Ukraine in 1648. They offered as well an alternative to the failed Messianism of the Sabbatean movement, a movement that had erupted among the Sephardim in 1665-66 but the

effects of which were felt long after among the Ashkenazim as well.

Mere compliance with the Torah and its interpreters did not meet the threat that Jews of Europe faced on the eve of the Technical Age. They were looking for solace and reinforcement at a personal level. They wanted mediaries who could both assure and uplift them. Hasidism produced such unusual men in the forms of *rebbes* and *zaddiks*, extraordinary "fools for God." They could be labeled mystics, miracle workers, or heretics, but they were above all devout and accessible mediaries, at once integral to their communities and yet valued above other pious Jews.

To grasp their influence on Jewish fundamentalism it is necessary to understand the *rebbes* as both theological innovators and social revolutionaries. Each *rebbe* became the embodiment of piety for his community. The *rebbe* was reckoned to be as different from other men as the Torah was different from other books. In a vertical cosmology that conceived of heaven and earth on a single axis, God communicated with humanity through a process of descent and ascent. All Jewish history became sorted out and remembered in two periods of equal measure: pre-Hasidic and Hasidic, a kind of Jewish gloss on the Jaspers division of world history into the pre-Axial, Axial, and Technical Ages. In the pre-Hasidic period, the Book was handed down to Jews on Mount Sinai in order to lift them up to heaven. Scholars endeavored to make the Book accessible to the whole community. But with the advent of the Hasidim, the *rebbe* took the place of both the Torah and the Scholars: even though his authority implicitly rested on his knowledge of Torah and his ability to interpret it better than other rabbis, it was he who personified the Torah. He was the living Torah, and as such the *rebbe* was sent to show Jews the way back up to God.

In the quotation at the outset of this chapter, Dow Baer epitomizes the attitude of early Hasidic masters. He contrasts the simple acts of the *zaddiks* or *rebbes* with the creation of heaven and earth. In his view, the eating and drinking of the *rebbes* outshines even the creation of the universe! How can this be? Because through creation, according to Kabalistic teaching, the Almightly made something out of nothing in a single holistic act, but the *rebbes*, by their unique sacramental power, continuously render something into nothing, even causing the food they eat to "raise on high holy sparks."[5]

The social function of the *rebbes* derived from their theological revaluation of spiritual authority. As demonstrated by Jacob Katz and more recently by Menachem Friedman, there developed in Eastern Europe during the nineteenth century "a kind of division of labor between the Hasidic *rebbe* and the traditional rabbi. While the latter mediated between the Jew and *halakha*, the former mediated between the pious individual (the *hasid*) and God,"[6] much as the Sufi shaykh in premodern times mediated between Sunni Muslims, the Prophet, and God. At the same time, the Hasidic community, known as *'eda*, came to be differentiated from the traditional community (*kehilla*). The former had no geographical boundaries but close voluntary ties, while the latter was restricted in both its geographical and legal functions. If the *rebbe* was not like other men, he was also not like other religious leaders. In effect, the rebbe did more than complement the role of the traditional rabbi; for a large segment of East European Jewry he supplanted the appeal of rabbinical authority.

It is not surprising, therefore, that the first opponents of the *rebbes* were the traditional rabbis, at once their neighbors and their rivals. The internal dispute between *rebbes* and rabbis remained intense till about the mid-nineteenth century. Often depicted as polemical duels between the Hasidim and *mitnaggdim* (the opponents), these contests were nonetheless internal to Judaism. Both contestants were seeking the same high ground, to preserve the people of Israel, whether through the *kehilla* or the *'eda*, by invoking the Torah as the mainstay of Jewish identity.

But by the mid-nineteenth century, the Enlightenment ethos, which had wreaked havoc on Western European Jewry in its initial outburst, began to impinge on the already weakened Jewish communities of Eastern Europe. The Hasidim responded by coalescing the *'edot* (pl. of *'eda*), formalizing their own ritual disciplines, and challenging their opponents. However, the *mitnaggdim*, or opponents, were no longer other traditional rabbis. The *mitnaggdim* had become the *maskilim*, those Jews who referred to themselves as "enlightened men" but who, in the view of the *rebbes*, had sold their soul to an alien ethos and, therefore, were no longer Jews but apostates. Claiming to be enlightened, they had actually enveloped themselves in darkness. For the *rebbes* and their followers, Enlightenment and Emancipation were interchangeable. They were twin terms for the same negative reality: the separation of Jews from their collective observance of the *mitzvoth*, or commandments of the Torah. The Emancipation, in their view, connoted not freedom but a new form of exile, a latter-day Babylon. Resisting all efforts to redefine Jewish identity in terms of Enlightenment and Emancipation values, the *rebbes* also opposed the Ashkenazi embodiment of secular Jewish hope, that nationalist movement which led to the formation of the new Zion, the Third Commonwealth,[7] the state of Israel.

The Hasidim were not the only Jews of the late nineteenth century who opposed Zionism as a secular ideology. A century earlier, when Hasidism was still flourishing in Eastern Europe, Jewish Orthodoxy had come into being as a reaction to the first stirrings of the Great Western Transmutation among West European Jewry. Like the notion of scriptural inerrancy among Christian fundamentalists or the *nizam-i mustafa* (the Muhammadan system) among Sunni Muslim fundamentalists, the idea of Orthodoxy itself reflected modern influences. The word "orthodoxy" has no Hebrew equivalent. Derived from Christian usage, it prevailed in the Jewish context to describe those who opposed the Enlightenment or *Haskala*.[8] The irony of Orthodoxy in its Jewish formulation has been aptly pinpointed by Gideon Aran:

> Tradition itself was altered in the course of its confrontation with modernization and secularization. At about the end of the eighteenth century, the encounter gave birth to a new social phenomenon: Orthodoxy. While Orthodoxy represents itself as the sole legitimate heir of traditional Judaism, it is in fact only one steam among others—although it is arguably the closest to the original medieval rabbinic mold. Orthodoxy, in practice, is a defensive reaction against the other modern trends in Judaism which it views as contrary to tradition.[9]

The chief function of Orthodoxy is also defensive: to neutralize the acids of modernism that had begun to corrode the structures of Jewish religious and social life. Samson Raphael Hirsch, a Prussian rabbi, and Moses Sofer, better known as Hatam Soter, a German rabbi who migrated to Slovakia (Bratislava), both inspired movements among non-Hasidic Jews which were later labeled as Orthodox. It was followers of Hatam Sofer who became, in the early 1870s, the first body of European Jews to win recognition as "an officially recognized Orthodox subgroup." When a decade later Samson Raphael Hirsch secured a similar concession from the Prussian government for his Frankfurt community, Orthodoxy was firmly launched as an expression of Jewish ritual and creedal observance.[10] The separatist impulse of the Orthodox, to keep themselves pure by withdrawing form the dominant group, was often frustrated. Particularly when it came to schooling for their children, the temptations were numerous to teach secular subjects alongside the traditional halakhic curriculum. Only that group which later became identified as the *haredim* stood firm by the pronouncement of Hazon Ish, that "foreign learning (i.e., secular knowledge) was not to be taught to *yeshiva* students."[11]

Many Orthodox, while eager to emigrate to Palestine, refused to participate in efforts to establish a Jewish commonwealth. How could Israel as a self-proclaimed Jewish state *not* represent the best interests of all Jews? Most non-Jews assume that it does. The Orthodox opposition to Zionism begs for further explication. It is at core a religious opposition, rejecting as incompatible with Tamudic observance any state that seeks to represent the aspirations of world Jewry. It is not merely fear that a Jewish state would not honor the *mitzvoth* as they had been honored in the prenational *kehilla* and *'edot*; rather, it was, as Jacob Katz has made clear, that "Jewish tradition did not foresee a middle stage between Exile and Redemption."[12] To the *haredim*, the idea of a Jewish state implies that history has stalled, that the God of Abraham, Isaac, and Jacob is no longer moving humanity inexorably toward a messianic closure. Some Orthodox rabbis have gone so far as to declare that "Zionism [is] a greater danger than the Enlightenment. The latter only led individual Jews astray, but the former undermined the very foundations of Jewish life."[13] Since symbols embody the values of traditional Judaism, the Zionist movement, by revalorizing age-old symbols, has preempted rather than simply rivaled Orthodoxy. It has dressed secularism in religious garb. Secularization, to the extent that it connotes more than the privatization of ritual observance, accelerates the transfer of religious values from their original context to a new context in which they serve nontheocratic purposes. It is in this latter sense that "Zionism [as a secular ideology] did effect a transposition and hence a transformation of significant meanings derived from traditional Judaism."[14]

Numerous Orthodox Jews, perceiving its threat to their spiritual heritage as evolved during the Diaspora, opposed Zionism. In Europe they formed organizations that challenged the advocacy of a Jewish state, at first passively and later actively. Just before the outbreak of World War I, successors to Samson Raphael Hirsch established the principal anti-Zionist organization, Agudat Israel. "This group declared its purpose to be the application, to all problems facing the Jews, of the perspective of traditionalism, i.e., the spirit of Torah. Thus it emerged as the Orthodox counterweight to the Zionist movement."[15] After the Holocaust, and in no small measure because of it, most of the Agudat Israel opted to migrate to Palestine or to settle in North America. Those in Palestine later became reluctant albeit permanent citizens of the state of Israel. To this day they continue to have separate schools (*yeshivot*) and refuse to acknowledge the public celebration of Independence Day. At the same time, however, most Agudat Israel members benefit from state-provided services. Only extreme Orthodox separatists, such as Neturei Karta, "actually refrain from any structural contact with the state's agencies." Most of them live a sequestered, if protected, existence in the heart of Jerusalem in the Meah Shearim quarter.[16]

Source: Bruce B. Lawrence. *Defenders of God: The Fundamentalist Revolt Against the Modern Age.* New York: Harper & Row, 1989. Copyright © 1989 by Bruce B. Lawrence. Reprinted by permission of HarperCollins Publishers, Inc.

Notes

[1] Eliezer Schweid, *Israel at the Crossroads*, trans. A. M. Winters (Philadelphia: Jewish Publication Society of America, 1973), p.21.

[2] Emile Marmorstein, *Heaven at Bay: The Jewish Kulturkampf in the Holy Land* (London: Oxford University Press, 1969), 195. The quote itself indicates the disparity of viewpoint in the sources. Zucker tells the same story of Brother Daniel, a Jewish convert to Catholicism, but does not include the provocative remark here cited from the Neturei Karta newspaper account of the event. See Norman L. Zucker, *The Coming Crisis in Israel: Private Faith and Public Policy* (Cambridge: MIT Press, 1973), pp.179-80.

[3] Charles S. Leibman, in his article "Extremism as a Religious Norm" (*Journal for the Scientific Study of Religion*, 22 (1983): 75-86), calls attention to two groups, Gush Emunim and Eda Haredit, the umbrella name for Neturei Karta, as extremists. The general points he makes are valid, but the context to which they relate is Israel as a secular polity. Secularism is the implied center, the privileged norm, for Israel as for other nation-states, and so the word "extremism," unlike fundamentalism, prejudges the character and also the significance, of both Gush Emunim and Neturei Karta as religious movements. "Ultraorthodox" is an apt term to describe Neturei Karta but *not* Gush Emunim. Only "fundamentalism" permits both groups to be framed within a rubric that addresses their paradoxical interrelatedness.

[4] See Joseph Dan, "Hasidism," in *The Encyclopedia of Religion*, ed., M. Eliade, (New York: Macmillan, 1987), 6: 208.

[5] Jacobs, *Hasidic Thought*, p.75.

[6] Not only for this quotation but for detailing the complex relationships between traditional rabbis and the emergent *rebbes* I am indebted to the insightful article of Menachem Friedman, "The Changing Role of the Community Rabbinate," *The Jerusalem Quarterly* 25 (Fall 1982): 79-99. The quotation just given is found on p.82.

[7] "Commonwealth" refers to the successive kingdoms that Israel has established in the Holy Land. The first extended from Kind David to the Babylonian exile (586 B.C.). The second began with the completion of the rebuilt temple (515 B.C.) and lasted till the Roman destruction of Jerusalem in A.D. 70. The "Third Commonwealth" is the most controversial. Many assert that it began in 1948 with the modern state of Israel. Others have argued that it did not begin till 1967, with the conquest of all Jerusalem, while still others believe that it has yet to come into being.

[8] Jacob Katz, "Orthodoxy in Historical Perspective," in *Studies in Contemporary Jewry*, ed. Peter Y. Medding (Bloomington: Indiana University Press, 1986), 2: 3-17, summarizes the origin and variability of the term "Orthodox," with special attention to pre-1948 developments outside Palestine.

[9] Gideon Aran, "The Roots of Gush Emunim," in Medding (ed.), *Studies*, 2: 124.

[10] See Katz, "Orthodoxy," p.8, for this quote. The overlap between these developments and changes in the Hasidic communities of Eastern Europe are brought out in his seminal study, *Tradition and Crisis: Jewish Society at the End of the Middle Ages* (New York: The Free Press, 1961), especially pp.225-44.

[11] The citation from Hazon Ish is provided in Menachem Friedman, "Changing Role," p.95.

[12] Katz, "Origins," p.15.

[13] Eliezer Goldman, "Responses to Modernity in Orthodox Jewish Thought," in Medding (ed.), *Studies*, 2: 65. No specific attributions are given, but almost any Neturei Karta spokesman would say something similar about the Zionist "threat."

[14] Aran, "Roots," p.123. The tense and last phrase have been slightly altered to suit the argument of this paragraph.

[15] Katz, "Orthodoxy," pp.11-12.

[16] Ibid., p.15.

Mobilization, Not Liberation: Trends in the "Pro-Family" Movement

Sara Diamond

SARA DIAMOND *is an investigative journalist who has taught journalism at the University of California at Santa Cruz. Currently she is pursuing her Ph.D. in sociology at the University of California, Berkeley.*

The women's contingent of the Christian Right is not without role models. In her book, *Who But a Woman?*, Concerned Women for America president Beverly LaHaye introduces the need for right-wing women's activism by telling an ironic story. She describes the defeat of "communism" in Brazil during the early 1960s, without ever mentioning that the elected administration of João Goulart was overthrown by a U.S.-backed military coup in 1964. In Beverly LaHaye's revised version of history, the defeat took place after "several prominent businessmen began meeting informally in 1961 to halt Brazil's plunge into totalitarianism."[1] They formed the Institute for Economic and Social Research, which LaHaye herself describes as an "intelligence network." Its purpose was to hunt for subversives in positions of leadership, to establish a television network and to mobilize women to take action against the government. These women—whom LaHaye lauds as role models—formed cell groups to organize prayer meetings, patriotic protest marches, and the purchase of television airtime and newspaper space to proclaim their anticommunist message. Ultimately, she says, it was the efforts of these anticommunist women that made the businessmen successful. The result was a military dictatorship installed in 1964, which lasted twenty years and resulted in the torture and murder of thousands of Brazilian citizens.[2]

Whether or not Beverly LaHaye is fully aware of the implications of her little story, she conveys an important message: right-wing women activists mobilized by their male leaders play a crucial role in the destabilization or manipulation of a society headed in a progressive direction.[3] Though the fight against legalized abortion, women's economic and employment rights, gay rights and academic freedom in public schools top the Concerned Women for America's agenda, Beverly LaHaye has been candid about the anticommunist focus of her movement.

The function of the so-called "pro-family" movement has been twofold. On one level, the movement has pressed—sometimes successfully—for policy changes that would turn back the clock on a wide array of progressive and liberal institutional reforms. On another level, the movement links diverse issues and creates an ideological climate in which intense nationalism and xenophobia can flourish. Most media and activist attention on the Christian Right has focused on the movement's efforts to outlaw abortion, to legislate against gay rights, to reinstitute prayer in public schools and to censor textbooks and other publications. But in addition to its obsession with "moral" issues, the leadership of the "pro-family" movement is also active in the foreign and military policy arena. Why else would Lt. Col. Oliver North have been a keynote speaker at the 1986 Concerned Women for America convention where he urged Christian Right women to press for contra aid?[4] Why else would major Christian Right women's leader in California, Barbara Alby, have co-sponsored a fundraising tribute for contra leader Adolfo Calero?[5]

This is not to slight the very real focus of the Christian Right on eliminating reproductive rights, pay equity for women, etc., but rather to stress that issues do not emerge in isolation within the movement. Unfortunately, some analysts have focused almost exclusively on the social agenda of the movement, without recognizing that conservatism on the domestic front is used as a bridge to build support for anticommunist military intervention.

Secular Humanism: the Christian Right's Boogey-Man

The "pro-family" issues are derived from an ongoing ideological struggle over which sector of the U.S. public will draw the official American portrait, both in the history books and in legislation. To a large extent, the Christian Right is engaged in a drive to reinvigorate fading symbols representing marital relations, parental authority and the sanctity and purity of the neighborhood movie theatre and public school. The right to determine how and by whom the minds of children are molded is the most valued prize in the tug of war between the Christian Right and secular society.

Nowhere has the struggle for the minds of children been so great as in the Christian Right's battle against "secular humanist" education. The term "secular humanist" is a catch-all phrase for a human-centered rather than God-centered philosophy. Secular humanists, according to their Christian detractors, believe that human beings shape their own destiny and solve their own problems through concrete physical means rather than through reliance on the supernatural.

Among Christian Right leaders, the primary advocate of war on secular humanism has been Tim LaHaye, one of the founders of the Moral Majority and head of the American Coalition for Traditional Values. In 1979, LaHaye published *The Battle for the Mind*, a treatise circulated widely by the Moral Majority. LaHaye, a fundamental Baptist, proclaims what he calls "humanist domination" as a sign that the "Great Tribulation"—the seven-year period of social chaos preceding Christ's return—is at hand. LaHaye defines secular humanism:

> Simply defined, humanism is man's [sic] attempt to solve his problems independently of God. Since moral conditions have become worse and worse in direct proportion to humanism's influence, which has moved our country from a biblically based society to an amoral "democratic" society during the past forty years, one would think that humanists would realize the futility of their position. To the contrary, they treacherously refuse to face the reality of their failures, blaming them instead on traditional religion or ignorance or capitalism or religious superstitions.[6]

LaHaye proceeds to develop an elaborate theory on the humanist conspiracy, linking the ACLU, the NAACP, the National Organization for Women, Hollywood movie producers and even Unitarianism to the impending downfall of modern civilization. The solution, LaHaye argues, is for Christian moralists to seize control of political and ideological institutions.

> Such leaders need to be returned to office and joined by others who share their moral persuasion. Only then will we halt the tragic breakdown that finds us murdering, by abortion, more babies every four years than Adolf Hitler killed in World War II.[7]

Aside from the philosophical debate, once broadly defined, secular humanism becomes a convenient label for anything and everything the Christian Right opposes. For years, TV preachers and Christian Right activists have blamed secular humanism for a host of social evils: declining public school standards, unwanted teen pregnancy, sexually transmitted diseases, loss of parental authority over children, high divorce rates and so forth.

Battling Secular Humanist Textbooks

Since 1975, Mel and Norma Gabler of Longview, Texas have become two of the most influential people in the field of education. As self-appointed Christian Right textbooks screeners, the Gablers' Education Research Analysts is a national clearinghouse for Christian Right complaints about textbook content. The Gablers believe that the function of education is to impart "factual knowledge, basic skills and cultural heritage," best accomplished through a "traditional curriculum of reading, math, and grammar, as well as patriotism, high moral standards, dress codes, and strict discipline, with respect and courtesy demanded from all students."[8]

Because they work out of Texas, the Gablers are in a position to influence textbook adoption nationwide. Texas is one of the largest states purchasing books, and its selections make an impression on textbook publishers. The Texas schoolbook adoption process is unique in that citizens who object to proposed curriculum material are invited to attend annual adoption hearings, and the Gablers have perfected the art of detailing and representing Christian Right objections to textbook material. The Gablers help like-minded activists in other states by issuing reams and reams of suggested book lists, detailed analyses of the pros and cons of the various publishers' latest editions and how-to materials on influencing textbook selection processes.

Textbooks that make it past the adoption process are still not safe from Christian Right censors. In the 1980s, anti-secular humanism brigades took their fight to the courts. The opening salvo was fired in Tennessee when a group of fundamentalist parents filed suit over a series of reading textbooks. Vicky Frost, the primary plaintiff in the case, contended that one of the second-grade textbook stories, which dealt with a magical trip to Mars, effectively advocated mental telepathy which she considered a positive portrayal of occultism.[9]

The case was prosecuted through the legal and financial support of Concerned Women for America, with CWA attorney Michael Farris pleading the case. In October 1986, a federal district court judge in Greenville, Tennessee ruled that the school district had indeed violated the families' civil rights by requiring children to read books they considered "anti-Christian." In December 1986, the same court awarded $50,521.59 to the Frost family and their co-plaintiffs as reimbursement for legal expenses incurred.[10]

While the Vicky Frost case was in litigation, another group of 600 fundamentalist parents sued the Alabama public school system over its use of textbooks deemed objectionable. They sought to remove all traces of "secular humanism" from state curriculum materials, contending that secular humanism is a religion. If Christianity as a religion cannot be taught in the public schools in any way, shape or form, they argued, then neither should teachers be allowed to indoctrinate students with "secular humanist" philosophy. Again, CWA led the fight, with the financial assistance of Pat Robertson's National Legal Foundation.

"There's a widespread feeling amongst conservative Christians that the religion of secular humanism has permeated public education," said attorney Michael Farris, general counsel for Concerned Women for America.[11]

The litigants were fortunate to get a judge who had a track record of opposing secular humanism. In January 1983, Judge Brevard Hand had upheld an Alabama law authorizing a moment of silent prayer in public schools. Although an appeals court reversed his decision, Hand went on to restructure the case so that the original single plaintiff was replaced by 624 fundamentalist Christians and the central argument of the case became not prayer but secular humanism.[12]

The case was heated, with numerous "expert witnesses" appearing on both sides of the secular humanism-as-religion argument. One of those testifying on behalf of the Christian Right was prominent University of Virginia sociologist, James D. Hunter. He argued that secular humanism is the functional equivalent of a religion and ought to have the same legal status in the public schools.[13]

On March 4, 1987, a federal judge in Mobile, Alabama banned 44 textbooks from the local public schools system on grounds that they promoted the "religion" of "secular humanism."[14] Several weeks later a federal appeals court overrode the decision.

Defeated on the humanism-as-religion front, the textbook crusaders are likely to redirect their energies toward influencing the textbook selection process and the policies of local school boards.[15] Upon his withdrawal from the 1988 presidential race, Pat Robert-

son's aides said the TV preacher planned to help born-again Christians take control of local school boards. Citizens for Excellence in Education, headed by Robert Simonds, specializes in training Christian Right parents to pressure local public schools administrators and to run for school board positions themselves.

Source: Sara Diamond. *Spiritual Warfare: The Politics of the Christian Right.* Boston: South End, 1989. Reprinted with permission.

Notes

[1] Beverly LaHaye, *Who But a Woman?* (Nashville: Thomas Nelson Publishers, 1984), p.9.

[2] See Joan Dassin, ed., *Torture in Brazil: A Shocking Report on the Pervasive Use of Torture by Brazilian Military Governments 1964-1979* (New York: Vintage Books, 1986); and A. J. Langguth, *Hidden Terrors: The Truth about U.S. Police Operations in Latin America,* (New York: Pantheon Books, 1978).

Readers interested in the role of right-wing women's movements in the Third World might consult two articles: Michele Mattelart, "Chile: The Feminine Side of the Coup or When Bourgeois Women Take to the Streets," NACLA's *Report on the Americas,* September 1975; and Maria de los Angeles Crummett, "El Poder Feminino: The Mobilization of Women Against Socialism in Chile," *Latin American Perspectives,* Issue 15, Fall 1977, Vol. IV No. 4.

[4] Don Lattin, "North's tough talk to right wing," *San Francisco Examiner,* December 7, 1986. North asked CWA members to lobby Congress in support of contra aid, which, as a National Security Council staffer, he was not allowed to do.

[5] April 22, 1988, Sacramento California, fundraising reception for Nicarao Relief Fund, the northern California affiliate of the FDN contras. At the event, Alby made a special point of embracing Calero's brother Mario and pledging her support.

[6] Tim LaHaye, *The Battle for the Mind* (Old Tappan, New Jersey: Fleming H. Revell Co., 1979), p.26.

[7] Ibid., p.177.

[8] Quoted in Carol Flake, *Redemptorama* (New York: Penguin, 1984), pp.39-40.

[9] "A Reprise of Scopes," *Newsweek,* July 28, 1986.

[10] *New York Times,* December 16, 1986, p.10.

[11] *New York Times,* February 28, 1988.

[12] "A Courtroom Clash over Textbooks," Time, October 27, 1986.

[13] Ibid.

[14] *New York Times,* March 5, 1987.

[15] See "Censorship tactics shifting," *United Press International,* August 31, 1988.

American Jeremiahs

Michael Lienesch

MICHAEL LIENESCH *is professor of political science at the University of North Carolina at Chapel Hill.*

Within the New Christian Right, the most prominent members of the movement practice a prophetic brand of politics. Believing Americans to be the modern chosen people, they think of them as following in the footsteps of the Israelites, who also broke the covenant by falling from faith into sin and secularity. It follows that they see themselves as modern versions of the ancient prophets who denounced their country's decline, exhorted the people to repent of their sins and reform their unrighteous ways, and promised either deliverance or destruction. The preachers in particular make repeated references to Jeremiah and Isaiah, Daniel and Ezekiel, even to John the Baptist and "the prophet Jonah, who cried out, 'Repent or perish'."[1] More often, they adopt the rhetorical style associated with what Sacvan Bercovitch called the American jeremiad, the late-seventeenth-century sermon condemning corruption and calling for moral reform. Applying the style to their own times, and echoing the radio preachers of the 1930s and 1940s, they create a contemporary rhetoric of renewal, a prophetic form of speech appropriate to present-day politics. Falwell is a master of the medium: "Now is the time to begin calling America back to God, back to the Bible, back to morality!"[2] Nevertheless, the prophetic style is by no means limited to the preachers. Thus Senator Helms, writing in his *When Free Men Shall Stand*, provides one of the best examples of it:

> The Old Testament teaches that Israel had a predictable relationship with God. Israel would prosper in the days it lived by the Word of God. Then when it fell away from God's law, through immorality and unbelief, Israel suffered civil strife, inability to maintain peace and security, and finally captivity. But Israel in its affliction would realize the error of its ways and would beseech the Lord to come to the aid of His chosen people. And God would hear His people and would deliver them from their enemies.

Applying the message to America, and aiming at its enemies, Helms concludes with a call for political action: "Americans as a people must once again rise up and reclaim their nation from the slothful, divisive, prodigal, and treacherous individuals who have bartered away our freedoms for a mess of pottage."[3]

The Causes of Corruption

According to these books, cultural corruption can be traced to the coming of humanist thinking in the Western world. Although the authors are never precise in defining the term (John Eidsmore suspects that "often they are unable to give a clear definition of the term because they do not really understand it"), they do make it clear that humanism is an attitude or philosophy that sees "man as the center of the universe."[4] Says Francis Schaeffer, in what is probably the definitive statement, "Humanism is the placing of Man at the center of all things and making him the measure of all things."[5] At least a few of them consider the term to be synonymous with original sin. John Whitehead, in any event, sees Adam as the "first humanist."[6] Others associate it closely with paganism. Thus Tim LaHaye traces humanist thinking back to "Babylon, the source of all religions." (LaHaye considers Confucianism, Buddhism, "Muhammadinism," "Babylonian Mysticism," and "Humanism" to be "pagan" religions.)[7] More commonly, the writers locate the beginning of humanism in the Roman empire, seeing it not only as the source of the persecution of the early Christians, but also as the reason for Rome's eventual decline and fall.[8] From the Romans, the connection to the modern world is fairly direct, being carried along by a thousand years of Roman Catholicism. Says John Whitehead, "Ultimately, Roman Catholics very largely compromised with humanism, leaving the criticism of humanism to the Protestants of the Reformation."[9] The rationalist scholastic St. Thomas Aquinas comes in for special scorn. Writes LaHaye, "It is an irony of history that a man who was sainted by his church as a scholar was responsible for reviving an almost dead philosophy, which has become the most dangerous religion in the world today—humanism."[10]

As the authors tell it, the history of humanism reached a turning point after Aquinas, when European thought divided dramatically into two lines, the humanism of the Renaissance and the biblical theism of the Reformation. In Francis Schaeffer's *How Should We Then Live?* (a history of Western culture produced by his son Franky Schaeffer as both an illustrated book and a feature-length movie), he focuses on the Renaissance strain, which he sees as the source of the antagonism to absolute truths that has been the hallmark of humanist thought.[11] Emphasizing the break between humanism and theism, Schaeffer argues that what came to be called "Christian humanism," as represented by Erasmus, was not Christian at all. Other like-minded writers have reiterated the point. "What of this term, 'Christian humanism'?" asks Rus Walton. "Is it not simply another of those 'inherent contradictions'? Is it not another snare, another delusion, another trap to draw man away from God?" Christianity and humanism, Walton explains, answering his own rhetorical question, "cannot be combined; they do not match."[12] Nor was the absence of absolutes the only evil to emerge from the Renaissance. In a thoughtful treatment of Renaissance art, Schaeffer sees the seeds of an individualistic and ultimately narcissistic approach to culture. While lacking Schaeffer's sophistication, Tim LaHaye treats the same theme in a slightly different way, offering his views of Michelangelo's statue of David: "The Renaissance obsession with nude 'art forms' was the forerunner of the modern humanist's demand for pornography in the name of freedom. Both resulted in a self-destructive lowering of moral standards."[13]

From Renaissance to Enlightenment, the corrupting course of humanist thinking continued and intensified. Describing the Enlightenment as an era of deism, illuminism, and rampant rationalism, the authors see it as an antitheistic age, in which belief gave way to doubt and religion to skepticism. Far from the conventional descriptions, which celebrate the Enlightenment as an era in which Europeans emerged from the darkness of superstition into the light of rationality, these writers see it as a period of retrogression, a return to paganism, in which "the men of the Enlightenment pushed aside the Christian base and heritage and looked back to the old pre-Christian times."[14] Although mentioning some of the early modern scientists, the writers tend to see philosophers such as Rousseau and Voltaire as particularly significant in setting the tone for their times. Tracing the influence of these thinkers, they blame them for what they see as some of the worst aspects of modernity, including the French Revolution, Darwin "and the mythology of evolution," and the Russian Revolution.[15] Rousseau is considered to be particularly culpable, since his philosophy is seen as inspiring many of the revolutions of the modern world. Citing his influence on French, Russian, and Third World revolutionaries, several of the authors see him as a kind of radical Rasputin, whose insidious influence extends even to today. Rousseau, says Tim LaHaye, is "a most influential writer-philosopher for today's college

youth. They study him vigorously, and most humanistic college professors are well versed in his thinking."[16] All told, the authors agree that the Enlightenment was a disastrous era, a spawning ground for most of the evils of the modern world. Writes LaHaye:

> The age of enlightenment and the skepticism of the Frenchmen Voltaire and Rousseau helped to propagate the naturalism and deism that permeated England and spread to the Colonies. Political ambition, greed, and the natural result of libertine living had a catastrophic effect on the morals of western civilization. In fact, the tragedies which have plagued Central Europe for the past 175 years and ultimately embroiled America in two world wars can be traced directly to this "free thinking" humanism.[17]

Continuing the story, these conservative authors describe the course of European civilization in the nineteenth and twentieth centuries as a scene of ongoing corruption and eventual disaster. Led by the bookish Francis Schaeffer, they tell of thinkers and of theories—Kant's dualism, Hegel's dialectical theory of history, Kierkegaard's irrationality—that encouraged the replacement of theistic absolutism with humanistic relativism. Throughout, they decry the decline of European philosophy, which they see as following an inexorable course "from optimism to pessimism."[18] Citing the creation of schools of thought such as behaviorism, determinism, evolutionism, and pragmatism, along with scientism of various kinds, they tell how European thinkers, while seeking to elevate humanity, in fact devalued it. Particularly important in this process was Darwinian evolutionism, in which human life came to be seen as only another kind of animal existence. Other forces contributed as well. (Tim LaHaye, who does not claim to be among the most sophisticated members of the movement, includes in this category "the wild art that goes under the guise of 'impressionism'.")[19] Eventually, having destroyed any possibility for personal redemption, Europeans were forced to turn to collectivist solutions, including Marxism, socialism, and fascism.[20] For these thinkers, who consider all forms of collectivism to be essentially the same, the culmination of humanism must always be totalitarianism, including the scientific socialism of Marx and Engels, the Bolshevistic communism of Lenin, Stalin, and Mao, and the fascism of the "humanist Adolph Hitler."[21]

[1.] LaHaye, Tim. *Battle for the Mind: You are Engaged in A Battle for the Mind, A Subtitle Warfare*(Grand Rapids, MT: Revell) 1982, p.202.

[2.] Falwell, Jerry. *Listen, America!* (Garden City, N.Y.: Doubleday and

Company, 1980), p 265. See Sacvan Bercovitch, *The American Jeremiad* (Madison: University of Wisconsin Press, 1978).

3. Helms, Jesse. *When Free Men Shall Stand* (Grand Rapids, MICH: Zondervan Publishing House, 1964) pp.120, 121.

4. Eidsmore, John. *God and Caesar: Biblical Faith and Political Action (Westchester: Ill: Crossways Books, 1984) p.131.*

5. Schaeffer, Francis. *A Christain Manifesto* (Westchester: Ill: Crossways Books, 1981) p.23. According to LaHaye, "Humanists have a basic misunderstanding of the nature of man. They consider man to be inherently good, whereas the Bible pictures humanity as fallen, sinful, and untrustworthy." LaHaye, *Battle for the Mind*, p.92.

6. Whitehead, John, *The Second American Revolution* (Westchester, Ill.: Crossway Books, 1982) p.27.

7. LaHaye, *Battle for the Mind*, pp.132, 133.

8. See Francis A. Schaeffer, *How Should We Then Live? The Rise and Decline of Western Thought and Culture* (Old Tappan, N.J.: Fleming H. Revell Company, 1976), p.22. LaHaye sees Roman humanism as derived from Greek humanism: "Unfortunately for history, the Romans were not given to much original thought, so they adopted the philosophy, art, architecture, and social customs of Greece, merged them with their own, and propagated Hellenistic culture throughout the Roman world." LaHaye, *Battle for the Mind*, p.28.

9. Whitehead, *Second American Revolution*, p.38.

10. LaHaye, *Battle for the Mind*, p.29.

11. See Francis Schaeffer, *How Should We Then Live?*, p.55.

12. Walton, Rus. *FACSI: Fundamentals for American Christians* (Nyack, N.Y.: Parson Publishing, 1979) pp.176, 177.

13. LaHaye, *Battle for the Mind*, p.30.

14. Schaeffer, Francis. *How Should We Then Live?*, p.122. LaHaye tells the same story with a populist slant: "In most countries of Europe, there were two classes of people, the elite ruling class, predominantly secularist in their thinking, and the masses, who were religious." The "elitists" he writes, were "ideal spawning grounds for skepticism, rationalism, illuminism, Enlightenment theories, and eventually socialism and Marxism." The masses, by contrast, "were not attracted to the secularistic fads." LaHaye, *Faith of Our Founding Fathers*, p.17.

15. Rushdoony, R. J. *This Independent Republic: Studies in the Nature and Meaning of American History* (Nutley, N.J.: Craig Press, 1964) p.137.

16. LaHaye, *Battle for the Mind*, p.69.

17. LaHaye, *Bible's Influence*, p.13.

18. Schaeffer, *How Should We Then Live?*, p.152. Schaeffer calls this change "The Breakdown." See ibid., pp.144-66. In his *Christian Manifesto*, he describes the shift "toward a world view based upon the idea that the final reality is impersonal matter or energy shaped into its present form by impersonal chance." Francis Schaeffer, *Christian Manifesto*, pp.17-18.

19. LaHaye, *Bible's Influence*, p.55.

20. John Whitehead includes racism in the same category. See Whitehead, *Stealing of America*, pp.8-16.

21. LaHaye, *Battle for the Mind*, p.119.

11

Feminism

The Ideal of Gender Equality

Feminism, so frequently viewed as a late twentieth century movement, has older roots. One might go so far as to say these roots can be traced to Plato's *Republic* and its depiction of the "guardian class". Less remotely, the roots of feminism are evidenced in the writings of Mary Wollstonecraft in the eighteenth century. She maintains, contrary to the prevailing opinion of her day, that women are as capable as men in their ability to attain those characteristics deserving of respect.

Drawing upon existentialist themes, including those of her partner Jean-Paul Sartre, Simone de Beauvoir describes the present subordinate condition of women and goes on to affirm their future independence. Perhaps more striking than anything else is her opening comment that one is not born, but rather *becomes* a woman. This is a position compatible with that of other feminists who have advocated androgyny.

Betty Friedan was among the first modern American feminists, and, as her extract shows, one who was strongly influenced by Simone de Beauvoir. Friedan succeeds in vividly describing the "problem with no name"—the problem previously identified by Wollstonecraft and refined by de Beauvoir.

What Wollstonecraft sees is male-female equality, but as Jean Bethke Elshtain says, to call for equality is the beginning, not the end, of the debate. For some feminists, such as Shulamith Firestone, the structural imperatives necessary to achieve this equality include freeing women from the tyranny of their reproductive biology by every means available. Ann Ferguson explores this search for equality in terms of the androgenous person: one who is neither masculine nor feminine but human. In her view, the ideal androgenous person would be industrious, autonomous and affectionate. According to Ferguson, this redefinition of gender would permit humans to transcend old categories and to develop positive human potentialities unrealized in the pre-

sent social systems. Ferguson looks analytically at a counter-argument to the androgenous view and finds it—in spite of Rousseau and Gilder—lacking.

Alison Jaggar addresses the issue of equality as it relates to the role assigned in the Western philosophical tradition to emotion and cognition. She makes a convincing case for the proposition that this tradition has tended to dismiss the epistemic authority of women on the grounds of their association with emotion. She argues, with success, that reinterpreting and refining our emotions is necessary to establishing a more credible base for theoretical investigation. Jaggar's analysis of emotion and epistemic authority could be construed as but one line of inquiry suggested by Ann Ferguson in discussing feminists' pursuit of equality. However, Jaggar has a tendency to forget that the story of passions (emotions) and their connection with reason plays a different role in the work of philosophers from Plato to Hume than it does in those after Hume.

In a very different vein, Judith Butler attempts to deconstruct the subject of feminism, partly in the expectation that this process will help to prevent the factionalization of women that will result from an effort to give universal and specific content to the category of women. By keeping open the referent of "women", new possibilities appear, possibilities different from the maternal or racial ontologies of the past. Butler claims that what is needed is "a resignification of the term 'women'", thereby enhancing a sense of agency and non-subordination. While there is undoubtedly food for thought in what Butler says, one cannot help but wish for greater clarity of style, perhaps along the lines offered by Ferguson or Jaggar, especially in Butler's discussion of "subordination" and "referent". One has a sense in reading her that her language soffers from the same episodic opaqueness that one encounters in the writings of Jea-Paul Sartre. This being said, few have ever claimed that Jean-Paul Sartre was not worth reading and the same could be said of Butler.

The Prevailing Opinion of a Sexual Character Discussed

Mary Wollstonecraft

MARY WOLLSTONECRAFT (1759-1797) earned her living teaching and working for a publisher. She married the anarchist William Godwin. She died September 1797 upon the birth of her daughter who was later to become Shelley's wife.

To account for, and excuse the tyranny of man, many ingenious arguments have been brought forward to prove, that the two sexes, in the acquirement of virtue, ought to aim at attaining a very different character; or, to speak explicitly, women are not allowed to have sufficient strength of mind to acquire what really deserves the name of virtue. Yet it should seem, allowing them to have souls, that there is but one way appointed by Providence to lead mankind to either virtue or happiness.

If then women are not a swarm of ephemeron triflers, why should they be kept in ignorance under the specious name of innocence? Men complain, and with reason, of the follies and caprices of our sex, when they do not keenly satirise our headstrong passions and grovelling vices. Behold, I should answer, that natural effect of ignorance! The mind will ever be unstable that has only prejudices to rest on, and the current will run with destructive fury when there are no barriers to break its force. Women are told from their infancy, and taught by the example of their mothers, that a little knowledge of human weakness, justly termed cunning, softness of temper, *outward* obedience, and a scrupulous attention to a puerile kind of propriety, will obtain for them the protection of man; and should they be beautiful, everything else is needless, for at least twenty years of their lives.

Thus Milton describes our first frail mother; though when he tells us that women are formed for softness and sweet attractive grace, I cannot comprehend his meaning, unless, in the true Mahometan strain, he meant to deprive us of souls, and insinuate that we were beings only designed by sweet attractive grace, and docile blind obedience, to gratify the senses of man when he can no longer soar on the wing of contemplation.

How grossly do they insult us who thus advise us only to render ourselves gentle, domestic brutes! For instance, the winning softness so warmly and frequently recommended, that governs by obeying. What childish expressions, and how insignificant is the being—can it be an immortal one?—who will condescend to govern by such sinister methods? "Certainly," says Lord Bacon, "man is of kin to the beasts by his body; and if he be not of kin to God by his spirit, he is a base and ignoble creature!" Men, indeed, appear to me to act in a very unphilosophical manner, when they try to secure the good conduct of women by attempting to keep them always in a state of childhood. Rousseau was more consistent when he wished to stop the progress of reason in both sexes, for if men eat of the tree of knowledge, women will come in for a taste; but, from the imperfect cultivation which their understandings now receive, they only attain a knowledge of evil.

Children, I grant, should be innocent; but when the epithet is applied to men, or women, it is but a civil term for weakness. For if it be allowed that women were destined by Providence to acquire human virtues, and, by the exercise of their understandings, that stability of character which is the firmest ground to rest our future hopes upon, they must be permitted to turn to the fountain of light, and not forced to shape their course by the twinkling of a mere satellite. Milton I grant, was of a very different opinion; for he only bends to the indefeasible right of beauty, though it would be difficult to render two passages which I now mean to contrast, consistent. But into similar inconsistencies are great men often led by their senses:

> To whom thus Eve with *perfect beauty* adorn'd.
> My author and disposer, what thou bid'st
> *Unargued* I obey; so God ordains;
> God is *thy law, thou mine*: to know no more
> Is woman's *happiest* knowledge and her *praise*.

These are exactly the arguments that I have used to children; but I have added, your reason is now gaining strength, and, till it arrives at some degree of

MARY WOLLSTONECRAFT (1759—1797)

MARY WOLLSTONECRAFT was a writer of both fiction and non-fiction and the leading critic of the patriarchical mores of the English society in which she lived. Often referred to as the "patron saint of feminism," Wollstonecraft's best-known work on the subject is *A Vindication of the Rights of Woman*, which she published in 1792. Her works of fiction, including *Mary: A Fiction* (1788) and *The Wrongs of Woman* (published posthumously in 1799) also contain overt attacks on English social customs.

Scholars have noted in Wollstonecraft's writing the classic Enlightenment faith in the possibility of human improvement. In her writings on education, such as *Thoughts on the Education of Daughters* (1787), she stressed that learning should be enjoyed and not done simply through memorization. In the *Vindication*, Wollstonecraft supports her contention that eighteenth-century Englishwomen were subject to a trivialized "acculturation" that stressed fragility, refinement and beauty while teaching them nothing of lasting and practical value. She advocated a "revolution in female manners" that would enable women to study important matters and to seek employment outside the home.

Wollstonecraft was also a keen student of the political events of her day. In 1791, she wrote and published *A Vindication of the Rights of Man* in response to Burke's *Reflections of the Revolution in France* which had appeared one year earlier. In 1792 she went to France to observe the revolutionary happenings there more closely, and in 1794 published *An Historical and Moral View of the Origin and Progress of the French Revolution*.

In 1797, shortly after marrying the radical English author William Godwin, Mary Wollstonecraft died after giving birth to the couple's second child. *The Wrongs of Women* was edited by Godwin and published in 1799.

---

maturity, you must look up to me for advice,—then you ought to *think*, and only rely on God.

Yet in the following lines Milton seems to coincide with me, when he makes Adam thus expostulate with his Maker:

> Hast Thou not made me here Thy substitute,
> And these inferior far beneath me set?
> Among *unequals* what society
> Can sort, what harmony or true delight?
> Which must be mutual, in proportion due
> Given and received; but in *disparity*
> The one intense, the other still remiss
> Cannot well suit with either, but soon prove
> Tedious alike: of *fellowship* I speak
> Such as I seek, fit to participate
> All rational delight—

In treating therefore of the manners of women, let us, disregarding sensual arguments, trace what we should endeavour to make them in order to co-operate, if the expression be not too bold, with the Supreme Being.

By individual education, I mean, for the sense of the word is not precisely defined, such an attention to a child as will slowly sharpen the senses, form the temper, regulate the passions as they begin to fer-ment, and set the understanding to work before the body arrives at maturity; so that the man may only have to proceed, not to begin, the important task of learning to think and reason.

To prevent any misconstruction, I must add, that I do not believe that a private education can work the wonders which some sanguine writers have attributed to it. Men and women must be educated, in a great degree, by the opinions and manners of the society they live in. In every age there has been a stream of popular opinion that has carried all before it, and given a family character, as it were, to the century. It may then fairly be inferred, that, till society be differently constituted, much cannot be expected from education. It is, however, sufficient for my present purpose to assert that, whatever effect circumstances have on the abilities, every being may become virtuous by the exercise of its own reason; for if but one being was created with vicious inclinations, that is positively bad, what can save us from atheism? or if we worship a God, is not that God a devil?

Consequently, the most perfect education, in my opinion, is such an exercise of the understanding as is best calculated to strengthen the body and form the heart. Or, in other words, to enable the individual to attain such habits of virtue as will render it independent. In fact, it is a farce to call any being virtuous whose virtues do not result from the exercise of its own reason. This was Rousseau's opinion respecting men; I extend it to women, and confidently assert that they have been drawn out of their sphere by false refinement, and not by an endeavour to acquire masculine qualities. Still the regal homage which they receive is so intoxicating, that until the manners of the times are changed, and formed on more reasonable principles, it may be impossible to convince them that the illegitimate power which they obtain by degrading themselves is a curse, and that they must return to nature and equality if they wish to secure the placid satisfaction that unsophisticated affections impart. But for this epoch we must wait—wait perhaps till kings and nobles, enlightened by reason, and, preferring the real dignity of man to childish state, throw off their gaudy hereditary trappings; and if then women do not resign the arbitrary power of beauty—they will prove that they have *less* mind than man.

I may be accused of arrogance; still I must declare what I firmly believe, that all the writers who have written on the subject of female education and manners, from Rousseau to Dr. Gregory, have contributed to render women more artificial, weak characters, than they would otherwise have been; and consequently, more useless members of society. I might have expressed this conviction in a lower key, but I am afraid it would have been the whine of affectation, and not the faithful expression of my feelings, of the clear result which experience and reflection have led me to draw. When I come to that division of the subject, I shall advert to the passages that I more particularly disapprove of, in the works of the authors I have just alluded to; but it is first necessary to observed that my objection extends to the whole purport of those books, which tend, in my opinion, to degrade one-half of the human species, and render women pleasing at the expense of every solid virtue.

Source: Mary Wollstonecraft. *The Rights of Woman.* Originally published in 1829.

The Second Sex

Simone De Beauvoir

SIMONE DE BEAUVOIR *(1908–86) was a French writer and leftist activist who became well known for her book* The Second Sex *(1949; trans 1953), a primer of the radical feminist movement. Along with Jean Paul Sartre, she was a leading advocate of existential ideas. DeBeauvoir also expressed her feminist and existentialist ideas through novels, including* She Came to Stay *(1943) and* The Mandarins *(1954).*

The women of today are in a fair way to dethrone the myth of femininity; they are beginning to affirm their independence in concrete ways; but they do not easily succeed in living completely the life of a human being. Reared by women within a feminine world, their normal destiny is marriage, which still means practically subordination to man; for masculine prestige is far from extinction, resting still upon solid economic and social foundations. We must therefore study the traditional destiny of woman with some care. In this book I shall seek to describe how woman undergoes her apprenticeship, how she experiences her position, in what kind of universe she is confined, what modes of escape are vouchsafed her. Then only—with so much understood—shall we be able to comprehend the problems of women, the heirs of a burdensome past, who are striving to build a new future. When I use the words *woman* or *feminine* I obviously refer to no archetype, no changeless essence whatever; the reader must understand the phrase "in the present state of education and custom" after most of my statements. It is not our concern here to proclaim eternal verities, but rather to describe the common basis that underlies every individual feminine existence.

Childhood

One is not born, but rather becomes, a woman. No biological, psychological, or economic fate determines the figure that the human female presents in society; it is civilization as a whole that produces this creature, intermediate between male and eunuch, which is described as feminine. Only the intervention of someone else can establish an individual as an *Other*. In so far as he exists in and for himself, the child would hardly be able to think of himself as sexually differentiated. In girls as in boys the body is first of all the radiation of a subjectivity, the instrument that makes possible the comprehension of the world: it is through the eyes, the hands, that children apprehend the universe, and not through the sexual parts. The dramas of birth and of weaning unfold after the same fashion for nurslings of both sexes; these have the same interests and the same pleasures; sucking is at first the source of their most agreeable sensations; then they go through an anal phase in which they get their greatest satisfaction from the excretory functions, which they have in common. Their genital development is analogous; they explore their bodies with the curiosity and the same indifference; from clitoris and penis they derive the same vague pleasure. As their sensibility comes to require an object, it is turned towards the mother: the soft, smooth resilient feminine flesh is what arouses sexual desires, and these desires are prehensile; the girl, like the boy, kisses, handles, and caresses her mother in an aggressive way; they feel the same jealousy if a new child is born, and they show it in similar behaviour patterns: rage, sulkiness, urinary difficulties; and they resort to the same coquettish tricks to gain the love of adults. Up to the age of twelve the little girl is as strong as her brothers, and she shows the same mental powers; there is no field where she is debarred from engaging in rivalry with them. If, well before puberty and sometimes even from early infancy, she seems to us to be already sexually determined, this is not because mysterious instincts directly doom her to passivity, coquetry, maternity; it is because the influence of others upon the child is a factor almost from the start, and thus she is indoctrinated with her vocation from her earliest years.

The world is at first represented in the newborn infant only by immanent sensations; he is still immersed in the bosom of the Whole as he was when he lived in a dark womb; when he is put to the breast or the nursing bottle he is still surrounded by the warmth of maternal flesh. Little by little he learns to perceive objects as distinct and separate from himself, and to distinguish himself from them. Meanwhile he is separated more or less brutally from the nourishing body. Sometimes the infant reacts to this separation by a violent crisis; [1] in any case, it is when the separation is accomplished at about the age of six months, perhaps, that the child begins to show the desire to attract others, through acts of mimicry that in time become real showing off. Certainly this attitude is not established through a considered choice; but it is not necessary to *conceive* a situation for it to *exist*. The nursling lives directly the basic drama of every existent; that of his relation to the Other. Man experiences with anguish his being turned loose, his forlornness. In flight from his freedom, his subjectivity, he would fain lose himself in the bosom of the Whole. Here, indeed, is the origin of his cosmic and pantheistic dreams, of his longing for oblivion, for sleep, for ecstasy, for death. He never succeeds in abolishing his separate ego, but at least he wants to attain the solidity of the in-himself, the *en-soi*, to be petrified into a thing. It is especially when he is fixed by the gaze of other persons that he appears to himself as being one.

It is in this perspective that the behaviour of the child must be interpreted: in carnal form he discovers finiteness, solitude, forlorn desertion in a strange world. He endeavours to compensate for this catastrophe by projecting his existence into an image, the reality and value of which others will establish. It appears that he may begin to affirm his identity at the time when he recognizes his reflection in a mirror—a time that coincides with that of weaning:[2] his ego becomes so fully identified with this reflected image that it is formed only in being projected. Whether or not the mirror actually plays a more or less considerable part, it is certain that the child commences towards the age of six months to mimic his parents, and under their gaze to regard himself as an object. He is already an autonomous subject, in transcendence towards the outer world; but he encounters himself only in a projected form.

When the child develops further, he fights in two ways against his original abandonment. He attempts to deny the separation: rushing into his mother's arms, he seeks her living warmth and demands her caresses. And he attempts find self-justification through the approbation of others. Adults seem to him like gods, for they have the power to confer existence upon him. He feels the magic of the regard that makes of him now a delightful little angel, now a monster. His two modes of defence are not mutually exclusive: on the contrary, they complement each other and interpenetrate. When the attempt at enticement succeeds, the sense of justification finds physical confirmation in the kisses and caresses obtained: it all amounts to a single state of happy passivity that the child experiences in his mother's lap and under her benevolent gaze. There is no difference in the attitudes of girls and boys during the first three or four years; both try to perpetuate the happy condition that preceded weaning; in both sexes enticement and showing-off behaviour occur: boys are as desirous as their sisters of pleasing adults, causing smiles, seeking admiration.

It is more satisfying to deny the anguish than to rise above it, more radical to be lost in the bosom of the Whole than to be petrified by the conscious egos of others: carnal union creates a deeper alienation than any resignation under the gaze of others. Enticement and showing off represent a more complex, a less easy stage than simple abandon in the maternal arms. The magic of the adult gaze is capricious. The child pretends to be invisible: his parents enter into the game, trying blindly to find him and laughing; but all at once they say: "You're getting tiresome, you are not invisible at all." The child has amused them with a bright saying; he repeats it, and this time they shrug their shoulders. In this world, uncertain and unpredictable as the universe of Kafka, one stumbles at every step.[3] That is why many children are afraid of growing up; they are in despair if their parents cease, taking them on their knees or letting them get into the grown-ups' bed. Through the physical frustration they feel more and more cruelly the forlornness, the abandonment, which the human being can never be conscious of without anguish.

Source: Simone De Beauvoir, *The Second Sex*, Translated from the French and edited by H.M Parshley, New English Library, 1960. Reprinted by permission of Hodder & Stoughton Publishers.

Notes

[1] Judith Gautier relates in her memoirs that she wept and pined so pitifully when taken from her nurse that they had to bring her back, and she was not weaned until much later.

[2] This theory was proposed by Dr. Lacan in *Les Complexes familiaux dans la formation de l'individu.* This observation, one of primary importance, would explain how it is that in the course of its development "the ego retains the ambiguous aspect of a spectacle."

[3] In her *Orange, bleue*, Yassu Gauelère relates anecdotes of childhood illustrating the inconsistent behaviour of both her father and mother; her childish conclusion was that "the conduct of grown-ups is decidedly incomprehensible."

The Problem that Has No Name

Betty Friedan

BETTY FRIEDAN (1921-) has been the senior spokesperson for women's rights in the USA over the past quarter of a century. Her book The Feminine Mystique (1963) was responsible for starting a nationwide feminist movement. She was a founder and the first president (1966–70) of the National Organization for Women (NOW).

The problem lay buried, unspoken, for many years in the minds of American women. It was a strange stirring, a sense of dissatisfaction, a yearning that women suffered in the middle of the twentieth century in the United States. Each suburban wife struggled with it alone. As she made the beds, shopped for groceries, matched slipcover material, ate peanut butter sandwiches with her children, chauffeured Cub Scouts and Brownies, lay beside her husband at night—she was afraid to ask even of herself the silent question—"Is this all?"

For over fifteen years there was no word of this yearning in the millions of words written about women, for women, in all the columns, books and articles by experts telling women their role was to seek fulfilment as wives and mothers. Over and over women heard in voices of tradition and of Freudian sophistication that they could desire no greater destiny than to glory in their own femininity. Experts told them how to catch a man and keep him, how to breastfeed children and handle their toilet training, how to cope with sibling rivalry and adolescent rebellion; how to buy a dishwasher, bake bread, cook gourmet snails, and build a swimming pool with their own hands; how to dress, look, and act more feminine and make marriage more exciting; how to keep their husbands from dying young and their sons from growing into delinquents. They were taught to pity the neurotic, unfeminine, unhappy women who wanted to be poets or physicists or presidents. They learned that truly feminine women do not want careers, higher education, political rights—the independence and the opportunities that the old-fashioned feminists fought for. Some women, in their forties and fifties, still remembered painfully giving up those dreams, but most of the younger women no longer even thought about them. A thousand expert voices applauded their femininity, their adjustment, their new maturity. All they had to do was devote their lives from earliest girlhood to finding a husband and bearing children.

By the end of the nineteen-fifties, the average marriage age of women in America dropped to 20, and was still dropping, into the teens. Fourteen million girls were engaged by 17. The proportion of women attending college in comparison with men dropped from 47 per cent in 1920 to 35 per cent in 1958. A century earlier, women had fought for higher education; now girls went to college to get a husband. By the mid-fifties, 60 per cent dropped out of college to marry, or because they were afraid too much education would be a marriage bar. Colleges built dormitories for "married students," but the students were almost always the husbands. A new degree was instituted for the wives—"Ph.T." (Putting Husband Through).

Then American girls began getting married in high school. And the women's magazines, deploring the unhappy statistics about these young marriages, urged that courses on marriage, and marriage counsellors, be installed in the high schools. Girls started going steady at twelve and thirteen, in junior high. Manufacturers put out brassieres with false bosoms of foam rubber for little girls of ten. And an advertisement for a child's dress, sizes 3–6x, in the *New York Times* in the fall of 1960, said: "She Too Can Join the Man-Trap Set."

By the end of the fifties, the United States birthrate was over-taking India's. The birth-control movement, renamed Planned Parenthood, was asked to find a method whereby women who had been advised that a third or fourth baby would be born dead or defective might have it anyhow. Statisticians were especially astounded at the fantastic increase in the number of babies among college women. Where once they had two children, now they had four, five, six. Women who had once wanted careers were now making careers out of having babies. So rejoiced *Life* magazine in a 1956 paean to the movement of American women back to the home.

In a New York hospital, a woman had a nervous breakdown when she found she could not breastfeed her baby. In other hospitals, women dying of cancer refused a drug which research had proved might save their lives: its side effects were said to be unfeminine. "If I have only one life, let me live it as a blonde," a larger-than-life-sized picture of a pretty, vacuous woman proclaimed from newspaper, magazine, and drugstore ads. And across America, three out of every ten women dyed their hair blonde. They ate a chalk called Metrecal, instead of food, to shrink to the size of the thin young models. Department-store buyers reported that American women, since 1939, had become three and four sizes smaller. "Women are out to fit the clothes, instead of vice-versa," one buyer said.

Interior decorators were designing kitchens with mosaic murals and original paintings, for kitchens were once again the center of women's lives. Home sewing became a million-dollar industry. Many women no longer left their homes, except to shop, chauffeur their children, or attend a social engagement with their husbands. Girls were growing up in America without ever having jobs outside the home. In the late fifties, a sociological phenomenon was suddenly remarked: a third of American women now worked, but most were no longer young and very few were pursuing careers. They were married women who held part-time jobs, selling or secretarial, to put their husbands through school, their sons through college, or to help pay the mortgage. Or they were widows supporting families. Fewer and fewer women were entering professional work. The shortages in the nursing, social work, and teaching professions caused crises in almost every American city. Concerned over the Soviet Union's lead in the space race, scientists noted that America's greatest source of unused brain power was women. But girls would not study physics: it was "unfeminine." A girl refused a science fellowship at Johns Hopkins to take a job in a real-estate office. All she wanted, she said, what every American girl wanted—to get married, have four children and live in a nice house in a nice suburb.

The suburban housewife—she was the dream image of the young American women and the envy, it was said, of women all over the world. The American housewife—freed by science and labour-saving appliances from the drudgery, the dangers of child-birth and the illnesses of her grandmother. She was healthy, beautiful, educated, concerned only about her husband, her children, her home. She had found true feminine fulfilment. As a housewife and a mother, she was respected as a full and equal partner to man in his world. She was free to choose automobiles, clothes, appliances, supermarkets; she had everything that women ever dreamed of.

In the fifteen years after World War II, this mystique of feminine fulfilment became the cherished and self-perpetuating core of contemporary American culture.

Millions of women lived their lives in the image of those pretty pictures of the American suburban housewife, kissing their husbands goodbye in front of the picture window, depositing their stationwagons-full of children at school, and smiling as they ran the new electric waxer over the spotless kitchen floor. They baked their own bread, sewed their own and their children's clothes, kept their new washing machines and dryers running all day. They changed the sheets on the beds twice a week instead of once, took the rug-hooking class in adult education, and pitied their poor frustrated mothers, who had dreamed of having a career. Their only dream was to be perfect wives and mothers; their highest ambition to have five children and a beautiful house, their only fight to get and keep their husbands. They had no thought for the unfeminine problems of the world outside the home; they wanted the men to make the major decisions. They gloried in their role as women, and wrote proudly on the census blank: "Occupation: housewife."

For over fifteen years, the words written for women, and the words women used when they talked to each other, while their husbands sat on the other side of the room and talked shop or politics or septic tanks, were about problems with their children, or how to keep their husbands happy, or improve their children's school, or cook chicken or make slipcovers. Nobody argued whether women were inferior or superior to men; they were simply different. Words like "emancipation" and "career" sounded strange and embarrassing; no one had used them for years. When a Frenchwoman named Simone de Beauvoir wrote a book called *The Second Sex*, an American critic commented that she obviously "didn't know what life was all about," and besides, she was talking about French women. The "woman problem" in America no longer existed.

If a woman had a problem in the 1950s and 1960s, she knew that something must be wrong with her marriage, or with herself. Other women were satisfied with their lives, she thought. What kind of a woman was she if she did not feel this mysterious fulfilment waxing the kitchen floor? She was so ashamed to admit her dissatisfaction that she never knew how many other women shared it. If she tried to tell her husband, he didn't understand what she was talking about. She did not really understand it herself. For over fifteen years women in America found it harder to talk about this problem than about sex. Even the psychoanalysts had no name for it. When a woman went to psychiatrist for help, as many women did, she would say, "I'm so ashamed," or "I must be hopelessly neurotic." "I don't know what's wrong with women today," a suburban psychiatrist said uneasily. "I only know something is wrong because most of my patients happen to be women. And their problem isn't sexual." Most women with this problem did not go to see a psychoanalyst, however. "There's nothing wrong really," they kept telling themselves. "There isn't any problem."

But on an April morning in 1959, I heard a mother of four, having coffee with four other mothers in a suburban development fifteen miles from New York, say in a tone of quiet desperation, "the problem." And the others knew, without words, that she was not talking about a problem with her husband, or her children, or her home. Suddenly they realized they all shared the same problem, the problem that has no name. They began, hesitantly, to talk about it. Later, after they had picked up their children at nursery school and taken them home to nap, two of the women cried, in sheer relief, just to know thy were not alone.

Gradually I came to realize that the problem that has no name was shared by countless women in America. As a magazine writer I often interviewed women about problems with their children, or their marriages, or their houses, or their communities. But after a while I began to recognize the telltale signs of this other problem. I saw the same signs in suburban ranch houses and split-levels on Long Island and in New Jersey and Westchester County; in colonial houses in a small Massachusetts town; on patios in the Midwest. Sometimes I sensed the problem, not as a reporter, but as a suburban housewife, for during this time I was also bringing up my own three children in Rockland County, New York. I heard echoes of the problem in college dormitories and semi-private maternity wards, at PTA meetings and luncheons of the League of Women Voters, at suburban cocktail parties, in station wagons waiting for trains, and in snatches of conversation overheard at Schrafft's. The groping words I heard from other women, on quiet afternoons when children were at school or on quiet evenings when husbands worked late, I think I understood first as a woman long before I understood their larger social and psychological implications.

Androgyny as an Ideal for Human Development

Ann Ferguson

ANNE FERGUSON *is Professor of philosophy and women's studies at the University of Massachessets—Amherst. She is the author of* Blood and the Root *and many articles in feminist political theory.*

Androgyny: The Ideal Defined

The term "androgyny" has Greek roots: *Andros* means man and *gyne* woman. An androgynous person would combine some of each of the characteristic traits, skills, and interests that we now associate with the stereotypes of masculinity and femininity. It is not accurate to say that the ideal androgynous person would be both masculine and feminine, for there are negative and distorted personality characteristics associated in our minds with these ideas.[1] Furthermore, as we presently understand these stereotypes, they exclude each other. A masculine person is active, independent, aggressive (demanding), more self-interested than altruistic, competent and interested in physical activities, rational, emotionally controlled, and self-disciplined. A feminine person, on the other hand, is passive, dependent, nonassertive, more altruistic than self-interested (supportive of others), neither physically competent nor interested in becoming so, intuitive but not rational, emotionally open, and impulsive rather than self-disciplined. Since our present conceptions of masculinity and feminity thus defined exclude each other, we must think of an ideal androgynous person as one to whom these categories do not apply—one who is neither masculine nor feminine, but human: who transcends those old categories in such a way as to be able to develop positive human potentialities denied or only realized in an alienated fashion in the current stereotypes.

The ideal androgynous being, because of his or her combination of general traits, skills, and interests, would have no internal blocks to attaining self-esteem. He or she would have the desire and ability to do socially meaningful productive activity (work), as well as the desire and ability to be autonomous and to relate lovingly to other human beings. Of course, whether or not such an individual would be able to *achieve* a sense of autonomy, self-worth, and group contribution will depend importantly on the way the society in which he/she lives is structured. For example, in a classist society characterized by commodity production, none of these goals is attainable by anyone, no matter how androgynous, who comes from a class lacking the material resources to acquire (relatively) nonalienating work. In a racist and sexist society there are social roles and expectations placed upon the individual which present him/her with a conflict situation: Either express this trait (skill, interest) and be considered a social deviant or outcast, or repress the trait and be socially accepted. The point, however, is that the androgynous person has the requisite skills and interests to be able to achieve these goals if only the society is organized appropriately.

Limits to Human Development: The Natural Complement Theory

There are two lines of objection that can be raised against the view that androgyny is an ideal for human development: first, that it is not possible, given the facts we know about human nature; and second, that even if it is possible, there is no reason to think it particularly desirable that people be socialized to develop the potential for androgyny. In this section I shall present and discuss natural complement theories of male/female human nature and the normative conclusions about sex roles.

There are two general facts about men and women and their roles in human societies that must be taken into account by any theory of what is possible in social organization of sex roles: first, the biological differences between men and women—in the biological reproduction of children, in relative physical strength, and in biological potential for aggressive (dominant, demanding) behavior; and second, the fact that all known human societies have had a sexual division of labor.

According to the natural complement theory, there are traits, capacities, and interests which inhere in men and women simply because of their biological differences, and which thus define what is normal "masculine" and normal "feminine" behavior. Since men are stronger than women, have bodies better adapted for running and throwing, and have higher amounts of the male hormone androgen, which is linked to aggressive behavior (cf. Maccoby, 1966), men have a greater capacity for heavy physical labor and for aggressive behavior (such as war). Thus it is natural that men are the breadwinners and play the active role in the production of commodities in society and in defending what the society sees as its interests in war. Since women bear children, it is natural that they have a maternal, nurturing instinct which enables them to be supportive of the needs of children, perceptive and sensitive to their needs, and intuitive in general in their understanding of the needs of people.

The natural complement theory about what men and women should do (their moral and spiritual duties, ideal love relations, etc.) is based on this conception of what are the fundamental biologically based differences between men and women. The universal human sexual division of labor is not only natural, but also desirable: Men should work, provide for their families, and when necessary, make war; women should stay home, raise their children, and, with their greater emotionality and sensitivity, administer to the emotional needs of their men and children.

The ideal love relationship in the natural complement view is a heterosexual relationship in which man and woman complement each other. On this theory, woman needs man, and man, woman; they need each other essentially because together they form a whole being. Each of them is incomplete without the other; neither could meet all their survival and emotional needs alone. The woman needs the man as the active agent, rationally and bravely confronting nature and competitive social life; while the man needs the woman as his emotional guide, ministering to the needs he doesn't know he has himself, performing the same function for the children, and being the emotional nucleus of the family to harmonize all relationships. Love between man and woman is the attraction of complements, each being equally powerful and competent in his or her own sphere—man in the world, woman in the home—but each incompetent in the sphere of the other and therefore incomplete without the other.

The validity of the natural complement theory rests on the claim that there are some natural instincts (drives and abilities) inherent in men and women that are so powerful that they will determine the norm of masculine and feminine behavior for men and women under any conceivable cultural and economic conditions. That is, these natural instincts will determine not only what men and women can do well, but also what will be the most desirable (individually satisfying and socially productive) for them.

Even strong proponents of the natural complement theory have been uneasy with the evidence that in spite of "natural" differences between men and women, male and female sex roles are not inevitable.

Not only are there always individual men and women whose abilities and inclinations make them exceptions to the sexual stereotypes in any particular society, but there is also a wide cross-cultural variation in just what work is considered masculine or feminine. Thus, although all known societies indeed do have a sexual division of labor, the evidence is that what behavior is considered masculine and what feminine is learned through socialization rather than mandated through biological instincts. So, for example, childcare is said by the proponents of the natural complement theory to be women's work, supposedly on the grounds that women have a natural maternal instinct that men lack, due to women's biological role in reproduction. And it is true that in the vast majority of societies in the sexual division of labor women do bear a prime responsibility for childcare. However, there are some societies where that is not so. The Arapesh have both mother and father play an equally strong nurturant role (cf. Mead, 1963). A case of sex-role reversal in childcare would be the fabled Amazons, in whose society those few men allowed to survive past infancy reared the children. In the case of the Amazons, whose historical existence may never be conclusively proved, what is important for the purposes of our argument is not the question of whether such a culture actually existed. Rather, insofar as it indicated that an alternative sexual division of labor was possible, the existence of the myth of the Amazon culture in early Western civilizations was an ongoing challenge to the natural complement theory.

It is not only the sexual division of labor in childcare that varies from society to society, but also other social tasks. Natural complement theorists are fond of arguing that because men are physically stronger than women and more aggressive, it is a natural division of labor for men to do the heavy physical work of society as well as that of defense and war. However, in practice, societies have varied immensely in the ways in which heavy physical work is parcelled out. In some African societies women do all the heavy work of carrying wood and water, and in most South American countries Indian men and women share these physical chores. In the Soviet Union women do the heavy manual labor involved in construction jobs, while men do the comparatively light (but higher-status) jobs of running the machinery ("Political Economy of Women," 1973). In predominantly agricultural societies, women's work overlaps men's. From early American colonial times, farm women had to be prepared to fight native Americans and work the land in cooperation with men. Israeli women make as aggressive and dedicated soldiers as Israeli men. Furthermore, if we pick any one of the traits supposed to be primarily masculine (e.g., competitiveness, aggressiveness, egotism), we will find not only whole societies of both men and women who seem to lack these traits, but also whole societies that exhibit them.[2]

Further evidence that general sex-linked personality traits are learned social roles rather than inevitable biological developments is found in studies done on hermaphrodites (Maccoby, 1966). When children who are biological girls, but because of vestigial penises are mistaken for boys, are trained into male sex roles, they develop the cultural traits associated with males in their society and seem to be well adjusted to their roles.

Faced with the variability of the sexual division of labor and the evidence that human beings as social animals develop their self-concept and their sense of values from imitating models in their community rather than from innate biological urges, the natural complement theorists fall back on the thesis that complementary roles for men and women, while not inevitable, are desirable. Two examples of this approach are found in the writings of Jean-Jacques Rousseau (in *Emile*) and in the contemporary writer George Gilder (1973). Both of these men are clearly male supremacists in that they feel women ought to be taught to serve, nurture, and support men.[3] What is ironic about their arguments is their belief in the biological inferiority of men, stated explicitly in Gilder and implicitly in Rousseau. Rousseau's train of reasoning suggests that men can't be nurturant and emotionally sensitive the way women can, so if we train women to be capable of abstract reasoning, to be self-interested and assertive, women will be able to do both male and female roles, and what will be left, then, for men to excel at? Gilder feels that men need to be socialized to be the breadwinners for children and a nurturant wife, because otherwise men's aggressive and competitive tendencies would make it impossible for them to cooperate in productive social work.

The desirability of complementary sex roles is maintained from a somewhat different set of premises in Lionel Tiger's book *Men in Groups* (1969). Tiger argues that the earliest sexual division of labor in hunting and gathering societies required men to develop a cooperative division of tasks in order to achieve success in hunting. Therefore, men evolved a biological predisposition toward "male bonding" (banding together into all-male cohort groups) that women lack (presumably because activities like gathering and childcare didn't require a cooperative division of tasks that would develop female bonding). Because of this lack of bonding, women are doomed to subjection by men, for this biological asset of men is a trait necessary for achieving political and social power.

It is hard to take these arguments seriously. Obviously, they are biased toward what would promote male interests and give little consideration to female interests. Also, they reject an androgynous ideal for human development, male and female, merely on the presumption that biological lacks in either men or women make it an unattainable ideal. It simply flies in the face of counterevidence (for example, single fathers in our society) to argue as Gilder does that men will not be providers and relate to family duties of socializing children unless women center their life around the nurturing of men. And to argue as Tiger does that women cannot bond ignores not only the present example of the autonomous women's movement, but also ethnographic examples of women acting as a solidarity group in opposing men. The women of the Ba-Ila in southern Africa may collectively refuse to work if one has a grievance against a man (Smith and Dale, 1920). A more likely theory of bonding seems to be that it is not biologically based but learned through the organization of productive and reproductive work.

Source: Mary Vetterling-Braggin, Frederick Elliston and Jane English, eds. *Feminism and Philosophy.* Totwa, N.J.: Rowman and Allanheld, 1977, pp.45-51. Copyright © 1977 by Littlefield, Adams & Co.

Notes

[1] I owe these thoughts to Jean Eishtain and members of the Valley Women's Union in Northampton, Massachusetts, from discussions on androgyny.

[2] Contrast the Stone Age tribe recently discovered in the Philippines, where competition is unknown, with the competitive male and female Dobus from Melanesia. See Ruth Benedict (1934).

[3] Rousseau says, in a typical passage from *Emile*, "When once it is proved that men and women are and ought to be unlike in constitution and in temperament, it follows that their education should be different." And on a succeeding page he concludes, "A woman's education must therefore be planned in relation to man. To be pleasing in his sight, to win his respect and love, to train him in childhood, to tend him in manhood, to counsel and console, to make his life pleasant and happy, these are the duties of woman for all time, and this is what she should be taught while she is young. The further we depart from this principle, the further we shall be from our own good, and all our precepts will fail to secure her happiness or our own" (Rousseau, 1911, pp.326, 328). Gilder's conclusion is as follows: "But at a profounder level the women are tragically wrong. For they fail to understand their own sexual power; and they fail to perceive the sexual constitution of our society, or if they see it, they underestimate its importance to our civilization and to their own interest in order and stability. In general across the whole range of the society, marriage and careers—and thus social order—will be best served if most men have a position of economic superiority over the relevant women in his [sic] community and if in most jobs in which colleagues must work together, the sexes tend to be segregated either by level or function" (Gilder, 1973, p.108).

References

Benedict, Ruth (1934), *Patterns of Culture,* Boston, Haughton Mifflin.

Gilder, George (1973). *Sexual Suicide,* New York, Bantam.

Maccoby, Eleanor, E., ed. (1966). *The Development of Sex Differences.* Stanford, Stanford University Press.

Mead, Margaret (1963). *Sex and Temperament,* New York, William Morrow.

"Political Economy of Women" issue (1973). *Review of Radical Political Economics* (Summer 1973).

Rousseau, Jean-Jacques (1911). *Emile,* New York, E.P. Dutton.

Smith, Edwin W., and Andrew M. Dale (1920). *The Ila-speaking Peoples of Northern Rhodesia,* London, Macmillan.

Tiger, Lionel (1969). *Men in Groups,* New York, Random House.

Christianity and Patriarchy: The Odd Alliance

Jean Bethke Elshtain

JEAN BETHKE ELSHTAIN *is Professor in the Departments of Political Science and Philosophy at Vanderbilt University.*

In one sense the title of my paper is odd. For surely there is nothing at all odd about an alliance between Christianity and patriarchy given the social and historical context in which Christianity took root and began to flourish. That world was not only "patriarchal," a term that is by no means self-evident and can be understood a number of different ways, but structured along lines that *guaranteed* sex segregation, on the one hand, and *required* sex collaboration, on the other.

Let me explain. If one goes back to the Greeks, one sees that war from the beginning was construed as the natural state of humankind. The Greek city-state was a community of warriors whose political rights were determined by the fundamental privilege of the soldier to decide his own fate. There was a direct line of descent from the Homeric warrior assemblies to Athenian naval democracy. Civic identity was restricted to those who bore arms. The formal definition of justice, repeated by Thrasymachus in his sparring with Socrates in the first book of Plato's *Republic,* was "the interest of the stronger." The Greek citizen army was an expression of the Greek *polis;* its creation was one of the chief concerns and chief consequences of the formation of the city-state. In Sparta, the army organized in mess groups was substituted for the family as the basic element of the state. Another custom of the male group, homosexuality, was developed and institutionalized, most systematically at Thebes in the 4th century, to create a Sacred Band of lovers fighting side by side. Such institutions served to ensure that sense of fellowship which was deemed a prerequisite of disciplined courage in war, of willingness to risk death together.[1]

Not having the bodies of protectors, of men constituted as warriors, women were those who had to be defended, whose role in the household, the *oikos*, was a necessary precondition for, but not an integral part of, the structure of the dominant political warrioring world. Needless to say, these presumptions were geared rigidly towards preserving sex segregation even as they required sex collaboration to hold the overall system intact.

The human body in Greek, then Roman, antiquity was wholly conscripted into society, an insight I owe to the great historian of late antiquity, Peter Brown. His is an important point and I shall repeat it. Brown's story goes like this. The pre-Christianized individual was not free to withhold his or her body from conscription into the extant social order. One could, with Socrates, endorse withdrawal of the soul from the body but one could not take oneself out of the group—one could not constitute one's body as a protest against its conscription as a social body in the form of the warrior, the slave, or the producer of children for the city. The classical, pre-Christian view, then, is that the city-state should have *complete control of human bodies* for the purpose of labor, procreation and war.[2]

The human body, hence the self, existed at the behest of the wider social order. Protest was rare. Augustine argues that Rome perfected the regime of *cupiditas* run rampant, the triumph of a lust to dominate. The distinctive mark of Roman life as a *civitas terrena,* an earthly city, was greed and lust for possession which presumed a right of exploitation. This became a foundation for human relationships, warping and perverting personality, marriage, family, indeed all things.

We will return to Augustine from time to time, but first let us look to Christianity's emergence in this world of the triumphant *Pax Romana*. Securing the historic context as a preliminary to making judgements is essential. Christ's mission began and ended in a dreary outpost of a corrupt, power-drunk empire already on a path from state worship to emperor deification to all the sordid evils of Caesarism. The Roman Empire, through guile and even genocide, had extended its sway over the then-known world. The only politics in the Empire was the passivity of subjects quashed by fear and hopelessness or the power-machinations of those spurred by greed and ambition. Those few voices from the past who rose to condemn Caesarism and to lament the loss of the *res publica* passed or were forced from the scene.

In my book, *Public Man, Private Woman,*[3] I issued

a salvo and I shall repeat it here: Christianity ushered a moral revolution into the world which dramatically, and for the better, transformed the prevailing images of the human person, male and female, and the relations between various human activities and the creation of shared social life. Christianity redeemed and sanctioned each individual life as well as everyday life, especially the lives of society's victims, and granted each a new-found dignity. The warrioring politics of the ancient world found itself put on trial, and convicted, for its violence and its perverted celebration of domination and acquisition.

The heady drama of this moral revolution, with its politically jarring implications, is a story that has lost none of its excitement. The legitimacy once accorded automatically to the claims of the city-state and the empire upon the human body of each and every one now had to make its case and could not be assumed unproblematically. The human body could withdraw from the demands placed upon it by society. The sexual-social contract could be broken. One was free to withhold or to surrender the body. Freedom of the will could be brought to bear on the body as a tangible locus, a sign, of a newfound relation of the self to the social world. One need not become a social body in the warrioring and householding ways. One could set the body apart as the temple of God. An elemental freedom was endorsed. Liberated individuals formed groups to validate their newfound individualities and to shore up the transformed and symbolically charged good represented by the new social body.

Women were implicated in the scheme of things from the start. The life of Jesus is peopled with women at many of its crucial stages and both men and women are involved in the spread of His message after His death and resurrection. Jesus displays His divine origins by signs and healing. He heals both men and women. People of both sexes are baptized. The dedication of men and women to Christ's work is evident throughout the New Testament. There is, of course, the oft-quoted passage in Galatians 3:28 that in Christ there is neither male nor female, Jew nor Gentile, slave nor free, but all are one. Some scholars have argued that in early Christianity the initial burst of human liberation extended to women as well as to men in a very high degree. I think this judgement is essentially correct but that does not make Jesus or the early Christians forerunners in some direct sense of our modern, secular notions of what equality between the sexes is or requires—a point I shall return to.

What does emerge is a new image of the human body and the body social, a radical notion of loving thy neighbor, a breakdown of old strictures of taboo and uncleanness, knowing violations of the Law to reaffirm its spirit at a deeper level, a sense of hidden-ness, mystery, surprise, discovery and joy of life. Jesus meant to put the security of the secure in jeopardy. The aim of the gospel, René Girard has suggested, was to liberate human beings from the need to have victims and to sacralize the victims they have.[4] It is to have life and to have it more abundantly. Jesus in this sense threatened "the system" through a mission and a gospel that made visible the ugly passions that hold intact ossified systems of power.

Jesus rejected the notion that one must rule others tyrannically or submit and be tyrannized—the Roman vision of governing. Early Christians worked to extirpate the barbarism of the Roman arena, ended infanticide and the abandonment of infants (disproportionately female), dictated that children should not be maimed, and devirilized the warrior. The Council of Nicea declared that the Christian who abandoned warrioring and returned to it "as dogs to their vomit" had to do penance. The priest foreswore use of his sexual instrument. It is impossible to overemphasize the drama and importance of these matters. They helped to lay the basis for the idea of human society based on the sacredness of the individual and the ideal of inviolate human personality.[5]

The best we can do today is to provide intimations of Christ's extraordinary appeal in a world in which force and violence had debased politics and there was no such thing as active participation in public life. How could one possibly speak of a common good in a world composed of victors and victims, imperialists and colonialists? The early Christians did endorse rendering unto Caesar that which was Caesar's, but that turned out to be minimal: obedience to laws aimed at public peace, payment of taxes, at first a refusal to serve in armies. What was not Caesar's was control of life's ultimate purpose and meaning and the human being's vocation and calling on this earth. Christian doctrine drained the empire of its claims to divinity and omnipotence. Possessing free will, the bearers of responsible moral agency, Christians could and might be called upon to act against the state, to resist its claims and impositions upon individuals, their bodies, their minds. This was something new under the sun: principled resistance to public power. The notion of moral revolt against public power opened up a range of options, duties, responsibilities, dilemmas and reassessments not possible in pre-Christian epochs—for males and females alike.

Welcomed into the new community, the *res publica Christiana,* the woman shared in the activities and ideals that were its living tissue. She found that qualities most often associated with her activities as mother—giving birth to and sustaining human life, an ethic of responsibility toward the helpless, the vulnerable, the weak, gentleness, mercy and compassion—were celebrated. The realm of necessity generated its own sanctity.[6] Women, like men, might be called upon to die for a cause, not as Homeric heroes wielding great swords, but as witnesses to the strength of their convictions.

Recall the rigidity of classical presumptions, including the notion that women and men were confined to entirely separate spheres on the basis of what their innate being enabled them to realize: this was the reigning view with few exceptions. Christianity defied this rigid separation of human beings by declaring that every human being is equal in God's eyes. The new Christian community included as central two groups excluded from the classical city—women and the poor. As Peter Brown argues in his book, *The Cult of the Saints,* women took on a public role in their own right in their relation to poor and sick. They founded shrines and poorhouses in their own names and got to pick some of their own kin—their special saints—and to go into the public world out of devotion to these self-chosen kin.[7]

God's grace was available to all. God's love, Christian Agape, very different from the classical Eros, infused human life. We must love one another. We are, argued Augustine, well advised to judge ourselves and others not by our acquisitions, or our power to compel, but by what it is we and they love. The new Christian community was available to any who had a hunger and thirst for righteousness. The Christian city of God on pilgrimage on this earth is "set apart by a holy yearning," in Augustine's phrase.[8] And that yearning includes hope: hope lodged in the capacity of human beings to long for something different, to examine the nature of their relationship with their immediate environment, above all, to establish their identities by refusing to be engulfed in the unthinking habits of their fellows.

The Christian recognizes an intimate dependence on the life around him or her and is aware of the tenacity of the links that bind us to the world. What is "our business within this common moral life," Augustine queried, and that is where I shall turn next. But, for a moment, one brief additional moment of honor for our early forebears: How different were the Christian band of men, women, children, the infirm, the possessed, the crippled from the warrior-citizen of the city-state? That Christianity failed to live up to the promise of its early mission in some utopian sense surprises none of us in our skeptical and cynical time. We know the world is a most intractable place. But that Christianity secured a moral revolution and established a set of claims which must be faced and answered today is an essential feature of any current exploration of men, women and human society and of that "odd alliance" signalled by the title of my paper.

All mass, charismatic movements, once they begin to take institutional form and lay plans for the long haul, lose the edge of their early enthusiasm and radicalism. Human beings are open to change and surprise but desirous, as well, especially in a world of such heightened human vulnerability as late classical antiquity, for safety and security. There were institutions in place, set up, at least ostensibly, to guarantee that safety and security, including armies and city-states and empires. For Rome, as horrible as its rule had been, had provided order.

It is difficult for us to understand late antiquity's obsessions with order living, as we do, in a society which has been mercifully spared much of the traumatic disorder of the twentieth century. Confronted with social and economic dislocation, barbarian invasions, corruption and debauchery in high places, it is small wonder indeed that Christians looked to and for order. The early bands of believers awaiting Christ's second coming gave way to settled, rule-governed forms of social life. People brought to this enterprise both the old and the new. None of us can ever leap out of his or her historic skin. Order got re-created, an uneven amalgam of old and new. Men, not surprisingly, had the advantage in terms of traditional orderings of authority. Women had newfound strength and purpose. The educated of both sexes had efficacy the nonliterate majority lacked. Those who knew Roman law shaped Christian life legalistically in ways that simultaneously safeguarded and veered away from the heady promise of Jesus' transvaluation of ancient virtues.

It would be foolish to look for a "key" here—either some clear-cut evidence of evil male intent to reenslave women or a definitive moment when Christianity made its peace with the inherited hierarchism of antiquity. The process was fitful, uneven, filled with anomalies. I can but indicate the lineaments of a much longer, much richer story. Could Christians be pacifists in a world in which others were committed to collective violence? Would that not guarantee the destruction of the Christian community?

The solution: a partial compromise, the notion of the just war as adumbrated by Augustine. Yes, violence is evil. Yes, the Christian must put it on trial. Yes, it is to be eschewed whenever possible. But no, it is not possible to evade violence altogether, for one's responsibility to protect a way of life or to spare the innocent from certain harm may commit the Christian, in the earthly city, to a lesser evil in order to prevent a greater one. Our Christian forebears could find no institutional forms to "hold" intact and guarantee the continuance of a stance of pure, collective non-violence. The warrior got partially resurrected as a just warrior, not the lustfully destructive warrior of old. He must do penance for his warrioring but he must sometimes be called upon to do evil to prevent evil.[9]

Similarly, there was no available social form to hold

a radically transformed vision of the full implications of ontological sex equality once the early utopian Christian communities made way for more routinized life. Rather than return to the rigidly sexually compartmentalized institutions of classical antiquity, a Christian notion of the family, of male and female helpmeets, and of conjugal sexual equality emerged. Conjugal equality, that is, placing the same sexual strictures on male and female and seeing in violations equal sins for each, did not imply absolute parity in male and female authority. The husband remained the head of the household. He was enjoined to "govern" gently, to avoid domination and cruelty, knowing his mate and children were equally children of God.

Why lodge final authority in the male head of household? The force of tradition explains much if not most. But there is more. Authority was construed as singular and descending, from the God-head and emanating downward. Earthly authority must emulate that Godly authority. This pushed towards verticality in human constructions of authoritative relationships. Hierarchism is present inside female communities as well. Over time the crust of custom became hardened, so many sedimented layers separating levels from one another. This isn't all that happened, but it is one major development and it guaranteed that over time, as Roman law became engrafted onto ecclesiastical institutions, the "naturalness" of hierarchical order got enshrined and became difficult to challenge.

Hence the odd alliance, though, as I indicated, it is not odd at all considering the historic moment and available institutional forms. What is remarkable is that the notion of ontological sexual equality was sustained even as institutional forms replicated much, though by no means all, of what had preceded. It is important to remember that women had weapons with which to fight—if you will forgive the martial metaphor. Their *dignitatis* was secure, although their earthly status might be shaky. Augustine is a fascinating transitional figure in all of this because he shares the view of a fundamental equality between the sexes, women being equals with men in the most important human capacity—free will—thus making them responsible human agents. Yet he also endorses the unitary model of authority, emanating towards a single head.[10]

Forgive me an extended Augustinian moment—for I think what Augustine struggled with helps to illuminate many current debates and concerns and shows how women may have sustained losses in Western history as it moved towards secular modernity. For example, Augustine defends the violated virtues of women raped in war, insisting that women should not punish themselves, although inevitably such an event engenders a sense of shame. Violation without the will's consent cannot pollute the character—a claim

"forgotten" to later history. In *The City of God*, Book 1, 19, he writes: "We have given clear reason for our assertion that when physical violation has involved no change in the intention of chastity by any consent to the wrong, then the guilt attaches only to the ravishers, and not at all to the woman forcibly ravished without any consent on her part. We are defending the chastity not only of the minds but even of the bodies of ravished Christian women. Will our opponents dare to contradict us?"[11]

Augustine goes on to tell us, in Book 11, 2, that in his pastoral tasks he administered consolation to women who "felt the pangs of shame," urging them "not to be ashamed at being alive, since they have no possible reason for being ashamed at having sinned.[12] Here Augustine challenges the constant attention to reputation required of Roman women, a constraining and oppressive demand that called upon women who had been violated to maintain their reputations by committing suicide. This is one of many points at which Augustine is remarkably enlightened, not just for his time but ours. Think about how oppressed women have been by the lurid insistencies of "reputation" in many historic epochs. "What will the neighbors think?"

He also attacks the *Lex Vaconia*, which forbade the appointment of a woman, even an only daughter, as heir. "I cannot quote, or even imagine, a more inequitable law."[13] He repudiates the Roman cult of Fortuna in which propitiation was offered to an unpredictable, arbitrary, erratic and, to the Romans, prototypically female goddess. Perhaps most importantly, whatever his acquiescence in the received social arrangements of this time, Augustine left as a permanent legacy a condemnation of that lust for dominion which distorts the personality, marriage, the family and all other aspects of political and social life. "He who desires the glory of possession," Augustine notes, " would feel that his power were diminished if he were obliged to share it with any living associate," he is one who cherishes his own manhood.[14] Women can be citizens of both the city of God and the earthly city. They, too, can be dominated by *caritas or cupiditas*. They can choose either to be dominated by "the flesh" or to embrace the ensouled body, joining other pilgrims in their sojourn on this earth. The blame lies not in our flesh—no one is evil by nature[15]—but in our capture by the " rule of the flesh" which is a fault of the mind and heart, not so much a failure of the body and certainly not a foreordained "given" of human existence.

Whether, and to what extent, women have been powerful or powerless, silenced or heard, revered or reviled in past societies, Western and non-Western, is an assignment for a lifetime. But we do have evidence, according to Peggy Reeves Sanday in her important work, *Female Power and Male Dominance*, that women's economic and political power and authority is most likely to appear where one finds a magico-religious association between maternity and social good."[16] Catholic Christianity valorized this association through veneration of the Holy Mother, thus contributing to a tangled skein that offers pictures of formal male power being balanced, or even undermined, by informal female power.

In societies, past and present, in which the home is the hub of human life, an arena of economic production as well as human procreation, a school, a hospice, a symbolically and actually potent place, women are often the repositories of several understandings of power associated with that sphere. Such female power is complementary to the more institutionalized, juridical authority of men. The roles and power ascribed to women are informal and not institutionalized, in contrast with the legitimated statuses and authority attributed to men. How interesting and how necessary to our odd alliance!

What are we to make of all this? First, it helps us to understand that secular male dominance is most visible and extreme in societies in which complementarity of powers has given way to an enhancement and expansion of institutionalized male authority accompanied by a simultaneous diminution in women's domestic, sacral and informal authority. As the world of female power recedes, the sphere of male power encroaches, absorbing more and more features of social life into the orbit of the jurido-political, the bureaucratized, the "legitimately" powerful. This has happened in North America and Western Europe given the cultural delegitimation of the mother," hence of the evocative power of her most cherished symbol.[17]

Women in secular society are left with few apparent options: to acquiesce in their historic loss of symbolic-domestic authority, to manipulate their diminished social role as mothers inside increasingly powerless families, or to join forces with the men, assuming "masculine" roles and identities and competing for power on established, institutionalized terms, whether inside churches or not. In other words, one ends the odd alliance by turning the new woman into the old man: we all become patriarchs, that is, beings vested with hierarchical and legalistic power and authority.

If one were to summarize current feminist demands, inside and outside churches, it would be for "equality." Presumably, if equality existed, patriarchal imbalance would not. But equality is an essentially contested concept. Interpretations over its meaning fill rows and rows of library shelves and lie at the heart of many political stories, both glorious and terrible. Do we have in mind formal-legalistic equality? Equality of opportunity? Equality of respect? Equality of results? These are the nasty questions political

theorists ask and may explain why we are sometimes a drag at social gatherings.

Each of these equalities shares some features with the others, yet each also diverges importantly. Each requires different things of us as citizens, believers, thinkers, men and women. To call for equality is the beginning, not the end of the debate. Why? Because, for example, a standard North American understanding of an essentially liberal version of equality commingling of formal-legalistic equality with equality of opportunity is wholly *compatible* with social hierarchies and widely disparate power and privilege. There is no inherent reason why women, at least those of the relatively privileged, well-educated classes, cannot become runners of the liberal procedural race as, in fact, more and more are doing. Much of the demand for equality *inside* churches comes from this essentially liberal construction.

Source: Jean Bethke Elshtain. "Christianity and Patriarchy: The Odd Alliance." *Modern Theology* 9, No. 2 (1993): 109-122. Reprinted with the permission of Basil Blackwell, Ltd.

Notes

[1] For the full story, see Jean Bethke Elshtain, *Women and War* (New York: Basic Books, 1987).

[2] See Brown's, *The Body and the Society* (New York: Columbia University Press, 1988).

[3] Princeton: Princeton University Press, 1981.

[4] See René Girard, "The Extinction of Social Order" in *Salmagundi* (Spring-Summer, 1984) pp.204-237; see also Margaret R. Miles, *Fullness of Life* (Philadelphia: The Westminster Press, 1981).

[5] See the discussion by Glenn Tinder, *The Political Meaning of Christianity* (Baton Rouge: Louisiana State University Press, 1989).

[6] Charles Taylor argues that the affirmation of everyday life is one feature of postReformation Europe and modernity. I have argued for the "redemption of everyday life" in *Public Man, Private Woman*. My argument here is that intimation of this affirmation can be found as a continuing theme in Hebrew covenantal and early Christian communities. See Taylor, *Sources of the Self* (Cambridge, Mass.: Harvard University Press, 1989).

[7] Peter Brown, *The Cult of the Saints* (Chicago: University of Chicago Press, 1981).

[8] For the Augustine material, in general, I rely upon my readings of *The City of God* (New York: Viking Penguin, 1984) and Peter Brown's wonderful biography, *Augustine of Hippo* (Berkeley: University of California Press, 1969).

[9] The classic text is, of course, Book XIX of *The City of God*.

[10] See my discussion in Chapter 2 of *Public Man, Private Woman*.

[11] Penguin Edition, p. 28.

[12] Penguin Edition, p. 49.

[13] Penguin Edition, Book III, 21, p.122.

[14] Here I refer the reader to the discussion and citations in *Women and War*, Chapter 4.

[15] Penguin Edition, Book XIV, 5, pp.554-555.

[16] Cambridge: Cambridge University Press, 1981.

[17] See the discussion in my essay, "The Power and Powerlessness of Women" in *Power Trips and Other Journeys* (Madison: University of Wisconsin Press 1991).

The Ultimate Revolution

Shulamith Firestone

SHULAMITH FIRESTONE *was born in Ottawa, Canada. She published* The Dialectic of Sex, *from which this article was taken, in 1970 at the age of 25. Firestone was one of the founders of the Women's Liberation Movement.*

Before we talk about revolutionary alternatives, let's summarize—to determine the specifics that must be carefully excluded from any new structures. Then we can go on to "utopian speculation" directed by at least negative guidelines.

We have seen how women, biologically distinguished from men, are culturally distinguished from "human." Nature produced the fundamental inequality—half the human race must bear and rear the children of all of them—which was later consolidated, institutionalized, in the interests of men. Reproduction of the species cost women dearly, not only emotionally, psychologically, culturally but even in strictly material (physical) terms: before recent methods of contraception, continuous childbirth led to constant "female trouble," early aging, and death. Women were the slave class that maintained the species in order to free the other half for the business of the world—admittedly often its drudge aspects, but certainly all its creative aspects as well.

This natural division of labor was continued only at great cultural sacrifice: men and women developed only half of themselves, at the expense of the other half. The division of the psyche into male and female to better reinforce the reproductive division was tragic: the hypertrophy in men of rationalism, aggressive drive, the atrophy of their emotional sensitivity was a physical (war) as well as a cultural disaster. The emotionalism and passivity of women increased their suffering (we cannot speak of them in a symmetrical way, since they were victimized as a class by the division). Sexually men and women were channeled into a highly ordered—time, place, procedure, even dialogue—heterosexuality restricted to the genitals, rather than diffused over the entire physical being.

I submit, then, that the first demand for any alternative system must be:

(1)*The freeing of women from the tyranny of their reproductive biology by every means available, and the diffusion of the childbearing and childrearing role to the society as a whole, men as well as women.* There are many degrees of this. Already we have a (hard-won) acceptance of "family planning," if not contraception for its own sake. Proposals are imminent for day-care centers, perhaps even twenty four-hour child-care centers staffed by men as well as women. But this, in my opinion, is timid if not entirely worthless as a transition. We're talking about radical change. And though indeed it cannot come all at once, radical goals must be kept in sight at all times. Day-care centers buy women off. They ease the immediate pressure without asking why that pressure is on women.

At the other extreme there are the more distant solutions based on the potentials of modern embryology, that is, artificial reproduction, possibilities still so frightening that they are seldom discussed seriously. We have seen that the fear is to some extent justified: in the hands of our current society and under the direction of current scientists (few of whom are female or even feminist), any attempted use of technology to "free" anybody is suspect. But we are preparing to talk about speculative systems, and for the purpose of our discussion we must assume flexibility and good intentions in those working out the change.

To thus free women from their biology would be to threaten the *social* unit that is organized around biological reproduction and the subjection of women to their biological destiny, the family. Our second demand will come also as a basic contradiction to the family, this time the family as an *economic* unit:

2)*The full self-determination, including economic independence, of both women and children.* To achieve this goal would require fundamental changes in our social and economic structure. This is why we must talk about a feminist socialism: in the immediate future, under capitalism, there could be at best a token integration of women into the labor force. For women have been found exceedingly useful and cheap as a transient, often highly skilled labor supply,[1] not to mention the economic value of their traditional function, the reproduction and rearing of the next generation of children, a job for which they are now patronized (literally and thus figuratively) rather than paid. But whether or not officially recognized, these are essential economic functions. Women, in this present capacity, are the very foundation of the economic superstructure, vital to its existence[2]. The paeans to self-sacrificing motherhood have a basis in reality: Mom *is* vital to the American way of life, considerably more than apple pie. She is an institution without which the system really would fall apart. In official capitalist terms, the bill for her economic services[3] might run as high as one-fifth of the gross national product. But payment is not the answer. To pay her, as is often discussed seriously in Sweden, is a reform that does not challenge the basic division of labor and thus could never eradicate the disastrous psychological and cultural consequences of that division of labor.

As for the economic independence of children, that is really a pipe dream, realized as yet nowhere in the world. And, in the case of children too, we are talking about more than a fair integration into the labor force; we are talking about the abolition of the labor force itself under a cybernetic socialism, the radical restructuring of the economy to make "work," i.e., wage labor, no longer relevant. In our post-revolutionary society adults as well as children would be provided for independent of their social contributions in the first equal distribution of wealth in history.

We have now attacked the family on a double front, challenging that around which it is organized: reproduction of the species by females and its outgrowth, the physical dependence of women and children. To eliminate these would be enough to destroy the family, which breeds the power psychology. However, we will break it down still further.

(3) *The total integration of women and children into all aspects of the larger society.* All institutions that segregate the sexes, or bar children from adult society, e.g., the modern school, must be destroyed.

These three demands predicate a feminist revolution based on advanced technology. And if the male/female and the adult/child cultural distinctions are destroyed, we will no longer need the sexual repression that maintains these unequal classes, allowing for the first time a "natural" sexual freedom. Thus we arrive at:

(4) *The freedom of all women and children to do whatever they wish to do sexually.* There will no longer be any reason not to. (Past reasons: Full sexuality threatened the continuous reproduction neces-

sary for human survival, and thus, through religion and other cultural institutions, sexuality had to be restricted to reproductive purposes, all nonreproductive sex pleasure considered deviation or worse; The sexual freedom of women would call into question the fatherhood of the child, thus threatening patrimony; child sexuality had to be repressed because it was a threat to the precarious internal balance of the family. These sexual repressions increased proportionately to the degree of cultural exaggeration of the biological family.) In our new society, humanity could finally revert to its natural "polymorphously perverse" sexuality—all forms of sexuality would be allowed and indulged. The fully sexuate mind, realized in the past in only a few individuals (survivors), would become universal. Artificial cultural achievement would no longer be the only avenue to sexuate self-realization: one could now realize oneself fully, simply in the process of being and acting.

Notes

[1] Most bosses would fail badly had they to take over their secretaries' job, or do without them. I know several secretaries who sign without a thought their bosses' names to their own (even brilliant) solutions. The skills of college women especially would cost a fortune reckoned in material terms of male labor.

[2] Margaret Benston ("The Political Economy of Women's Liberation," *Monthly Review*, September 1969), in attempting to show that women's oppression is indeed economic—though previous economic analysis has been incorrect—distinguishes between the male superstructure economy based on *commodity* production (capitalist ownership of the means of production, and wage labor), and the pre-industrial reduplicative economy of the family, production for immediate use. Because the latter is not part of the official contemporary economy, its function at the basis of that economy is often overlooked. Talk of drafting women into the superstructure commodity economy fails to deal with the tremendous amount of necessary production of the traditional kind now performed by women without pay: Who will do it?

[3] Juliet Mitchell, in "Women: The Longest Revolution" *(New Left Review,* December 1966), states that "domestic labor is enormous if qualified in terms of productive labor. In Sweden, 2,340 million hours a year are spent by women in housework compared with 1,290 million hours spent by women in industry." The Chase Manhattan Bank estimates a woman's over-all domestic work week at 99.6 hours. Margaret Benston gives her minimal estimate for a *childless* married woman at 16 hours, close to half of a regular work week; a mother must spend at least six or seven days a week working close to 12 hours.

Love and Knowledge: Emotion in Feminist Epistemology

Alison M. Jaggar

ALISON M. JAGGAR *is a professor of philosophy at the University of Colorado, where she also teaches women's studies. Her areas of specialization include philosophical method, analytical philosophy, and social and political philosophy. Her books include* Feminist Politics and Human Nature *(1983) and* Gender/Body Knowledge: Feminist Reconstructions of Being and Knowing, *co-edited with Suan R. Bordo (1989). Presently she is writing* Feminism and Moral Theory.

The Ideological Function of the Myth

So far, I have spoken very generally of people and their emotions, as though everyone experienced similar emotions and dealt with them in similar ways. It is an axiom of feminist theory, however, that all generalizations about "people" are suspect. The divisions in our society are so deep, particularly the divisions of race, class, and gender, that many feminist theorists would claim that talk about people in general is ideologically dangerous because such talk obscures the fact that no one is simply a person but instead is constituted fundamentally by race, class, and gender. Race, class, and gender shape every aspect of our lives, and our emotional constitution is not excluded. Recognizing this helps us to see more clearly the political functions of the myth of the dispassionate investigator.

Feminist theorists have pointed out that the Western tradition has not seen everyone as equally emotional. Instead, reason has been associated with members of dominant political, social, and cultural groups and emotion with members of subordinate groups. Prominent among those subordinate groups in our society are people of color, except for supposedly "inscrutable Orientals", and women.[1]

Although the emotionality of women is a familiar cultural stereotype, its grounding is quite shaky. Women appear to be more emotional than men because they, along with some groups of people of color, are permitted and even required to express emotion more openly. In contemporary Western culture, emotionally inexpressive women are suspect as not being real women[2] whereas men who express their emotions freely are suspected of being homosexual or in some other way deviant from the masculine ideal. Modern Western men, in contrast with Shakespeare's heroes, for instance, are required to present a facade of coolness, lack of excitement, even boredom, to express emotion only rarely and then for relatively trivial events, such as sporting occasions, where the emotions expressed are acknowledged to be dramatized and so are not taken entirely seriously. Thus, women in our society form the main group allowed or even expected to express emotion. A woman may cry in the face of disaster, and a man of color may gesticulate, but a white man merely sets his jaw.[3]

White men's control of their emotional expression may go to the extremes of repressing their emotions, failing to develop emotionally or even losing the capacity to experience many emotions. Not uncommonly, these men are unable to identify what they are feeling, and even they may be surprised, on occasion, by their own apparent lack of emotional response to a situation, such as a death, where emotional reaction is perceived to be appropriate. In some married couples, the wife is implicitly assigned the job of feeling emotion for both of them. White, college-educated men increasingly enter therapy in order to learn how to "get in touch with" their emotions, a project other men may ridicule as weakness. In therapeutic situations, men may learn that they are just as emotional as women but less adept at identifying their own or others' emotions. In consequence, their emotional development may be relatively rudimentary; this may lead to moral rigidity or insensitivity. Paradoxically, men's lacking awareness of their own emotional responses frequently results in their being more influenced by emotion rather than less.

Although there is no reason to suppose that the thoughts and actions of women are any more influenced by emotion than the thoughts and actions of men, the stereotypes of cool men and emotional women continue to flourish because they are confirmed by an uncritical daily experience. In these circumstances, where there is a differential assignment of reason and emotion, it is easy to see the ideological function of the myth of the dispassionate investigator. It functions, obviously, to bolster the epistemic authority of the currently dominant groups, composed largely of white men, and to discredit the observations and claims of the currently subordinate groups including, of course, the observations and claims of many people of color and women. The more forcefully and vehemently the latter groups express their observations and claims, the more emotional they appear and so the more easily they are discredited. The alleged epistemic authority of the dominant groups then justifies their political authority.

The previous section of this paper argued that dispassionate inquiry was a myth. This section has shown that the myth promotes a conception of epistemological justification vindicating the silencing of those, especially women, who are defined culturally as the bearers of emotion and so are perceived as more "subjective", biased and irrational. In our present social context, therefore, the ideal of the dispassionate investigator is a classist, racist, and especially masculinist myth.[4]

Emotional Hegemony and Emotional Subversion

As we have seen already, mature human emotions are neither instinctive nor biologically determined, although they may have developed out of presocial, instinctive responses. Like everything else that is human, emotions in part are socially constructed; like all social constructs, they are historical products, bearing the marks of the society that constructed them. Within the very language of emotion, in our basic definitions and explanations of what it is to feel pride or embarrassment, resentment or contempt, cultural norms and expectations are embedded. Simply describing ourselves as angry, for instance, presupposes that we view ourselves as having been wronged, victimized by the violation of some social norm. Thus, we absorb the standards and values of our society in the very process of learning the language of emotion, and those standards and values are built into the foundation of our emotional constitution.

Within a hierarchical society, the norms and values that predominate tend to serve the interests of the dominant groups. Within a capitalist, white supremacist, and male-dominant society, the predominant values will tend to be those that serve the interests of rich white men. Consequently, we are all likely to develop an emotional constitution that is quite inappropriate for feminism. Whatever our color, we are likely to feel what Irving Thalberg has called "visceral racism"; whatever our sexual orientation, we are likely to be homophobic; whatever our class, we are likely to be at least somewhat ambitious and competitive; whatever our sex, we are likely to feel contempt for women. Such emotional responses may be rooted in us so deeply that they are relatively impervious to intellectual argument and may recur even when we pay lip service to changed intellectual convictions.[5]

By forming our emotional constitution in particular ways, our society helps to ensure its own perpetuation. The dominant values are implicit in responses taken to be precultural or acultural, our so-called gut responses. Not only do these conservative responses hamper and disrupt our attempts to live in or prefigure alternative social forms but also, and in so far as we take them to be natural responses, they blinker us theoretically. For instance, they limit our capacity for outrage; they either prevent us from despising or encourage us to despise; they lend plausibility to the belief that greed and domination are inevitable human motivations; in sum, they blind us to the possibility of alternative ways of living.

This picture may seem at first to support the positivist claim that the intrusion of emotion only disrupts the process of seeking knowledge and distorts the results of that process. The picture, however, is not complete; it ignores the fact that people do not always experience the conventionally acceptable emotions. They may feel satisfaction rather than embarrassment when their leaders make fools of themselves. They may feel resentment rather than gratitude for welfare payments and hand-me-downs. They may be attracted to forbidden modes of sexual expression. They may feel revulsion for socially sanctioned ways of treating children or animals. In other words, the hegemony that our society exercises over people's emotional constitution is not total.

People who experience conventionally unacceptable, or what I call "outlaw" emotions often are subordinated individuals who pay a disproportionately high price for maintaining the *status quo*. The social situation of such people makes them unable to experience the conventionally prescribed emotions: for instance, people of color are more likely to experience anger than amusement when a racist joke is recounted, and women subjected to male sexual banter are less likely to be flattered than uncomfortable or even afraid.

When unconventional emotional responses are experienced by isolated individuals, those concerned may be confused, unable to name their experience; they may even doubt their own sanity. Women may come to believe that they are "emotionally disturbed" and that the embarrassment or fear aroused in them by male sexual innuendo is prudery or paranoia. When certain emotions are shared or validated by others, however, the basis exists for forming a subculture defined by perceptions, norms, and values that systematically oppose the prevailing perceptions, norms, and values. By constituting the basis for such a subculture, outlaw emotions may be politically because epistemologically subversive.

Outlaw emotions are distinguished by their incompatibility with the dominant perceptions and values, and some, though certainly not all, of these outlaw emotions are potentially or actually feminist emotions.

Emotions become feminist when they incorporate feminist perceptions and values, just as emotions are sexist or racist when they incorporate sexist or racist perceptions and values. For example, anger becomes feminist anger when it involves the perception that the persistent importuning endured by one woman is a single instance of a widespread pattern of sexual harassment, and pride becomes feminist pride when it is evoked by realizing that a certain person's achievement was possible only because that individual overcame specifically gendered obstacles to success.[6]

Outlaw emotions stand in a dialectical relation to critical social theory: at least some are necessary for developing a critical perspective on the world, but they also presuppose at least the beginnings of such a perspective. Feminists need to be aware of how we can draw on some of our outlaw emotions in constructing feminist theory, and also of how the increasing sophistication of feminist theory can contribute to the re-education, refinement, and eventual reconstruction of our emotional constitution.

Outlaw Emotions and Feminist Theory

The most obvious way in which feminist and other outlaw emotions can help in developing alternatives to prevailing conceptions of reality is by motivating new investigations. This is possible because, as we saw earlier, emotions may be long-term as well as momentary; it makes sense to say that someone continues to be shocked or saddened by it situation, even if she is at the moment laughing heartily. As we have seen already, theoretical investigation is always purposeful, and observation always selective. Feminist emotions provide a political motivation for investigation and so help to determine the selection of problems as well as the method by which they are investigated. Susan Griffin makes the same point when she characterizes feminist theory as following "a direction determined by pain, and trauma, and compassion and outrage" (Griffin [1979, p.31]).

As well as motivating critical research, outlaw emotions may also enable us to perceive the world differently from its portrayal in conventional descriptions. They may provide the first indications that something is wrong with the way alleged facts have been constructed, with accepted understandings of how things are. Conventionally unexpected or inappropriate emotions may precede our conscious recognition that accepted descriptions and justifications often conceal as much as reveal the prevailing state of affairs. Only when we reflect on our initially puzzling irritability, revulsion, anger or fear may we bring to consciousness our 'gut-level' awareness that we are in a situation of coercion, cruelty, injustice or danger. Thus, conventionally inexplicable emotions, particularly though not exclusively those experienced by women, may lead us to make subversive observations that challenge dominant conceptions of the *status quo.* They may help us to realize that what are taken generally to be facts have been constructed in a way that obscures the reality of subordinated people, especially women's reality.

But why should we trust the emotional responses of women and other subordinated groups? How can we determine which outlaw emotions are to be endorsed or encouraged and which rejected? In what sense can we say that some emotional responses are more appropriate than others? What reason is there for supposing that certain alternative perceptions of the world, perceptions informed by outlaw emotions, are to be preferred to perceptions informed by conventional emotions? Here I can indicate only the general direction of an answer, whose full elaboration must await another occasion.[7]

I suggest that emotions are appropriate if they are characteristic of a society in which all humans (and perhaps some non-human life too) thrive, or if they are conducive to establishing such a society. For instance, it is appropriate to feel joy when we are developing or exercising our creative powers, and it is appropriate to feel anger and perhaps disgust in those situations where humans are denied their full creativity or freedom. Similarly, it is appropriate to feel fear if those capacities are threatened in us.

This suggestion, obviously, is extremely vague and may even verge on the tautologous. How can we apply it in situations where there is disagreement over what is or is not disgusting or exhilarating or unjust? Here I appeal to a claim for which I have argued elsewhere: the perspective on reality that is available from the standpoint of the subordinated, which in part at least is the standpoint of women, is a perspective that offers a less partial and distorted and therefore more reliable view (Jaggar [1983, ch. 11]). Subordinated people have a kind of epistemological privilege in so far as they have easier access to this standpoint and therefore a better chance of ascertaining the possible beginnings of a society in which all could thrive. For this reason, I would claim that the emotional responses of subordinated people in general, and often of women in particular, are more likely to be appropriate than the emotional responses of the dominant class. That is, they are more likely to incorporate reliable appraisals of situations. Even in contemporary science, where the ideology of dispassionate inquiry is almost overwhelming, it is possible to discover a few examples that seem to support the claim that certain emotions are more appropriate than others in both a moral and epistemological sense. For instance, Hilary Rose claims that women's practice of caring, even though warped by its containment in the alienated context of a coercive sexual division of labor, has nevertheless generated more accurate and less oppressive understandings of women's bodily functions, such as menstruation (Rose [1983]). Certain emotions may be both morally appropriate and epistemologically advantageous in approaching the non-human and even the inanimate world. Jane Goodall's scientific contribution to our understanding of chimpanzee behavior seems to have been made possible only by her amazing empathy with or even love for these animals (Goodall [1986]). In her study of Barbara McClintock, Evelyn Fox Keller describes McClintock's relation to the objects of her research—grains of maize and their genetic properties—as a relation of affection, empathy and "the highest form of love: love that allows for intimacy without the annihilation of difference". She notes that McClintock's "vocabulary is consistently a vocabulary of affection, of kinship, of empathy" (Keller [1984, p.164]). Examples like these prompt Hilary Rose to assert that a feminist science of nature needs to draw on heart as well as hand and brain.

Some Implications of Recognizing the Epistemic Potential of Emotion.

Accepting that appropriate emotions are indispensable to reliable knowledge does not mean, of course, that uncritical feeling may be substituted for supposedly dispassionate investigation. Nor does it mean that the emotional responses of women and other members of the underclass are to be trusted without question. Although our emotions are epistemologically indispensable, they are not epistemologically indisputable. Like all our faculties, they may be misleading, and their data, like all data, are always subject to reinterpretation and revision. Because emotions are not presocial, physiological responses to unequivocal situations, they are open to challenge on various grounds. They may be dishonest or self-deceptive, they may incorporate inaccurate or partial perceptions, or they may be constituted by oppressive values. Accepting the indispensability of appropriate emotions to knowledge means no more (and no less) than that discordant emotions should be attended to seriously and respectfully rather than condemned, ignored, discounted or suppressed.

Just as appropriate emotions may contribute to the development of knowledge, so the growth of knowledge may contribute to the development of appropriate emotions. For instance, the powerful insights of feminist theory often stimulate new emotional responses to past and present situations. Inevitably, our emotions are affected by the knowledge that the women on our faculty are paid systematically less than the men, that one girl in four is subjected to sexual abuse from heterosexual men in her own family, and that few women reach orgasm in heterosexual intercourse. We are likely to feel different emotions toward older women or people of color as we re-evaluate our standards of sexual attractiveness

or acknowledge that black is beautiful. The new emotions evoked by feminist insights are likely in turn to stimulate further feminist observations and insights, and these may generate new directions in both theory and political practice. There is a continuous feedback loop between our emotional constitution and our theorizing such that each continually modifies the other and is in principle inseparable from it.

The ease and speed with which we can re-educate our emotions is unfortunately not great. Emotions are only partially within our control as individuals. Although affected by new information, they are habitual responses not quickly unlearned. Even when we come to believe consciously that our fear or shame or revulsion is unwarranted, we may still continue to experience emotions inconsistent with our conscious politics. We may still continue to be anxious for male approval, competitive with our comrades and sisters and possessive with our lovers. These unwelcome, because apparently inappropriate emotions, should not be suppressed or denied; instead, they should be acknowledged and subjected to critical scrutiny. The persistence of such recalcitrant emotions probably demonstrates how fundamentally we have been constituted by the dominant world view, but it may also indicate superficiality or other inadequacy in our emerging theory and politics.[8] We can only start from where we are—beings who have been created in a cruelly racist, capitalist and male-dominated society that has shaped our bodies and our minds, our perceptions, our values and our emotions, our language, and our systems of knowledge.

The alternative epistemological models that I suggest would display the continuous interaction between how we understand the world and who we are as people. They would show how our emotional responses to the world change as we conceptualize it differently and how our changing emotional responses then stimulate us to new insights. They would demonstrate the need for theory to be self-reflexive, to focus not only on the outer world but also on ourselves and our relation to that world, to examine critically our social location, our actions, our values, our perceptions, and our emotions. The models would also show how feminist and other critical social theories are indispensable psychotherapeutic tools because they provide some insights necessary to a full understanding of our emotional constitution. Thus, the models would explain how the reconstruction of knowledge is inseparable from the reconstruction of ourselves.

A corollary of the reflexivity of feminist and other critical theory is that it requires a much broader construal than positivism accepts of the process of theoretical investigation. In particular, it requires acknowledging that a necessary part of theoretical process is critical self-examination. Time spent in analyzing emotions and uncovering their sources should be viewed, therefore, neither as irrelevant to theoretical investigation nor even as a prerequisite for it; it is not a kind of clearing of the emotional decks, "dealing with" our emotions so that they will not influence our thinking. Instead, we must recognize that our efforts to reinterpret and refine our emotions are necessary to our theoretical investigation, just as our efforts to reeducate our emotions are necessary to our political activity. Critical reflection on emotion is not a self-indulgent substitute for political analysis and political action. It is itself a kind of political theory and political practice, indispensable for an adequate social theory and social transformation.

Finally, the recognition that emotions play a vital part in developing knowledge enlarges our understanding of women's claimed epistemic advantage. We can now see that women's subversive insights owe much to women's outlaw emotions, themselves appropriate responses to the situations of women's subordination. In addition to their propensity to experience outlaw emotions, at least on some level, women are relatively adept at identifying such emotions, in themselves and others, in part because of their social responsibility for caretaking, including emotional nurturance. It is true that women, like all subordinated peoples, especially those who must live in close proximity with their masters, often engage in emotional deception and even self-deception as the price of their survival. Even so, women may be less likely than other subordinated groups to engage in denial or suppression of outlaw emotions. Women's work of emotional nurturance has required them to develop a special acuity in recognizing hidden emotions and in understanding the genesis of those emotions. This emotional acumen can now be recognized as a skill in political analysis and validated as giving women a special advantage both in understanding the mechanisms of domination and in envisioning freer ways to live.

Source: Alison M. Jaggar. "Love and Knowledge: Emotion in Feminist Epistemology." *Inquiry* 32: 151-176. Reprinted with the permission of Scandinavian University PRess, Oslo, Norway.

Notes

[1] E. V. Spelman (1982) illustrates this point with a quotation from the well-known contemporary philosopher R. S. Peters. who wrote "we speak of emotional outbursts, reactions, upheavals and women" *(Proceedings of the Aristotelian Society,* New Series, vol. 62).

[2] It seems likely that the conspicuous absence of emotion shown by Mrs Thatcher is a deliberate strategy she finds necessary to counter the public perception of women as too emotional for political leadership. The strategy results in her being perceived as a formidable leader, but as an Iron Lady rather than a real woman. Ironically, Neil Kinnock, leader of the British Labour Party and Thatcher's main opponent in the 1987 General Election, was able to muster considerable public support, through television commercials portraying him in the stereotypically feminine role of caring about the unfortunate victims of Thatcher economics. Ultimately, however, this support was not sufficient to destroy public confidence in Mrs Thatcher's "masculine" competence and gain Kinnock the election.

[3] On the rare occasions when a white man cries, he is embarrassed and feels constrained to apologize. The one exception to the rule that men should be emotionless is that they are allowed and often even expected to experience anger. Spelman (1982) points out that men's cultural permission to be angry bolsters their claim to authority.

[4] Someone might argue that the viciousness of this myth was not a logical necessity. In an egalitarian society, where the concepts of reason and emotion were not gender-bound in the way they still are today, it might be argued that the ideal of the dispassionate investigator could be epistemologically beneficial. Is it possible that, in such socially and conceptually egalitarian circumstances, the myth of the dispassionate investigator could serve as a heuristic device, an ideal never to be realized in practice but nevertheless helping to minimize "subjectivity" and bias? My own view is that counterfactual myths rarely bring the benefits advertised and that this one is no exception. This myth fosters an equally mythical conception of pure truth and objectivity, quite independent of human interests or desires, and in this way it functions to disguise the inseparability of theory and practice, science and politics. Thus, it is part of an antidemocratic worldview that mystifies the political dimension of knowledge and unwarrantedly circumscribes the arena of political debate.

[5] Of course, the similarities in our emotional constitutions should not blind us to systematic differences. For instance, girls rather than boys are taught fear and disgust for spiders and snakes, affection for fluffy animals and shame for their naked bodies. It is primarily, though not exclusively, men rather than women whose sexual responses are shaped by exposure to visual and sometimes violent pornography. Girls and women are taught to cultivate sympathy for others: boys and men are taught to separate themselves emotionally from others. As I have noted already, more emotional expression is permitted for lower-class and some non-white men than for ruling-class men, perhaps because the expression of emotion is thought to expose vulnerability. Men of the upper classes learn to cultivate an attitude of condescension, boredom, or detached amusement. As we shall see shortly, differences in the emotional constitution of various groups may be epistemologically significant in so far as they both presuppose and facilitate different ways of perceiving the world.

[6] A necessary condition for experiencing feminist emotions is that one already be a feminist in some sense, even if one does not consciously wear that label. But many women and some men, even those who would deny that they are feminist, still experience emotions compatible with feminist values. For instance, they may be angered by the perception that someone is being mistreated just because she is a woman, or they may take special pride in the achievement of a woman. If those who experience such emotions are unwilling to recognize them as feminist, their emotions are probably described better as potentially feminist or prefeminist emotions.

[7] I owe this suggestion to Marcia Lind.

[8] Within a feminist context, Berenice Fisher suggests that we focus particular attention on our emotions of guilt and shame as part of a critical re-evaluation of our political ideals and our political practice (Fisher [1984]).

References

Fisher, Berenice 1984. "Guilt and Shame in the Women's Movement: The Radical Ideal of Action and Its Meaning for Feminist Intellectuals." *Feminist Studies* 10, 185-212.

Goodall, Jane 1986. *The Chimpanzees of Bombe: Patterns of Behavior* Cambridge, MA: Harvard University Press.

Griffin, Susan 1979. *Rape: The Power of Consciousness.* San Francisco: Harper & Row.

Jaggar, Alison M. 1983. *Feminist Politics and Human Nature.* Totawa, NJ: Rowman & Allanheld.

Keller, E.F. 1984. *Gender and Science.* New Haven, CT: Yale University Press.

Rose, Hilary 1983. "Hand, Brain, and Heart: A Feminist Epistemology for the Natural Sciences." *Signs: Journal of Women in Culture and Society* 9, No. 1, 73-90.

Spelman, E. V. 1982. "Anger and Insubordination." Manuscript; early version read to midwestern chapter of the Society for Women in Philosophy, spring, 1982.

Wierzbicka, Anna 1986. "Human Emotions: Universal or Culture-Specific?" *American Anthropologist* 88, 584-94.

Young, R. M. 1985. *Darwin's Metaphor: Nature's Place in Victorian Culture.* Cambridge: Cambridge University Press.

Contingent Foundations

Judith Butler

JUDITH BUTLER *currently is a professor in the Department of Rhetoric at the University of California at Berkeley.*

For the subject to be a pregiven point of departure for politics is to defer the question of the political construction and regulation of the subject itself; for it is important to remember that subjects are constituted through exclusion, that is, through the creation of a domain of deauthorized subjects, presubjects, figures of abjection, populations erased from view. This becomes clear, for instance, within the law when certain qualifications must first be met in order to be, quite literally, a claimant in sex discrimination or rape cases. Here it becomes quite urgent to ask, who qualifies as a "who," what systematic structures of disempowerment make it impossible for certain injured parties to invoke the "I" effectively within a court of law? Or less overtly, in a social theory like Albert Memmi's *The Colonizer and the Colonized,* an otherwise compelling call for radical enfranchisement, the category of women falls into neither category, the oppressor or the oppressed.[1] How do we theorize the exclusion of women from the category of the oppressed? Here the construction of subject-positions works to exclude women from the description of oppression, and this constitutes a different kind of oppression, one that is effected by the very *erasure* that grounds the articulation of the emancipatory subject. As Joan Scott makes clear in *Gender and the Politics of History,* once it is understood that subjects are formed through exclusionary operations, it becomes politically necessary to trace the operations of that construction and erasure.[2]

The above sketches in part a Foucaultian reinscription of the subject, an effort to resignify the subject as a site of resignification. As a result, it is not a "bidding farewell" to the subject per se, but, rather, a call to rework that notion outside the terms of an epistemological given. But perhaps Foucault is not really postmodern; after all, his is an analytics of *modern* power. There is, of course, talk about the death of the subject, but which subject is that? And what is the status of the utterance that announces its passing? What speaks now that the subject is dead? That there is a speaking seems clear, for how else could the utter-

ance be heard? So clearly, the death of that subject is not the end of agency, of speech, or of political debate. There is the refrain that, just now, when women are beginning to assume the place of subjects, postmodern positions come along to announce that the subject is dead (there is a difference between positions of poststructuralisim which claim that the subject never existed, and postmodern positions which claim that the subject *once* had integrity, but no longer does). Some see this as a conspiracy against women and other disenfranchised groups who are now only beginning to speak on their own behalf. But what precisely is meant by this, and how do we account for the very strong criticisms of the subject as an instrument of Western imperialist hegemony theorized by Gloria Anzaldua,[3] Gayatri Spivak[4] and various theorists of postcoloniality? Surely there is a caution offered here, that in the very struggle toward enfranchisement and democratization, we might adopt the very models of domination by which we were oppressed, not realizing that one way that domination works is through the regulation and production of subjects. Through what exclusions has the feminist subject been constructed, and how do those excluded domains return to haunt the "integrity" and "unity" of the feminist "we?" And how is it that the very category, the subject, the "we," that is supposed to be presumed for the purpose of solidarity, produces the very factionalization it is supposed to quell? Do women want to become subjects on the model which requires and produces an anterior region of abjection, or must feminism become a process which is self-critical about the processes that produce and destabilize identity categories? To take the construction of the subject as a political problematic is not the same as doing away with the subject; to deconstruct the subject is not to negate or throw away the concept; on the contrary, deconstruction implies only that we suspend all commitments to that to which the term, "the subject," refers, and that we consider the linguistic functions it serves in the consolidation and concealment of authority. To deconstruct is not to negate or to dismiss, but to call into question and, perhaps most importantly, to open up a term, like the subject, to a reusage or redeployment that previously has not been authorized.

Within feminism, it seems as if there is some political necessity to speak as and for *women,* and I would not contest that necessity. Surely, that is the way in which representational politics operates, and in this country, lobbying efforts are virtually impossible without recourse to identity politics. So we agree that demonstrations and legislative efforts and radical movements need to make claims in the name of women.

But this necessity needs to be reconciled with another. The minute that the category of women is invoked as *describing* the constituency for which feminism speaks, an internal debate invariably begins over what the descriptive content of that term will be. There are those who claim that there is an ontological specificity to women as childbearers that forms the basis of a specific legal and political interest in representation, and then there are others who understand maternity to be a social relation that is, under current social circumstances, the specific and cross-cultural situation of women. And there are those who seek recourse to Gilligan and others to establish a feminine specificity that makes itself clear in women's communities or ways of knowing. But every time that specificity is articulated, there is resistance and factionalization within the very constituency that is supposed to be *unified* by the articulation of its common element. In the early 1980s, the feminist "we" rightly came under attack by women of color who claimed that the "we" was invariably white, and that "we" that was meant to solidify the movement was the very source of a painful factionalization. The effort to characterize a feminine specificity through recourse to maternity, whether biological or social, produced a similar factionalization and even a disavowal of feminism altogether. For surely all women are not mothers; some cannot be, some are too young or too old to be, some choose not to be, and for some who are mothers, that is not necessarily the rallying point of their politicization in feminism.

I would argue that any effort to give universal or specific content to the category of women, presuming that that guarantee of solidarity is required *in advance,* will necessarily produce factionalization, and that "identity" as a point of departure can never hold as the solidifying ground of a feminist political movement. Identity categories are never merely descriptive, but always normative, and as such, exclusionary. This is not to say that the term "women" ought not to be used, or that we ought to announce the death of the category. On the contrary, if feminism presupposes that "women" designates an undesignatable field of differences, one that cannot be totalized or summarized by a descriptive identity category, then the very term becomes a site of permanent openness and resignifiability. I would argue that the rifts among women over the content of the term ought to be safeguarded and prized, indeed, that this constant rifting ought to be affirmed as the ungrounded ground of feminist theory. To deconstruct the subject of feminism is not, then, to censure its usage, but, on the contrary, to release the term into a future of multiple significations, to emancipate it from the maternal or racialist ontologies to which it has been restricted, and to give it play as a site where unanticipated meanings might come to bear.

Paradoxically, it may be that only through releasing the category of women from a fixed referent that something like "agency" becomes possible. For if the term permits of a resignification, if its referent is not fixed, then possibilities for new configurations of the term become possible. In a sense, what women signify has been taken for granted for too long, and what has been fixed as the "referent" of the term has been "fixed," normalized, immobilized, paralyzed in positions of subordination. In effect, the signified has been conflated with the referent, whereby a set of meanings have been taken to inhere in the real nature of women themselves. To recast the referent as the signified, and to authorize or safeguard the category of women as a site of possible resignifications is to expand the possibilities of what it means to be a woman and in this sense to condition and enable an enhanced sense of agency.

One might well ask: but doesn't there have to be a set of norms that discriminate between those descriptions that ought to adhere to the category of women and those that do not? The only answer to that question is a counter-question: who would set those norms, and what contestations would they produce? To establish a normative foundation for settling the question of what ought properly to be included in the description of women would be only and always to produce a new site of political contest. That foundation would settle nothing, but would of its own necessity founder on its own authoritarian ruse. This is not to say that there is no foundation, but rather, that wherever there is one, there will also be a foundering, a contestation. That such foundations exist only to be put into question is, as it were, the permanent risk of the process of democratization. To refuse that contest is to sacrifice the radical democratic impetus of feminist politics. That the category is unconstrained, even that it comes to serve antifeminist purposes, will be part of the risk of this procedure. But this is a risk that is produced by the very foundationalism that seeks to safeguard feminism against it. In a sense, this risk is the foundation, and hence is not, of any feminist practice.

In the final part of this paper, I would like to turn to a related question, one that emerges from the concern that a feminist theory cannot proceed without presuming the materiality of women's bodies, the materiality of sex. The chant of antipostmodernism runs, if everything is discourse, then is there no reality to bodies? How do we understand the material violence that women suffer? In responding to this criticism, I would like to suggest that the very formulation misconstrues the critical point.

I don't know what postmodernism is, but I do have some sense of what it might mean to subject notions of the body and materiality to a deconstructive critique. To deconstruct the concept of matter or that of bodies is not to negate or refuse either term. To deconstruct these terms means, rather, to continue to use them, to repeat them, to repeat them subversively, and to displace them from the contexts in which they have been deployed as instruments of oppressive power. Here it is of course necessary to state quite plainly that the options for theory are not exhausted by *presuming* materiality, on the one hand, and *negating* materiality, on the other. It is my purpose to do precisely neither of these. To call a presupposition into question is not the same as doing away with it; rather, it is to free it up from its metaphysical lodgings in order to occupy and to serve very different political aims. To problematize the matter of bodies entails in the first instance a loss of epistemological certainty, but this loss of certainty does not necessarily entail political nihilism as its result.[5]

If a deconstruction of the materiality of bodies suspends and problematizes the traditional ontological referent of the term, it does not freeze, banish, render useless, or deplete of meaning the usage of the term; on the contrary, it provides the conditions to *mobilize* the signifier in the service of an alternative production.

Consider that most material of concepts, "sex," which Monique Wittig calls a thoroughly political category, and which Michel Foucault calls a regulatory and "fictitious unity." For both theorists, sex does not *describe* a prior materiality, but produces and regulates the *intelligibility* of the *materiality* of bodies. For both, and in different ways, the category of sex imposes a duality and a uniformity on bodies in order to maintain reproductive sexuality as a compulsory order. I've argued elsewhere more precisely how this works, but for our purposes, I would like to suggest that this kind of categorization can be called a violent one, a forceful one, and that this discursive ordering and production of bodies in accord with the category of sex is itself a material violence.

The violence of the letter, the violence of the mark which establishes what will and will not signify, what will and will not be included within the intelligible, takes on a political significance when the letter is the law or the authoritative legislation of what will be the materiality of sex.

So what can this kind of poststructural analysis tell us about violence and suffering? Is it perhaps that forms of violence are to be understood as more pervasive, more constitutive, and more insidious than prior models have allowed us to see? That is part of the point of the previous discussion of war, but let me now make it differently in yet another context.

Consider the legal restrictions that regulate what does and does not count as rape: here the politics of violence operate through regulating what will and will not be able to appear as an effect of violence.[6] There is, then, already in this foreclosure a violence at work, a marking off in advance of what will or will not qualify under the signs of "rape" or "government violence," or in the case of states in which twelve separate pieces of empirical evidence are required to establish "rape," what then can be called a governmentally facilitated rape.

A similar line of reasoning is at work in discourses on rape when the "sex" of a woman is claimed as that which establishes the responsibility for her own violation. The defense attorney in the New Bedford gang rape case asked the plaintiff, "If you're living with a man, what are you doing running around the streets getting raped?"[7] The "running around" in this sentence collides grammatically with "getting raped": "getting" is procuring, acquiring, having, as if this were a treasure she was running around after, but "getting raped" suggests the passive voice. Literally, of course, it would be difficult to be "running around" and be "getting raped" at the same time, which suggests that there must be an elided passage here, perhaps a directional that leads from the former to the latter? If the sense of the sentence is, "running around [looking to get] raped," which seems to be the only logical way of bridging the two parts of the sentence, then rape as a passive acquisition is precisely the object of her active search. The first clause suggests that she "belongs" at home, with her man, that the home is a site in which she is the domestic property of that man, and the "streets" establish her as open season. If she is looking to get raped, she is looking to become the property of some other, and this objective is installed in her desire, conceived here as quite frantic in its pursuit. She is "running around," suggesting that she is running around looking under every rock for a rapist to satisfy her. Significantly, the phrase installs as the structuring principle of her desire "getting, raped," where "rape" is figured as an act of wilful self-expropriation. Since becoming the property of a man is the objective of her "sex," articulated in and through her sexual desire, and rape is the way in which that appropriation occurs "on the street" [a logic that implies that rape is to marriage as the streets are to the home, that is, that "rape" is street marriage, a marriage without a home, a marriage for homeless girls, and that marriage is domesticated rape], then "rape" is the logical consequence of the enactment of her sex and sexuality outside domesticity. Never mind that this rape took place in a bar, for the "bar" is, within this imaginary, but an extension of the "street," or perhaps its exemplary moment, for there is no enclosure, that is, no protection, other than the *home* as domestic marital space. In any case, the single cause of her violation is here figured as her "sex" which, given its natural propensity to seek expropriation, once dislocated from domestic propriety, naturally pursues its rape and is thus responsible for it.

The category of sex here functions as a principle of production and regulation at once, the cause of the violation installed as the formative principle of the body is sexuality. Here sex is a category, but not merely a representation; it is a principle of production, intelligibility, and regulation which enforces a violence and rationalizes it after the fact. The very terms by which the violation is explained *enact* the violation, and concede that the violation was under way before it takes the empirical form of a criminal act. That rhetorical enactment *shows* that "violence" is produced through the foreclosure effected by this analysis, through the erasure and negation that determines the field of appearances and intelligibility of crimes of culpability. As a category that effectively produces the political meaning of what it describes, "sex" here works its silent "violence" in regulating what is and is not designatable.

I place the terms "violence" and "sex" under quotation marks: is this the sign of a certain deconstruction, the end to politics? Or am I underscoring the iterable structure of these terms, the ways in which they yield to a repetition, occur ambiguously, and am I doing that precisely to further a political analysis? I place them in quotation marks to show that they are under contest, up for grabs, to initiate the contest, to question their traditional deployment, and call for some other. The quotation marks do not place into question the urgency or credibility of sex or violence as political issues, but, rather, show that the way their very materiality is circumscribed is fully political. The effect of the quotation marks is to denaturalize the terms, to designate these signs as sites of political debate.

If there is a fear that, by no longer being able to take for granted the subject, its gender, its sex, or its materiality, feminism will founder, it might be wise to consider the political consequences of keeping in their place the very premises that have tried to secure our subordination from the start.

Source: Judith Butler. "Contingent Foundations." In *Feminists Theorize the Political.* Edited by Judith Butler and Joan W. Scott. New York: Routledge, 1992. Originally appearing as "Contingent Foundations: Feminism and the Question of 'Postmodernism'" in *Praxis International* 11 (1991) 150-156. Reprinted by permission of Basil Blackwell.

Notes

[1] "At the height of the revolt," Memmi writes," the colonized still bears the traces and lessons of prolonged cohabitation (just as the smile or movements of a wife, even during divorce proceedings, remind one strangely of those of her husband)." Here Memmi sets up an analogy which presumes that colonizer and colonized exist in a parallel and separate relation to the divorcing husband and wife. The analogy simultaneously and paradoxically suggests the feminization of the colonized, where the colonized is presumed to be the subject of men, *and* the exclusion of the women from the category of the colonized subject. Albert Memmi, *The Colonizer and the Colonized*, (Boston: Beacon Press, 1965), p.129.

[2] Joan W. Scott, *Gender and the Politics of History.* (New York: Columbia University Press), 1988, introduction.

[3] Gloria Anzaldua, *La Frontera/Borderlands.* (San Francisco: Spinsters Ink. 1988).

[4] Gayatri Spivak. "Can the Subaltern Speak?" in *Marxism and the Interpretation of Culture*, eds. Nelson and Grossberg, (Chicago: University of Illinois Press, 1988).

[5] The body posited as prior to the sign, is always *posited* or *signified* as prior. This signification works through producing an *effect* of its own procedure, the body that it nevertheless and simultaneously claims to discover as that which *precedes* signification. If the body signified as prior to signification is an effect of signification, then the mimetic or representational status of language, which claims that signs follow bodies as their necessary mirrors, is not mimetic at all; on the contrary, it is productive, constitutive, one might even argue *performative*, inasmuch as this signifying act produces the body that it then claims to find prior to any and all signification.

[6] For an extended analysis of the relationship of language and rape, see Sharon Marcus' contribution, "Fighting Bodies, Fighting Words: A Theory and Politics of Rape Prevention" in Judith Butler and Joan W. Scott eds., *Feminists Theorize the Political.* (New York: Routledge, 1992), pp.385-403.

[7] Quoted in Catharine MacKinnon, *Toward a Feminist Theory of the State*, (Boston: Harvard University Press, 1989), p.171.

12

Environmentalism

The Ideal of a Renewed Environment

In 1990, thirty-two world-renowned scientists joined with 370 well-known spiritual leaders to issue an appeal for the preservation and cherishing of the earth. This appeal is a testimony to the widespread and urgent concerns that persons in the last decade of the twentieth century have for the environment. These concerns embrace the problems created by global warming, the depletion of the ozone layer, the extinction of species, the destruction of forests, the contamination of ground water, soil erosion, acid rain, and population explosion. The breadth and depth of these matters has given birth to a movement called environmentalism.

It is a sobering thought to be reminded that a much earlier warning had been sounded about some of the aforementioned impending environmental disasters. In the 1960s, Rachel Carson warned that unless people were willing to make major and immediate changes in their attitude and approach to the management of the earth, humanity would destroy this planet. Her conclusions are not unique to the 1960s. In her writings, she quotes Albert Schweitzer who also believed that humans would end up demolishing the earth.

Schweitzer's position on the environment was predicated on his deep moral principle of reverence for life, a principle articulated long in advance of the time when it would receive tacit support, first in the animal rights movement and then in the deep-ecology movement. In part, Anne and Paul Ehrlich develop Schweitzer's belief by arguing in favour of biodiversity on the basis of ethical, aesthetic and economic notions. One might with fairness say that Schweitzer's belief is more accurately reflected in the writing of Arne Naess when he speaks in defence of an articulate platform for a well-defined deep-ecology movement. Naess challenges conventional ideologies in saying that what is called for is ideological change which appreciates the intrinsic value of both human and non-human life. This ideological change is partly reflected in Alison Clayson's analysis of the OECD Environment Report Card.

Perhaps what is called for is more direct action in the courageous form in which it was manifested in the life of Chico Mendes, union leader and ecological activist who was assassinated on December 22, 1988 in Brazil as he attempted to stop the destruction of the Brazilian rain forest. From a somewhat different perspective, but picking up on a point raised by the Ehrlichs, Goran Ohlin argues that there is little that governments can do to change population policy as it is not something to be turned on and off at will. Ohlin does stress, however, that governments can direct their efforts toward promoting and developing the technologies that will minimize the environmental destruction caused by the demands of surging populations. In arguing in this way, Ohlin offers a more specific route to some of the objectives identified by the *United Nations Brundtland Report* when it talks about institutional and legal changes necessary for a sustainable environment. Finally, Carl Sagan offers an appeal that he launched for the preservation of the Earth. This appeal is signed by 32 distinguished scientists.

Civilization and Ethics

Albert Schweitzer

ALBERT SCHWEITZER (1875-1965) was a French theologian, philosopher, organist, doctor and recipient of the 1952 Nobel Peace Prize.

With Descartes, philosophy starts from the dogma: "I think, therefore I exist." With this paltry, arbitrarily chosen beginning, it is landed irretrievably on the road to the abstract. It never finds the right approach to ethics, and remains entangled in a dead world- and life-view. True philosophy must start from the most immediate and comprehensive fact of consciousness, which says: "I am life which wills to live, in the midst of life which wills to live." This is not an ingenious dogmatic formula. Day by day, hour by hour, I live and move in it. At every moment of reflection it stands fresh before me. There bursts forth from it again and again as from roots that can never dry up, a living world- and life-view which can deal with all the facts of Being. A mysticism of ethical union with Being grows out of it.

As in my own will-to-live there is a longing for wider life and for the mysterious exaltation of the will-to-live which we call pleasure, with dread of annihilation and of the mysterious depreciation of the will-to-live all around me, whether it can express itself before me, or remains dumb.

Ethics consist, therefore, in my experiencing the compulsion to show to all will-to-live the same reverence as I do to my own. There we have given us that basic principle of the moral which is a necessity of thought. It is good to maintain and to encourage life; it is bad to destroy life or to obstruct it.

As a matter of fact, everything which in the ordinary ethical valuation of the relations of men to each other ranks as good can be brought under the description of material and spiritual maintenance or promotion of human life, and of effort to bring it to its highest value. Conversely, everything which ranks as bad in human relations is in the last analysis material or spiritual destruction or obstruction of human life, and negligence in the endeavour to bring it to its highest value. Separate individual categories of good and evil which lie far apart and have apparently no connection at all with one another fit together like the pieces of a jig-saw puzzle, as soon as they are comprehended and deepened in this the most universal definition of good and evil.

The basic principle of the moral which is a necessity of thought means, however, not only an ordering and deepening, but also a widening of the current views of good and evil. A man is truly ethical only when he obeys the compulsion to help all life which he is able to assist, and shrinks from injuring anything that lives. He does not ask how far this or that life deserves one's sympathy as being valuable, nor, beyond that, whether and to what degree it is capable of feeling. Life as such is sacred to him. He tears no leaf from a tree, plucks no flower, and takes care to crush no insect. If in summer he is working by lamplight, he prefers to keep the window shut and breathe a stuffy atmosphere rather than see one insect after another fall with singed wings upon his table.

If he walks on the road after a shower and sees an earthworm which has strayed on to it, he bethinks himself that it must get dried up in the sun, if it does not return soon enough to ground into which it can burrow, so he lifts it from the deadly stone surface, and puts it on the grass. If he comes across an insect which has fallen into a puddle, he stops a moment in order to hold out a leaf or a stalk on which it can save itself.

He is not afraid of being laughed at as sentimental. It is the fate of every truth to be a subject for laughter until it is generally recognized. Once it was considered folly to assume that men of colour were really men and ought to be treated as such, but the folly has become an accepted truth. To-day it is thought to be going too far to declare that constant regard for everything that lives, down to the lowest manifestations of life, is a demand made by rational ethics. The time is coming, however, when people will be astonished that mankind needed so long a time to learn to regard thoughtless injury to life as incompatible with ethics.

Ethics are responsibility without limit towards all that lives.

As a general proposition the definition of ethics as a relationship within a disposition to reverence for life, does not make a very moving impression. But it is the only complete one. Compassion is too narrow

ALBERT SCHWEITZER (1875-1965)

Albert Schweitzer's combination of intellectual achievement and practical morality has not been equalled in the 20th century. He set his course early in life, when, at the age of twenty-one, he vowed that he would live for science and art until he was thirty and then devote the rest of his life to serving humanity. In 1889, Schweitzer obtained a doctorate in theology and became a curate in a Strasbourg church. In 1903 he became principal of the theological college in the same city. His biography of Bach and an edition of Bach's organ music made him a leading authority in this field as well.

In 1906 Schweitzer set about fulfilling the second part of his vow by resigning from the college to pursue a doctorate in medicine at the University of Strasbourg. In 1913, along with his new wife who was a qualified nurse, he set off for French Equatorial Africa (now Gabon) where he set up a hospital to fight leprosy and sleeping sickness. He remained here essentially for the rest of his life, making only brief visits Europe and America to raise funds and to lecture.

Schweitzer used the term "Reverence for Life" to describe a universal concept of ethics in which he believed altruism and egoism could be directed by combining respect for all life with the highest development of individual human potential. In his own life he was able to actualize these ideals to an uncompromising extent. In 1952, Schweitzer was awarded the Nobel Prize for Peace.

---

to rank as the total essence of the ethical. It denotes, of course, only interest in the suffering will-to-live. But ethics include also feeling as one's own all the circumstances and all the aspirations of the will-to-live, its pleasure, too, and its longing to live itself out to the full, as well as its urge to self-perfecting. ...

I can do nothing but hold to the fact that the will-to-live in me manifests itself as will-to-live which desires to become one with other will-to-live. That is for me the light that shines in the darkness. The ignorance in which the world is wrapped has no existence for me; I have been saved from the world. I am thrown, indeed, by reverence for life into an unrest such as the world does not know, but I obtain from it a blessedness which the world cannot give. If in the tenderheartedness produced by being different from the world another person and I help each other in understanding and pardoning, when otherwise will would torment will, the division of the will-to-live is at an end. If I save an insect from a puddle, life has devoted itself to life, and the division of life against itself is ended. Whenever my life devotes itself in any way to life, my finite will-to-live experiences union with the infinite will in which all life is one, and I enjoy a feeling of refreshment which prevents me from pining away in the desert of life.

Source: Albert Schweitzer. *Civilization and Ethics*, London: Adam & Charles Black, 1949. Reprinted by permission of Rhena Schweitzer Miller.

The Obligation to Endure

Rachel Carson

RACHEL CARSON *(1907-1964) was a writer and scientist who was employed by the U.S. Fish and Wildlife Service for about sixteen years. She wrote* The Sea Around Us *(1951) and* Silent Spring *(1962) among other works. Carson is widely regarded as one of the founders of the modern environmental movement.*

To Albert Schweitzer, who said

"Man has lost his capacity to foresee and forestall.
He will end by destroying the earth."

The history of life on earth has been a history of interaction between living things and their surroundings. To a large extent, the physical form and the habits of the earth's vegetation and its animal life have been molded by the environment. Considering the whole span of earthly time, the opposite effect, in which life actually modifies its surroundings, has been relatively slight. Only within the moment of time represented by the present century has one species—man—acquired significant power to alter the nature of his world.

During the past quarter century this power has not only increased to one of disturbing magnitude but it has changed in character. The most alarming of all man's assaults upon the environment is the contamination of air, earth, rivers, and sea with dangerous and even lethal materials. This pollution is for the most part irrecoverable; the chain of evil it initiates not only in the world that must support life but in living tissues is for the most part irreversible. In this now universal contamination of the environment, chemicals are the sinister and little-recognized partners of radiation in changing the very nature of the world—the very nature of its life. Strontium 90, released through nuclear explosions into the air, comes to earth in rain or drifts down as fallout, lodges in soil, enters into the grass or corn or wheat grown there, and in time takes up its abode in the bones of a human being, there to remain until his death. Similarly, chemicals spayed on croplands or forests or gardens lie long in soil, entering into living organisms, passing from one to another in a chain of poisoning and earth. Or they pass mysteriously by underground streams until they emerge and, through the alchemy of air and sunlight, combine into new forms that kill vegetation, sicken cattle, and work unknown harm on those who drink from once pure wells. As Albert Schweitzer has said, "Man can hardly even recognize the devils of his own creation."

It took hundreds of millions of years to produce the life that now inhabits the earth—eons of time in which that developing and evolving and diversifying life reached a state of adjustment and balance with its surroundings. The environment, rigorously shaping and directing the life it supported, contained elements that were hostile as well as supporting. Certain rocks gave out dangerous radiation; even within the light of the sun, from which all life draws its energy, there were short-wave radiations with power to injure. Given time—time not in years but in millennia—life adjusts, and a balance has been reached. For time is the essential ingredient; but in the modern world there is no time.

The rapidity of change and the speed with which new situations are created follow the impetuous and heedless pace of man rather than the deliberate pace of nature. Radiation is no longer merely the background radiation of rocks, the bombardment of cosmic rays, the ultraviolet of the sun that have existed before there was any life on earth; radiation is now the unnatural creation of man's tampering with the atom. The chemicals to which life is asked to make its adjustment are no longer merely the calcium and silica and copper and all the rest of the minerals washed out of the rocks and carried in rivers to the sea; they are the synthetic creations of man's inventive mind, brewed in his laboratories, and having no counterparts in nature.

To adjust to these chemicals would require time on the scale that is nature's; it would require not merely the years of a man's life but the life of generations. And even this, were it by some miracle possible, would be futile, for the new chemicals come from our laboratories in an endless stream; almost five hundred annually find their way into actual use in the United States alone. The figure is staggering and its implications are not easily grasped—500 new chemicals to which the bodies of men and animals are required somehow to adapt each year, chemicals totally outside the limits of biologic experience.

Among them are many that are used in man's war against nature. Since the mid-1940s over 200 basic chemicals have been created for use in killing insects, weeds, rodents, and other organisms described in the modern vernacular as "pests"; and they are sold under several thousand different brand names.

These sprays, dusts, and aerosols are now applied almost universally to farms, gardens, forests, and homes—nonselective chemicals that have the power to kill every insect, the "good" and the "bad," to still the song of birds and the leaping of fish in the streams, to coat the leaves with a deadly film, and to linger on in soil—all this though the intended target may be only a few weeds or insects. Can anyone believe it is possible to lay down such a barrage of poisons on the surface of the earth without making it unfit for all life? They should not be called "insecticides," but "biocides."

The whole process of spraying seems caught up in an endless spiral. Since DDT was released for civilian use, a process of escalation has been going on in which ever more toxic materials must be found. This has happened because insects, in a triumphant vindication of Darwin's principle of the survival of the fittest, have evolved super races immune to the particular insecticide used, hence a deadlier one has always to be developed—and then a deadlier one than that. It has happened also because, for reasons to be described later, destructive insects often undergo a "flareback," or resurgence, after spraying, in numbers greater than before. Thus the chemical war is never won, and all life is caught in its violent crossfire.

Along with the possibility of the extinction of mankind by nuclear war, the central problem of our age has therefore become the contamination of man's total environment with such substances of incredible potential for harm—substances that accumulate in the tissues of plants and animals and even penetrate the germ cells to shatter or alter the very material of heredity upon which the shape of the future depends.

Some would-be architects of our future look toward a time when it will be possible to alter the human germ plasm by design. But we may easily be doing so now by inadvertence, for many chemicals, like radiation, bring about gene mutations. It is ironic to think that man might determine his own future by something so seemingly trivial as the choice of an insect spray.

All this has been risked—for what? Future historians may well be amazed by our distorted sense of proportion. How could intelligent beings seek to control a few unwanted species by a method that contaminated the entire environment and brought the threat of disease and death even to their own kind?

Yet this is precisely what we have done. We have done it, moreover, for reasons that collapse the moment we examine them. We are told that the enormous and expanding use of pesticides is necessary to maintain farm production. Yet is our real problem not one of overproduction? Our farms, despite measures to remove acreages from production and to pay farmers not to produce, have yielded such a staggering excess of crops that the American taxpayer in 1962 is paying out more than one billion dollars a year as the total carrying cost of the surplus-food storage program. And is the situation helped when one branch of the Agriculture Department tries to reduce production while another states, as it did in 1958, "It is believed generally that reduction of crop acreages under provisions of the Soil Bank will stimulate interest in use of chemicals to obtain maximum production on the land retained in crops."

All this is not to say there is no insect problem and no need of control. I am saying, rather, that control must be geared to realities, not to mythical situations, and that the methods employed must be such that they do not destroy us along with the insects.

Source: Rachel Carson. *Silent Spring.* The Riverside Press: Cambridge, Mass., 1962.

A Platform of the Deep Ecology Movement

Arne Naess

ARNE NAESS *is Professor at the Council for Environmental Studies, University of Oslo.*

(1) The flourishing of human and non-human life on Earth has intrinsic value. The value of non-human life forms is independent of the usefulness these may have for narrow human purposes.

(2) Richness and diversity of life forms are values in themselves and contribute to the flourishing of human and non-human life on Earth.

(3) Humans have no right to reduce this richness and diversity except to satisfy vital needs.

(4) Present human interference with the non-human world is excessive, and the situation is rapidly worsening.

(5) The flourishing of human life and cultures is compatible with a substantial decrease of the human population. The flourishing of non-human life requires such a decrease.

(6) Significant change of life conditions for the better requires change in policies. These affect basic economic, technological, and ideological structures.

(7) The ideological change is mainly that of appreciating *life quality* (dwelling in situations of intrinsic value) rather than adhering to a high standard of living. There will be a profound awareness of the difference between big and great.

(8) Those who subscribe to the foregoing points have an obligation directly or indirectly to participate in the attempt to implement the necessary changes.

The eight formulations are of course in need of clarification and elaboration. A few remarks:

Re (1) Instead of "biosphere" we might use the term "ecosphere" in order to stress that we of course do not limit our concern for the life forms in a biologically narrow sense. The term "life" is used here in a comprehensive non-technical way to refer also to things biologists may classify as non-living: rivers (watersheds), landscapes, cultures, ecosystems, "the living earth". Slogans such as "let the river live" illustrate this broader usage so common in many cultures.

Re (2) So-called simple, lower, or primitive species of plants and animals contribute essentially to the richness and diversity of life. They have value in themselves and are not merely steps toward the so-called higher or rational life forms. The second principle presupposes that life itself, as a process over evolutionary time, implies an increase of diversity and richness.

Why talk about diversity *and* richness? Suppose humans interfere with an ecosystem to such a degree that 1000 vertebrate species are each reduced to a survival minimum. Point (2) is not satisfied. *Richness*, here used for what some others call "abundance", has been excessively reduced. The maintenance of richness has to do with the maintenance of habitats and the number of individuals (size of populations). No exact count is implied. The main point is that life on Earth may be excessively interfered with even if complete diversity is upheld.

What is said above about species holds also for habitats and ecosystems which show great similarity so that it makes sense to count them.

Re (3) This formulation is perhaps too strong. But, considering the mass of ecologically irresponsible proclamations of human rights, it may be sobering to announce a norm about what they have no right to do.

The term "vital need" is vague to allow for considerable latitude in judgement. Differences in climate and related factors, together with differences in the structures of societies as they now exist, need to be considered. Also the difference between a means to the satisfaction of the need and the need must be considered. If a whaler in an industrial country quits whaling he may risk unemployment under the present economic conditions. Whaling is for him an important means. But in a rich country with a high standard of living whaling is not a vital need.

Re (4) Status of interference. For a realistic assessment of the global situation, see the unabbreviated version of the IUCN's *World Conservation Strategy* (1980). There are other works to be highly recommended such as Gerald Barney's *Global 2000 Report to the President* of the United States (1980).

People in the materially richest countries cannot be expected to reduce their excessive interference with the non-human world to a moderate level overnight. Less interference does not imply that humans should not modify some ecosystems as do other species. Humans have modified the Earth and will continue to do so. At issue is the nature and extent of such interference.

The fight to preserve and extend areas of wilderness or near-wilderness should continue and should focus on the general ecological functions of these areas (one such function: large wilderness areas are required by the biosphere to allow for continued evolutionary speciation of animals and plants). Present designated wilderness areas and game preserves are not large enough to allow for speciation of large birds and mammals.

Re (5) Limitation of population. The stabilisation and reduction of the human population will take time. Interim strategies need to be developed. But this in no way excuses the present complacency. The extreme seriousness of our current situation must first be more widely recognised. But the longer we wait the more drastic will be the measures needed. Until deep changes are made, substantial decreases in richness and diversity are liable to occur; the rate of extinction of species will be greater than in any other period of Earth history.

A legitimate objection may be that if the present billions of humans deeply change their behaviour in the direction of ecological responsibility, non-human life could flourish. Formulation (5) presupposes that the probability of a deep enough change in economics and technology is too small to take into account.

Re (6) Policy changes required. Economic growth as conceived and implemented today by the industrial states is incompatible with points (1) to (5).

Present ideology tends to value things because they are scarce and because they have a commodity or market value. There is prestige in vast consumption and waste, to mention only two of many relevant factors. Economic growth registers mainly growth in marketable values, not in values generally, including ecological values. Whereas "self-determination", "local community", and "think globally, act locally" will remain key slogans, the implementation of deep changes nevertheless requires increasingly global action in the sense of action across every border, perhaps contrary to the short-range interests of local communities.

Support for global action through nongovernmental organisations becomes increasingly important. Many of these organisations are able to act locally from grass roots to grass roots, thus avoiding negative governmental interference.

Cultural diversity today requires advanced technology, that is, techniques that advance the basic goals of each culture. So-called soft, intermediate, and appropriate technologies are steps in this direction.

Re (7) Some economists criticise the term "quality of life" because it is supposed to be too vague. But, on closer inspection, what they consider to be vague is actually the non-quantifiable nature of the term. One cannot quantify adequately what is important for the quality of life as discussed here, and there is no need to do so.

Re (8) There is ample room for different opinions about priorities. What should be done first, what next? What is most urgent? What is necessary as opposed to what is highly desirable? Different opinions in these matters should not exclude vigorous cooperation.

What is gained from tentatively formulating basic views shared today by most or all supporters of the deep ecology movement? Hopefully it makes it a little easier to localise the movement among the many "alternative" movements. Hopefully this does not lead to isolation but rather to even better cooperation with many other alternative movements. It might also make some of us more clear about where we stand, and more clear about which disagreements might profitably be reduced and which ones might profitably be sharpened. After all, as we shall see, "diversity" is a high-level norm!

Source: Arne Ness and David Rothenberg (Eds.), *Ecology, Community and Lifestyle.* Cambridge: Cambridge University Press, 1989.

The State of the Environment: A Report Card for OECD Countries

Alison Clayson

ALISON CLAYSON *resides in France and is an occasional contriutor to the science journal,* Ambio.

Every six years the Organization for Economic Cooperation and Development (OECD) publishes a report on *The State of the Environment* in its twenty-four member countries.[1] This year's document differs form its predecessors in two ways: it reviews the progress achieved in attaining environmental objectives over the whole of the past two decades—about the lifetime of most environmental policies and institutions, and it includes for the first time a 76-page supplement of twenty-five *Environmental Indicators*. The supplement has been produced at the specific request of the Heads of State attending the G-7 summits in Paris (July 1989) and Houston (July 1990). It allows a country-by-country comparison of "achievements" for indicators ranging from CO_2 emissions, wastewater treatment and use of forest resources—to threatened species, energy supplies, transport trends and demographics.[2]

Mixed Results

The report card, as one might expect, is mixed. For every area where particular pollutants have been reduced, there are other areas where no risk assessment exists or where prior accumulations of chemicals and gases are posing additional threats; where growth in certain sectors such as transport has simply outpaced the benefits derived from environmental policies that were otherwise positive.

Thus, great strides have been made in controlling release into the environment of such persistent chemicals as DDT, polychlorinated biphenyls (PCBs) and mercury compounds. But the bad news is that there are still another 100,000 chemical compounds in current commercial use for which no risk assessment has been made, and several thousand new ones must be screened as they come onto the market each year.

Urban air pollution from sulfur dioxide, particulate matter and lead also have been greatly reduced. Yet according to the 1991 report, OECD countries are still responsible for 45% of world CO_2 emission, 40% of sulfur oxides and 50% of nitrogen oxides. These and other gases contribute to the greenhouse effect and global impacts on climate change, sea level, and agriculture.

The report signals the virtual elimination of microbial contamination of drinking water in OECD countries during the last two decades, yet it also reveals that chemical pollution of water remains a major problem since 330 million people—about 40% of the OECD population—live in areas not served by wastewater treatment stations at all.

Some 130 million people in OECD countries are subjected to unacceptable noise levels (over 65 decibels) on a daily basis.

As a result of management policies, forest resources of the OECD as a whole are actually increasing, with both the amount of timber and average annual growth having improved since 1970. Welcome news, indeed. Unfortunately, however, massive deforestation in the tropics is offsetting these gains. Besides the local consequences of erosion, water-balance disturbance, loss of valuable genetic and economic resources, deforestation on this scale may contribute to global climate problems. *The State of the Environment* confirms that the "major challenge in the years to come is to extend, across the world, the principles of management and sustainable development that the OECD area has successfully applied. As the leading consumers and importers of wood the OECD countries have a very large responsibility in safeguarding the world's forests."

One of the greatest environmental disappointments throughout OECD countries concerns transportation. Over the past twenty years, improved motor vehicle standards and technological developments incorporated by the automotive industry have helped to mitigate the effects of noise and gas emissions on the environment. But, despite this progress, "the contribution from the transport sector to total emissions of air pollutants is both higher than in the past, and high compared with contributions from other sectors," for the number of vehicles and related problems of traffic congestion have grown continuously.

Another disappointing result is registered for waste

generation and disposal. The good news is that in most OECD countries, municipal-waste-collection services, at least, have become available to the whole population during the past 20 years. Unfortunately, the quantity of wastes produced has increased steadily, raising a number of management problems. OECD figures estimate that in 1990 alone, 9 billion tonnes were produced. These included 420 million tonnes of municipal wastes, and close to 1500 tonnes of industrial wastes (including over 300 million tonnes of hazardous wastes). Additionally, about 7 billion tonnes of other wastes—residues from energy production, mining, agriculture, sewage sludge and demolition debris—were generated. What to do with it? Despite measures taken, the quantity, the toxicity and/or the complexity of waste have overtaken policy planner's ability to deal with it at an acceptable cost. The OECD concludes that "It is vital, therefore, that prevention of waste formation... become a major aspect of the concept of sustainable development."

Lessons for the Future.

In reviewing the results of the OECD survey, a number of observations stand out:

- that within the OECD club itself there is tremendous variation, from one country to another and from one region to another, in responding to environmental problems, The *Environmental Indicators* supplement provides an invaluable breakdown of the details.

- that much pollution is of a transboundary nature, whether it be the release of fluorocarbons into the atmosphere, the contamination of groundwater supplies, acid rain, soil erosion and degradation, or the dumping of wastes into waterways and seas.

- that environmental progress requires not only a reduction in the yearly output of pollution, but also reductions in the backlog of pollutants accumulated in soil, air and water.

- that a compartmentalized approach to studying human exposure to pollution is no longer adequate. New, integrated strategies—that treat the complexities of multiple exposure and the interactions of so-called cross-media pollution on health and environment—must be devised.

- that pollution abatement policy, which has usually focused on outside environmental conditions, should now also look at people's exposure to pollutants inside homes, vehicles, commercial and industrial premises.

- that the international dimension of environmental and economic conditions are increasingly apparent. OECD countries may represent only 16% of the world's population (down from 19% two decades ago) and 24% of its land area; but their market economies account for about 72% of world gross product, 78% of all road vehicles, and 50% of global energy use. They generate about 76% of world trade, including 73% of chemical product exports and about 73% of forest product imports. Some 95% of bilateral development assistance comes from OECD members.

Conclusion

In assessing the state of the environment in member countries, the OECD reveals an uneven track record. For the situation to improve, the report suggests, there must be a better integration of environmental and economic factors in decision-making, whether concerning trade, manufacturing, or aid. Bringing this about will require structural changes at all levels so that economic forces do not undermine the benefits to be gained from environmental regulation and technological innovation. As an example, the OECD report cites the pricing of natural resources, which often do not reflect their true value. In future, recommends the OECD, the cost of pollution prevention or of cleanup should be built into the equation. Water prices, OECD economists say "are too low in most OECD countries and water, accordingly, is inefficiently used."

Another challenge for the 1990s will be to translate the numerous international and regional agreements into environmental realties. International environmental law must be expanded to take account of new concerns such as climate change, and national legislation must be strengthened and enforced. The OECD recommends a greater effort towards quantifying liabilities and targets, and certainly this report, with its wealth of comparative data and other statistics, shows how this might be accomplished. Compendia of environmental data are now published fairly regularly in seventeen OECD countries, although the international comparability of results is still imperfect and mechanisms for the integrating information into policy-making are still quite primitive.

Finally, the OECD concludes that the direct costs of protecting environmental quality of the past twenty years have not been unduly high. The price tag is estimated in the range of 0.8 to 1.5% of GDP, whereas benefits are significant. However, those countries that have deferred pollution abatement and now face an important backlog "might have to consider relatively costly options in order to restore their environment." The good news, according to OECD sources, is that public opinion in the United States, Japan and 14

European countries shows clear support for environmental protection, even at the expense of reduced
economic growth. Public awareness and demands for
a better environment may even have provided that
main impetus to industry and lawmakers for what
progress has already been achieved. It remains to be
seen, however, if the more complex and intractable
problems of the 1990s will fare as well.

Source: Alison Clayson. "The State of the Environment: A Report Card
for OECD Countries." *Ambio* 20, No. 3-4 (1991): 163-4. Reprinted with
permission.

Notes

[1] Australia, Austria, Belgium, Canada, Denmark, Finland, France,
Greece, Iceland, Ireland, Italy, Luxembourg, the Netherlands, New
Zealand, Norway, Portugal, Spain, Sweden, Switzerland, Turkey, the
Untied Kingdom, the United States of America. Plus the Commission
of the European Communities and, sometimes, Yugoslavia.

[2] Copies of The State of the Environment and its supplement Environmental Indicators. A Preliminary Set (Paris 1991) may be ordered for
180 FF from: OECD Publications, 2 rue André-Pascal, 75775 Paris
Cedex 16, France.

Chico Mendes: The Pioneer Frontier Martyr

Julie Wheelwright

JULIE WHEELWRIGHT *is a Canadian journalist living in London.*

Outside Brazil, Francisco Chico Mendes was known as an ecological activist intent on preserving the Amazon rainforest. Inside his own country he was known to the rural landowners as a union troublemaker, and—to the small but growing percentage of middle-class Brazilians in southern cities, increasingly concerned by their country's appalling record for environmental issues—as a hero.

In fact, in the context of Brazil's pioneer frontier along the southern fringes of the Amazon forest, Chico Mendes was just one more "little man" who had attempted to stand up for his rights in the face of powerful interest groups intent on his land.

All along this pioneer front, from Acre and Rondônia in the west, through Mato Grosso and Goiás in central Brazil, and to southern Pará in the east, such "little" men and women have been fighting a losing battle to establish their land-claims against powerful land-owning lobbies. His death is just one of over 1,000 assassinations in connection with land rights since 1980, documented in the 1988 Amnesty International report on human rights. Chico's struggle goes back to the late 1970s, when he and his fellow *seringueiros*, or rubber-tappers, in the Xapuri area of the Western Amazon state of Acre, began to organize themselves into a Union to fight against the near-slavery conditions of their trade. With the help of the fledgeling Partido do Trabalhadores, or Worker's Party, the *seringueiros* were able to win certain basic rights: the right to work the forest within which their rubber trees grew; a fair market price for their balls of smoked latex rubber, and the elimination of the middleman, who, by overcharging for basic necessities, had reduced the *seringueiros* to a state of permanent indebtedness. As the Union grew in numbers, the *seringueiros* established small co-operatively-run schools and medical facilities within their forest *seringais*, or rubber-tapping areas.

Since its acquisition from Bolivia at the turn of the century, Acre had always been the centre for Brazil's rubber-tappers. After the international collapse of the rubber market in the early decades, Acre experienced a slight renaissance during the Second World War, when demand for rubber increased significantly. Of Acre's present population of 380,000, almost a third are still dependent upon the extraction of latex for their own livelihood.

With the increasing success of the Union, Chico and his fellows hoped to extend their cause to the other isolated rubber-tapping communities scattered over the Amazon basin. Their struggle, however, became a head-on collision with far more powerful "interest groups" intent on exploiting the resources of one of the world's last remaining wilderness frontiers. These "interest groups" gave short shrift to the interests of a small, relatively powerless group of "primitive" people depending on an outdated method of gaining their livelihood from the forest.

Until the mid-1980s Acre, isolated by immense distances and a lack of road access from the south, largely escaped the kind of conflicts wracking the other Amazon states along the pioneer frontier. However, with the completion of the BR 364 highway to Porto Velho, capital of the neighbouring state of Rondônia to the south, and the planned extension of the road to Acre's capital of Rio Branco, the state came increasingly under the rapacious gaze of land-hungry outsiders. And while foreigners see the Amazon basin as an area of wilderness to be preserved, to the majority of Brazilians—those living far away in the developed cities to the south, and those in charge of Brazil's onward march to prosperity and development—the Amazon basin represents a huge area of untapped riches. The lack of development is simply symbolic of the country's backwardness.

As the battle hotted-up for control of Acre's forests, the *seringueiros* found themselves under increasing pressure from large landowners, intent on clearing forests for cattle-ranchers, or for lucrative re-sale to prospective colonists. Although rubber-tappers are active in most of the forest, the cattle-ranchers own the land titles—often forgeries, according to the rubber-tappers.

With Federal Government incentives for agricultural projects within the Amazon, the price of land in the areas bordering the new road rocketed. Cleared land was sold for ten times the value of the original virgin forest, regardless of the suitability of its soils for agriculture or ranching. With the immense value to loggers of the tropical hardwoods, it is not difficult to see how fortunes could be made—the eventual agricultural worth of the land became irrelevant.

Since the early 1980s, faced with the increased chances that a democratic Brazilian Government would actually implement some kind of land reform, the large landowners, and principally those owning large tracts of land along the pioneer frontier, have allied themselves in a group called the "União Democrático Rural", the Democratic rural Union, or UDR. The group wielded such power that, by successful lobbying, it was able to modify the 1986s Land Reform Bill to such an extent as to render it virtually toothless. The UDR does not operate as a separate political party, but rather by throwing its support behind any state or federal politician sufficiently sympathetic to its aims. This has led to some bizarre political alliances in the state politics along the pioneer front. One of the UDR's recent successes has been the creation of the State of Tocatins, carved out of the north of Goiás state, and controlled by UDR members owning most of this virgin land. This move has been guaranteed by Brasilia's constituent assembly, presently hammering out Brazil's new constitution.

Fortunately for Acre's *seringueiros*, their fight to establish rights in the rainforest coincided with a focusing of the world's attention on the destruction of the rainforest habitat, and all its attendant horror-stories of oxygen-depletion and climatic changes. Chico Mendes was adopted by international environmentalist groups as a champion of ecological good sense. The *seringueiro*, with his dependence on a large area of forest within which to tap his trees, is a natural defender of the rainforest; both the *seringueira* tree, and the *castanheira* or Brazil-nut tree, depend on the complex ecology of the rainforest to survive, as lone trees become sterile and die.

Allied with the political and financial clout of the environmentalist groups, the rubber-tappers could use their intricate knowledge of the forest to come up with an alternative plan for exploitation of the Amazon, one which would simultaneously safeguard the forest itself.

Thus was born the "extractive reserve" project. In 1988, funded by the Washington-based Inter-American Development Bank and the World Wide Fund for Nature (WWF), three such forest reserves were set up by the state and government in Acre. Of the state's 15 million hectares, 3.5 million hectares of the most accessible land were targeted for state appropriation: one million hectares of the most fertile soils were set aside for colonization, and the reminder for the creations of the extractive reserves is to establish further ways of extracting renewable resources, without entailing destruction of the habitat.

It was into one of these extractive reserves, a rubber-tapping area supporting various *seringueiro* families with a small community school, where he himself had worked all his life, that Chico Mendes led various representatives of the world's press and members of environmentalist groups last July. His knowledge of the forest, its extractive products and medicinal plants, contrasted sharply with the large landowners' ignorance of not only forest-management, but even the most basic conservation measures necessary on their own ranches.

Sadly, Chico's international fame was not enough to guarantee his life. He was shot down in his simple wooden house in Xapuri on 22 December 1988; police suspect the two sons of a local rancher.

Whether the state government has the political will, or even power, to continue its policy of rational exploitation of the forest remains to be seen. International pressure made the Federal Government cut off incentives for agricultural development in the Amazon.

There are signs that the outrage felt over Sr Mendes' death is provoking hitherto complacent middle-class Brazilians into demanding changes in their government's attitude to environment policies.

Moreover, as Sr Mendes joins a long list of pioneer frontier martyrs, there is a growing realization that further environmental degradation can only be avoided if tackled in conjunction with a more rational and just policy of land distribution.

Source: Julie Wheelwright. "The Rain Forest Myth." *Geographical Magazine*, April 1989: 22-24.

Towards Common Action: Proposals for Institutional and Legal Change

Gro Harlem Brundtland

GRO HARLEM BRUNDTLAND *(1913-) is the Prime Minister of Norway. She is a physician and democratic socialist who headed the United Nations Commission investigating the political, social, and ecological difficulties associated with sustained global economic growth.*

In the middle of the 20th century, we saw our planet from space for the first time. Historians may eventually find that this vision had a greater impact on thought than did the Copernican revolution of the 16th century, which upset humans' self-image by revealing that the Earth is not the centre of the universe. From space, we see a small and fragile ball dominated not by human activity and edifice but by a pattern of clouds, oceans, greenery, and soils. Humanity's inability to fit its activities into that pattern is changing planetary systems fundamentally. Many such changes are accompanied by life-threatening hazards, from environmental degradation to nuclear destruction. These new realities, from which there is no escape, must be recognized—and managed.

The issues we have raised in this report are inevitably of far-reaching importance to the quality of life on earth—indeed, to life itself. We have tried to show how human survival and well-being could depend on success in elevating sustainable development to a global ethic. In doing so, we have called for such major efforts as greater willingness and co-operation to combat international poverty, to maintain peace and enhance security world-wide, and to manage the global commons. We have called for national and international action in respect of population, food, plant and animal species, energy, industry, and urban settlements. The previous chapters have described the policy directions required.

The onus for action lies with no one group of nations. Developing countries face the challenges of desertification, deforestation, and pollution, and endure most of the poverty associated with environmental degradation. The entire human family of nations would suffer from the disappearance of rain forests in the tropics, the loss of plant and animal species, and changes in rainfall patterns. Industrial nations face the challenges of toxic chemicals, toxic wastes, and acidification. All nations may suffer from the releases by industrialized countries of carbon dioxide and of gases that react with the ozone layer, and from any future war fought with the nuclear arsenals controlled by those nations. All nations will also have a role to play in securing peace, in changing trends, and in righting an international economic system that increases rather than decreases inequality, that increases rather than decreases numbers of poor and hungry.

The time has come to break out of past patterns. Attempts to maintain social and ecological stability through old approaches to development and environmental protection will increase instability. Security must be sought through change. The Commission has noted a number of actions that must be taken to reduce risks to survival and to put future development on paths that are sustainable.

Without such reorientation of attitudes and emphasis, little can be achieved. We have no illusions about "quick-fix" solutions. We have tried to point out some pathways to the future. But there is no substitute for the journey itself, and there is no alternative to the process by which we retain a capacity to respond to the experience it provides. We believe this to hold true in all the areas covered in this report. But the policy changes we have suggested have institutional implications, and it is to these we now turn—emphasizing that they are a complement to, not a substitute for, the wider policy changes for which we call. Nor do they represent definitive solutions, but rather first steps in what will be a continuing process.

In what follows we put forward, in the first place, what are essentially conceptual guidelines for institutions at the national level. We recognize that there are large differences among countries in respect of population size, resources, income level, management capacity, and institutional traditions; only governments themselves can formulate the changes they should make. Moreover, the tools for monitoring and evaluating sustainable development are rudimentary and require further refinement.

We also address, in more specific terms, the question of international institutions. The preceding chapters have major implications for international co-operation and reforms, both economic and legal. The international agencies clearly have an important role in making these changes effective, and we endeavour to set out the institutional implications, especially as regards the United Nations system.

I. The Challenge for Institutional and Legal Change

Shifting the Focus to the Policy Sources

The next few decades are crucial for the future of humanity. Pressures on the planet are now unprecedented and are accelerating at rates and scales new to human experience: a doubling of global population in a few decades, with most of the growth in cities; a five- to tenfold increase in economic activity in less than half a century; and the resulting pressures for growth and changes in agricultural, energy, and industrial systems. Opportunities for more sustainable forms of growth and development are also growing. New technologies and potentially unlimited access to information offer great promise.

Each area of change represents a formidable challenge in its own right, but the fundamental challenge stems from their systemic character. They lock together environment and development, once thought separate; they lock together "sectors," such as industry and agriculture; and they lock countries together as the effects of national policies and actions spill over national borders. Separate policies and institutions can no longer cope effectively with these interlocked issues. Nor can nations, acting unilaterally.

The integrated and interdependent nature of the new challenges and issues contrasts sharply with the nature of the institutions that exist today. These institutions tend to be independent, fragmented, and working to relatively narrow mandates with closed decision processes. Those responsible for managing natural resources and protecting the environment are institutionally separated from those responsible for managing the economy. The real world of interlocked economic and ecological systems will not change; the policies and institutions concerned must.

This new awareness requires major shifts in the way governments and individuals approach issues of environment, development, and international co-operation. Approaches to environment policy can be broadly characterized in two ways. One, characterized as the "standard agenda," reflects an approach to environmental policy, laws, and institutions that focuses on environmental effects. The second reflects an approach concentrating on the policies that are the sources of those effects.[1] These two approaches represent distinctively different ways of looking both at the issues and at the institutions to manage them.

The effects-oriented "standard agenda" has tended to predominate as a result of growing concerns about the dramatic decline in environmental quality that the industrialized world suffered during the 1950s and 1960s. New environmental protection and resource management agencies were added on to the existing institutional structures, and given mainly scientific staffs.[2]

These environment agencies have registered some notable successes in improving environmental quality during the past two decades.[3] They have secured significant gains in monitoring and research and in defining and understanding the issues in scientific and technical terms. They have raised public awareness, nationally and internationally. Environmental laws have induced innovation and the development of new control technologies, processes, and products in most industries, reducing the resource content of growth.[4]

However, most of these agencies have been confined by their own mandates to focusing almost exclusively on the effects. Today, the sources of these effects must be tackled. While these existing environmental protection policies and agencies must be maintained and even strengthened, governments now need to take a much broader view of environmental problems and policies.

Central agencies and major sectoral ministries play key roles in national decision making. These agencies have the greatest influence on the form, character, and distribution of the impacts of economic activity on the environmental resource base. It is these agencies through their policies and budgets, that determine whether the environmental resource base is enhanced or degraded and whether the planet will be able to support human and economic growth and change into the next century.

The mandated goals of these agencies include increasing investment, employment, food, energy, and other economic and social goods. Most have no mandate to concern themselves with sustaining the environmental resource capital on which these goals depend. Those with such mandates are usually grouped in separate environment agencies or, sometimes, in minor units within sectoral agencies. In either case, they usually learn of new initiatives in economic and trade policy, or in energy and agricultural policy, or of new tax measures that will have a severe impact on resources, long after the effective decisions have been taken. Even if they were to learn earlier, most lack the authority to ensure that a given policy is implemented.

Environmental protection and sustainable development must be an integral part of the mandates of all agencies of governments, of international organizations, and of major private-sector institutions. These must be made responsible and accountable for ensuring that their policies, programmes, and budgets encourage and support activities that are economically and ecologically sustainable both in the short and longer terms. They must be given a mandate to pursue their traditional goals in such a way that those goals are reinforced by a steady enhancement of the environmental resource base of their own national community and of the small planet we all share.

New Imperatives for International Co-operation

National boundaries have become so porous that traditional distinctions between local, national, and international issues have become blurred. Policies formerly considered to be exclusively matters of "national concern" now have an impact on the ecological bases of other nations' development and survival. Conversely, the growing reach of some nations' policies—economic, trade, monetary, and most sectoral policies—into the "sovereign" territory of other nations limits the affected nations' options in devising national solutions to their "own" problems. This fast-changing context for national action has introduced new imperatives and new opportunities for international co-operation.

The international legal framework must also be significantly strengthened in support of sustainable development. Although international law related to environment has evolved rapidly since the 1972 Stockholm Conference, major gaps and deficiencies must still be overcome as part of the transition to sustainable development. Much of the evidence and conclusions presented in earlier chapters of this report calls into question not just the desirability but even the feasibility of maintaining an international system that cannot prevent one of several states from damaging the ecological basis for development and even the prospects for survival of any other or even all other states.

However, just at the time when nations need increased international co-operation, the will to co-operate has sharply declined. By the mid-1980s, multilateral institutions were under siege for many, and often contradictory, reasons. The UN system has come under increasing attack for either proposing to do too much or, more frequently, for apparently doing too little. Conflicting national interests have blocked significant institutional reforms and have increased the need for fundamental change.[5] By the mid-1980s, funds for many international organizations had levelled off or declined in both relative and absolute terms.

Bilateral development assistance has declined as a percentage of gross national product (GNP) in many countries, falling even further below the targets proposed in the early 1970s.[6] The benefits and effectiveness of aid have come under serious question, in part because of criticism based on environmental considerations.[7] Yet, sustainable development creates the need for even greater international aid and co-operation.

Nations must now confront a growing number, frequency, and scale of crises. A major reorientation is needed in many policies and institutional arrangements at the international as well as national level. The time has come to break away. Dismal scenarios of mounting destruction of national and global potential for development—indeed, of the Earth's capacity to support life—are not inescapable destiny. One of the most hopeful characteristics of the changes the world is racing through is that invariably they reflect great opportunities for sustainable development, providing that institutional arrangements permit sustainable policy options to be elaborated, considered, and implemented.

II. Proposals for Institutional and Legal Change

The ability to choose policy paths that are sustainable requires that the ecological dimensions of policy be considered at the same time as the economic, trade, energy, agricultural, industrial, and other dimensions—on the same agendas and in the same national and international institutions. That is the chief institutional challenge of the 1990s.

There are significant proposals for institutional and legal change in previous chapters of our report. The Commission's proposals for institutional and legal change at the national, regional, and international levels are embodied in six priority areas:
- getting at the sources,
- dealing with the effects,
- assessing global risks,
- making informed choices,
- providing the legal means, and
- investing in our future.

Together, these priorities represent the main directions for institutional and legal change needed to make the transition to sustainable development. Concerted action is needed under all six.

Source: Gro Harlem Brundtland. *Our Common Future.* New York: Oxford University Press, 1987. © World Commission on Environment and Development 1967. Reprinted from *Our Common Future* (1967) by permission of Oxford University Press.

Notes

[1] The characteristics and differences of the two approaches are described in our inaugural report, "Mandate for Change: Key Issues, Strategy and Workplan," Geneva, 1985.

[2] L.G. Uy, "Combating the Notion of Environment as Additionality: A study of the Integration of Environment and Development and a Case for Environmental Development as Investment," Centre for Environmental Studies, University of Tasmania, Hobart, Tasmania, 1985 (to be published).

[3] OECD, *Environment and Economics, Vols I and II*, Background Papers for the International Conference on Environment and Economics (Paris: 1984).

[4] OECD, "The Impact of Environment Policies on Industrial Innovation," in *Environment and Economics, Vol. III, op. cit.*

[5] R. Bertrand, "Some Reflections on Reform of the United Nations," Joint Inspection Unit, UN, Geneva, 1985.

[6] V. Fernando, "Development Assistance, Environment and Development," prepared for WCED, Geneva, 1985.

[7] "List of Projects with Possible Environmental Issues," transmitted to Congress by US Agency for International Development, 1987, as included in Public Law 99-591.

The Value of Biodiversity

Paul R. Ehrlich and Anne H. Ehrlich

PAUL R. EHRLICH *is Bing Professor of Population Studies and Professor of Biological Sciences at Standford University. He has published extensively primarily in the field of ecology and evolution.*
ANNE H. EHRLICH *is a senior Research Associate in Biological Sciences at Stanford University. She has co-authored with Paul Ehrlich several books including* Extinction, The Population Explosion, *and* Healing the Planet.

One problem facing ecologists and economists today is how to measure the value of environmental goods whose destruction (associated with the ever-increasing scale of the human enterprise) generates vast externalities. A prime example of one of those goods is biodiversity—the variety of genetically distinct populations and species of plant, animals, and microorganisms with which *Homo sapiens* shares Earth, and the variety of ecosystems of which they are functioning parts.

Economists and ecologists agree that biodiversity has value to humanity, although whether it has value independent of human needs is less clear. Both groups also agree that the value of biodiversity to humanity has both use and non-use components. Biodiversity can be important because it supplies us with food (fishing and hunting), direct enjoyment (scenic values, bird watching), or ecosystem services (recycling of nutrients): all use values. It also provides non-use values, especially so-called existence values, for example, the pleasure an American who will never travel to Africa may get from knowing that free-living black rhinos exist there.

This paper does not address the question of how to measure the economic values of biodiversity; that is a task primarily for economists. Rather, we wish to summarize two ecologists' views of those values qualitatively to provide economists with background they need to carry out the evaluation. One can conveniently divide those values into four categories: *ethical*; *esthetic*; *direct economic*; and *indirect economic*.

Ethical Values

The ethical values of biodiversity are based on the religious or quasi-religious feelings of many people in many cultures that other lifeforms have intrinsic value and deserve some degree of protection from destruction by humanity. These views differ from society to society and are not applied equally to all organisms. Buddha questioned whether human beings have a right to kill other animals *at all*. A religious Buddhist may strive to avoid stepping on ants when he walks, since he considers all life sacred. A nonreligious American might contend that people should never kill whales, but would swat a mosquito without a second thought.

There has been a historic precedent for extending the notion of *rights* to include animals other than human beings. Two centuries ago it was permissible to beat your horse to death. Today, horses are legally protected against abuse, and regard for other domestic animals is encoded in humane laws. That such sentiments are being extended to nondomestic animals is suggested by increasing opposition to hunting, laws to protect birds, the movement to protect whales and dolphins, and the general revulsion at such spectacles as the Canadian slaughter of baby seals.

Our own view, and that of many biologists and environmentalists, is that, as the dominant species on the planet, *Homo sapiens* has an ethical responsibility to preserve biodiversity. This means opposing intentional exterminations of other species and supporting conservation efforts. One cannot assert this ethical responsibility on scientific grounds. It clearly arises from essentially religious feelings; we believe that our only known living companions in the universe have a right to exist. Biologist David Ehrenfeld[1] called this the *Noah Principle*, naming it after the best-known practitioner of conservation. In Ehrenfeld's view, species and communities should be preserved "because they exist and because this existence is itself but the present expression of a continuing historic process of immense antiquity and majesty. Longstanding existence in Nature carries with it the unimpeachable right to continued existence." We suspect that the basic problem of conserving biodiversity is not likely to be solved until and unless a much large proportion of the human population comes to share this view.

Esthetic Values

The beauty of birds, tropical fishes, butterflies, and flowering plants is widely acknowledged and supports extensive economic activity including bird-watching and feeding, scuba diving, butterfly collection, photography, and the making of nature films. But many less familiar organisms have a little-appreciated beauty. For instance, some tiny wasps and flies, when seen under the microscope, appear to be fashioned out of solid gold. The algae known as diatoms have glasslike shells that are as exquisite and varied as snowflakes. Indeed, *all* organisms at least exhibit the beauty of design. Even the tiniest beetles, some of which are scarcely bigger than a period on this page, have complete external skeletons, nervous and digestive systems, and complex musculature. Such insects show a degree of sophisticated miniaturization as yet unapproached by human engineers. They also exhibit complicated behaviours and intricate relationships with other organisms, giving them what we have called a *beauty of interest*.[2] In fact, insects display the kind of beauty, intricacy, and diversity that captivates gun collectors, airplane and railroad buffs, philatelists, computer hackers, bibliophiles, and so one. Even a single insect species can, and has, provided a human being with a lifetime of fascinating study. So even if insects didn't play critical roles in the ecosystems that support humanity, to the degree that we lose their diversity, the world becomes a less interesting place. Each species of bug is, as the great French anthropologist Claude Levi-Strauss wrote, "an irreplaceable treasure, equal to the works of art which we religiously preserve in museums."[3] Each one dwarfs in interest and intricacy works like the Mona Lisa which are valued at tens of millions of dollars, yet humanity exterminates them without a qualm.

Direct Economic Values

Natural ecosystems, of course, also directly provide people with food and innumerable materials of all sorts, from maple syrup and truffles to teak. Most notably, a crucial portion of the protein in our diets comes straight from nature in the form of fishes and other animals harvested from the seas. This service is provided by the oceans in conjunction with coastal wetland habitats, which serve as crucial nurseries for marine life that is either harvested directly or serves as a food supply for sea life that we eat.

The timber and other wood products that we harvest from forests are also provided free by natural ecosystems. People do replant trees in managed forests and tree farms, but the quality and variety of timbers from such sources is generally inferior to that from old-growth forests. Rubber, many kinds of oils and organic chemicals, spices and herbs, wild berries and game are provided by natural ecosystems. The active ingredients in at least a third of the prescription drugs used by civilization come directly from or were derived from chemical compounds found in wild plants, fungi, or other organisms, especially in tropical forests—digitalis, morphine, quinine, and antibiotics being among the most familiar.

Natural ecosystems maintain a vast *genetic library* from which *Homo sapiens* has already withdrawn the very basis of civilization and which promises untold future benefits. That library of millions of different species and billions of genetically distinct populations is what biologists are referring to when they speak of biotic diversity, or biodiversity.

Wheat, rice, and corn (maize) were scruffy wild grasses before they were borrowed from the library and developed by selective breeding into the productive crops that now form much of humanity's feeding base. Wild relatives of those and dozens of other crops still represent important reservoirs of genes that are essential for improving the crops or developing new strains to keep them from being overwhelmed by stresses such as changing climate or the evolution of new pest or diseases. All crops and all domestic animals, of course, originated from that library.

The capacity of the genetic library to supply more of the same is still largely untapped. The potential for biodiversity to supply new and vitally needed foods and medicines alone is enormous.[4,5] Recently, scientists have found another medically useful compound, gliotoxin, among the lowly fungi, which gave humanity penicillin and cyclosporin A (the latter is used routinely by surgeons to guard against rejection of organ transplants). Gliotoxin shows promise of providing a way to make transplanted organs invisible to the body's immune system without compromising their other functions.[6] That could relieve transplant patients the dangers of taking drugs (like cyclosporin A) that suppress the immune system and protect the transplant but also expose the patient to a serious risk of infection. Gliotoxin also has characteristics that may make it a powerful tool in designing anti-cancer drugs.

Similarly, wild plants and animals could be sources of new foods to augment the human food supply, which in the last generation or two has seen shrinkage in the variety of foodstuffs entering the economy as agricultural systems have shifted to the *big three* (wheat, rice an maize) and other widely grown and improved crops at the expense of many traditional varieties and species. The narrowing of the genetic base of major crops is a serious concern that has been addressed (although how adequately is questioned by many agronomists and geneticists). But the neglect of potential food plants that have never been domesticated and of many traditional foods in tropical regions is also a serious matter, especially as tropical forests, the prime potential source of new foods, drugs, and other useful materials, vanish at accelerating rates.[7] Furthermore, the tropical regions where such new foods might be found are the regions where people are hungriest and most in need of new food resources.[8,9]

Indirect Economic Values

Humanity, of course, is dependent for its very existence on other organisms, but in ways that are rarely recognized in formal economic analyses. It must be emphasized that it is not just preserving samples of the world's genetic diversity (as might conceivably, but not practically, be done through a vast network of seed banks, botanic gardens, and zoos) that is important. Other organisms, in all their extraordinary variety, are part and parcel of a global life-support system that benefits them and humanity as well. We not only sprang from other life ourselves, we are completely dependent on it to maintain the habitability of this planet.

Perhaps the most basic dependence of humanity on other organisms is through the process of photosynthesis. That is the process by which green plants, algae, and some microorganisms bind solar energy into chemical bonds of carbohydrate molecules (sugars, starches, cellulose). That chemical energy can be used to drive the life processes of organisms, mostly by combining it with oxygen in a slow burning process known as cellular respiration (or just respiration). The vast majority of non-photosynthesizers—human beings and other animals, fungi, and many microorganisms—must obtain their energy from photosynthesizers, either by eating them or by eating other animals that do.

Members of biological communities, the collection of organisms living in an area, interact continuously with their nonliving surroundings, and the interacting complexes are what biologists call ecosystems. Every kind of organism exchanges gases with its physical environment. The rosebush in your garden takes in carbon dioxide (CO_2) and gives off oxygen when the sun shines (and the reverse at night). Indeed, all photosynthesizing plants remove carbon dioxide from the atmosphere and water from the soil, and use the carbon from the carbon dioxide and the hydrogen from the water to build carbohydrates. The excess oxygen is released to the atmosphere. In contrast, human beings and other animals take in oxygen and carbohydrates (as well as other molecules necessary for life), and give off carbon dioxide, water, and heat. The latter are the exhaust products of respiration: plants also produce CO_2 as they respire and use it in their photosynthesis.

Rooted plants remove a steady stream of water from the soil and release it into the atmosphere as water vapor. The volume of this water flow, which holds plants without woody stems upright and prevents wilting of the leaves of trees and shrubs, is little appreciated. A single corn plant with a dry weight of a pound at maturity transfers some sixty gallons of water from soil to atmosphere during its lifetime of a few months. The amount of water that a single rainforest tree returns to the atmosphere in its lifetime of 100 years or more is truly prodigious—on the order of 2.5 million gallons.

Plants also help to break apart rocks and form soil, and change patterns of low-level winds (as anyone who has moved from an open meadow into a woodland on a windy day can attest). Various organisms, especially bacteria, help run vast chemical cycles in which elements such as carbon, nitrogen, sulfur, and phosphorus circulate on a global scale.

The interdependence of the biological and physical worlds can be seen in the story of how our distant ancestors migrated ashore from the sea. Until perhaps 450 million years ago (about one tenth of Earth's age), life was confined to the oceans. Then in what, geologically speaking, was a relatively short period—perhaps 40 million years—plants, arthropods (insects and their relatives), and amphibians (ancestors of frogs and salamanders) colonized the land. That sudden emergence from the deep was made possible by the activities of photosynthesizers in the oceans.

The first photosynthetic bacteria appeared in the sea 3 billion years or more before the land was occupied. Oxygen is a byproduct of photosynthesis, and all the oxygen in Earth's oceans and atmosphere was put there by that process. Today, oxygen is the second most common gas in the atmosphere (after nitrogen), comprising about a fifth of it, and it was all put there by living beings over billions of years.

Ozone is a special type of oxygen molecule formed of three (rather than two) oxygen atoms. It is formed in the stratosphere when ultraviolet radiation from the sun splits a normal O_2 molecule and one of the resultant atoms latches on to another O_2 molecule to form a molecule of ozone, O_3. Ozone absorbs solar radiation in a portion of the ultraviolet part of the spectrum known as UV-B.[10] That is lucky for life on land, since UV-B is extremely damaging to life, and no other atmospheric molecule effectively blocks it out (UV-B does not penetrate water beyond 15 to 60 feet, depending on the clarity of the water).[11]

It took marine photosynthesizers billions of years to enrich the oceans and then the atmosphere with enough oxygen (and thus ozone) to create an ozone layer high in the stratosphere to shield Earth's surface from most of the income UV-B. So early organisms in the oceans critically modified the physical world by giving Earth an oxygen-rich atmosphere. This enabled living things, including our distant ancestors (those amphibians), to leave the sea. And ozone, a product of chemical processes in both living and nonliving systems, is itself an important greenhouse gas in the troposphere (lower atmosphere), influencing Earth's surface temperature and climate.

Because of the crucial importance of interactions between living and nonliving portions of the biosphere, they can be viewed as two components of a single worldwide ecosystem. Ecologists consider the entire biosphere to be an ecosystem, and they view local biotic communities and the physical environments, with which the organisms in the communities interact, as ecosystems as well.

Two kinds of ecosystems are crucial to the functioning of human society today. The first kind is agricultural ecosystems, whose importance to society is obvious. Basically, they are simplified versions of natural ecosystems, artificially maintained by humanity to increase the production of commodities people need and desire. The importance of natural ecosystems is much less widely appreciated, but society depends upon them every bit as much as it depends on agricultural ecosystems. That is true in large part because agricultural ecosystems are embedded in natural ones and depend on the natural components for their sustained productivity. ...

Substituting for Ecosystem Services

As should be apparent by now, living organisms in natural and agricultural ecosystems play enormous and critical roles in making Earth a suitable habitat for *Homo sapiens*. They have already stored enough oxygen in the atmosphere for us to breathe for thousands of years even if no more were produced;[12] they supply all our food (directly or indirectly), and they help to keep the climate equable and fresh water flowing steadily. Furthermore, these services are provided on such a grand scale that there is usually no real possibility of substituting for them, even in cases where scientists might know how.[13] In short, their destruction is in large measure irreversible. Even where restoration is possible, it requires a great deal of effort and a long time to accomplish; even then, the result is likely to be an impoverished version of the original. This irreversibility thus raises important questions of intergenerational equity, among others.

People have tried substitutions, sometimes with a measure of success, at least initially. In developing the productive agricultures of the North American Midwest, humanity, with apparent success, has substituted corn and wheat for perennial prairie grasses (plants whose vegetative parts survive several winters and which reproduce over several summers). But the crops are annuals (they go through a complete generation each year, starting form seed), and annuals do not develop the extensive root systems of perennials. They therefore do not participate in the soil-generating service of ecosystems to the same degree as perennials; soil nutrient stores are gradually depleted, and soil itself is more readily eroded away. Inorganic fertilizers are used to replace some important nutrients, but they contribute little toward maintaining the structure of soil or its component micro-organisms. Whether the depth and fertility of the prairie soils can be maintained indefinitely under cultivation remains to be seen. So far, the signs are not encouraging.[14,15] Meanwhile, native prairie grasses that might be essential elements in restoring more productive pastures in the Midwest are barely hanging on in places like cemeteries and railroad embankments.

The loss of ecosystem services following deforestation is especially rapid and dramatic. Ecologist F.J. Bormann explained the substitution dilemma as follows:[16]

> We must find replacements for wood products, build erosion control works, enlarge reservoirs, upgrade air pollution control technology, install flood control works, improve water purification plants, increase air conditioning, and provide new recreational facilities. These substitutes represent an enormous tax burden, a drain on the world's supply of natural resources, and increased stress on the natural system that remains. Clearly the diminution of solar-powered natural systems and the expansion of fossil-powered human systems are currently locked in a positive feedback cycle. Increased consumption of fossil energy means increased stress on natural systems, which in turn means still more consumption of fossil energy to replace lost natural functions if the quality of life is to be maintained.

The loss of the *genetic library* service is particularly severe when tropical rain forests are cleared, and crops, pastures, scrub, or other types of vegetation substituted for them, since those forests are home to somewhere between 50 and 90% of all of Earth's species (distinct kinds) of organisms.[17]

In fact, one could conclude that virtually all human attempts at complete or large-scale substitution for ecosystem services are ultimately unsuccessful, whether it be substitutions of synthetic pesticides for natural pest control, inorganic fertilizers for natural ones, chlorination for natural water purification, or whatever.[18] Substitutes generally require a large energy subsidy, which adds to humanity's general impact on the environment. And most substitutes are not completely satisfactory even in the short run. In sum, there is little to suggest that humanity will be able to substitute adequately for the ecosystem services that will be lost as the epidemic of extinctions now under way escalates. And escalate it seems bound to do. No one knows for certain how fast genetically distinct populations and species of other organisms are vanishing, but all biologists who deal with the problem know the rates are far too high and are rising.

The Extinction Epidemic

How do biologists know? First, they are watching the flora and fauna fading away before their very eyes. Coral reefs on which we studied the behaviour of fascinating fishes have been destroyed by the sewage from "love boat" cruise ships. Many places where we once studied butterflies have been converted to freeways, parking lots, or farm fields. We have searched in vain for once abundant frogs in Costa Rica. In the last hundred years, ichthyologists have seen 27 species of freshwater fishes become extinct in North America. Ornithologists watch in distress as populations of many forest birds of the eastern United States decline rapidly.[19]

That evidence, however, is anecdotal. More important, and more scientific evidence is what biologists know: that organisms are highly adapted to their habitats. Many eastern warblers require extensive tracts of forest to maintain their populations; the neon tetras so prized by aquarists will only breed in acid water (in which trout cannot breed); caterpillars or Bay checkerspot butterflies require certain plants to eat, and those plants require certain kinds of soils to grow on. The list is endless; populations of organisms are honed by evolution to thrive in their home environments, and they often have very specific requirements for survival. If a habitat is dramatically changed, most or all the plants, animals, and microorganisms that once inhabited it will consequently be wiped out.

Humanity today is on a rampage of changing natural habitats dramatically: cutting them down, plowing them up, overgrazing them, paving them over, damming and diverting water, flooding or draining areas, spraying them with pesticides and acid rain, pouring oil into them, changing their climates, exposing them to increased ultraviolet radiation, and on and on. And the process is accelerating: the rate of destruction of tropical forests almost doubled in the 1980s.[20]

Consequently, ecologists know that Earth's biota is being slaughtered at an escalating pace, but it is not possible to count populations and species as they vanish.[21] For one thing, the true extent of biodiversity is unknown. Estimates of the total number of existing species range from an extremely conservative 2 million (some 1.4 million have been described and given Latin names) to well over 50 million.[22] Assuming there are 10 million species more or less, and that on average each species consists of several hundred genetically distinct populations, one can easily postulate the existence of billions of populations.[23]

How fast is this diversity now disappearing? Although it is impossible to say with precision, the answer clearly is "frighteningly fast."[24] More than a decade ago, we estimated that mammal and bird species were becoming extinct 40 to 400 times as fast as they normally have since the great extinction spasm that affected the dinosaurs and many other life-forms 65 million years ago.[25] In 1989, Harvard's Craaford Laureate ecologist, E.O. Wilson, conservatively estimated the annual extinction rate at 4000 to 6000 species, some 10,000 times the background rate before *Homo sapiens* started practicing agriculture. It is conceivable that the rate is actually 60 000 to 90 000 species annually; 150 000 times background.[26,27]

Of course, biotic diversity is constantly generated by the natural process that eventually creates new species. That process of the differentiation of populations (speciation) normally operates on a time scale of from thousands to millions of years. All estimates of present day extinction rates show them to be vastly higher than the rates at which the natural process that creates biodiversity could be expected to compensate for the losses.[28] The extinction *outputs* far exceed the speciation *inputs*, and Earth is becoming biotically impoverished because of it.

To biologists, perhaps the most ominous data pointing to the urgency of dealing with the extinction problem are those relating to the human impact on the planet's total supply of energy produced in photosynthesis—global net primary production.[29] Net primary production (NPP) is the energy fixed by photosynthesis, minus that required by the plants themselves for their life processes.[30] One can think of NPP basically as the total food supply of all animals and decomposers. Almost 40% of all potential NPP generated on land is now directly consumed, diverted, or forgone because of the activities of only one of millions of animal species, *Homo sapiens*. Although the human impact on NPP in oceanic ecosystems is very small (c. 2%), that on land is so huge that we appropriate altogether about 25% of global NPP.

Human beings use NPP directly when they eat plants or feed them to domestic animals and when they harvest wood and other plant products. Human beings divert NPP by altering entire systems, redirecting NPP towards human ends, as when natural ecosystems are converted to cropland or pasture. And people *reduce* potential NPP by converting highly productive natural systems into less productive ones: tropical forests to pastures; savannas and grasslands to deserts; deciduous forests and prairies to farms; and farms to homes, shopping centers, and parking lots.

Since the great majority of the world's species (probably over 95%) now exist on land, the 40% human appropriation and loss of NPP there go far to explain the extinction crisis. The amount of energy available to support the millions of other kinds of animals on Earth clearly has been drastically reduced. Plant diversity too, is reduced because much less land, especially land with suitable soils and climate, remains to support plant growth outside human-controlled or degraded areas. One, probably conservative, estimate made on the basis of this reduction of available energy is that 3 to 9% of Earth's species may be extinct or endangered by 2000, an estimate in the same ballpark as the higher ones above.[31] If the current accelerating trends continue, half of Earth's species might easily disappear by 2050.

The amount of terrestrial NPP available to accommodate further expansion of the human enterprise is not that great, considering that humanity has already taken over some 40% and the human population is projected to double in the next half-century or so. Yet expectations are for massive economic growth to meet the needs and aspirations of that exploding population. One important international study, the Brundtland Report, advocated a five- to tenfold increase in global economic activity in the next several decades in an effort to eliminate poverty.[32] What a substantial expansion of both the population *and* its mobilization of resources implies for the redirection and further loss of terrestrial NPP by humanity is obvious: people will try to take over all of it and lose more in the process.

Harvard policy analyst William Clark was being extremely conservative when he wrote, "The implications of this desperately needed economic growth for the already stressed planetary environment are at least problematic and are potentially catastrophic."[33] Indeed, if anything remotely resembling the Brundtland population-economic growth scenario is played out, we can kiss goodbye to most of the world's biodiversity, and perhaps civilization along with it.

The Economic Value of Biodiversity

The ravaging of biodiversity, in our view, is the most serious single environmental peril facing civilization. Biodiversity is a resource for which there is absolutely no substitute; its loss is irreversible on any time-scale of interest to society. The loss can be viewed as one of the (if not *the*) most single serious externality associated with human economic activity. But it is an externality so vast and pervasive that finding ways to evaluate (let alone internalize) it will be difficult in the extreme. All we will offer here is a few comments on possible approaches.

First, there are clearly some species whose value is amenable to rather routine cost-benefit analyses—those, for example, that are harvested commercially. The value of species with high esthetic, interest, or rarity values, such as beautiful birds, *Morpho* butterflies, great whales or black rhinoceros can also be monetized by techniques such as assessment of willingness to pay travel costs to see them or asking people how much they would be willing to donate to save them. Such methods will provide only partial values for those species, however. They would not ordinarily encompass their roles in food chains or their potential values to future generations.

Furthermore, methods focusing on the values of individual species, especially scarce ones, will not ordinarily capture the critical ecosystem services value of biodiversity in aggregate. For example, one might be able to demonstrate that the role of a given plankton-eating whale species in an oceanic food chain was not critical to the ecosystem's stability. If that species were exterminated. populations of other plankton-feeding whales might increase and fill the role of the extinct species. But the extermination of one such whale species would increase the probability that all the other would go extinct, as whaling pressures were transferred to them. Even the loss of a second whale species might cause significant changes in oceanic ecosystems (perhaps including deleterious impacts on fisheries).

This is an example of what we call the "rivet-popper" problem.[34] The removal of a single rivet from an airplane's wing is unlikely to cause a crash; airplanes have failsafe designs including considerable redundancy. But the continuous removal of numerous rivets will sooner or later lead to disaster. The timing of the disaster would be difficult to predict, since it would depend both on only partially understood structural factors in the wing and on unpredictable future environmental events (e.g., rough landings, turbulent flying conditions). For similar reasons, the precise impacts of deleting species (or genetically distinct populations) from an ecosystem are difficult to predict, but the eventual costs of continuing to do so are crystal clear.

Economists, with the help of ecologists, face the unenviable task of assigning value to biodiversity in such a way that the costs of the loss of a small portion of a vast machinery are reasonably assessed.

More, they need to account for the enormous losses that have occurred before now, reflecting the reality that the remaining biodiversity is a fast-fading (though otherwise self-renewable) essential resource. When a few hectares of degraded seminatural habitat, say in the vicinity of Siena, are converted into another roadway, how can one evaluate the cost in decreased flood control, reduced photosynthesis, increased soil erosion, and disruption of other local ecosystem services? How can one assess the loss of attractive birds to watch, the curtailed opportunities for local children to learn how nature works, and so on? The task may be extremely difficult, but it is also overridingly important. After all, a market system can hardly function to the ultimate benefit of humanity if it must classify the capacity for Earth to support life as an externality that cannot be properly internalized.[35,36]

Source: Paul R. Ehrlich and Anne H. Ehrlich. "The Value of Biodiversity." *Ambio* 21, No. 3 (1992): 219-226. Reprinted with permission.

Notes

[1] Ehrenfeld, D. 1978. *The Arrogance of Humanism.* Oxford: Oxford University Press.

[2] Ehrlich, P. and Ehrlich, A. 1981. *Extinction: The Causes and Consequences of the Disappearance of Species.* Random House, New York, p.38.

[3] Discussion of the Special Commission on Internal Pollution, London, October 1975.

[4] Ehrlich and Ehrlich. 1951; and Myers, N. 1979. *The Sinking Ark.* Pergamon, New York.

[5] Myers, N. 1983. *A Wealth of Wild Species.* Westview Press, Boulder.

[6] Waring, P. and Müllbacher, A. 1990. Fungal warfare in the medicine chest. *New Scientist,* 27 October, 41-44.

[7] Myers, N. 1989. *Deforestation Rates in Tropical Forests and Their Climatic Implications.* Friends of the Earth. London

[8] Ehrlich, P. and Ehrlich, A. 1990. *The Population Explosion.* Simon & Schuster. New York.

[9] World Bank. 1990. *World Development Report 1990.* (Special edition on poverty). Washington. DC.

[10] Technically, solar radiation between the wavelengths of 0.23 and 0.32 microns.

[11] Worrest, R. and Grant, L. 1989. Effects of ultraviolet-B radiation on terrestrial plants and marine organisms. In: *Ozone Depletion.* Jones, R. and Wigley, T. (eds). (New York: Wiley) p.197-206.

[12] Of course, if no more oxygen were being produced, photosynthesis would have ceased, and we would all promptly starve to death.

[13] Ehrlich, P. and Mooney, H. 1983. Extinction, substitution, and ecosystem services. *Bioscience* 33, 248-254.

[14] National Research Council, Committee on the Role of Alternative Farming Methods in Modern Production Agriculture, Board on Agriculture (J. Pesek, Chairman), 1989. *Alternative Agricultural,* National Academy Press, Washington DC. New York.

[15] Francis, C. A., Flora, C. B. and King, L. D. (eds). 1990. *Sustainable Agriculture in Temperate Zones.* John Wiley & Sons, New York.

[16] Bormann. F. 1976. An inseparable linkage; conservation of natural ecosystems and the conservation of fossil energy. *BioScience* 26, 754-760.

[17] The percentage depends on the diversity of small arthropods in tropical forests, which at the moment has only been *very* roughly estimated. See May, R. 1989. How many species are there on Earth? *Science* 241, 1441-1449.

[18] Chlorination, although clearly an important barrier against waterborne disease where supplies are polluted, does not kill some disease organisms and chlorine compounds (such as chloroform) formed in the water may be carcinogenic or damaging in other ways. See Wilson, R. and Crouch, E. 1987. Risk assessment and comparisons: an introduction. *Science* 236, 267-270.

[19] Talbot, F. 1990. *Earth, Humankind and Our Responsibility,* Plenary Address to the American Association of Museums, June (mimeo).

[20] Myers, N. 1989.

[21] Raven, P., The scope of the plant conservation problem world-wide. In: *Botanic Gardens and the World Conservation Strategy,* 1987, Academic Press, London.

[22] Ehrlich and Ehrlich. 1981; and for a fine overview, see Wilson, E. 1989. Threats to biodiversity. *Scientific American,* September, 108-116. See also (17).

[23] This very rough estimate depends heavily on how one defines both population and "genetically distinct." Based on our research group's experience with herbivores insects (which may themselves number millions of species) and a survey of the literature, this number seems to be in the ballpark.

[24] A fine book putting the extinction epidemic in a context of human evolution is Diamond, J. 1991. *The Rise and Fall of the Third Chimpanzee.* Harper and Collins, New York.

[25] For more details on soils and technical citations on what follows, see Ehrlich, P. and Ehrlich, A. and Holdren, J. 1977. *Ecoscience; Population, Resources, Environment.* W.H. Freeman & Co., San Francisco.

[26] Assuming T. Erwin's estimates (1988. The tropical forest canopy. In: *Biodiversity.* Wilson, E. (ed). National Academy Press, Washington, DC, p.123-129.) of tropical rainforest diversity are correct, the base of the estimate is a non-conservative total of 30 million species instead of Wilson's "very conservative" 2 million.

[27] Ehrlich, P. and Wilson, E. 1991. Biodiversity studies: science and policy. *Sciences.* (In press).

[28] For an overview of the differentiation of populations (which leads to speciation), see Ehrlich, 1986. (15). A more technical treatment can be found in Futayama, D. 1986. Evolutionary Biology. Second Edition, Sinaver Assoc., Sunderland, Mass.

[29] Vitousek, P., Ehrlich, P., Ehrlich, A. and Matson, P. 1986. Human appropriation of the products of photosynthesis. *BioScience* 36, 368-373.

[30] Technically, NPP is the energy remaining after subtracting the respiration of the primary producers (mostly green plants, algae, and bacteria) from the total amount of energy fixed biologically (virtually all solar). NPP is the energy that supports all organisms animals, fungi, parasitic plants, and other consumers and decomposers except primary producers.

[31] Wright, D. 1990. Human impacts on energy flow through natural ecosystems, and implications for species endangerment. *Ambio* 19, 189-194. Under the higher estimates listed above, one might assume that roughly one or two million species could be extinct by 2000. That would be 5% of the 24-40 million species, a not unreasonable estimate of organic diversity. But all such estimates obviously, are only the crudest of approximations.

[32] World Commission on Environment and Development. 1987. *Our Common Future.* Oxford University Press, New York.

[33] Managing planet Earth. *Scientific American,* September 1989, 46-54.

[34] Ehrlich and Ehrlich. 1981, p.38.

[35] This basic point comes from Daly H. and Cobb, J. Jr. 1989. *For the Common Good.* Beacon Press, Boston, p.37.

[36] This paper is dedicated to the memory of our dear friend. LuEsther T. Mertz, who did so much to support the efforts of Stanford's Center for Conservation Biology to preserve biodiversity. It has benefited greatly from discussion with Partha Dasgupta (Cambridge University) and Lawrence Goulder (Department of Economics, Stanford), Lisa and Timothy Daniel (Bureau of Economic Research, Federal Trade Commission), and Harold Mooney and Peter Vitousek (Department of Biological Sciences, Stanford University), all of whom have criticized the manuscript. A large portion of the paper was developed in the course of writing a section on biodiversity for a chapter of our book, *Healing the Planet,* Addison Wesley (1991).

The Population Concern

Göran Ohlin

GÖRAN OHLIN *is professor of economics, University of Uppsala, Sweden, currently serving as Assistant Secretary-General at the United Nations. Ever since his dissertation (Harvard, 1954) about population in economic history, he has sporadically followed developments in economic demography. This paper expresses his personal views and should in no way be attributed to the United Nations or any of its affiliated organs.*

Is there a Global Population Problem?

The growth of the world population in this century is so spectacular that it is obviously one of the most noteworthy aspects of modern history. But this is only the culmination of a phenomenon that began some centuries ago. It can safely be asserted that it will not go on for ever, but for the time being this surge of population is a source of great upset.

Not just population growth but virtually every aspect of population change is regarded in one quarter or another as a problem with ominous consequences:

- The rapid population growth in poor countries is seen as a threat to their development and even to global welfare.

- In many industrialized countries, reproduction rates have long been less than one, pointing to declining natural increase. This too has inspired concern, not only about the economic consequences but also about the reasons why people do not want children.

- The great inequalities of income in the world, as well as political disruption and violence, have already given rise to extensive international migration, legal and illegal. There are fears of new waves of it in the years to come. Some countries worry about emigration, especially of highly educated people, and others about immigration, especially of unskilled manpower.

What is common to these issues is that they inspire worry or even fear. The nature of these concerns are familiar to all. It is less well known that professional students of population tend to find many of the arguments behind those concerns unsubstantiated, scientifically unfounded, and misleading in terms of policy concerns. I shall try to explain some of the reasons for this skepticism, but I shall confine myself to the subject of population growth.

Even if one holds a skeptical view of much of what is said about the harmfulness of population growth, this does not imply a refusal to recognize that population is important. The growth of the world population is obviously an extraordinary phenomenon. But precisely what the importance of population growth is in the overall scheme of historical change is not so obvious as many think. I will suggest some of the complexities of the subject and the conflicts of opinion that it gives rise to. After a brief sketch of the predominant postwar opinions about population and development in the industrial countries and in international organizations, I shall discuss first the intellectual controversies and then the political conflicts that have arisen.

Postwar Attitudes Towards Population Growth

It is interesting and may be somewhat surprising to many that in the immediate postwar period there was practically no worry about population growth. I say practically, because a few demographers had made a life-long vocation of it but they found few listeners at the time.

One of the first things the United Nations Secretariat did after its creation at the end of World War II was to provide the first comprehensive picture of living conditions all over the world. The management of decolonization and the promotion of development was to become one of the major tasks of the UN system. The UN produced projections which showed populations growing at a bit more than 1% around the world. There was much discussion about how to provide the capital and know-how that underdeveloped countries needed, and some rather sophisticated discussions about what is today called human development and governance. But in the beginning there was no excitement about the population problem.

The change came when it was realized that populations in the poorer parts of the world were growing very much faster than previously thought—not at 1% but closer to 3% a year. That means doubling in 24 years rather than 72. From that time on and to this day much of the argumentation about population growth has been unduly dominated by mere numbers and by scary extrapolations based on compound interest, which easily baffles unaided common sense. In addition, some very primitive economic reasoning tends to stick to population alarmism. If India is so poor today, the reasoning might go, how is it going to feed and support a population that will be twice as large in the next generation and four times as large the generation after that? There are also many variations on the theme that "we" will be swamped by "them." "They" might be the peoples of Asia and Africa and Latin America who threaten to displace the peoples of the rich and industrialized countries from their already shrinking role in the world, or "they" might be the masses in the poor countries who would overwhelm their traditional rulers.

In its crudest form, those who proclaim population crises simply forget that with every mouth there are two arms and two legs and a brain. It is not the present generation that will support future generations; they will have to do that themselves. The question is whether they will find it harder if the total population is larger. Harder, or perhaps easier, as has for the most part been the case in the past.

In the context of the developing countries where almost all of global population growth is now concentrated, three distinct preoccupations have in turn dominated the attempts to provide a rationale for the new Malthusianism and to show that the present rates of population growth are inimical to development. A growing population will obviously not suffer from a shortage of manpower, so they all emphasize the shortage of factors of production complementary to labor: the first capital, the second land, and the third one environment and resources at large. Each of these approaches emerged in response to the policy preoccupations of the day.

In the late 1950s, foreign-aid programs were getting under way. Questions were raised about how to raise the amount of capital per head in developing countries and what difference population growth would make. One very reasonable suggestion was that even if a growing population brought its own labor supply, it would be difficult to provide it with the capital equipment that it needed. Savings would be smaller because parents with many children would save less. Demographic investments, as Alfred Sauvy used to call them, investments in schools and hospitals; and widening investments as Alvin Hansen called them, investments which simply maintained the stock of capital per head in a growing population these would preempt the deepening investments that would raise capital per head in the productive sectors of the economy.

Around 1960, elaborate models emerged to show that with lower birthrates there would be more savings available for investments in productive equipment and per capita growth.[1] There were even attempts to estimate the economic benefit of one prevented birth. When this substantial benefit was compared with the puny estimated cost of preventing the birth by government-sponsored family planning, the conclusion was that investments in family planning were vastly superior to those in mundane projects such as power plants or irrigation as a means of raising per capita incomes.

These arguments were fashionable for a while. The trouble was that it was impossible to find empirical evidence in support of them. They were based on a priori notions about the influence of population growth on savings and on the efficiency of capital use which did not seem to be correct. Even small changes in these parameters would make it possible to meet the needs of man-made capital for a growing population and somehow that seemed to be happening in many places. There was no apparent relationship between population growth and economic growth.

In the 1960s, a serious food crisis was occurring in India and Asia as a whole. The idea that overpopulation causes food shortages and famines is ancient—and, in many local and historical cases, undoubtedly correct. The *Geography of Hunger* was the title of one of the earliest postwar books in the neo-Malthusian vein. In the 1960s the time was ripe for this theme, and there was a flood of confident reports about the shortage of arable land and food. It suddenly seemed self-evident that growing populations were outstripping the capacity of poor countries to feed themselves, to use a standard phrase in such writings.

Once again, reality proved troublesome, even at crude inspection. To be sure, Africa has continued its economic decline to this day, but the Asian agricultural crisis was turned around although populations continued to grow. Somehow there were reserves, if not of land then of technological potential for irrigation and numerous other improvements. And there were many other things involved, such as bad and even atrocious agricultural policies which would make for food shortages no matter what the state of population of population growth.

By the 1970s, the scope of concern about development and the future of the world economy had broadened to encompass the environment and the ecology—the outer limits to expansion, whether demographic or economic. The Malthusian worry had in the past often been put in terms of the balance between population and resources. Now the concept of the resources needed to sustain life on earth sprang to life, as scientists began to spell out in much greater detail than before the intricate ecological cycles and their global dimension. The biosphere was under threat, and so was the biogenetic legacy and its multitude of species. The environmental agenda expanded from year to year.

The environmental concern was hardly even present in the first postwar decades, and when it emerged it was first linked more to pollution than to population. But as new dimensions of environmental destruction, such as desertification and deforestation, attracted political attention, they were laid at the door of population growth. The looming water shortage in many parts of the world seemed to raise an even more insuperable barrier than the shortage of land. Above all, energy which is at the heart of economic progress, moved up on the agenda of global concerns in two giant leaps. First there was a decade or so of worry about how long fossil fuels would last and whether nuclear power was safe. Then, by the time nuclear energy was under a cloud on account of the waste problem and Chernobyl, the issue of climate change raised the question, not whether it could be safely used.

In the four decades since these discussions began, the population in most of the developing countries has increased threefold. To many people, at least in the rich countries, it seems obvious, with no further proof needed, that this growth of population has been a major cause of environmental destruction, increasing poverty, and widespread famines. They believe, very sincerely, that something could, should, or even must, be done to slow down the growth of population in developing countries. They are surprised, even incredulous, to hear that anyone can dispute something so self-evident. That brings me to the intellectual and academic, or professional, disputes.

The Intellectual Controversy

Professional demographers have not been in the front line of those who have proclaimed population crises, bombs, or explosions. But a great deal of the financing of demographic research projects in the 1960s and 1970s emanated from institutions which were committed to projects and policies of population restraint—the Population Council, USAID and other donor agencies, the Ford Foundation, the World Bank, UNFPA, etc. The question inevitably arises to what extent this swayed the orientation of research. There certainly was an energetic search for evidence that would support the strong policy positions already taken, but in the end it was not overly successful. The World Bank's World Development Report 1984 focussed on population growth but concluded, rather lamely, that "for most countries, for any given amount of resources, a slower rate of population growth would help to promote economic and social development."[2]

Other surveys in the mid-1980s reached similar results. There seemed in fact, as Geoffrey McNicoll put it, to be "fundamental disagreement about the net impact of one of the most profound changes in social circumstances in the modern world."[3] The US National Academy of Science undertook a major review and found that the negative impact of population growth on such things as resource exhaustion, savings, urbanization, and unemployment had been exaggerated.[4]

The result was the appearance of what has been called a revisionist interpretation of the role of population in development. Only a few go so far as to welcome population growth but many suggest that its significance must be found in other linkages than the direct impact of population growth.

This is perhaps less surprising in a historical perspective. To begin with, from the time of Malthus, many red alerts have been issued about population growth but the expected disasters have failed to materialize. The Malthusian forecast itself was wrong. Not just slightly off but magnificently wrong. Europe and North America embarked on the industrial revolution and the most extraordinary economic advance on a broad front that the world had ever seen, virtually erasing poverty in the sense of the permanent semi-starvation that prevailed among the poor when Malthus was writing.

Those alarmists who are at all aware of the past say that, yes Malthus was wrong, he was crying wolf too early, but this time it is serious. Of course they are right in saying that high rates of population growth cannot go on forever in a limited world. Some people equipped with a logarithm table or a calculator have amused themselves by showing that with any population growth at all, the world would eventually be covered by human bodies piled one on top of the other.

To serious demographers, such extrapolation is meaningless because the prevailing hypothesis about the relationship between general economic progress and population change is that of the demographic transition. A decline in mortality will eventually be followed by a decline in fertility, as had happened in the industrialized world. But during this demographic transition, a vast bulge of population growth is bound to occur. In most of the countries of Europe the population increased from its pre-industrial to its present stage by a factor of ten. In the US in the 19th century it increased faster than in most of the developed countries today.

Forgetful of their own past, observers in industrial countries view the growth of population in poor countries with deep alarm. Not infrequently they fantasize about the high and unrestrained fertility those countries. But the rising growth rates in developing countries are the product of lower death rates, declining mortality, and increasing life expectancy, all of them suggesting that at least in some ways conditions of life have improved.

The logic of the grand approach of the demographic transition is simply that it takes time for parents to realize that mortality conditions have changed and that they do not need to produce six children to have at least two surviving ones. It takes a generation or so for social patterns to change.

In the meantime population will grow fast. But there is reason to see this as a sign of improved social health and not as a sinister disease. That used to be the view in earlier historical times. Today, there is a tendency in rich countries to believe that the reasons for high fertility in poor countries are ignorance, irresponsibility, and improvidence. There is evidence, of course, in developing countries, as in the industrial countries, past and present, of breakdowns in the control of fertility through the family system. This is especially likely if the benefits of a large family are great and evident to parents, while the costs of rapid population growth devolve on others. This is the kind of situation which economists describe as one of externalization of costs or benefits. But such situations are not likely to be repaired by appeals to family planning which will only work when parents want fewer children.

As to the impact of population growth as such, regardless of its causes, research findings have been weak. It is in the nature of the hypothesis of the demographic transition that a certain amount of economic pressure relative to their ambitions is what will induce parents to reduce the number of children. Migration, local, long-distance, or international, has always been an important element in population growth. Some have seen it as evidence of overpopulation, others as evidence of ambition. What would the modern world look like without it?

Problems frequently attributed to population growth, such as famines and unemployment turn out, on closer inspection, to be very much more due to policies penalizing trade, agriculture, and enterprise. It is now frequently argued that rapid population growth brings other problems to a head sooner, and thus perhaps forces a more rapid response to them, and also that population growth has induced people to become more innovative and settle new lands.

One intellectual issue that remains particularly unclear is whether the problem is the rate of growth of population or the level of population. Those who think in terms of rates of adjustment, of capital formation, of the time needed for institutional change, worry about the rate of change. Those who think in terms of total global resources worry more about the total size of world population.

But population is not the only force that strains the world's ecological carrying capacity. The other force is technology. It is not difficult to show that the bulk of environmental stress is due to technology rather than to population growth.

Political Controversy

Population is a subject that evokes strong emotions, conscious or subconscious. It contains every Freudian ingredient one can think of: sex, death, and the complex relations between in-groups and out-groups with economic, social, or even racial components. So it is not surprising that it is an area where political debate tends to be rather passionate.

In the 1960s, population became a hot international political issue and it has remained one ever since. Politicians and governments in rich countries were confidently asserting that population growth in developing countries was a principal threat to the development of those countries. Increasingly, it also came to be implied that rapidly growing countries were increasing their claims on the limited resources of the world as a whole. Governments in the Third World had to do something about it.

Opinions in developing countries themselves were more hesitant and divided. The hectoring by donor countries was resented. Even where there were family-planning programs these were usually justified in terms of spacing and protection of mothers' health or in terms of family welfare and not as deliberate population-control policies. In some countries, family planning was aggressively pursued by governments which were sincerely convinced that the growth of the poor had to be stemmed. India, cheered on by Western supporters, stepped up its approach in the 1970s, with mass sterilization campaigns and plans for compulsory sterilization as part of the emergency program for development that had been proclaimed. A surge of discontent then temporarily brought Mrs. Gandhi down, and even into jail, which put an end to that particular approach.

Population is simply an area where the limits of government are particularly apparent. It is an expression of the irony of history that western countries should now exhort the rest of the world to control fertility. Their own record in that regard was in the past one of persistent persecution of advocates of family planning, and it would be impossible to claim that the fertility decline in industrial countries was promoted by government policy.

Is population growth really a policy variable? Does

it make any sense to think that governments in developing countries have the power to do something that donor governments never did but instead opposed bitterly? The record suggests that well-run family-planning programs do have a influence on fertility, though a marginal one. They may have a much greater pay-off in maternal health and social benefits, and they are an indispensable part of health and welfare policies, but they do not constitute a device for "population control."

In Latin America and Asia, the powerful force of the fertility transition is already clearly at work. In Africa, the situation is more dubious, but then so are the economic trends. The economic hardships of the 1980s may even have raised infant mortality in Africa. The evidence is weak but the hypothesis remains likely. The demographic impact of AIDS is under intense study. In spite of the deterioration of health conditions and health-care systems in the stricken areas the impact on the growth of population may be relatively limited, but the opposite cannot be ruled out.

Certainly many governments in developing countries would like to slow down their population growth, if only they could see a way to do more than they are already doing. They should do more, and the donors who urge them on so eloquently should help them more. The amounts are trifling. Birth rates will come down, with or without these efforts, but in the best of circumstances it will take time, and this will accentuate the problem of sharing the carrying capacity of a limited biosphere.

Conclusion

It is sometimes confidently asserted that the population of the world could not be raised to the levels of consumption of the rich countries without disastrous consequences for the environment. However, this is not as obvious as it seems to many. If the lifestyles of the rich countries are taken to include their present wasteful technology it would certainly be impossible to replicate it throughout the world, but the potential of technology has proved immense in the past. In the 19th century it was argued that London could not grow much bigger because there would not be room for the horses. Of course technology must change, will change, and is already changing. Population growth is slowing down too, and in the rich countries some people are surprised to find that it does not asymptotically settle down for zero growth and stability. Instead birth rates have been heading down towards levels where populations might decline, and how could anybody really expect anything else, given the ineluctable fact that the production of children is one of the most democratic aspects of social life.

Everyone is now agreed that the prospects of mankind are uncertain; the stakes are enormous. From the point of view of the poorer countries the perspective is obvious: the rich countries have polluted the earth by population growth and above all by their technology, leaving little or no room for development along the same lines for the rest of the world, where the population will grow a great deal.

What should governments do in the face of the two forces that will decide the future: population and technology? The obvious answer is to work on both, but one should be under no illusions as to the powers of government to restrain population at will. It is often said that whatever is done to solve environmental problems will be of no avail unless something is done about population, and that therefore population policy must be a first priority. I think that is a serious misunderstanding. Population growth is not, in any country, an uncontrolled force. It is everywhere subject to a great many social constraints, and governments cannot do much about it without genuine social and economic change. Even so the change will be slow, and populations will continue to grow, probably even in the countries where AIDS is rampant. The area of population policy that deserves particular attention is that of migration where there is little readiness for the great pressures for redistribution that are building up.

But the change in technology that is necessary to reduce ecological strain is something that governments can and must do something about right away. It is what development is about: education, infrastructure, and enterprise.

These matters of development and environment are no longer of purely national concern. A world of 10 or 15 billion people some time in the next century is quite likely, but it is neither constructive nor warranted to see this inevitable increase as a frightening flood of humanity that will spell the end of civilization. It will pose vast institutional and political problems, but it will also mean that there will be an increased pool of human ingenuity, talent, and will to survive.

Source: Göran Ohlin, "The Population Concern." *Ambio* 21, No. 1 (1992): 6-9. Reprinted with permission.

[1] The work of reference for this approach was Coale, A.J. and Hoover, E.M. 1958. *Population Growth and Economic Development in Low-Income Countries*. Princeton University Press, Princeton.

[2] World Bank. 1984. *World Development Report*. New York.

[3] McNicoll, G. 1984. Consequences of rapid population growth: An overview and assessment. Center for Policy Studies, The Population Council, *Working Paper No. 105*.

[4] National Research Council, Committee on Population, 1986. *Report of the Working Group on Population Growth and Economic Development*. US National Academy of Sciences, Washington, DC.

Preserving and Cherishing the Earth

Carl Sagan

CARL SAGAN, a distinguished astrophysicist, *organized this document and presented it at the Moscow meeting of the Global Forum of Spiritual and Parliamentary Leaders, January 15-19, 1990. Three hundred seventy well-known spiritual leaders from 83 countries—Patriarchs, Lamas, Chief Rabbis, Grand Muftis, Cardinals, Mullahs, Archibishops, professors of theology—signed their names to this urgent appeal from 32 world-renowned scientists.*

The Earth is the birthplace of our species and, so far as we know, our only home. When our numbers were small and our technology feeble, we were powerless to influence the environment of our world. But today, suddenly, almost without anyone noticing, our numbers have become immense and our technology has achieved vast, even awesome, powers. Intentionally or inadvertently, we are now able to make devastating changes in the global environment—an environment to which we and all the other beings with which we share the Earth are meticulously and exquisitely adapted.

We are now threatened by self-inflicted, swiftly moving environmental alterations about whose long-term biological and ecological consequences we are still painfully ignorant—depletion of the protective ozone layer; a global warming unprecedented in the last 150 millennia; the obliteration of an acre of forest every second; the rapid-fire extinction of species; and the prospect of a global nuclear war which would put at risk most of the population of the Earth. There may well be other such dangers of which, in our ignorance, we are still unaware. Individually and cumulatively they represent a trap being set for the human species, a trap we are setting for ourselves. However, principled and lofty (or naive and shortsighted) the justifications may have been for the activities that brought forth these dangers, separately and together they now imperil our species and many others. We are close to committing—many would argue we are already committing—what in religious language is sometimes called Crimes against Creation.

By their very nature these assaults on the environment were not caused by any one political group or any one generation. Intrinsically, they are transnational, transgenerational and transideological. So are all conceivable solutions. To escape these traps requires a perspective that embraces all the peoples of the planet and all the generations yet to come.

Problems of such magnitude, and solutions demanding so broad a perspective must be recognized from the outset as having a religious as well as scientific dimension. Mindful of our common responsibility, we scientists—many of us long engaged in combatting the environmental crisis—urgently appeal to the world religious community to commit, in world and deed, and as boldly as is required, to preserve the environment of the Earth.

Some of the short-term mitigations of these dangers—such as greater energy efficiency, rapid banning of chlorofluorocarbons or modest reductions in the nuclear arsenal—are comparatively easy and at some level are already underway. But other, more far-reaching, more long term, more effective approaches will encounter widespread inertia denial, and resistance. In this category are conversion from fossil fuels to a non-polluting energy economy, a continuing swift reversal of the nuclear arms race and a voluntary halt to world population growth—without which many of the other approaches to preserve the environment will be nullified.

As on issues of peace, human rights and social justice, religious institutions can here too be a strong encouraging national and international initiatives in both the private and public sectors, and in the diverse world of commerce, education, culture and mass communication.

The environmental crisis requires radical changes not only in public policy, but also in individual behaviour. The historical record makes clear that religious teaching, example, and leadership are powerfully able to influence personal conduct and commitment.

As scientists, many of us have had profound experience of awe and reverence before the universe. We understand that what is regarded as sacred is more likely to be treated with care and respect. Our planetary home should be so regarded. Efforts to safeguard and cherish the environment need to be infused with a vision of the sacred. At the same time, a much wider and deeper understanding of science and technology is needed. If we do not understand the problem, it is unlikely we will be able to fix it. Thus, there is a vital role for both religion and science.

We know that the well-being of our planetary environment is already a source of profound concern in your councils and congregations. We hope this Appeal will encourage a spirit of common cause and joint action to help preserve the Earth.

List of Signatories

Carl Sagan
Cornell University, Ithaca, New York
Hans A. Bethe
Cornell University, Ithaca, New York
Elise Boulding
University of Colorado, Boulder, Colorado
M. I. Budyko
State Hydrological Inst., Leningrad, USSR
S. Chandrasekhar
University of Chicago, Chicago, Illinois
Paul J. Crutzen
Max-Planck Inst. for Chemistry, Mainz, W. Germany
Margaret B. Davis
University of Minnesota, Minneapolis, Minnesota
Freeman J. Dyson
Inst. for Advanced Study, Princeton, New Jersey
Richard L. Garwin
IBM Corporation, Yorktown Heights, New York,
Gyorgi S. Golitsyn
Academy of Sciences of the USSR, Moscow, USSR
Stephen Jay Gould
Harvard University, Cambridge, Massachusetts
James E. Hansen
NASA Goddard Institute for Space Studies, New York, New York
Mohammed Kassas
University of Kairo, Egypt
Henry W. Kendall
Union of Concerned Scientists, Cambridge, Massachusetts
Motoo Kimura
National Institute of Genetics, Mishima, Japan
Thomas Malone
St. Joseph College, West Hartford, Connecticut
Lynn Marjulis
University of Massachusetts, Amherst, Massachusetts

Peter Raven
Missouri Botanical Garden, St. Louis, Missouri
Roger Revelle
University of California, San Diego La Jolla, California
Walter Orr Roberts
National Center for Atmospheric Research, Boulder, Colorado
Abdus Salam
International Center for Theoretical Physics, Trieste, Italy
Stephen H. Schneider
National Center for Atmospheric Research, Boulder, Colorado
Hans Suess
University of California, San Diego La Jolla, California
O. B. Toon
NASA Ames Research Center, Moffett Field, California
Richard P. Turco
University of California, Los Angeles, California
Yevgeniy P. Velikhov
Academy of Sciences of the USSR, Moscow, USSR
Carl Friedrich von Weizsäcker
Max-Planck Institute, Starnberg, W. Germany
Sir Frederick Warner
Essex University, Colchester, U. K.
Victor F. Weisskopf
Massachusetts Institute of Technology, Cambridge, Massachusetts
Jerome B. Wiesner
Massachusetts Institute of Technology, Cambridge, Massachusetts
Robert R. Wilson
Cornell University, Ithaca, New York
Alexy V. Yablokov
Academy of Sciences of the USSR, Moscow, USSR

(Affiliations for identification purposes only.)

Source: Carl Sagan. "Preserving and Cherishing the Earth: An Appeal for Joint Commitment in Science and Religion." *Ambio* 19, No. 4 (1990): 226. Reprinted with permission.

13

Communitarianism

The Ideal of the Common Good

In recent years, partly in reaction to the veneration of individual rights and partly in reaction to the decay of communities in the modern world, there has occurred a renewed interest in the common good of the body politic. The position usually associated with this renewed interest is that of communitarianism.

In the following readings on communitarianism I have includes two earlier writers, namely Jean-Jacques Rousseau and Georg Willhelm Friedrich Hegel. Rousseau recognizes the need for each nation to have its own particular system of institutions, institutions which ought to be modified by local situations. The parameter of these social structures is, however, compliance with two objects: liberty and equality. Since he recognizes that liberty cannot exist without equality, the greatest good seems to rest upon the common good as suggested by other communitarians.

Hegel, writing during the nineteenth century, acknowledges a system of complete interdependence wherein the livelihood, happiness and legal status of one person is interwoven with the livelihood, happiness and rights of all. What emerges is a system of interdependent needs that comprises civil society.

Picking up on some of the foregoing, Sibyl Schwarzenbach calls Hegel the original mouthpiece of modern communitarianism. She thinks that Rawls's theory is not far from Hegel's, but that it distances itself from the liberalism of Hobbes. Further she maintains that Rawls's notion of reflective equilibrium must be extended into the private sphere, where women perform the communal activities she emphasizes.

Michael Sandel draws a contrast between the politics of rights and the politics of the common good and by so doing contrasts the liberal with the communitarian. He reminds us of Hegel's criticism of Kant in placing rights ahead of the common good, and of Aristotle's position that the justification of political arrangements lies in common purposes and ends. And in a few short paragraphs Sandel manages to situate Rawls, utilitarians and relativists on the communitarian's map.

The dialectical connection between communitarianism and liberalism is neatly explored by Michael Walzer, although he is quick to point out that criticisms of the latter by the former are contradictory, for they rely on both a criticism of liberal theory and liberal practice. He attempts to support his position by looking at what he calls the four mobilities: geographic, social, marital, and political. In doing so he attempts to criticize the communitarian position of MacIntryre and others.

Allen Buchanan distinguishes between the liberal political thesis requiring the state to protect basic individual civil and political rights and various justifications that have been given for that thesis. He then proceeds to discuss effectively the connection between communitarianism, justice and pluralism. Such a discussion is long overdue for it forces the reader to demand from the communitarian a better account of the common good.

Displaying originality, Alasdair MacIntyre grounds moral reasoning and rationality in the life of a community—a body which has *shared* beliefs about goods. According to him, to be a rational individual is to participate in a social life that embraces a rational tradition, so that individual rationality becomes defined in terms of a communal phenomenon. MacIntyre develops many of these notions elsewhere, but here he presents just enough to whet our appetites.

The search for the common good undertaken by communitarians is not some abstract undertaking but a practical—albeit reflective—activity of attempting to find public interests in the life of communities. In a sense the communitarian approach is a throwback, not simply to Rousseau, but to Aristotle and his claim that *common* views on matters of good and evil are needed to make a state.

The Different Systems of Legislation

Jean-Jacques Rousseau

JEAN-JACQUES ROUSSEAU *(1712-1778) was a Swiss thinker who wrote philosophy, novels, essays, and music. The Social Contract,* Discourse on the Origin and Bases of Inequality among Men, *and* Confessions *were his most famous writings; the first, from which the present selection is taken, is his major work on society and politics.*

If we ask precisely wherein consists the greatest good of all, which ought to be the aim of every system of legislation, we shall find that it is summed up in two principal objects, *liberty* and *equality*—liberty, because any individual dependence is so much force withdrawn from the body of the State; equality, because liberty cannot subsist without it.

I have already said what civil liberty is. With regard to equality, we must not understand by this word that the degrees of power and wealth should be absolutely the same; but that, as to power, it should fall short of all violence, and never be exercised except by virtue of station and of the laws; while, as to wealth, no citizen should be rich enough to be able to buy another, and none poor enough to be forced to sell himself, which supposes, on the part of the great, moderation in property and influence, and, on the part of ordinary citizens, repression of avarice and covetousness.[1]

It is said that this equality is a chimera of speculation which cannot exist in practical affairs. But if the abuse is inevitable, does it follow that it is unnecessary even to regulate it? It is precisely because the force of circumstances is ever tending to destroy equality that the force of legislation should always tend to maintain it.

But these general objects of every good institution ought to be modified in each country by the relations which arise both from the local situation and from the character of the inhabitants; and it is with reference to these relations that we must assign to each nation a particular system of institutions, which shall be the best, not perhaps in itself, but for the State for which it is designed. For instance, if the soil is unfruitful and barren, or the country too confined for its inhabitants, turn your attention to arts and manufactures, and exchange their products for the provisions that you require. On the other hand, if you occupy rich plains and fertile slopes, if, in a productive region, you are in need of inhabitants, bestow all your cares on agriculture, which multiples men, and drive out the arts, which would only end in depopulating the country by gathering together in a few spots the few inhabitants that the land possesses.[2] If you occupy extensive and convenient coasts, cover the sea with vessels and foster commerce and navigation; you will have a short and brilliant existence. If the sea on your coasts bathes only rocks that are almost inaccessible, remain fish-eating barbarians; you will lead more peaceful, perhaps better, and certainly happier lives. In a word, besides the maxims common to all, each nation contains within itself some cause which influences it in a particular way, and renders its legislation suitable for it alone. Thus the Hebrews in ancient times, and the Arabs more recently, had religion as their chief object, the Athenians literature, Carthage and Tyre commerce, Rhodes navigation, Sparta war, Rome valor. The author of the *Spirit of the Laws* has shown in a multitude of instances by what arts the legislator directs his institutions towards each of these objects.

What renders the constitution of a State really solid and durable is the observance of expediency in such a way that natural relations and the laws always coincide, the latter only serving, as it were, to secure, support, and rectify the former. But if the legislator, mistaken in his object, takes a principle different from that which springs from the nature of things; if the one tends to servitude, the other to liberty, the one to riches, the other to population, the one to peace, the other to conquests, we shall see the laws imperceptibly weakened and the constitution impaired; and the State will be ceaselessly agitated until it is destroyed or changed, and invincible nature has resumed her sway.

Source: Jean-Jacques Rousseau. *The Social Contract.* Originally published in 1762.

Notes

[1] If, then, you wish to give stability to the State, bring the two extremes as near together as possible; tolerate neither rich people nor beggars. These two conditions, naturally inseparable, are equally fatal to the general welfare; from the one class spring tyrants, from the other, the supporters of tyranny; it is always between these that the traffic in public liberty is carried on; the one buys and the other sells.

[2] Any branch of foreign commerce, says the Marquis d'Argenson, differs merely a deceptive utility through the kingdom generally; it may enrich a few individuals, even a few towns, but the nation as a whole gains nothing, and the people are none the better for it.

JEAN-JACQUES ROUSSEAU (1712-1778)

JEAN-JACQUES ROUSSEAU, although born in Geneva, is widely known as an important French (he came to Paris in 1741) philosopher and political thinker (he also wrote novels and operas). His most important political work is *The Social Contract* (1762) which has been called "The Bible of the French Revolution," because of its tremendous influence on the leaders of that uprising. Rousseau also contributed important writing on education in *Emile* (1762), and on philosophy in the *Discourse on the Origin of Inequality* (1755).

Rousseau stood apart from the French rationalist philosophers of the eighteenth century. These so-called "Encyclopedists," like Montesquieu and Voltaire, stressed a sceptical, scientific and rational approach within their criticism of society. Rousseau, on the other hand, emphasized the importance of the sentimental and emotional elements of the human personality.

It is for this reason that he is often viewed as a predecessor of many nineteenth-century romantics.

Rousseau's *The Social Contract* opens with the famous first line "Man was born free and everywhere he is in chains." This represents Rousseau's assertion that people, once they come to live within a society, have lost the opportunity to live as "natural" entities. Consequently, for Rousseau, any inquiry into the political life of people is an investigation into the kinds of agreements, or "social contracts" they form with one another. Once people have agreed to live in this way, they are subject to what he called the "general will" which Rousseau believed to be absolute and unerring. Rulers are simply instruments of this popular will, and can and should be removed if their authority fails to embody this will. It is evident, then, that this kind of ideology is perfectly suited to the revolutionary thought prevalent in France in the late eighteenth century.

When combined with Rousseau's insistence on the primacy of the emotions, it is also not surprising that he was also an advocate of an eighteenth-century brand of nationalism that utilized a shared myth to unify and strengthen nations. *Considerations on the Government of Poland* (1770) was his most forceful enunciation in this area.

Civil Society

Georg Wilhelm Friedrich Hegel

GEORGE HEGEL *(1770-1831) was a German idealist who was born in Stuttgart. In 1818 he was appointed Professor at the University of Berlin where he became famous and influential largely owing to his writings which included* Phenomenology of Mind *and* Science of Logic.

182. The concrete person,[1] who is himself the object of his particular aims, is, as a totality of wants and mixture of caprice and physical necessity, one principle of civil society. But the particular person is essentially so related to other particular persons that each establishes himself and finds satisfaction by means of the others, and at the same time purely and simply by means of the form of universality, the second principle here.

183. In the course of the actual attainment of selfish ends—an attainment conditioned in this way by universality—there is formed a system of complete interdependence, wherein the livelihood, happiness, and legal status of one man is interwoven with the livelihood, happiness, and rights of all. On this system, individual happiness, &c., depend, and only in this connected system are they actualized and secured. This system may be prima facie regarded as the external state,[2] the state based on need, the state as the Understanding envisages it.

184. The Idea in this stage of division imparts to each of its moments a characteristic embodiment; to particularity it gives the right to develop and launch forth in all directions; and to universality the right to prove itself not only the ground and necessary form of particularity, but also the authority standing over it and its final end. It is the system of the ethical order, split into its extremes and lost, which constitutes the Idea's abstract moment, its moment of reality. Here the Idea is present only as a relative totality[3] and as the inner necessity behind this outward appearance.

185. Particularity by itself, given free rein in every direction to satisfy its needs, accidental caprices, and subjective desires, destroys itself and its substantive concept in this process of gratification. At the same time, the satisfaction of need, necessary and accidental alike, is accidental because it breeds new desires without end, is in thoroughgoing dependence on caprice and external accident, and is held in check by the power of universality. In these contrasts and their complexity, civil society affords a spectacle of extravagance and want as well as of the physical and ethical degeneration common to them both.

The development of particularity to self-subsistence...is the moment which appeared in the ancient world as an invasion of ethical corruption and as the ultimate cause of that world's downfall. Some of these ancient states were built on the patriarchal and religious principle, others on the principle of an ethical order which was more explicitly intellectual, though still comparatively simple; in either case they rested on primitive unsophisticated intuition. Hence they could not withstand the disruption of this state of mind when self-consciousness was infinitely reflected into itself; when this reflection began to emerge, they succumbed to it, first in spirit and then in substance, because the simple principle underlying them lacked the truly infinite power to be found only in that unity which allows both sides of the antithesis of reason to develop themselves separately in all their strength and which has so overcome the antithesis[4] that it maintains itself in it and integrates it in itself.

In his *Republic,* Plato displays the substance of ethical life in its ideal beauty[5] and truth; but he could only cope with the principle of self-subsistent particularity, which in his day had forced its way into Greek ethical life, by setting up in opposition to it his purely substantial state. He absolutely excluded it from his state, even in its very beginnings in private property...and the family, as well as in its more mature form as the subjective will, the choice of a social position, and so forth. It is this defect which is responsible both for the misunderstanding of the deep and substantial truth of Plato's state and also for the usual view of it as a dream of abstract thinking, as what is often called a "mere ideal." The principle of the self-subsistent inherently infinite personality of the individual, the principle of subjective freedom, is denied its right in the purely substantial form which Plato gave to mind in its actuality. This principle dawned in an inward form in the Christian religion and in an external form (and therefore in one linked with abstract universality) in the Roman world. It is historically subsequent to the Greek world, and the philosophic reflection which descends to its depth is likewise subsequent to the substantial Idea of Greek philosophy.

186. But in developing itself independently to totality, the principle of particularity passes over into universality, and only there does it attain its truth and the right to which its positive actuality is entitled. This unity is not the identity which the ethical order requires, because at this level, that of division…both principles are self-subsistent. It follows that this unity is present here not as freedom but as necessity, since it is by compulsion that the particular rises to the form of universality and seeks and gains its stability in that form.

187. Individuals in their capacity as burghers[6] in this state are private persons whose end is their own interest. This end is *mediated* through the universal which thus *appears* as a *means* to its realization. Consequently, individuals can attain their ends only in so far as they themselves determine their knowing, willing, and acting in a universal way and make themselves links in this chain of social connexions. In these circumstances, the interest of the Idea—an interest of which these members of civil society are as such unconscious—lies in the process whereby their singularity and their natural condition are raised, as a result of the necessities imposed by nature as well as of arbitrary needs, to formal freedom and formal universality of knowing and willing—the process whereby their particularity is educated up to subjectivity.

The idea that the state of nature is one of innocence and that there is a simplicity of manners in uncivilized *(ungebildeter)* peoples, implies treating education *(Bildung)* as something purely external, the ally of corruption. Similarly, the feeling that needs, their satisfaction, the pleasures and comforts of private life, and so forth, are absolute ends, implies treating education as a mere means to these ends. Both these views display lack of acquaintance with the nature of mind and the end of reason. Mind attains its actuality only by creating a dualism within itself, by submitting itself to physical needs and the chain of these external necessities, and so imposing on itself this barrier and this finitude, and finally by maturing (*bildet*) itself inwardly even when under this barrier until it overcomes it and attains its objective reality in the finite. The end of reason, therefore, is neither the manners of an unsophisticated state of nature, nor, as particularity develops, the pleasure for pleasure's sake which education procures. On the contrary, its end is to banish natural simplicity, whether the passivity which is the absence of the self, or the crude type of knowing and willing, i.e., immediacy and singularity, in which mind is absorbed. It aims in the first instance at securing for this, its external condition, the rationality of which it is capable,

i.e., the form of universality or the Understanding *(Verstandigkeit)*. By this means alone does mind become at home with itself within this pure externality. There, then, mind's freedom is existent and mind becomes objective to itself in this element which is implicitly inimical to mind's appointed end, freedom; it has to do there only with what it has itself produced and stamped with its seal. It is in this way then that the form of universality comes explicitly into existence in thought, and this form is the only worthy element for the existence of the Idea. The final purpose of education, therefore, is liberation and the struggle for a higher liberation still; education is the absolute transition from an ethical substantiality which is immediate and natural to the one which is intellectual and so both infinitely subjective and lofty enough to have attained universality of form. In the individual subject, this liberation is the hard struggle against pure subjectivity of demeanour, against the immediacy of desire, against the empty subjectivity of feeling and the caprice of inclination. The disfavour showered on education is due in part to its being this hard struggle; but it is through this educational struggle that the subjective will itself attains objectivity within, an objectivity in which alone it is for its part capable and worthy of being the actuality of the Idea.

Moreover, this form of universality—the Understanding, to which particularity has worked its way and developed itself, brings it about at the same time that particularity becomes individuality genuinely existent in its own eyes. And since it is from this particularity that the universal derives the content which fills it as well as its character as infinite self-determination, particularity itself is present in ethical life as infinitely independent free subjectivity. This is the position which reveals education as a moment immanent in the Absolute and which makes plain its infinite value.

188. Civil society contains three moments:

(A) The mediation of need and one man's satisfaction through his work and the satisfaction of the needs of all others—the *System of Needs.*

(B) The actuality of the universal principle of freedom therein contained—the protection of property through the *Administration of Justice.*

(C) Provision against contingencies still lurking in systems (A) and (B), and care for particular interests as a common interest, by means of the *Police* and the *Corporation.*

Source: George W.F. Hegel. *Naturrecht und Staatswissenschaft im Grundrisse* and *Grundlinien der Philosophie des Rechts.* Originally published in 1821.

Rawls, Hegel, and Communitarianism

Sibyl A. Schwarzenbach

SIBYL A. SCHWARZENBACH *is Assistant Professor of Philosophy at Baruch College of the City University of New York. She has published numerous articles in moral and political theory and is presently at work on a book entitled* On Civic Friendship.

Political, Not Metaphysical

I shall begin my comparison of the political thought of Rawls and that of Hegel by stressing what remains, no doubt, the fundamental difference between them: their respective stances in regard to metaphysics in general. My thesis shall be, in broadest outlines, that A *Theory of Justice* retains much of the fundamental structure of Hegel's political theory while detaching this structure from its background metaphysics of absolute idealism—from Hegel's monism and his talk of "world spirit," from the doctrines of absolute knowledge and concrete universals, from the concept of the self as alienation and return, and so on. Many will here surely object that such a reading will result in but an evisceration of Hegel. In defense of my project, however, I shall try to show that Rawls nonetheless retains the *import* of many of the most significant strands of Hegel's metaphysics; Rawls does this, however, in what he now takes to be a *practical,* and no longer metaphysical, form.

I do not mean to minimize the profound differences between the two thinkers. It is well known, for example, that Hegel viewed his political philosophy as but one subpart of his more comprehensive metaphysical system, as set forth (in skeletal form) in his *Enzyklopaedie* (1830). Although scholars dispute the sense in which Hegel claims his *Philosophy of Right* can actually be "deduced" from the more general system, agreement does exist that some form of "necessary connection" is being propounded between the general metaphysics and the political theory.[1] More recently, of course, scholars have begun to question whether any such necessary connection de facto exists, but this was clearly not Hegel's problem.[2] Hardcore "Hegelians," moreover, continue to stress Hegel's uncompromising holism; on the Continent, at least, it is considered improper to study Hegel's political thought without first spending semesters, if not years, on the *Science of Logic.*[3] The Hegelian horse pill, it seems, must be swallowed whole or not at all.

John Rawls, on the other hand, posits an explicit separation between his political philosophy and any comprehensive, "metaphysical" system.[4] In this respect, Rawls is decidedly "un-Hegelian; " he stands closer here to the positivist, or more accurately, to the American pragmatist tradition. For Rawls's claim is not so much that metaphysical systems ultimately reduce to "nonsense" (that metaphysical claims are without purpose or meaning), but rather that such systems generally *underdetermine* (they may support, but they do not entail) one's substantive position in ethics or political philosophy. In regard to his own theory, Rawls writes,

> If metaphysical presuppositions are involved, ... they are so general that they would not distinguish between the distinctive metaphysical views—Cartesian, Leibnizian, or Kantian; realist, idealist or materialist—with which [modern] philosophy traditionally has been concerned. In this case, they would not appear to be relevant for the structure and content of a political conception of justice one way or the other. *(PNM, 240)*

Rawls's insight, although not altogether novel,[5] is important, for it acknowledges that one might well be an ontological materialist (as was Hegel) or an absolute idealist (as was Hegel) and yet still be a political monarchist rather than a democrat in both cases. Moreover, there appears to be no inconsistency involved. By taking such a normative, "practical" approach to the study of political issues, the metaphysical similarities or differences between any two theorists will be minimized for the express purpose of focusing on the structure and content of their substantive, ethical positions.

In rejecting Hegel's extreme holism, however, and in claiming that moral theory retains a certain "independence" from further questions of metaphysics, ontology, or semantics, Rawls denies a major tenet of Hegelianism.[6] The question thus remains as to the respect in which (if any) his theory is similar to

Hegel's. I propose to identify three areas in which Rawls's position may be considered typically "Hegelian." By this I mean that in each case, the move originally introduced by Hegel and accepted by Rawls differs markedly not only from positions held within the Anglo-American, predominantly utilitarian tradition but from positions held by Kant. The three areas I assemble under the headings of the task of political philosophy (including its method and justification), the conception of the political person, and finally, the conception of human community and the state. If I am correct, Rawls's theory may appropriately be labeled "Hegelian" in these important areas, once we have granted, that is, the possible separation of political theory from a full-blown metaphysics. ...

The Owl of Minerva

We have seen that Rawls's theory is not so far from the original mouthpiece of modern communitarianism as is commonly believed. In regard to political philosophy's aim as conflict resolution or reconciliation, its method as the attempt to "bring order" and to gain an "overview" of our moral life, its "expressive" conception of the political person with two minimal moral powers, and its vision of the well-ordered society as a "social union of social unions," Rawls's theory (like Hegel's) has greatly distanced itself from the Hobbesian strand of liberalism. In the reading presented here, Rawls and Hegel even share a common weakness: Both still allow the Hobbesian strand too unbridled a rein in the economic realm—in "private" or "civil society." This brings me to a final similarity between the two.

In Hegel's view, the owl of Minerva—philosophy—spreads her wings only at dusk; only when an action has already been completed or a way of life grown old is it possible to grasp it fully in thought (PR, "Preface"). This conception of philosophy as a "looking backwards" holds, with some qualification, for Rawls's theory as well.[7] That is, just as Marx criticized Hegel for failing to recognize, at the beginning of the nineteenth century in Germany, the movement toward democracy in the political domain, so I believe Rawls's theory has not taken seriously the call for democracy in the economic domain in this century.[8] Certainly, the radical implications of the women's movement have yet to capture his attention.[9] And I believe in both cases, the reason is the same: Similar to the political employment of Hegel's dialectic, reflective equilibrium starts from the data of our philosophical tradition and "public political culture." Although Rawls here intends to highlight our shared political tradition (in contrast to the individualistic economic domain), examining this tradition alone would appear insufficient; radical new developments may emerge elsewhere first, for example, within the workplace. Or again, examining our philosophical tradition and public political culture, although necessary and important, cannot be sufficient; the realm until recently has been composed entirely of males. This suggests that for a more "adequate" account of the well-ordered society, reflective equilibrium must be "radicalized" and extended into new (in particular, into the so-called private) domains.[10]

My own view is that if we are to think deeply about community (about what it is that holds a just society together), we can no longer overlook the important communal activities which women have traditionally performed within the private sphere, for instance, interpreting and responding to the concrete needs of others, an activity that goes far toward binding people to one another. Further, as women move into the public sphere (and as feminists have begun to argue), a new demand emerges that our political institutions henceforth acknowledge this activity. A conception of the "modern state," for instance, traditionally conceived in terms of maintaining law and order, a military prepared for war, and a policing of citizenry and competition, could give way to a different conception whereby the state is fundamentally conceived as a flexible provider of services, an educator and satisfier of need.

In conclusion, I believe much of the contemporary "communitarian" attack on Rawls is a red herring; either the attack is misconceived or Rawls from the start acknowledged the point. Perhaps this much the comparison of his thought with Hegel's has clarified. But so, too, my comparison has hopefully suggested that, particularly in the area of moral and political philosophy, many of the slandered Hegelian notions appear to have a certain appropriateness; the tradition of analytic philosophy, in discarding all of Hegel, threw out the baby with the bathwater. The doctrine of "internal relations," for instance, far from proclaiming its legitimacy across the board, has a definite appeal when dealing with relations between persons.[11] When I hear of a child abused next door, the death of a loved one, or of a peoples' rights being systematically violated, I am (or at least I should be) altered. Similarly, the idea of "dialectic" or "synthesis," that knowledge of the person is to be attained not simply by reflection (as in Descartes) nor by mere empirical observation (as for Hume) nor by the direct intuition of some mysterious faculty (Moore) but rather (like reflective equilibrium) is *mediated* and indirect, the hard-earned result of concrete experience, subtle reflection, and the interaction between a variety of particular, historically situated selves—this complex approach leads *away,* in my view, from the smug self-certainty that accompanies all dogmatism. Finally, the fact that the focus is again on the person, not on the person conceived as an isolated organism (as in, say, a biological reading) but on the person considered as a political and "cultural" being, as one whose desires and actions have an essential connection to the background institutions and social conditions amid which it was schooled; that the focus is again on the person—not merely in the sense of focusing on what kind of beings we are but on what kind of persons we aspire and ought to be—this is only a part of the legacy of Hegel which remains alive and well in the thought of Rawls.

Source: Sibyl A. Schwarzenbach. "Rawls, Hegel, and Communitarianism." *Political Theory* 19, No. 4 (1991): 539-571. Reprinted by permission of Sage Publications, Inc.

Notes

[1] See *Hegel's Philosophy of Right*, translated by T. M Knox (Oxford: Oxford University Press, 1977), para. 2. All further references to this text will be indicated by PR followed by paragraph number. "R" after a paragraph number refers to Hegel's remarks immediately following the main paragraph, "A" to later additions culled from notes taken at Hegel's lectures.

[2] Professor U. Steinforth, for instance, recently defended such a separation between Hegel's metaphysical doctrines and his political theory (lecture at Columbia University, Spring 1987).

[3] *Wissenschaft der Logik (Berlin, 1812)*. This work espouses what the Anglo-American world would call Hegel's "metaphysics."

[4] And this is the case, Rawls intends, for any of the standard meanings of the term "metaphysics." See "Justice as Fairness: Political not Metaphysical," *Philosophy and Public Affairs* 14, No. 3 (Summer 1985): 223-51 (hereafter "PNM").

[5] Wittgenstein, for instance, makes a similar point: "But the idealist will wish to teach his children the word 'chair,' after all, for of course he wants to teach them to do this and that, e.g., to fetch a chair. Where then will the difference lie between how the idealist-educated children speak and the realist ones? Won't the difference only be one of battle cry?" (Zettel, para. 414, translation mine). Whereas Wittgenstein's is a pragmatic point, Rawls's theory may be viewed as extending this insight into the normative domain.

[6] See "The Independence of Moral Theory." *Proceedings and Addresses of the American Philosophical Association* 48 (1974-75): 5-22, where Rawls argues that moral theory (the study of structures, as these relate to our moral sensibilities and natural attitude) is independent of the theory of meaning, epistemology and philosophy of mind.

[7] I believe it holds generally, although one finds such "utopian" or forward-looking passages in Rawls as "until we bring ourselves to conceive how this [a public understanding of mutual respect] could happen, it can't happen" (John Rawls., "Justice as Fairness: Political not Metaphysical," *Philosophy and Public Affairs* 14 (1985): 223-51, p.231).

[8] This is not to say that certain "left-wing Rawlsians" have not made such a call; I include the work of J. Cohen and J. Rogers, *On Democracy* (New York: Penguin Books, 1983), chap. 6, Doppelt (1981), and myself (1988) in this category.

[9] I might here add that the women's movement of the past century, and all the gains women have thereby won, lends renewed credence to Hegel's view of history as the struggle for "the realization of freedom." It may just be that Rawls' theory, although implicitly operating with certain assumptions about the nature of historical progress, needs to elaborate such assumptions more fully to better ground his own position.

[10] Why, for instance, should our common "shared" precepts about family life, the treatment of children, animals, principles of friendships, trust, and so on not be elaborated and critically relevant for our public political life? An approach developing such a reflective equilibrium of the private real, as well as its implications for our public life, is developed in the author's forthcoming *On Civic Friendship*.

[11] Things are "internally related" to each other if (as Bradley typically expresses it) the terms are "altered necessarily" by the relations into which they enter. Again, if it is necessary of me that I stand in a certain relation to a certain object, so that I would not be what I am if I did not, then this relation is "internal" to me. See Hylton, Russell, Idealism, 44ff.

The Political Theory of the Procedural Republic

Michael J. Sandel

MICHAEL J. SANDEL *is Associate Professor Government at Harvard University. He is the author of* Liberalism and the Limits of Justice.

I

Liberals often take pride in defending what they oppose—pornography, for example, or unpopular views.[1] They say the state should not impose on its citizens a preferred way of life, but should leave them as free as possible to choose their own values and ends, consistent with a similar liberty for others. This commitment to freedom of choice requires liberals constantly to distinguish between permission and praise, between allowing a practice and endorsing it. It is one thing to allow pornography, they argue, something else to affirm it.

Conservatives sometimes exploit this distinction by ignoring it. They charge that those who would allow abortions favor abortion, that opponents of school prayer oppose prayer, that those who defend the rights of communists sympathize with their cause. And in a pattern of argument familiar in our politics, liberals reply by invoking higher principles; it is not that they dislike pornography less, but rather that they value toleration, or freedom of choice, or fair procedures more.

But in contemporary debate, the liberal rejoinder seems increasingly fragile, its moral basis increasingly unclear. Why should toleration and freedom of choice prevail when other important values are also at stake? Too often the answer implies some version of moral relativism, the idea that it is wrong to "legislate morality" because all morality is merely subjective. "Who is to say what is literature and what is filth? That is a value judgment, and whose values should decide?".

Relativism usually appears less as a claim than as a question ("Who is to judge?"). But it is a question that can also be asked of the values that liberals defend. Toleration and freedom and fairness are values too, and they can hardly be defended by the claim that no values can be defended. So it is a mistake to affirm liberal values by arguing that all values are merely subjective. The relativist defense of liberalism is no defense at all.

What, then, can be the moral basis of the higher principles the liberal invokes? Recent political philosophy has offered two main alternatives—one utilitarian, the other Kantian. The utilitarian view, following John Stuart Mill, defends liberal principles in the name of maximizing the general welfare. The state should not impose on its citizens a preferred way of life, even for their own good, because doing so will reduce the sum of human happiness, at least in the long run; better that people choose for themselves, even if, on occasion, they get it wrong. "The only freedom which deserves the name," writes Mill, "is that of pursuing our own good in our own way, so long as we do not attempt to deprive others of theirs, or impede their efforts to obtain it." He adds that his argument does not depend on any notion of abstract right, only on the principle of the greatest good for the greatest number. "I regard utility in the largest sense, grounded on the permanent interests of man as a progressive being."[2]

Many objections have been raised against utilitarianism as a general doctrine of moral philosophy. Some have questioned the concept of utility, and the assumption that all human goods are in principle commensurable. Others have objected that by reducing all values to preferences and desires, utilitarians are unable to admit qualitative distinctions of worth, unable to distinguish noble desires from base ones. But most recent debate has focused on whether utilitarianism offers a convincing basis for liberal principles, including respect for individual rights.

In one respect, utilitarianism would seem well-suited to liberal purposes. Maximizing utility does not require judging people's values, only aggregating them. And the willingness to aggregate preferences without judging them suggests a tolerant spirit, even a democratic one. When people go to the polls, we count their votes whatever they are.

But the utilitarian calculus is not always as liberal as it first appears. If enough cheering Romans pack the Coliseum to watch the lion devour the Christian, the collective pleasure of the Romans will surely outweigh the pain of the Christian, intense though it be. Or if a big majority abhors a small religion and wants it banned, the balance of preferences will favor suppression, not toleration. Utilitarians sometimes defend individual rights on the ground that respecting them now will serve utility in the long run. But this calculation is precarious and contingent. It hardly secures the liberal promise not to impose on some the values of others. As the majority will is an inadequate instrument of liberal politics—by itself it fails to secure individual rights—so the utilitarian philosophy is an inadequate foundation for liberal principles.

The case against utilitarianism was made most powerfully by Kant. He argued that empirical principles, such as utility, were unfit to serve as basis for the moral law. A wholly instrumental defense of freedom and rights not only leaves rights vulnerable, but fails to respect the inherent dignity of person. The utilitarian calculus treats people as means to the happiness of others, not as ends in themselves, worthy of respect.[3]

Contemporary liberals extend Kant's argument with the claim that utilitarianism fails to take seriously the distinction between persons. In seeking above all to maximize the general welfare, the utilitarian treats society as a whole as if it were a single person; it conflates our many, diverse desires into a single system of desire, and tries to maximize. It is indifferent to the distribution of satisfactions among persons, except insofar as this may affect the overall sum. But this fails to respect our plurality and distinctness. It uses some as a means to the happiness of all, and so fails to respect each as an end in himself.

Modern-day Kantians reject the utilitarian approach in favor of an ethic that takes rights more seriously. In their view, certain rights are so fundamental that even the general welfare cannot override them. As John Rawls writes, "Each person possesses an inviolability founded on justice that even the welfare of society as a whole cannot override ... the rights secured by justice are not subject to political bargaining or to the calculus of social interests."[4]

So Kantian liberals need an account of rights that does not depend on utilitarian considerations. More than this, they need an account that does not depend on any particular conception of the good, that does not presuppose the superiority of one way of life over others. Only a justification neutral about ends could preserve the liberal resolve not to favor any particular ends, or to impose on its citizens a preferred way of life.

But what sort of justification could this be? How is it possible to affirm certain liberties and rights as fundamental without embracing some vision of the good life, without endorsing some ends over others? It would seem we are back to the relativist predicament—to affirm liberal principles without embracing any particular ends.

The solution proposed by Kantian liberals is to draw a distinction between the "right" and the "good"—between a framework of basic rights and liberties, and the conceptions of the good that people may choose to pursue within the framework. It is one thing for the state to support a fair framework, they argue, something else to affirm some particular ends. For example, it is one thing to defend the right to free speech so that people may be free to form their own opinions and choose their own ends, but something else to support it on the grounds that a life of a political discussion is inherently worthier than a life unconcerned with public affairs, or on the grounds that free speech will increase the general welfare. Only the first defense is available on the Kantian view, resting as it does on the ideal of a neutral framework.

Now the commitment to a framework neutral among ends can be seen as a kind of value—in this sense the Kantian liberal is no relativist—but its value consists precisely in its refusal to affirm a preferred way of life or conception of the good. For Kantian liberals, then, the right is prior to the good, and in two senses. First, individual rights cannot be sacrificed for the sake of the general good, and second, the principles of justice that specify these rights cannot be premised on any particular vision of the good life. What justifies the rights is not that they maximize the general welfare or otherwise promote the good, but rather that they comprise a fair framework within which individuals and groups can choose their own value and ends, consistent with a similar liberty for others.

Of course, proponents of the rights-based ethic notoriously disagree about what rights are fundamental, and about what political arrangements the ideal of the neutral framework requires. Egalitarian liberals support the welfare state, and favor a scheme of civil liberties together with certain social and economic rights—rights to welfare, education, health care, and so on. Libertarian liberals defend the market economy, and claim that redistributive policies violate people's rights; they favor a scheme of civil liberties combined with a strict regime of private property rights. But whether egalitarian or libertarian, rights-based liberalism begins with the claim that we are separate, individual persons, each with our own aims, interests, and conceptions of the good, and seeks a framework of rights that will enable us to realize our capacity as free moral agents, consistent with a similar liberty for others.

II

Within academic philosophy, the last decade or so has seen the ascendance of the rights-based ethic over the utilitarian one, due in large part to the influence of John Rawls' important work, *A Theory of Justice*. In the debate between utilitarian and right-based theories, the rights-based ethic has come to prevail. The legal philosopher H.L.A. Hart recently described the shift from "the old faith that some form of utilitarianism must capture the essence of political morality" to the new faith that "the truth must lie with a doctrine of basic human rights, protecting specific basic liberties and interests of individuals... Whereas not so long ago great energy and much ingenuity of many philosophers were devoted to making some form of utilitarianism work, latterly such energies and ingenuity have been devoted to the articulation of theories of basic rights."[5]

But in philosophy as in life, the new faith becomes the old orthodoxy before long. Even as it has come to prevail over its utilitarian rival, the rights-based ethic has recently faced a growing challenge from a different direction, from a view that gives fuller expression to the claims of citizenship and community than the liberal vision allows. Recalling the arguments of Hegel against Kant, the communitarian critics of modern liberalism question the claim for the priority of the right over the good, and the picture of the freely choosing individual it embodies. Following Aristotle, they argue that we cannot justify political arrangements without reference to common purposes and ends, and that we cannot conceive our personhood without reference to our role as citizens, and as participants in a common life.

This debate reflects two contrasting pictures of the self. The rights-based ethic, and the conception of the person it embodies, were shaped in large part in the encounter with utilitarianism. Where utilitarians conflate our many desires into a single system of desires, Kantians insist on the separateness of persons. Where the utilitarian self is simply defined as the sum of its desires, the Kantian self is a choosing self, independent of the desires and ends it may have at any moment. As Rawls writes, "The self is prior to the ends which are affirmed by it; even a dominant end must be chosen from among numerous possibilities."[6]

The priority of the self over its ends means I am never defined by my aims and attachments, but always capable of standing back to survey and assess and possibly to revise them. This is what it means to be a free and independent self, capable of choice.

And this is the vision of the self that finds expression in the ideal of the state as a neutral framework. On the rights-based ethic, it is precisely because we are essentially separate, independent selves that we need a neutral framework, a framework of rights that refuses to choose among competing purposes and ends. If the self is prior to its ends, then the right must be prior to the good.

Communitarian critics of rights-based liberalism say we cannot conceive ourselves as independent in this way, as bearers of selves wholly detached from our aims and attachments. They say that certain of our roles are partly constitutive of the persons we are—as citizens of a country, or members of a movement, or partisans of a cause. But if we are partly defined by the communities we inhabit, then we must also be implicated in the purposes and ends characteristic of those communities. As Alasdair MacIntyre writes, "what is good for me has to be the good for one who inhabits these roles."[7] Open-ended though it be, the story of my life is always embedded in the story of those communities from which I derive my identity—whether family or city, people or nation, party or cause. On the communitarian view, these stories make a moral difference, not a only a psychological one. They situate us in the world, and give our lives their moral particularity.

What is at stake for politics in the debate between unencumbered selves and situated ones? What are the practical differences between a politics of rights and a politics of the common good? On some issues, the two theories may produce different arguments for similar policies. For example, the civil rights movement of the 1960s might be justified by liberals in the name of human dignity and respect for persons, and by communitarians in the name of recognizing the full membership of fellow citizens wrongly excluded from the common life of the nation. And where liberals might support public education in hopes of equipping students to become autonomous individuals, capable of choosing their own ends and pursuing them effectively, communitarians might support public education in hopes of equipping students to become good citizens, capable of contributing meaningfully to public deliberations and pursuits.

On other issues, the two ethics might lead to different policies. Communitarians would be more likely than liberals to allow a town to ban pornographic bookstores, on the grounds that pornography offends its way of life and the values that sustain it. But a politics of civic virtue does not always part company with liberalism in favor of conservative policies. For example, communitarians would be more willing than some rights-oriented liberals to see states enact laws regulating plant closing, to protect their communities from the disruptive effects of capital mobility and sudden industrial change. More generally, where the liberal regards the expansion of individual rights and entitlements as unqualified moral and political progress, the communitarian is troubled by the tendency of liberal programs to displace politics from smaller forms of association to more comprehensive ones. Where libertarian liberals defend the private economy and egalitarian liberals defend the welfare state, communitarians worry about the concentration of power in both the corporate economy and the bureaucratic state, and the erosion of those intermediate forms of community that have at times sustained a more vital public life.

Liberals often argue that a politics of the common good, drawing as it must on particular loyalties, obligations, and traditions, opens the way to prejudice and intolerance. The modern nation-state is not the Athenian *polis*, they point out; the scale and diversity of modern life have rendered the Aristotelian political ethic nostalgic at best and dangerous at worst. Any attempt to govern by a vision of the good is likely to lead to a slippery slope of totalitarian temptations.

Communitarians reply that intolerance flourishes most where forms of life are dislocated, roots unsettled, traditions undone. In our day, the totalitarian impulse has sprung less from the convictions of confidently situated selves than from the confusions of atomized, dislocated, frustrated selves, at sea in a world where common meanings have lost their force. As Hannah Arendt has written, "What makes mass society so difficult to bear is not the number of people involved or at least not primarily, but the fact that the world between them has lost its power to gather them together, to relate and to separate them."[8] Insofar as our public life has withered, our sense of common involvement diminished, we lie vulnerable to the mass politics of totalitarian solutions. So responds the party of the common good to the party of rights. If the party of the common good is right, our most pressing moral and political project is to revitalize those civic republican possibilities implicit in our tradition but fading in our time.

Source: Michael J. Sandel. "The Political Theory of the Procedural Republic." *Revue de Metaphysique et de Morale* 93, No. 1 (1988): 57-68. Reprinted with permission.

Notes

[1] In this and the following section, I draw on the introduction to Sandel, ed., *Liberalism and Its Critics*, Oxford, Basil Blackwell, 1984.

[2] Mill, *On Liberty*, ch. 1.

[3] See KANT, *Groundwork of the Metaphysics of Morals*, trans. H. J. Paton, New York, Harper and Row, 1956, and "On the Common Saying: This May be True in Theory, But It Does Not Apply in Practice," "in Hans Reiss, ed., *Kant's Political Writings*, Cambridge, Cambridge University Press, 1970.

[4] Rawls, *A Theory of Justice*, Oxford, Oxford University Press, 1971, p.3-4.

[5] Hart, "Between Utility and Rights," in Alan Ryan, ed., *The Idea of Freedom*, Oxford, Oxford University Press, 1979, p.77.

[6] Rawls, *A Theory of Justice*, p.560.17

[7] MacIntyre, *After Virtue*, Notre Dame, University of Notre Dame Press, 1981, p.205.

[8] Arendt, *The Human Condition*, Chicago, University of Chicago Press, 1958, p.52-53.

The Communitarian Critique of Liberalism

Michael Walzer

MICHAEL WALZER *(1935-) is Professor in the School of Social Sciences, Institute for Advanced Study, Princeton University. He is the author of numerous books and articles in political philosophy.*

I

Intellectual fashions are notoriously short-lived, very much like fashions in popular music, art, or dress. But there are certain fashions that seem regularly to reappear. Like pleated trousers or short skirts, they are inconstant features of a larger and more steadily prevailing phenomenon—in this case, a certain way of dressing. They have brief but recurrent lives; we know their transience and expect their return. Needless to say, there is no afterlife in which trousers will be permanently pleated or skirts forever short. Recurrence is all.

Although it operates at a much higher level (an infinitely higher level?) of cultural significance, the communitarian critique of liberalism is like the pleating of trousers: transient but certain to return. It is a consistently intermittent feature of liberal politics and social organization. No liberal success will make it permanently unattractive. At the same time, no communitarian critique, however penetrating, will ever be anything more than an inconstant feature of liberalism. Someday, perhaps, there will be a larger transformation, like the shift from aristocratic knee-breeches to plebian pants, rendering liberalism and its critics alike irrelevant. But I see no present signs of anything like that, nor am I sure that we should look forward to it. For now, there is much to be said for a recurrent critique, whose protagonists hope only for small victories, partial incorporations, and when they are rebuffed or dismissed or coopted, fade away for a time only to return.

Communitarianism is usefully contrasted with social democracy, which has succeeded in establishing a permanent presence alongside of and some times conjoined with liberal politics. Social democracy has its own intermittently fashionable critics, largely anarchist and libertarian in character. Since it sponsors certain sorts of communal identification, it is less sub-ject to communitarian criticism than liberalism is. But it can never escape such criticism entirely, for liberals and social democrats alike share a commitment to economic growth and cope (although in different ways) with the deracinated social forms that growth produces. Community itself is largely an ideological presence in modern society; it has no recurrent critics of its own. It is intermittently fashionable only because it no longer exists in anything like full strength, and it is criticized only when it is fashionable.

The communitarian critique is nonetheless a powerful one; it would not recur if it were not capable of engaging our minds and feelings. In this essay, I want to investigate the power of its current American versions and then offer a version of my own—less powerful, perhaps, than the ones with which I shall begin, but more available for incorporation within liberal (or social democratic) politics. I do not mean (I hardly have the capacity) to lay communitarianism to rest, although I would willingly wait for its reappearance in a form more coherent and incisive than that in which it currently appears. The problem with communitarian criticism today—I am not the first to notice this—is that it suggests two different, and deeply contradictory, arguments against liberalism. One of these arguments is aimed primarily at liberal practice, the other primarily at liberal theory, but they cannot both be right. It is possible that each one is partly right—indeed, I shall insist on just this partial validity—but each of the arguments is right in a way that undercuts the value of the other.

II

The first argument holds that liberal political theory accurately represents liberal social practice. As if the Marxist account of ideological reflection were literally true, and exemplified here, contemporary Western societies (American society especially) are taken to be the home of radically isolated individuals, rational egotists, and existential agents, men and women protected and divided by their inalienable rights. Liberalism tells the truth about the asocial society that liberals create—not, in fact, *ex nihilo* as their theory suggests, but in a struggle against traditions and communities and authorities that are forgotten as soon as they are escaped, so that liberal practices seem to have no history. The struggle itself is ritually celebrated but rarely reflected on. The members of liberal society share no political or religious traditions; they can tell only one story about themselves and that is the story of *ex nihilo* creation, which begins in the state of nature or the original position. Each individual imagines himself absolutely free, unencumbered, and on his own—and enters society, accepting its obligations, only in order to minimize his risks. His goal is security, and security is, as Marx wrote, "the assurance of his egoism." And as he imagines himself, so he *really is,*

> that is, an individual separated from the community, withdrawn into himself, wholly preoccupied with his private interest and acting in accordance with his private caprice ... The only bond between men is natural necessity, need, and private interest.[1]

(I have used masculine pronouns in order to fit my sentences to Marx's. But it is an interesting question, not addressed here, whether this first communitarian critique speaks to the experience of women: Are necessity and private interest their only bonds with one another?)

The writings of the young Marx represent one of the early appearances of communitarian criticism, and his argument, first made in the 1840s, is powerfully present today. Alastair MacIntyre's description of the incoherence of modem intellectual and cultural life and the loss of narrative capacity makes a similar point in updated, state-of-the-art, theoretical language.[2] But the only theory that is necessary to the communitarian critique of liberalism is liberalism itself. All that the critics have to do, so they say, is to take liberal theory seriously. The self-portrait of the individual constituted only by his willfulness, liberated from all connection, without common values, binding ties, customs, or traditions—sans eyes, sans teeth, sans taste, sans everything—need only be evoked in order to be devalued: It is already the concrete absence of value. What can the real life of such a person be like? Imagine him maximizing his utilities, and society is turned into a war of all against all, the familiar rat race, in which, as Hobbes wrote, there is "no other goal, nor other garland, but being foremost."[3] Imagine him enjoying his rights, and society is reduced to the coexistence of isolated selves, for liberal rights, according to this first critique, have more to do with "exit" than with "voice."[4] They are concretely expressed in separation, divorce, withdrawal, solitude, privacy, and political apathy. And finally, the very fact that individual life can be de-

scribed in these two philosophical languages, the language of utilities and the language of rights, is a further mark, says MacIntyre, of its incoherence: Men and women in liberal society no longer have access to a single moral culture within which they can learn how they ought to live.[5] There is no consensus, no public meeting-of-minds, on the nature of the good life, hence the triumph of private caprice, revealed, for example, in Sartrean existentialism, the ideological reflection of everyday capriciousness.

We liberals are free to choose, and we have a right to chose, but we have no criteria to govern our choices except our own wayward understanding of our wayward interests and desires. And so our choices lack the qualities of cohesion and consecutiveness. We can hardly remember what we did yesterday; we cannot with any assurance predict what we will do tomorrow. We cannot give a proper account of ourselves. We cannot sit together and tell comprehensible stories, and we recognize ourselves in the stories we read only when these are fragmented narratives, without plots, the literary equivalent of atonal music and nonrepresentational art.

Liberal society, seen in the light of this first communitarian critique, is fragmentation in practice; and community is the exact opposite, the home of coherence, connection, and narrative capacity. But I am less concerned here with the different accounts that might be provided of this lost Eden than I am with the repeated insistence on the reality of fragmentation after the loss. This is the common theme of all contemporary communitarianisms: neoconservative lamentation, neo-Marxist indictment, and neoclassical or republican hand-wringing. (The need for the prefix "neo" suggests again the intermittent or recurrent character of communitarian criticism.) I should think it would be an awkward theme, for if the sociological argument of liberal theory is right, if society is actually decomposed, without residue, into the problematic coexistence of individuals, then we might well assume that liberal politics is the best way to deal with the problems of decomposition. If we have to create an artificial and ahistorical union out of a multitude of isolated selves, why not take the state of nature or the original position as our conceptual starting point? Why not accept, in standard liberal fashion, the priority of procedural justice over substantive conceptions of the good, since we can hardly expect, given our fragmentation, to agree about the good? Michael Sandel asks whether a community of those who put justice first can ever be more than a community of strangers.[6] The question is a good one, but its reverse form is more immediately relevant: If we really are a community of strangers, how can we do anything else but put justice first?

III

We are saved from this entirely plausible line of argument by the second communitarian critique of liberalism. The second critique holds that liberal theory radically misrepresents real life. The world is not like that nor could it be. Men and women cut loose from all social ties, literally unencumbered, each one the one and only inventor of his or her own life, with no criteria, no common standards, to guide the invention—these are mythical figures. How can any group of people be strangers to one another when each member of the group is born with parents, and when these parents have friends, relatives, neighbors, comrades at work, coreligionists, and fellow citizens—connections, in fact, which are not so much chosen as passed on and inherited? Liberalism may well enhance the significance of purely contractual ties, but it is obviously false to suggest, as Hobbes sometimes seemed to do, that all our connections are mere "market friendships," voluntarist and self-interested in character, which cannot outlast the advantages they bring.[7] It is in the very nature of a human society that individuals bred within it will find themselves caught up in patterns of relationship, networks of power, and communities of meaning. That quality of being caught up is what makes them persons of a certain sort. And only then can they make themselves persons of a (marginally) different sort by reflecting on what they are and by acting in more or less distinctive ways within the patterns, networks, and communities that are willy-nilly theirs.

The burden of the second critique is that the deep structure even of liberal society is in fact communitarian. Liberal theory distorts this reality and, insofar as we adopt the theory, deprives us of any ready access to our own experience of communal embeddedness. The rhetoric of liberalism—this is the argument of the authors of *Habits of the Heart* limits our understanding of our own heart's habits, and gives us no way to formulate the convictions that hold us together as persons and that bind persons together into a community.[8] The assumption here is that we are in fact persons and that we are in fact bound together. The liberal ideology of separatism cannot take personhood and bondedness away from us. What it does take away is the *sense* of our personhood and bondedness, and this deprivation is then reflected in liberal politics. It explains our inability to form cohesive solidarities, stable movements and parties, that might make our deep convictions visible and effective in the world. It also explains our radical

dependence (brilliantly foreshadowed in Hobbes's *Leviathan*) on the central state.

But how are we to understand this extraordinary disjunction between communal experience and liberal ideology, between personal conviction and public rhetoric, and between social bondedness and political isolation? That question is not addressed by communitarian critics of the second sort. If the first critique depends on a vulgar Marxist theory of reflection, the second critique requires an equally vulgar idealism. Liberal theory now seems to have a power over and against real life that has been granted to few theories in human history. Plainly, it has not been granted to communitarian theory, which cannot, on the first argument, overcome the reality of liberal separatism and cannot, on the second argument, evoke the already existing structures of social connection. In any case, the two critical arguments are mutually inconsistent; they cannot both be true. Liberal separatism either represents or misrepresents the conditions of everyday life. It might, of course, do a little of each— the usual muddle—but that is not a satisfactory conclusion from a communitarian standpoint. For if the account of dissociation and separatism is even partly right, then we have to raise questions about the depth, so to speak, of the deep structure. And if we are all to some degree communitarians under the skin, then the portrait of social incoherence loses its critical force.

IV

But each of the two critical arguments is partly right. I will try to say what is right about each, and then ask if something plausible can be made of the parts. First, then, there cannot be much doubt that we (in the United States) live in a society where individuals are relatively dissociated and separated from one another, or better, where they are continually separating from one another—continually in motion, often in solitary and apparently random motion, as if in imitation of what physicists call Brownian movement. Hence we live in a profoundly unsettled society. We can best see the forms of unsettlement if we track the most important moves. So, consider (imitating the Chinese style) the Four Mobilities:

1. *Geographic mobility.* Americans apparently change their residence more often than any people in history, at least since the barbarian migrations, excluding only nomadic tribes and families caught up in civil or foreign wars. Moving people and their possessions from one city or town to another is a major industry in the United States, even though many people manage to move themselves. In another sense, of course, we are

all self-moved, not refugees but voluntary migrants. The sense of place must be greatly weakened by this extensive geographic mobility, although I find it hard to say whether it is superseded by mere insensitivity or by a new sense of many places. Either way, communitarian feeling seems likely to decline in importance. Communities are more than just locations, but they are most often successful when they are permanently located.

2. *Social mobility*. This article will not address the arguments about how best to describe social standing or how to measure changes, whether by income, education, class membership, or rank in the status hierarchy. It is enough to say that fewer Americans stand exactly where their parents stood or do what they did than in any society for which we have comparable knowledge. Americans may inherit many things from their parents, but the extent to which they make a different life, if only by making a different living, means that the inheritance of community, that is, the passing on of beliefs and customary ways, is uncertain at best. Whether or not children are thereby robbed of narrative capacity, they seem likely to tell different stories than their parents told.

3. *Marital mobility*. Rates of separation, divorce, and remarriage are higher today than they have ever been in our own society and probably higher than they have ever been in any other (except perhaps among Roman aristocrats, although I know of no statistics from that time, only anecdotes). The first two mobilities, geographic and social, also disrupt family life, so that siblings, for example, often live at great distances from one another, and later as uncles and aunts, they are far removed from nephews and nieces. But what we call "broken homes" are the product of marital breaks, of husbands or wives moving out—and then, commonly, moving on to new partners. Insofar as home is the first community and the first school of ethnic identity and religious conviction, this kind of breakage must have counter-communitarian consequences. It means that children often do not hear continuous or identical stories from the adults with whom they live. (Did the greater number of children ever bear such stories? The death of one spouse and the remarriage of the other may once have been as common as divorce and remarriage are today. But, then, other sorts of mobility have to be considered: Both men and women are more likely today to marry across class, ethnic, and religious

lines; remarriage will therefore often produce extraordinarily complex and socially diverse families—which probably are without historical precedent.)

4 *Political mobility*. Loyalty to leaders, movements, parties, clubs, and urban machines seems to decline rapidly as place and social standing and family membership become less central in the shaping of personal identity. Liberal citizens stand outside all political organizations and then choose the one that best serves their ideals or interests. They are, ideally, independent voters, that is, people who move around; they choose for themselves rather than voting as their parents did, and they choose freshly each time rather than repeating themselves. As their numbers increase, they make for a volatile electorate and hence for institutional instability, particularly at the local level where political organization once served to reinforce communal ties.

The effects of the Four Mobilities are intensified in a variety of ways by other social developments which we are likely to talk about in the common metaphor of movement: the advance of knowledge, technological progress, and so on. But I am concerned here only with the actual movement of individuals. Liberalism is, most simply, the theoretical endorsement and justification of this movement.[9] In the liberal view, then, the Four Mobilities represent the enactment of liberty, and the pursuit of (private or personal) happiness. And it has to be said that, conceived in this way, liberalism is a genuinely popular creed. Any effort to curtail mobility in the four areas described here would require a massive and harsh application of state power. Nevertheless, this popularity has an underside of sadness and discontent that are intermittently articulated, and communitarianism is, most simply, the intermittent articulation of these feelings. It reflects a sense of loss, and the loss is real. People do not always leave their old neighborhoods or hometowns willingly or happily. Moving may be a personal adventure in our standard cultural mythologies, but it is as often a family trauma in real life. The same thing is true of social mobility, which carries people down as well as up and requires adjustments that are never easy to manage. Marital breaks may sometimes give rise to new and stronger unions, but they also pile up what we might think of as family fragments: single-parent households, separated and lonely men and women, and abandoned children. And independence in politics is often a not-so-splendid isolation: Individuals with opinions are cut loose from groups with programs. The result is a decline in "the sense of efficacy," with accompanying effects on commitment and morale.

All in all, we liberals probably know one another less well, and with less assurance, than people once did, although we may see more aspects of the other than they saw, and recognize in him or her a wider range of possibilities (including the possibility of moving on). We are more often alone than people once were, being without neighbors we can count on, relatives who live nearby or with whom we are close, or comrades at work or in the movement. This is the truth of the first communitarian argument. We must now fix the limits of this truth by seeking what is true in the second argument.

In its easiest version, the second argument—that we are really, at bottom, creatures of community—is certainly true but of uncertain significance. The ties of place, class or status, family, and even politics survive the Four Mobilities to a remarkable extent. To take just one example, from the last of the Four: It remains true, even today in this most liberal and mobile of societies, that the best predictor of how people will vote is our knowledge of how their parents voted.[10] All those dutifully imitative young Republicans and Democrats testify to the failure of liberalism to make independence or waywardness of mind the distinctive mark of its adherents. The predictive value of parental behavior holds even for independent voters: They are simply the heirs of independence. But we do not know to what extent inheritances of this sort are a dwindling communal resource; it may be that each generation passes on less than it received. The full liberalization of the social order, the production and reproduction of self-inventing individuals, may take a long time, much longer indeed, than liberals themselves expected. There is not much comfort here for communitarian critics, however; while they can recognize and value the survival of older ways of life, they cannot count on, and they must have anxieties about, the vitality of those ways.

But there is another approach to the truth of the second critical argument. Whatever the extent of the Four Mobilities, they do not seem to move us so far apart that we can no longer talk with one another. We often disagree, of course, but we disagree in mutually comprehensible ways. I should think it fairly obvious that the philosophical controversies that MacIntyre laments are not in fact a mark of social incoherence. Where there are philosophers, there will be controversies, just as where there are knights, there will be tournaments. But these are highly ritualized activities, which bear witness to the connection, not the disconnection, of their protagonists. Even political conflict in liberal societies rarely takes forms so extreme as to

set its protagonists beyond negotiation and compromise, procedural justice, and the very possibility of speech. The American civil rights struggle is a nice example of a conflict for which our moral/political language was and is entirely adequate. The fact that the struggle has had only partial success does not reflect linguistic inadequacy but rather political failures and defeats.

Martin Luther King's speeches evoked a palpable tradition, a set of common values such that public disagreement could focus only on how (or how quickly) they might best be realized.[11] But this is not, so to speak, a traditionalist tradition, a *Gemeinschaft* tradition, a survival of the preliberal past. It is a liberal tradition modified, no doubt, by survivals of different sorts. The modifications are most obviously Protestant and republican in character, though by no means exclusively so: The years of mass immigration have brought a great variety of ethnic and religious memories to bear on American politics. What all of them bear on, however, is liberalism. The language of individual rights—voluntary association, pluralism, toleration, separation, privacy, free speech, the career open to talents, and so on—is simply inescapable. Who among us seriously attempts to escape? If we really are situated selves, as the second communitarian critique holds, then our situation is largely captured by that vocabulary. This is the truth of the second critique. Does it make any sense then to argue that liberalism prevents us from understanding or maintaining the ties that bind us together?

It makes some sense, because liberalism is a strange doctrine, which seems continually to undercut itself, to disdain its own traditions, and to produce in each generation renewed hopes for a more absolute freedom from history and society alike. Much of liberal political theory, from Locke to Rawls, is an effort to fix and stabilize the doctrine in order to end the endlessness of liberal liberation. But beyond every current version of liberalism, there is always a super liberalism, which, as Roberto Unger says of his own doctrine, "pushes the liberal premises about state and society, about freedom from dependence and governance of social relations by the will, to the point at which they merge into a large ambition: the building of a social world less alien to a self that can always violate the generative rules of its own mental or social constructs."[12] Although Unger was once identified as a communitarian, this ambition—large indeed!—seems designed to prevent not only any stabilization of liberal doctrine but also any recovery or creation of community. For there is no imaginable community that would not be alien to the eternally transgressive self. If the ties that bind us together do not *bind* us, there can be no such thing as a community. If it is anything at all, communitarianism is antithetical to transgression. And the transgressive self is antithetical even to the liberal community which is its creator and sponsor.[13]

Liberalism is a self-subverting doctrine; for that reason, it really does require periodic communitarian correction. But it is not a particularly helpful form of correction to suggest that liberalism is literally incoherent or that it can be replaced by some preliberal or antiliberal community waiting somehow just beneath the surface or just beyond the horizon. Nothing is waiting; American communitarians have to recognize that there is no one out there but separated, rights-bearing, voluntarily associating, freely speaking, liberal selves. It would be a good thing, though, if we could teach those selves to know themselves as social beings, the historical products of, and in part the embodiments of, liberal values. For the communitarian correction of liberalism cannot be anything other than a selective reinforcement of those same values or, to appropriate the well-known phrase of Michael Oakeshott, a pursuit of the intimations of community within them.

Source: This essay was first given as the John Dewey lecture at Harvard Law School in September 1989. It was republished as: Michael Walzer, "The Communitarianism Critique of Liberalism," *Political Theory* 18, No. 1, (1990): 6-23. Reprinted by permission of Sage Publications, Inc.

Notes

[1] Karl Marx, "On the Jewish Question," in *Early Writings*, ed. by T.B. Bottomore (London: C.A. Watts, 1963), P. 26.

[2] Alsadair MacIntyre, *After Virtue* (Notre Dame: University of Notre Dame Press, 1981).

[3] Thomas Hobbes, *The Elements of Law*, Part I, ch. 9, para. 21. I have noticed that the two favourite writers of communitarian critics of this first kind are Hobbes and Sartre. Is it possible that the essence of liberalism is best revealed by these two, who were not, in the usual sense of the term, liberals at all?

[4] See Albert Hirschman's *Exit, Voice, and Loyalty* (Cambridge, MA: Harvard University Press, 1970).

[5] MacIntyre, *After Virtue*, chs. 2, 17.

[6] This is Richard Rorty's summary of Sandel's argument: "The Priority of Democracy to Philosophy," in *The Virginia Statue for Religious Freedom*, ed. by Merrill D. Peterson and Robert C. Vaughan (Cambridge: Cambridge University Press, 1982).

[7] Thomas Hobbes, *De Cive*, ed. by Howard Warrender (Oxford: Oxford University Press, 1983), Part, ch. 1.

[8] Robert Bellah et al., *Habits of the Heart* (Berkeley: University of California Press, 1985), pp. 21, 290; see Rorty's comment, "Priority," p. 275, n. 12.

[9] And also its practical working out, in the career open to talents, the right of free movement, legal divorce, and so on.

[10] See A. Campbell et al., *The American Voter* (New York: Wiley, 1960), pp. 147–148.

[11] See the evocation of King in *Habits of the Heart*, pp. 249, 252.

[12] Roberto Mangabeira Unger, *The Critical Legal Studies Movement* (Cambridge, MA: Harvard University Press, 1986), p. 41.

[13] Cf. Buff-Coat (Robert Everard) in the Putney debates: "Whatsoever ... obligations I should be bound unto, if afterwards God should reveal himself, I would break it speedily, if it were an hundred a day." In *Puritanism and Liberty*, ed. by A.S.P. Woodhouse (London: J.M. Dent, 1938), p. 34. Is Buff-Coat the first superliberal or Unger a latter-day Puritan saint?

Assessing the Communitarian Critique of Liberalism

Allen E. Buchanan

ALLEN E. BUCHANAN *is Professor at the University of Wisconsin. He has written in the fields of economics and ethics, including his book* Ethics, Efficiency, and the Market.

Introduction

As liberal political regimes have been the dominant form of political organization in the West, so liberalism has prevailed in Anglo-American political philosophy. In the past few years, however, a vigorous challenge to liberal political philosophy—and by implication to the political institutions it attempts to legitimize—has arisen under the banner of "communitarianism." The communitarian challenge achieves its most powerful expression in the works of Alasdair MacIntyre, Charles Taylor, and Michael Sandel.[1] My task here is to articulate some of the most central elements of the communitarian critique of liberalism and then to assess their merits by seeing whether liberalism has the resources to respond to them effectively.

There are perhaps almost as many communitarian positions as there are communitarian writers. Nevertheless, some common threads run through most of the important communitarian works.[2] The fundamental communitarian criticisms seem to be these:

i) Liberalism devalues, neglects, and/or undermines community, and community is a fundamental and irreplaceable ingredient in the good life for human beings.

ii) Liberalism undervalues political life—viewing political association as a merely instrumental good, it is blind to the fundamental importance of full participation in political community for the good life for human beings.

iii) Liberalism fails to provide, or is incompatible with, an adequate account of the importance of certain types of obligations and commitments—those that are not chosen or explicitly undertaken through contracting or promising—such as familial obligations and obligations to support one's community or country.

iv) Liberalism presupposes a defective conception of the self, failing to recognize that the self is "embedded" in and partly constituted by communal commitments and values which are not objects of choice.

v) Liberalism wrongly exalts justice as being "the first virtue of social institutions," failing to see that, at best, justice is a remedial virtue, needed only in circumstances in which the higher virtue of community has broken down. (My purpose, however, is not exegetical. I aim to reconstruct and evaluate the most interesting position which could be called communitarian, not limiting myself to the explicit views of any particular communitarian writers.) ...

The Status of Justice and the Pluralist Assumption

A good deal of what makes communitarian thought exciting and provocative is its critical attitude toward justice. Yet here, too, there are serious ambiguities as to the nature and import of the arguments. To the extent that justice is thought of as being a matter of individual rights, we have already examined in some depth the communitarian's complaints about justice, arguing in reply that liberal individual rights have considerable value for community.

A different, though closely related, aspect of the communitarian critique of justice is advanced by Sandel. He contends that liberals have failed to recognize a fundamental limitation on justice. For justice, according to Sandel, is not the highest virtue a society can hope to achieve; it is at best a remedial virtue and one whose value is proportional to the presence of that defect whose job it is to remedy.[3] It is only because our (liberal) society suffers so grievously from this defect that we value justice so highly. The defect for which justice is the remedy is the absence of community or, more accurately, it is pluralism, the lack of a shared conception of the common good.

Hence, a prominent feature of the circumstances of justice is pluralism, and pluralism is a matter of degree. As pluralism proliferates, appeals to principles of justice become more urgent and the virtue of justice comes to be more highly prized. As pluralism diminishes and a greater convergence on a conception of the good is attained, the need for principles of justice dwindles and the status of justice as a virtue diminishes proportionately.

Once again, two claims ought to be distinguished: the thesis that justice is a remedial virtue (the remedial thesis) and the thesis that the need for and value of principles of justice vary with the extent of pluralism or divergence in conceptions of the common good (the proportionality thesis).

The proportionality thesis may be unexceptionable. At any rate, an advocate of the liberal political thesis need not deny its truth. She can simply note that most modern societies, including our own, are in fact sufficiently pluralistic to make reliance on principles of justice, including those that articulate liberal individual rights, quite valuable. In addition, however, the liberal can argue that virtually any feasible and desirable society will require principles of justice, including liberal individual rights, even if there exists in it a much greater consensus on the common good than modern societies typically exhibit.

As I have urged elsewhere, individual rights can play a valuable role even in societies in which there is unanimous agreement as to what the common good is and a universal commitment to pursuing it.[4] For even in such a society there could be serious, indeed violent, disagreements either about how the common good is to be specified concretely and in detail or about the proper means and strategies for achieving it. Individual rights, especially rights of political participation, freedom of expression, and association can serve to contain and channel such disagreements and to preserve community in spite of their presence. So even if the proportionality thesis is true—even if the need for and value of principles of justice vary with the extent of pluralism—justice may still be extremely important, indeed indispensable, even in societies which enjoy a remarkable measure of agreement on the common good.

Once this point is appreciated, the remedial thesis, at least if it is supposed to be a criticism of the liberal political theses, appears to be quite implausible. To say that justice is a remedial virtue because it is only needed where community is lacking or incomplete is to imply that the sorts of disagreements that lead us to rely on principles of justice are unfortunate defects, lamentable flaws. In other words, the implication is that justice, being a remedy, is second-best. It would be better to live in a society in which the flaw that requires the remedy did not exist. This, however, seems simply false. Why should the extremely minimal sort of disagreement (on the concrete specification of the common good or the proper means for achieving it) that makes justice valuable be considered any sort of defect at all? Only the acceptance of an ideal of absolute harmony and a refusal to accord any positive value, no matter how limited, to diversity would make a flaw of that extremely minimal pluralism which the circumstances of justice include.

If such an extraordinarily strict ideal of homogeneity were granted, it would follow that justice is a remedial virtue. But then the claim that justice is a remedial virtue would have no sting. Since societies in our world fall so far short of the ideal of the thoroughgoing convergence of values, justice is still extremely important for us. And to the extent that justice includes individual rights, the claim that respect for such rights is "only" a remedial virtue rings hollow.

Source: Allen E. Buchanan. "Assessing the Communitarian Critique of Liberalism." *Ethics* 99 (1989): 852-882. Reprinted with permission.

Notes

[1] A. MacIntyre, *After Virtue: A Study in Moral Theory* (London: Duckworth, 1981); C. Taylor, *Hegel and Modern Society* (Cambridge: Cambridge University Press, 1979); M. Sandel, *Liberalism and the Limits of Justice* (Cambridge: Cambridge University Press, 1982).

[2] I have chosen here not to include Roberto Unger among the communitarians whose views I examine, partly because some features of his work cast doubt on whether he should be considered a communitarian and partly because he focuses much more heavily on the critique of liberal legal systems than the authors I do examine. Nor does this article deal explicitly with the work of Michael Walzer, who, though perhaps sharing some tenets with major communitarians such as MacIntyre and Sandel, seems to me in some respects to be much closer to liberalism.

[3] Sandel, *Liberalism and the Limits of Justice*, pp.31, 183.

[4] Buchanan, *Marx and Justice*, (Totowa, N. J.: Rowman & Allanheld, 1982) pp.164-68.

Moral Arguments and Social Contexts

Alasdair MacIntyre

ALASDAIR MACINTYRE *was Professor at Vanderbilt University and more recently at Notre Dame University. He has written many articles and within the past few years has published three well known books, namely* After Virtue *(1981),* Whose Justice? Which Rationality? *(1988), and* Three Rival Versions of Moral Inquiry *(1990).*

Virginia Held believes it possible for intellectuals to speak from a point of view independent of existing social arrangements and interests, from which as purely external critics they should articulate for society the standards that genuine moral and aesthetic worth decree. The issue between her and Richard Rorty turns on whether a necessary precondition of this possibility can be satisfied. Held's thesis requires that conclusions concerning genuine moral worth can be devised and justified, independently of any appeal to *de facto* beliefs, conventions, and institutions. This is what Rorty denies. Held's thesis also requires that everyone else, plain persons who are not intellectuals, have good reason to attend to declarations by intellectuals. This I deny for reasons which undermine Rorty's argument as well as Held's.

What precludes modern intellectuals from being justly accorded the role and the responsibilities assigned to them by Held is the extent of intellectual and social dissensus. On every substantive social and moral issue intellectuals appear on opposing sides: Sowell versus Thurow, Scholem versus Arendt, Bethe versus Teller. If Held's thesis is that plain persons should attend only to intellectuals whose arguments are sound, then the intellectual task of identifying sound arguments devolves on the plain person, and any clear distinction between intellectuals and nonintellectuals is obliterated.

In place of the hierarchical relationship of intellectuals to plain persons we might entertain the hope of developing a form of social conversation in which professors are as likely to learn from farmers or coalminers as *vice versa*. But on what resources could such conversation draw? Rorty's answer is that, given the failure of all attempts to construct the kind of rationally-justifiable-as-such morality presupposed by Held's thesis, it has nothing to draw upon but our common stock on conventions and anecdotes. But once again dissensus is the obstacle. There are too many rival conventions, too many conflicting anecdotes; and the repetition of assertions and denials does not constitute conversation. What postmodern bourgeois liberalism exhibits is not moral argument freed from unwarranted philosophical pretensions, but the decay of moral reasoning.

That decay is unsurprising in a society whose world view, oscillating between *Moralität* and *Sittlichkeit*, obscures the connection between the possibility of moral reasoning and the existence of a certain type of tradition-bearing community. Any particular piece of practical reasoning has rational force only for those who both have desires and dispositions ordered to some good and recognize that good as furthered by doing what that piece of practical reasoning bids. Only within a community with shared beliefs about goods and shared dispositions educated in accordance with those beliefs, both rooted in shared practices, can practical reason-giving be an ordered, teachable activity with standards of success and failure. Such a community is rational only if the moral theory articulated in its institutionalized reason-giving is the best theory to emerge so far in its history. The best theory so far is that which transcends the limitations of the previous best theory by providing the best explanation of that previous theory's failures and incoherences (as judged by the standards of that previous theory) and showing how to escape them.

The succession of such institutionalized theories in the life of a community constitute a rational tradition whose successive specifications of human good point forward to a never finally specifiable human *telos*. To be a rational individual is to participate in social life informed by a rational tradition. It is when modern societies reject this kind of rootedness in rational tradition that moral theorists either with the Enlightenment and Held attempt to construct a morality from the resources of reason-as-such or with Rorty seek to come to terms with the fragmented *status quo*.

Source: Alasdair MacIntyre. "Moral Arguments and Social Contexts." *The Journal of Philosophy* 70, No. 12 (1983): 590-591. Reprinted with permission of Alasdair MacIntyre and *The Journal of Philosophy*.

Suggested Reading

General Introduction

Baradar, Leon P. *Political Ideologies*, 5th ed. (Englewood Cliffs, N.J.: Prentice Hall, 1994)

Goodwin, Barbara. *Using Political Ideas* 2nd ed. (New York: John Wiley and Sons, 1987)

Heywood, Andrew. *Political Ideologies* (London: Macmillan Education Ltd, 1992)

Ingersoll, David E. and Richard K. Matthews. *The Philosophic Roots of Modern Ideology* 2nd ed. (Englewood Cliffs: Prentice Hall, 1991)

Macridis, Roy. *Contemporary Poltical Ideologies* 5th ed. (New York: HarperCollins Publishers Inc., 1992)

Sargent, Lyman Tower. *Contemporary Political Ideologies* 7th ed. (Chicago: The Dorsey Press, 1987)

Classical Liberalism

Barry, N. *On Classical Liberalism and Libertarianism* (London: Macmillan, 1986)

Brittan, S. *A Restatement of Economic Liberalism* (London: Macmillan, 1988)

Laski, Harold. *The Rise of European Liberalism* (London: George Allen and Unwin, 1936)

Macpherson, C.B. *The Political Theory of Possessive Individualism* (Oxford: Oxford University Press, 1962)

Reform Liberalism

Berkowitz, Edward and Kim McQuaid. *Creating the Welfare State: The Political Economy of Twentieth-Century Reform* (New York: Praeger, 1988)

Dworkin, R. *A Matter of Principle* (London: Harvard University Press, 1985)

Gauthier, *Morals By Agreement* (Oxford: Oxford University Press, 1986)

Gray, J. *Liberalism* (Milton Keynes: Open University, 1986)

Avineri, Shlomo and Avner de-Shalit, eds. *Communitarianism and Individualism* (Oxford: Oxford University PRess, 1992)

Kymlicka, Will. *Liberalism, Community and Culture* (Oxford: Clarendon Press, 1989)

Lowi, Theordore. *The End of Liberalism: Ideology, Policy and the Crisis of Public Authority* (New York: W.W. Norton and Co., 1969)

Conservatism

Forbes, Duncan. *Hume's Philosophical Politics* (Cambridge: 1975)

Hayek, F.A. *The Constitution of Liberty* (London: Routledge and Kegan Paul, 1960)

Honderich, T. *Conservatism* (London: Hamish Hamilton, 1990)

Kirk, Russell. *The Conservative Mind* (Chicago: Henry Regnery, 1960)

Neo-Conservatism

Gamble, A. *The Free Economy and the Strong State* (London: Macmillan, 1988)

King, Desmond. *The New Right* (London: Macmillan, 1987)

Levitas, R. ed. *The Ideology of the New Right* (Cambridge: Polity Press, 1986)

Self, Peter. *Political Theories of Modern Government* (London: Unwin Hyman, 1985)

Marxism

Cohen, G.A. *History, Labour and Freedom* (Oxford: Oxford University Press, 1988)

McLellan, David. *Karl Marx: His Life and Thought* (New York: Harper and Row, 1973)

Miliband, Ralph. *The State in Capitalist Society* (London: Quartet Books, 1973)

Nielsen, K. *Marxism and the Moral Point of View* (Boulder: Westview Press, 1989)

Stephenson, Carl. *Mediaeval Feudalism* (Ithaca: Cornell University Press, 1956)

Socialism

Brucan, Silviu. *World Socialism at the Crossroads: An Insider's View* (Westport, Conn: Greenwood Press, 1990)

Crosland, C.A.R. *The Future of Socialism* (London: Jonathan Cape, 1956)

Dunn, J. *The Politics of Socialism* (Cambridge: Cambridge University Press, 1984)

Harrington, Michael. *Socialism: Past and Future* (New York: Little, Brown, 1989)

Lichtheim, G. *A Short History of Socialism* (London: Fontana-Collins, 1975)

Markovic, M. *Democratic Socialism: Theory and Practice* (New York: St. Martin's Press, 1982)

Fascism

Bullock, Alan. *Hitler: A Study in Tyranny* (New York: Harper and Row, 1971).

Karsten, F.L. *Rise of Fascism* (Berkeley: University of California Press, 1980).

Lee, Stephen J. *The European Dictatorships*, 1918-1945 (New York: Routledge, 1987).

O'Sullivan, N. Fascism (London: Dent, 1984)

Anarchism

Carr, E.H. *Michael Bakunin* (New York: Vintage Books, 1961)

Ehrlich, H.J. et al. eds. *Reinventing Anarchy* (London: Routledge and Kegan Paul, 1979)

Woodcock, G. *A History of Libertarian Ideas and Movements* (Harmondsworth: Penguin, 1986)

Ritter, A. *Anarchism: A Theoretical Analysis* (New York: Cambridge University Press, 1980)

Nationalism

Gellner, Ernest. *Nations and Nationalism* (Oxford: Basil Blackwell, 1983)

Hobsbawm, E.J. *Nations and Nationalism Since 1780* (Cambridge: Cambridge University Press, 1990)

Kedourie, E. *Nationalism* (London: Hutchinson, 1985 revised edition)

Minogue, K.R. *Nationalism* (New York: Basic Books, 1967)

Fundamentalism

Aveneri, Shlomo and Avner de-Shalit, eds. *Communitarianism and Individualism* (Oxford University Press, 1992)

Berryman, Philip. Liberation Theology (New York: Pantheon, 1987)

Esposito, John. *The Straight Path* (New York: Oxford University Press, 1991)

Hadden, Jeffrey and Anson Shupe. *Televangelism, Power and Politics* (Boston: Beacon Hill, 1988)

Wills, Gary. *Under God: Religion and American Politics* (New York: Simon and Schuster, 1990)

Feminism

Dworkin, Andrea. *Right-wing Women* (New York: Coward-McCann, 1983)

Elshtain, Jean Bethke. *Public Man, Private Women* (Princeton: Princeton University Press, 1981)

Goldman, Emma. *The Traffic in Women and Other Essays on Feminism.* (Albion, Calif.: Time Change Press,1970).

Harding, Sandra. *The Science Question in Feminism.* (Ithaca: Cornell University Press, 1986)

Jaggar, Alison. *Feminist Politics and Human Nature* (Totowa, N.J.: Rowman and Allanheld, 1983)

Spivak, Gayatri Chakravorty. *In Other Worlds* (New York: Methuen, 1987)

Stanton, Gloria. *History of Woman Suffrage.* (New York: Arno Press, 1969)

Environmentalism

Corson, Walter H. (ed.). *The Global Ecology Handbook.* (Boston: Beacon Press, 1990)

Leggett, Jeremy (ed.). *Global Warming: The Greenpeace Report* (New York: Oxford University Press, 1991)

Lovelock, J. *Gaia: A New Look at Life on Earth* (Oxford: Oxford University Press, 1982)

Parkin, Sara. Green Parties: An International Guide (London: Heretic Books, 1988)

Communitarianism

Kymlicka, Will. *Liberalism, Community and Culture* (Oxford: Clarendon Press, 1989).

Contemporary Political Philosophy (New York: Oxford Univeristy Press, 1990)

MacIntyre, Alasdair. *Whose Justice? Which Rationality?* (Notre Dame: Notre Dame University, 1988)

Three Rival Versions of Moral Inquiry (Notre Dame: Notre Dame University, 1990)

Glossary

Alienation

Being estranged from one's essential nature, or from one's work or fellow human beings. This idea played a role in the writings of Hegel and Marx.

Anarchism

Political movement which advocates the abolition of authority on the grounds that coercion is evil. It aims to achieve social harmony without government. By the end of the nineteenth century, many anarchists became interested in the revolutionary potential of anarcho-syndicalism or revolutionary trade-unionism.

Androgyny

The condition of possessing both male and female characteristics.

Anti-Semitism

Discrimination against the Jews which became institutionalised by the Nazis during the years 1939-45.

Apartheid

Racial segregation as practised by the National Party in South Africa from 1948 to 1993.

Aristocracy

Rule by the best.

Aryans

In Nordic mythology a pure and noble-blooded race of Nothern Europe.

Autarky

An economic policy that emphasizes self-sufficiency through the reduction of imported goods. In pre-Nazi Germany this idea was used to explain the failures of economic policies based on free trade and to attack the positions of Smith, Cobden, and Ricardo.

Balfour Declaration

The promise of a Jewish homeland in Palestine as made in a letter from A.J. Balfour, UK Foreign Secretary, to Lord Rothschild of the Zionist Federation in 1917.

Bolshevism

From the Russian word 'bolshinstvo' meaning 'majority'. In 1903 the Russian Social-Democratic Party split into the Bolsheviks headed by Lenin and the Mensheviks or minority. The first of these was radical and the other moderate.

Bourgeoisie

Term used by Marx to refer to the owners of the means of production in a capitalist society. In common parlance it refers to the middle class, in particular that which has commercial, financial or industrial connections.

Bureaucracy

That part of government comprising the civil service i.e., the nonelected officials.

Capitalism

An economic system in which the means of production and the apparatus of distribution are controlled by a narrow class of owners. In principle, free competition characterizes such a system.

Caste

A rigid hereditary class. It refers to a system often associated with Hinduism in India where rigid social divisions as determined by occupations are strictly enforced.

Civil Disobedience

Non-violent resistance of the law. This type of action was advocated by Mohandas K. Gandhi in the independence movement in India against the British in the 1940s and by Martin Luther King Jr. in the civil rights movement in the USA during the 1960s.

Civil Rights

Rights which include entitlements to equal treatment in public places, hotels, restaurants, shops and public transport. Such rights are often grouped with political rights which include entitlement to the franchise. Civil and political rights contrast with economic and social rights which would embrace among other things the right to equal employment, health and educational opportunities and services.

Class Struggle

Marxist term describing the tension or contradiction between one class and another. During the economic phase called capitalism, Marx thought the contradiction was between the capitalists (the bourgeoisie) as the owners of the means of production and the workers (the proletariat) as the creators of goods.

Classical Liberalism

A version of liberalism advocated by John Lock and Adam Smith. Locke emphasized the rights of individuals to life, liberty and property while Smith emphasized the rights of individuals to economic freedom.

Communism

Political movement inspired by Marx in the nineteenth century advocating collective ownership of property including importantly the means of production.

Communitarianism

Political philosophy which emphasizes the role of community and tradition in defining the interests and rights of persons. This position has ancient roots but has been recently advanced by Alasdair MacIntyre.

Comparative Advantage

Theory of Adam Smith's, developed by David Ricardo, to the effect that nations should trade that which they produce efficiently and import that which they do not.

Conservatism

Political philosophy wedded to the idea of preserving traditions, practices, and institutions.

Constitutionalism

Belief in government working within a framework of a constitution which defines the duties and powers of government institutions. It may also embrace the idea of entrenched individual rights.

Corporatism

System of government in which trade and professional groups are incorporated into the processes of government. This economic system was used by fascists in Italy and resulted in the formation of syndicates or unions, regional organizations and national corporations controlled by the state.

Cultural Revolution

Movement in China in 1960s to purge that country of the opponents of Mao Tse-Tung. Leaders of this movement comprised the Red Guard.

Democracy

Derived from the Greek word 'demokratia' meaning 'rule by the people'. In contemporary discussions this takes two forms: participatory democracy and representative democracy, the former being the type found in some of the city states of ancient Greece and the latter being the type found in present day western industrialised nations.

Democratic Centralism

Lenin's theory that in the policies of the party, the central leadership is to permit free and open discussions prior to but not after policy decisions.

Dialectic

The art of critical examination into the truth of an opinion. Plato's dialectical thinking made use of the method of questions and answers. Hegel's dialectical metaphysics postulated a struggle between the thesis and anti-thesis of an idea. Marx turned Hegel on his head and postulated a dialectic of matter, thereby adopting a positon called dialectical materialism.

Dictatorship

From the Latin word 'dictator' meaning ' the absolute rule of a person or group without the consent of the governed'.

Dictatorship of the Proletariat

According to Marxism-Leninism, the transitory period of rule by the proletariat following the overthrow of the bourgeoisie.

Division of Labour

The practice of specialisation in labour, noted respectively by Adam Smith and David Ricardo in the eighteenth and nineteenth centuries but also recognised by Plato in the fourth century B.C.

Ecology

Study of the interaction between plants and animals and their environment. It emphasizes the close relationship which sustains all forms of life.

Economic Determinism

The theory that economic matters such as modes and relations of production determine social and political matters such as legal and religious institutions.

Elitism

Belief in rule by a minority justified either on the gounds of desirability, i.e. merit, or on the grounds of inevitability, other methods of leadership being inefficient, impractical, or unattainable.

Enabling Bill

A bill passed in March 1933 in Germany that transferred all legislative powers to Hitler's cabinet, including the power to amend the constitution. The third clause of the bill provided that laws enacted by the Government (cabinet) should be drafted by the Chancellor (Hitler) and should come into effect one day after publication.

Environmentalism

Philosophy aiming to place environmental considerations at the top of the political agenda. Perhaps the best-known group advocating this idea is Greenpeace.

Equality

Ideal in political philosophy. What is sought is either procedural equality (equality in the administration of the law) or substantive equality (equality of rights including the right to equal opportunity).

Fascism

Movement established by Benito Mussolini in 1919 calling for the abandonment of liberal and communist ideals to be replaced by totalitarian ideals of leadership, ethno-national unity, myth, irrationality and the corporate state.

Federalism

Constitutional system in which legislative powers are divided between the central government and regional governments at the state or provincial level. The citizen is thus subject to the legislative authority of at least two levels of government.

Feminism

Movement aimed at advancing women's interests. Several philosphical positions have emerged from this movement including liberal, socialist and radical ones. These positions deal variously with the dichotomy between public man and private woman, patriarchy, sex and gender.

Feudalism

The peculiar association of vassalage with fief-holding that was developed in the Carolingian Empire and subsequently spread to other parts of Europe.

Fiscal Policy
The spending and revenue-producing (e.g. taxation) policies of a government.

Freedom
The state of being able to think, act and associate as one wishes. Negative freedom is characterized by the absence of constraints while positive freedom is characterized by development of one's abilities.

Führer
Literally "leader" but in practice the chief or supreme leader in Third Reich.

Führerprinzip
Leadership principle adhered to in Nazi Germany and fascist Italy which required absolute obedience to the leader and correspondingly to his subordinates as in a military chain of command.

Fundamentalism
Movement which emphasizes commitment to the basic ideas of a creed.

GATT
The General Agreement on Tariffs and Trade established in 1948 which aims at the reduction of trade barriers through the operation of the principle of the most favoured nation.

Gestapo
The Geheime Staatspolizei or secret police in Hitler's Third Reich.

Gnosticism
A syncretic religious and philosophical movement in the 2nd century A.D. that emphasized esoteric knowledge.

Halakhah
Hebrew expression for 'in the proper way'. It refers to the accumulated laws and ordinances as they evolved from Old Testament times.

Humanism
A secular philosophy which emphasizes the basic needs and interests of human beings. This idea was extant during classical times but was rediscovered during the Renaissance.

Ideologue
Intransigent supporter of an ideology.

Il Duce
Supreme leader in fascist Italy; term used to refer to Benito Mussolini.

Imperialism
The practice by a country of acquiring and adminstering colonies and dependencies. Lenin thought of imperialism as the highest stage of capitalism.

IMF
International Monetary Fund established by the UN in 1945. The purposes of the Fund are to expand international trade and thereby establish a high level of employment, real income and production as well as to create stable exchange rates.

Industrial Revolution
Dramatic industrial change in the 18th and 19th century which profoundly shaped modern man. This period witnessed the transformation of the modes of production from handcrafted work to mechanization and still later to automation.

Invisible Hand
Notion advanced by Adam Smith to describe the tendency of individual interest in the free market to advance the interest of society as a whole. Sometimes thought of as the tendency of supply and demand towards self-correction.

Iron Law of Oligarchy
Theory of Robert Michel that organizations are controlled by the few active people in them because of the requirements of efficiency and organization.

Iron Law of Wages
Theory of David Ricardo to the effect that owners of the means of production, the capitalists, would pay workers no more than they needed to survive.

Labour Theory of Value
An idea developed by David Ricardo stating that prices of goods are proportional to the value of labour embodied in them.

Laissez Faire
Literally 'to let things be'. This is a principle of capitalism espoused by Adam Smith according to whom economic activity should be free of government interference.

League of Nations
International organization established in 1920 under a covenant found in the Treaty of Versailles, which ended World War I. The idea of the League was found in President Wilson's Fourteen Points although the US Senate refused to ratify the Treaty or to join the League.

Lebensraum
German word meaning 'living space'. The term was used by the Nazis betweeen 1933 and 1945 as a slogan to justify German acquisition of territory particularly that in Eastern Europe.

Liberalism
A political philosophy emphasizing the rights of individuals within society. The first version of this philosophy was articulated by John Locke who stood in favour of the rights of individuals to life, liberty and property and by Adam Smith who stood in favour of economic freedoms. The second, and later version, was spelled out by T.H. Green and John Dewey who believed that political institutions should facilitate the goal of personal self-realization.

Liberation Theology
Latin American movement in the Catholic Church aimed at advancing the cause of social justice among the poor and dispossessed in that part of the world.

Libertarianism

Philosophical position advanced by such writers as Robert Nozick and Jan Narveson which advocates the widest possible domain of freedom for the individual. The position differs from anarchism in subscribing to the notion of the minimal state.

Lumpenproletariat

According to Marx, a marginalized part of the proletariat (nowadays sometimes referred to as the "underclass"). This group of marginal citizens is not in general, thinks Marx, disposed to support the interests of the working class in its struggle with the bourgeoisie. More often it is co-opted by the latter for reactionary purposes.In the theory of Marx all rogues, vagabonds and prostitutes.

Maoism

Political philosophy of Mao Tse-tung (1893-1976) which adapted Marxism-Leninism to serve China's needs. The term is sometimes used to refer to the cult surrounding Chairman Mao, a cult which reached its climax in the Cultural Revolution (1966-1969).

Marshall Plan

Popular name for the European Recovery Program. This was a proposal made by George Marshall, US Secretary of State, in 1947, to assist in the recovery of war-torn Europe.

Marxism

School of political thought advocated by Marx and Engels and developed by Lenin and others. According to this ideology the relations of production constitute the economic structure of society upon which are built the political and legal superstructures. In the capitalist phase of history, Marxists believe the bourgeoisie is in control of the means of production. Since the bourgeoisie will not relinquish this control, the proletariat will have to seize it.

Materialism

The belief that natural resources or modes of production are the primary explanation of social and political structures and activity.

Mercantilism

Economic theory common in the fifteenth and sixteenth centuries. According to this theory, power of a given country was determined by its wealth as measured by gold and silver. Accordingly, state power would be enhanced if these metals could be monopolised.

Meritocracy

Social system in which social position and advancement are determined by ability and industry.

Monetarism:

School of thought which believes that the control of money supply is the most important mechanism for controlling the national economy and avoiding inflation.

Multilateralism

In international affairs, a commitment by three or more nation-states to the joint pursuit of specific goals.

Munich Agreement

The agreement made between France, Germany, Italy and the UK in 1938 which provided for the cession of parts of Czechoslovakia to Germany.

Nationalism

Movement of a nation which venerates the idea of the nation. This idea is sometimes distinguished from that of the state especially where the state embraces different ethnic groups. Nationalism played a particular important role in the fascism of Germany during the Third Reich and of Italy under Mussolini.

Natural Law

Principles discoverable by reason that pertain to human conduct. It precedes all human or enacted law.

Neo-conservatism

Political philosophy which reverts back to the economic ideals of classical liberalism and couples these with the practice of monetarism and privatisation.

New Deal

Name given in 1930s to policies of Franklin Delano Roosevelt affecting business, collective bargaining, social security, housing loan guarantees and welfare assistance. It underpinned the electoral dominance of the Democrats from 1932 to 1980.

NEP

New Economic Policy introduced by Lenin in 1921 in the USSR to rebuild the economy. Small factories and agriculture were once again privatised.

Nihilism

The radical rejection of values. This idea was advanced by Nietzsche in the nineteenth century.

Paris Commune

A government of Jacobins, anarchists, and socialists in Paris in 1871 that was soon overthrown by conservative forces.

Participatory Democracy

Form of democracy in which those affected by decisions participate in the making of them. This form usually contrasts with representative democracy.

Patriarchy

Rule by the father. A social system in which men dominate women.

Permanent Revolution

Trotsky's theory that revolution should be continuous and international. The effect of this in theory was to institutionalise revolution.

Pluralism

A theory which maintains that political power is distributed among interest groups in a civil society. Such groups include unions, churches, professional organizations, and ethnic groups. Government policy is the result of the resolution of conflict among these competing groups.

Plutocracy

Rule by the wealthy.

Pragmatism

In the theory of knowledge, contrasts with empiricism and rationalism. In political theory it refers to the practice of determining political action on the basis of the practical and expedient rather than on the basis of rigid principles.

Progressive Taxation

System of taxation in which the per centage of income tax paid increases with earned income.

Proletariat

The class of wage earners with no property who subsist through the sale of their labour. In Marx's dialectical materialism, the proletariat would ultimately be victorious over the bourgeoise but only after a violent revolution.

Property

That which is owned. Things owned are those things to which one has a right or rights (an entitlement or entitlements) to their use or enjoyment. Private property is owned by individuals whilst public property is owned by the state.

Protection Association

Term used by Robert Nozick to refer to protective organizations which would naturally form if man were placed in a Hobbesian or Lockean state of nature.

Radicalism

Political philosophy looking for far-reaching and sometimes immediate change. Jacobins and Marxists are illustrative of this school of thinking.

Reactionary

The intransigent resistance to change or, occasionally, the desire to return to the past.

Reform Liberalism

A version of liberalism that developed in the nineteenth century and twentieth centuries. T.H. Green of England was the first spokesperson of this movement but John Dewey of the USA and John Maynard Keynes of England soon followed. What these three shared was a recognition of the importance of individual liberties and of the need for forceful state action to create conditions favourable to the enhancement of these liberties.

Revolution

Radical or dramatic social and political change in a country. Illustrations of such events include the French, American and Bolshevik Revolutions.

Rights

Justifiable claim on legal or moral ground to have something or to act in a certain way. Positively enacted rights are those that have been created by legislation whilst natural rights are those which one has by virtue of being a human being or being sentient. Both Hobbes and Locke made use of the notion of natural rights and in time this concept became incorporated into the Declaration of Independence.

Seneca Falls Convention

Conference held in 1848 in Seneca Falls, New York, which marked the birth of the American Women's Rights Movement. The convention adopted Elizabeth Stanton's Declaration of Sentiments and called for female suffrage.

Sephardim

Jews who have come to Israel from Arab lands. The ancestors of these people originally lived in Spain until expelled in 1492.

Social Contract

The agreement found at the base of all civil society, according to Hobbes and Locke. It is the agreement that moves man from a state of nature to a condition of civilization.

Social Darwinism

School of thought which attempts to transfer Darwin's ideas regarding natural selection in biology to the cultural, social and economic domains. Herbert Spencer in the 19th century and William Sumner in the 20th century are names associated with this school.

Socialism

Political philosophy which advocates public ownership of some means of production. Frequently this results in the nationalisation of key industries or modes of transportation.

State of Nature

Hobbesian and Lockean term which refers to the pre-political condition of humanity. Out of this condition there emerges a social contract between a sovereign and her people (Hobbes) or between equally free individuals (Locke).

Sunni

The dominant branch of Islam which embraces the traditional social and legal practices of the Muslim community.

Superstructure

Those dimensions of social life which are explained in terms of the substructure or means of production. The superstructure includes religion, law, philosophy, science, culture and the family.

Survival of the Fittest

Term used by Herbert Spencer to capture the meaning of the term 'natural selection' as used by Darwin.

Syndicalism

Trade-unionism. It specifically refers to the version of trade unionism before 1914 in Spain and Italy.

Third Reich

The Nazi regime in Germany from 1933 to 1945. The passing of the Enabling Law in February 1933 ended the Weimar Republic and established a new political order. The First Reich was the Holy Roman Empire (962-1806) and the Second Reich was the German empire (1871-1918). Hitler expected the Third Reich to last a thousand years.

Third World

The developing countries of Africa, Asia and Latin America. The First and Second Worlds comprise respectively the industrialized democratic nations and the orthodox communist countries.

Totalitarian

Political system in which all aspects of society are controlled by the state. Such a system would result in the state's control of such fundamental institutions as schools, churches, the courts, the family, the workplace, and even recreational organizations. Such a system emerges typically at the far left and far right of the political spectrum.

Utilitarianism

School of ethics claiming that the value of actions is to be measured in terms of its utility to produce pleasure or pain. Early members of this school included Bentham, James Mill and J.S. Mill. According to the first of these the proper course of action was that which produced the greatest happiness for the greatest number.

War Crimes

Acts of soldiers or civilians which may be considered breaches of the laws or customs of war. At the conclusion of WW II an International Military Tribunal was established to investigate crimes against peace, war crimes and crimes against humanity as committed by Germany and its allies.

Weimar Republic

German Republic created after WWI and destroyed by the Third Reich in 1933. Its presidents were Friedrich Ebert and Field Marshal Paul von Hindenburg.

Welfare State

Political state which has a social safety net in the form of such programs as unemployment insurance, old age security, medical coverage, and assistance for those with individual challenges.

Zionism

Jewish nationalist movement having as its goal the creation of a Jewish state in Palestine. This movement originated in Eastern Europe during the nineteenth century and the first Zionist Congress was convened in 1897 by Theodore Herzl.